Readers in Neurodiversity

Edited by
Damian Milton

The Double Empathy Reader

Exploring Theory, Neurodivergent Lived Experience and Implications for Practice

Pavilion
PUBLISHING

The Double Empathy Reader

Published by:
Pavilion Publishing and Media Ltd
Blue Sky Offices, 25 Cecil Pashley Way, Shoreham by Sea, West Sussex, BN43 5FF

Tel: +44 (0)1273 434943
Email: info@pavpub.com
Web: www.pavpub.com

Published 2025

A catalogue record for this book is available from the British Library.

ISBN: 978-1-803882-95-6

Pavilion Publishing and Media is a leading publisher of books, training materials and digital content in mental health, social care and allied fields. Pavilion and its imprints offer must-have knowledge and innovative learning solutions underpinned by sound research and professional values.

Editor: Damian Milton
Copyeditor: Roger Bullen
Cover design: Emma Dawe, Pavilion Publishing and Media Ltd
Page layout and typesetting: Phil Morash, Pavilion Publishing and Media Ltd
Printing: Independent Publishers Group (IPG)

Contents

Biographies

Kay Louise Aldred is an experienced educator with a Postgraduate Certificate in Education (PGCE) and a theologian holding a Master's degree (MA) focused on embodiment spirituality, needs, and care. A published author, she specialises in embodied education, and the bottom-up 'fleshy knowing' rooted in the lived neurodivergent experience of the bodymind. Her work as Development Lead at Neurodiverse Connection is centred on neuro-inclusive, nervous-system-focused, trauma-informed, relational, and creative approaches to training and resources. Kay's approach aims to enhance individual and collective well-being, while also fostering positive change in organisational culture and outcomes.

Katherine Arrowsmith has a Postgraduate Certificate in Autism and Asperger Syndrome from Sheffield Hallam University for which she received a distinction. The chapter included in this book is a revised version of an essay submitted as part of this. She recently completed a Foundation course in Art Therapy with the British Association of Art Therapists, combining her love of drawing and painting with an interest in therapeutic work. She hopes to pursue this further. As a peer mentor for Neurodiverse Self-Advocacy (NDSA) for four years, Katherine provided support to autistic adults on the *Tool Up for Employment* course and also on the *Pathway* post-diagnostic support program. She currently works as a Specialist Mentor for neurodivergent university students and is an Autism Mentor with Hendrickx Associates (www.asperger-training.com).

Consuelo Martínez Astorga is a Psychologist, Professor, and Writer. She holds a master's degree from the University of Chile and is a PhD candidate in Psychology at the Universidad Internacional Iberoamericana, supported by a FUNIBER scholarship. Her academic, research, and professional career has focused on studying neurodiversity and neurodivergence, with a particular emphasis on assessing and supporting adults on the autism spectrum. She has extensive training in the field of the Autism Spectrum, addressing both its clinical dimensions and its sociocultural implications. She has also dedicated herself to scientific outreach and disseminating specialized information on autism and neurodivergence, actively contributing to raising awareness and building accessible knowledge in various academic and public spaces.

Dr. Harriet Axbey is an early career researcher at Swansea University in the Faculty of Medicine, Health and Life Science looking at the reproductive and gynaecological health of autistic people with wombs. She has a PhD in Education from Durham University looking at neurodiverse interactions between autistic and non-autistic people, and has published two books: one a children's book *My Brother Tom Has Superpowers* (YouCaxton Publications, 2021), and another a guide for autistic people starting university titled *University: The Autistic Guide, Everything you need to survive and thrive* (Pavilion Publishing, 2024). Harriet qualified as a teacher before completing her PhD, and her research interests include inclusive education, supporting the development of autistic children, reproductive healthcare, and tackling inequality in education and healthcare.

Sofie Boldsen is a postdoctoral researcher in philosophy at the University of Jyväskylä. Her current work explores the phenomenological structure of autistic sensory experiences, with a particular emphasis on touch. Driven by a broader interest in how experiential variations can expand and challenge phenomenological analyses, Boldsen investigates how autistic experiences shed light on the role of touch in shaping selfhood and intersubjectivity. She holds a PhD in psychology from Roskilde University and brings an interdisciplinary background rooted in phenomenology as an approach to philosophical and psychological inquiry. Her primary research focuses on developing a phenomenology of autism, emphasizing embodiment, sensory experience, and intersubjectivity. Additionally, she has published on topics such as intersubjectivity, development, perception, materiality, phenomenological methodology, and issues related to autism and schizophrenia.

Spencer Brower (she/her/hers) is a Queer, neurodivergent, white cisgender woman who provides psychological services for youth and families with a focus on increasing equity and access across lines of intersectional marginalization. Her current research interests include affirming treatment and assessment, the construct of belonging, adolescent mental health and identity, and multidisciplinary collaboration and consultation. She is particularly interested in qualitative research for its potential to promote the inclusion and representation of voices often excluded from research and increase social validity. Prior to doctoral studies and training to become licensed psychologist, Spencer earned her master's degree in Inclusive Teaching at Teachers' College, Columbia University and taught special education and English Language Arts for several years at public and private schools in the Northeast. In addition to being a certified educator, Spencer is certified in teaching twice exceptional youth and has completed courses towards advanced certification focused on Autism. She also spent a year between her undergraduate and master's degrees teaching English in Taiwan through a Fulbright Fellowship.

Amandine Catala is a Full Professor in the Department of Philosophy at the Université du Québec à Montréal (UQAM), where she holds the Canada Research Chair on Epistemic Injustice and Agency (CRC-IAE) and runs the Lab for the Exploration of Epistemic Justice in Action (LEJEA). She is also a Senior Research Associate at the African Centre for Epistemology and Philosophy of Science (ACEPS) at the University of Johannesburg. Her research interests lie in feminist, social, and political philosophy as well as philosophy of race and philosophy of disability, and include epistemic injustice and agency, territory, colonialism, racism, migration, linguistic justice, cultural minorities, and neurodiversity. Her monograph titled *The Dynamics of Epistemic Injustice: Situating Epistemic Power and Agency* was published by Oxford University Press in 2025. She is the co-founder of the Autistic Collective of UQAM, an initiative that aims to bring together and support Autistics who study, work, or teach at UQAM.

Jill Corbyn (they/them) is the Founder and Director of Neurodiverse Connection CIC. Jill started the organisation with the overarching aim of delivering better outcomes for neurodivergent people. Neurodiverse Connection is currently a proud delivery partner for the Culture of Care Programme. This aims to promote a culture shift within psychiatric inpatient settings. Neurodiverse Connection contributed to the creation of 12 core standards that inform this bold, new vision and now works with the programme governance and delivery teams to promote Autism-informed care. Jill is an experienced facilitator, advocate and innovator with a particular interest in autism, sensory environments, collaborative working practices and health and social care. They were the lead author on the co-produced 'It's Not Rocket Science' report, which centres on the experiences of children and young people who have experienced Mental Health inpatient environments. They were also lead author for the co-produced LGA paper 'Supporting autistic flourishing at home and beyond: considering and meeting the sensory needs of autistic people in housing'.

Paul Davies is an independent researcher, Autistic (with a capital 'A') autism trainer, trainee psychotherapist, Clinical Hypnotherapist and Life Coach. He received his autism diagnosis late in life. He has spent 25 years working within a range of equality projects, now focussing on a human-rights based, least restrictive, autism positive approach to Autistic human beings and communication. He has delivered sessions on 'autism and trauma informed care' for a wide range of organisations including the NHS. As a Visiting Lecturer, Paul worked alongside Dr Allison Moore to co-create and co-deliver the 'cutting edge' Critical Autism Studies at Edge Hill University and a keen supporter of PARC. In 2020, Paul contributed a chapter to "The Neurodiversity Reader" Ed. Dr Damian Milton. This chapter seeks to demonstrate that communication can take many forms and still make a contribution to disrupting the primacy of the spoken word.

Giorgio De Acutis is a qualified educator, having graduated from Roma Tre University, and a cultural mediator. Over the years, he has worked as an educator in the field of child neuropsychiatry and intercultural activities in schools, as well as a cultural mediator in projects supporting the inclusion of asylum seekers, homeless individuals, and unaccompanied foreign minors. He has a strong passion for neuroscience and cultural anthropology.

Marjorie Désormeaux-Moreau (they/them) is a full-time faculty member in the Occupational Therapy program at Université de Sherbrooke. Their work focuses on fostering empowerment, whether through the identity development or through engagement and participation in meaningful activities and occupations. They are particularly interested in participatory and citizen-driven methodologies, as well as critical autism studies and, more broadly, critical disability studies. Marjorie's research program emphasizes the experiential knowledge of autistic adults, the development of "by and for" initiatives and services, and the realities and experiential knowledge of neurodivergent and disabled occupational therapists. Marjorie is also actively involved in community work and advocacy, exemplified by their role as co-founder of Autisme Soutien, a Québec (Canada)-based non-profit organization led by and for autistic Francophones.

Dr. Laura DeThorne, PhD CCC-SLP, has worked in the academic field of Communication Sciences and Disorders for over twenty years and recently founded Neurodiverse by Design, LLC. Her scholarship focuses on communication, autism, and neurodiversity. Through her various roles as researcher, administrator, teacher, mentor, and parent, she's gained a deep appreciation for the importance of neurodivergent perspectives, thoughtful communication practices, compassionate accountability, and the need to think outside the box.

Sarah Douglas is a late-diagnosed AuDHD, neurosparkly, AFAB cis woman who has multiple lived experiences of abuse, coercion, and control. She also has ME/CFS, depression and anxiety and is recovering from eating disorders, self-harm, and suicidality, but is living proof that with the right support, a disabled person can have a good quality of life and do amazing things. Energy allowing, Sarah's work includes advising participatory autism research studies and support services for survivors of abuse. Sarah is also a published author, co-writing *Understanding Autistic Relationships Across the Lifespan* with Dr Felicity Sedgewick and is conducting her own research into the intersection of spiritual abuse and autism. Current interests include theatre, metal/rock music and red squirrels, the latter ironically coinciding with her ADHD diagnosis at the ripe old age of 52.

Dr. Raymi Doyle is a consultant psychotherapist and coach at 'the space between us', providing clinical, educational and supervisory support internationally to neurodivergent individuals, professionals & organisations since 2005. Raymi opened a private practice in 2011 to provide clinical and supervisory support for both neurodivergent children, adults & couples. Noticing a gap in training professionals he developed a bespoke autism training programme delivered through higher education to a range of professionals. This has exponentially grown to presenting and chairing on national/international conferences as well as guest peer reviewed international articles for over a decade, where he has won awards for his service. Raymi self-funded and completed his doctorate in 2022 called "Bridging the Gap between the Autistic, the Therapist, and the Theoretical Perspective", in an attempt to understand the relational space between neurotypes across numerous clinical practices. This was one of the first studies to explore neurodivergent therapists. This ultimately led to developing his conceptual framework on 'neurotransception' and ultimately identifying himself as neurodivergent. Raymi has since developed a relational debriefing model that he has successfully piloted, and has integrated this within his neuroinclusive consultancy service, as well supporting novice neurodivergent researcher-practitioners, that he offers adjacent to his clinical practice.

Danny Dunn is an autistic second year Psychology Ph.D. student at The University of Texas at Dallas, studying under Dr. Noah Sasson. The primary focus of their research is to better understand the disconnects between autistic and non-autistic people, and how to cultivate friendship and connection across neurotypes. As an emerging scholar they are exploring many facets of this topic, and have been conducting studies to investigate the issues of double empathy, friendship, camouflaging, and the experiences of autistic people with multiple intersecting marginalizations. In addition to their work in academia they have been involved in autistic advocacy and community for ten years, as part of organizations like AANE, and For Autistic Empowerment. Ultimately, the goal of their advocacy and their professional work is the same: to improve the lives of autistic people through increased connection, understanding, and support.

David Ekdahl is an Assistant Professor at the Department of Public Health at Aarhus University. His main research areas are embodiment, virtuality, autism, and phenomenological methodology, including the relationship between the neurodiversity movement and applied phenomenology. He leads several research projects, including the Carlsberg-funded project 'Shelter from the Norm', which investigates the bodily significance of online spaces for autistic people. His research also explores professional esports performance, sensory perception in virtuality, and how digital environments challenge traditional understandings of embodied experience. Ekdahl has held visiting researcher positions at the University of Copenhagen's Center for Subjectivity Research and the University of Exeter's Department of Sociology, Philosophy, and Anthropology. His research has been presented across the public sphere, including on national television and before the Danish Parliament.

Dr. Rebecca Ellis is an early career researcher based in Nottingham. She completed her PhD in Human and Health Sciences at Swansea University, focusing on improving autism care pathways in Wales. She is passionate about improving healthcare for the autistic and wider disabled communities. They are currently working as a research officer at Swansea University for the autistic-led Autism from Menstruation to Menopause project, funded by the Wellcome Trust. She cares greatly about science communication, especially through creative methods such as poetry, comedy, art, and improv. She is an advocate for the neurodivergent community through her science communication account on Instagram (@Neuro_Divers). She loves food, plants, crime podcasts and foggy weather.

Fiona Ferris has worked with AsIAm, Ireland's Autism Charity, since 2017, initially in the role of Early Years Specialist. Fiona assumed the role of Deputy CEO in 2019 and oversees the Training and Accreditation Department within AsIAm. Fiona delivers talks both nationally and internationally about Autism, neurodiversity and disability, while contributing her own experiences as an Autistic adult and a parent to an Autistic child. In her talks, Fiona aims to give practical, relatable knowledge and strategies to assist others in supporting the Autistic community to be afforded the same chance to succeed, thrive and fully participate in their community. Fiona's expertise covers a broad range of topics including Autism and Women, Neurodiversity, Disability Rights, Early Years Development, Employment, Accessibility and Education.

Dr. Erinn H. Finke is a researcher and educator specializing in autism, friendship development, and augmentative and alternative communication (AAC). Currently a Research and Teaching Fellow at Calvin University, Dr. Finke's research explores the complexities in friendship, and specifically, the friendships of autistic people, underscoring the importance of individualized, evidence-based supports that foster meaningful social connections. Funded by organizations such as the U.S. Department of Education and the American Speech-Language-Hearing Association, her work integrates qualitative and experimental methodologies to understand and support social outcomes for autistic people, including those with significant communication support needs. Dr. Finke has published extensively on friendship, social interventions, and the role of videogaming as a social context for autistic individuals. Recognized as a Fellow of the American Speech-Language-Hearing Association, her work emphasizes the importance of understanding individual preferences and tailored supports that respect the unique viewpoints of autistic people.

David Gray-Hammond is an independent academic, author, and Advocate whose work focuses heavily on Autistic mental health, neurodivergent rights, and neuroqueer theory and practice. He is co-founder of the Autistic Substance Use Network, an organisation set up to advance research into Autistic experiences of substance use. He is well known in online Autistic spaces. His most popular books are "A Guide to Autism and Psychosis", "Unusual Medicine", and "The New Normal".

Dr. Aimee Grant is a Senior Lecturer and Wellcome Trust Career Development Fellow at Swansea University Centre for Lactation, Infant Feeding and Translation. She has researched marginalised pregnancy and early motherhood for more than a decade, including those living in poverty, stigmatised locations and Disabled women. Aimee's current research includes an 8 year Wellcome Trust funded longitudinal qualitative study using creative methods to understand Autistic experiences "from menstruation to menopause". She is the author of two Documentary Analysis texts (Routledge, 2019; Policy Press, 2022) and The Autism Friendly Guide to Pregnancy, birth and the fourth trimester (Jessica Kingsley, 2025). She is a non-executive director of Disability Wales and was added to the Disability Power 100 list in 2023.

Josie Green is a musician, writer and educator with an honours degree in performing arts. She continues to support and advocate for her children in special and mainstream education who have experienced long periods out of school, and embraces; optimistically, the potential long-term benefits of outdoor activity, books and the creative arts.

Elise Guthrie Stirling is an autistic researcher, professional and parent of three autistic daughters, as well as being an advocate and spokesperson for the autistic community and parents of children with additional support needs. Formerly an autism specialist teacher, Elise has diverged into further and higher education, valuing opportunities to support teacher learning and critical reflection and debate around the dominant discourse of autism and inclusion, and hopes to engage a wider audience in recognising the value and importance of autistic authenticity.

Dr. Emine Gurbuz completed her PhD at Durham University in 2020 and is a Senior Lecturer at the School of Psychology, Sport and Health Sciences at University of Portsmouth UK. She is a part of the Centre for Interaction, Development and Diversity Research Center (CIDD) which investigates social interactions in all aspects of human development. Dr. Gurbuz's work mainly focuses on understanding social and academic experiences of autistic students at university using qualitative and quantitative methods. In her research, she uses community based participatory research (CBPR) approach and collaborates with autistic and non-autistic university students and support professionals as co-researchers to design and validate inclusive measures of support needs.

Lorna Hamilton is Professor of Developmental Psychology and Inclusive Education at York St John University. Using longitudinal designs and participatory, accessible methods, her research focuses on understanding the challenges experienced by neurodivergent learners in order to inform inclusive and affirming educational practice in school and university settings. Lorna is a Principal Fellow of the Higher Education Academy and a Chartered Psychologist.

Dr. Nathan Keates is a Lecturer in the Health and Social Care department at the University of Sunderland in London. Their scholarly work centres on autistic people, neurodiversity and disability, education, and theatre, with a particular emphasis on the lived experiences of autistic individuals and the broader neurodivergent community. As a key contributor to the emerging field of Critical Neurodiversity and Autism Studies, Dr. Keates's research explores the intersections of theatre, mental distress, language, and the life course of neurodivergent individuals. Their work has contributed to understanding and supporting autistic lives, fostering meaningful change both within academic contexts and society at large. Dr. Keates is committed to amplifying autistic voices in research and advocating for active citizenship. Through their work, they seek to promote inclusivity and understanding, bridging the gap between academic inquiry and practical societal applications.

Ghafaria Khan has worked for the past 5 years as a specialist mentor in mental health and autism, supporting higher education students remotely. She has completed her undergraduate degree in Honours Psychology, followed by a Masters in Mental Health studies obtained at King's College London. Currently, Ghafaria is pursuing a doctorate at the University College London, where her research is in autism and mental health, focusing on the South Asian population.

Ruth Knight (she/her) is an autistic researcher and a Senior Lecturer in Psychology at York St John University. She has a particular interest in how neurodivergence influences mental health experiences, especially when this intersects with other experiences of marginalization. Following completing her PhD at the University of York, she worked with Converge at YSJ to explore the impact of arts education for people living with different mental health conditions and experiences. She is especially passionate about coproduced research, and uses mixed methods throughout her work. In her teaching practice she is driven to create a more equitable dynamic in the classroom, considering how forming collaborative relationships can help both teachers and students. She especially enjoys working with students on research projects to explore different experiences in innovative ways.

Prof Beatriz López is a developmental psychologist, working at the University of Portsmouth. Her main research interests fall within the area of cognitive development with a particular focus on how socio-cultural factors affect cognitive development in autism. Recently, her research has focused on documenting the heterogeneity of cognitive profiles across domains and across development. The ultimate aim of this research is to inform personalised care plans for autistic children and adults. She is the founder of the Autism Research Network, a network aimed at bringing together academics, practitioners and people with autism and their families. She is also the founder of the Autism Centre for Research on Employment which has been set up in collaboration with four local authorities and funded by the Department of Health.

Rayan Magon is a Master's student in Psychology at Villanova University. She previously completed her bachelor's in Psychology and Philosophy at the University of Toronto as a Pearson Scholar. Rayan aspires to earn a PhD in Educational/School Psychology, focusing on talent development and using cognitive developmental theory to enhance educational practices that promote creativity and human flourishing. She is dedicated to developing strategies that foster resilience, hope, self-efficacy, and academic achievement, particularly for disadvantaged students (low-SES, disabilities, mental illness), while helping all students reach their full potential. Rayan is also an advocate for understanding Autism Spectrum

Disorder (ASD) and plans to continue researching social cognition, empathy in Autism, and language development in the future. Outside of academics, she enjoys reading philosophy, dancing, making music, and singing.

Eleonora Marocchini is a neurodivergent psycholinguist and an independent researcher in Social Sciences at the Institute for Globally Distributed Open Research and Education (IGDORE). She obtained her PhD in Psychology and Cognitive Science at the University of Genova in 2022. While writing her PhD thesis on empathy and pragmatic communication in autism, she got in contact with critical works in Disability and Neurodiversity Studies, as well as Science and Technology Studies, challenging traditional and pathologising approaches to cognitive diversity. As a result, she left traditional academia and started conducting and promoting independent and participatory research while working as a freelance science communicator and consultant. Her first book, "Neurodivergente. Capire e coltivare la diversità dei cervelli umani" (Tlon, 2024), an introduction to neurodiversity for Italian readers, has been listed among the 10 best science communication books in Life Sciences of 2024 by the Italian National Prize for Science Communication (Giancarlo Dosi).

Roberto Mastropasqua is an autistic activist, trainer, and volunteer in the third sector. He is a board member of Neuropeculiar APS and is dedicated to studying and disseminating sociocultural issues related to neurodivergence through the lenses of social sciences, Disability Studies, Critical Autism Studies, and Neurodiversity Studies. He collaborates in the co-design and implementation of projects aimed at fostering a culture of diversity and overcoming social barriers that lead to the exclusion and marginalization of minority groups.

Damian Milton is a sociologist and social psychologist who specialises in autism research, and an autism rights advocate. He is a Senior Lecturer at the University of Kent and chair of the Participatory Autism Research Collective (PARC). He has been teaching in the Further and Higher Education sectors since 2000 in a range of subject areas relating to autism and learning disabilities. His interest in autism began when his son was diagnosed as autistic in 2005 at two years old. He was diagnosed with Asperger Syndrome in 2009 at the age of 36. His work is influenced by the social model of disability, and many of his publications deconstruct and critically analyse past theories.

Larissa Minner (she/they) is a multi-award-winning researcher, scholar, trainer, speaker, and consultant whose work centres neurodiversity, inclusive research, and accessible healthcare, education, and workplaces. As an autistic person with multiple disabilities, Larissa integrates lived experience with research expertise to advance systemic change. Their work has focused on healthcare disparities, strengths-based mental health models, and participatory approaches that honor disabled voices. A seasoned trainer and international keynote speaker, Larissa is frequently invited to present on topics including neuro-affirming practices, trauma-informed care, and accessible program design. Across all areas of their work, Larissa is committed to building a world where all bodies and minds are valued.

Allison Moore is a Reader in Social Sciences at Edge Hill University. She researches in the areas of Critical Autism Studies and Critical ADHD Studies and adopts a constructionist perspective read through a feminist lens. She is also interested in ecological approaches that see individuals as active agents in a network of dynamic and interrelated relationships. She supervises MRes and PhD students, primarily in the area of autism. Her research interests include autism and sexuality, representations of autism in popular culture, and autism and trauma.

Katie Munday is an ESRC-funded PhD student at the University of Portsmouth. Their study is titled: Exploring Trans and Gender Diverse Autistic Adults' Experiences of Health and Social Care Inequity. They have worked with Disabled children and young people in the youth sector since 2015. Katie is a community researcher exploring cancer care inequity for both transgender and Disabled people and they have published on Autistic people's experiences of cancer services, substance use services, and gender identity healthcare. Katie is a co-founder of the Autistic Substance Use Network (ASUN), which hopes to address the knowledge gap of Autistic substance use and its impact on policy and services. Katie is Autistic, Disabled, trans and queer and they advocate for harm reduction, trans liberation, and neuro-anarchy.

Carol-Anne Murphy is a researcher and lecturer in Speech and Language therapy at the University of Limerick (UL), Ireland. She enjoys working collaboratively with diverse groups through research and teaching, to support children and young people with developmental speech, language and communication needs to achieve optimal outcomes. She is particularly interested in the mechanisms of action involved in and the outcomes of speech, language and communication supports; and in the practices and policies that impact how these supports are delivered to children and young people within and across contexts. She is a member of the Health Research Institute (HRI) and Centre for Implementation Research (CIRcUL) at UL and works with national and international collaborators seeking to generate new knowledge and effect change.

Alexandra Newson PhD (she/her) is a neurodivergent and disabled researcher, advocate, and educator who received her doctorate in special education from the University of Oregon. Her current research interests include utilizing equitable neuroinclusive research methodologies to promote and empower disabled and neurodivergent educator and student lived experiences and perspectives. Her passion for this research stems from her experiences as a special educator to youth with co-occurring disabilities, mental health needs, and trauma histories. She has seen how the use of trauma-informed neurodiversity-affirming practices with neurodivergent and disabled individuals is more than just best practice, but a social justice issue. Her current projects focus on Autistic educator experiences of burnout and flourishing, supporting neurodivergent and disabled preservice educators, and training educators on ways to implement neurodiversity-affirming practices in K-12 settings. Before beginning her doctoral studies, Dr. Newson received a Master of

Science at the University of Oregon in Special Education with K-12 licensure. Dr Newson has taught in private and public-school settings in the Pacific Northwest as a certified Special Educator and educational assistant. As an educator, advocate and researcher, Alex hopes to bridge the gap in current educational systems to better empower practitioners to disrupt their communities while holding systems accountable.

Dr. Michelle O'Donoghue, PhD MSc MIASLT, is a Speech and Language Therapist, Academic and Researcher. She is a member of the University of Limerick's Health Research Institute. Her research explores inclusion and creating neuro-affirmative environments, using participatory approaches and implementation science.

Maisie Roberts (she/they) is a writer with an interest in critical neurodiversity studies, focusing on neurodivergent cultures and social spaces, and neurodivergent advocacy. Maisie initially trained as a sociologist of the workplace and completed her PhD in this area. They now work as an equality, diversity and inclusion manager and are also a coach. As a neurodivergent person, Maisie draws on her lived experiences of challenging marginalisation through self-advocacy and enjoys supporting others through mentoring, peer support and coaching to develop their own self-advocacy skills.

Liz Roscoe is an experienced teacher with a Postgraduate Certificate in Education, the National Professional Qualification for Headship and a Master's degree in Psychology. During her primary and secondary teaching career, she specialised in teaching and co-ordinating Literacy and Drama and was a primary school Writing Moderator. She is a PhD psychology candidate and demonstrator at Sheffield Hallam University. Her research aims to investigate how autistic adults process and respond to information during social communication, in light of the Double Empathy Problem and through the lens of the social model of disability. An overarching aim of the project is to address these questions using participatory research, which is co-produced with members of autistic communities. This is her first publication.

Alice Running is an autistic woman and parent to autistic children. She is an author and writer with a particular interest in the use of (parent-carer) blame within autism public services.

Dr. Siva priya Santhanam is an Assistant Professor in the Department of Communication Sciences and Disorders at Bowling Green State University, USA. She is a licensed speech and language therapist. Dr. Santhanam directs the Interactive and Neurodiversity-Affirming Communication Supports (INACS) program at the BGSU Speech and Hearing Clinic. Her research focuses on (1) developing and evaluating strengths-based social communication supports for autistic adults that leverage their special interests, (2) investigating factors that influence autistic self-advocacy in educational settings, and (3) increasing understanding and appreciation of autistic communication among non-autistic people.

Alice Sodi is the founder and vice president of Neuropeculiar APS, an association committed to promoting the rights of neurodivergent people. She is a scholar of Disability Studies and Critical Autism Studies, as well as a trainer, and a science communicator. She has co-organised events such as AUTcamp and research and training projects on Neurodiversity, anti-oppressive educational practices, accessibility, and disability rights, in collaboration with universities, third-sector organisations, institutions, and companies. She participates in various institutional technical working groups. As an author of essays and articles on disability and neurodiversity, she has contributed to collective volumes and policy documents advocating for the rights of autistic people.

Caehryn Tinker is an autistic, ADHDer, dyslexic PhD student at The University of Brighton. Their research focuses on collaborative drawing with autistic young people as a way to express ideas and emotions, as well as reducing the demands of spoken interactions. Caehryn has 30 years of experience working with autistic young people and their families and has always had a person centred, creative approach. They currently work as a senior specialist intervention advisor with Aspens Charities and are a member of the exhibitions committee for the arts charity Outside In. Caehryn is a practising artist who draws as a way to express their thoughts and feelings. They recently contributed a chapter about drawing with autistic young people in *Drawing in Health and Wellbeing Marks, Signs and Traces*, edited by Philippa Lyon & Curie Scott, published by Bloomsbury.

Verónica Vidal is an assistant professor at the School of Education at Universidad de Los Andes, Chile. She is a Speech Language Pathologist graduated from University of Chile. She completed her Master's in Neuroscience at Universidad de Chile and her Ph.D. in Speech & Hearing Sciences from the University of Illinois at Urbana-Champaign. Her research focuses on the inclusion and support of neurodivergent population, with particular focus on autistic children in educational contexts. Currently, she is the principal investigator in several studies with governmental and other external funding. She is an active member of the Chilean society of Speech Language Pathologists and editor of the chapter on childhood communication at the Revista Chilena de Fonoaudiología.

Dr. Gemma L. Williams is an academic researcher, consultant and public speaker focussed on improving autistic and neurodivergent people's quality of life. Originally trained as a linguist, her research interests have extended to more social justice-related issues, including: autistic people's experiences of loneliness, barriers to healthcare for neurodivergent people, neurodivergence and homelessness, the sensory environments of public spaces, neurodivergent sensory processing, autistic experiences of reproductive health and autistic flow states. In addition to her academic posts she has worked with the Westminster Commission on Autism and National Development Team for Inclusion, contributing to a number of commissioned reports, projects and inquiries aimed at improving service provision for autistic and neurodivergent people. Her book, *Understanding Others in a Neurodiverse World,* was published by Pavilion Publishing in July 2024.

Kathryn Williams is a PhD student in the School of Social Sciences at Cardiff University researching communication and healthcare access for autistic adults. Kathryn is also the research director for Autistic UK CIC, an autistic-led organisation that seeks to promote the rights of autistic people in research, policy, and practice. Kathryn's research interests include studying healthcare inequalities faced by autistic adults through the lens of epistemic injustices, with a particular focus on hermeneutical injustices faced by autistic adults within healthcare settings. Kathryn critically examines normative expectations of the performance of illness and seeks to challenge structural inequalities through her research and systems advocacy work with Autistic UK CIC. She is a proponent of co-production, lived experience, and emancipatory approaches to research, and has also conducted research on behalf of the Wales Centre for Public Policy into the role of co-production and lived experience evidence in disability policy making in Wales.

Meghan Wilson Duff, PsyD (they/them) is an associate professor of psychology in the Psychology and Community Studies Program at University of Maine at Machias. They coordinate and teach courses for the Mental Health and Rehabilitation Minor for University of Maine. Previously, they worked as a child and family therapist and adolescent addiction treatment provider. They also write children's books, including the picture book *How Are You, Verity?*, illustrated by Taylor Barron and released by Magination/APA, which features a nonbinary neurodivergent (autistic/AuDHD/ADHD coded) main character who loves sea life.

An introduction to the Neurodiversity Readers Series

Originating with *The Neurodiversity Reader* published in 2020, the Neurodiversity Readers Series looks to bring together work from pioneering research and practice within and beyond the neurodiversity movement to critically explore its associated concepts and how they might be translated into practice. We now bring you *The Double Empathy Reader* which brings together a substantial collection of work from leading researchers, theorists and practitioners, with first-hand accounts of neurodivergent people, to explore this growing area of study. The next Reader to follow on from these in the series will be *The Monotropism Reader* which will explore the theory generated by the seminal work of Dinah Murray, Mike Lesser and Wenn Lawson relating to neurodivergent perceptual interest and attention.

Section 1: Theoretical Accounts

Chapter 1:
An Introduction to The Double Empathy Reader

Damian Milton

The Double Empathy Reader

The Double Empathy Reader collection brings together work from leading researchers, theorists and practitioners, with first-hand accounts of neurodivergent people, to explore this growing area of study within the neurodiversity movement. This comprehensive handbook explores the 'Double Empathy Problem': the breakdown in mutual understanding that can happen between any two people, yet is more likely to occur when people of differing dispositions attempt to interact. It challenges the traditional view that in exchanges between autistic and non-autistic people, this breakdown is simply the result of autistic people being inherently deficient in empathy. Thirteen years after the theory was first published, *The Double Empathy Reader* brings together a substantial volume of work to explore the research that has developed in that time, as well as the many gaps in our understanding that still exist, with the aim of understanding the potential of this theory to aid a reframing of autism itself and the radical change this could bring when considering best-practice models for supporting autistic people in different settings. In keeping with *The Neurodiversity Reader*, this volume also explores how the concept of the 'Double Empathy Problem' may be of use in theory and practice regarding neurodiversity more generally.

Theoretical antecedents

I first coined the term 'the Double Empathy Problem' in the late 2000s to help give voice to the social disjuncture and difficulties experienced by autistic people regarding mutual reciprocity with others (particularly with those who were not autistic). Grounded in my own personal experiences growing up as an undiagnosed autistic person and the accounts

I had read by others, the concept was also influenced by my academic background, especially that of sociology, and also several philosophers and social psychologists. Perhaps the encounter with such theorists was through the philosophical fiction of Robert Pirsig (see Milton, 2017) and the sociology of Howard Becker (1963) who pioneered work on 'labelling theory' and, in doing so, described the career path of a social 'outsider'. It was through such work that I became engaged with these disciplines and became a student of sociology and philosophy in the mid-1990s. It was here that I discovered the works of Erving Goffman (which I revisit in Chapter 8 of this reader) and of Harold Garfinkel (1967; see Milton, 2012), who played a crucial role in developing my own understanding of everyday social interactions, and whose work helped me to develop the concept of the Double Empathy Problem in relation to the experiences of autistic people.

In the mid-1990s I also studied philosophical works such as Thomas Nagel's *What Would It Be Like to Be a Bat?* (Nagel, 1980) and Ludwig Wittgenstein's (2009) thought experiment of a 'beetle-in-a-box'. For Nagel (1980), consciousness is not something that can be seen as exclusively human, but something shared by many, if not all, animals. Nagel (1980) argues that what we share with other organisms is sensory perceptions and a subjective nature of experience, 'qualia', irreducible to objective measurement and explanation. From such a perspective, experiences cannot be explained by functional and intentional states, but consciousness is intimately connected with a particular 'point of view'. Nagel (1980) uses the example of bats with highly developed sensory systems to highlight that though we might be able to imagine what it is like to be a bat, this is hardly the same as having the perspective of a bat. Even if one were to somehow be able to change oneself into a bat, one would not have developed as a bat and have the mindset of a bat. Logically speaking then, it would not be possible for two human beings to take on the perspective of another, reducing theory of mind to assumptions, predictions and projections.

Wittgenstein's (2009) beetle-in-a-box thought experiment suggests that one can imagine a group of people who each had a box containing a beetle, but where no one could look at what was inside each other's box, and where everyone claims they can know what a beetle is by looking at it. In such a scenario, it is possible that each person had something completely different in their box, thus showing the content of the box to be irrelevant to whatever 'language game' it is being used in. For Wittgenstein (2009), we cannot access each other's subjective experience, and all that could be discussed is what is available to us through language.

My own engagement with the academic literature regarding autism came later in my life, when my son was diagnosed as autistic in 2005. It was from here that I discovered the works of Uta Frith and Simon Baron-Cohen and the hypothesis of a theory of mind deficit in autistic people. As an autistic sociologist who had been analysing social interaction and social outsiders for much of their early career, it became painfully obvious to me that such seminal works that had shaped my own understanding of the social world regarding social interaction had rarely, if ever, been applied in relation to autistic people. It was upon frequenting a parent group of those with autistic children, that I began to use the phrase 'the Double Empathy Problem' to try and explain that the social disjuncture between autistic and non-autistic people was of a mutual nature and not solely located in the mind of the autistic person.

The structure and content of *The Double Empathy Reader*

As I was to later discover, I was not alone in my thinking regarding these issues, as can be seen in Chapter 2 of this reader – a republication of an editorial piece that reflects on ten years of work since the Double Empathy Problem was first discussed in an academic publication. In Chapter 2, I also detail how the theory developed and blossomed within varying academic disciplines and how more contemporary theorists influenced the development of the Double Empathy Problem as a concept.

As with *The Neurodiversity Reader* (Milton et al., 2020) before it, this reader has been structured into three main sections. The reader is designed so that it can be read as a flow of topics from beginning to end, yet also easily allow for a 'dip-in-and-out' style of engagement with the chapters. The first section of the reader explores theoretical accounts of the Double Empathy Problem. In Chapter 3, Eleonora Marocchini explores autistic people's social communication and linguistic pragmatics and reframes such issues in relation to the Double Empathy Problem, and in doing so raises important questions as to whether research in social communication and its core concepts hold as scientifically sound. In Chapter 4, Ekdahl and Boldsen examine phenomenological autism research and suggest the importance of considering autistic perspectives as expressions of phenomenological diversity and the avoidance of deficiency-based models of autism. They argue that phenomenological frameworks and concepts used to analyse autistic perspectives need to be open to critical self-reflection, revision and expansion when confronted with experiences that might in different ways diverge from classical phenomenological descriptions of subjectivity and its essential structures. In Chapter 5, Désormeaux-Moreau and Catala contend that the Double Empathy Problem is not only a matter of interpersonal communication, but also a source of epistemic injustice and systemic oppression for autistic people and other neurominorities. Drawing on their own experiences as autistic scholars, advocates and activists, they present two 'microstories' that illustrate how the Double Empathy Problem can lead to the exclusion and marginalization of autistic experiences and perspectives in various contexts. They then analyse how these stories reveal the phenomenon of 'Neurodiversity Lite', which involves a superficial and tokenistic use of neurodiversity-related concepts, a display of fake(d) empathy and a lack of genuine respect and understanding for autistic perspectives. In Chapter 6, Finke and Dunn explore the concept of 'intellectual humility' in relation to the Double Empathy Problem and distinguish it from approaches based on perspective-taking. In Chapter 7, Rayan Magon looks to (re) integrate a Lacanian psychoanalytic perspective into theorizing autism while also proposing practical ways to bridge the double empathy divide, involving the concept of empathy as language-mediated intersubjectivity. In Chapter 8, I return to discuss the influence of the seminal work of Erving Goffman on the development of the Double Empathy Problem as a theory and how this might contribute to an understanding of 'autistic masking'. In Chapter 9, Raymi Doyle puts forward the concept of 'neurotransception' as a framework for negotiating relational and power dynamics. Chapter 10 reports on a participatory research study by Liz Roscoe that explored how autistic people communicate with both autistic and non-autistic others and what impacted the success of these interactions. Chapter 11 completes this section with Maisie Roberts building a working conceptualization of autistic sociality within autistic spaces and culture. Roberts suggests that how autistic people socialize within autistic spaces and cultures is key to understanding how current inequalities may be overturned, thereby cultivating a greater sense of autistic culture, joy, solidarity and community.

In the second section of this reader we hear direct personal accounts and phenomenology of the Double Empathy Problem, and what it is like to experience social disjuncture. The section begins with Chapter 12 by Paul Davies, which takes an 'angry poetic response' to the Double Empathy Problem. In Chapter 13, David Gray-Hammond argues that the structural oppression of autistic people is perpetuated by the Double Empathy Problem and misunderstandings of autistic communication. In Chapter 14, Josie Green gives an autobiographical account, that included 'rebelling against a monumental lack of empathy'. In Chapter 15, Meghan Wilson Duff tackles the Double Empathy Problem from 'three angles', not just social interaction breakdown, but the negative impact that such breakdowns have on the lives of autistic people, and the recognition (or lack thereof) of the existence and vitality of autistic communities and culture. In Chapter 16, Alice Running investigates the relationship between the Double Empathy Problem and the scrutiny that autistic families are often subjected to by professionals. In Chapter 17, Sarah Douglas discusses 'spiritual abuse' in relation to the Double Empathy Problem and the importance of creating inclusive church cultures that validate autistic ways of being and communicating. This section finishes with Chapter 18, by Kathryn Williams, that explores how the Double Empathy Problem and hermeneutical injustices contribute to disparate health care access for autistic people.

In the third section of this reader, the implications of the Double Empathy Problem in practice and in working with neurodivergent people is explored as a primary focus. Chapter 19, by Newson and Brower, investigates autistic flourishing in the context of the Double Empathy Problem and gives guidance for valuing and promoting autistic experience and communication. In Chapter 20, Sodi, Mastropasqua and De Acutis present a proposal to approach relational difficulties from the perspective of what they term 'neurocultural mediation', which consists of supporting the relationship between people characterized by substantial mutual differences, symmetrically with respect to the parties, with the aim of giving both parties tools for self-awareness and awareness of the variety of 'human kinds'. In Chapter 21, O'Donoghue et al. use the Double Empathy Problem to reframe supports for peer interaction by drawing on first-person autistic perspectives, participatory research and international models of educational service provision to reframe the role of adult as a 'cultural broker' when supporting peer interactions involving autistic and non-autistic children, particularly within educational settings. In Chapter 22, Elise Guthrie Stirling reflects upon their Doctoral research regarding the play of autistic children, and the interpretive dissonance produced by the Double Empathy Problem in misunderstandings of authentic autistic play. In Chapter 23, Corbyn and Aldred examine critically important embodied aspects of the Double Empathy Problem. In this chapter, the discussion moves 'the problem' beyond mind, by focusing on the less explored embodied experience (emotionality, sensation, feelings, nervous system and regulation states) of the Double Empathy Problem and its practical implications. In Chapter 24, Katherine Arrowsmith interrogates diagnostic practice and tools such as the Empathy Quotient (EQ) test. In Chapter 25, Caehryn Tinker discusses collaborative character and narrative drawing as a way for autistic children and young people to construct their own experiences and reduce communication misunderstandings with practitioners. Chapter 26 by Williams et al. brings together a collective of autistic AFAB (assigned female at birth) researchers from the UK to explore how the Double Empathy Problem intersects with structural misogyny within health care, leading to dangerously inadequate services for autistic AFAB people and an urgent need for more research. In Chapter 27, Nathan Keates explores the connection between autistic theatre performers and the Double Empathy Problem, focusing on the interpersonal disparities that could be experienced by autistic theatre performers. Chapter 28, by Gurbuz and Santhanam, discuss self-advocacy as it relates to the Double Empathy Problem and the complexities associated with self-advocacy and barriers encountered. Chapter 29, by Ghafaria Khan investigates mentoring practices in relation to the Double Empathy Problem through their own experiences as a mentor in higher education settings. In Chapter 30, Katie Munday explores the 'double rainbow' intersection between autistic and trans identity and experience. Munday looks at how there is a Double Empathy Problem between cisgender neuronormative professionals and transgender and gender diverse autistic patients, and how this affects experiences of health care. Chapter 31, by Larissa Minner, explores the concept of universal design and how, by implementing such principles in practice, environments can be created where communication and sensory barriers can be reduced, and empathy enhanced for individuals with diverse communication styles. Chapter 32, by Hamilton and Knight, investigates the practical implications of the Double Empathy Problem within higher education settings. Two case studies of third-year modules within a psychology BSc programme are given, that sought to reduce double empathy barriers in the classroom using universal design for learning (UDL) techniques, interest- and strength-based approaches, and the removal of forced participation. Finally, in Chapter 33, Allison Moore explores the Double Empathy Problem in relation to people with dementia. Moore argues that if understood as neurodivergence, although still acknowledging dementia as pathology, it becomes possible to see how people with dementia experience the Double Empathy Problem whereby 'difficulties' in communication are attributed to their cognitive decline, rather than an interactional failure.

Responding to critique and moving forward

Since its inception, the Double Empathy Problem has gained much popularity, not only within the autistic community and broader neurodivergent communities, but also among families, practitioners and researchers spanning a wide array of disciplines. Last year, however, the theory received its first formal academic critique (Livingston et al., 2024). It was suggested in this article that, in terms of psychological science, the Double Empathy Problem was poorly conceptualized and had a weak derivation chain (explanation of causal mechanisms) and often conflated with other conceptual constructs. They also contended that it was difficult to translate theoretical claims into testable predictions and evidence, and suggested that the theory needs reconsideration, particularly through better synthesis with literature in cognitive neuroscience regarding social interaction. Until such times, they suggest caution in the translation of research on the Double Empathy Problem into applied settings.

In response to these criticisms, I would start by pointing out that the theory did not originate within psychological science but was grounded in the phenomenological experiences of autistic people and influenced in the main by microsociological theorists. While the theory has become an umbrella term for a host of work within psychological science (see Chapter 2), to me there seems little issue with conflation of concepts, but rather complementary investigations into issues that could be at work within social interactions, such as work relating to first impressions, metacognition or mutual perspective-taking. For me, the translation of theoretical claims into empirical predictions gathers apace with ongoing synthesis, with cognitive neuroscientific theory largely absent in the critique rather than in the literature (for example, see Bervoets et al., 2021; Bolis et al., 2018; Dingamanse et al., 2023). While one could argue that work in the field of psychological science is in its early stages, the same cannot be said of work regarding a theory of mind deficit in autistic people. While derivation chains for such a deficit have been theorized, it is highly debatable that they have stood up to scrutiny (Gernsbacher & Yergeau, 2019; Long et al., 2025). Meanwhile, as for caution regarding the translation of research regarding the Double Empathy Problem into applied settings, I would obviously wholeheartedly disagree. The reason being that the consequences of the theory for practice largely pertain to humility in the face of others – reducing the imposition of normative social expectations, accommodating diverse sensory needs, and emphasizing the importance of rapport and relationship building and how this can be a difficult and drawn-out process situated within unequal power relations with misunderstandings regarding neurodivergent people that have often led to a reduction in agency rather than empowerment.

In terms of empirical testing of the Double Empathy Problem, a useful complementary concept would be that of the 'Mind-Space Framework' (Long et al., 2025). This framework is similarly founded on the notion that different minds will give rise to different mental states in the same situation. This framing suggests that information (or indeed assumptions) about the traits of another person or their cognitive abilities is used when inferring mental states and can be represented as a location in a multidimensional 'mind-space', where each dimension represents a different trait. Long et al. (2022) also produced empirical research to test out the Mind-Space Framework through an 'interview task'. In this task, participants watch videos of a practice job interview and report their inferences about the traits and mental states of the interviewer and the candidate. Importantly, the interviewers and candidates were not actors but were instead recruited as study participants. Interviewers and candidates engaged in the unscripted practice job interviews, which formed the interview task stimuli, and reported their mental states along the same dimensions as participants later used to report their inferences.

> *The Mind-space framework, then, makes clear predictions about possible ways in which ToM [Theory of Mind] inference might differ between autistic and neurotypical minds.* (Long et al., 2025)

The framework can also be used to make direct comparisons between predictions made by accounts of the Double Empathy Problem and those of a theory of mind deficit.

Moving forward, I would hope that the theory of the Double Empathy Problem and related issues across disciplines and applied settings continue to be a source of inspiration for research and practice innovations and *The Double Empathy Reader* may help assist the laying of a foundation for such future work.

References

Becker, H. (1963). *Outsiders: Studies in the Sociology of Deviance*. The Free Press.

Bervoets, J., Milton, D., & Van de Cruys, S. (2021). Autism and intolerance of uncertainty: an ill-fitting pair. *Trends in Cognitive Sciences, 25*(12), 1009–1010. https://doi.org/10.1016/j.tics.2021.08.006

Bolis, D., Balsters, J., Wenderoth, N., Becchio, C., & Schilbach, L. (2018). Beyond autism: Introducing the dialectical misattunement hypothesis and a Bayesian account of intersubjectivity. *Psychopathology, 50*(6), 355–372. https://doi.org/10.1159/000484353

Dingemanse, M., Liesenfeld, A., Rasenberg, M., Albert, S., Ameka, F. K., Birhane, A., ... & Wiltschko, M. (2023). Beyond single-mindedness: A figure-ground reversal for the cognitive sciences. *Cognitive Science, 47*(1), e13230. https://doi.org/10.1111/cogs.13230

Garfinkel, H. (1967). *Studies in Ethnomethodology*. Polity Press.

Gernsbacher, M. A., & Yergeau, M. (2019). Empirical failures of the claim that autistic people lack a theory of mind. *Archives of Scientific Psychology, 7*(1), 102. https://doi.org/10.1037/arc0000067

Livingston, L. A., Hargitai, L. D., & Shah, P. (2024). The double empathy problem: A derivation chain analysis and cautionary note. *Psychological Review. 132*(3), 744–757. https://doi.org/10.1037/rev0000468

Long, E. L., Cuve, H. C., Conway, J. R., Catmur, C., & Bird, G. (2022). Novel theory of mind task demonstrates representation of minds in mental state inference. *Scientific Reports, 12*(1), 21133. https://doi.org/10.1038/s41598-022-25490-x

Long, E. L., Catmur, C., & Bird, G. (2025). The theory of mind hypothesis of autism: A critical evaluation of the status quo. *Psychological Review*. Advance online publication. https://doi.org/10.1037/rev0000532

Milton, D. (2012). On the ontological status of autism: The 'double empathy problem'. *Disability & Society, 27*(6), 883–887. https://doi.org/10.1080/09687599.2012.710008

Milton, D. E. (2017). Zen and the art of aut-ethnography: a tribute to Robert M. Pirsig. *Disability & Society, 32*(10), 1671–1676. https://doi.org/10.1080/09687599.2017.1368889

Milton, D., Ridout, S., Murray, D., Martin, N., & Mills, R., eds. (2020). *The Neurodiversity Reader: Exploring Concepts, Lived Experiences and Implications for Practice*. Pavilion.

Nagel, T. (1980). What is it like to be a bat?. In N. Block (ed.) *Readings in Philosophy of Psychology (Volume I)* (pp. 159–168). Harvard University Press.

Wittgenstein, L. (2009). *Philosophical Investigations*. John Wiley & Sons.

Chapter 2:
The 'Double Empathy Problem': 10 Years On[1]

Damian Milton, Emine Gurbuz and Beatriz López

In simple terms, the 'Double Empathy Problem' refers to a breakdown in mutual understanding (that can happen between any two people) and hence a problem for both parties to contend with, yet more likely to occur when people of very differing dispositions attempt to interact. Within the context of exchanges between autistic and non-autistic people, however, the locus of the problem has traditionally been seen to reside in the brain of the autistic person. This results in autism being primarily framed in terms of a social communication disorder, rather than interaction between autistic and non-autistic people as a primarily mutual and interpersonal issue.

It has been ten years since the 'Double Empathy Problem' as a term was first described within the pages of an academic journal (Milton, 2012). Although, importantly, the conceptualization of the issue has, since its inception, been influenced by and framed within a broader history of academic theorizing (particularly from the disciplines of Sociology and Philosophy). Yet, this coining of the term helped express an issue that had long been discussed within autistic community spaces. The initial conceptualizing of the Double Empathy Problem was critical of theory of mind accounts of autism and suggested that the success of an interaction partly depended on two people sharing similar experiences of ways of being in the world. This is not to say that autistic people will automatically be able to connect and feel empathy with other autistic people they meet any more than two random non-autistic people would; however, there is greater

1 This chapter was first published as an editorial in *Autism: The International Journal of Research and Practice* on 20 October 2022, available online: https://journals.sagepub.com/doi/10.1177/13623613221129123 https://doi.org/10.1177/13623613221129123

potential for such, at least in how being autistic (or not) shapes experiences of the social world. An obvious example would be how differing sensory perceptions would impact communicating with others and shared understanding.

While the theorizing behind the concept of the Double Empathy Problem was initially derived through a combination of personal experience, anecdotal accounts and limited qualitative data, this area of concern has since been approached by numerous research projects, not only within the field of Psychology (e.g., Chen et al., 2021; Crompton et al., 2020; Heasman & Gillespie, 2018; Sasson et al., 2017; Sheppard et al., 2016), but also more broadly in the disciplines of Neuroscience (Bolis et al., 2017), Philosophy (Chapman, 2019), Linguistics (Williams et al., 2021), Film Studies (Eastwood et al., 2022) and Design (Gaudion et al., 2014). For instance, Gaudion et al. (2014) explored how to develop shared experiences with autistic adults and non-autistic designers to develop empathic understanding of autistic experience to enhance their designs. While the findings of these studies can be seen to support the concept of the Double Empathy Problem, many of the researchers involved were initially unaware of the concept (including post-publication). In recent years, however, researchers have begun to explicitly frame their findings in terms of the Double Empathy Problem, and both conference and online symposia dedicated to the topic have been held. This interest has been more than matched by that found among the autistic community.

This year saw the first of a series of British Psychological Society (BPS)-funded seminars on the Double Empathy Problem. The first seminar[2], hosted by the University of Portsmouth and University of Kent, gathered fifteen Established and Early Career Researchers from across the world. The first part of the seminar focused on the theoretical background of the Double Empathy Problem, including previous work regarding how the Double Empathy Problem emerges (e.g., second-person interactions), while the second part consisted of talks documenting recent behavioural, neurological, questionnaire and qualitative evidence investigating the Double Empathy Problem. The seminar ended with a panel discussion around language regarding disability and normality, addressing topics such as moving beyond the binary of autistic/neurotypical toward a more continuous understanding of neurodiversity and 'recognition' rather than 'diagnosis' of autism. The panel also explored how the Double Empathy Problem might be used to inform support and bridge the gap between autistic and non-autistic people, and more generally examined the future of autism knowledge production. This seminar opened an ongoing conversation, between the approximately 500 researchers and members of the autistic community attending, around theories and evidence-based

2 The recording of the full seminar can be found here: https://sites.google.com/port.ac.uk/autismemploymenttoolkit/bps-seminar-series?authuser=0

research findings concerning the Double Empathy Problem. This continued dialogue will be crucial for creating a research agenda informed by autistic people themselves and developing good practice.

Despite great strides being taken in this area of research, there remain large gaps in our understanding and avenues to explore. Current work shows that, in brief encounters, autistic people are routinely perceived more negatively than their non-autistic peers in terms of being less 'likeable', more awkward or less trustworthy (Alkhaldi et al., 2021; Lim et al., 2022; Sasson et al., 2017). In fact, autistic adults report frequent experiences of misunderstandings by others and little acceptance by the non-autistic community, which has negative effects on their mental health (Camus et al., 2022). These misunderstandings could partially be due to different expectations from, or preferences for, social interactions, such as friendships (e.g., Finke, 2022). Further empirical research into the mental health consequences of misunderstandings and misperceptions experienced by autistic people (e.g., camouflaging, loneliness) is required. However, it is most important to identify the sources of these misunderstandings by examining 'cross-neurotype' interactions systematically. An important step in this process is to gain a developmental understanding of how differences in the social lifeworld of autistic and non-autistic people unfold at both the macro (i.e., lifespan/development) and micro scale (i.e., within social relationships at work or school). The inclusion of both autistic and non-autistic stakeholders in every stage of future research about the Double Empathy Problem must be a priority.

It is also vital to remember how the Double Empathy Problem, as initially conceived, was heavily influenced by sociological theory and that such social interactions happen within a continually negotiated and mutually constructed context, albeit one infused by unequal power relations (Milton, 2016). An account of the Double Empathy Problem cannot ignore such relationships. An obvious example would be how intersectional oppressions would impact social interaction. We have yet to understand, for instance, how two people of different ethnicities, as well as different neurotypes, experience an interaction. As such, an alternative account of autistic development is needed that is not rooted in notions of a social communication disorder, but as a different embodied way of being that can lead to effects on social interactions and understanding. Work examining what has been called 'participatory sense-making' (De Jaegher, 2021) may also be fruitful as this framework not only conceptualizes autism at an interactional rather than individual level, but also places an emphasis on the understanding of how the active 'online' coordination that occurs between people is at the root of their mutual understanding and becoming.

While there is much work to be done to explore these issues across multiple disciplines, the concept of the Double Empathy Problem has the potential to aid a reframing of autism itself from a social communication disorder to a description of a broad range of developmental differences and embodied experiences, and how they play out in specific social and cultural contexts. If this were so, it would lead to a radical change to current diagnostic criteria. This is most important, however, when considering best practice models for supporting autistic people in a variety of settings. We already know that interpretations about autistic sociality from observations alone may not be accurate (Doherty et al., 2022; Mitchell et al., 2021). Instead of focusing on perceived social deficits and normative remediation, the concept suggests a position of humility in the face of difference, and the need to build rapport and understanding and not to assume a lack of capacity for understanding. Ultimately, the concept reminds us of the social situatedness of the lives of autistic people and those who support them.

References

Alkhaldi, R. S., Sheppard, E., Burdett, E., & Mitchell, P. (2021). Do neurotypical people like or dislike autistic people? Autism in Adulthood, 3(3), 275–279. https://doi.org/10.1089/aut.2020.0059

Bolis, D., Balsters, J., Wenderoth, N., Becchio, C., & Schilbach, L. (2017). Beyond autism: Introducing the dialectical misattunement hypothesis and a Bayesian account of intersubjectivity. Psychopathology, 50(6), 355–372. https://doi.org/10.1159/000484353

Camus, L., Macmillan, K., Rajendran, G., & Stewart, M. (2022). 'I too, need to belong': Autistic adults' perspectives on misunderstandings and well-being. PsyArXiv. https://doi.org/10.31234/osf.io/5mysh

Chapman, R. (2019). Autism as a form of life: Wittgenstein and the psychological coherence of autism. Metaphilosophy, 50(4), 421–440. https://doi.org/10.1111/meta.12366

Chen, Y. L., Senande, L. L., Thorsen, M., & Patten, K. (2021). Peer preferences and characteristics of same-group and cross-group social interactions among autistic and non-autistic adolescents. Autism, 25(7), 1885–1900. https://doi.org/10.1177/13623613211005918

Crompton, C. J., Ropar, D., Evans-Williams, C. V., Flynn, E. G., & Fletcher-Watson, S. (2020). Autistic peer-to-peer information transfer is highly effective. Autism, 24(7), 1704–1712. https://doi.org/10.1177/1362361320919286

De Jaegher, H. (2021). Seeing and inviting participation in autistic interactions. Transcultural Psychiatry, 60(5), 852–865. https://journals.sagepub.com/doi/abs/10.1177/13634615211009627

Doherty, M., Neilson, S., O'Sullivan, J., Carravallah, L., Johnson, M., Cullen, W., & Shaw S. C. (2022). Barriers to healthcare and self-reported adverse outcomes for autistic adults: A cross-sectional study. BMJ Open, 12(2), Article e056904. https://doi.org/10.1136/bmjopen-2021-056904

Eastwood, S., Evans, B., Gaigg, S., Harbord, J., & Milton, D. (2022). Autism through cinema: Co-creation and the unmaking of knowledge. International Journal of Qualitative Studies in Education, 1–18. https://www.tandfonline.com/doi/full/10.1080/09518398.2022.2025492

Finke, E. H. (2022). The kind of friend I think I am: Perceptions of autistic and non-autistic young adults. Journal of Autism and Developmental Disorders, 53, 3074–3064. https://link.springer.com/article/10.1007/s10803-022-05573-4

Gaudion, K., Hall, A., Myerson, J., & Pellicano, L. (2014). Design and wellbeing: Bridging the empathy gap between neurotypical designers and autistic adults. Design for Sustainable Wellbeing and Empowerment, 2014, 61–77.

Heasman, B., & Gillespie, A. (2018). Perspective-taking is two-sided: Misunderstandings between people with Asperger's syndrome and their family members. Autism, 22(6), 740–750. https://doi.org/10.1177/1362361317708287

Lim, A., Young, R. L., & Brewer, N. (2022). Autistic adults may be erroneously perceived as deceptive and lacking credibility. Journal of Autism and Developmental Disorders, 52(2), 490–507. https://doi.org/10.1007/s10803-021-04963-4

Milton, D. (2012). On the ontological status of autism: The 'double empathy problem'. Disability and Society, 27(3), 883–887. https://doi.org/10.1080/09687599.2012.710008

Milton, D. (2016). Disposable dispositions: Reflections upon the work of Iris Marion Young in relation to the social oppression of autistic people. Disability and Society, 31(10), 1403–1407. https://doi.org/10.1080/09687599.2016.1263468

Mitchell, P., Sheppard, E., & Cassidy, S. (2021). Autism and the double empathy problem: Implications for development and mental health. British Journal of Developmental Psychology, 39(1), 1–18. https://doi.org/10.1111/bjdp.12350

Sasson, N. J., Faso, D. J., Nugent, J., Lovell, S., Kennedy, D. P., & Grossman, R. B. (2017). Neurotypical peers are less willing to interact with those with autism based on thin slice judgments. Scientific Reports, 7, 40700. https://doi.org/10.1038/srep40700

Sheppard, E., Pillai, D., Wong, G. T. L., Ropar, D., Mitchell, P. (2016). How easy is it to read the minds of people with autism spectrum disorder? Journal of Autism and Developmental Disorders, 46(4), 1247–1254. https://doi.org/10.1007/s10803-015-2662-8

Williams, G. L., Wharton, T., & Jagoe, C. (2021). Mutual (mis)understanding: Reframing autistic pragmatic 'impairments' using relevance theory. Frontiers in Psychology, 12, Article 616664. https://doi.org/10.3389/fpsyg.2021.616664

Chapter 3:

Reframing Social Communication through the Double Empathy Lens: Implications for Pragmatics in Autism

Eleonora Marocchini

Introduction

When we talk about social communication, we refer to a complex and broad concept not only encompassing social cognition and social interaction, but also language and, specifically, the pragmatic dimension of language. This dimension is rarely discussed outside the realm of linguistics and psychology of language; it tends to be perceived as a very technical and specific field, but in reality, it is particularly important when reflecting on communication between neurotypes.

Pragmatics, in fact, focuses on the way language is used in context, describing processes of production and comprehension of implied meanings, i.e., how a speaker can imply certain meanings beyond the literal meaning of utterances, and how a listener can infer or deduce them. As such, social cognition and pragmatics have traditionally been conceived of as inextricably intertwined, and, subsequently, as impaired in autistic people.

Pragmatics also has different subfields, with different aims and core ideas: while pragmatic research on neurotypical people evolved towards a framework of individual differences and co-construction of meaning and discourse, the influential theory of mind deficit hypothesis by Baron-Cohen, which is probably well known to the readers of this book, informed the subfield of clinical pragmatics to the point where a 'unitary pragmatic impairment' was predicted to be found in autism, prompting the production of a wealth of experimental research aimed at testing whether the comprehension of specific pragmatic phenomena or abilities would be 'preserved' in autistic people.

In this contribution, I will retrace the history of the main concepts in social cognition and pragmatics research in an attempt to reframe social communication (between neurotypes) in light of the Double Empathy Problem.

The ambiguity of 'empathy'

Although frequently mentioned in science and the media, empathy is an ambiguous construct, with various meanings and implications. Caroline Bollen recently mapped these meanings within autism research and found 31 unique definitions and 52 different methods to test it in the 111 articles she took into account for the analysis (Bollen, 2023). As Fletcher-Watson and Bird (2020) point out, the way we define empathy has strong implications on theories of empathy in autism and therefore, sometimes, on autism as a whole.

For the scope of this contribution, we will just mention that most of the scientific literature agrees on the fact that empathy encompasses both cognitive and affective states of the subject and of others, sometimes referring to these two components as cognitive empathy or theory of mind and affective empathy. Theory of mind per se is traditionally defined as the ability to impute mental states to oneself and other people (Wimmer & Perner, 1983) where mental states include desires, beliefs, intentions and sometimes even emotions. This variety of definitions and boundaries between these concepts raises a number of questions. Particularly relevant to theories of autism and cross-neurotype communication are (1) whether empathy is an implicit and automatic process or an explicit and intentional one, (2) whether emotion recognition has to be considered part of empathy or not (and in case it is not, whether it is a necessary previous step, or a source of information), and (3) whether emotional and behavioural responses are included in the concept of empathy itself or have to be considered just as related consequences.

Some propose that empathy relies on two sources of input, derived from two different processes/components of the 'empathy system', i.e., the situation understanding system and the affective cue classification system (Bird & Viding, 2014). These would contribute, for instance, to the attribution of emotional states to others: cues from them (e.g., tone, facial expressions) would be processed by the affective cue classification system and cues from the situation (e.g., where these others are and talk) by the situation understanding system; the latter would even allow for emotion recognition and attribution without personal cues. This would mean that emotions could be recognized and attributed via 'learned situational cues to emotion' (Bird & Viding, 2014), that some authors acknowledge to be socially constructed cues (Bollen, 2023).

Social constructions also seem to operate in the domain of emotional and behavioural responses to empathy, as they would entail the elicitation of a feeling that is 'simply appropriate' to the other person's emotion (Baron-Cohen & Wheelwright, 2004) and potentially the appropriate behavioural response. A question we leave for later is: appropriate according to whom?

It is not surprising that testing empathy is not particularly straightforward. A considerable number of studies rely on self-report scales, that are inherently biased given the social desirability of empathy as a characteristic to have (Fultz & Bernieri, 2022), and tests with relevant validity issues for both empathy (Harrison et al., 2022) and theory of mind (Quesque & Rossetti, 2020). It is therefore interesting to note that these tests have been used to characterize the autistic population, regardless of their validity: a relevant case in point would be that of the 2007 edition of the 'Reading the Mind in the Voice' test, where the items from the previous version (2002), where autistic participants had performed similarly to controls, were removed (Chevallier, 2012). The assumption of an empathy or theory of mind deficit in the autistic population was so strong that tests not revealing it were identified as unsuitable (Rajendran & Mitchell, 2007). This attitude toward core concepts in the social cognition domain influenced views of pragmatics in autism as well.

The roots of pragmatics in autism

We defined pragmatics as a field and level of language that describes the processes of implying figurative, indirect or ironic meanings beyond the literal or direct meaning of an utterance, which are left to the listener to infer or deduce.

Pragmatics evolved from a view of pragmatic competence as a communication-specific module of theory of mind (Sperber & Wilson, 2002), built to comprehend these meanings through intention recognition mechanisms, to more complex accounts of these processes as relying on linguistic skills, theory of mind and other abilities depending on the task (Bosco et al., 2018).

This evolution did not change the biased roots of the subfield, i.e., a presumed unitary pragmatic deficit in the autistic population; it just shifted the research aims to test whether specific pragmatic phenomena (metaphor, lexical ambiguity resolution, scalar implicature, irony, humour, speech acts, detection, etc.) were 'preserved' in autism. Many of them actually are, even from that point of view: autistic participants have performed similarly to neurotypical ones in several paradigms testing lexical ambiguity resolution (Brock et al. 2008), scalar implicatures (Chevallier et al., 2010; Hochstein et al., 2017), indirect requests comprehension (Marocchini et al., 2022) and deception detection (van Tiel et al., 2021). However, in many of these studies the ableist lens through which most of this literature looks at the available evidence manifests in the discussion of the results: in fact, the interpretation of any finding that would not confirm the expected impairment has historically been linked to alternative or compensatory strategies to safeguard performance rather than actual pragmatic competence (Marocchini, 2023).

Similarly to what has happened with theory of mind and empathy, then, research on the domains of figurative language and pragmatics in general suffered from a bias towards autistic performance and way of functioning, to the point where even in the context of neuroimaging studies, both lower and higher activity in specific brain areas (implicated in pragmatics) of autistic participants, as compared to those of neurotypical participants, ended up being interpreted as an autistic deficit or a mechanism to compensate a deficit (Gernsbacher & Pripas-Kapit, 2012).

The fact itself that autistic people are systematically compared to a neurotypical group in almost all research paradigms in clinical and experimental pragmatics can be problematized. It is not specific to autism: any population that is conceived of as a clinical population gets this scientific treatment. However, this practice entails losing insights on cognitive diversity and individual differences, both in the neurodivergent and the typical population: it is highly improbable that all neurotypical people use the same exact strategy to understand pragmatic phenomena; in fact, we know this is hardly ever the case, even in childhood (Matthews et al., 2018). Other subfields of pragmatics seem to show higher awareness of the variability of both individuals and elements in conversations that can lead to miscomprehension without appealing to supposed deficits and compensatory strategies: research in pragmatics outside of the experimental and clinical subfields builds on concepts such as co-constructed discourse and meaning negotiation that could be useful in autism research as well. Of course, for this to happen, it is necessary to consider autistic people (and potentially any clinical population, from a neurodiversity-informed perspective) as equal conversation partners, and to focus on differences rather than impairments.

The disruptive potential of the Double Empathy Theory

As readers of this book will know, traditional views of empathy are not the only theories available to look at autistic communication. Through the lens of the Double Empathy Problem, cross-neurotype interaction and communication is framed as *'a disjuncture in reciprocity between two differently disposed social actors'* (Milton, 2012). To put it in simpler terms, the Double Empathy Problem can be defined as a *'breakdown in mutual understanding'* (Milton et al., 2022). The two main implications of the Double Empathy Problem, namely the hypotheses that (1) neurotypical people could have difficulties in understanding autistic people and (2) autistic people have less to no difficulties in understanding other autistic people, are not entirely theoretical anymore: there is some empirical evidence in favour of both.

On the one hand, neurotypical people seem to have difficulties in inferring autistic people's mental states, both affective and cognitive (Brewer et al., 2016; Edey et al., 2016; Heasman and Gillespie, 2017; Sheppard et al., 2016); on the other, autistic people can communicate effectively and display good and fine-grained communicative abilities when talking to one another (Chen et al., 2021; Crompton et al., 2020a; Crompton et al., 2020b; Heasman and Gillespie, 2019; Morrison et al., 2020; Williams et al., 2021).

The Double Empathy Problem raises important questions as to whether research in social communication and its core concepts hold as scientifically sound once observed from a symmetrical epistemic posture. Moreover, as briefly shown here, theoretical and empirical contributions from autistic researchers and studies making use of participatory research paradigms provide preliminary yet important answers to some of these questions, showing cross-neurotype communication as a mutual (mis)understanding process where all participants in the conversation are equally responsible of the co-constructed discourse and of the potential lack of comprehension, thus highlighting the potential for the double empathy lens to reshape these concepts by posing new and possibly more relevant questions.

We have already raised one of these questions earlier in this chapter, when introducing emotional and behavioural responses to empathy: who gets to decide what emotional response is appropriate? We can elaborate new ones in the light of this theory and these data. Most importantly, on the social cognition level: (1) is neurotypical people's theory of mind an actual ability to infer other people's mental states if it only holds when these other people are neurotypical? And at the same time, on the social communication level: (2) if pragmatics focuses on the way language is used by speakers in context, why is clinical pragmatics invariably testing and framing mutual miscomprehension as an impairment on the interlocutor's side?

A new way to look at empathy and pragmatics

Two main points emerge from the analysis so far: on the one hand, there seems to be a role for (social) learning in recognizing emotions and intentions, as people can rely on learned situational cues (Bird & Viding, 2014) to understand the situation they are in (this could possibly be true for considering how to 'appropriately' react, as well); on the other hand, being part of the same group or 'sharing similar experiences of being in the world' (Milton et al., 2022) seems to play an important part in mutual understanding.

Although the two points may seem to be unrelated, they might in fact intersect: if social learning has a role in feeling and displaying empathy 'appropriately', then belonging to a specific social group or sharing similar experiences to the group or person we learn from through interaction can have an impact on how implicit and clear the learning can be. This is an issue that has been discussed in neurotypical research as well, as it seems that empathy and mutual understanding is reduced by possibly any mismatch in sociocultural or ethnic identity in general, due to outgroup prejudices and ingroup favouritism (Eres & Molenberghs, 2013; Szanto & Krueger, 2019). There is empirical evidence of the fact that it is more difficult to attribute, perceive and 'read' minds in outgroup faces (as compared to ingroup faces), which seem to require stronger emotional expressions to be understood (Hackel et al., 2014). Even regardless of neurotype, then, there is evidence that people's empathy is stronger for (or biased toward) people they feel close or similar to, with implications for morality and equity (Fowler et al., 2021).

This observation does not speak of an inescapable limit of the human brain: it is possible that increasing familiarity, along with awareness and comprehension of (neuro)diversity, can reduce prejudices and improve the quality of communicative interactions (Davis & Crompton, 2021). However, it is important to note that while most autistic people are (sometimes painfully) aware of being different from most (neurotypical) people they would interact with and how this might shape their interactions, neurotypical people hardly ever take this possibility into account while communicating, and end up discriminating autistic people, both knowingly and unknowingly (Alkhaldi et al., 2019; Cage et al., 2019; Sasson et al., 2017).

The concept and testing of '*faux pas*' is a case on point here: a faux pas is defined in theory of mind and pragmatics research as a situation where '*a speaker says something without considering if it is something that the listener might not want to hear or know, and which typically has negative consequences that the speaker never intended*' (Baron-Cohen et al., 1999). Stories including a *faux pas* (or not) are used as theory of mind tests, as they entail different knowledge or mental states between the protagonists of the story and the need to detect the potential emotional impact of a statement on another person or to foresee the embarrassment the 'awkward situation' would create in '*all those involved in a particular situation who realize a faux pas has occurred*' (Thiébaut et al., 2016). An important thing to note here is that embarrassment is known to be a complex emotion that has both biological, intrapersonal and, crucially, socially constructed bases (Withers, 2016); as a consequence, different social groups might have different conceptions of what an 'awkward situation' is and might feel embarrassed according to different social rules. The second important thing is that researchers ideating the stories for testing *faux pas* create them according to the social rules of the neurotypical group. Nevertheless, autistic adults can detect (neurotypically-determined) *faux pas* in these tests; however, they tend to over-detect them (Thiébaut et al., 2016). One possible explanation put forward by researchers is that detection of *faux pas* might proceed through a process of trial-and-error of fitting experience-based social schemas of situations that turned out to be (perceived as) embarrassing to the current situation or stimuli. Autistic people have probably been told several times in life that their differences in *faux pas* perception exist and lead them to understate potential embarrassment in neurotypical people. As a consequence, they might decide to be cautious and frame as a potential *faux pas* a conversational interaction that is not, which in the words of the researchers are referred to as 'false negatives'. This rigidity in evaluating a *faux pas* as present or not is a perfect example of neuronormativity in pragmatics: the Double Empathy Problem would suggest that different values, different neurotypes and different lived experiences might shape what we perceive as a *faux pas* or, even, lead us to commit to being truthful rather than to avoid embarrassment. Moreover, the consideration that people might base their evaluation of a *faux pas* on experience-based social schemas, seems to suggest agreement in the literature about how important learned social constructions are in communicating and reacting 'appropriately' and, crucially, in anticipating reactions in conversation as a result of a generalization of observed and experienced reactions and behaviour. It is reasonable to assume that this learned generalization is easier whenever the observed reaction and behaviour has also been experienced in first person, as is the case with people sharing the same neurotype of the majority of people they interact with.

Sharing the same neurotype does not, however, mean that the interlocutor will infer or deduce any implied meaning correctly, that is, the way the speaker actually implied them. In fact, interactional pragmatics also deals with a concept known as 'unwanted inferences', that is, inferences that the interlocutor might derive that the speaker does not want them to derive, so they resort to explicit cancellation of the potential implicature (Elder & Haugh, 2023). An example of this discourse strategy is following a statement with the addition: *'but of course I do not mean that…'*. This can be used whenever the speaker perceives the risk of misunderstanding (or when they want to frame the interlocutor's interpretation of what they said as a misunderstanding), as a preventative conversational repair (i.e., correcting and clarifying eventual troubles in understanding that have actually occurred). This line of research, in light of the Double Empathy Problem, seems to possibly hint that 'mind-reading' is heavily based on processes of generalization of both the speaker's point of view and previous experience of conversations: in fact, in these cases the speaker is anticipating the way the interlocutor could potentially interpretate what they are saying, even before the interlocutor has responded.

The timing of these cases makes it clear that the speaker's mind-reading cannot be based on anything the specific interlocutor said in that specific moment, and that the interlocutor's assumed mind-reading is expected to follow very general rules, so much so that it can be anticipated. Moreover, the scientific literature on the Double Empathy Problem highlights failure of the neurotypical mind-reading strategies or functioning when the mind of the interlocutor does not function in the same way as the speaker's. Taken together, these elements seem to suggest a negative answer to the question of whether neurotypical people's theory of mind can be conceived of as an actual ability to infer other people's mental states. A new way to look at it through the double empathy lens would be to conceive it as a sociocognitive function that attempts at constructing other people's mental states by generalizing the person's point of view, informed by the person's neurotype and sociocultural identity and previous interactions they have had, which have probably, primarily, been with people with the same neurotype and a similar sociocultural identity. As a result, theory of mind abilities only hold when the other people whose mental states the person is trying to infer are neurotypical and, possibly, reflect their sociocultural identity.

These observations have implications for pragmatics as well: once we make space for the possibility that empathy and theory of mind are much more linked to different dispositions of the social actors involved, shared experiences, socially constructed concepts and unwritten rules of a social group than to purely cognitive abilities, we also leave room to discuss the need for a 'clinical' pragmatics to exist or, to say the least, to be applied to autism. As briefly discussed in the Introduction, pragmatics focuses on the way language is used by speakers in context, and the sociocultural aspects of the context and the identity of the speakers are known to have a role both in the production of pragmatic phenomena and in mutual comprehension. These aspects are usually taken into account in sociolinguistics and intercultural pragmatics, but they are hardly ever considered or thought of when dealing with data from populations that are considered clinical populations, as if being part of a group that is framed as clinical – mainly on the basis of their social communication – could not be considered a sociocultural factor in itself.

The disruptive potential of the Double Empathy Problem, then, also resides in the possible implication that cross-neurotype pragmatics could be framed as intercultural pragmatics, rather than clinical pragmatics. This would mean stopping the testing and framing of mutual miscomprehension between neurotypes as the result of an impairment on the autistic interlocutor's side, and starting to consider autistic means of communication as equally valid, just coming from a different background of functioning, culture and lived experience.

This is not a novel proposal – but it is a rather new and unfrequented framework for cross-neurotype communication. A comprehensive view of what this account could add to the conversation is offered by Hillary (2020), who points out how proactive attitudes toward misunderstandings can flourish whenever a cultural difference is recognized and how, crucially, *'autism doesn't get a culture'* – therefore, the issue of comprehending (neurotypical) others and making themselves comprehensible to (neurotypical) others is framed as a problem that the autistic person has to solve on their own. Thinking of autistic culture(s) could be confusing, though many definitions of culture include social, linguistic, personal and political aspects – the autistic identity is arguably both different from the neurotypical identity and definable in terms of all of these aspects, and it can and does intersect with other cultures a person is a part of. Stones (2023), for instance, notes the existence of four cultural categories that people identifying as neurodivergent recognize as significant: interest systems, sensory sensitivity, affect display and social interactions.

One of the practical consequences of such a theoretical position is that cultural differences, once they are explicit, are expected as well as framed as mutual (though cultural supremacy must be taken into account, too). Another one would be that they can be taught by, and learned from, people of different cultures, while in the case of neurocognitive differences 'learning' is currently confined to neuropsychological training and behavioural therapy provided to neurodivergent people, aimed at helping them fit into the neurotypical culture.

Even though the idea of cross-(neuro)cultural communication training seems to be more equitable, it is not easy to describe what autistic communication (let alone neurodivergent communication in general) entails and teach 'appropriate' ways to interact. In fact, autism in its current formulation is a spectrum including people with very different abilities and preferences in terms of language, sensory input and sociality. Coming back to a question and issue formulated earlier in this chapter ('appropriate according to whom?'), any kind of normative approach to interaction risks impoverishing the diversity of human communication and leaving those who communicate differently from said norm behind, even when the 'norm' in that specific context is a description of neurodivergent functioning. This is even more relevant when trying to generalize the Double Empathy Problem to other neurotypes beside autism, particularly when considering multiple neurodivergences can coexist within the same brain. However, anecdotal evidence can be found, in neurodivergent communities, that communication seems to be easier between people of different neurotypes that do not align with the neurotypical norm than it is for them to communicate with neurotypical people, even when they do not share the same communicative features. I would argue that this might be the case precisely because they reject the norm or, at least, that they are consciously aware of the fact that the interlocutors will probably not align with it: this is what it would mean to communicate within a conversational space where, as suggested, (neuro)cultural differences are expected and framed as mutual.

Conclusion

Reframing social communication through the double empathy lens can, ironically, *'mean different things to different people'*. The Double Empathy Problem already had the merit of shedding a new light on empathy and theory of mind as neuronormative concepts and prompting discussions leading to more equitable ways to look at autistic social interactions.

The disruptive potential of this view resides in the fact that on the one hand it can be used to reflect on what theory of mind and social cognition in general really is for neurotypical people as well, and what this means for social communication and specifically for (clinical or intercultural) pragmatics; on the other hand it can be a first important step to move beyond the binary of autistic and neurotypical social communication toward a conceptualization of cross-neurotype communication (regardless of the neurotypes involved) as a cross-(neuro)cultural process where divergence from the norm(s) and diversity (as well as individual differences) are expected and respected, in line with the neurodiversity paradigm.

In sum, the double empathy lens puts forward *'a position of humility in the face of difference'* (Milton et al., 2022), and, potentially, of human (neuro)diversity as a whole.

References

Alkhaldi, R. S., Sheppard, E., & Mitchell, P. (2019). Is there a link between autistic people being perceived unfavorably and having a mind that is difficult to read? *Journal of Autism and Developmental Disorders, 49,* 3973–3982.

Baron-Cohen, S., & Wheelwright, S. (2004). The empathy quotient: An investigation of adults with Asperger syndrome or high functioning autism, and normal sex differences. *Journal of Autism and Developmental Disorders, 34*(2), 163–175. https://doi.org/10.1023/b:jadd.0000022607.19833.00

Baron-Cohen, S., O'Riordan, M., Stone, V., Jones, R., & Plaisted, K. (1999). Recognition of faux pas by normally developing children and children with Asperger syndrome or high-functioning autism. *Journal of Autism and Developmental Disorders, 29,* 407–418.

Bird, G., & Viding, E. (2014). The self to other model of empathy: Providing a new framework for understanding empathy impairments in psychopathy, autism, and alexithymia. *Neuroscience & Biobehavioral Reviews, 47,* 520–532. https://doi.org/10.1016/j.neubiorev.2014.09.021

Bollen, M. (2023). A reflective guide on the meaning of empathy in autism research. *Methods in Psychology, 8,* 100109. https://doi.org/10.1016/j.metip.2022.100109

Bosco, F. M., Tirassa, M., & Gabbatore, I. (2018). Why pragmatics and theory of mind do not (completely) overlap. *Frontiers in Psychology, 9,* 1453.

Brewer, R., Biotti, F., Catmur, C., Press, C., Happé, F., Cook, R., & Bird, G. (2016). Can neurotypical individuals read autistic facial expressions? Atypical production of emotional facial expressions in autism spectrum disorders. *Autism Research, 9*(2), 262–271.

Brock, J., Norbury, C., Einav, S., & Nation, K. (2008). Do individuals with autism process words in context? Evidence from language-mediated eye-movements. *Cognition, 108*(3), 896–904.

Cage, E., Di Monaco, J., & Newell, V. (2019). Understanding, attitudes and dehumanisation towards autistic people. *Autism, 23*(6), 1373–1383.

Chen, Y. L., Senande, L. L., Thorsen, M., & Patten K. (2021). Peer preferences and characteristics of same-group and cross-group social interactions among autistic and non-autistic adolescents. *Autism, 25*(7), 1885–1900.

Chevallier, C. (2012). Theory of mind and autism: Revisiting Baron-Cohen et al.'s Sally-Anne study. In A. M. Slater, & P. C. Quinn (Eds.), *Developmental Psychology: Revisiting the Classic Studies* (pp. 148–163). SAGE.

Chevallier, C., Wilson, D., Happé, F., & Noveck, I. (2010). Scalar inferences in Autism spectrum disorders. *Journal of Autism and Developmental Disorders, 40*(9), 1104–1117.

Crompton, C. J., Ropar, D., Evans-Williams, C. V., Flynn, E. G., & Fletcher-Watson, S. (2020a). Autistic peer-to-peer information transfer is highly effective. *Autism, 24*(7), 1704–1712.

Crompton, C. J., Sharp, M., Axbey, H., Fletcher-Watson, S., Flynn, E. G., & Ropar, D. (2020b). Neurotype-matching, but not being autistic, influences self and observer ratings of interpersonal rapport. *Frontiers in Psychology, 11,* 586171. https://doi.org/10.3389/fpsyg.2020.586171

Davis, R., & Crompton, C. J. (2021). What do new findings about social interaction in autistic adults mean for neurodevelopmental research? *Perspectives on Psychological Science, 16*(3), 649–653. https://doi.org/10.1177/1745691620958010

Edey, R., Cook, J., Brewer, R., Johnson, M. H., Bird, G. and Press, C. (2016). Interaction takes two: Typical adults exhibit mind-blindness towards those with autism spectrum disorder. *Journal of Abnormal Psychology, 125*(7), 879–908.

Elder, C-H., & Haugh, M. (2023). Exposing and avoiding unwanted inferences in conversational interaction. *Journal of Pragmatics, 218*, 115–132. https://doi.org/10.1016/j.pragma.2023.09.014

Eres, R., & Molenberghs, P. (2013). The influence of group membership on the neural correlates involved in empathy. *Frontiers in Human Neuroscience, 7*, 176.

Fletcher-Watson, S., & Bird, G. (2020). Autism and empathy: What are the real links? *Autism, 24*(1), 3–6. https://doi.org/10.1177/1362361319883506

Fowler, Z., Law, K. F., & Gaesser, B. (2021). Against empathy bias: The moral value of equitable empathy. *Psychological Science, 32*(5), 766–779. https://doi.org/10.1177/0956797620979965

Fultz, A. A., & Bernieri, F. J. (2022). Observer descriptions of the empathic person: A look at the Davis IRI and Hogan empathy scales. *The Journal of Social Psychology, 162*(1), 26–40. https://doi.org/10.1080/00224545.2021.1985416

Gernsbacher, M. A., & Pripas-Kapit, S. R. (2012). Who's missing the point? A commentary on claims that autistic persons have a specific deficit in figurative language comprehension. *Metaphor and Symbol, 27*(1), 93–105. https://doi.org/10.1080/10926488.2012.656255

Hackel, L. M., Looser, C. E., & Van Bavel, J. J. (2014). Group membership alters the threshold for mind perception: The role of social identity, collective identification, and intergroup threat. *Journal of Experimental Social Psychology, 52*, 15–23.

Harrison, J. L., Brownlow, C. L., Ireland, M. J., & Piovesana, A. M. (2022). Empathy measurement in autistic and nonautistic adults: A COSMIN systematic literature review. *Assessment, 29*(2), 332–350. https://doi.org/10.1177/1073191120964564

Heasman, B., & Gillespie, A. (2017). Perspective-taking is two-sided: Misunderstandings between people with Asperger's syndrome and their family members. *Autism, 22*(6), 740–750.

Heasman, B., & Gillespie, A. (2019). Neurodivergent intersubjectivity: Distinctive features of how autistic people create shared understanding. *Autism, 23*(4), 910–921.

Hillary, A. (2020). Neurodiversity and cross-cultural communication. In H. Bertilsdotter Rosqvist, N. Chown, & A. Stenning (Eds.), *Neurodiversity Studies: A New Critical Paradigm* (pp. 91–107). Routledge. https://doi.org/10.4324/9780429322297-10

Hochstein, L., Bale, A., & Barner, D. (2017). Scalar implicature in absence of epistemic reasoning? The case of autism spectrum disorder. *Language Learning and Development, 14*(3), 224–240.

Marocchini, E., Di Paola, S., Mazzaggio, G., & Domaneschi, F. (2022). Understanding indirect requests for information in high-functioning autism. *Cognitive Processing, 23*, 129–153. https://doi.org/10.1007/s10339-021-01056-z

Marocchini, E. (2023). Impairment or difference? The case of theory of mind abilities and pragmatic competence in the autism spectrum. *Applied Psycholinguistics, 44*(3), 365–383. https://doi.org/10.1017/S0142716423000024

Matthews, D., Biney, H., & Abbot-Smith, K. (2018). Individual differences in children's pragmatic ability: A review of associations with formal language, social cognition, and executive functions. *Language Learning and Development, 14*(3), e186–e223. https://doi.org/10.1080/15475441.2018.1455584

Milton, D. (2012). On the ontological status of autism: The double empathy problem. *Disability & Society, 27*(6), 883–887.

Milton, D., Gurbuz, E., & López, B. (2022). The 'double empathy problem': Ten years on. *Autism, 26*(8), 1901–1903. https://doi.org/10.1177/13623613221129123

Morrison, K. E., DeBrabander, K. M., Jones, D. R., Faso, D. J., Ackerman, R. A., & Sasson, N. J. (2020). Outcomes of real-world social interaction for autistic adults paired with autistic compared to typically developing partners. *Autism, 24*(5), 1067–1080.

Quesque, F., & Rossetti, Y. (2020). What do theory-of-mind tasks actually measure? Theory and practice. *Perspectives on Psychological Science, 15*(2), 384–396. https://doi.org/10.1177/1745691619896607

Rajendran, G., & Mitchell, P. (2007). Cognitive theories of autism. *Developmental Review, 27*(2), 224–260.

Sasson, N. J., Faso, D. J., Nugent, J., Lovell, S., Kennedy, D. P., & Grossman, R. B. (2017). Neurotypical peers are less willing to interact with those with autism based on thin slice judgments. *Scientific Reports, 7*, 40700. https://doi.org/10.1038/srep40700

Sheppard, E., Pillai, D., Wong, G. T-L., Ropar, D., & Mitchell, P. (2016). How easy is it to read the minds of people with autism spectrum disorder? *Journal of Autism and Developmental Disorders, 46*(4), 1247–1254.

Sperber, D., & Wilson, D. (2002). Pragmatics, modularity and mind-reading. *Mind and Language, 17* (1–2), 3–23.

Stones, E. (2023). Cross-neurotype communication competence. In M. S. Jeffress, J. M. Cypher, J. Ferris, & J-A. Scott-Pollock (Eds.), *The Palgrave Handbook of Disability and Communication* (pp. 45–65). Springer International Publishing.

Szanto, T., & Krueger, J. (2019). Introduction: Empathy, shared emotions, and social identity. *Topoi, 38*, 153–162. https://doi.org/10.1007/s11245-019-09641-w

Thiébaut, F. I., White, S. J., Walsh, A., Klargaard, S. K., Wu, H. C., Rees, G., & Burgess, P. W. (2016). Does faux pas detection in adult autism reflect differences in social cognition or decision-making abilities? *Journal of Autism and Developmental Disorders, 46*(1), 103–112. https://doi.org/10.1007/s10803-015-2551-1

van Tiel, B., Deliens, G., Geelhand, P., Murillo Oosterwijk, A., & Kissine, M. (2021). Strategic deception in adults with autism spectrum disorder. *Journal of Autism and Developmental Disorders, 51*, 255–266. https://doi.org/10.1007/s10803-020-04525-0

Williams, G. L., Wharton, T., & Jagoe, C. (2021). Mutual (mis)understanding: Reframing autistic pragmatic 'impairments' using relevance theory. *Frontiers in Psychology, 12*, 616664. https://doi.org/10.3389/fpsyg.2021.616664

Wimmer, H., & Perner, J. (1983). Beliefs about beliefs: Representation and constraining function of wrong beliefs in young children's understanding of deception. *Cognition, 13*, 103–128.

Withers, L. A. (2016). Embarrassment. In V. Zeigler-Hill, & T. Shackelford (Eds.) *Encyclopedia of Personality and Individual Differences*. Springer. https://doi.org/10.1007/978-3-319-28099-8_506-1

Chapter 4:

The Double Empathy Problem: Methodological Lessons for Future Phenomenological Autism Research

David Ekdahl and Sofie Boldsen

In this contribution, we identify and discuss two core lessons emerging from the double empathy problem which, we argue, carry special significance to phenomenological autism research moving forward. For one, the double empathy problem highlights the need for phenomenological research to engage with the actual, subjective and intersubjective experiences of autistic individuals in their full richness and nuance, interrogating not only typical but also atypical and diverging modes of social being in their own right. In this regard, we stress the importance of considering autistic perspectives as expressions of phenomenological diversity and avoid deficiency-based models of autism which have historically been influential, including in phenomenological autism research. Second, phenomenological frameworks and concepts used to analyse autistic perspectives need to be open to critical self-reflection, revision and expansion when confronted with experiences that might in different ways diverge from classical phenomenological descriptions of subjectivity and its essential structures. These lessons, while distinct, are not separate, and highlight the need for phenomenology to cultivate a critical self-reflective stance towards its own tacit assumptions of normality, echoing calls for theoretical and methodological introspection similarly emphasized in critical phenomenology. Incorporating these lessons into phenomenological research allows not only for richer and more veridical accounts of autistic life, it also, we argue, sets the stage for a phenomenological research programme able to realise its structural ambitions of accounting for subjectivity and intersubjectivity more fully.

Introduction

The double empathy problem arose in large part as a response to a widespread idea among autism researchers that social dysfunction is a core characteristic of autism. The double empathy problem as a framework for social disjunctures in a neurodiverse world emphasizes that intersubjective salience centrally revolves around reciprocity of social norms and expectations, which shape how we navigate and make sense of the social spaces around us and when we fail to. On the model proposed in the double empathy problem, the oft-occurring breakdowns in social salience between allistic and autistic individuals result from social disjunctures that emerge within the intersubjective setting itself, rather than because of social dysfunction 'inside' any one interlocutor. Conversely, the double empathy problem predicts that for purely autistic interactions, similar to purely non-autistic interactions, such social disjunctures will be less prevalent.

For the purposes of this contribution, the double empathy problem, at its core, can be seen to reflect a growing call to respect or take seriously both non-autistic and autistic perspectives in their own right – especially when exploring autistic intersubjectivity and social capability. In this regard, the double empathy problem adds significant considerations of *heterogeneity* to questions of sociality and autistic existence. Unsurprisingly, the double empathy problem has been significant both in sparking a new range of research into autistic social capabilities (Chown, 2014; Crompton et al., 2020; Heasman & Gillespie, 2019; Morrison et al., 2020) and in moving away from the widespread picture of autism as social dysfunction.

Our aim here is to show how core features of the double empathy problem, in different ways, stand to specifically improve and refine future *phenomenological* autism research, which, historically, has been rooted in the tradition of psychopathology, and, consequently, has approached autism and autistic intersubjectivity largely absent of considerations of heterogeneity, as well as neurodiversity more broadly.

After providing a brief introduction to phenomenology, we spell out two overarching lessons for future phenomenological autism research, drawing on what we argue are core features of the double empathy problem. First, phenomenological research needs to engage fully with autistic embodiment as expressions of subjective diversity, treating autistic experience as, phenomenologically speaking, functional expressions of subjectivity and thus providing autistic perspectives with what we here refer to as phenomenological justice. Second, phenomenological autism research needs to cultivate an awareness of its own structural or transcendental assumptions of normality, allowing autistic subjectivity into the fold of subjectivity and, in doing so, letting autistic experiences expand and refine phenomenological frameworks and concepts.

Phenomenological research

Phenomenology is a philosophical movement initiated by Edmund Husserl in the beginning of the twentieth century. Initially, phenomenology was conceived as a radical epistemological project defined by the method of suspending metaphysical and scientific beliefs in favour of describing phenomena as they are given to an experiencing subject (Husserl, 1983). Since its inception as a science of consciousness, one of the most common critiques of phenomenology has been charges of solipsism and introspectionism (Dennett, 2018). Contrary to such claims, the object of phenomenology is defined not merely by what is given to a subject, but by *subjectivity* itself – something still intrinsically open to intersubjective validation (Varela & Shear, 1999, p. 2). Phenomenology deals not only with how phenomena are experienced but also with the very nature of phenomena and subjectivity. In the oft-cited words of Shaun Gallagher and Dan Zahavi, phenomenology is *'an account of subjective experience'* rather than *'a subjective account of experience'* (Gallagher & Zahavi, 2008, p. 19). An important problem, which this article takes up, is on what ground phenomenology develops its analyses of the nature of themes such as embodiment, subjectivity and intersubjectivity: Which subjectivity is described and in what ways are phenomenological analyses open to accommodating alternative or divergent expressions?

These questions warrant some consideration of the relationship between philosophical thinking and empirical cases. *First*, one can think of phenomenology as an invitation to consider the subjective experience of the diverse and multifarious objects of empirical sciences, e.g., mental illness, cultural phenomena, the physical body or cognitive processes. For example, in the qualitative psychological methodology of *interpretative phenomenological analysis* (IPA), phenomenology is mainly understood as an attempt to *'explore/understand/make sense of the subjective meanings of events/experiences/states of the individual participants themselves'* (Smith & Osborn, 2004, p. 229). *Second*, phenomenology has been understood as a distinctive philosophical method, which can be adapted to fit empirical inquiry in a variety of fields. Such a strategy has been undertaken, for example, in the *descriptive phenomenological method* developed by Amedeo Giorgi, where phenomenology is considered a rigorous method of analysis enabling not merely the study of subjective experience of various phenomena but also analysis of the structural features of such phenomena themselves (Giorgi, 2009; Englander & Morley, 2021).

While these first two strategies emphasize the epistemological impetus of phenomenology to found knowledge on experience, we will also consider here two additional strategies that understand phenomenology mainly as a set of philosophical analyses and concepts. In this regard, a *third* strategy focuses on applying phenomenological insights and concepts to the analysis of empirical phenomena. Here, a notable example is the tradition of *phenomenological psychopathology*, where phenomenological analyses (of, for example, time-consciousness, self-awareness or affectivity) are employed to understand the experiential structures of clinical psychiatric phenomena (Fuchs, 2013; Sass & Parnas, 2003). Finally, a *fourth* strategy consists in supposing a somewhat opposite directionality between phenomenological philosophy and empirical cases by considering how phenomenology can itself be nuanced and enriched by empirical research. Here, it has been argued by Ravn and Høffding (2016) that qualitative research on exceptional cases of bodily practice can enrich phenomenological thinking, and by Fernandez (2017) that empirical research may challenge and nuance philosophical analyses of the ontological structures of existence.

Considering our aim of describing the ways in which the double empathy problem should inform phenomenological research in the field of autism studies, we will deal most explicitly with the third and fourth strategies as our main focus is the methodological preconditions for allowing phenomenology, as a philosophical account of intersubjectivity, to adapt to autistic forms of social engagement. Thus, we focus on the phenomenological notion of intersubjectivity as the philosophical framework to be put in dialogue with autism as a divergent range of social relatedness.

It is also through discussions on the nature of intersubjectivity that phenomenology has most explicitly engaged with autism research previously. Running in partial tandem with core tenets of the double empathy problem, phenomenological scholars have critiqued the dominant theory of mind paradigm in autism research for assuming that social understanding is a purely cognitively driven process (Gallagher & Zahavi, 2008; Tanaka, 2015). As an account of social cognition, theory of mind relies on the idea that knowledge of other people's intentions, beliefs and emotions is mediated by a higher-order cognitive and inferential process where the behaviour of others is interpreted through the application of mental state concepts (Leslie, 1987; Premack & Woodruff, 1978; Carruthers, 1996). Contrary to such an account, phenomenological scholars have argued that social understanding relies on the direct perception of the other's behaviour as bodily *expressive* (Merleau-Ponty, 2012; Scheler, 1954). In other words, we experience others intuitively, directly and perceptually through our embodied engagement with them without the need to rely on processes of inference.

Phenomenologists have not only critically responded to theory of mind as an account of intersubjectivity but also as an account of autism (Fuchs, 2015; Zahavi & Parnas, 2003). In this way, critical assessment of theory of mind is a shared access point for both phenomenology and the double empathy problem to develop alternative accounts of social understanding that align with autistic experience. While phenomenological accounts of autism make important headway in taking seriously autistic experience for understanding autism, we are suspicious of the tendency of such accounts to lean on an understanding of autism as a pathology, albeit on a phenomenological level. In the following, we review and critically assess existing phenomenological approaches to autism. Drawing on insights of heterogeneity and reciprocity as emphasized by the double empathy problem, we flesh out two methodological lessons for future phenomenological research.

Lesson 1: Autistic embodiment and phenomenological justice

Similar to its central place and role in cognitive science more broadly, the theory of mind approach has strongly influenced the trajectory of autism research over the last thirty years. The theory of mind hypothesis of autism proposes that the nature of autism is an impairment in the cognitive mechanism responsible for inferring the mental states of others, rendering autistic persons unable to form a 'theory of mind' and ultimately leaving them blind to the emotions, intentions and beliefs of others (Baron-Cohen, 1995; Baron-Cohen et al., 1985; Leslie, 1994). Not only this, an important aspect of some theory of mind accounts is that our access to our own mental states is mediated by metarepresentation and inference in the same way as our knowledge of others' (e.g., Gopnik, 1993). As autistic persons are proposed to lack a theory of mind altogether, a controversial consequence of the theory of mind framework is that autistic persons lack experiential access to their own mental states as well as others' (Frith & Happé, 1999). As has been argued by McGeer (2005), such an account constructs autistic persons as unreliable knowers of their own experiences and would render it futile to consult subjective reports of autistic persons to gain knowledge of autism. The double empathy problem, in contrast, underscores the significance of stepping back from assumptions of cognitive deficiency and dysfunction, and instead recognize and pay attention to the entire social context itself, including the first-person perspective of the autistic interlocutors, when accounting for intersubjective salience and mismatches.

Yet, recognition of the first-person perspective of autistic individuals has been far from a staple in the history of autism research, which has from its inception been framed largely by medical and psychopathological approaches (American Psychiatric Association, 2013; Baron-Cohen, 2002; Baron-Cohen et al., 1985; Baron-Cohen et al., 1986). Critics of such approaches have stressed that autistic perspectives have historically been unduly dismissed in ways that undermine autistic agency and dignity. Most centrally, these dismissals of autistic perspectives have been contextualized and explored as instances of *epistemic injustice* (Catala et al., 2021; Chapman & Carel, 2022; Fricker, 2007). In this context, epistemic injustice refers to cases where autistic individuals' testimonies are unduly dismissed due to biases about autism, as well as cases where the very structure of certain communities' shared vocabulary warps its understanding of autism (Chapman & Carel,

2022). Concerning autistic sociability specifically, Catala et al. (2021) point out that the gap between first- and third-person accounts of the nature and character of autistic sociability, or lack thereof, is itself a source of epistemic harm as autistic needs for and approaches to social connectedness are discounted and discredited. As a consequence, autistic existence and especially clashes in social saliency between autistic and non-autistic individuals have often been framed by models of pathology rather than divergence and disability – a distinction of significance increasingly emphasized by neurodiversity researchers (Chapman, 2020).

Enter the phenomenological tradition, which, as outlined above, has prided itself on being a uniquely radical method that gives fundamental priority to the world as it appears before and correlates with subjectivity rather than starting from explanation, theory or superstition. Such a methodological framework would seem a suitable starting point from which to engage more fully with autistic experiences of and approaches to social interaction. In this context, phenomenological scholars have argued that the defining feature of autism is not an impaired ability to represent the mental states of others as theory of mind would have it – that is, a higher-order cognitive problem of metarepresentation – but rather a disturbance on the pre-reflective level of subjective and intersubjective experience. Here, Thomas Fuchs focuses on autism as *'a disorder of primary or embodied intersubjectivity'* (Fuchs, 2015, p. 196, italics in original), which has also been argued by Shaun Gallagher to arise through sensorimotor problems affecting social interaction already at the level of primary intersubjectivity (Gallagher, 2004). According to Till Grohmann, such sensorimotor problems can be understood as transformations of a person's bodily intentionality, indicating that *'in autism the intentional body has less plasticity and fewer capacities to creatively adapt to new bodily tasks'* (Grohmann, 2018a, p. 7).

According to Dan Zahavi and Josef Parnas (2003, see also Zahavi, 2005), such disturbances at the level of embodiment and embodied self-awareness are at the root of autistic persons' difficulty with intuitively and immediately grasping the emotional expressions of other persons, forcing them to depend on more reflexively driven and cognitively laborious strategies for understanding others. Concerning social experience in autism, Valeria Bizzari (2018) similarly argues that autism is a disturbance on the level of intercorporeality and interaffectivity with the consequence of rendering autistic persons unable to feel complex social emotions such as shame (Bizzari & Spremberg, 2019). Focusing on empathy as an intentional act that allows for the experience of another person as a subject, Kathleen Haney proposes that autistic persons are unable to engage in empathic acts of consciousness, and consequently, that they are trapped in a solipsistic world of 'mere things' (Haney, 2013, p. 49).

While dealing with autistic experiences and subjectivity as their central object of study, available phenomenological accounts of autism are often firmly situated in a psychopathological framework committed to exploring the nature of autistic disturbances. Such a framework runs the risk of retaining the basic idea of autism as a social impairment. Notwithstanding profound differences in how knowledge of autism is developed and founded, one of the main differences between the available phenomenological framework and the predominant theory of mind hypothesis is the question of *'where the impairment lies'* (Bizzari, 2018, p. 161); on a higher-order cognitive level or on the level of embodied intersubjectivity. That is, while subjectivity and embodiment are taken seriously as conceptual frameworks for understanding autistic difficulties navigating social settings, the need remains to critically rethink phenomenological approaches to autism in a way that takes the concept of diversity as a basis for understanding such notions.

Another prominent feature of the above summarized phenomenological accounts of autism is that they are rarely, or only sporadically, based on empirical investigation of actual autistic experiences. That is, phenomenology functions primarily as a conceptual framework for clarifying core notions related to the thematic focus of the analyses in question, such as affectivity, bodily intentionality, intersubjectivity, etc. In effect, the available phenomenological framework for understanding autism seems aimed more at conceptual analysis rather than committed to empirical exploration, and autism is often discussed as a psychopathological concept rather than an empirically experienced phenomenon.

Lending weight to autistic perspectives, we suggest, is pivotal for phenomenological researchers, whether hermeneutic, existential or more structurally motivated, as well as whether mostly conceptual or at least in part data-driven. As expressed by the double empathy problem, when it comes to autistic perspectives on sociality, it is of great importance not to miss out on insights concerning the ways in which autistic persons actually do experience and navigate social settings, albeit in possible, qualitatively different ways, rather than inheriting the supposition that autism is characterized by social impairment.

In this regard, future phenomenological research stands to benefit from engaging more directly with the double empathy problem and its tenets of heterogeneity and reciprocity. Here, the core idea that heterogeneity in how autistic and non-autistic persons experience the world can be the cause of breakdowns of reciprocal social understanding necessitates a fuller understanding of autistic experience and subjectivity from a first-person perspective. By stressing the heterogeneous manners in how individuals, whether autistic or not, meet each other and make sense of each other, the double empathy problem emphasizes that what might be taken to be breakdowns or deficiencies on the side of the autistic individual, can actually be attributed to disjunctures in the aforementioned heterogeneity rather than mere deficiency on the side of any one social interlocutor. For a fuller picture of why autistic and non-autistic individuals can struggle understanding each other, seriously considering the diversity that characterizes social understanding is therefore essential. If phenomenological autism research is to accurately reflect autistic subjectivity and intersubjectivity, and afford autistic persons epistemic justice, autistic perspectives themselves need to be afforded what we might call *phenomenological justice*: they need to be treated as, phenomenologically speaking, functional expressions of (inter)subjectivity in their full richness and nuance (see also Donnellan et al., 2013).

In other words, to more veridically describe autistic (inter)subjectivity, phenomenological researchers need to recognize and consider especially the lived, embodied perspectives of actual, autistic individuals in full richness and nuance. The connection between embodiment and the double empathy problem is notably clear, and both concepts have been 'eclectically' explored in a shared context (Milton, 2014). As a concept that in various ways and different degrees stresses the significance of the sensing, practical and felt body to our sense- or meaning-making capabilities in the world and around others, embodiment has notably seen an increased prevalence within autism research over the last decade (Boldsen, 2022a; Boldsen, 2022b; de Jaegher, 2013; Krueger, 2021a; Krueger, 2021b), with researchers emphasizing the significance of *autistic styles* of embodiment to the often divergent ways in which autistic individuals navigate and make sense of the world and its social spaces compared to non-autistic persons. However, as pointed out in our discussion of phenomenological approaches to autism, it is crucial to be mindful of how the distinction between disturbance and diversity is negotiated in one's account of the autistic body. In other words, differences in autistic embodiment are not expressive of malfunctioning sensory and motor systems but profound variance in how the world is felt and made sense of on a basic bodily level.

Embodied perspectives on autism are significant because they allow autism researchers to explore a range of questions hitherto ignored (see de Jaegher, 2013). With the double empathy problem in mind, embodied perspectives allow autism researchers to, for example, approach the social disjunctures and difficulties that arise between autistic and non-autistic interlocutors with an eye towards embodied heterogeneity, and to consider the interactional impact of these differences on the social salience of the encounter. Just as the double empathy problem emphasizes overlaps in social expectations and norms for social salience, so too classical phenomenological contributors have stressed the significance of *bodily familiarity* between interlocutors for social salience (Husserl, 2001, pp. 455, 475–476; Merleau-Ponty, 2012, p. 370; Stein, 1989, p. 66; see also Ekdahl, 2023; Zahavi, 2014). Recognizing the importance of bodily familiarity for social understanding is furthermore a central methodological task for phenomenological autism researchers as heterogeneous styles of embodied expression and communication may hinder the immediate understanding between researcher and research participant.

The double empathy problem stands as a reminder that researchers looking to phenomenologically investigate autistic perspectives need to cultivate an awareness of the ground from which their conceptual or structural investigations proceed. The veridicality of phenomenological accounts of autistic embodiment and bodily familiarity is centrally dependent on the degree to which they are grounded upon actual autistic perspectives. It is thus worthwhile to consider relevant, first-person-driven sources of autistic embodiment and the manners in which they are capable of affording autistic persons phenomenological justice. Below, we discuss three sources, while again emphasizing the necessity of engaging with these as intact expressions of subjectivity in their full richness rather than as expressions of underlying impairment regardless of phenomenological level.

First, autistic autoethnographic studies and similar first-person-based research drawing on one's own lived experiences as an autistic person may draw out phenomenological insights. While not necessarily engaging directly with phenomenological theory and method, such accounts have highlighted, from a first-person perspective, the meaning of embodiment for the experience of autism while at the same discussing the autistic body as a normative and ideological site (Yergeau, 2013).

Second, autistic autobiographies offer a wealth of insight on autistic embodiment, subjectivity and intersubjectivity (Gerland, 1996; Grandin, 1996; Lawson, 2001; Mukhopadhyay, 2011; Prince-Hughes, 2004; Tammet, 2007; Williams, 1992). While researchers should be careful of the danger of tokenizing segments of written accounts of autism in support of general theories of autism, autistic autobiographies offer the possibility of in-depth phenomenological engagement with autistic lives as singular experiences are described in the context of larger life-narratives. Thus, autistic autobiographies may present a wealth of nuance and depth, including by emphasizing the felt, bodily dimensions of autistic existence.

Third, interview studies that adopt a qualitative and phenomenological research design may elicit highly detailed and rich descriptions of autistic experiences, provided they strive to embrace an empathetic second-person perspective towards the first-person perspectives of the autistic informants. As stated previously, the empathetic encounter between non-autistic researcher and autistic person can itself be marred by double empathy problems, including the researcher failing to grasp divergent forms of communicative pacing and expressivity, as well as underestimating autistic social capability. Taking these issues into consideration on a practical level presupposes a certain degree of bodily and social familiarity between interviewer and informant(s) – something which itself depends on the researcher(s) acquiring familiarity with autistic culture and embodiment through exposure and interaction.

Regardless of which of the above three entry points for phenomenologically studying autism one chooses, we want to emphasize the importance of striving toward autistic participation in the research process to ensure the relevance of the research conducted for autistic persons themselves and the resonance of analyses and results with actual autistic experiences and perspectives (see, for example, Pellicano et al., 2022). When dealing with written accounts, such as autoethnographies and autobiographies, participation can also mean allowing the themes and problems raised by the text itself to shape the object of research. This also serves to highlight the premise that conducting phenomenological research with autistic persons also means giving up some of one's power over the object of study. That is, as a non-autistic autism researcher, one should not attempt to be able to set the agenda completely. In the following, we will discuss this issue from the conceptual point of view of how phenomenology itself should be open to autistic participation and impact in theoretical analyses.

Lesson 2: A critical phenomenology of autism

We have so far argued that, from a historical perspective, phenomenological research has often failed to approach autism and autistic intersubjectivity as expressions of subjective and intersubjective diversity. To remedy this, following the heterogeneous picture of intersubjectivity expressed by the double empathy problem, we have argued that phenomenology needs to engage in a richer and more nuanced manner with actual, first-person lived perspectives of autistic persons, with an eye especially toward autistic embodiment. This is important, we have argued, if phenomenological justice is to be afforded autistic subjectivity and intersubjectivity, and, relatedly, if phenomenological accounts of autism are to merit descriptive and analytic veridicality.

In this regard, a significant weakness of failing to afford phenomenological justice to autistic persons is that it is simultaneously a relinquishment of phenomenology's own stated, transcendental ambition of accounting for *subjectivity per se* (Merleau-Ponty, 2012). That is to say, phenomenological approaches to autism and autistic intersubjectivity starting out from assumptions of pathology or deficiency risk treating autistic perspectives as already distinct or separate from ('normal') subjectivity, rather than as adding phenomenological nuance and complexity to the overall picture. When this happens, autistic perspectives are, in lieu of in different ways diverging from classical phenomenological accounts of (neurotypical) subjectivity, notably not treated as expressive of robust or functional subjectivity. In this way, distinct but not separate from Lesson 1, likewise correlated with the heterogeneous and neurodiversity-affirming tenets of the double empathy problem, is a second, overarching methodological lesson for phenomenological researchers which merits further consideration.

Phenomenological research aspiring to afford phenomenological justice to autistic perspectives presupposes not only an increased mindfulness of *how* autism and autistic perspectives are deployed as neurodivergent cases of embodied subjectivity and intersubjectivity, but also the degree to which such neurodivergent perspectives are allowed to feed back into and shape the deployed phenomenological frameworks and concepts themselves. Methodologically speaking, phenomenological researchers need to cultivate a mindfulness of the implied power structure that lies in the intersection between their chosen phenomenological insights deployed as an analytical framework, and autism as the case to be analysed using said framework. If the deployed phenomenological framework is treated too rigidly as a range of insights into otherwise normal or robust subjectivity, this, methodologically speaking, leaves little room for heterogeneous or neurodiverse expansion or refinement on the side of the phenomenological framework itself when confronted with divergent forms of subjectivity that might not comply with classical, phenomenological accounts of subjectivity and intersubjectivity. In other words, a consequence of placing one's phenomenological framework on a pedestal and treating autistic subjectivity and intersubjectivity as expressions of deficiency from the perspective of said pedestal is that the phenomenological framework itself is placed in an insulated position when it comes to actually engaging with and learning from autistic perspectives. Put simply, if phenomenological research is to claim descriptive authority on subjectivity and its correlation with the world and others, it needs to recognize subjectivity and intersubjectivity – in all its facticity – as much more heterogeneous or neurodiverse than has historically been the case.

Allowing neurodiverse perspectives into the phenomenological fold of subjectivity in a manner that might inform classical, phenomenological concepts opens up a rich array of new questions and considerations for phenomenological researchers to consider and explore. Following the double empathy problem, phenomenological concepts previously deployed in the context of autism and empathy research, often to showcase supposed deficiencies in autistic social capabilities, can themselves be placed under a novel critical light. We might, as an example, reflect critically on the assumed normality of neurotypical styles of embodiment implied in phenomenological analyses, and instead recognize and make room for the significance of autistic styles of embodiment (de Jaegher, 2013). For example, using autobiographical accounts, Grohmann (2018b) highlights how autistic persons' experiences of sensory absorption presents phenomenology with a non-objectifying form of perception. We might let such insights *expand* classical phenomenological descriptions of the lived body as a structural feature of subjectivity, but a structural feature with a multitude of neurodiverse expressions.

Treating autistic perspectives and experiences as expressions of subjective diversity not only allows phenomenological researchers to expand and refine classical, phenomenological concepts and frameworks, it also allows researchers to appreciate the often-disabling impact of neurotypical norms and spaces on autistic existence. As an example, building on extensive fieldwork and in-depth interviews with autistic adolescents and young adults, Sofie Boldsen (2022a; 2022b) has described alternative forms of social experience and practice in autism that both question the assumed psychopathological division between 'social' and 'non-social' dimensions of autism as well as the philosophically assumed primacy of the embodied face-to-face encounter for a sense of social connectedness. In this context, prolonged engagement with autistic persons can enable a reconsideration of both fundamental understandings of what autism is in the field of psychiatry, but also the phenomenological structures of embodiment, perception and intersubjectivity that one relies on for developing such understandings.

Another example that focuses specifically on autism in relation to the normativity and politics of space is Joel Krueger's (2021b) phenomenological analysis of the experiences of disorientation that can emerge when, for example, autistic persons need to navigate neurotypical spaces and norms. Krueger's phenomenological approach notably does not start out from assumptions of pathology on the side of the autistic person, but instead explores the disruptive and disorienting effects of being an autistic body in spaces dominated by neurotypical norms and design. As similarly emphasized by the double empathy problem, neurotypicality is generally the name of the game when it comes to society's social expectations and shared social spaces, for which reason clashes with autistic styles of embodiment are often unfairly treated as a result of dysfunctionality on the side of the autistic person. In this way, acknowledging the place and role of autistic embodiment can importantly illuminate significant, overlooked features of neurotypical embodiment too, including its pre-reflective, oft-assumed *normality* on the side of the neurotypical person – continuously reaffirmed by the very neurotypical norms and spaces themselves.

We here suggest that phenomenological researchers stand to benefit from drawing on objections similarly raised by critical and feminist phenomenologists (Ahmed, 2006; Butler, 1988; Fisher, 2010; Marder, 2014; Young, 1980). Critical phenomenology as a multifarious movement has often sought inspiration from queer theory, critical race theory and feminist thought, taking as its departure people on *'the margins of society: for example, people of colour and queer people'* (Dyring, 2020). In the context of autism specifically, phenomenological research has long had a vested interest in exploring real-life cases of divergence, but usually to ascertain invariant features of 'normal' subjectivity. This has traditionally been done under the heading of *factual variation* (Froese & Gallagher 2010; Gallagher 2005), a suggested methodological supplement or alternative to phenomenology's imaginatively grounded cousin *eidetic variation*. Whereas the latter was intended by early phenomenologists as a process whereby the phenomenologist uses their free, imaginative faculties to zoom in on structural or invariant features of subjectivity, factual variation instead revolves around phenomenologists seeking out empirical cases to probe these otherwise imaginatively designated invariant features. In this way, the phenomenological motivation for engaging with factual variations is straightforwardly that our imaginative faculties are limited; that the world and others often surprise, resist and challenge the limits of our imagination. In this regard, non-autistic phenomenological researchers' faculties of imagination are arguably a highly limited source of insight when it comes to grasping autistic (inter)subjectivity in all its richness and diversity.

A related approach outlined by Anthony Fernandez revolves around considering the subject matter of phenomenology as consisting of three layers: existentials, modes and prejudices (Fernandez, 2017). Here, empirical cases, such as autism, present particular modes that potentially enable *'general insights regarding the structure of the existential to which the mode belongs'* (Fernandez, 2017, p. 3555). In this context, autistic modes of social engagement may productively enlighten the study of the general features of intersubjectivity as a fundamental structure of existence. While our approach here is much in line with this proposal, more work needs to be done in order to develop it into a more concrete methodological strategy. One suggestion offered by Havi Carel is using illness or pathology more generally as phenomenological tools that potentially reveal the full spectrum of human experience by adding to 'normal' experiences of, for example, embodiment and intersubjectivity (Carel, 2021). Notably, Carel's account relies on a conception of illness as a process of 'falling ill', understood as a change or a modification of a person's habituated way of being in the world that invites reflexive attention to tacitly assumed norms of experience and embodiment. However, autism is not an illness, and it is futile to understand autism as something that 'happens' to a person (see Martiny, 2015, for a parallel critique of phenomenological approaches to disability).

As factual variation, rather than exploring and analysing autistic experiences with an eye toward identifying pathology, dysfunction or deficiency in the hopes of more clearly ascertaining 'normal', non-autistic (inter)subjectivity and embodiment, we suggest that autistic embodied experiences be deployed as factual variations of *(inter)bodily diversity* (Boldsen, 2023). Following the critical phenomenological writings of Gayle Salamon (2010), the challenge for future phenomenological autism research is thus to account, in a non-pathologizing manner, for autistic bodies which might manifest intersubjectivity in ways that 'exceed or confound' assumed normality. In the spirit of the double empathy problem, future phenomenological autism research, in short, needs to be better at accommodating and learning from autistic forms of intersubjectivity.

References

Ahmed, S. (2006). *Queer Phenomenology: Orientations, Objects, Others*. Duke University Press Books.

American Psychiatric Association (2013). *Diagnostic and Statistical Manual of Mental Disorders* (5th ed.). American Psychiatric Publishing. https://doi.org/10.1176/appi.books.9780890425596

Baron-Cohen, S. (1995). *Mindblindness. An Essay on Autism and Theory of Mind.* The MIT Press. https://doi.org/10.7551/mitpress/4635.001.0001

Baron-Cohen, S. (2002). The extreme male brain theory of autism. *Trends in Cognitive Sciences* 6(6), 248–254. https://doi.org/10.1016/S1364-6613(02)01904-6

Baron-Cohen, S., Leslie, A. M., & Frith, U. (1985). Does the autistic child have a "theory of mind"? *Cognition, 21*(1), 37–46. https://doi.org/10.1016/0010-0277(85)90022-8

Baron-Cohen, S., Leslie, A. M., & Frith, U. (1986). Mechanical, behavioural and I = intentional understanding of picture stories in autistic children. *British Journal of Developmental Psychology, 4*(2), 113–125. https://doi.org/10.1111/j.2044-835X.1986.tb01003.x

Bizzari, V. (2018). 'Like in a shell': Interaffectivity and social cognition in Asperger's Syndrome. *Thaumàzein/Rivista di Filosofia, 6*, 158–179.

Bizzari, V. & Spremberg, A. (2019). Shame as a resonant emotion: The case of autism spectrum disorder. *Rivista de Filosofia Aurora, 31*(54). https://doi.org/10.7213/1980-5934.31.054.ds02

Boldsen, S. (2022a). Material encounters: A phenomenological account of social interaction in autism. *Philosophy, Psychiatry, & Psychology, 29*(3), 191–208. https://doi.org/10.1353/ppp.2022.0039

Boldsen, S. (2022b). Autism and the sensory disruption of social experience. *Frontiers in Psychology, 13*, 874268. https://doi.org/10.3389/fpsyg.2022.874268

Boldsen, S. (2023). Autisme, fænomenologi og kropslig diversitet. In S. Køppe, J. Toft, & H. Winther (Eds.), *Krop-psyke* (pp. 181–208). Hans Reitzels Forlag.

Butler, J. (1988). Performative acts and gender constitution: An essay in phenomenology and feminist theory. *Theatre Journal, 40*(4), 519–531. https://doi.org/10.2307/3207893

Carel, H. (2021). Pathology as a phenomenological tool. *Continental Philosophy Review, 54*(2), 201–217. https://doi.org/10.1007/s11007-021-09538-9

Carruthers, P. (1996). Simulation and self-knowledge: A defence of the theory-theory. In P. Carruthers, & P. K. Smith (Eds.), *Theories of Theories of Mind* (pp. 22–38). Cambridge University Press.

Catala, A., Faucher, L., & Poirier, P. (2021). Autism, epistemic injustice, and epistemic disablement: A relational account of epistemic agency. *Synthese, 199*, 9013–9039. https://doi.org/10.1007/s11229-021-03192-7

Chapman, R. (2020). Defining neurodiversity for research and practice. In H. Bertilsdottir Rosqvist, N. Chown, & A. Stenning (Eds.), *Neurodiversity Studies: A New Critical Paradigm* (pp. 218–220). Routledge.

Chapman, R., & Carel, H. (2022). Neurodiversity, epistemic injustice, and the good human life. *Journal of Social Philosophy, 53*(4), 614–631. https://doi.org/10.1111/josp.12456

Chown, N. (2014). More on the ontological status of autism and double empathy. Disability & Society, 29(10), 1672–1676. https://doi.org/10.1080/09687599.2014.949625

Crompton, C. J., Ropar, D., Evans-Williams, C. V. M., Flynn, E. G., & Fletcher-Watson, S. (2020). Autistic peer-to-peer information transfer is highly effective. *Autism, 24*(7), 1704–1712. https://doi.org/10.1177/1362361320919286

de Jaegher, H. (2013). Embodiment and sense-making in autism. *Frontiers in Integrative Neuroscience, 7*, 15. https://doi.org/10.3389/fnint.2013.00015

Dennett, D. C. (2018). The fantasy of first-person science. In S. Wuppuluri and F. A. Doria (Eds.), *The Map and the Territory: Exploring the Foundations of Science, Thought and Reality* (pp. 455-473). Springer. https://doi.org/10.1007/978-3-319-72478-2_26

Donnellan, A. M., Hill, D. A., & Leary, M. R. (2013). Rethinking autism: Implications of sensory and movement differences for understanding and support. *Frontiers in Integrative Neuroscience, 6*, 124. https://doi.org/10.3389/fnint.2012.00124

Dyring, R. (2020). Critical phenomenology. In: *Oxford Research Encyclopedia of Anthropology*. https://doi.org/10.1093/acrefore/9780190854584.013.461

Ekdahl, D. (2023). The double empathy problem and the problem of empathy: Neurodiversifying phenomenology. *Disability & Society*, https://doi.org/10.1080/09687599.2023.2220180

Englander, M., & Morley, J. (2021). Phenomenological psychology and qualitative research. *Phenomenology and the Cognitive Sciences, 22*(1), 25–53. https://doi.org/10.1007/s11097-021-09781-8

Fernandez, A. V. (2017). The subject matter of phenomenological research: Existentials, modes, and prejudices. *Synthese, 194*(9), 3543–3562. https://doi.org/10.1007/s11229-016-1106-0

Fisher, L. (2010). Feminist phenomenological voices. *Continental Philosophical Review, 43*(1), 83–95. https://doi.org/10.1007/s11007-010-9132-y

Fricker, M. (2007). *Epistemic Injustice: Power and the Ethics of Knowing*. Oxford University Press. https://doi.org/10.1093/acprof:oso/9780198237907.001.0001

Frith, U., & Happé, F. (1999). Theory of mind and self-consciousness: What is it like to be autistic? *Mind & Language, 14*(1), 82–89. https://doi.org/10.1111/1468-0017.00100

Froese, T. & Gallagher, S., (2010). Phenomenology and artificial life: Toward a technological supplementation of phenomenological methodology. *Husserl Studies*, http://dx.doi.org/10.1007/s10743-010-9071-9

Fuchs, T. (2013). The phenomenology of affectivity. In K. W. M. Fulford, M. Davies, R. G. T. Gipps, G. Graham, J. Z. Sadler, G. Stanghellini, & T. Thornton (Eds.), *The Oxford Handbook of Philosophy and Psychiatry* (pp. 612–631). Oxford University Press. https//doi.org/10.1093/oxfordhb/9780199579563.013.0038

Fuchs, T. (2015). Pathologies of intersubjectivity in autism and schizophrenia. *Journal of Consciousness Studies*, 22(1), 191–214.

Gallagher, S. (2004). Understanding interpersonal problems in autism: Interaction theory as an alternative to theory of mind. *Philosophy, Psychiatry, & Psychology, 11*(3), 199–217. https://doi.org/10.1353/ppp.2004.0063

Gallagher, S. (2005). *How the Body Shapes the Mind*. Oxford University Press. https://doi.org/10.1093/0199271941.001.0001

Gallagher, S., & Zahavi, D. (2008). *The Phenomenological Mind: An Introduction to Philosophy of Mind and Cognitive Science*. Routledge. https://doi.org/10.4324/9780203086599

Gerland, G. (1996). *A Real Person: Life on the Outside*. Souvenir Press.

Giorgi, A. (2009). *The Descriptive Phenomenological Method in Psychology: A Modified Husserlian Approach*. Duquesne University Press.

Gopnik, A. (1993). How we know our own minds: The illusion of first-person knowledge of intentionality. *Behavioral and Brain Sciences, 16*, 1–14. https://doi.org/10.1017/S0140525X00028636

Grandin, T. (1996). *Thinking in Pictures: And Other Reports from My Life with Autism*. Vintage.

Grohmann, T. (2018a). A phenomenological account of sensorimotor difficulties in autism: Intentionality, movement, and proprioception. *Psychopathology, 50*(6), 408–415. https://doi.org/10.1159/000481949

Grohmann, T. (2018b). Hypnotic experience and the autism spectrum disorder: A phenomenological investigation. *Phenomenology and the Cognitive Sciences, 17*(5), 889–909. https://doi.org/10.1007/s11097-018-9563-1

Haney, K. M. (2013). Edith Stein and autism. In L. Embree, & T. Nenon (Eds.). *Husserl's Idéen*. Springer.

Heasman, B., & Gillespie, A. (2019). Neurodivergent Intersubjectivity: Distinctive features of how autistic people create shared understanding. *Autism, 23*(4), 910–921. https://doi.org/10.1177/1362361318785172

Husserl, E. (1983). *Ideas Pertaining to a Pure Phenomenology and to a Phenomenological Philosophy: First Book: General Introduction to a Pure Phenomenology*. Springer.

Husserl, E. (2001). *Zur Phänomenologie der Intersubjektivität: Texte aus dem Nachlass Erster Teil: 1905–1920: 13*. Edited by I. Kern. Softcover reprint of the original 1st ed. 1973 edition. Springer.

Krueger, J. (2021a). Enactivism, other minds, and mental disorders. *Synthese, 198*(S1), 365–389. https://doi.org/10.1007/s11229-019-02133-9

Krueger, J. (2021b). Finding (and losing) one's way: Autism, social impairments, and the politics of space. *Phenomenology & Mind , 21*(December), 20–33. https://doi.org/10.17454/pam-2102

Lawson, W. (2001). *Understanding and Working with the Spectrum of Autism: An Insider's View*. Jessica Kingsley Publishers.

Leslie, A. M. (1987). Pretense and representation: The origins of "theory of mind". *Psychological Review, 94*(4), 412-426. https://doi.org/10.1037/0033-295X.94.4.412

Leslie, A. M. (1994). Pretending and believing: Issues in the theory of ToMM. *Cognition, 50*(1–3), 211–238. https://doi.org/10.1016/0010-0277(94)90029-9

Marder, M. (2014). *Phenomena--critique--logos: The Project of Critical Phenomenology*. Rowman & Littlefield International.

Martiny, K. M. M. (2015). *Embodying Investigations of Cerebral Palsy: A Case of Open Cognitive Science*. Det Humanistiske Fakultet.

McGeer, V. (2005). Out of the mouths of autistics: Subjective report and its role in cognitive theorising. In A. Brook & K. Akins (Eds.), *Cognition and the Brain: The Philosophy and Neuroscience Movement* (pp. 98–130). Cambridge University Press.

Merleau-Ponty, M. (2012). *Phenomenology of Perception* (Trans. D. Landes). Routledge.

Milton, D. (2014). Embodied sociality and the conditioned relativism of dispositional diversity. *Autonomy, the Critical Journal of Interdisciplinary Autism Studies, 1*(3), 1–7.

Morrison, K. E., DeBrabander, K. M., Jones, D.R., Faso, D. J., Ackerman, R.A., and Sasson, N. J. (2020). Outcomes of real-world social interaction for autistic adults paired with autistic compared to typically developing partners. *Autism*, *24*(5), 1067–1080. https://doi.org/10.1177/1362361319892701

Mukhopadhyay, T. R. (2011). *How Can I Talk If My Lips Don't Move: Inside My Autistic Mind.* Arcade Publishing.

Pellicano, E., Lawson, W., Hall, G., Mahony, J., Lilley, R., Heyworth, M., Clapham, H., & Yudell, M. (2022). "I knew she'd get it, and get me": Participants' perspectives of a participatory autism research project. *Autism in Adulthood*, *4*(2), 120–129. https://doi.org/10.1089/aut.2021.0039

Premack, D., & Woodruff, G. (1978). Does the chimpanzee have a theory of mind? *Behavioral and Brain Sciences*, *1*(4), 515–526. https://doi.org/10.1017/S0140525X00076512

Prince-Hughes, D. (2004). *Songs of the Gorilla Nation: My Journey through Autism.* Crown.

Ravn, S., & Høffding, S. (2016). The promise of 'sporting bodies' in phenomenological thinking: How exceptional cases of practice can contribute to develop foundational phenomenological concepts. *Qualitative Research in Sport, Exercise and Health*, *9*, 1–13. https://doi.org/10.1080/2159676X.2016.1187663

Salamon, G. (2010). *Assuming a Body: Transgender and Rhetorics of Materiality.* Columbia University Press.

Sass, L., & Parnas, J. (2003). Schizophrenia, consciousness, and the self. *Schizophrenia Bulletin*, *29*(3), 427–444. https://doi.org/10.1093/oxfordjournals.schbul.a007017

Scheler, M. (1954). *The Nature of Sympathy* (Trans. P. Heath). Routledge and Kegan Paul.

Smith, J. A., & Osborn, M. (2004). Interpretative phenomenological analysis. In G. M. Breakwell (Ed.), *Doing Social Psychology Research* (pp. 229–254). Blackwell Publishing; British Psychological Society.

Stein, E. (1989). *On the Problem of Empathy* (Trans. W. Stein, 3rd ed.). ICS Publications.

Tammet, D. (2007). *Born on a Blue Day: Inside the Extraordinary Mind of an Autistic Savant.* Simon and Schuster.

Tanaka, S. (2015). Intercorporeality as a theory of social cognition. *Theory & Psychology*, *25*(4), 455–472. https://doi.org/10.1177/0959354315583035

Varela, J. F. & Shear, J. (1999). First-person methodologies: What, why, how? *Journal of Consciousness Studies*, *6*(2-3), 1–14.

Williams, D. (1992). *Nobody Nowhere: The Remarkable Autobiography of an Autistic Girl.* Doubleday.

Yergeau, M. (2013). Clinically significant disturbance: On theorists who theorise theory of mind. *Disability Studies Quarterly*, *33*(4). https://doi.org/10.18061/dsq.v33i4.3876

Young, I. M. (1980). Throwing like a girl: A phenomenology of feminine body comportment motility and spatiality. *Human Studies*, *3*, 137–156. https://doi.org/10.1007/BF02331805

Zahavi, D. (2005). *Subjectivity and Selfhood: Investigating the First-Person Perspective.* The MIT Press. https://doi.org/10.7551/mitpress/6541.001.0001

Zahavi, D. (2014). *Self and Other: Exploring Subjectivity, Empathy, and Shame.* Illustrated edition. Oxford University Press.

Zahavi, D., & Parnas, J. (2003). Conceptual problems in infantile autism research: Why cognitive science needs phenomenology. *Journal of Consciousness Studies*, 10(9–10), 53–71.

Chapter 5:

How *Not* to Solve the Double Empathy Problem: Neurodiversity Lite and the Fake(d) Empathy Problem

Marjorie Désormeaux-Moreau and Amandine Catala

In this chapter, we explore the challenges and consequences of the Double Empathy Problem in the context of diversity, equity and inclusion (DEI), as well as within neuroinclusion initiatives. We contend that the Double Empathy Problem is not only a matter of interpersonal communication, but also a source of epistemic injustice and systemic oppression for Autistic[3] people and other neurominoritized groups. Drawing on our own experiences as Autistic scholars, advocates and activists, we present two microstories that illustrate how the Double Empathy Problem can lead to the exclusion and marginalization of Autistic experiences and perspectives in various contexts. We then analyse how these stories reveal the phenomenon of Neurodiversity Lite, which involves a superficial and tokenistic use of neurodiversity-related concepts, a display of fake(d) empathy, and a lack of genuine respect and understanding for Autistic perspectives. We conclude by offering some suggestions on how to overcome the Double Empathy Problem and foster genuine neuroinclusion.

3 In this chapter, we use the term 'Autistic' (upper case 'A') when referring to individuals. This choice reflects the deep connection of the chapter's content to our own experiences and identities as Autistic academics engaged in advocacy work. In capitalizing the word, we aim to emphasize the importance of moving away from the dominant pathologizing perspective of autism, and to centre autism as an integral part of identity and culture, which is crucial to the equity and justice lens discussed.

Ideal for the role, but only if you conform to our way of doing and thinking: Two microstories

First microstory: A non-inclusive diversity committee

Imagine that you have been asked to serve on a committee specifically as an Autistic person. This might be an institutional committee devoted to diversity, equity and inclusion (DEI) or a local committee focusing on disability in general or on autism in particular. The people chairing the committee are not disabled or autistic, and neither are most other committee members. Committee meetings take place online on Teams and all members are expected to always have their cameras on, or to provide a 'valid' reason if they do not. No one takes the time to ask what concrete measures might be taken to facilitate your inclusion as an Autistic person on the committee.

Over the course of a few months, the committee meets multiple times. At one point, one of the items on the agenda is the language that the committee, along with the institution or organization the committee is a part of, should use when referring to autism and Autistics. As an Autistic self-advocate who is attuned to the perspectives of Autistic communities, you explain that most Autistics prefer terms like 'Autistic person', 'neurodiversity' and 'neuronormativity',[4] and hence reject terms like 'autism spectrum disorder' (ASD), 'deficits' or 'people with autism'. An allistic person counters that they have an autistic child in their family who uses the term ASD. You suggest that perhaps the fact that this person is a child and that adults around them constantly refer to autism as ASD might explain why the child uses that term; and you point out that even if they were an adult, the term 'ASD' still would not reflect the preference of most Autistics. Another allistic person adds that terminological decisions should not be made by Autistic communities alone, but should instead be discussed jointly with allistics in a democratic manner. You explain that the choice of language is a matter of respecting the dignity and agency of Autistics, and that such respect should not be the object of a democratic vote, but is rather the precondition for any democratic deliberation. You are then cautioned that your insistence is not helping the case of Autistic people and instead alienates allistics, who should have an equal say in the matter. Another allistic person concludes the discussion by stating that changing the language we use takes time and asks you to be patient, arguing that it is unreasonable to expect swift changes, especially when *'there are so many other things to take care of'* besides language. The meeting ends, leaving you exhausted and knocked out by a terrible headache for the next 12 hours. This awful conversation occupies your thoughts for days and you dread the next meeting.

4 We understand neuronormativity as 'the prevalent, neurotypical set of assumptions, norms, and practices that construes [so-called] neurotypicality as the sole acceptable or superior mode of cognition, and that stigmatizes attitudes, behaviors, or actions that reflect neuroatypical modes of cognition as deviant or inferior. Neuronormative assumptions, norms, and practices uphold standards regarding, for example, (what is neurotypically considered) appropriate eye contact, facial expressions, prosody, conversational flow, processing, and responsiveness – all of which can be difficult for autistic individuals to understand, sense, or apply, due to neurocognitive differences' (Catala et al., 2021, p. 9016).

When you receive the meeting minutes a few weeks later, you are surprised to find that they do not include any of your contributions, even though you did partake in the conversation and took great care to be clear and to address the points under discussion. As usual, the email encourages committee members to reach out with any queries, so you contact the committee chair to inquire about this omission. Over a month later, you receive a response explaining that most of your input at that meeting was provided via the chat (which is true, as it is your preferred mode of communication in those meetings) but that committee members should contribute only orally, and that you cannot revisit points raised earlier in the conversation. This is all news to you, as no such guidelines were previously communicated to committee members. Perplexed, you ask if it would be possible to dedicate a moment at an upcoming meeting to discuss communication modalities, since, after all, you were recruited as an Autistic person, and Autistics often have preferences for certain communication modalities that may differ from those of allistics. You underline that addressing communication modalities is important, since the input of Autistic members will be excluded if their communication modalities are deemed inadequate. You are told, however, that this is not feasible as there is too much on the agenda already, and committee members are too busy to prolong the meeting or to add another meeting. Instead, you are 'graciously' offered the option to record a video of your thoughts for the committee, which committee members can then watch, if or when they have time. (At this point, readers might think that you cannot make that stuff up, and they would be right). After enduring similar experiences in subsequent meetings, you eventually decide to withdraw from the committee.

Second microstory: The emotional toll of neuronormative research on an Autistic evaluator

Now, imagine receiving an invitation to join a review committee for a pioneering research project. In this context, you act as an external reviewer and are responsible for evaluating the study proposal submitted by an interdisciplinary research team. Their research project is dedicated to the implementation of neuroinclusive educational strategies within the context of elementary education. Your expertise in participatory research, critical autism studies and critical disability studies has singled you out as an asset to the committee. As an Autistic person, your unique insight and perspectives are perceived has having the potential to enrich the committee's understanding and approach to the project.

Upon reviewing the research proposal, you are immediately struck by the choice of language. The terminology and concepts paint a pathologizing and deficit-oriented picture of neurominoritized students[5] as defective, a stark reminder of the misconceptions and

5 In this chapter, the concept of 'neurominoritized' refers to neurocognitive profiles that are often labeled as 'neurodivergent' (or 'neuroatypical'). This concept is to be contrasted with the concept of 'neuronormalized', which describes neurocognitive profiles that are often labeled as 'neurotypical'. These terms emphasize the power dynamics and the dimensions of privilege and marginalization that underlie the production and differentiation of neurocognitive categories (Catala, 2023).

biases that persist in society. You also notice numerous conceptual and methodological inconsistencies. The argument directly contradicts neuroinclusive principles and does not align with the neurodiversity paradigm. Despite the research team's claim to the contrary, the proposed study does not reflect a participatory approach. These inconsistencies, glaringly apparent to you, indicate a fundamental misunderstanding of the subject matter and a lack of rigour in the research methodology. Despite encountering several passages that are deeply hurtful and invalidating – both for yourself and for your Autistic peers, you take the time to formulate constructive feedback. You end up dedicating an entire day – a significant rearrangement of your schedule, as you had not anticipated devoting so much time to this evaluation – to articulate your feedback, elucidate the concepts involved, provide resources and references, and suggest concrete avenues for improvement. You pinpoint prejudicial formulations and propose alternatives; you explain the conceptual inconsistencies between the neuroinclusive approaches the team claims to follow and the content of educational strategies it proposes to implement and document; and you highlight methodological limitations while suggesting ways to avoid them. When you eventually meet with the other reviewers to discuss the research project, you discover that all other members are neuronormalized professors who lack experiential or scientific knowledge regarding inclusive education or participatory research. All three of them consider the research proposal to be excellent, whereas you deem it mediocre. You spend a considerable amount of time explaining your perspective, relying on methodological and conceptual arguments, but it feels like you are talking to a brick wall. The emotional labour of struggling to secure recognition and uptake from your fellow committee members is exhausting, leaving you feeling isolated, misunderstood and invalidated.

At one point, an evaluator dryly responds, '*It's ironic that as an Autistic person, you perceive this project as a failure. You, of all people, should understand the significance and challenge of such a research project.*' This statement strikes a nerve. It's not just a dismissal of your expertise; it's a negation of your identity. It feels like a betrayal, a devaluation of both your lived experience as well as your professional and scientific expertise. The sheer discrepancy between your stance and that of all other members eventually leads you to question and doubt your conclusions, prompting you to reassess the whole proposal. Perhaps, you think, you were overly critical. Upon revisiting the research proposal, however, it still seems just as problematic. At the next committee meeting, you reassert your unfavourable evaluation of the project, elucidating your arguments once more, supplemented with a list of relevant readings. Some members concur that the project, as proposed, could benefit from your suggestions and it is decided that recommendations will be sent to the research team, inviting them to ensure their research is rooted in neuroinclusive approaches. When, a few days later, you receive (in bcc) the message sent to the research team, you are shocked to find that it conveys the exact opposite of everything you articulated during the meeting. Deeply disturbed, you ponder how this is possible. Did they pay any attention to what you said at the last meeting? Did they even read your written feedback? At this point, you begin to wonder whether, and at what cost, you could handle the emotional labour and the feelings of invalidation and discredit you are experiencing. You conclude that the best way to take care of yourself is to resign from the committee.

Neurodiversity Lite, the Double Empathy Problem, and epistemic injustice: Or how to understand what connects these two microstories

What do these two microstories have in common? How could things have gone so drastically wrong in committees explicitly dedicated to DEI, disability or autism? How could these committees, through their very modes of operation and the very articulation of their intentions, so thoroughly miss the core objectives of all equity and inclusion efforts? The short answer: Neurodiversity Lite, the Double Empathy Problem and epistemic injustice.

'Neurodiversity Lite': Surfing on a trendy concept

At first glance, one could assume that these two microstories are rooted in what Milton (2012) has called the Double Empathy Problem. Indeed, the Autistic committee members featured in each of the microstories, exhibit a distinct mode of communication from the other committee members. For instance, in both scenarios, they articulate their perspectives in writing. Moreover, their perspectives diverge from that of their colleagues, a divergence that is not solely attributable to their being Autistic and the intersection of their professional expertise with their experiential knowledge. This divergence also stems from their critical stance toward the traditionally individualistic, deficit-focused, neuronormative discourse and approaches prevalent in autism research. While explaining these microstories in terms of different communication preferences and perspectives is accurate to some extent (a point we will delve into later), interpreting them solely in these terms would be a reductive oversimplification. Upon closer scrutiny, it appears that what is at stake in both these microstories stems from what can be referred to as Neurodiversity Lite.

Neurodiversity Lite (Neumeier, 2018) refers to the superficial use of neurodiversity-related concepts as mere buzzwords. This approach outwardly proclaims a commitment to neuroinclusion, while simultaneously exhibiting a lack of any genuine interest in, engagement with, or substantial knowledge of, neurodiversity and neuroinclusion, as well as a reluctance to transform existing habits and practices. In other words, 'Neurodiversity Lite' is a purely performative, surface-level endeavour that seeks to enhance an institution or organization's reputation under the guise of diversity and inclusion, without making any substantial contribution to either. The key move, here, is to appear as though one cares. A central aspect of a Neurodiversity Lite approach is feigned empathy toward Autistics (and other neurominoritized individuals), without any genuine respect for neurodiversity, nor any understanding or compassion toward neurominoritization. Real empathy – *genuine empathy – would require acknowledging and valuing the experiences, needs and perspectives of Autistics*, which is glaringly absent in both microstories, where the opinions expressed by the Autistic committee members were entirely discredited and ignored, and their communicative needs were completely neglected. Under these circumstances, the inclusion of Autistic individuals on those committees seems to be merely symbolic and it appears that in both instances, they were recruited as a token gesture of inclusivity. Indeed, as Autistics, they were 'welcome' on the committee – serving to enhance the committee's image and 'tick the autism box', but only under the condition that their ideas conform to those of the other members. This leads us to conclude that the initiatives/committees described in the microstories were more driven by image-related (i.e., tokenistic) motives than by a sincere desire to effect change. These motives are intrinsically tied to a form of fake(d) empathy, which results in the adoption of pseudo-solutions, by individuals from the dominant group, unfortunately at the expense of those who are personally and directly impacted by DEI and the requirements of neuroinclusive practice. As Milton pointed out in 2012, when outlining the Double Empathy Problem, while autism has gained in public attention, Autistic people are still silenced from all but tokenistic participation. More than ten years later, silencing, tokenism and the exclusion of Autistic people contribute to the maintenance of epistemic injustices and the perpetuation of discriminative and oppressive practices. Rooted in tokenism, such exclusions exemplify an approach deeply rooted in a pity-charity dynamic rather than genuine empathy.

The Double Empathy Problem and the display of fake(d) empathy

The *Double Empathy Problem* can be observed in social interactions involving individuals with different dispositions, as illustrated in the two microstories we discussed. In each story, an Autistic individual's contributions to the group are grounded in their experiential, practical and scientific knowledge related to autism, marginalization, exclusion and other forms of injustice. Conversely, other members, who lack experiential knowledge of autism or disability in general, base their contributions on scientific or administrative knowledge. In both microstories, this knowledge is not only misaligned with the committee's mandate, but also stems from a biomedical and neuronormative understanding of autism. For instance, committee members in the first microstory include allistic human resources representatives, while committee members in the second microstory include researchers with expertise in didactics and education, who all exhibit a limited understanding of DEI-related concepts as well as a traditional and pathologizing understanding of autism. This dichotomy leads to a significant gap in communication preferences (Autistic versus allistic) and in understanding the issues at hand (deep and experiential for Autistics; superficial, unrelated or even erroneous knowledge for allistics). The absence of a shared understanding, particularly in relation to autism and equity, obstructs dialogue and interaction in both examples.

This is highly problematic, especially given the socially situated nature of communication and reciprocity – a fundamental premise of the Double Empathy Problem. Social interactions occur within contexts permeated by unequal power relations that cannot be ignored (Milton et al., 2022). Indeed, in our two microstories, Autistics were outnumbered (1:12 in the first microstory and 1:4 in the second), and their contributions to the committee were discredited. The diminished credibility given to Autistics by committee members, due to conscious or subconscious neuronormative biases, constitutes what is known as 'epistemic injustice'.

Epistemic injustice

Epistemic injustice is a type of injustice that a person faces specifically in their capacity as a knower or epistemic agent, for instance, as someone who produces, uses or transmits knowledge or information. Epistemic injustice occurs when a person is either inadequately consulted or believed, or inadequately represented or understood, due to individual, societal or institutional biases that result in unjustly reduced levels of credibility or intelligibility for members of non-dominant groups. In this context, the neuronormative biases that structure mainstream or dominant systems of knowledge production end up discrediting or rendering unintelligible the experiences and perspectives of Autistics. We contend that this is deeply problematic.

Consider the issue of using pathologizing and stigmatizing language to describe autism – terms such as disorder, deficits, deficiency, risk, suffers from, affected by, fix, cure, treatment and intervention – which is at work in both microstories. This language creates an aura of tragedy around autism, leading to two problematic implications. First, these terms contribute to a stigmatizing image of autism, which results in the misinterpretation and misrepresentation of Autistic individuals and perspectives in mainstream allistic society. Philosophers call this 'hermeneutical injustice' (Fricker, 2007), which captures a problem with the dominant *interpretation* of the experiences or situations of marginalized social groups. Second, the negative portrayal of Autistics as deficient human beings leads to the dismissal of their position on certain issues, because of conscious or subconscious prejudice on the part of their interlocutors. This phenomenon is known as 'testimonial injustice' (Fricker, 2007), where someone's testimony or contribution is not given the credibility it deserves due to conscious or subconscious biases on the part of their interlocutors. Both microstories are glaring cases of testimonial injustice, as Autistics in neither case are taken seriously due to neuronormative biases, and their experiences, needs and perspectives are utterly ignored.

Let's now examine the imposition of communication modalities, such as the emphasis on oral, synchronous communication and the prohibition of written, asynchronous modes of communication – as illustrated in the first microstory. Two further problems arise here. First, the Autistic member is not even consulted on the matter: they are not perceived as the kind of person who might have important and useful insight into this issue. This phenomenon is referred to as 'preemptive testimonial injustice' (Fricker, 2007), or as 'testimonial quieting' (Dotson, 2011), where members of minoritized groups are prevented from contributing to an exchange, which results in their silencing or quieting. Second, this imposition of communication modalities reflects neuronormative assumptions regarding how knowledge should be produced or transmitted, as well as who might be able to contribute and how. This is known as 'metaepistemic injustice' (Catala, 2020), or an injustice that concerns the biased and exclusionary ways in which we conceive of knowledge and knowers.

Moreover, both microstories illustrate how allistics expect Autistics to educate them about why certain habits and practices (such as pathologizing language or neuronormative communication modalities) are problematic, only to dismiss their concerns and leave the problem unaddressed. In other words, allistics expect Autistics to perform significant cognitive and emotional labour, and hence to spend valuable time and energy that they can then no longer invest in their own projects, while ultimately disregarding their input and leaving the system unchanged. This phenomenon – which involves a burden of proof, an opportunity cost, and scepticism resulting in indifference or inertia – has been called 'epistemic exploitation' (Berenstain, 2016).

Additionally, both microstories demonstrate how the concept of neurodiversity becomes extracted, appropriated and instrumentalized by an institution or organization to project an image of diversity and inclusion. However, this is done while detaching the concept from its community of origin, depoliticizing it to the point where it becomes virtually useless and ineffective for real change, while taking credit for the work or ideas of others, or profiting from them with little to no regard for the neurodiversity movement or its ideals. This encompasses several issues which philosophers have called 'epistemic extractivism' (Alcoff, 2022) and 'epistemic appropriation' (Davis, 2018).

Finally, in both microstories, the sole Autistic member eventually withdraws from the committee. However, this departure is more accurately characterized as forced (self-) exclusion rather than as a voluntary exit due to insidious discrimination. Indeed, in both stories the Autistic person leaves because they have learned from experience that their contributions will not be taken seriously due to neuronormative biases on the part of fellow committee members. In both stories, the person anticipates a lack of uptake on the part of their biased interlocutors, and hence decides not to engage as they otherwise would in a given conversation or exchange. This phenomenon is referred to as 'testimonial smothering' (Dotson, 2011).

From fake(d) empathy and tokenism to exclusion, epistemic injustices and perpetuating discriminative and oppressive practices

The Double Empathy Problem (Milton, 2012) has primarily been addressed as it emerges at the micro or individual level (e.g., between an Autistic and an allistic person) or at the meso or group level (e.g., between Autistics and allistics more generally). Much less attention, if any, has been paid to the Double Empathy Problem as it arises at the macro level of systems of knowledge production. When referring to systems of knowledge production, we mean institutions, practices and criteria that aim to define what constitutes knowledge, validate research methods or questions, and identify who is considered a legitimate holder and contributor of knowledge.

In the two microstories, the impact of the Double Empathy Problem is evident at the personal and interpersonal level. Autistics are often silenced, their perspectives sidelined, resulting in further harms. These 'misunderstandings' and the committee's lack of uptake negatively affected their physical well-being and mental health, took a significant emotional toll and generated doubts about the value of one's expertise as well as about their place and belonging within the committee and more broadly within the organization – all of which echoes the reflections of other authors (Camus et al., 2022; Milton et al., 2022). It is easy to grasp how these situations can also negatively impact the overall well-being, productivity and job satisfaction of the Autistics involved in these committees. Furthermore, such circumstances have likely tarnished their reputation within the organization, as other committee members may have erroneously assumed that their Autistic colleagues are difficult to collaborate with, leading to social isolation within the workplace and exacerbating exclusion. Moreover, withdrawing – or rather, being excluded – from their respective committees has likely resulted in missed opportunities for development or career advancement, as participation in committees often provides exposure to new ideas, skills and networks, which are crucial for career progression.

What is even more concerning, and potentially missed in a superficial reading of these stories, are the profound and far-reaching macro and societal consequences of the exclusionary practices at play in these microstories, as the committees in each case exerted significant influence over institutional rules and practices, as well as national or even international educational knowledge and practices. Both the 'misunderstandings' outlined above and a lack of openness led to the exclusion of Autistics from processes that could have influenced the very policies, rules, norms and expectations that often devalue, marginalize and penalize them. This exclusion thus amounts to testimonial injustice or quieting, and to hermeneutical marginalization.

Moreover, the power of these committees is not only epistemic, but also social and political. Indeed, the numerous and cascading implications and ramifications of their exclusion from these committees can easily be imagined. Some examples include the maintenance of neuronormative practices in schools and workplaces, which creates barriers for Autistic individuals, inducing stress and anxiety, and potentially hinders the pursuit of their interests and talents. Such obstacles can discourage, exclude or marginalize Autistic people from certain fields of study or work, reducing their potential and contribution. Furthermore, these obstacles contribute to reduced access to certain employment opportunities, leading to a scarcity of Autistic role models in various employment fields. This lack of representation in hiring, promotion and leadership roles limits the visibility, influence and empowerment of Autistic people in the workplace and society at large. Secondary harms/wrongs, such as the impact on income and purchasing power within Autistic communities, also arise from not considering Autistic perspectives in committees like those of the microstories. This can affect Autistic people and communities' quality of life, access to services and resources, and participation in civic and social activities, thereby creating economic and social disparities and inequalities.

Conclusion

This chapter began with two microstories, inspired by the experiences of the authors of this chapter, that suggest that the Double Empathy Problem is not only a matter of interpersonal communication, but also a source of epistemic injustice and systemic oppression for Autistic people and other neurominoritized groups. Specifically, we argued that these two microstories illustrate the approach of Neurodiversity Lite, which involves both fake(d) empathy and epistemic injustice.

By its very definition, Neurodiversity Lite remains a superficial enterprise. Indeed, both committees in our microstories thought they could tackle neurodiversity or DEI initiatives without recognizing that doing so fundamentally requires changing their current (neuronormative) presuppositions, habits and practices. Such changes cannot be implemented or realized without understanding neuronormativity and without taking into account the first-person experiences and perspectives of Autistics. Indeed, addressing questions of neurodiversity or DEI requires acknowledging that these are lived realities for minoritized groups, including neurominoritized individuals such as Autistics, and that dominant groups do not have direct access to that lived experience. Our social position (e.g., as allistic/neuronormalized or Autistic/neurominoritized) directly affects our experience of the world (e.g., of neuronormativity) and by extension our knowledge and understanding of the world: what we notice in it or not, what we find important and relevant or not, and so on. Whereas Autistics experience the negative effects of neuronormativity every day, neuronormalized people may not even notice it. This is because neuronormativity is not an obstacle that harms and marginalizes neuronormalized people: instead, it is a system that benefits and privileges them.

When our social position limits our experience and understanding of certain realities in this way, we must acknowledge that differently positioned others know more about these realities they experience every day. That is, we must recognize that our social position comes with epistemic limitations and adopt a posture of *epistemic humility*: i.e., acknowledge that there are certain things that we do not know, realize or understand because of our limited experience. When dominant groups fail to recognize their epistemic limitations and reject or resist the contributions of Autistics – as illustrated in our two microstories – they engage in active ignorance and display epistemic arrogance (Medina, 2013). By actively ignoring the perspectives of Autistics, including their understandings of the neuronormative world, neuronormalized people continue to marginalize Autistics and to render our perspectives incomprehensible or unintelligible, which is a case of hermeneutical injustice.

Because their active ignorance inherently involves a lack of understanding of Autistic perspectives, neuronormalized people continue to empathize only with members of their in-groups, who share similar positions, experiences and understandings. This sort of allistic echo-chamber, where genuine empathy is reserved for in-group members, serves to maintain the status quo of neuronormative power relations, while pretending to work toward neuroinclusion and displaying fake(d) empathy toward out-group members. Here we can appreciate the gap between empathy as a concept or an ideal, and empathy as applied and practiced in contexts that are characterized by unjust power relations, such as neuronormativity. This lack of genuine empathy toward differently situated others reinforces epistemic arrogance and vice versa.

Nevertheless, we firmly believe that we can collaboratively build a future where neurodiversity is not only acknowledged but also celebrated, where Autistics are not only tolerated but also truly valued, and where neuronormativity is not only scrutinized but also fundamentally transformed. Achieving this requires genuine empathy toward Autistics, which in turn can only be achieved through epistemic humility from neuronormalized individuals and communities. In other words, neuronormalized people must be willing to engage with and learn from Autistics and other neurominoritized people. This kind of engagement and learning is possible only when people acknowledge the different epistemic limitations and privileges that attach to different social positions. If we want to work together to challenge and change the neuronormative system that oppresses and excludes neurominorized people, it is essential that we meet each other and establish a meaningful dialogue that is based on epistemic humility and genuine empathy. Only then can we realistically hope to overcome the Double Empathy Problem.

References

Alcoff, L. M. (2022). Extractivist epistemologies. *Tapuya: Latin American Science, Technology and Society*, *5*(1), 212–231. https://doi.org/10.1080/25729861.2022.2127231

Berenstain, N. (2016). Epistemic exploitation. *Ergo, an Open Access Journal of Philosophy*, *3*, 569–590. http://dx.doi.org/10.3998/ergo.12405314.0003.022

Camus, L., Macmillan, K., Rajendran, G., & Stewart, M. (2022). 'I too, need to belong': Autistic adults' perspectives on misunderstandings and well-being. *PsyArXiv*, https://doi.org/10.31234/osf.io/5mysh

Catala, A. (2020). Metaepistemic injustice and intellectual disability: A pluralist account of epistemic agency. *Ethical Theory and Moral Practice*, *23*(5), 755–776. https://doi.org/10.1007/s10677-020-10120-0

Catala, A. (2023, April 11). Understanding Neurodiversity, Unlearning Neuronormativity. Blog of the APA. https://blog.apaonline.org/2023/04/11/understanding-neurodiversity-unlearning-neuronormativity/

Catala, A., Faucher, L., & Poirier, P. (2021). Autism, epistemic injustice, and epistemic disablement: A relational account of epistemic agency. *Synthese*, *199*(3–4), 9013–9039. https://doi.org/10.1007/s11229-021-03192-7

Davis, E. (2018). On epistemic appropriation. *Ethics*, *128*(4), 702–727. https://doi.org/10.1086/697490

Dotson, K. (2011). Tracking epistemic violence, tracking practices of silencing. *Hypatia*, *26*(2), 236–527. https://doi.org/10.1111/j.1527-2001.2011.01177.x

Fricker, M. (2007). *Epistemic Injustice: Power and the Ethics of Knowing*. Oxford University Press.

Medina, J. (2013). *The Epistemology of Resistance: Gender and Racial Oppression, Epistemic Injustice, and the Social Imagination*. Oxford University Press.

Milton, D. E. M. (2012). On the ontological status of autism: The 'double empathy problem'. *Disability & Society*, *27*(6), 883–887. https://doi.org/10.1080/09687599.2012.710008

Milton, D., Gurbuz, E., & López, B. (2022). The 'double empathy problem': Ten years on. *Autism*, *26*(8), 1901–1903.

Neumeier, S. M. (2018, February 9). 'To Siri with Love' and the problem with Neurodiversity Lite. *Rewire News*. https://rewire.news/article/2018/02/09/siri-love-problem-neurodiversity-lite/

Chapter 6:

Intellectual Humility and Double Empathy Theory: Challenges and Opportunities

Erinn H. Finke and Danny H. Dunn

Intellectual humility

Intellectual humility (IH) is a psychological and philosophical concept that refers to the recognition of one's own cognitive limitations, the willingness to acknowledge gaps in knowledge or understanding, the openness to consider alternative viewpoints and the willingness to engage in respectful dialogue with others (Hopkin et al., 2014; Krumrei-Mancuso & Rouse, 2016; Leary et al., 2017; McElroy et al., 2014; Porter & Schumann, 2017). Intellectual humility is different from perspective-taking. Perspective-taking is the ability to recognize and understand an alternative point of view, whereas IH is the ability to recognize and consider shortcomings in one's own point of view (Porter et al., 2022b).

At its core, IH involves recognizing no individual possesses perfect knowledge or complete understanding of the world (Krumrei-Mancuso, 2017) and acknowledging one's beliefs and opinions should be subject to revision based on new evidence or insights (e.g., Hopkin et al., 2014; McElroy et al., 2014). Ways of thinking that reflect low or high IH have been associated with specific motives, emotions and behaviours (Leary, 2018). Individuals with high IH are more likely to actively seek out new information, perspectives and evidence, even if it challenges their existing beliefs (Krumrei-Mancuso & Rouse, 2016). They are confident in their beliefs, and yet open to alternative information or evidence. Individuals with high IH are willing to admit when they don't know something or when they've made a mistake, without feeling threatened or defensive.

Defining IH has been a topic of discussion among researchers. Scholars generally agree on the core elements but a complete description of IH is more complicated and nuanced. Porter and colleagues (2022a) systematically reviewed the psychological and philosophical literature related to IH and identified 18 distinct definitions. From this review, these researchers proposed a new, integrated, framework for conceptualizing IH. This framework was intended to support the development of a uniform description of the components of IH. This framework contextualizes the reciprocal influences of internal versus expressed variables, as well as self versus other variables centring recognition of intellectual limitations as the core factor of the framework. Internal (self) variables include awareness of ignorance and awareness of fallibility. Internal (other) variables include awareness of value in other people's intellect. Expressed (self-public) variables include admitting ignorance and fallibility. Expressed (self-private) variables include redressing ignorance and fallibility. Expressed (other-public) variables include listening to other people's ideas. Expressed (other-private) variables include openness to corrective feedback. This framework is the first attempt to integrate the rapidly expanding research exploring the nature and characteristics of IH. Understanding how to foster or increase IH in any capacity depends on a shared conceptualization of IH.

Correlates of intellectual humility

State (situation-specific) and trait (general, across situations) IH have been associated with a wide range of psychological variables (cognitive, social, personality; Porter et al., 2022b). Cognitive variables with clear and consistent relationships include dogmatism (e.g., Christen et al., 2019; Haggard et al., 2018; Krumrei-Mancuso, 2018; Leary et al., 2017), cognition (e.g., Davis et al., 2016; Krumrei-Mancuso et al., 2020; Leary et al., 2017; Porter & Schumann, 2017) and open-mindedness/curiosity (e.g., Brienza et al., 2018; Haggard, et al., 2018; Krumrei-Mancuso & Newman, 2020; Krumrei-Mancuso et al., 2020; Leary et al., 2017; Meagher et al., 2021; Porter & Schumann, 2017; Zmigrod et al., 2019). Individuals who are more dogmatic, who are more likely to follow a set of rules without exception, tend to exhibit lower IH. Those with higher cognitive abilities, and those who are open-minded/ curious are more likely to exhibit higher IH (Porter et al., 2022b).

Social variables with clear and consistent relationships with IH include empathetic concern (Krumrei-Mancuso, 2017, 2018), emotional diversity (Grossmann et al., 2016; Grossmann et al., 2019), forgiveness of others (Brienza et al., 2018; Grossmann et al., 2016; Hodge et al., 2020; McElroy et al., 2014), general humility (Davis et al., 2016; Krumrei-Mancuso & Rouse, 2016; Porter & Schumann, 2017), perspective-taking (Brienza et al., 2018; Grossmann et al., 2016; Grossmann et al., 2019; Kross & Grossmann, 2012; Krumrei-Mancuso, 2017, Krumrei-

Mancuso,2018; Peetz & Grossmann, 2021), positive perception/value of other people (e.g., Bowes et al., 2022; Hodge et al., 2020; Jarvinen & Paulus, 2017; Krumrei-Mancuso & Rouse, 2016; Stanley et al., 2020; Zachry et al., 2018), prosociality (Krumrei-Mancuso, 2017; Krumrei-Mancuso & Newman, 2020; McElroy et al., 2014) and compromise (Brienza et al., 2018; Grossmann et al., 2016; Grossmann et al., 2019; Peetz & Grossmann, 2021). These social variables are positively correlated to IH. People who have more of these social characteristics are more likely to exhibit higher IH (Porter et al., 2022).

Personality variables with clear and consistent relationships with IH include agreeableness (Bowes et al., 2022; Davis et al., 2016; Haggard et al., 2018; Krumrei-Mancuso, 2018; Leary et al., 2017; McElroy et al., 2014; Meagher et al., 2019; Porter & Schumann, 2017), neuroticism (Brienza et al., 2018; Haggard et al., 2018; Jarvinen & Paulus, 2017; Meagher et al., 2015) and openness to experience (Bowes et al., 2022; Brienza et al., 2018; Davis et al., 2016; Haggard et al., 2018; Krumrei-Mancuso & Rouse, 2016; Leary et al., 2017; McElroy et al., 2014; Meagher et al., 2021; Porter & Schumann, 2017). Individuals who are more neurotic (who experience higher levels of anxiety, negativity and self-doubt) exhibit lower IH. Those with higher agreeableness, and who are open to new experiences are more likely to exhibit higher IH (Porter et al., 2022a).

Trait and state intellectual humility

Intellectual humility has far-reaching impacts on individual and societal well-being. Leary stated *'there is no contradiction or conflict in viewing IH both as a state (how intellectually humble a person is in a particular situation at a particular time) and a trait (how intellectually humble a person is in general, across situations)'* (Leary, 2018, p. 5). Despite this, almost all research on IH to date has focused on studying IH as a trait or personality characteristic.

There are some investigations of the effects of IH on interpersonal interactions and relationships. At a trait level, people with higher IH are more likely to display tolerance of differing ideological views (e.g., political or religious) and are less likely to degrade people who differ from themselves (Bowes et al., 2020; Hook et al., 2017). Higher IH predisposes a willingness to listen to others and fosters an attitude receptive to constructive dialogue (Bowes et al., 2020; Hook et al., 2017). People high in IH are less likely to become defensive or confrontational when their beliefs or ideas are challenged; they are more willing to consider alternative viewpoints (Colombo et al., 2021). People with higher IH are more willing to befriend outgroup members and connect with them on social media platforms (Bowes et al., 2022; Porter & Schumann, 2017).

State and trait IH have been linked to greater cooperation. In professional settings and collaborative endeavours, IH creates a more productive and harmonious environment that is open to diverse ideas, leading to innovation and effective problem-solving (Grossmann et al, 2017; Porter et al., 2022b). In situations of disagreement or conflict, IH allows individuals to approach disagreements with an open and empathetic mindset – willing to consider alternative viewpoints and seek common ground (Porter & Schumann, 2017; Porter et al., 2022b).

State IH is closely linked to empathy. Acknowledging limitations and valuing others' perspectives can enhance the capacity for understanding and caring about the experiences, beliefs and well-being of others (Krumrei-Mancuso, 2017). This strengthens interpersonal relationships. Finally, IH has been shown to contribute to a culture of learning and personal growth. Some research shows intellectually humble individuals seek out new information, consider different perspectives, and adapt their beliefs when confronted with valid evidence or counterarguments (Krumrei-Mancuso et al., 2020).

Intellectual humility as a social structure

In contrast to the research investigating IH as an individual mindset, disposition or even an interpersonal construct, Dunning asserted *'intellectual humility resides not only within the individual but also the collectives and social structures that the individual belongs to'* (Dunning, 2023, p. 264). From this perspective, IH is an engrained value of a social environment. This perspective on IH is founded on the idea that attitudes are culturally ingrained, not of the individual, but a result of the environment, settings and societies in which a person resides and interacts (e.g., LeVine, 1973).

According to Dunning (2023), the study of implicit biases supports this perspective. Because implicit bias is outside the awareness, intention and control of the individual person (Kurdi et al., 2019), it can only really be reliably studied and understood at the cultural or societal level (Hehman et al., 2019). This has resulted in new views that implicit bias may not represent personal attitudes, but rather those of the social environment in which a person lives, works and learns (Payne & Hannay, 2021). From this perspective, research on IH should explore the role of cultural and collective ideologies on levels of IH. Dunning (2023) suggested several interesting directions for future inquiry including understanding of the habits of IH professions or organizations. What interventions are in place in these spaces to limit or discourage intellectual arrogance? Would interventions be more effective at a collective level rather than at the level of the individual?

While it is valuable to contemplate the origins of IH, it is more interesting and useful to understand the aspects of IH that are learned and can be cultivated in specific situations and how this type of IH varies across events and interactions (Leary, 2018). There is a large body of research that shows beliefs can change (e.g., Friedman, 2004; James & Barton, 2004). Leary (2018) hypothesized IH can be increased through both personal decisions and through intervention.

Improving intellectual humility

The research investigating methods for improving IH is limited. Most intervention studies have documented short-term improvements using literacy tasks to stimulate reflection. These studies have shown activities that afford a person the ability to distance themselves from a situation and contemplate the experience from the vantage point of an observer have greater impact on IH than similar activities completed from the perspective of being immersed in a scenario (Kross & Grossmann, 2012).

Other interventions have used comparison writing tasks. Participants are asked to write about their knowledge of a specific operation or policy and then compare that to the formal procedural documents or policy statements to provide direct evidence of gaps in knowledge of the procedures or policies in question (e.g., Johnson et al., 2016). Other interventions have used reading tasks (e.g., reading about the benefits of IH or about intelligence being malleable) to increase short-term, self-reported state IH (Porter & Schumann, 2017; Porter et al., 2020). These small-scale interventions show IH can be increased, albeit temporarily, using fairly simple and cost-effective interventions.

Finally, two studies investigated the impact of direct instruction on changes in IH with mixed effects. In one study, students in an undergraduate philosophy course were provided direct instruction on IH at the beginning of their class. Outcomes indicated the students who received the lesson demonstrated greater levels of compromise during conflicts and were seen as having higher IH by their peers (Meagher et al., 2019). The other study provided direct instruction to middle school and high school students at a week-long philosophy camp. Results showed the students who received the IH instruction reported higher IH compared to untrained students who attended the same camp (Anderson et al., 2021).

These studies provide some evidence that IH can change. This is consistent with the psychological literature that shows beliefs can change. Based on this literature it is reasonable to expect IH can be affected by outside interventions, as well as through a person's decision to become more intellectually humble (Leary, 2018). For a person to decide to become more intellectually humble, they would need to believe that approaching the world in a more intellectually humble manner is beneficial and has no notable down sides (Leary, 2018).

Continuing to develop evidence-based interventions to support changes in IH is dependent on the ability to determine baseline levels of IH accurately and efficiently through assessment. Assessment of IH has also been a topic of much discussion in the literature. As a result, there are several different scales and methods of measurement used regularly to assess IH.

Assessing intellectual humility

The most commonly used assessments of IH take slightly different approaches to quantifying the ability to recognize intellectual limitations. Some use self-report measures of general trait IH (Alfano et al., 2017; Haggard et al., 2018; Krumrei-Mancuso & Rouse, 2016; Leary et al., 2017; Meagher et al., 2015); while others use peer measurement (McElroy et al., 2014; Meagher et al., 2015). One measures IH with respect to specific domains, topics and issues (Hoyle et al., 2016).

Self-report measures

One question regarding the validity of self-report measures concerns whether an individual can accurately report their own IH. At the crux of this question is whether an intellectually humble person will accurately report the intensity of their strengths in seeking out information and willingness to change their mind. A second, but related, concern is the potential for intellectually arrogant people to overreport these same virtues. In fact, when this relationship was studied, a significant positive relationship was found between measures of self-enhancement and ratings of intellectual humility (Meagher et al., 2015).

The one study that compared self-reports of IH and intellectual arrogance (IA) with peer-reports found inconsistent results indicating self and other reports were not significantly correlated for IH and were only moderately correlated for IA (Meagher et al., 2015). This may indicate self-report measures are not accurate, but this should be considered with caution. This study did not use one of the psychometrically validated measures for assessing IH, but instead used a four-item scale developed for the investigation (Meagher et al., 2015). Thus, more research is needed to address the question of the efficacy of self-report measures of IH and how the outcomes relate to observable behavioural tendencies.

Over Claiming Questionnaire

One tool used in several investigations to link IH to an observable behavioural correlate is the Over Claiming Questionnaire (OCQ). This questionnaire asks participants to indicate their familiarity with a variety of topics, some of which are fabrications (Feeney & Goffin, 2015). Participants who claim knowledge of fabricated topics are objectively identified as either having misrepresented or misremembered their knowledge. Misrepresenting one's knowledge is clearly associated with intellectual arrogance. The results of this assessment can be difficult to clearly interpret, however, as it is impossible to account for mistaking fabricated items for another topic they have, indeed, been exposed to previously (Feeney & Goffin, 2015). Many of the fabricated topics are created using common prefixes, suffixes and existing words which may sound familiar to some participants (e.g., mistaking 'megaphrenia', consumer apparatus, plates of parallax for 'schizophrenia', consumer price index, angles of parallax). This clouds the interpretation of selection of fabricated items as an indication of deliberate misrepresentation (Feeney & Goffin, 2015). Use of this tool is further complicated by the fact that the OCQ correlates well to some measures of general trait IH (Alfano et al., 2017) and not to others (Deffler et al., 2016).

General Intellectual Humility Scale

The General Intellectual Humility Scale (GIHS), created by Leary and colleagues, is tightly focused on IH as a person's ability to admit their beliefs can be wrong, with some items that branch into domains like changing one's mind when presented with new information, seeking out disconfirmatory evidence, and respecting the differing beliefs of others (Leary et al., 2017).

When compared, the GIHS did not significantly correlate to the OCQ (Deffler et al., 2016), but did have associations with items related to recognition memory. Those with higher IH on the GIHS were better at distinguishing between familiar and unfamiliar beliefs in a specific old–new recognition task (Deffler et al., 2016). The GIHS is a unique scale because it identifies arguments for controversial topics. Participants with high IH remember the arguments they have seen before and those they have not, even when the arguments in question disagree with their stance or opinion (Deffler et al., 2016).

The original paper describing the development of the GIHS examined the relationship between IH and processing and perceiving persuasive arguments (Leary et al., 2017). Results indicated when the beliefs of participants with high IH were challenged they rated strong arguments as stronger and weak arguments as weaker than those with low IH (Leary et al., 2017). When the beliefs of the participants were confirmed, participants consistently rated strong arguments as stronger than the weak arguments, regardless of IH level (Leary et al., 2017). These results confirm the GIHS measures a person's ability to recognize their beliefs and choices may be wrong.

Limitations Owning Intellectual Humility Scale

Haggard and colleagues (2018) developed the Limitations Owning Intellectual Humility Scale (L-OIHS). This scale measures IH in terms of the tendency to recognize one's intellectual or epistemic limitations and then seek to ameliorate those limitations. The measure assesses three factors: owning one's intellectual limitations, comfort/discomfort with intellectual limitations and love of learning. The L-OIHS significantly predicted openness and close-mindedness over and above education, social desirability and other IH scales such as the GIHS, the Comprehensive Intellectual Humility Scale (CIHS) and an additional unpublished intellectual humility scale (Haggard et al., 2018). The L-OIHS was positively correlated with other self-reported personality traits including agreeableness, extraversion, openness and conscientiousness, as well as significant negative correlations with dogmatism and neuroticism (Haggard et al., 2018).

Comprehensive Intellectual Humility Scale

The remaining psychometrically validated self-report scales for IH have four factors each and assess IH from a broad theoretical definition. The four factors assessed by the CIHS (Krumrei-Mancuso & Rouse, 2016) are independence of intellect and ego, openness to revising one's viewpoint, respect for others' viewpoints and lack of intellectual overconfidence. Outcomes research suggests the CIHS predicts open-mindedness better than the other scale available at the time of the analysis (McElroy et al., 2014). However, since that time, research has shown the L-OIHS predicts open-mindedness even better than the CIHS (Haggard et al., 2018). Caution is needed in interpreting this comparison, however, because the L-OIHS and the CIHS were developed based on different theoretical perspectives of IH. The L-OIHS focuses closely on IH as recognizing, owning and working to ameliorate intellectual and epistemic limitations, while the CIHS takes a broad theoretical perspective, aiming to capture the balance between intellectual arrogance and intellectual servility (Krumrei-Mancuso &Rouse, 2016).

Multi-dimensional Intellectual Humility Scale

In contrast to the CIHS, the four factors assessed by the Multi-dimensional Intellectual Humility Scale (MIHS) (Alfano et al., 2017) include: open-mindedness (versus arrogance), intellectual modesty (versus vanity), corrigibility (versus fragility) and engagement (versus boredom). Each factor reflects a different facet of IH and includes interpersonal and intrapersonal social dimensions. Corrigibility, for example, is an interpersonal factor that measures an individual's emotional response to having their views directly challenged or corrected. People low in corrigibility generally report feeling angry, annoyed, humiliated, frustrated or embarrassed at such a challenge. Intellectual modesty also has an interpersonal social dimension. This factor measures the desire to be perceived as intelligent by others. A person who seeks to be known as the smartest person in the room is low in intellectual modesty, and high in intellectual vanity. The dimensions of open-mindedness and engagement are intrapersonal measures. Open-mindedness measures the willingness to learn from other people, especially those who hold different views. Engagement assesses the willingness to seek out various sources of information to fill in gaps in knowledge or understanding (Alfano et al., 2017).

Intellectual Humility Scale

The remaining IH scales were designed to assess IH in relation to a specific population, occupation, or perspective. Originally the Intellectual Humility Scale (IHS) was developed to assess the IH of religious leadership (McElroy et al., 2014). Since the time of its development, however, it has been adapted for use in the general population as a self-report measure (Davis et al., 2016; McElroy et al., 2014). Though none of the items explicitly mention religion in their wording, the topics covered in the questions may be more likely to be encountered by religious leaders than members of the general population (McElroy et al., 2014). For example, one item asks whether the respondent *'is good at mediating controversial topics'* (McElroy et al., 2014, p. 23). Many individuals in the general population likely have less opportunity to engage in this type of task than a religious leader might.

There are other limitations to adapting a scale for use outside of the original purpose that should be considered. Wording of items not originally intended for self-report may be impacted by self-enhancement bias when adapted for self-report. On the IR-HIS, items like *'Makes fun of people with different viewpoints.'*; *'Acts like a know-it-all.'*; and *'Gets defensive if others do not agree with them.'* (McElroy et al., 2014, p.23) exhibit this concern. Although the issue of self-enhancement bias can apply to all scales of IH; scales originally developed for self-report mitigate this by using value-neutral phrasing as much as possible (Alfano et al., 2017; Leary et al., 2017).

Specific Intellectual Humility Scale

The Specific Intellectual Humility Scale (SIHS) was developed as a self-report tool but does not measure overall trait IH. It evaluates IH with respect to a specific domain, topic or issue. The SIHS was psychometrically validated on the domains of politics and religion, the topic of gun control and the issues of background checks for gun purchases, vaccinations and abortion (Hoyle et al., 2016). It was found to be reliable, to reflect a single factor, to be negatively associated with dogmatism, and positively associated with openness (Hoyle et al., 2016). Some items on the full version of the 9-item scale appear to be susceptible to a lack of discriminant validity. For example, answers to the item *'My sources for information about _______ might not be the best.'* are subjective based on the understanding of levels of evidence of the respondent. A participant who gets their information from social media would hopefully answer this differently than a participant who gets their information from peer reviewed meta-analyses. This is not, however, an issue with the items included in the 3-item abridged scale.

Choosing a measure of intellectual humility

The deciding factor in choosing a scale to measure IH should be the theoretical conception or definition best suited to address the research question. The L-OIHS is ideal for quantifying a person's willingness to understand their limitations and seek to acquire new information (Haggard et al., 2018). The GIHS is ideal to assess a person's willingness to accept they may be wrong (Leary et al., 2017). The CIHS and the MIHS could both be used for capturing a broad inclusive definition of IH, or individual subscales from these scales could be used to pinpoint more specific aspects of IH (Alfano, et al., 2017; Krumrei-Mancuso & Rouse 2016). The SIHS should be used in research on topics or situations where specific views are relevant (Hoyle et al., 2016). Future research on IH should be meticulous in choosing what definition of IH is most appropriate to the research question being asked so a more nuanced understanding of IH and the implications of IH on other situations and interactions can be obtained.

Issues for consideration

While IH is framed most often as a virtue, there may be potential pitfalls to certain conceptualizations of IH, especially examining the role of IH in debates on topics where there is an established, scientifically proven, response. For example, most scientists would agree that having a debate on topics, such as whether vaccines cause autism, or the validity of climate change, would be unproductive and regressive. The science on these issues is settled, and further debate does not support intellectual progress. In fact, positioning these topics as debate topics may, in and of itself, legitimize an unscientific opinion by juxtaposing it against a scientific theory.

This is not, however, a killing blow to IH. Some conceptions of IH, like the ones used in the L-OIHS or the GIHS, avoid this issue. The L-OIHS avoids the topic of other's beliefs, except for one item that asks about reactions to having a mistake in reasoning pointed out. The items in the GIHS are phrased carefully, using 'belief', 'attitude' and 'opinion', such that factually settled issues are not in question. The CIHS, however, does have several items which may fall into this trap. For example, item 49 states *'When someone disagrees with ideas that are important to me, it feels as though I'm being attacked.'* (Krumrei-Mancuso & Rouse, 2016, p. 213). This item would reflect low IH on a topic such as whether pineapple belongs on pizza, but would be interpreted differently in response to statements such as *'I'm opposed to genocide against [my demographic]'*. This may seem like an extreme example, but it highlights a problematic feature of the scale in that there is nothing to differentiate between ideas worthy of debate and those which should be unacceptable to debate. It also, crucially, focuses on the emotional response to being challenged or questioned, not the behavioural response. Questions on IH scales that focus on feelings are loaded on the first factor: independence of intellect and ego. All the other factors in the CIHS avoid this issue.

Double empathy theory and intellectual humility

The relationship between IH and double empathy lies in their shared emphasis on understanding and acknowledging different perspectives and experiences. While IH focuses on recognizing cognitive limitations and being open to alternative viewpoints (e.g., Leary, 2018), double empathy applies this concept to interpersonal and social interactions with autistic people. The Double Empathy Theory, proposed by Milton (2012), suggests the difficulties in social communication and interaction between autistic and non-autistic individuals arise from a reciprocal lack of understanding and empathy. It challenges the traditional assumption that difficulties are a result of autistic deficits and instead focuses on the mutual need for understanding and empathy by both individuals in an interaction.

Autism and double empathy

Autistic people are a socially marginalized minority group (Botha & Frost, 2020) who because of their preferences related to social interactions and communication are stigmatized by non-autistic people (e.g., Gillespie-Lynch et al., 2021; Jones et al., 2021a). Traditional interpretations of autistic ways of being have classified differences as autistic 'deficits' (Kapp et al., 2013). Responses to these 'deficit' interpretations have resulted in the application of interventions focused on training autistic people to act more neurotypical, a process that has been shown to teach autistic people to 'mask' their authentic selves, resulting in trauma (Pearson & Rose, 2021). This is especially traumatic since behaviours considered socially 'normative' are subjective and shift based on context, culture and interactional dynamics (Milton, 2017).

Recent research has taken a different approach to understanding autistic sociality and social interactions. Many studies in this emerging line of research have investigated how stigma and social judgements affect interpersonal and relational outcomes for autistic people (Alkhaldi et al., 2021; DeBrabander et al., 2019; Dunn et al., 2023; Morrison et al., 2020; Sasson & Morrison, 2019; Sasson et al., 2017). Outcomes of this research suggest neurotypical adults tend to have less favourable first impressions (DeBrabander et al., 2019) and lower rapport with autistic others in social interactions (Crompton et al., 2020) compared to non-autistic partners. These data do not seem to represent 'deficits' in the social cognitive skills or social motivation of autistic people (Morrison et al., 2020) because when autistic individuals are interacting with each other these patterns are disrupted. Although autistic observers do rate autistic others as more awkward than non-autistic others, they do not report reduced social interest (DeBrabander et al., 2019). This discrepancy may be explained by differences in the value assigned to awkwardness by autistic and non-autistic people (Dunn et al., 2023).

Many of the social norms and standards autistic individuals commonly violate are arbitrary (Milton, 2012). Recognizing this may be difficult for neurotypicals who have internalized these norms and are incentivized to maintain them for their self-image as the normal and natural default (Milton, 2012). Greater IH may disrupt this conditioning.

Intellectual humility and double empathy

Intellectual humility aligns with the principles of the Double Empathy Theory by promoting an open-minded and humble approach to understanding the experiences and perspectives of others, including the experiences and perspectives of autistic and other neurodivergent people. Cultivating IH would include recognizing the biases, assumptions and limitations, which affect the ability to understand and empathize with people whose lived experiences differ from one's own. In this way, neurotypical people with higher IH can develop a greater appreciation for the ways autistic people perceive and experience the world. This, in turn, may result in increased willingness to engage in open and empathetic cross-neurotype communication, which could lead to improved mutual understanding, reduced prejudice and enhanced social interactions.

Intellectual humility may be one contributing factor to bridging the empathy gap in neurodiverse interactions. To acknowledge one's knowledge is incomplete may facilitate mutual understanding and collective meaning-making (Finke & Dunn, 2023). Altering one's viewpoints to better align with the experiences and perspectives of someone different from oneself is difficult. The natural tendency, especially in the current cultural climate, is to confirm one's own perspective by surrounding oneself with people who think about and experience the world similarly to oneself (e.g., Jones & Sugden, 2001; Mercier, 2022). Accepting as valid the perspective of someone whose lived experiences, perspectives, values and beliefs are different from oneself implicitly necessitates intellectual humility.

Increasing intellectual humility to improve neurodiverse interactions

At the time of this writing there are no studies examining the subject of IH as it relates to autism stigma, double empathy or neurodiverse interactions. There are, however, studies exploring the relationship between IH and stigma toward neurodivergent, disabled or otherwise marginalized individuals.

The most pertinent of these is a study by Schmitt and Huynh (2023) examining IH and stigma towards post-traumatic stress disorder (PTSD). Results indicated, when controlling for demographic variables, including the participant having a diagnosis of PTSD or knowing someone with a diagnosis of PTSD, IH as measured by the CIHS accounted for a significant amount of the variance in stigma over and above these other variables. This self-report survey study did not, however, include variables focused on interpersonal interactions, nor did it include observable behavioural measures. Nonetheless it is an excellent starting point from which to begin pursuing such studies.

Further support for the idea that increasing IH could ameliorate the double empathy divide comes from studies examining IH and stigma more broadly. Worachek and Leibham (2018) found higher scores on the CIHS predicted more positive attitudes toward disability in a sample of college students. Additionally, Bell (2021) found higher scores on the GIHS were associated with lower levels of dispositional attributions toward a hypothetical roommate who was either obese or showing signs of alcohol use disorder. Higher levels of IH also predicted greater forgiveness of a hypothetical roommate who had committed a transgression against the participant.

Although there is a dearth of direct investigation of the impact of IH on the Double Empathy Problem as it appears in interaction between autistic and non-autistic people, the preliminary evidence suggests a promising effect on stigma, judgement and attitudes toward those perceived as other. The evidence related to interventions to increase IH is also promising, with a wide range of strategies and interventions easily adapted to specifically focus on topics relevant to neurodiversity.

Increasing state intellectual humility: Direct persuasion

There seem to be two primary methods for increasing IH. One is direct persuasion. Interventions, like reading a persuasive article on the malleability of intelligence or reading about the benefits of IH, were sufficient to increase state IH (Porter et al., 2022c). Other persuasive interventions may be less direct, but still effective, such as reflecting on and affirming one's personal values (Hanel et al., 2023), or engaging in repeated guided diary writing sessions (Porter et al., 2022c). Diary writing was shown to be effective when guidelines were provided for the diary entries that encouraged IH without naming it as IH or discussing IH directly (Porter et al., 2022c). Another intervention increased IH and compassion through a voluntary online program. Results of this project replicated the finding that those who are motivated to increase their IH can do so through guided practice (Mendonça et al., 2023).

Ideally, interventions as simple as informing the public about the virtues of IH and recommending IH be practiced would bring about widespread change, but none of the published intervention studies have examined the long-term stability of these effects. Further, these data suggest participants who were more interested and motivated to increase IH showed the greatest improvements. Motivation to participate in an intervention designed specifically to challenge thinking and understanding may be low for experts who have spent a lifetime building a career and reputation studying a topic or group of people, such as experts on autism and other forms of neurodiversity. Changes in IH for these individuals, however, would have far reaching effects.

Increasing state intellectual humility: Demonstrating limits

Another common method of increasing IH involves directly demonstrating the limits of an individual's knowledge. This could involve requesting participants explicitly list what they do or do not know about a given subject (Porter et al., 2022c). This approach may again run into roadblocks with experts who find their confidence increased by reflecting on what they do know, and may highlight universal unknowns rather than what they do not know (e.g., they do not know the exact aetiology of autism versus a topic like neurodiversity or masking). One possible workaround would be to combine techniques and have the expert write down everything they know about a relevant or important subdiscipline within autism research (e.g., how autism manifests differently by gender, the long-term effects of masking and camouflaging), then providing an opportunity for gaining new or additional information, and finally providing additional time to reflect on what was learned.

Increasing state intellectual humility: Preservice training and education

It may also be possible to cultivate increased IH in future generations of clinicians, experts and laypeople via the education system utilizing direct persuasion approaches. At any level, educational approaches could be modified to encourage IH by rewarding humble acknowledgements of ignorance just as much as confident declarations of knowledge. This falls in line with principles of universal design for education, like encouraging revision, multiple attempts at mastering knowledge, low stakes knowledge checks to guide further instruction, and opportunities to work one-on-one with an instructor or tutor on areas of growth (Bernacchio & Mullen, 2007).

At the higher education level, those seeking careers as clinicians, scientists, doctors or teachers could be explicitly instructed about IH, its benefits, and the importance of IH for those in positions of epistemic authority. These types of broad systemic changes in education are unlikely to arrive overnight, but programmes, or even individual instructors, can begin implementing these strategies without waiting for systemic change.

For clinicians, doctors and teachers actively working the field already, there are opportunities for intervention through continuing education credit courses which are required for licensing. Additionally, some larger institutions which provide services to autistic people may require their employees to undergo training and intervention if it could be shown such training would improve their job performance or retention. This type of institutional support will require a higher standard of evidence than currently available in support of increasing IH. With greater interest towards this question in the field, that goal could be achievable.

Increasing state intellectual humility: Parent training and education

Another population that may benefit from intervention, should increasing IH prove beneficial to ameliorating the double empathy divide, would be non-autistic parents of autistic children. Although parents are typically regarded as the authority on their children, the double empathy divide does not disappear because of blood relations. Parents who have their child's best interest at heart may still cause inadvertent harm because they do not understand their autistic child's experience of the world (Offit, 2010). Increases in IH may both aid them in learning more about autism and help them avoid falling for misinformation. It may also give them a sense of humility toward their child and their child's behaviour, as they may be more resistant to their initial impressions of a behaviour and may, in turn, seek out more information to check their assumptions. These parents may also be more likely to ask their children about their experiences directly (Haggard et al., 2018). These hypothesized effects require further study to explore. The potential benefits make a compelling case for conducting further research.

While there are, at the time of this writing, no studies examining IH in the context of autistic and non-autistic interactions, there is sufficient adjacent evidence to believe it may be a fruitful area of research. If the potential benefits can be produced, and replicated, increasing IH may be one step in the journey to bridge the double empathy gap.

References

Alfano, M., Iurino, K., Stey, P., Robinson, B., Christen, M., Yu, F., & Lapsley, D. (2017). Development and validation of a multi-dimensional measure of intellectual humility. *PloS One, 12*(8), e0182950. https://doi.org/10.1371/journal.pone.0182950

Alkhaldi, R. S., Sheppard, E., & Mitchell, P. (2019). Is there a link between autistic people being perceived unfavorably and having a mind that is difficult to read? *Journal of Autism and Developmental Disorders, 49*, 3973–3982. https://doi.org/10.1007/s10803-019-04101-1

Anderson, D. J., Holte, P. N., Maffly-Kipp, J., Conway, D., Katz, C. E., & Schlegel, R. J. (2021). The development of intellectual humility as an impact of a week-long philosophy summer camp for teens and tweens: Preliminary results. *Precollege Philosophy and Public Practice, 3*, 41–65. https://doi.org/10.5840/p4202151418

Bell, K. (2021). *Who am I to Judge? Intellectual Humility and Dispositional Attributions* {Dissertation, The University of Oklahoma]. ShareOK.

Bernacchio, C., & Mullen, M. (2007). Universal design for learning. *Psychiatric Rehabilitation Journal, 31*(2), 167–169. https://doi.org/10.2975/31.2.2007.167.169

Botha, M., & Frost, D. M. (2020). Extending the minority stress model to understand mental health problems experienced by the autistic population. *Society and Mental Health, 10*(1), 20–34. https://doi.org/10.1177/2156869318804297

Bowes, S. M., Blanchard, M. C., Costello, T. H., Abramowitz, A. I., & Lilienfeld, S. O. (2020). Intellectual humility and between-party animus: Implications for affective polarization in two community samples. *Journal of Research in Personality, 88*, 103992. https://doi.org/10.1016/j.jrp.2020.103992

Bowes, S. M., Costello, T. H., Lee, C., McElroy-Heltzel, S., Davis, D. E., & Lilienfeld, S. O. (2022). Stepping outside the echo chamber: Is intellectual humility associated with less political myside bias? *Personality and Social Psychology Bulletin, 48*(1), 150–164. https://doi.org/10.1177/0146167221997619

Brienza, J. P., Kung, F. Y., Santos, H. C., Bobocel, D. R., & Grossmann, I. (2018). Wisdom, bias, and balance: Toward a process-sensitive measurement of wisdom-related cognition. *Journal of Personality and Social Psychology, 115*(6), 1093. https://doi.org/10.1037/pspp0000171

Christen, M., Alfano, M., & Robinson, B. (2019). A cross-cultural assessment of the semantic dimensions of intellectual humility. *AI & Society, 34*, 785–801. https://doi.org/10.1007/s00146-017-0791-7

Colombo, M., Strangmann, K., Houkes, L., Kostadinova, Z., & Brandt, M. J. (2021). Intellectually humble, but prejudiced people. a paradox of intellectual virtue. *Review of Philosophy and Psychology, 12*, 353–371. https://doi.org/10.1007/s13164-020-00496-4

Crompton, C.J., Sharp, M., Axbey, H., Fletcher-Watson, S., Flynn, E. G., & Ropar, D. (2020) Neurotype-matching, but not being autistic, influences self and observer ratings of interpersonal rapport. *Frontiers in Psychology, 11*, 586171. https://doi.org/10.3389/fpsyg.2020.586171

Davis, D. E., Rice, K., McElroy, S., DeBlaere, C., Choe, E., Van Tongeren, D. R., & Hook, J. N. (2016). Distinguishing intellectual humility and general humility. *The Journal of Positive Psychology, 11*(3), 215–224. https://doi.org/10.1080/17439760.2015.1048818

DeBrabander, K. M., Morrison, K. E., Jones, D. R., Faso, D. J., Chmielewski, M., & Sasson, N. J. (2019). Do first impressions of autistic adults differ between autistic and nonautistic observers? *Autism in Adulthood, 1*(4), 250–257. http://doi.org/10.1089/aut.2019.0018

Deffler, S. A., Leary, M. R., & Hoyle, R. H. (2016). Knowing what you know: Intellectual humility and judgments of recognition memory. *Personality and Individual Differences, 96*, 255–259. http://doi.org/10.1016/j.paid.2016.03.016

Dunn, D., de la Garza, J. D., Jones, D. R., & Sasson, N. J. (2023). Awkward but so what: Differences in social trait preferences between autistic and non-autistic adults. *Neurodiversity, 1*. https://doi.org/10.1177/27546330231203833

Dunning, D. (2023). Where does intellectual humility reside? *The Journal of Positive Psychology, 18*(2), 264–266. https://doi.org/10.1080/17439760.2022.2155220

Feeney, J. R., & Goffin, R. D. (2015). The Overclaiming Questionnaire: A good way to measure faking? *Personality and Individual Differences, 82,* 248–252. https://doi.org/10.1016/j.paid.2015.03.038

Finke, E. H. & Dunn, D. H. (2023). Neurodiversity and double empathy: Can empathy disconnects be mitigated to support autistic belonging? *Disability & Society*. 1–24. https://doi.org/10.1080/09687599.2023.2295802

Friedman, S. (2004). Learning to make more effective decisions: Changing beliefs as a prelude to action. *The Learning Organization, 11*(2), 110–128. https://doi.org/10.1108/09696470410521583

Gillespie-Lynch, K., Daou, N., Obeid, R., Reardon, S., Khan, S., & Goldknopf, E. J. (2021). What contributes to stigma towards autistic university students and students with other diagnoses? *Journal of Autism and Developmental Disorders, 51*, 459–475. https://doi.org/10.1007/s10803-020-04556-7

Grossmann, I., Gerlach, T. M., & Denissen, J. J. (2016). Wise reasoning in the face of everyday life challenges. *Social Psychological and Personality Science, 7*(7), 611–622. https://doi.org/10.1177/1948550616652206

Grossmann, I., Brienza, J. P., & Bobocel, D. R. (2017). Wise deliberation sustains cooperation. *Nature Human Behaviour, 1*(3), 0061. https://doi.org/10.1038/s41562-017-0061

Grossmann, I., Oakes, H., & Santos, H. C. (2019). Wise reasoning benefits from emodiversity, irrespective of emotional intensity. *Journal of Experimental Psychology: General, 148*(5), 805. https://doi.org/10.1037/xge0000543

Haggard, M., Rowatt, W. C., Leman, J. C., Meagher, B., Moore, C., Fergus, T., Whitcomb, D., Battaly, H., Baehr, J., & Howard-Snyder, D. (2018). Finding middle ground between intellectual arrogance and intellectual servility: Development and assessment of the limitations-owning intellectual humility scale. *Personality and Individual Differences, 124,* 184–193. https://doi.org/10.1016/j.paid.2017.12.014

Hanel, P. H., Roy, D., Taylor, S., Franjieh, M., Heffer, C., Tanesini, A., & Maio, G. R. (2023). Using self-affirmation to increase intellectual humility in debate. *Royal Society Open Science, 10*(2), 220958. https://doi.org/10.1098/rsos.220958

Hehman, E., Calanchini, J., Flake, J. K., & Leitner, J. B. (2019). Establishing construct validity evidence for regional measures of explicit and implicit racial bias. *Journal of Experimental Psychology: General, 148*(6), 1022. https://doi.org/10.1037/xge0000623

Hodge, A. S., Mosher, D. K., Davis, C. W., Captari, L. E., Hook, J. N., Davis, D. E., & Van Tongeren, D. R. (2020). Political humility and forgiveness of a political hurt or offense. *Journal of Psychology and Theology, 48*(2), 142–153. https://doi.org/10.1177/0091647120911112

Hook, J. N., Farrell, J. E., Johnson, K. A., Van Tongeren, D. R., Davis, D. E., & Aten, J. D. (2017). Intellectual humility and religious tolerance. *The Journal of Positive Psychology, 12*(1), 29–35. https://doi.org/10.1080/17439760.2016.1167937

Hopkin, C. R., Hoyle, R. H., & Toner, K. (2014). Intellectual humility and reactions to opinions about religious beliefs. *Journal of Psychology and Theology, 42,* 50–61. https://doi.org/10.1177/009164711404200106

Hoyle, R. H., Davisson, E. K., Diebels, K. J., & Leary, M. R. (2016). Holding specific views with humility: Conceptualization and measurement of specific intellectual humility. *Personality and Individual Differences, 97,* 165–172. https://doi.org/10.1016/j.paid.2016.03.043

James, I. A., & Barton, S. (2004). Changing core beliefs with the continuum technique. *Behavioural and Cognitive Psychotherapy, 32*(4), 431–442. https://doi.org/10.1017/S1352465804001614

Jarvinen, M. J., & Paulus, T. B. (2017). Attachment and cognitive openness: Emotional underpinnings of intellectual humility. *The Journal of Positive Psychology, 12*(1), 74–86. https://doi.org/10.1080/17439760.2016.1167944

Johnson, D. R., Murphy, M. P., & Messer, R. M. (2016). Reflecting on explanatory ability: A mechanism for detecting gaps in causal knowledge. *Journal of Experimental Psychology: General, 145*(5), 573. https://doi.org/10.1037/xge0000161

Jones, M., & Sugden, R. (2001). Positive confirmation bias in the acquisition of information. *Theory and Decision, 50,* 59–99. https://doi.org/10.1023/a:1005296023424

Jones, D. R., DeBrabander, K. M., & Sasson, N. J. (2021). Effects of autism acceptance training on explicit and implicit biases toward autism. *Autism, 25*(5), 1246–1261. https://doi.org/10.1177/1362361320984896

Kapp, S. K., Gillespie-Lynch, K., Sherman, L. E., & Hutman, T. (2013). Deficit, difference, or both? Autism and neurodiversity. *Developmental Psychology, 49*(1), 59. https://doi.org/10.1037/a0028353

Kross, E., & Grossmann, I. (2012). Boosting wisdom: Distance from the self enhances wise reasoning, attitudes, and behavior. *Journal of Experimental Psychology: General, 141*(1), 43. https://doi.org/10.1037/a0024158

Krumrei-Mancuso, E. J. (2017). Intellectual humility and prosocial values: Direct and mediated effects. *The Journal of Positive Psychology, 12,* 13–28. https://doi.org/10.1080/17439760.2016.1167938

Krumrei-Mancuso, E. J. (2018). Intellectual humility's links to religion and spirituality and the role of authoritarianism. *Personality and Individual Differences, 130,* 65–75. https://doi.org/10.1016/j.paid.2018.03.037

Krumrei-Mancuso, E. J., & Newman, B. (2020). Intellectual humility in the sociopolitical domain. *Self and Identity, 19*(8), 989–1016. https://doi.org/10.1080/15298868.2020.1714711

Krumrei-Mancuso, E. J., & Rouse, S. V. (2016). The development and validation of the Comprehensive Intellectual Humility Scale. *Journal of Personality Assessment, 98*, 209–221. https://doi.org/10.1080/00223891.2015.1068174

Krumrei-Mancuso, E. J., Haggard, M. C., LaBouff, J. P., & Rowatt, W. C. (2020). Links between intellectual humility and acquiring knowledge. *The Journal of Positive Psychology, 15*(2), 155–170. https://doi.org/10.1080/17439760.2019.1579359

Kurdi, B., Seitchik, A. E., Axt, J. R., Carroll, T. J., Karapetyan, A., Kaushik, N., Tomezsko, D., Greenwald, A. G., & Banaji, M. R. (2019). Relationship between the Implicit Association Test and intergroup behavior: A meta-analysis. *American Psychologist, 74*(5), 569–586. https://doi.org/10.1037/amp0000364

Leary, M. R. (2018). *The Psychology of Intellectual Humility*. John Templeton Foundation, 3.

Leary, M. R., Diebels, K. J., Davisson, E. K., Jongman-Sereno, K. P., Isherwood, J. C., Raimi, K. T., Deffler, S. A., & Hoyle, R. H. (2017). Cognitive and interpersonal features of intellectual humility. *Personality and Social Psychology Bulletin, 43*, 793–813. https://doi.org/10.1177/0146167217697695

LeVine, R. A. (1973). *Culture, Behavior, and Personality*. Transaction Publishers.

McElroy, S. E., Rice, K. G., Davis, D. E., Hook, J. N., Hill, P. C., Worthington, E, L., Jr., & Van Tongeren, D. R. (2014). Intellectual humility: Scale development and theoretical elaborations in the context of religious leadership. *Journal of Psychology and Theology, 42*, 19–30. https://doi.org/10.1177/009164711404200103

Meagher, B. R., Leman, J. C., Bias, J. P., Latendresse, S. J., & Rowatt, W. C. (2015). Contrasting self-report and consensus ratings of intellectual humility and arrogance. *Journal of Research in Personality, 58*, 35–45. https://doi.org/10.1016/j.jrp.2015.07.002

Meagher, B. R., Gunn, H., Sheff, N., & Van Tongeren, D. R. (2019). An intellectually humbling experience: Changes in interpersonal perception and cultural reasoning across a five-week course. *Journal of Psychology and Theology, 47*(3), 217–229. https://doi.org/10.1177/0091647119837010

Meagher, B. R., Leman, J. C., Heidenga, C. A., Ringquist, M. R., & Rowatt, W. C. (2021). Intellectual humility in conversation: Distinct behavioral indicators of self and peer ratings. *The Journal of Positive Psychology, 16*(3), 417–429. https://doi.org/10.1080/17439760.2020.1738536

Mendonça, S. E., Dykhuis, E. M., & Jayawickreme, E. (2023). Examining the possibilities for volitional character change in compassion and intellectual humility through a three-month online intervention. *Journal of Research in Personality, 104*, 104373. https://doi.org/10.1016/j.jrp.2023.104373

Mercier, H. (2022). Confirmation bias-myside bias. In R. F. Pohl (Ed.), *Cognitive Illusions: Intriguing Phenomena in Thinking, Judgment, and Memory* (pp. 78–91). Routledge.

Milton, D. E. (2012). On the ontological status of autism: The 'double empathy problem'. *Disability & Society, 27*(6), 883–887. https://doi.org/10.1080/09687599.2012.710008

Milton, D. (2017). *Autism: Impaired Compared to What?*

Morrison, K. E., DeBrabander, K. M., Jones, D. R., Ackerman, R. A., & Sasson, N. J. (2020). Social cognition, social skill, and social motivation minimally predict social interaction outcomes for autistic and non-autistic adults. *Frontiers in Psychology, 11*, 591100. https://doi.org/10.3389/fpsyg.2020.591100

Offit, P. A. (2010). *Autism's False Prophets: Bad Science, Risky Medicine, and the Search for a Cure*. Columbia University Press.

Shaver, & L. S. Wrightsman (Eds.), *Measures of Personality and Social Psychological Attitudes* (pp. 17–59). Academic Press.

Payne, B. K., & Hannay, J. W. (2021). Implicit bias reflects systemic racism. *Trends in cognitive sciences, 25*(11), 927–936. https://doi.org/10.1016/j.tics.2021.08.001

Pearson, A., & Rose, K. (2021). A conceptual analysis of autistic masking: Understanding the narrative of stigma and the illusion of choice. *Autism in Adulthood, 3*(1), 52–60. https://doi.org/10.31219/osf.io/6rwa5

Porter, T., & Schumann, K. (2017). Intellectual humility and openness to the opposing view. *Self and Identity, 17*(2), 139–162. https://doi.org/10.1080/15298868.2017.1361861

Porter, T., Baldwin, C. R., Warren, M. T., Murray, E. D., Cotton Bronk, K., Forgeard, M. J., Snow, N. E., & Jayawickreme, E. (2022a). Clarifying the content of intellectual humility: A systematic review and integrative framework. *Journal of Personality Assessment, 104*(5), 573–585. https://doi.org/10.1080/00223891.2021.1975725

Porter, T., Elnakouri, A., Meyers, E. A., Shibayama, T., Jayawickreme, E., & Grossmann, I. (2022b). Predictors and consequences of intellectual humility. *Nature Reviews Psychology, 1*(9), 524–536. https://doi.org/10.1038/s44159-022-00081-9

Porter, T., Molina, D. C., Lucas, M., Oberle, C., & Trzesniewski, K. (2022c). Classroom environment predicts changes in expressed intellectual humility. *Contemporary Educational Psychology, 70,* 102081. https://doi.org/10.1016/j.cedpsych.2022.102081

Sasson, N. J., & Morrison, K. E. (2019). First impressions of adults with autism improve with diagnostic disclosure and increased autism knowledge of peers. *Autism, 23*(1), 50–59. https://doi.org/10.1177/1362361317729526

Sasson, N. J., Faso, D. J., Nugent, J., Lovell, S., Kennedy, D. P., & Grossman, R. B. (2017). Neurotypical peers are less willing to interact with those with autism based on thin slice judgments. *Scientific Reports, 7*(1), 40700. https://doi.org/10.1038/srep40700

Schmitt, R. M., & Huynh, H. P. (2023). Stay (close to) humble: Intellectual humility negatively predicts stigma toward and social distance from individuals with posttraumatic stress disorder. *Psychological Reports, 128*(2), 827–851. https://doi.org/10.1177/00332941231157233

Stanley, M. L., Sinclair, A. H., & Seli, P. (2020). Intellectual humility and perceptions of political opponents. *Journal of Personality, 88*(6), 1196–1216. https://doi.org/10.1111/jopy.12566

Worachek, K., & Leibham, M. B. (2018). *A Preliminary Study of College Students' Levels of Humility and Disability Attitudes.* University of Wisconsin Eau Claire. https://minds.wisconsin.edu/bitstream/handle/1793/79302/WoracheckSpr18.pdf?sequence=1&isAllowed=y

Zachry, C. E., Phan, L. V., Blackie, L. E., & Jayawickreme, E. (2018). Situation-based contingencies underlying wisdom-content manifestations: Examining intellectual humility in daily life. *The Journals of Gerontology: Series B, 73*(8), 1404–1415. https://doi.org/10.1093/geronb/gby016

Zmigrod, L., Zmigrod, S., Rentfrow, P. J., & Robbins, T. W. (2019). The psychological roots of intellectual humility: The role of intelligence and cognitive flexibility. *Personality and Individual Differences, 141,* 200–208. https://doi.org/10.1016/j.paid.2019.01.016

Chapter 7:

Realizing Autistic Individuation and Bridging the Double Empathy Divide: Insights from a Lacanian Perspective

Rayan Magon

Autism isn't something a person has, or a "shell" that a person is trapped inside. There's no normal child hidden behind the autism. Autism is a way of being. It is pervasive; it colors every experience, every sensation, perception, thought, emotion, and encounter, every aspect of existence. It is not possible to separate the autism from the person – and if it were possible, the person you'd have left would not be the same person you started with.

(Sinclair, 1993)

Introduction

The Lacanian psychoanalytic metapsychology of autism, as propounded by scholars such as Rosine Lefort, Robert Lefort, Jean-Claude Maleval, Éric Laurent and Leon Brenner, establishes a distinct theoretical framework for the comprehension of autism as a unique mode of subjective functioning, yielding profound insights. This chapter aims to provide insight into fundamental questions about the core nature of autism, empathy challenges, differences in social cognition, the intrinsic nature of autistic subjectivity and the potential for individuation. The goal is to reintegrate a psychoanalytic perspective into the exploration of autism while proposing practical ways to bridge the double empathy divide, which involves an examination of the concept of 'empathy' as language-mediated intersubjectivity.

There have been notable instances of misjudgements concerning the existence of empathy deficits in people with autism, which regrettably overlook the profound implications of differences in communication and social cognition - such as differences in processing social information - on social connection. These discrepancies specifically hinder meaningful communication and mutual understanding between neurotypical and autistic individuals. This phenomenon is notably exemplified by Milton's articulation of the Double Empathy Problem, positing empathy as a 'two-way street' where issues seem to emerge due to bidirectional differences in communication styles between neurotypicals and autistics (Milton, 2012a, p. 4).[6] Milton's framework attributes the empathy-based challenges to breakdowns in mutual understanding between individuals with distinct dispositions (i.e., autistics and neurotypicals). He states:

> *The 'double empathy problem': A disjuncture in reciprocity between two differently disposed social actors which becomes more marked the wider the disjuncture in dispositional perceptions of the lifeworld – perceived as a breach in the 'natural attitude' of what constitutes 'social reality' for 'neuro-typical' people and yet an everyday and often traumatic experience for 'autistic people'.* (Milton, 2012a, p. 3)

This chapter thus contends against the contextualization of autism in terms of empathy 'deficits' and endeavours to scrutinize the dyadic factors integral to empathy (convergences and differences), aligning with Milton's assertion that this breakdown ensues organically owing to disparities in information processing, resulting in a state of mutual perplexity for both the parties involved.

6 This understanding moves beyond the medical model that focuses on deficits, and embraces how differences in ways of empathizing, and the differences in language use and comprehension, as well as the differences in life worlds, can make empathizing across these differences 'difficult'.

> *Rather than lacking a theory of mind, it is argued here that due to differences in the way autistic people process info, they are not socialized into the same shared ethno as neurotypical people, and thus breaches in understanding happen all the time, leaving both in a state of confusion. The difference is that the neurotypical person can repair the breach, by the reassuring belief that ~99 out of 100 people still think and act like they do, and remind themselves that they are the normal ones.* (Milton, 2011, p. 4)

The present discourse endeavours to delineate a comprehensive perspective on autism, which commences with an examination of the historical metamorphosis of the term 'autism'. Subsequently, a Lacanian psychoanalytic framework is employed to categorize the essence of autism, thereby elucidating insights into the autistic subject. The analysis then proceeds to an assessment of the Double Empathy Problem and scrutinizes individual differences. Conclusively, an attempt is made to proffer a potential resolution of this problem by contextualizing 'empathy' within the framework of language-mediated intersubjectivity. The ultimate objective of this enquiry is to furnish a nuanced understanding that facilitates the genuine individuation of autism and enables the realization of its full potential.

Moreover, the pervasive influence of behaviourism has significantly shaped the formulation and application of interventions for autism, often resulting in initiatives focused on normative assimilation that systematically neglect individual differences (Milton, 2017; Milton & Moon, 2012). The triumphs of behaviourism in inducing autistics to exhibit a semblance of 'non-autistic' normalcy have, regrettably, yielded deleterious consequences, as illustrated by Williams, who lamented:

> *I had virtually no socially-shared nor consciously, intentionally expressed, personhood beyond this performance of a non-autistic 'normality' with which I had neither comprehension, connection, nor identification. This disconnected constructed facade was accepted by the world around me when my true and connected self was not. Each spoonful of its acceptance was a shovel full of dirt on the coffin in which my real self was being buried alive.* (Williams, 1996, p. 243)

To ameliorate these adverse outcomes and provide genuine support to individuals on the autism spectrum, it becomes imperative to cultivate a comprehensive understanding of the internal aspects of autism. This chapter endeavours to address these internal aspects, through the lens of Lacanian psychoanalysis. Although, Lacan did not extensively explore the subject of autism, subsequent Lacanian psychoanalysts like Jean-Claude Maleval pioneered the concept that autism is a mental phenomenon; contributing to the development of a psychoanalytic clinic of autism. Brenner's (2020) seminal work encapsulates this Lacanian approach to autism as well, reframing it not as a pathology but as a distinct *mode of being*, resonating with Sinclair's (1993) conceptualization of autism as a 'way of being'. Brenner's scholarship also unveils the crucial mechanism of 'autistic foreclosure', integral to the formation of the unique subjective structure, associated with autism.

The discourse on autism is presently gradually shifting away from behaviourism, with initiatives like the Critical Autism Forum, University of Nottingham, UK, endorsing a psychoanalytic model aligned with neurodiversity and the autism rights movement (Evans, 2017). This paradigm shift holds promise of radically answering enquiries regarding the subjective structure, inner being and ontological status of autism. Embracing this approach creates a potential avenue for the flourishing and individuation of the autistic identity within the broader sociocultural milieu.

What is the *essence* of autism?

It is incredibly difficult to pin down any specific definition of autism, because even though autism has likely existed throughout human history, it was not formally recognized or studied until the twentieth century. Additionally, a semantic metamorphosis of this term can be noted historically (Evans 2013; Evans, 2017). This historical change in psychological categories begs the question of whether a universal psychology and categorization, is even truly possible. Consequently, the question, 'What is autism?' lacks a straightforward response; rather the understanding of this category is contingent upon the framework of interpretation one uses.

In this section, I explore the historical evolution of the term 'autism', and following that, in the next section, I emphasize its reclassification as a *mode of being* within the psychoanalytic framework (Brenner, 2020).[7] This shift holds the potential to surmount the inherent limitations of behaviourism. Thus, viewing autism spectrum disorder (ASD) as a *mode of being* allows for the identification of the unique subjective structure inherent in autism, promoting an appreciation of individual differences. Consequently, it offers the potential to devise an ideal developmental trajectory that genuinely enhances the well-being and quality of life of autistic individuals.

---

7 A fundamental summary of Leon Brenner's book *The Autistic Subject* is presented, along with its correlation to other followers of Lacanian theory.

Early and late classifications of autism

In the early 1900s, Swiss psychiatrist Eugen Bleuler (1911/1950) used the term 'autism' to describe the self-focused behaviour seen in some individuals with schizophrenia, in response to Freud's work on *autoerotic* thinking. Bleuler derived the term 'autism' from 'autoerotism', which focuses on detachment from reality in schizophrenia. Evans (2017) addresses how Freud challenged Bleuler's interpretation of autism, and extended psychoanalytic principles to explain early infantile cognition by introducing the concept of primary narcissism, highlighting a diverse early infantile thinking present in the developmental phase where a child primarily focuses on oneself before fully recognizing others. Piaget (1923/2015) also adopted the term 'autism' to create a more detailed description of infantile thought that went beyond traditional concepts of intelligence. In his work *The Language and Thought of the Child*, he introduced a novel concept called 'egocentric' thought. Autism, therefore, was perceived as a temporary and 'primitive' way of thinking that would naturally fade away as individuals grew older. Evans (2017) writes that *'The inherent contradiction* [was] *between Bleuler and Piaget's claim that autism was a normal stage of all child development, versus the claim that autism was "inborn" in a select group of children'*.

Furthermore, it was the work of Leo Kanner (1943) that marked a significant milestone in autism's history, where his paper titled 'Autistic Disturbances of Affective Contact', identified a group of children who exhibited distinct patterns of 'behaviour', including difficulties in social interactions, language and repetitive behaviours. He coined the term 'early infantile autism' to describe this condition.[8] Evans's (2017) book, describes how the category of autism grew and new models were developed that were against the theories of the infantile unconscious, where this new English *epidemiological* autism of the 1960s, appropriated these psychoanalytic terms and rebuilt them. Evans quotes that,

> *From the mid-1960s onwards, child psychologists in Britain used the word 'autism' to describe the exact opposite of what it had meant up until that time. Whereas 'autism' in the 1950s referred to excessive hallucinations and fantasy in infants, 'autism' in the 1970s referred to a complete lack of an unconscious symbolic life.* (Evans, 2017)

The original psychoanalytic theory centred on human instincts and impulses. In contrast, early behaviourists departed from this perspective, proudly formulating their theories exclusively based on observable and measurable behaviours. They rejected mentalism, dismissing the investigation of subjectivity and selfhood in the field of psychology (Evans,

8 Kanner was the first one to describe autism as a distinct set of symptoms or behavioural problems.

2017; Richards, 1996).[9] Before the 1950s, autism was conceptualized as a category of imagination and inwardness. However, in the late twentieth century, there was a notable shift towards the impairment model and assessment of behavioural symptoms. This behavioural approach was considered more 'scientific' and 'ideal', as it avoided unsupported metaphysical assertions regarding the ontological status of autism. This also led to the 'deficit' and 'impairment' model of classifying autism. Evans discusses:

> *Whereas the Piagetian, Isaacian and Kleinian theories of autism that had dominated until the 1950s had constructed autism and primary narcissism as the 'pre-social' stages of development that later re-emerged in pathological psychosis, the psychology of 'autistic spectrum disorders' would regard these early stages of thought in infancy as a defect, deficiency or shortcoming that could only be surmounted via a full-blown interaction with the social world. As it blossomed in the 1980s and 1990s, Wing's autistic spectrum psychology organised theories of mental development around the contention that infants and children could be 'deficient' or 'impaired' in their ability to engage in the social world.* (Evans, 2017)

Furthermore, the introduction of statistical and epidemiological methods was a crucial point that led to the complete reversal of the meaning of autism. Evans's book seeks to explain why the conceptual change of autism is important, as in the present day, the varied presentations of autism make it difficult to attribute any specific 'cause' to autism and require substantial clarification. Regarding this shift, Evans further quotes:

9 Mentalism and behaviourism differ from each other fundamentally, and behaviourism rejects that inferences to mental phenomena have any explanatory significance and calls them 'explanatory fictions'.

> *Although the psychoanalytic theory was influential within government policy in the 1960s and 1970s, it was simultaneously being stripped of its descriptive terminology and the language that supported all of its major contentions concerning childhood psychopathology. The science of 'mental defect' posed a challenge to these psychoanalytically influenced all-too-perfect constructions of children's social and emotional development, and it was a challenge that was virtually impossible to overcome. New 'styles of reasoning' around autism took account of multiple and varied forms of child development, but they did so in a way that was restricted by the scientific models used to formulate them.* (Evans, 2017)

This book also accentuates critiques by Isaacs and other British psychologists against behaviourism. They contend that behaviourism neglected the crucial aspects of a child's relationship to reality and society, which the earlier psychoanalytic models actively addressed. Rather, behaviourism emphasized behavioural management as its focal point.

This historic analysis highlights a notable deficiency in behaviourism and its classification of ASD, as it fails to adequately address the imperative task of understanding and acknowledging the internal subjective and experiential aspects of autistic individuals. While behavioural interventions can effectively manage specific aspects of the condition, a singular focus on behaviour modification may fall short of addressing the root causes and of comprehensively supporting the overall well-being of individuals. Therefore, exploration of the 'causal mechanisms' underlying autism through a Lacanian psychoanalytic approach becomes imperative.

Discussions and critiques surrounding psychoanalytic assertions regarding the mother's role in the onset of autism have been thoroughly debated and challenged in contemporary times.

However, historically, psychoanalytic theory has been deficient in its understanding of autism, emphasizing environmental causes such as inadequate parenting leading to aberrant behaviour, rather than recognizing the individuality of autism (Waltz, 2013). For example, Klein (1961), Bettelheim (1967) and Bowlby (1940, 1951) all held mothers responsible, even though their psychoanalytic models were not identical.[10] Notwithstanding, the Lacanian psychoanalytic approach directs its attention to the subject's relationship

10 Klein was influenced by Karl Abraham who believed extreme deprivation caused children to withdraw and exhibit stimming behavior (Waltz, 2013, p. 45). Historically, clinicians were unwilling to explore alternative causes to behavioural issues, rather than those stemming from childhood neglect – which while impactful may not always be the cause (Waltz, 2012. p. 46). Autism must thus be viewed as a *mode of being*.

with language instead, presenting a more apt framework for the examination of autism. Revisiting psychoanalysis necessitates a critical examination and departure from the outdated practice of assigning blame to mothers. Many new initiatives seek to reembrace a psychoanalytic model in the study of autism (e.g., the Critical Autism Forum, University of Nottingham, UK), in light of the neurodiversity movement (Evans, 2017). The departure from behaviourism thus holds the potential to provide insights into the subjective structure, essential being and ontological status of ASDs.

Autism as a *mode of being*: A Lacanian perspective

Despite the extensive historic study and analysis of the subject of autism, we are yet to crystallize a sufficiently clear conceptual 'essence'. In his book, *The Autistic Subject*, Brenner observes a divergence between the scientific comprehension of autism and the subjective testimonies of autistic individuals. This disjunction arises from the qualitative disparity between these two descriptive paradigms, as encapsulated in his quote:

> *There remains an acute disparity between, on the one hand, the theoretical and practical frameworks developed in these fields and, on the other hand, the subjective testimonies of 'high-functioning' autistic individuals presented in books and popular media. This disparity is not rooted in the use of different terminologies but rather is a manifestation of a qualitative difference between these two descriptive paradigms. While scientists designate autism as a mental or physical disorder to be objectively studied – and as a result to be contained – many autistic individuals attribute autism to their sense of selfhood, defining it as a unique mode of openness to the world that is an immanent aspect of their subjectivity. They describe autism as a* mode of being, *fundamentally linked to their identity and basic practices of existence.* (Brenner, 2020, p. 7)

Brenner's work further underscores the internal dynamics and causality underlying autism. He accomplishes this by anchoring the conceptualization in Freud and Lacan's psychoanalytic notion of a mental or subjective structure, elucidating an individual's *mode of being*, that structures their whole psychic reality (Brenner, 2020, pp. 9–10). Accounting for autism as a 'singular subjective structure', originally introduced by Rosine Lefort and Robert Lefort, Brenner examines the constitutive psychic mechanism, which he calls 'autistic foreclosure'.[11] This enables us to transcend the limited recognition of autism, which often reduces it merely to behavioural symptoms that are varied and challenging to essentialize. Instead, we can now recognize the singularity of autism (Brenner, 2020, p. 16).[12] The epoch-making significance of this framework is that it allows us to finally demarcate the essence of autism, which is identified with the *'structural conditions that enable autistic symptoms to manifest in the first place'* (Brenner, 2020, p. 274). Seeking an affirmative designation of autism, Brenner asserts that the Lacanian psychoanalytic clinic of autism supports their being rather than seeking a 'cure' for it (Brenner, 2020, p. 275).

There have been several Lacanian psychoanalysts who have contributed to the understanding of autism. Rosine Lefort and Robert Lefort examined a child with severe autism, that led them to infer two core concepts that are prominent in the Lacanian clinic of autism today. Effectively, there was neither an indicator of the function of the Big Other, nor a correct introduction of the drive functionality (Lefort & Lefort, 1998, pp. 311–320).[13] The term Big Other refers to the symbolic system of laws and rules that govern sociolinguistic arrangements. It mediates individual subjectivity by influencing how we understand ourselves and our place in society. These structural symbolic laws, which include things like language, cultural norms and societal expectations, are what make our social existence possible. Thus, the Big Other is inscribed in the symbolic order as 'the collectively imagined third-party adjudicator passing symbolic judgements on our behaviour' (Salter & Dutta, 2023). To elaborate further, the entry into language (particularly the realm of the Big Other and signifier) socializes individuals into culture, which thereby leads to a symbolic castration (Lacan, 2014, pp. 275–276) of the autoerotic *jouissance*, leading to the subjects' alienation from themselves.[14] This symbolic castration is not a literal act, but a symbolic process, which refers to the moment when a child, particularly during the Oedipal phase, recognizes the authority of the symbolic order and undergoes a symbolic loss or lack. For Lacan castration means, *'that jouissance has to be refused in order to be attained on the inverse scale of the law of desire'* (Lacan, 2002, p. 311). The set of laws governing signifiers is demarcated by Lacan as the 'Other of language' (Brenner, 2020, p. 215; Lacan, 2019, p. 226). The subject, as influenced or occupied by the linguistic Other, incorporates otherness within itself. Thus, the barred subject ($) in Lacan, represents the split introduced between the conscious and the unconscious mind, due to the mediating influence of the Other via language (Lacan, 2002, p. 288).[15] The subject is split by the very fact that they are a speaking being (Lacan, 2002, p. 269).

11 This will be elaborated upon further in this section

12 This singularity of autism emphasizes internal causality, rather than external factors such as parental influence.

13 The difference in drive functionality is later expounded in the discussion of the invocatory drive circuit.

14 Understanding the role of the Big Other in socializing individuals is crucial. Autistic individuals often resist and rebel against societal norms, as seen in their struggle with gender socialization.

15 The symbol $, is used to designate the status of the subject as a barred subject in Lacanianism.

In elucidating the intricacies of autistic subjectivity, Lefort and Lefort accentuate the pivotal absence of their fundamental connection to a symbolic order. The deficiency arises from the autistic individual's lack of alienation within the signifier, resulting in the absence of castration (Lefort & Lefort, 2003, pp. 27, 52). The distinctive trait of autistic subjectivity lies in a resolute refusal to undergo alienation within the signifier, as highlighted by Lefort and Lefort (2003) and Maleval (2009, 2015), manifesting notably in the impoverished nature of babbling (Maleval, 2018).[16] Lefort and Lefort, in *The Birth of the Other*, state that individuals with autism lack a vital connection between the concept of authority, represented by the 'Name-of-the-Father', and the signifier in the symbolic order, governing language and social norms (Lefort & Lefort, 1994, p. 341).[17] Maleval mentions that the signifier *'breaks the link with what it signifies'*, but the *signs 'do not efface the thing represented'*, leaving no room for the possibility of metaphoric and metonymic exchange, that is typical of signifiers (Maleval, 2012, pp. 40–42). The signifier is devoid of a specific referent; it lacks reference to any specific entity yet shares a fundamental characteristic with the trace – which is a marker of absence, establishing 'effacing' is a distinctive feature of the signifier. Maleval (2012) posits a reliance on the sign over the signifier, in autism, drawing from Temple Grandin's experiential account in *Thinking in Pictures*, where Grandin underscores this by asserting, *'The easiest words for an autistic child to learn are nouns, because they directly relate to pictures'* (Grandin, 2006, p. 14).

The unique manner in which autistic individuals access language by giving preference to signs, rather than signifiers, makes their language appear inflexible and rigid. Brenner (2023) observes that autistic subjects utilize iconic signs to encode complex concepts. This linguistic orientation is intricately linked to the absence of repression in autism.[18] Within the linguistic network of signs in autism, Brenner identifies the construction of a supplementary or synthetic Other, attributing it to the absence of a split and repression in the autistic unconscious:

16 This is in a way a foreclosure of castration.

17 The Name-of-the-Father indicates the laws and prohibitions of the symbolic order, representing a symbolic authoritarian father.

18 This lack of repression makes denial of one's unconscious impossible and the autistic topology is such that it doesn't differentiate between the internal and the external, akin to a child prior to the development of the ego.

> *In this sense, one can speculate that the autistic unconscious is structured like a language that is not composed of signifiers but is composed of other linguistic units. As will be elaborated in the following section, these linguistic units are 'signs'. In cases where signs are organized into a linguistic network, they construct what later in this chapter will be called the 'supplementary' or 'synthetic Other'. ... Maleval (2009) agrees that in autism there is a total 'absence of repression' (p. 211). With no repression, not even primal repression, the subject is not rendered as split between consciousness and the unconscious. Therefore, if we assume that there is an autistic unconscious, we infer that it is always accessible to consciousness – brought 'out into the open' (à ciel ouvert).* (Brenner (2020, p. 217)

Brenner associates this reliance on the sign and loss of access to the Other, with the mechanism he calls 'autistic foreclosure'. This is also foreclosed at a prior level, that leaves no possibility for the inscription of the signifier (Brenner, 2020, p. 121).[19]

> *The subject loses access to Other in all of its symbolic modalities. Accordingly, in autism we say that there is no Other through whom the image is inscribed; no Other who is the bearer of the drive object and the mediator of jouissance; no Other as language; no symbolic Other giving access to the social bond; and no unconscious composed of signifiers and split from consciousness.* (Brenner, 2020, p. 215)

Moreover, within the Lacanian clinic of autism, autism is linked to the retention of drive objects – a concept expounded by Lacan (2001, 2015) in Seminars X and XI. Specifically, these drive objects, notably the voice object or invocatory drive, necessitate relinquishment or 'castration' upon entering the symbolic order of language (Brenner, 2020, pp. 15, 126, 195–199). Brenner designates the object of autistic foreclosure as the *rim*, in the invocatory drive circuit, which he describes through Maleval's (2012, pp. 37–38) description of the subject's 'retention of the voice' where he links it to a deliberate rejection of establishing the Other, referring to the symbolic order as the space where signifiers reside, as the location where the voice object is to be recorded (Brenner, 2020, p. 195). Éric Laurent posits that a prominent characteristic of autistic functioning involves the resurgence of *jouissance*

19 For instance, it is foreclosed at the level of the 'symbol of negation' that is prior to the inscription of the signifier.

at the rim, an intense experience that infiltrates the subject without the regulatory presence of a rim (Laurent, 1992, p. 156).[20] Brenner further explores Maleval's account of retaining the voice object and links it explicitly to the absence of a rim in the autistic drive circuit (Brenner, 2020, pp. 166–168) and quotes,

> *According to Maleval's dynamic interpretation, autism originates in the retention of the voice object from the field of the Other; in other words, in autism we originally find an active refusal to yield invocatory jouissance and inscribe it in the Other … Accordingly, I argue that the symbolic inscription of the rim in the circuit of the invocatory drive can be designated as the object of autistic foreclosure. Without the rim, the drive circuit is 'short-circuited' – lacking a source and unable to return to its goal, thus hindering the inscription of the voice object in the Other. Without the voice object inscribing a void in the Other, the dimension of lack cannot be instated in the Other, as well as on the subject's body … the foreclosure of the rim in the drive circuit hinders the symbolic inscription of the void in the Other, causing it to reappear in the real and give rise to an unbearable anxiety that is experienced by the subject as mutilation.* (Brenner, 2020, p. 197–199)

In Brenner's work, the primary focus is on illustrating the distinctive and unique mode of access to language in autism. Despite the absence of access to signifiers, autistic individuals are not in any way outside of language (Maleval, 2009, p. 99). Contrarily, they are characterized as remarkably verbose (Brenner, 2020, pp. 219-223; Lacan, 1989, p. 19) and inclined to express themselves without taking linguistic ease (Lacan, 1975, p. 3). Lacan contends that autistic subjects are, in fact, subjects of language, inherently *speaking beings* (Brenner, 2020, pp. 14, 283). The crucial aspect is that autistic individuals tend to develop this language in 'isolation', lacking the typical communicative function, resulting in the manifestation of a verbose linguistic style.[21]

Conclusively, Brenner's work illuminates that, within the Lacanian clinic, autism is a distinctive mode of subjective functioning arising from foreclosure, contrasting it with a mere behavioural disorder. In the Lacanian diagnostic framework, autism is primarily

20 A rim for Lacan, is essentially what initiates and maintains the connection between the body and language, and in the next passage I explain how despite the foreclosure in autism, autistic subjects possess a supplementary access to this. Previously in the chapter, the concept of a supplementary and synthetic Other has been examined through Brenner's work.

21 Since autistic individuals develop language in isolation, they rely on signs that are pointillistic and directly represent the signified meaning. Whereas neurotypical individuals are more likely to hastily generalize.

defined by structural criteria rather than symptomatology, rooted in the subject's intricate interplay with *jouissance* and language (Brenner, 2020, p. 237). Concerning this relationship, the autistic subject possesses supplementary access (Brenner, 2020, p. 237; Laurent, 2012, pp. 69–70; Maleval, 2012, pp. 54, 102). Moreover, this nuanced relationship with language accentuates potential challenges in empathizing. Rather than constituting a deficit in autistic individuals, the difficulty lies in the limited access to the signifier, making it arduous to articulate emotional states, understanding, and compassion, at the vocalized level (Brenner, 2020, p. 282).

Implications for the Double Empathy Problem: A possible resolution?

In this examination thus far, the Lacanian clinic of autism has provided invaluable insights into the nuances of autistic subjectivity, the intricacies of language and the social order, and the foundational psychogenic mechanisms shaping the autistic disposition. However, when confronting Milton's (2012a) Double Empathy Problem, the contribution of this psychoanalytic perspective to the discourse remains unclear, thus far. I aim to propose a resolution to the Double Empathy Problem by highlighting the gleanings from the Lacanian framework and further elucidate the individual differences that underpin this divide. These individual differences give us insight into the causes of breakdowns in mutuality and reciprocity, thereby illuminating how a common ground can be found between differences, based on our shared humanity. The central objective of this exploration lies in comprehending the significance of language-mediated intersubjectivity in empathy within the Double Empathy Problem and identifying how communication and connection across this divide is possible. Litowitz underscores the vital role of faith in communication processes, expressing it as *'faith in communication such that he or she can better maintain a private self within an intersubjective world'* (Litowitz, 2014, p. 309).[22]

I endeavour to propose that a particular type of empathy can bridge these differences, which emphasizes intersubjectivity over theory of mind. To achieve this, I will draw upon Ratcliffe's (2012) concept of 'radical empathy' that was emphasized in Dant (2014), as a means of connection with individuals despite apparent variations in their lived experiences: *'empathizing with others involves suspending, to varying degrees, a world of norms, roles, artifact functions, and various other contents. Phenomenologically speaking, this ... is to stop presupposing aspects of what is more usually given as our world'* (Ratcliffe, 2012, p. 478). The challenges of achieving intersubjective understanding in cases of diverse subjectivities are addressed in this section. As Dant aptly states, *'for intersubjectivity, there is no*

22 In addressing the Double Empathy Problem, I believe a crucial solution involves clear communication and explanation to foster mutual understanding, allowing us to escape the alienation of the self within the socialization of language and culture (the Big Other). Given that the issue stems from communication gaps leading to misunderstandings, it is essential to have faith in the potential for effective communication across differences, ultimately achieving mutual understanding.

prerequisite of a "theory of mind" and no cognitive structure or other capacity that must be in place beyond the need to recognize that as human beings they share the life-world' (Dant, 2014, p. 9). Furthermore, the autistic forms of connection are emphasized based on shared interests and experiences, by Dant:

> *Rather than 'reading' or 'mentalizing' what is in someone's mind they are more likely to be trying to find common interests and understanding with the people around them and coping with the stress and anxiety of sensory overload or particular types of situations.* (Dant, 2014, p. 12)

Dant further highlights that autistic people have a different intentionality that may be difficult to pair with across differences, as such establishing common grounds such that the other person's life-world becomes co-present (highlighting Husserl's notion of *appresentation* which transfers personal experience to others) is what is difficult (Dant, 2014, p. 11). Since autistic individuals are in the minority, it is tempting to blame them for the difficulties in empathizing, labelling them as 'deficient'.[23] Instead, Dant emphasizes how 'radical empathy' must go both ways:

> *From both directions an approach of 'radical empathy' would increase the capacity to engage in intersubjectivity more successfully. It is in effect what those people with autism who 'get by' successfully in the social world do as they learn by a conscious effort to accept the world as others see it.* (Dant, 2014, p. 10)

In this chapter, I argue that autistic people do have a sense of intersubjectivity, although it may appear different than others. Heasman and Gillespie's exploration delves into the distinctions in autistic social sharing and relationality as compared to neurotypicals, shedding light on pivotal characteristics of neurodivergent intersubjectivity. They claim that this neurodivergent intersubjectivity can be encouraged in the hegemonic neurotypical environment as well, *'future research should examine the varieties of neurodivergent intersubjectivity, with associated problems and potentials, and how those forms of intersubjectivity can be enabled to flourish, particularly in autistic-to-neurotypical encounters'* (Heasman & Gillespie, 2019, p. 1). They also explore the situational resources that facilitate this neurodivergent intersubjectivity, examining, for instance:

23 Therefore, establishing common ground fundamentally requires us to see both life-worlds and individualities as valid, instead of labelling one or the other as defective or wrong.

> *For example, the difficulties autistic people experience in indexing sociocultural meaning (Ochs and Solomon, 2010) are not so problematic when sociocultural conventions are relaxed because some autistic adults are able to delve into their own repositories of symbolic resources to generate localised meanings and develop mutual understanding. Likewise, fragmentation of the interaction coherence by attending to different aspects of the interactional context (Bottema-Beutel, 2017) is less of a problem when norms permit the spontaneous interchange of private and social speech.* (Heasman & Gillespie, 2019, p. 11)

By examining the contextual elements of interactions, Heasman and Gillespie investigate the potential for intersubjectivity. They specifically highlight two aspects of neurodivergent intersubjectivity: a generous assumption of common ground, which, if unsuccessful, leads to discoordination and may come across as egocentric; and a low demand for coordination (Heasman & Gillespie, 2019, pp. 6–7). For example, this assumption of common ground is evident in instances of information dumping, a behaviour that may appear egocentric (c.f. Frith & De Vignemont, 2005), where the autistic individual assumes a shared ground but when not reciprocated, can be perceived as fragmented.

Furthermore, the low demand for coordination in autistic-to-autistic exchanges, allowed for the ability to quickly move on from disconnected and disruptive turns (Heasman & Gillespie, 2019). These low forms of coordination have also been addressed in terms of coherence, pragmatics and detecting sociocultural cues (Baltaxe, 1977; Heasman & Gillespie, 2019; Kremer-Sadlik, 2004; Tager-Flusberg & Anderson, 1991; Volden et al., 1997). It is important to note that intersubjectivity can still exist without the strict requirement for 'coordination', as intersubjectivity differs from 'coordination'; this is a departure from the emphasis on 'coordination' in neurotypical discourse. Heasman and Gillespie (2019) emphasize the significance of these findings, suggesting that instances of failed coordination in autistic individuals might actually be endeavours to bridge 'subjectivities' and consequently, could lead to intersubjectivity. This perspective is crucial as previous discussions on intersubjectivity in autism have primarily focused on autistic-to-neurotypical interactions, often overlooking the distinctions that contribute to empathy challenges:

> *Intersubjectivity differs from coordination, in that coordination focuses on consensus, whereas intersubjectivity characterizes the diversity of ways people create shared understanding. For example, an interlocutor may share information that is not reciprocated or acknowledged by another interlocutor in the next conversational turn. This may be deemed a failure to coordinate but equally count as a moment of intersubjectivity because it is an attempt to bridge 'subjectivities', an act which may be reciprocated, or become useful, at a later stage of the interaction … Studies of intersubjectivity in autism have been primarily based on autistic-to-neurotypical interactions. These have highlighted difficulties such as shared intentionality (Tomasello et al., 2005) and reciprocating nonverbal cues (García-Pérez et al., 2007; Hobson and Lee, 1998). However, autistic divergence from the neurotypical norm for interacting (i.e., neurodivergent behaviour) can result in a gap in mutual understanding which makes empathy (Milton, 2012a), perspective-taking (Heasman and Gillespie, 2017; Sheppard et al., 2016), and social perception (Sasson et al., 2017; Sasson and Morrison, 2017) difficult for both parties.* (Heasman & Gillespie, 2019)

Sinclair (1993) describes that autistic individuals feel like foreigners as they are expected to share the systems, language and meanings of the hegemonic neurotypical population. Sinclair suggests that instead of this expectation, the communication should be reframed, and their differences should be understood by the neurotypical individual. In the next section, I once again delve into the Lacanian perspective, unveiling critical distinctions in the relationship – or the absence thereof – to the Other, distinguishing autistics from neurotypicals. I therefore suggest implications for the individuation of autism to its full potential. Subsequently, I explore how this recognition of individual differences opens avenues for fostering mutual understanding and reciprocity.

Language and intersubjectivity

The mind is distributed via language because words are common to other minds, and this forms the basis of intersubjectivity (Colapietro 1989, pp. 102–104). Litowitz (2014) observes a desire to break free from the prison-house-of-language, driven by our misinterpretations and imperfect understandings. Litowitz shares that preverbal procedural knowledge is one avenue toward transcending the limitations of language. This underscores an unmediated engagement with the world, leading to veridical representations, which is eventually supplanted by a shared mediated system of language (Litowitz, 2014, p. 303). This linguistic mediation essentially represents all the loss of 'meaning' due to the alienation in the signifier. This is why we seek to escape the constraints of language. Alternatively, this pursuit involves aspiring to create an ideal linguistic system (c.f. Eco, 1995), envisioning effortless understanding facilitated by language. These are the two ways of seeking to move beyond language. Litowitz (2014) also contends that language plays a dual role in maintaining both a sense of self and a connection to a broader sense of belonging:

> *But to move from shared rhythm to meaning requires that rhythm be a part of a communicational system such as a human language. I have tried to show how the unique properties of language provide the necessary conditions for both our individual identity (our subjectivity) and our intersubjective encounters with others. The uniqueness of the acquisition of the same language system for each of us, plus the limited sloppiness of this perfectly imperfect system as it has evolved, ensures that we must keep communicating if we are to maintain a sense both of self and of belonging.* (Litowitz, 2014)

At the core of understanding the double empathy divide is the crucial distinction between the sign and signifier in the communication dynamics between autistic and allistic individuals, as outlined by the psychoanalytic framework. This distinction, prominently highlighted, illuminates the differences in communication styles that give rise to the double empathy challenge. Insights from the Lacanian psychoanalytic clinic further suggest that embracing the true essence of autism involves promoting growth by acknowledging the unique subjective structure of autism. It becomes essential for us to identify and explore channels for communication across these divides, fostering the collaborative construction of meaning. Given that language may be our sole hope for reconciling differences across this divide, it is crucial to understand how intersubjectivity can be facilitated through communicative acts that foster shared meaning.

Individual differences and overcoming the double empathy divide

Chapple et al. (2021) explore strategies to address the Double Empathy Problem by concentrating on fundamental human similarities that transcend individual differences. It is crucial, however, to preserve individual differences, preventing the sacrifice of our unique identities in the pursuit of unity with others. In the quest for a double empathy understanding, Chapple et al. underscore the necessity of embracing (instead of a strictly scientific methodology) creative and open approaches that facilitate immersive shared experiences. These open methodologies empower individuals to transcend their identities and comprehend differences. Highlighting these nuanced differences within the broader context of shared similarities becomes imperative in overcoming the Double Empathy Problem. Hence, the central proposition in this chapter is to accentuate individual differences to bridge the double empathy divide. Traditionally, when individuals with autism engage in non-autistic behaviours, they may give the impression of 'empathizing', yet they are, in reality, masking behaviours dictated by societal norms. Although it may appear that autistic individuals are assimilating and becoming more empathic, this is not an authentic display of empathy, as autistics may still lack a genuine understanding of the neurotypical experience.

Autistic individuals, much like everyone else, desire human connection and meaningful relationships, often experiencing loneliness and social ostracization that contributes to a poorly developed sense of self and self-esteem. Unfortunately, they often encounter more disconnection than connection during social interactions (Sinclair, 1993). Therefore, it is essential to grasp how both autistic and neurotypical individuals can acknowledge the differences that set them apart and learn how to respond to each other. The prevalent stigmatization and labelling of autistic individuals as odd or deviant hinder the potential for bridging this gap from both perspectives. Furthermore, Cooper et al. (2017) discovered that that a heightened sense of autistic social identity correlated with improved self-esteem. This underscores the significance of the psychoanalytic framework, which enables us to move beyond a deficit or impairment-focused model of autism. Brenner's work emphasizes an understanding of autism viewing it as nonadaptive or dysfunctional. This perspective calls upon scientists to transcend prevalent theories and comprehend the unique internal functioning of autism.

> *Accordingly, some of the most widespread theories of autism determine it in terms of a deficit of empathy (Baron-Cohen & Wheelwright, 2004), impairment of executive cognitive capabilities (Pennington & Ozonoff, 1996), weak central coherence or deficit in central processing of sensory data (Happé & Frith, 2006), and even as mindblindness (Baron-Cohen, 1997; Frith, 2001). Designating autism on the basis of its affirmative features problematizes the way it is addressed in these scientific studies. It calls for scientists to implement their research with an aim toward explaining what autism is – to provide empirical evidence for the singularity of its internal functioning and not its dependence on the failure of other mental or physiological faculties.* (Brenner, 2020, p. 275)

Williams et al. (2021) delve into the intricacies of autistic challenges in social communication, framing it as a bidirectional issue through the lens of relevance theory. They contend that effective communication hinges on the reciprocal sharing of relevance and assert that disparities exist between autistics and allistics in determining what they deem relevant.

> *What is and is not relevant, which facts and assumptions are manifest at any given time, and the way in which representations are organized and accessible, may be more markedly different than those of a non-autistic interlocutor, or indeed, a different autistic interlocutor. The degree of cognitive effort required to generate certain cognitive effects will therefore also be different.* (Williams et al., 2021)

In this study conducted by Williams et al., it was observed that most participants successfully achieved mutual understanding, facilitated by a universally shared topic of loneliness. Notably, the study also highlighted the bridging of gaps across cross-dispositional differences, incorporating dispositional preferences from both neurotypical and autistic individuals. This integration involved accommodating the neurotypical preference for minimized interruptions and addressing the autistic preference by allowing more time for information processing.

> *Less common, but equally as important, are the moments where the gap between sometimes very different dispositions are bridged. The familiar cross-dispositional conversations involving A1, A6, and A8, while low on flow and at times asymmetrical, demonstrate how the familiarity of an interlocutor (X1, X6, and X8, respectively) can be functionally supportive where the autistic speaker struggles. In these conversations additional processing time was given, interruptions minimized and misspeaks accommodated for. Yet it was during the conversations with non-autistic strangers where some of the most surprising moments of connection and mutual understanding were made. A6 and A7, with their respective unfamiliar cross-dispositional interlocutors managed to reach a state of attunement, flow, and rapport through the establishing of affective common ground. In the first instance this was achieved through warm curiosity manifesting in frequent questioning about the other's experiences, and in the second through the volunteering of personal information and emotional openness. One potential reason for the high levels of mutual understanding across all conversations may be because speakers were orientated around a central topic (loneliness) which, having agreed to participate, they had an intrinsic motivation to address.*
> (Williams et al., 2021)

These instances illustrate fundamental ways in which communication and language, when navigating interactions between autistic and neurotypical individuals, can transcend inherent differences and create an open space for shared understanding. Another straightforward example involves an autistic person who, while maintaining clarity and directness, learns to be more tactful, while the neurotypical person learns to be less ambiguous and indirect – a simple yet effective means of bridging communication divides. It is evident that, often, the most profound connections thrive among individuals of shared dispositions. Autistics, for instance, often find a sense of resonance and belonging when communicating with others who share their neurotype, challenging the notion of a lack of social motivation (Chevallier et al., 2012; Williams et al., 2021, p. 17). Williams et al.'s study delves into dyadic factors between individuals with varying dispositions, revealing that while mutual understanding is more straightforward among shared dispositions, it is still achievable across differing dispositions by accommodating each other's individual differences and communication styles.

Moreover, Shah and Frith (1983, 1993) discovered that autistic individuals excel in tasks emphasizing detail focus over overall meaning/context, potentially leading to the misconception that they overlook the big picture. Milton (2012b) challenges the 'weak central coherence' theory (Happe, 1994) in autism, highlighting its contestation in the works of Mottron et al. (1999) and Baron-Cohen (2008), as autistic individuals can indeed infer the big picture but are naturally drawn to details. This inference aligns with the sign–signifier relationship in autism, where they do not necessarily struggle to create a category from multiple particulars. Instead, they establish a system of rules to acquire language. Regarding this, Brenner states:

> *Not being able to spontaneously learn the grammar of language due to their isolated appropriation of signs, autistic individuals search for rules that organize the relationships between signs. They mainly find these rules in the order they discover in the world. This is why they find the immutability of these rules to be so important. Breaking the immutability of the order of the world damages the fragile organization of signs. The immutable circuits actualize the rules they invent for themselves and the regularities they observe in the world. Accordingly, Williams argues, that she was always 'under the rule of a lot of very strict principles.' She adds that she is aware that these were 'her own rules' and that they were 'not compatible with the carefree life of well-adjusted people' (Williams & Bartak, 1992, p. 139).*
> (Brenner, 2020)

The profound impact of Lacanian psychoanalytic theory on the Double Empathy Problem lies in its ability to illuminate the distinct levels at which the autistic and allistic subjects are oriented within language. This understanding opens avenues for hypothesizing potential methods of communication across these differences. The exact mechanisms of such communication remain uncertain and extend beyond the purview of this chapter. I thus leave the door open for further substantiation. In the subsequent section, I delve into how the Lacanian perspective contributes to shaping a pathway toward autistic individuation. This involves fostering a sense of self and interpersonal belonging, as opposed to the experience of social rejection. A pivotal aspect of the Lacanian framework is the imperative to support the *being* of autism rather than rejecting it in our interventions. Consequently, a clear trajectory emerges for individualizing the differences associated with autism, such as prioritizing the sign over the signifier. This insight can be effectively incorporated into the development of communication strategies for autistic individuals, as later demonstrated in Brenner's discussion of on/off conduct.

The individuation of autism: Lacanian contributions

Society would have us believe that the desire to fit in is the innate urge of every human being. This is not the case, rather it is to be accepted. However, almost all societies only grant acceptance to those who conform and comply, and thus the desire to fit in becomes the primary urge for most people. When individuals operate within groups, their behaviour often deviates significantly from their conduct in solitary situations, a phenomenon known as deindividuation (Festinger et al., 1952). This behavioural shift arises specifically from the influence of socialization. This is the kind of alienation in language, that the autistic individual fundamentally seeks to avoid.

In earlier sections, I have highlighted the experience of autistic individuals who feel a sense of diminished individuality (e.g., Sinclair, 1993), while attempting to assimilate into the prevailing norms of neurotypicals, often driven by behavioural training. Although behaviourism is credited for generating observable changes and adaptive outcomes, these apparent 'positive' effects may superficially appear as developmental milestones. However, they fundamentally restrict the individuation and authentic self-expression of the autistic individual, hindering genuine well-being and personal growth. This chapter has aimed to illustrate how insights from Lacanian theory on the subjective structure of autism can elucidate the underlying causal mechanisms of autism and ascertain potential pathways for achieving individuation and addressing the challenges posed by the Double Empathy Problem.

Brenner's (2020) book explores the concept of repetitive on/off conduct. This on/off behaviour employed by people with autism operates at a symbolic/sign level, which allows for their entry into the symbolic order (Maleval, 2009, pp. 144–145), which Brenner describes as:

> *In the on/off conduct, an object invested with jouissance is linked with a sign that is then effaced by the use of a linguistic negation. In other words, in the on/off conduct, the subject gains mastery over a sum of jouissance that is deposited in a simple autistic object by associating it with a sign that can be controlled by being linguistically negated. This coping strategy brings many autistic subjects to develop a growing 'vocabulary' of signs that are associated with different simple autistic objects that are coupled with bodily sensations. This vocabulary provides them with a way through which jouissance can be rendered tolerable … developing more intricate coping abilities, strengthening the protective rim and enriching its capacities.* (Brenner, 2020, p. 243)

This phenomenon is articulated as a means of assisting the autistic individual in transcending the limitations linked to the absence of the rim in autism, ultimately leading to mastery of *jouissance*. In the Lacanian clinic, linguistic access to the sign serves as a form of treatment, representing a crucial aspect and avenue of progress in conceptualizing individuation in autism. This underscores the need to move beyond conventional reinforcement learning (c.f. Skinner, 1957) and provide autistic individuals with developmental approaches that specifically address and accommodate their unique individualities.

Whitehead and Purvis (2023) underscore the pivotal issue of failing to achieve individuation within the autism spectrum, a predicament intricately tied to challenges in utilizing and comprehending symbolic language. This cyclic dilemma arises as the deficiency in social adjustment hampers overall development, while the ensuing stunted development, in turn, impedes social adjustment. Yet, amid this pattern, it becomes evident that certain individuals can surpass language-related limitations and even compensate for the absence of the rim. What factors contribute to the emergence of such instances of optimal developmental outcomes?

Whitehead and Purvis champion an approach to autism treatment grounded in the person-centred philosophy pioneered by Carl Rogers. This approach places a premium on prioritizing individuation within the broader humanistic perspective. To pave the way for individuating autism and fostering optimal development, understanding the unique mode of autistic subjective functioning is essential; notably facilitated by the Lacanian framework and emphasizing 'radical empathy' is crucial for fostering mutual understanding across differences. The individuation of autism is closely tied to social development, encompassing aspects like belonging, acceptance, communicational reciprocity and prosocial expression.

This paper's framework aims to achieve these social goals by uniquely supporting individuals, respecting their way of being rather than deindividuating them through social assimilation. Corden et al. (2021) found that increased dissatisfaction with being autistic correlated with lower self-esteem, whereas a heightened sense of pride in one's autistic identity was associated with greater self-esteem. Therefore, emphasizing the autistic identity is crucial in the pursuit of achieving developmental milestones. Overcoming the Double Empathy Problem hinges on focusing on individuating the autistic individual based on their essential being, diverging from a one-size-fits-all approach modelled after neurotypicals.

Conclusion

In conclusion, grasping autistic subjectivity aids researchers, clinicians, and caregivers in navigating challenges and embracing strengths. This insight is essential for creating targeted interventions and support systems aligned with autistic individuals' unique needs. It also promotes a societal shift towards valuing neurodiversity and acknowledging the valuable contributions individuals with autism offer. In this chapter, I traced autism's historical evolution, emphasizing the need for causal understanding and effective individuation. Leveraging a Lacanian psychoanalytic framework, particularly Brenner's 'autistic foreclosure', provided foundational insights. Furthermore, exploring intersubjectivity through language illuminated paths to overcome the Double Empathy Problem. Recognizing individual differences emerged as crucial for fostering double empathy and autism spectrum individuation. Last, embracing a comprehensive, person-centred perspective is deemed vital for advancing autism comprehension and developing supportive interventions that lead to autistic flourishing.

Future research may explore the distinction between coordination and intersubjectivity in autistic-to-neurotypical encounters, exploring how the latter can manifest even in the absence of coordination. Additionally, investigating how communication differences, stemming from the primacy of the sign versus signifier, can be addressed through clarity and transparent communication models is an intriguing avenue for exploration.

References

Baltaxe, C. A. M. (1977). Pragmatic deficits in the language of autistic adolescents. *Journal of Pediatric Psychology, 2*(4), 176–180. https://doi.org/10.1093/jpepsy/2.4.176

Baron-Cohen, S. (1997). *Mindblindness: An Essay on Autism and Theory of Mind.* MIT Press.

Baron-Cohen, S. (2008). *Autism and Asperger Syndrome: The Facts.* Oxford University Press.

Baron-Cohen, S., & Wheelwright, S. (2004). The empathy quotient: An investigation of adults with Asperger syndrome or high functioning autism, and normal sex differences. *Journal of Autism and Developmental Disorders, 34*(2), 163–175. https://doi.org/10.1023/B:JADD.0000022607.19833.00

Bettelheim, B (1967). *The Empty Fortress: Infantile Autism and the Birth of the Self.* The Free Press.

Bleuler E. (1950). *Dementia Praecox or the Group of Schizophrenias*. International Universities. (Original work published 1911)

Bowlby, J. (1940). The influence of early environment on the development of neurosis and neurotic character, *The International Journal of Psychoanalysis*, *21*, pp. 154–178.

Bowlby, J. (1951). *Maternal Care and Mental Health*. World Health Organization.

Brenner L. S. (2020). *The Autistic Subject: On the Threshold of Language*. Palgrave Macmillan.

Brenner, L. S. (2023). The autistic pseudosignifier: Imaginary dialectization of signs in the clinic of autism. *Theory & Psychology*, *33*(4), 535–554. https://doi.org/10.1177/09593543231176543

Chapple, M., Davis, P., Billington, J., Myrick, J. A., Ruddock, C., & Corcoran, R. (2021). Overcoming the double empathy problem within pairs of autistic and non-autistic adults through the contemplation of serious literature. *Frontiers in Psychology*, *12*, 708375. https://doi.org/10.3389/fpsyg.2021.708375

Chevallier, C., Kohls, G., Troiani, V., Brodkin, E. S., & Schultz, R. T. (2012). The social motivation theory of autism. *Trends in Cognitive Sciences*, *16*, 231–239. https://doi.org/10.1016/j.tics.2012.02.007

Colapietro, V. M. (1989). *Peirce's Approach to the Self: A Semiotic Perspective on Human Subjectivity.* SUNY Press.

Cooper, K., Smith, L. G. E., & Russell, A. (2017). Social identity, self-esteem, and mental health in autism. *European Journal of Social Psychology* 47, 844–854. https://doi.org/10.1002/ejsp.2297

Corden, K., Brewer, R., & Cage, E. (2021). Personal identity after an autism diagnosis: Relationships with self-esteem, mental wellbeing, and diagnostic timing. *Frontiers in Psychology*, *12*, 699335. https://doi.org/10.3389/fpsyg.2021.699335

Dant, T. (2014). In two minds: Theory of Mind, intersubjectivity, and autism. *Theory & Psychology, 25*(1), 45–62. https://doi.org/10.1177/0959354314556526

Eco, U. (1995). *The Search for the Perfect Language.* Blackwell.

Evans, B. (2013). How autism became autism: The radical transformation of a central concept of child development in Britain. *History of the Human Sciences*, *26*(3), 3–31. https://doi.org/10.1177/0952695113484320

Evans, B. (2017). *The Metamorphosis of Autism: A History of Child Development in Britain*. Manchester University Press.

Festinger, L., Pepitone, A., & Newcomb, T. (1952). Some consequences of de-individuation in a group. *The Journal of Abnormal and Social Psychology*, *47*, 382–389. https://doi.org/10.1037/h0057906

Frith, U. (2001). Mind blindness and the brain in autism. *Neuron*, *32*(6), 969–979. https://doi.org/10.1016/S0896-6273(01)00552-9

Frith, U., & De Vignemont, F. (2005). Egocentrism, allocentrism, and Asperger syndrome. *Consciousness and Cognition*, *14*(4), 719–738. https://doi.org/10.1016/j.concog.2005.04.006

García-Pérez, R. M., Lee, A., & Hobson, R. P. (2007). On intersubjective engagement in autism: A controlled study of nonverbal aspects of conversation. *Journal of Autism and Developmental Disorders*, *37*(7), 1310–1322. https://doi.org/10.1007/s10803-006-0276-x

Grandin, T. (2006). *Thinking in Pictures, Expanded Edition: My Life with Autism*. Vintage.

Happe, F. (1994). *Autism: An Introduction to Psychological Theory.* UCL Press.

Happé, F., & Frith, U. (2006). The weak coherence account: Detail-focused cognitive style in autism spectrum disorders. *Journal of Autism and Developmental Disorders*, *36*(1), 5–25. https://doi.org/10.1007/s10803-005-0039-0

Heasman, B., & Gillespie, A. (2017). Perspective-taking is two-sided: Misunderstandings between people with Asperger's syndrome and their family members. *Autism*, *22*(6), 740–750. https://doi.org/10.1177/1362361317708287

Heasman, B., & Gillespie, A. (2019). Neurodivergent intersubjectivity: Distinctive features of how autistic people create shared understanding. *Autism: The International Journal of Research and Practice*, *23*(4), 910–921. https://doi.org/10.1177/1362361318785172

Hobson, R. P., & Lee, A. (1998). Hello and goodbye: a study of social engagement in autism. *Journal of Autism and Developmental Disorders*, *28*(2), 117–127. https://doi.org/10.1023/A:1026088531558

Kanner, L. (1943). Autistic disturbances of affective contact. *Nervous Child*, *2*, 217–250.

Klein, M. (1961). *Narrative of a Child Analysis: The Conduct of Psycho-Analysis of Children as Seen in the Treatment of a Ten-Year-Old Boy*. Basic Books.

Kremer-Sadlik, T. (2004). How children with autism and Asperger syndrome respond to questions: a 'naturalistic' theory of mind task. *Discourse Studies*, *6*(2), 185–206. https://doi.org/10.1177/1461445604041767

Lacan, J. (1975). *Conferences and Conversations at North American Universities.* In Yale University, Kanzer Seminar (Vol. 4, pp. 5–66).

Lacan, J. (1989). Geneva lecture on the symptom. *Analysis,* (1), 7–26.

Lacan, J. (2001). In J.-A. Miller (Ed.), *The Seminar of Jacques Lacan, Book XI: The Four Fundamental Concepts of Psychoanalysis (1964).* Norton & Company.

Lacan, J. (2002). *Écrits: A Selection* (B. Fink, Trans.). W. W. Norton.

Lacan, J. (2014). In J. Miller (Ed.), *The Seminar of Jacques Lacan, Book X, Anxiety (1962–1963).* Polity.

Lacan, J. (2019). *The Seminar of Jacques Lacan, Book VI, Desire and Its Interpretation (1958–1959).* Polity.

Laurent, É. (1992). Discusion. In *L'Autisme et la Psychanalyse.* Presses Universitaires du Mirail.

Laurent, É. (2012). *La Bataille de l'Autisme.* Navarin.

Lefort, R., & Lefort, R. (1994). *The Birth of the Other.* University of Illinois Press.

Lefort, R., & Lefort, R. (1998). L'autisme, spécificité. In *Le Symptomcharlatan* (pp. 311–320). Threshold.

Lefort, R., & Lefort, R. (2003). *La Distinction de L'Autisme.* Seuil

Litowitz, B. E. (2014). Coming to terms with intersubjectivity: Keeping language in mind. *Journal of the American Psychoanalytic Association, 62*(2), 294–312. https://doi.org/10.1177/0003065114530156

Maleval, J.-C. (2009). *L'Autiste et sa Voix.* Seuil.

Maleval, J.-C. (2012). Why the hypothesis of an autistic structure? *Psychoanalytical Notebooks,* 25, 27–49.

Maleval, J.-C. (2015). Extension du spectre de l'autisme. *L'Évolution Psychiatrique, 90,* 764–781.

Maleval, J.-C. (2018). Da estrutura autista. *Revista ASEPHallus de Orientação Lacaniana, 13*(26), 4–38.

Milton, D. (2011) "Filling in the gaps", a micro-sociological analysis of autism. *Theorising Normalcy and the Mundane, 2nd International Conference.* Manchester Metropolitan University.

Milton, D. (2012a). On the ontological status of autism: The 'double empathy problem'. *Disability & Society, 27*(6), 883–887. https://doi.org/10.1080/09687599.2012.710008

Milton, D. (2012b). *So What Exactly is Autism?* Autism Education Trust.

Milton, D. (2017). *A Mismatch of Salience: Explorations of the Nature of Autism from Theory to Practice.* Pavilion Press.

Milton, D., & Moon, L. (2012). The normalisation agenda and the psycho-emotional disablement of autistic people. *Autonomy, the Critical Journal of Interdisciplinary Autism Studies, 1*(1).

Mottron, L., Burack, J. A., Stauder, J. E., & Robaey, P. (1999). Perceptual processing among high-functioning persons with autism. *Journal of Child Psychology and Psychiatry, and Allied Disciplines, 40*(2), 203–211. https://doi.org/10.1111/1469-7610.00433

Ochs, E., & Solomon, O. (2010). Autistic sociality. *Journal of the Society for Psychological Anthropology, 38*(1), 69–92. https://www.jstor.org/stable/40603401

Pennington, B. F., & Ozonoff, S. (1996). Executive functions and developmental psychopathology. *Journal of Child Psychology and Psychiatry, 37*(1), 51–87. https://doi.org/10.1111/j.1469-7610.1996.tb01380.x

Piaget, J. (2015). *The Language and Thought of the Child.* Routledge. (Original work published 1923)

Ratcliffe, M. (2012). Phenomenology as a form of empathy. *Inquiry: An Interdisciplinary Journal of Philosophy, 55*(5), 473–495. https://doi.org/10.1080/0020174X.2012.716196

Richards, G. (1996). *Putting Psychology in its Place: An Introduction from a Critical Historical Perspective.* Taylor & Frances/ Routledge.

Salter, L. A., & Dutta, M. J. (2023). The algorithmic big Other: Using Lacanian theory to rethink control and resistance in platform work. *Distinktion: Journal of Social Theory, 26*(1), 1–16. https://doi.org/10.1080/1600910X.2023.2224521

Sasson, N. J., & Morrison, K. E. (2017). First impressions of adults with autism improve with diagnostic disclosure and increased autism knowledge of peers. *Autism, 23*(1), 50–59. https://doi.org/10.1177/1362361317729526

Sasson, N. J., Faso, D. J., Nugent, J., Lovell, S., Kennedy, D. P., & Grossman, R. B. (2017). Neurotypical peers are less willing to interact with those with autism based on thin slice judgments. *Scientific Reports, 7,* 40700. https://doi.org/10.1038/srep40700

Shah, A., & Frith, U. (1983). An islet of ability in autistic children: A research note. *Journal of Child Psychology and Psychiatry, and Allied Disciplines, 24*(4), 613–620. https://doi.org/10.1111/j.1469-7610.1983.tb00137.x

Shah, A., & Frith, U. (1993). Why do autistic individuals show superior performance on the block design task? *Journal of Child Psychology and Psychiatry, and Allied Disciplines, 34*(8), 1351–1364. https://doi.org/10.1111/j.1469-7610.1993.tb02095.x

Sheppard, E., Pillai, D., Wong, G. T., Ropar, D., & Mitchell, P. (2016). How easy is it to read the minds of people with autism spectrum disorder? *Journal of Autism and Developmental Disorders, 46*(4), 1247–1254. https://doi.org/10.1007/s10803-015-2662-8

Skinner, B. F. (1957). *Verbal Behavior.* Appleton-Century-Crofts.

Sinclair, J. (1993). Don't mourn for us. *Our Voice, 1*(3), 1–7. Retrieved from https://www.autreat.com/dont_mourn.html

Tager-Flusberg, H., & Anderson, M. (1991). The development of contingent discourse ability in autistic children. *Journal of Child Psychology and Psychiatry, 32*(7), 1123–1134. https://doi.org/10.1111/j.1469-7610.1991.tb00353.x

Tomasello, M., Carpenter, M., Call, J., Behne, T., & Moll, H. (2005). Understanding and sharing intentions: The origins of cultural cognition. *Behavioral and Brain Sciences, 28*(5), 675–735. https://doi.org/10.1017/S0140525X05000129

Volden, J., Mulcahy, R. F., & Holdgrafer, G. (1997). Pragmatic language disorder and perspective taking in autistic speakers. *Applied Psycholinguistics, 18*(2), 181–198. https://doi.org/10.1017/S0142716400009966

Waltz, M. (2013). *Autism: A Social and Medical History*. Palgrave Macmillan.

Whitehead, P. M., & Purvis, K. (2023). Humanizing autism research and treatment: Facilitating individuation through person-centered therapy. *The Humanistic Psychologist, 51*(1), 71–86. https://doi.org/10.1037/hum0000249

Williams, D. (1996) *Autism: An Inside-Out Approach*. Jessica Kingsley.

Williams, D., & Bartak, L. (1992). *Si on me touche je n'existe plus: le témoignage exceptionnel d'une jeune autiste*. Robert Laffont.

Williams, G. L., Wharton, T., & Jagoe, C. (2021). Mutual (mis)understanding: Reframing autistic pragmatic "impairments" using relevance theory. *Frontiers in Psychology, 12*, 616664. https://doi.org/10.3389/fpsyg.2021.616664

Chapter 8:

Revisiting Goffman: The Presentation of an Autistic Self in Everyday Life

Damian Milton

Introduction

In developing the concept of the Double Empathy Problem there have been a range of theoretical influences that I have drawn upon (the breadth of which is discussed in Chapter 1 of this Reader). For the purposes of this chapter, however, I have decided to concentrate on one of the most salient of antecedents, the work of Erving Goffman, and in particular *The Presentation of Self in Everyday Life* (Goffman, 1959) and *Stigma: Notes on the Management of a Spoiled Identity* (Goffman, 1963). In recent years, there has been much discussion about the phenomenon of 'autistic masking', to which my all too often response was: *'Can you please read some Goffman'*. Unfortunately, with the notable exception of the work of Pearson and Rose (2021), the connection between Goffman's work and this topic are barely, if at all, mentioned. I came to realize, however, that it had been some years since I had read Goffman's work myself, despite its influence on my early career as a sociologist. In this chapter, I revisit these texts to reappraise their influence and value to work regarding both the Double Empathy Problem and autistic masking.

Goffman was a Canadian sociologist whose work spanned from the mid-1950s until his death in 1983. He pioneered the 'dramaturgical approach' to theorizing social interaction and was highly influential upon the use of qualitative methods in social science. In his first major publication, *The Presentation of Self in Everyday Life* (Goffman, 1959), he set out how, when a person comes into contact with another person, they will utilize their appearance and their manner, as well as the setting they are situated within, in order to manage the impressions they are presenting, while their partner in the interaction will simultaneously be trying to obtain information about them to form an impression of them. In this work, Goffman made an analogy between the performances that people portray in everyday life with that of a theatrical performance, the 'dramaturgical self'. He analyses settings and performances, frontstage and backstage, as well as the personal 'front' portrayed by individual social actors through their appearances and manner. As an example, one could take the role of a mental health professional, whose appearances and manner will follow certain expectations and scripts when performing 'on stage' (interacting with a patient), and yet is likely to interact quite differently 'backstage' with their colleagues in the staff room. An aspect of Goffman's analysis in this work that is of salience here was how he discussed breakdowns in social interaction:

> *By virtue of the same sign-accepting tendency, the audience may misunderstand the meaning that the cue was designed to convey or may read an embarrassing meaning into gestures or events that were accidental, inadvertent, or incidental and not meant by the performer to carry any meaning whatsoever.* (Goffman, 1959, p. 59)

In this passage, Goffman shows how a sense of social reality is mutually constructed by actors through the process of social interaction and, like many other sociological commentators (e.g., Becker, 1963; Garfinkel, 1967), indicates how fragile such constructions can be. Goffman also states, however, how people will often take precautions to prevent disruptions to expectations within interactions and how, in group culture, such disruptions can form the content of practical jokes, anecdotal stories and cautionary tales, and can be used for humour, catharsis or sanction.

Goffman (1959) describes how we come to see performances within interactions on something of a continuum between sincerity and cynicism/deception. While he saw all interactions as performative, this was indicating how such performances were viewed by an audience. It is interesting to note at this point the central feature of the ability to deceive others and understand deception within descriptions of what constitutes the performance of a 'theory of mind'. It also brings to mind associations of truth telling and honesty which are often made relating to autistic people, and the expectation of sincerity, as well as the common experience among autistic people of not being believed, when being as sincere as possible, for not 'performing' to normative social expectations. As an example, not having one's reporting of pain believed by a clinician.

Goffman, the Double Empathy Problem and power

> *We have then a kind of interactional modus vivendi. Together the participants contribute to a single overall definition of the situation which involves not so much a real agreement as to what exists but rather a real agreement as to whose claims concerning what issues will be temporarily honoured.* (Goffman, 1959, p. 21)

In the above passage, one can potentially see the influence of phenomenological theory on Goffman's work and the notion of the 'natural attitude'; that being the belief in one's own perceptual reality and that this reality is a shared one with others. While Goffman (1959) has been criticized for not situating his work in wider structural concerns and power relations within society, one can see in this passage the potential for power to influence the exchanges between people at a microsociological level between social actors in particular settings. Breakdowns in communication and interaction are, for example, more likely when the participants are vying for power to define a situation, while viewing said situation from very differing frameworks and perspectives.

Goffman (1959) was no doubt one of the earliest social scientists to give an in-depth analysis of interactive breakdowns and, thus, was a seminal influence on the theory of the Double Empathy Problem. Goffman detailed how performances can be disrupted by unmeant gestures and *faux pas*. Interestingly, he described such events in terms of 'incidents' which force upon the audience: '*...an image of the man behind the mask*' (Goffman, 1959, p. 206). While Goffman did not use the term 'masking' in a conceptual sense, but rather those of 'passing' and 'concealment' (Goffman, 1963), he indeed uses the phrase here in relation to performance and disruptions to that performance.

> *Given the fact that the individual effectively projects a definition of the situation when he enters the presence of others, we can assume that events may occur within the interaction which contradict, discredit, or otherwise throw doubt upon this projection. When these disruptive events occur, the interaction itself may come to a confused and embarrassed halt. Some of the assumptions upon which the responses of the participants had been predicted become untenable, and the participants find themselves lodged in an interaction for which the situation has been wrongly defined and is now no longer defined. At such moments the individual whose presentation has become discredited may feel ashamed while the others present may feel hostile, and all the participants may come to feel ill at ease, nonplussed, out of countenance, embarrassed, experiencing the kind of anomaly that is generated when the minute social system of face-to-face interaction breaks down.*
> (Goffman, 1959, pp. 23–24)

The above passage, indeed, neatly captures many aspects of the Double Empathy Problem – the projection of a definition of social context, how interactions can come to a grinding halt, the reactions for both parties, and, while an anomaly for many, an everyday experience in the lives of autistic people. I would also like to draw attention here to instances where a performance or attempt to 'mask' fails, or when an autistic person has little conception of being a performer and makes little attempt to 'mask' (although perhaps to 'conceal'). Where autistic people also have severe or profound learning disabilities, perceptions may turn to those of an affront to social expectations and sense of shared reality. We often see hostile assumptions made regarding the actions of autistic people and a problematic 'theory of autistic mind'. Goffman (1959) also spoke of the role of the 'non-person' in social life, present in an interaction, but one who does not take on the role of performer or audience. He gives the case of servants, who are expected to be present but not to involve themselves in interactions. Autistic people with learning disabilities are often reduced to a role of 'non-person', rarely present and to be talked about (and in deep contrast to the campaigning slogan of 'nothing about us, without us'). Yet, even from such a reduced positionality, the very presence of an autistic person can form a disruption to the normative order, as Deleuze and Guattari (1980) once observed in relation to autistic children:

> *An intensive trait starts working for itself, a hallucinatory perception, synaesthesia, perverse mutation, or play of images shakes loose, challenging the hegemony of the signifier. In the case of the child, gestural, mimetic, ludic, and other semiotic systems regain their freedom and extricate themselves from the "tracing," that is, from the dominant competence of the teacher's language – a microscopic event upsets the local balance of power.*
> (Deleuze and Guattari, 1980, p. 15)

Goffman, stigma and a sense of social identity

In his earlier work on *The Presentation of Self in Everyday Life* (Goffman, 1959), Goffman gives mention to issues of concealment and deception in social interaction, yet this aspect was to be given much more depth in his later work on *Stigma: Notes on the Management of Spoiled Identity* (Goffman, 1963). In this later work, he explores impression management and how people conceal aspects of their social identities when they deviate from socially approved norms. When not meeting the standards set by others, a person can feel disjuncture and shame, leading to concealment. It has long been thought that autistic people, due to deficiencies in social understanding and motivation, would not be capable of a high level of impression management. In the wake of this misperception, the issue of masking and concealment was almost totally lacking within the research literature. As phenomenological discourse of autistic experience has expanded, this has been shown to be quite false. It can also be shown that concealment is not confined to autistic people deemed to be 'high-functioning', as those with learning disabilities will still conceal aspects of their identity in the presence of others to avoid sanction and disapproval. The assumption of a lack of autistic sociality can thus be seen as part of a narrative and culture which had framed autistic people as 'non-persons', not even as credible speakers to their own experiences. Today, within the autistic community, issues of disclosure and masking loom large, leaving autistic people to navigate the consequences of having an othered identity (Milton & Sims, 2016).

In *Stigma* (Goffman, 1963), Goffman distinguishes between a person's 'actual' and 'virtual' social identity, whereby a virtual identity is that created by constructs that others associate with that person, often created by assumptions and stereotypes. A stigmatized person, therefore, has a role to play that is defined by others with subsequent expectations. A person's actual identity, when enacted, can also defy such expectations, often leading to social consequences. Goffman (1963) also discusses varying types of stigmas that can impact upon people, those of the physical body, those of character (often with a known record of misdemeanours) and those of a tribal nature referring to group associations and prejudices.

> *...we believe the person with a stigma is not quite human. On this assumption we exercise varieties of discrimination, through which we effectively, if often unthinkingly, reduce his life chances.* (Goffman, 1963, p. 15)

Stigma occurs not only when a particular norm is unsupported, but also when a norm is not enacted and 'realized'. Here we can see social interaction as a mutually orchestrated performance or 'dance' regarding the realization of social norms. When these are breached or broken, the consequences may vary greatly due to context but are not likely to favour those in the position of a minoritized other, particularly those deemed deficient in the realm of social interaction and communication. One can also draw a link here to how the Double Empathy Problem plays out between autistic and non-autistic people, and to another seminal theorist that influenced its conceptualization, Harold Garfinkel. Garfinkel (1967) suggested that when a person's 'natural attitude' was breached, the common response was to attempt to repair the breach as quickly as possible, to find a reason (or excuse) that fits with one's previous framing of the situation and keeps one's natural attitude intact.

> *The most fortunate of normals is likely to have his half-hidden failing, and for every little failing there is a social situation where it will loom large, creating a shameful gap between virtual and actual social identity.* (Goffman, 1963, p. 152)

Impression management relating to stigma (*à la* 'masking') is clearly not something confined to the experiences of autistic people alone. What can be said to be rather different though are the reasons why someone may be concealing and masking aspects of their identity and the consequences for them if this is unsuccessful. Masking, as a phenomenon, is not specific to any one group of people, but the stigma associated with being autistic is rather more so.

Autistic acceptance

An important concept within *Stigma* (Goffman, 1963) is passing, whereby a person with a stigma blends in with 'normals' by way of not disclosing personal attributes. So, one conceals to 'pass as normal' or at least 'normal enough' not to be sanctioned for not being so. In addition to this, Goffman (1963) suggested that a central feature in the lives of autistic people would be what one could call 'acceptance' of one's performance and virtual social identity, and its alignment with actual social identity. This would also be true in terms of social groupings and spaces, safe zones of belonging away from the possibility of stigmatized and negative associations. Indeed, breaking with commonly agreed upon 'reality', employing unconventional interpretations of the character of social identity and providing safe spaces for autistic community interaction, can all be said to be mainstays of autistic community and culture, along with campaigning for wider social 'acceptance', with this term often being used to supplant charity initiatives regarding 'autism awareness'.

> *In social situations with an individual known or perceived to have a stigma, we are likely, then, to employ categorizations that do not fit, and we and he are likely to experience uneasiness … And since the stigmatised person is likely to be more often faced with these situations than are we, he is likely to become the more adept at managing them.* (Goffman, 1963, p. 31)

In the above passage, Goffman (1963) again gives voice to the uneasiness of breakdowns in interaction, yet for the stigmatized person this will become a common experience and one they will become potentially more adept at managing than so-called 'normals'. This notion was echoed in my own work regarding the Double Empathy Problem (Milton, 2012), where I made the same argument in relation to interactive breakdowns between autistic and non-autistic people.

Goffman (1963) described how some who are stigmatized will seek out remediation and correction to repair their 'spoiled' social identity. However, he issues a warning that, in such cases, people do not acquire the status of 'normal' but that of a person with a known record for once having carried a stigma. When attaining a stigma, Goffman (1963) suggests that one is thrown into new relationships with old contacts, and into new relationships with those who share the stigma. This can be found in the accounts of autistic people upon self-identification and/or diagnosis, and upon encounters with the autistic community. Goffman (1963) also points out that those who carry a stigma in one regard can exhibit prejudices toward those who are stigmatized in another regard. An important reminder that intersectional relations within and beyond the autistic community may also lead to problematic divides and a Double Empathy Problem situated within unequal power relations.

In managing a stigmatized identity, Goffman (1963) makes an important distinction between what he describes as the 'discredited', those with a visible or well-known stigma, and the 'discreditable', whose stigma is not widely known about by others. Each situation has differing impacts upon how the stigmatized person will manage the impressions they make to others. For the discreditable, this means the management of information and disclosure, and issues of concealment and passing (and masking). Goffman (1963) shows how stigma can often be carried on the body, or that, much like a prestige or status 'symbol', one can have symbols of stigma. Such stigma symbols are often thus concealed.

> *The area of stigma management, then, might be seen as something that pertains mainly to public life, to contact between strangers or mere acquaintances, to one end of a continuum whose other pole is intimacy.* (Goffman, 1963, p. 69)

In the above passage, Goffman (1963) contrasts stigma with the acceptance one might find in an intimate relationship. Thus, if there is a solution to the Double Empathy Problem, then it is the building of relationships and rapport, mutual understanding through humility and shared respect. I have often noted that the Double Empathy Problem can be, at times, most problematic when dealing with complete strangers or new social situations. While breakdowns in understanding still occur in intimate relationships, at least one would hope there would be, if not more understanding, at least more acceptance.

Speakers for the stigmatized

An interesting aspect of Goffman's (1963) account is his discussion regarding what he called 'speakers' for the stigmatized, who appear in front of various audiences to present a case for the stigmatized, often providing a model of normal achievement, being 'heroes of adjustment', and providing moral tales to illustrate a normative desired code of conduct for the stigmatized. Here one can see parallels with the notion coined many years ago by Jim Sinclair of the autistic 'self-narrating zoo exhibit', positioned by non-autistic people at autism events to speak of their experience and answer personal questions, but without also having a position of a professional, and, even less so, allowed a critique of the status quo.

Goffman (1963) also talked about how, for some, becoming part of a 'movement' for the stigmatized could absorb one's existence until a stigmatized person finds that they have become a professional, with a career thrust upon them of 'representing their category'. Goffman (1963) could see, however, that such a positionality was a precarious one to inhabit.

> *To his other troubles he must add that of being simultaneously pushed in several directions by professionals who tell him what he should do and feel about what he is and isn't, and all this in purportedly his own interests.* (Goffman, 1963, p. 150)

One may find oneself juggling the expectations of professionals with those of one's community, branded non-representative when this was not a chosen role to begin with and so on. I am sure the above passage will resonate strongly with many an autistic advocate.

Goffman (1963) also described those who respond to stigma with defiance and rebellion – disaffiliates (whether loudly or quietly), deviants, eccentrics and group cultists:

> *Also, it seems possible for an individual to fail to live up to what we effectively demand of him, and yet be relatively untouched by this failure; insulated by his alienation, protected by identity beliefs of his own, he feels that he is a fully-fledged human being, and that we are the ones who are not quite human. He bears the stigma but does not seem to be impressed or repentant about doing so.* (Goffman, 1963, p. 17)

While I would obviously stop a long way short of seeing others as 'not quite human' in response, one could say the unrepentant deviant is perhaps the path that I have taken myself. This response is also reflected in cultural movements such as 'autistic pride', which is less a celebration of being 'autistic' but could be said to be celebrating having survived, and sometimes thrived, as an autistic person in an unfriendly society.

A word to the wise

In *Stigma* (Goffman, 1963), Goffman distinguishes between what he called the 'own and the wise'. The own being those who embodied and enacted a stigmatized identity and the wise being those who are privy to the secret life of the stigmatized and who were sympathetic to their plight. Allies one could say, or in common parlance today, the 'woke'. Goffman (1963) points out that the positionality of the 'wise' can lead, however, to stigma by association and gives, as one example, the loyal spouse of a mental patient, with the problems faced spreading out like waves with diminishing intensity to those in relationships with the stigmatized person. What is commonly referred to in sociological circles as 'courtesy stigma'.

In revisiting Goffman (1959; 1963), it should be noticeable that in the case of 'the stigmatized', and in this instance the case of autistic masking, one can be said to be '*damned if you do, and damned if you don't*', discredited at every juncture, but sometimes finding solace in one's own culture and community. So, for those wishing to understand the presentation of an autistic self in everyday life and the Double Empathy Problem, and who may see themselves as allies to the cause of autistic people's wellbeing, a word to the wise ... please read Goffman!

References

Becker, H. (1963). *Outsiders: Studies in the Sociology of Deviance.* The Free Press.

Deleuze, G., & Guattari, F. (1980). trans. B. Massumi (2004). *A Thousand Plateaus.* Continuum.

Garfinkel, H. (1967). *Studies in Ethnomethodology.* Polity Press.

Goffman, E. (1959). *The Presentation of Self in Everyday Life.* Penguin.

Goffman, E. (1963). *Stigma: Notes of the Management of a Spoiled Identity.* Penguin.

Milton, D. (2012). On the ontological status of autism: The 'double empathy problem'. *Disability & Society, 27*(6), 883–887. https://doi.org/10.1080/09687599.2012.710008

Milton, D., & Sims, T. (2016). How is a sense of well-being and belonging constructed in the accounts of autistic adults? *Disability & Society, 31*(4), 520–534. https://doi.org/10.1080/09687599.2016.1186529

Pearson, A., & Rose, K. (2021). A conceptual analysis of autistic masking: Understanding the narrative of stigma and the illusion of choice. *Autism in Adulthood, 3*(1), 52–60. https://doi.org/10.31219/osf.io/6rwa5

Chapter 9:

Neurotransception: A Conceptual Framework to Negotiate Relational and Power Dynamics that Exist across Divergent Neurotypes

Raymi Doyle

Introduction: The paradigm shift of intersubjectivity as a lens for looking at the relational dynamic of autistic experience

Historically, autism research has focused on individuals; however, it has been argued that the original author of autistic experience, Sukhareva, was interested in how children make connections with other (Zeldovich, 2018), which has a focus on understanding relational dynamics.

Psychoanalytic theories have moved away considerably from Bettleheim's (1967) belief that autism stemmed from refrigerator mothers and their frozen demeanour toward the child. There was a paradigm shift that had '*shaken the foundations of psychoanalysis*' (Thompson, 2005, p. 40) when intersubjective and relational perspectives were explored as an alternative to classical Freudian theory, where psychoanalysis was already phenomenological in its latency. This was an important concept to understand as it not only provided a rationale to begin to integrate different philosophies of intersubjectivity, but also the different theories of intersubjectivity that have since evolved (Gillespie & Cornish, 2010).

Decentred intersubjectivity suggests that it is through our interaction with others that we come to know ourselves, as self-knowledge is prone to inaccuracies through self-knowledge of the generalized other, and this is where decentring takes place (McKenzie, 2015). Cash further added that a double decentring can take place, which occurs across two stages and ultimately ends in the dulling down of the multidimensional aspect of the individual.

> *The first involves the tension between the I and the It, where the I must distinguish itself from an It. Meanwhile the second form of decentring involves the tension between the I and what Cash describes as 'the rules of the field of ideology'.*
> (Cash, 2003, p. 189)

McKenzie further suggested that we make subjectivity dependent on intersubjectivity rather than opposition of it.

> *By framing the relationship of subjective/intersubjective and conscious/unconscious into a matter of dependency rather than opposition, the task of understanding decentring becomes less about fixing the problem through 'recentring,' and more a matter of incorporating the concept of decentring into emotional experience.* (McKenzie, 2015, p. 76)

This could be argued as moving away from subjective positioning of self, where self is imposing power dynamics on other through the suggestion that other needs to be 'fixed', to creating space for a more intersubjective and incorporated emotional experience of other. This is especially relevant since autistic individuals have often been framed in a lens of disability and otherness that needs to be 'fixed' (Pearson & Rose, 2021), and a 'fix it' mentality imposed by professionals could be more related to the fixer's need to be less in a place of unknown, rather than the autistic individual's need (Doyle, 2023).

Although psychoanalysis had been suggested as having limited evidence and value toward autistic experience (Campbell et al., 1996; Howlin & Rutter, 1987, as cited in Howlin, 1998), this was related to treatment rather than a lens to reflect on the relational dynamics underlying the complex relationship between therapist and client. While the dilemma of imposing psychological theory on neurodivergence may be too generic, the flip side is that it is more understanding of relational dynamics.

Misrepresentation of the autistic experience and its influence on an empathic understanding of other

The Autistic Mutual Aid Society Edinburgh (AMASE) recently completed a review of adults' experiences of counselling (Hallett & Kerr, 2020). This indicated higher proportionate rates of mental ill health, but more barriers to access these services. These barriers included counselling experience, the therapeutic physical space, feelings and distress, working together, and how much was known about autism. What was apparent was how autistic individuals experienced therapy that was not adjusted to their autistic experience. While this research provided some insight into how therapy may be improved, it did not explore the underlying dynamics that were occurring between the therapist and the client.

There is a growing consensus from the autistic community that they have been misrepresented (Bottema-Beutel et al., 2021) by academic research with respect to the heterogeneity of the autistic individuals, by using a deficit medical model as opposed to positive attributes, which is an affront to the human dignity of the autistic individual (Milton et al., 2014), as a deficit model does not allow for autism being a natural variation in human evolution (O'Reilly et al., 2020). Although there is a growing presence of autistic authors in autism research, research has concentrated on methodologies, with a focus on reliability and validity rather than relevance (Jones, 2022).

Mitchell et al. (2021) have argued that autistic individuals had also been misrepresented through the belief that they lack empathy. It has been suggested that interneurotypes experience a mismatch, where non-autistic individuals may lack the capacity to empathize with autistic individuals and vice versa, defined as the Double Empathy Problem (Milton, 2012). The Double Empathy Problem contests the view that autistic and other neurodivergent individuals have a theory of mind deficit (Chapple et al., 2021) and offers an explanation that looks at difficulties with reciprocity and mutuality across divergent neurotypes (Milton, 2012; Milton et al., 2018).

There have been increasing levels of research to support the Double Empathy Problem (Brewer et al., 2016; Edey et al., 2016; Heasman & Gillespie, 2017; Hubbard et al., 2017; Sheppard et al., 2016). The Double Empathy Problem reframed the argument as being relational rather than individual (Milton et al., 2018), where autistic individuals felt more comfortable and less tired interacting together than interacting with non-autistic individuals (Crane et al., 2021; Crompton et al., 2020). The Double Empathy Problem has been referred to as a 'disjuncture in reciprocity between two differently disposed social actors'

(Milton, 2012, p. 884), which was harder for the autistic individual as this disjuncture was uncommon, as opposed to the non-autistic individual where, ultimately, the gap terminated the interaction. This increased anxiety and frustration lowered self-esteem and deteriorated mental health for autistic individuals (Milton et al., 2018).

Mitchell and colleagues (2021) believed that these misperceptions influenced the behaviour of the autistic individual by manifesting as barriers preventing them from experiencing social experiences. This encouraged autistic individuals to camouflage their experience and mirror the behaviour of the non-autistic, which further generated stress and anxiety, and resulted in them feeling undervalued, and separate from and a burden upon society. They proposed a social developmental account of autism, which was a transactional account of how another person's behaviour influences other, by reflecting on retrodictive mindreading as interpreting signals in another person's behaviour to infer their inner state. Gallese and Goldman (1998) suggested that accuracy was not only in receiving a signal but also emanating from it, which would suggest a bidirectional relationship within this signal. This fits the concept that autistic individuals are not emotionally detached, but rather send and receive emotional signals differently to neurotypicals (Nuske et al., 2013). However, stating that this was solely related to empathy was quite modular, where there could be numerous systems with many attributes associated (Korkmaz, 2011). Indeed, Bloom states that '*empathy is narrow in its focus, rendering it innumerate and subject to bias*' (Bloom, 2017, p. 24).

While Fletcher-Watson and Bird (2020) suggest that the conflation of empathy with other social cognitive processes results in empathy being misattributed as a central feature of autism, there is also a potential cost to trying to separate this aspect of interaction. If we try to separate integrated systems that are working in harmony, does this evoke the argument that the 'whole is greater than the sum of its parts', where we could be exploring something quite different by breaking it into the sum of its parts? It is also critical to recognize the importance of discussing empathy in the midst of the empathy deficit among autistic individuals (Fletcher-Watson & Bird, 2020), without forgetting that there has to be an emphasis on understanding empathy as part of a greater context of social processes (Kimber et al., 2023), and that we do not fully understand how different neurotypes experience an interaction (Milton et al., 2022), yet there is a clear need to understand why one neurotype may misperceive or perform snap judgements on another (Nicolaidis et al., 2019).

Empathy has also been questioned as being divergent in how it is experienced among victims, where some people are more empathic to one type of victim as opposed to others. Contrary to the belief that autistic individuals are more egocentric (Bodner et al 2015; Lombardo & Baron-Cohen, 2011), it is of the author's opinion that there may be more ego attached to neurotypicals who frame their empathy in positive terms, as focusing on a person as needing to be fixed may come from a place of ego (Doyle, 2023). On the other hand, spaciousness allows the ego to go somewhere else, where you witness both self, the other, and the connective space without all those interruptions (Doyle, 2021; 2023). Wayment and Bauer referred to this as the quiet ego:

> *The quiet ego is a way of construing the self that transcends egotism, not by neglecting the self but rather by facilitating a balance of concerns for the self and others as well as by facilitating the growth of the self and others.* (Wayment & Bauer, 2018, p. 881)

The application of predictive coding within a relational dynamic

When we think of people making inferences, it is understandable to think of Friston coding theory. Friston (2008) suggested that the brain was an active inference framework that applied hypothesis testing to minimize prediction errors. Since the brain was in the dark, its input came from prior experience or evolutionary knowledge (Froese & Ikegami, 2013). Exteroceptive and proprioceptive data from the senses were compared to prior knowledge (Fonaghy, 2021). Hohwy (2014) proposed a perceptual hierarchy, where lower-level processing occurred from this exteroceptive and proprioceptive input, producing a prediction error signal, and higher-level processing sent down signals that provided contextual modulation to dictate expectations of how the prediction error should be evaluated. This contextual signal determined how seriously the prediction error was taken, so that an epistemic trust/mistrust developed that could regulate/downregulate the prediction error (Fonaghy, 2021).

There have been increasing appeals to apply prediction coding theory to the cognitive, perceptual and neural processes occurring across autistic experience (Lawson et al., 2014; Pellicano & Burr, 2012; Qian & Lipkin, 2011; Rosenberg et al., 2015; Sinha et al., 2014; van Boxtel & Lu, 2013; Van de Cruys et al., 2014). These studies show an individualistic notion of biological changes occurring from accessing top-down prior knowledge to make predictions of bottom-up sensory information, which does not recognize the importance of the relational dynamic of a shared mechanism between two individuals, as discussed by Deschrijver and Palmer (2020).

Deschrijver and Palmer (2020) suggest that theory of mind is better studied in a relational framework, where they believe there is a misalignment as opposed to inferred mental representations in how theory of mind has often been viewed. Although there will always be a misalignment between self and other guiding interaction, they suggested that the human brain engaged the temporoparietal junction (TPJ) when observing an action that mismatched the observer's own. This established a neural mechanism for action conflict monitoring, which is essentially when there is mismatch in the prediction of other.

They suggested less monitoring of the misalignment among autistic individuals between self and other, and a suppression between self and other representations, as other people's mental representations conflicted with their own. The suppression was because other people's incongruent mental states hindered that of the autistic individual. Viewed as suppression rather than an absence, this moves away from a deficit model concept to something still being resolved. Executive function, along with cognitive control, aided in this suppression. While differences in theory of mind were related to a difference in a shared social-conflict monitoring mechanism that was best studied through a shared mechanism, they acknowledged the dilemma of differentiating between shared representational frameworks as opposed to that of the individual. This was essentially the difference between intrasubjective and intersubjective experience.

This study is relevant for a plethora of reasons. It first explains how a shared but differently experienced mechanism is related to that constant sense of feeling different often described within autistic experience. It provides insight as to how executive function may be a contributing mechanism, from deficit to coping mechanism. It also recognizes the importance of studying autistic interaction in the context of human interaction at a relational level, and how the other's experience may be contributing to the autistic self. Although there were differences in how action conflict monitoring (Friston's prediction error) was experienced between interneurotypes, it acknowledged the dilemma of separating a shared representational framework from the observer's own, differentiating the intrasubjective from the intersubjective.

Crompton and colleagues (2020) suggested that this type of shared information was 'shared equally effectively' in groups of autistic or non-autistic individuals, but not when there was a mixed interneurotype group. Considering they found there was less of a rapport suggests a more relational exchange that may not necessarily mean an exchange of empathy, but an exchange within the relational dynamic itself. When we focus on the relational dynamic, this allows for the heterogeneity of the empathic experience to occur across interneurotypes, and allows us to hold the elusive quality of empathy which has been hard to define (Coplan, 2011; Fletcher-Watson & Bird, 2020).

Rapport, defined as the quality of the interaction between two individuals, based on attentiveness, positivity and coordination, has been studied both within and between different neurotypes (Crompton et al., 2020; Rifai et al., 2022). Heasman and Gillespie suggest that intersubjectivity between autistic individuals goes beyond coordination, as coordination focuses on consensus, whereas intersubjectivity characterizes the shared understanding that is experienced between individuals. In this two-way gap of mutual understanding between autistic and neurotypical individuals, they suggest that double empathy occurs for both parties, highlighting the danger of '*interpreting neurodivergent behaviour on neurotypical terms*' (Heasman & Gillespie, 2019, p. 911).

Dialectical misattunement theory was proposed as a cumulative misattunement between persons, where researchers (Bolis et al., 2017) believed irrelevant information processing could lead to a perceptual overload, whereby the autistic individual may withdraw into themselves to reduce prediction errors, which could be described as autistic inertia. They suggested that their model in technical terms was '*studying potential dynamic and recurrent feedback loops across and within different levels of description, as well as temporal scales, driving both quantitative and qualitative changes*' (Bolis et al., 2017, p.368).

The paper was titled 'Beyond Autism' as it wanted to embrace the individual as well as socioculturally mediated interactions with other people by looking at the reciprocal alignment of individual and societal practices, as opposed to individual brain function. Although dialectical misattunement has been suggested as the mechanism behind the Double Empathy Problem (Rifai et al., 2022), it does not provide insight as to how these processes may be occurring outside of a hypothetical theorem. Although it further supports the shift in seeing autistic experience from an individual to a more relational dynamic, there is still an emphasis on an autistic brain having difficulty in making predictions. This begs the question of how relational dynamics may integrate with a Bayesian theorem. Wallace has commented on the issue of the individual self in relation to external events:

Our existence is invariably intersubjective, for we exist in a causal nexus in which we are constantly influenced by, and exert influence upon, the world around us, including other people. The individual self does not exist independently of the body and mind, but rather exists in reliance upon a myriad of physical and mental processes that are constantly changing. (Wallace, 2001, p. 209)

Wallace's (2001) statement is essentially claiming that many systems are integrated both within an individual as well as between individuals, and that separating these may prove difficult since they are constantly in a state of flux.

If we cannot fully understand autistic experience in how it is experienced as self, we could review autism using an intersubjective lens to help us see through the eyes of the client themselves (Sachs, 1995). Indeed, Shakespeare (2006) claimed that disability was neither the result of the individual nor society, but was rather a complex interaction between the two. When I listened carefully to autistic individuals' perspectives across the literature as well as within my research (Doyle, 2023), the term disability is often disabling to autistic individuals, as it separates and divides rather than includes. Therefore, it could be argued that there is a need for research to be developed that bridges the gap between different neurotypes interpreting research. This was the impetus for me, the author, to explore a range of methodologies, ultimately resulting in the development of my own methodology, shaped by a pilot study and by my understanding of autistic experience needs, as well as what I did not know. This required me to reflexively revisit my own relationship with autistic experience.

To know when one has entered an unknown intersubjective space, it is necessary to have an insight into our own subjective and intrasubjective space. Gallagher cited Di Paulo and colleagues stating, '*Just as it takes two to tango, one cannot accomplish interaction by oneself. Just as when two people dance the tango, something dynamic is created that neither one could create on one's own.*' (Gallagher, 2014, p. 496). The differentiation between these spaces may set aside Stein's dilemma (1916/1989) by asking to what extent does one need to be the same as the other to empathize, as through intersubjectivity and expanding space, we are connecting beyond empathy (Erskine, 1998) This was why it was important for me to ask the question, 'Why am I researching this topic?', from both a subjective and intrasubjective, leading to an intersubjective/mutual, understanding. While it is impossible to share every morsal of my reflexive journey, one particular client early in my career captured this idea profoundly.

Reflexive statement

I was introduced to an eight-year-old boy early in my career who on paper exhibited a myriad of autism-associated behaviours that were categorized, at the time, under a triad of impairment as a social inability which often resulted in challenging behaviour. When I first met him, he seemed to be quite content in his own space, until someone tried to pull him into their own dynamic, where these behaviours would manifest as a reaction. It felt like watching someone from another planet interact, and it was obvious that I was the foreigner coming into his world, which was as symbolic as it was literal, since I was an Irishman working in the US. Although I could see him, he felt distant, exploring his terrain, and I felt almost like I was intruding upon his space. I felt a sense of guilt trying to pull him into this other planet. Although I had treatment plans to develop that were based on psychological and educational assessments and I was behaviourally trained, here I was imposing interventions from goals that were designed by individuals who had never met him, just assessed him. Although that was my job, I realized the importance of his self-determinism, and realized that the psychotherapist in me wanted to develop our relationship, while the behaviourist in me was trained to develop interventions.

What this essentially taught me was how much we differ and how we are not able to fully interpret the other. However, we can still begin to co-construct meaning between self and other, if we are willing to understand how ourselves, both within and between neurotypes, impact our interpretation of other, both individually and collectively. This thought culminated alongside two conversations I had. The first being with a research methods expert in wondering if a more co-constructive means was needed and the second asking me how, within a research method, could I determine the difference between what was intrasubjective and intersubjective.

Therefore, a qualitative constructivist grounded theory adaptation using an intersubjective analysis embedded within an abductive reasoning paradigm was developed (Doyle, 2017) to analyse the intersubjective space between researcher and participant. This was called a 'co-constructivist grounded theory adaptation'. This was first trialled in a pilot study, readjusted to address any of the limitations, and then applied within a doctoral research project with 12 participants (Doyle, 2023). Several categories evolved around relational dynamics between divergent individuals, leading to a core category as a conceptual framework termed 'neurotransception'. I will endeavour to provide an overview of the findings but understand that further dissemination is required to fully comprehend the depth and impact this conceptual framework may have at both a pragmatic and academic level within the field of neurodivergence, as well as across a broader context.

Neurotransception

Neurotransception is a conceptual umbrella framework resulting from theorization (Jabareen, 2009) that has emerged from the findings of a doctoral piece of research (Doyle, 2023). It goes beyond interoception (Mahler, 2016), where a person is trying to interpret and predict their internal world (Barrett & Simmons, 2015); exteroception, where a person is trying to make sense of the world around them; context blindness (Vermeulen, 2012), where individuals struggle to understand social situations as a neurodivergent experience; and neuroception (Porges, 2004), where individual neural circuitry assesses the safety of individuals and situations.

Neurotransception is defined and conceptualized as the transmission and reception of neurobiological signals that could be consciously or unconsciously occurring between individuals, which are used to sense the safety of being in the space with other as part of the social hierarchy relationship within that group or interaction. The transmitter in this case is the neurotypical individual who is sending the signal, and the receptor is the autistic individual receiving either the signal itself, or the impact of the transmitter sending the signal. I discuss these terms generally in relation to the conceptual umbrella framework from the findings emerging from the data, as opposed to suggesting a fixed model of interaction. I have used the general terms transmitter and receptor in Figure 9.1, which refers to the neurotypical and autistic individuals respectively with those terms as interneurotypes, and below provide some excerpts from the doctorate research to substantiate these claims.

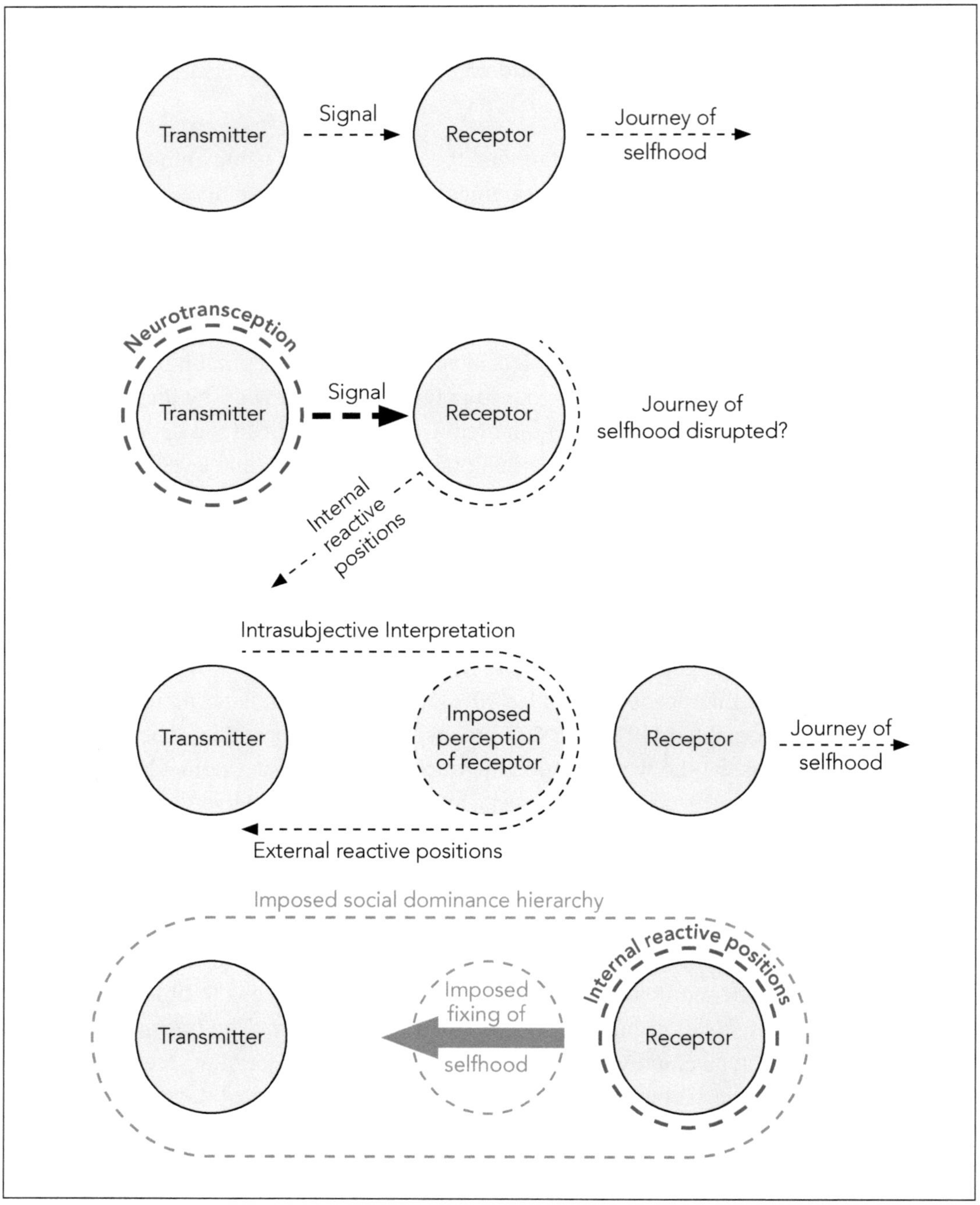

Figure 9.1: Theory of neurotransception (Doyle, 2023).

Signals are integrated within social interactions between individuals, where a neurotypical individual as transmitter is seeking a response signal that provides feedback about whether it is safe to engage with an individual as receptor. This is often through facial gestures (particularly smiles), eye contact (Pönkänen & Hietanen, 2012) and affect (Gaigg, 2012), which can modulate autonomic arousal states used in sensing safety. I was, however, interested in understanding how this occurred when there was an autistic individual as a receptor.

Crompton and colleagues (2020) have already recognized that autistic individuals are more comfortable with their own neurotype as opposed to mixed interneurotypes. In relation to the unconscious/conscious signalling as shown in Figure 9.1, Participant 12 (P12) in this research (Doyle, 2023) defined the concept of signalling when she claimed that if we remove preconceived judgement, and that affect is only one means of signalling, there is more safety for the neurotypical individual, which allows the autistic individual to feel a lot more '*comfortable because people can embrace them and they're not pinging off negative vibes.*' P12 recognized that she sensed a demanding pressure during social engagement from people smiling:

> *It's asking a lot when someone smiles at you. It's like, 'What do you need now?' Whereas, if it's part of an engagement it's different because you know where it's coming from.* (P12)

Clin and Kissine (2023) further alluded to how this discomfort can be projected in their study on how the neurotypical may be experiencing distress from the eye contact of the autistic individual and projecting that distress upon the autistic individual.

When both individuals within an interaction, as transmitter and receptor in general, are exchanging signals of safety, they can engage in optimal conditions for that relationship, which relates to the context of how therapeutic relationships can work on a systemic, neurobiological/somatic/sensorimotor, cognitive and behavioural level. This may also occur between autistic individuals as both transmitter and receptor:

> *It feels like I have got a pretty sharp autism radar these days, and I can spot things pretty easily, but I also inhabit this world, so I am talking from inside it.* (P1)

If the original transmitter did not receive a response signal indicating safety to engage, or a signal they could interpret from the other as safe to engage (Porges, 2004), then this potentially created a space of unknown. Pierce (1977) identified this as part of the cloud of unknowing, where we as social creatures are trying to surpass evolution. The more we move forward, the less we know, triggering the need to know more, and the less comfortable we can be in an unknown space. This was seen as a greater problem for neurotypical neurotypes as transmitters, as opposed to the autistic individual as transmitter:

> *I just think people really, really want to be safe and secure, and people are safe and secure in the things that they know, and anything that is unknown freaks them out.* (Participant 3 [P3])

This has also been recently postulated following the completion of this research by Clin and Kissine:

> *Based on a bidirectional perspective on interactional difficulties in autism, we speculate that the neurotypicals' distress when their attempts to eye contact are not reciprocated could make their behaviour insistent, which, in turn, could make the autistics uncomfortable.* (Clin & Kissine, 2023, p. 1949)

The neurotypical transmitter operates on a system that uses ego to work with all these disruptions of signals. However, ego's attempt to rebalance the imbalances is from a place of unknown, which means that the neurotypical individual's ego as transmitter uses context to make shortcut predictions. Context blindness has been used to explain why individuals struggle to interpret social situations (Vermeulen, 2012). In this instance, the misinterpretation by neurotypical neurotypes as transmitters of autistic individuals' behaviour could be seen as a form of reverse context blindness. These shortcut predictions are intrasubjective, and interrupt relational dynamics to justify their projections.

This has since been corroborated post-study, where Chapple et al. (2023) found that autistic readers were better able to hold on to detailed complexity, whereas non-autistic readers tended to reduce information down to key ideas for generalization.

The ego here is intrasubjective since it holds fictional representations and projections of the other (Evans, 1996). Porges (2020) defined projections as a misaligned top-down interpretation of a bottom-up experience, as opposed to vice versa. The misaligned top-down interpretation of that bottom-up experience was an attempt to reduce the prediction error (Friston, 2008) between self and other. Deschrijver and Palmer (2020) suggested that incongruence between divergent empathic experiences was part of the egocentric bias that was used to process social conflict, or what could be interpreted as minimizing the prediction error (Friston, 2008).

Therefore, the neurotypical individual as transmitter sends a signal to minimize their prediction error, which could occur both consciously or unconsciously depending on an individual's awareness. If they did not receive a response signal from the autistic individual as receptor, then their intrasubjective ego was misattuned both within self and self's experience of other, which may help explain the dialectical misattunement hypothesis (Bolis et al., 2017) that has been suggested to be an underlying mechanism of the Double Empathy Problem (Rifai et al., 2022). Within the neurotypical self as transmitter, there was an incongruence growing between what was experienced from a bottom-up fear and what was a top-down attempt to reduce the prediction error, which was akin to a decentred intersubjectivity (McKenzie, 2015).

Participant 6 (P6) provided an example of the above where a care assistant had a closed intrasubjective loop, and they perceived and interpreted the autistic individual's behaviour as aggressive and called the police, as opposed to seeing that the autistic individual was in distress (Doyle, 2023). The care assistant's intrasubjective ego may have inadvertently misinterpreted the distressed autistic neurotype as receptor requiring support and help. This is also visually represented by the dashed line surrounding the neurotypical neurotype transmitter in Figure 9.1.

The autistic individual as receptor experiences this misalignment of the neurotypical neurotype transmitter as two different languages. When the neurotypical transmitter is seeking safety, their conscious/unconscious systems may not realize there is incongruence within the neurotypical neurotype's signals, which the autistic receptor's conscious/unconscious systems receive and interpret as exhaustive and confusing due to hypersensitiveness, as Participant 5 (P5) eloquently explained:

> *It is like I can read two conversations, and I think that happens a lot with autistic and highly sensitive people. And that is why it is so exhausting, because I am taking in everything the person is saying, and I am taking in everything they are really not saying ... So it's what they are coming out of their mouth [sic], but what all the other sayings they are not saying, their fear, their judgement, their manipulation, whatever it is, all that other stuff I can sense. And then I am following two conversations at the same time* [sic]. (P5)

This is why it is important for a therapist to be reflexive with their own state of incongruence.

The neurotypical neurotype as transmitter's activated intrasubjective ego is a closed loop, where the neurotypical transmitter's interpretations are coming from within their own being as opposed to between them and an autistic individual as receptor. The neurotypical transmitter consciously/unconsciously interprets the response of the autistic receptor as one of two responses; either purposefully not responding, or unable to respond. This may explain why autistic individuals have often been misinterpreted as having challenging behaviour, e.g., (P6).

If the neurotypical transmitter had a more open loop signal, where they had the capacity to receive the signal of the autistic individuals as a transmitter, they may be able to receive feedback from the autistic individuals, and realize that their signal as a neurotypical transmitter is confusing for the autistic individual as receptor. However, since the neurotypical individual as transmitter has an activated intrasubjective ego, where they are projecting their internal experience on other because of the misalignment between a top-down and bottom-up experience, a threat response is activated in the neurotypical individual as transmitter as a means to cope with this dilemma, which can be both consciously and unconsciously experienced. This process could explain how the Double Empathy Problem occurs (Milton, 2012).

The concept of the neurotypical neurotype individual having an intrasubjective and closed focus to minimize the prediction error was alluded to by Chapple and colleagues (2021) when they proposed that the Double Empathy Problem was related to how autistic individuals had a more open-ended assessment of mental states. This was further supported by the principle of context blindness (Vermeulen, 2012). Since autistic individuals may struggle to make short-term predictions, it could be implied that the neurotypical individual as transmitter was making shortcut predictions which were intrasubjective, and therefore a closed loop of what they perceived the autistic receptor's needs to be.

This suggests that the autistic individual as a receptor is less likely to engage in closed intrasubjective interpretations of others' thought processes, as the autistic individual may have a propensity to be intersubjective from having more insight into other. This interpretation was based on Chapple and colleagues' (2021) concept of a more open assessment of other, and evidenced by P5's comment on reverse mindblindness:

> *I don't go out in the world and expect everybody to start thinking my way – but people expect me to start thinking their way, and I see it as a reverse mindblindness.* (P5)

This is important, as it not only refutes the myth that autistic individuals have an impaired theory of mind (Gernsbacher & Yergeau, 2019), but it also suggests there may be a more advanced capacity to engage from hyperawareness within an intersubjective space, in an open-ended loop, given the right context. This is extremely important when we are therapeutically interacting with an autistic individual as a neurotypical or allistic other, as the autistic individual may pick up things that the neurotypical individual may not actually be aware of.

The journey of selfhood

The journey of selfhood was used as a collective term to represent one's development as an individual within my doctoral research (Doyle, 2023). Neurotransception was ultimately identified as interrupting an autistic individual's journey of selfhood. Part of the journey of selfhood may involve developing an inhibitory/excitatory relationship with accepting a position of self in relation to other. Depending on the individual's journey, they may inhibit more awareness of self/other in relation to exciting their awareness of self/other.

If that was employed as a reactive position, as discussed in the next section, it manifested as underselved and overothered positions of self as an attempt to know how to react to others, while protecting self from being less connected to self. Overselving was an excessive focus on self to the detriment of other; underothering was less focused on other to maintain the integrity of the overselved position that was used for ego-based, overselved and intrasubjective justifications. The journey of selfhood may have involved applying a default overothering position as an attempt to generate more access to an overselved position. However, it may require reverting back to reactive positions to integrate new learning/meaning as part of that chaos. Participant 2 (P2) provided insight into being less reactive from engaging in therapeutic process, and no longer being '*a slave to her fear*', which would indicate reactivity was separate to being autistic, although intricately linked.

Participant 4 (P4) indicated that this should not always be interrupted, as it may be part of their own internal regulation within their homeostasis. Homeostasis is the purposeful regulation between the various systems in the body, critical to one's well-being (Cannon, 1945). However, it also may be how the individual gets back into a journey of selfhood:

> *I think one of the most positive things for families to understand sometimes is that sometimes you can't always make sense of chaos; sometimes there is chaos, and not trying to fix that chaos and going with the flow is part of it.* (P4)

Reactive positions in neurotransception

Internal reactive position

Internal reactive positions of autistic neurotype receptors as part of one's journey of selfhood became their own theme for autistic individuals as receptors when they were occurring as part of the individuals' defences in reaction to neurotransception, as opposed to further development of self (Figure 9.1). The 'repositioning of self' is one such category, which often occurs when the autistic individual as receptor is attempting to recalibrate how they are being impacted or how they will interact across neurotransceptive relational dynamics. Some examples of these are summarized in Table 9.1.

Table 9.1: Repositioning of self.

Repositioning of self
Underselving
Overothering
Blur between self and other

There was found to be an inhibitory–excitatory (IE) relationship with acceptance of positioning self in relation to other, where an autistic individual as receptor sought allostasis. This was where self was either exciting or inhibiting their focus on self/other. Allostasis was achieving stability through changing the defended levels of one or more forms of regulation to adapt to changing environments (Sterling & Eyer, 1988), and allostatic load referred to the cumulative cost for an individual dealing with psychosocial, behavioural and environmental demands (McEwen, 1998).

Underselving involved a lesser focus on self as opposed to the focus on other, which may have felt like a blur between self and other as a way to protect the integrity of self:

> *What I found is happening in the last five or six years … Is that I pick up on that other person's energy and their mind And I mirror them And I become, I can't tell where I begin, and they end in some places.* (P5)

Overothering was an excessive focus on other. Overothering became confusing when the other was in their own incongruence, which meant that the autistic individual neurotype potentially embodied the incongruence of other. Overothering within a neurotransception neutral place could be a powerful space within therapy, as it helped address projected incongruence within the dynamics. The IE relationship between underselving and overothering also fed into what participants experienced as a blur, where it was hard to separate between self and other as Participant 8 (P8) described:

> *Yeah. I absolutely think that for myself and especially those I know on the spectrum there is a weaker ... I don't know what to call it. I'd say barrier between our feelings and other people's feelings. So, I can very, very easily pick up other people's feelings without realising I've picked up their feelings and then I will start feeling it and carrying it for however many days and might not, at any point, realise that it was never mine to begin with. I've picked it up from somebody else and just been carrying it around.* (P8)

Miles (2014) suggested that cultural anchoring, which is the process where individuals incorporate less salient identities into their core identity, was important when predicting and describing behaviour.

External reactive positions

External reactive positions were the reactive positions of others external to the autistic neurotype within this research but could be associated with reactive positions of others in a broader context. The bottom-up processes that manifested as a sense of threat within the neurotypical neurotype as transmitter, within the concept of neurotransception as discussed above, whether conscious or unconscious, activated a social dominance status within the neurotypical neurotype as transmitter. This was due to the unknown being a threat to their position in the group, also exemplified in P3's response in the example below and visually represented via the dashed line surrounding the fourth row in Figure 9.1.

P3 spoke of her older sister trying to force her autistic sister to see the world through the older sister's perception. This was because she has '*very definite ideas about how the world is, and she wants it to fit that*'. This was the older sister's attempt to return to the status quo, which resolves her internal incongruence and therefore reduces the prediction error. What this means is that the neurotypical neurotype as transmitter could be imposing their perception on the autistic neurotypes as receptors, as opposed to what the autistic receptors position actually was, as shown in Figure 9.1.

This sense of threat may also be an internal threat to the neurotypical neurotype as transmitter, due to that level of incongruence they may have from the two paths of communication (what someone says and what someone is not saying), that P5 explained as receiving from neurotypical neurotypes, which they may or may not be consciously aware of.

Extreme external reactive positions could continue to evolve where the neurotypical neurotype as transmitter may engage in what becomes an intrasubjective neurotransceptive looping, which is where the neurotypical neurotype as transmitter makes an intrasubjective interpretation to justify their next response. If this looping is not interrupted, this may have the potential to lead to an escalation of threat-enhanced projections, which may have the following outcomes whether consciously or unconsciously intended:

- The transmitter may become coercively controlling.
- The transmitter may become defensive.
- The transmitter may lose their ability to engage and revert to more socially dominating processes in order to regain a sense of control. These may take the form of:
  - generating an alpha status or what appears to be an alpha status, creating more incongruence within self.
  - collaborative beta engagement in finding safety within beta separating or ostracizing the other within the pack.
- The transmitter may attempt to befriend the individual in a narcissistic way in order to negate a threat response as opposed to genuine attunement.

Social dominance from a neurotransceptive lens

Stevanovic and colleagues (2019) stated that both neurotypes require dominance to experience calm. Social dominance can be a default defence mechanism in the neurotypical neurotype, as a transmitter's attempt to regain control by imposing their social reality within that space of unknown, which is used to minimize their prediction error. This may not always be within the neurotypical transmitter's awareness. This is in part due to the concept that neurotypical neurotypes as individuals are often privileged as the dominant neurotype and social construct (Murray, 2020). This was defined when Participant 1 (P1) was instructed by a neurotypical individual to refer to himself as a person with autism, even when he did not identify with that term:

> *We had weekly PD [personal development] sessions on the counselling training, and the facilitator was quite insistent that I did not call myself autistic, but I called myself a person with autism. But it didn't work like that for me, and I didn't accept that, and I didn't want to, and people got really annoyed with me for calling myself autistic, but it was like that, it is so deep in me, it in some ways is me.* (P1)

This is consistent with atypical social ranking (Ogawa et al., 2019), where autistic individuals show more resistance to social rank recognition. While Ogawa and colleagues indicate this could be a response *'to compensate deficits from neural systems processing social information'* (Ogawa et al., 2019, p. 1), this could also be explained by the neurotypical neurotype as transmitter imposing a social ranking, as described in the example above with P3. The autistic neurotype as receptor may not respond initially because their neurotype does not perceive, consciously or unconsciously, any initial threat, as described by P1's example below and visually represented in Figure 9.1:

> *This person that I am talking about, is quite well known, and I acted like she could have been anyone, and maybe I was a bit disrespectful in that way, but emm that's autism for you.* (P1)

Haaker et al. (2016) stated that social ranking/dominance was activated when it was determined that an individual constituted a physical threat, although they recognized that the interaction between dominance and threat learning remained unknown.

Therefore, if individuals who work in a restrictive practice setting have an internalized threat, self-activated from their own incongruence and stemming from neurotransception, then what they perceive as supporting could be more related to trying to maintain a social hierarchy without fully being aware.

P4's example of working with staff supporting a distressed individual demonstrates how this internalized threat can manifest in a neurotypical neurotype as controlling behaviour:

> *The staff were terrified, saying, 'We don't feel in control.' I said, 'OK, you don't feel in control. How many instances of physical aggression have you had to restrain in the last six months?' And they actually said one, and it didn't last very long.* (P4)

The neurotypical neurotype as transmitters in this example (staff) internalized a threat that was incongruent with self, then projected this sense of threat onto the autistic neurotype as receptor (individual). The neurotypical individuals (staff) interpreted the threat which came from feeling out of control as coming from the autistic receptor, rather than realizing it was their own internal threat system that was activated due to that incongruence. When the neurotypical staff were questioned regarding their rationality for this fear, they acknowledged their rationality was flawed. When the autistic receptor is reacting to that sense of threat from neurotypical transmitter because of internal reactive positions, the neurotypical transmitter may justify that reaction as the threat they perceived from the beginning. Thus, a series of misinterpretations can begin. P4 described this as follows:

> *Sometimes you have to reflect on people [and ask] who's got the problem there. And it is actually people not thinking from the other person's perspective. They are not empathising, they are not seeing the world from that stressed trauma.* (P4)

P4 suggested this to be the case when referring to this autistic individual, as developmentally he is quite young and learning to regulate, which P6 also suggested in an example of working with a child. P8 also described having an emotional side that was interrupted, which is to this day quite young. These examples would suggest that some autistic neurotypes as receptors' reactive positions could be interruptions of their journey of self, as shown in Figure 9.1, where the autistic receptor was pulled into a state of chaos as represented by the dashed line around the receptor.

The fix-it mentality from a neurotransception lens

Within this social hierarchy, the neurotypical neurotype, in order to resolve the prediction error and also reduce the level of threat, activates this social dominance to elevate their social need at the expense of the autistic neurotype as receptor. Although this could occur through many processes, this research specifically identified how this was carried out through attempts to try and 'fix' the autistic neurotype as receptor, so that the neurotypical neurotype as transmitter was able to resolve all of the occurring internal dilemmas they were experiencing from activated neurotransception.

The fix-it mentality is where the neurotypical neurotype as transmitter attempts to put the autistic individual into 'a box' as a problem to be fixed. However, this may be more in relation to the neurotypical neurotype as transmitter trying to resolve their own internal prediction error. If the neurotypical neurotype as transmitter sends a signal within neurotransception that is not received back to provide the neurotypical neurotype with a sense of safety, then social hierarchy dominance is activated, which places the neurotypical neurotype as transmitter's sense of safety ahead of the needs of the autistic neurotype as receptor as the other. This has the potential impact of consciously or unconsciously suggesting that the autistic neurotype as receptor's need is lesser, as being fixed suggests that one is broken, and so intrasubjectively perceives the autistic individual as lesser. Hence, if the autistic receptor, from the neurotypical transmitter's perspective, is consciously or unconsciously fixed, this deactivates the social hierarchy dominance, which deactivates the sense of threat, which is also a justification that helps minimize the prediction error. It also resolves the dilemma of not receiving a response back from the neurotransception signalling, as now the need to fix imposes the concept that the autistic neurotype as receptor, from the perception of the neurotypical neurotype as transmitter, is a deficit.

The evidence for both positive and negative discrimination that autistic individuals have experienced (Heasman & Gillespie, 2019) may come from an intrasubjective need to resolve the prediction error within the neurotypicals' experience of neurotransception. While some neurotypicals may see the need to minimize the prediction error as an imposed sense of the autistic individual as lesser within a social hierarchy, other neurotypical attempts to minimize the prediction error may be generated due to a need to help and support. In both instances, neurotypicals perceive the autistic individual as lesser and that could be argued to be discriminatory. Indeed, the stigma and negative discrimination found from the disclosure of a diagnosis (Davidson & Henderson, 2010; Powell & Acker, 2016; Treweek et al., 2018) may be related to the need to see the individual as lesser as described above.

> *Heasman and Gillespie supported the idea that neurotypicals may be in a state of incongruence, where their projection is coming from this bottom-up and top-down misalignment, when they stated that 'over-estimating one's own helpfulness is understandable, since it protects the positive identity of the perceiver and brings their self-perception into line with their ideal Self.'* (Heasman & Gillespie, 2019, p. 11)

Examples of fix-it mentalities are imposed through various mechanisms identified within this research, such as pejorative language used to define autism from a professional viewpoint, social skills which are weaponized to impose social pretence engagement for the non-autistic transmitters to get the signal of safety, parents looking for the child to be fixed from attending therapy, and interventions used that imply the need to be fixed as opposed to having a functional divergent neurotype that is accepted. However, this research acknowledges that these are only some examples.

Future discussion and implications

These findings suggest that underlying relational dynamics occur throughout the autistic individual's life span, which may impact their mental health experiences and be misrepresented as part of autistic experience. This has implications for researching other misrepresented groups within a neurodivergent identity, as well as other marginalized groups. This may also involve a larger conversation around exploring diagnosis at a relational level, since a significant amount of the data collected and reviewed in this research explored the significance of what diagnosis meant to one's journey of selfhood.

The conceptual framework of this research was also limited in that it focused on the impact that neurotypicals neurotypes may be having as transmitters on the autistic neurotypes as receptors. However, it did not look in detail at the variation that exists across transmitters' responses (i.e., autistic neurotype transmitters and neurotypical neurotype receptors, apart from the generic variation between externalized reactive positions). Future research is already being considered to address this.

While this chapter is a flavour of the research, there is already extensive data within this research on the impact of neurotransception on traumatic experience and trauma-informed care, and variations in neurodivergent experiences across cultural and gender differences, as this was an international study. These findings will be reviewed in further publications and presentations.

It is the through further exploring how neurotransception may have an impact on a range of dynamics, as discussed but not limited to the above, that pragmatic ways of neutralizing neurotransception, that has already been developed within this research, may be applied in a working theory that can be integrated across existing theoretical constructs and accessed by a range of professionals.

References

Barrett, L. F., & Simmons, W. K. (2015). Interoceptive predictions in the brain. *Nature Reviews Neuroscience, 16*(7), 419–429. https://doi.org/10.1038/nrn3950

Bettleheim, B. (1967). *The Empty Fortress: Infantile Autism and the Birth of the Self.* The Free Press.

Bloom, P. (2017). Empathy and its discontents. *Trends in Cognitive Sciences, 21*(1), 24–31.

Bodner, K. E., Engelhardt, C. R., Minshew, N. J., and Williams, D. L. (2015). Making inferences: Comprehension of physical causality, intentionality, and emotions in discourse by high-functioning older children, adolescents, and adults with autism. *Journal of Autism and Developmental Disorders, 45*, 2721–2733. https://doi.org/10.1007/s10803-015-2436-3

Bolis, D., Balsters, J., Wenderoth, N., Becchio, C., & Schilbach, L. (2017). Beyond autism: Introducing the dialectical misattunement hypothesis and a Bayesian account of intersubjectivity. *Psychopathology, 50*(6), 355–372. https://doi.org/10.1159/000484353

Bottema-Beutel, K., Kapp, S. K., Lester, J. N., Sasson, N. J., & Hand, B. N. (2021). Avoiding ableist language: Suggestions for autism researchers. *Autism in Adulthood, 3*(1), 18–29. https://doi.org/10.1089/aut.2020.0014

Brewer, R., Biotti, F., Catmur, C., Press, C., Happé, F., & Cook, R. (2016). Can neurotypical individuals read autistic facial expressions? Atypical production of emotional facial expressions in autism spectrum disorders. *Autism Research, 9*(2), 262–271. https://doi.org/10.1002/aur.1508

Campbell, M., Schopler, E., Cueva, J. E., & Hollin, A. (1996). Treatment of autistic disorder. *Journal of American Academy of Child and Adolescent Psychiatry, 35*(2), 134-143. https://doi.org/10.1097/00004583-199602000-00005

Cannon, W. B. (1945). *The Way of an Investigator: A Scientist's Experiences in Medical Research.* Hafner Publishing Company.

Cash, J. (2003). Conclusion: Politics, history and the unconscious. In J. Damousi & R. Reynolds (Eds.), *Essays in History and Psychoanalysis* (pp. 188–198). Melbourne University Press.

Chapple, M., Davis, P., Billington, J., Myrick, J. A., Ruddock, C., & Corcoran, R. (2021). Overcoming the Double Empathy Problem within pairs of autistic and non-autistic adults through the contemplation of serious literature. *Frontiers in Psychology, 12,* Article 708375. https://doi.org/10.3389/fpsyg.2021.708375

Chapple, M., Davis, P., Billington, J., & Corcoran, R. (2023). Exploring the different cognitive, emotional and imaginative experiences of autistic and non-autistic adult readers when contemplating serious literature as compared to non-fiction. *Frontiers in Psychology, 14,* 1001268. https://doi.org/10.3389/fpsyg.2023.1001268

Clin, E., & Kissine, M. (2023). Neurotypical, but not autistic, adults might experience distress when looking at someone avoiding eye contact: A live face-to-face paradigm. *Autism: The International Journal of Research and Practice, 27*(7), 1949–1959. https://doi.org/10.1177/13623613221148553

Coplan, A. (2011). Will the real empathy please stand up? A case for a narrow conceptualization. *The Southern Journal of Philosophy, 49*(1), 40–65. https://doi.org/10.1111/j.2041-6962.2011.00056.x

Crane, L., Hearst, C., Ashworth, M., Davies, J., & Hill, E. L. (2021). Supporting newly identified or diagnosed autistic adults: An initial evaluation of an autistic-led programme. *Journal of Autism and Developmental Disorders, 51*(3), 892–905. https://doi.org/10.1007/s10803-020-04486-4

Crompton, C. J., Hallett, S., Ropar, D., Flynn, E., & Fletcher-Watson, S. (2020). 'I never realised everybody felt as happy as I do when I am around autistic people': A thematic analysis of autistic adults' relationships with autistic and neurotypical friends and family. *Autism: The International Journal of Research and Practice, 24*(6), 1438–1448. https://doi.org/10.1177/1362361320908976

Davidson, J., & Henderson, V. L. (2010). 'Coming out' on the spectrum: Autism, identity and disclosure. *Social & Cultural Geography, 11*(2), 155–170. https://doi.org/10.1080/14649360903525240

Deschrijver, E., & Palmer, C. (2020). Reframing social cognition: Relational versus representational mentalizing. *Psychological Bulletin, 146*(11), 941–969. https://doi.org/10.1037/bul0000302

Doyle, R. (2017, May 19–20). *Bridging the Gap, between the Autistic, the Therapist, and the Thetical Perspective: An Intersubjective Awareness* [Conference presentation]. 23rd Annual BACP Research Conference, Chester, UK.

Doyle, R. (2021, May 15). *Neurotransception: Negotiating the Intersubjective Space between Us, a Way of Being in Research* [Conference presentation]. 25th Annual BACP Research Conference, Online.

Doyle, R. (2023). *Bridging the Gap between the Autistic Individual, the Therapist, and the Theoretical Perspective: An Intersubjective Analysis* [DPsych thesis, Middlesex University]. Middlesex University Research Repository. https://repository.mdx.ac.uk/item/18y764

Edey, R., Cook, J., Brewer, R., Johnson, M. H., Bird, G., & Press, C. (2016). Interaction takes two: Typical adults exhibit mind-blindness towards those with autism spectrum disorder. *Journal of Abnormal Psychology, 125*(7), 879–908. https://doi.org/10.1037/abn0000199

Erskine, R. G. (1998). Attunement and involvement: Therapeutic responses to relational needs. *International Journal of Psychotherapy, 3*(3), 235–244. https://doi.org/10.4324/9780429479519-3

Evans, D. (1996). *An Introductory Dictionary of Lacanian Psychoanalysis.* Routledge.

Fletcher-Watson, S., & Bird, G. (2020). Autism and empathy: What are the real links? *Autism, 24*(1), 3–6. https://doi.org/10.1177/1362361319883506

Fonaghy, P. (2021, March 20) *Epistemic Trust and Free Energy: An Integrative Model for Psychological Therapy* [Conference presentation]. Still Face and Mirror Neurons: the Neuroscience of Psychotherapy, London.

Friston, K. (2008). Hierarchical models in the brain. *PLoS Computational Biology, 4*(11), e1000211. https://doi.org/10.1371/journal.pcbi.1000211

Froese, T., & Ikegami, T. (2013). The brain is not an isolated "black box," nor is its goal to become one. *Behavioral and Brain Sciences, 36*(3), 213–214. https://doi.org/10.1017/S0140525X12002348

Gaigg, S. B. (2012). The Interplay between emotion and cognition in autism spectrum disorder: Implications for developmental theory. *Frontiers in Integrative Neuroscience, 6,* Article 113. https://doi.org/10.3389/fnint.2012.00113

Gallagher, S. (2014). In your face: Transcendence in embodied interaction. *Frontiers in Human Neuroscience, 8,* Article 495. https://doi.org/10.3389/fnhum.2014.00495

Gallese, V., & Goldman, A. (1998). Mirror neurons and the simulation theory of mindreading. *Trends in Cognitive Sciences, 2*(12), 493–501. https://doi.org/10.1016/S1364-6613(98)01262-5

Gernsbacher, M. A., & Yergeau, M. (2019). Empirical failures of the claim that autistic people lack a theory of mind. *Archives of Scientific Psychology, 7*(1), 102–118. https://doi.org/10.1037/arc0000067

Gillespie, A., & Cornish, F. (2010). Intersubjectivity: Towards a dialogical analysis. *Journal for the Theory of Social Behaviour, 40*(1), 19-44. https://doi.org/10.1111/j.1468-5914.2009.00419.x

Haaker, J., Molapour, T., & Olsson, A. (2016). Conditioned social dominance threat: Observation of others' social dominance biases threat learning. *Social Cognitive and Affective Neuroscience, 11*(10), 1627–1637. https://doi.org/10.1093/scan/nsw074

Hallett, S., & Kerr, C. (2020). *'You need support, validation, good coping skills. You need and deserve acceptance': Autistic Adult Experiences of Counselling.* Autistic Mental Health & Autistic Mutual Aid Society Edinburgh (AMASE). https://www.autisticmentalhealth.uk/counsellingreport

Heasman B., & Gillespie A. (2017). Perspective-taking is two-sided: Misunderstandings between people with Asperger's syndrome and their family members. *Autism, 22*(6), 740–750. https://doi.org/10.1177/1362361317708287

Heasman, B., & Gillespie, A. (2019). Participants over-estimate how helpful they are in a two-player game scenario toward an artificial confederate that discloses a diagnosis of autism. *Frontiers in Psychology, 10*, Article 1349. https://doi.org/10.3389/fpsyg.2019.01349

Hohwy, J. (2014). The self-evidencing brain. *Noûs, 50*(2), 259-285. https://doi.org/10.1111/nous.12062

Howlin, P. (1998). *Children with Autism and Asperger Syndrome.* Wiley.

Howlin, P., & Rutter, M. (1987). *Treatment of Autistic Children.* Wiley.

Hubbard D. J., Faso D. J., Assmann P. F., & Sasson N. J. (2017). Production and perception of emotional prosody by adults with autism spectrum disorder. *Autism Research, 10*(12), 1991–2001. https://doi.org/10.1002/aur.1847

Jabareen, Y. (2009). Building a conceptual framework: Philosophy, definitions, and procedure. *International Journal of Qualitative Methods, 8*(4), 49-62. https://doi.org/10.1177/160940690900800406

Jones, S. C. (2022). Measuring the wrong thing the right way? Time to rethink autism research tools. *Autism in Adulthood: Challenges and Management.* 4(2), 104-109. https://doi.org/10.1089/aut.2021.0050

Kimber, L., Verrier, D., & Connolly, S. (2023). Autistic people's experience of empathy and the autistic empathy deficit narrative. *Autism in Adulthood.* http://doi.org/10.1089/aut.2023.0001

Korkmaz, B. (2011). Theory of mind and neurodevelopmental disorders of childhood. *Pediatric Research, 69*(5 Pt 2), 101–108. https://doi.org/10.1203/PDR.0b013e318212c177

Lawson, R. P., Rees, G., & Friston, K. J. (2014). An aberrant precision account of autism. *Frontiers in Human Neuroscience, 8*, Article 302. https://doi.org/10.3389/fnhum.2014.00302

Lombardo, M. V., & Baron-Cohen, S. (2011). The role of the self in mindblindness in autism. *Consciousness and Cognition, 20*(1), 130–140. https://doi.org/10.1016/j.concog.2010.09.006

Mahler, K. (2016). *Interoception The Eighth Sensory System: Practical Solutions for Improving Self-Regulation, Self-Awareness and Social Understanding of Individuals with Autism Spectrum and Related Disorders.* Blackwell.

McEwen, B. S. (1998). Protective and damaging effects of stress mediators. *The New England Journal of Medicine, 338*(3), 171–179. https://doi.org/10.1056/NEJM199801153380307

McKenzie, J. (2015). Recognizing decentered intersubjectivity in social experience. *Emotion Review, 7*(1), 73–78. https://doi.org/10.1177/1754073914545361

Miles, A. (2014). Addressing the problem of cultural anchoring: An identity-based model of culture in action. *Social Psychology Quarterly, 77*(2), 210–227. https://doi.org/10.1177/0190272514524062

Milton, D., Mills, R., & Pellicano, E. (2014). Ethics and autism: Where is the autistic voice? Commentary on Post et al. *Journal of Autism and Developmental Disorders, 44*(10), 2650–2651. https://doi.org/10.1007/s10803-012-1739-x

Milton, D., Heasman, B., & Sheppard E. (2018). Double empathy. In: F. R. Volkmar (Ed.) *Encyclopedia of Autism Spectrum Disorders* (pp. 1–8). Springer.

Milton, D., Gurbuz, E., & López, B. (2022). The 'double empathy problem': Ten years on. *Autism, 26*(8), 1901–1903. https://doi.org/10.1177/13623613221129123

Mitchell, P., Sheppard, E., & Cassidy, S. (2021). Autism and the double empathy problem: Implications for development and mental health. *The British Journal of Developmental Psychology, 39*(1), 1–18. https://doi.org/10.1111/bjdp.12350

Murray F. (2020). Neurodiversity is for everyone. In D. Milton, S. Ridout, N. Martin, R. Mills, & D. Murray (Eds.). *The Neurodiversity Reader*, (pp. 105–109). Pavilion.

Nicolaidis, C., Milton, D., Sasson, N. J., Sheppard, E. L., & Yergeau, M. (2019). An expert discussion on autism and empathy. *Autism in Adulthood: Challenges and Management, 1*(1), 4–11. https://doi.org/10.1089/aut.2018.29000.cjn

Nuske, H. J., Vivanti, G., & Dissanayake, C. (2013). Are emotion impairments unique to, universal, or specific in autism spectrum disorder? A comprehensive review. *Cognition and Emotion, 27*(6), 1042–1061. https://doi.org/10.1080/02699931.2012.762900

O'Reilly, M., Lester, J. N., & Kiyimba, N. (2020). Autism in the twentieth century: An evolution of a controversial condition. In S. J. Taylor & A. Brumby (Eds.), *Healthy Minds in the Twentieth Century* (pp. 137–165). https://doi.org/10.1007/978-3-030-27275-3_7

Ogawa, S., Iriguchi, M., Lee, Y. A., Yoshikawa, S., & Goto, Y. (2019). Atypical social rank recognition in autism spectrum disorder. *Scientific Reports, 9*(1), Article 15657. https://doi.org/10.1038/s41598-019-52211-8

Pearson, A., & Rose, K. (2021). A conceptual analysis of autistic masking: Understanding the narrative of stigma and the illusion of choice. *Autism in Adulthood: Challenges and Management, 3*(1), 52–60. https://doi.org/10.1089/aut.2020.0043

Pellicano, E., & Burr, D. (2012). When the world becomes 'too real': A Bayesian explanation of autistic perception. *Trends in Cognitive Sciences, 16*(10), 504–510. https://doi.org/10.1016/j.tics.2012.08.009

Pierce, J. C. (1977). *The Magical Child: Rediscovering Nature's Plan for Our Children.* Dutton.

Pönkänen, L. M., & Hietanen, J. K. (2012). Eye contact with neutral and smiling faces: Effects on autonomic responses and frontal EEG asymmetry. *Frontiers in Human Neuroscience, 6*, Article 122. https://doi.org/10.3389/fnhum.2012.00122

Porges, S. W. (2004). Neuroception: A subconscious system for detecting threats and safety. *Zero to Three, 24*(5), 19–24.

Porges, S. (2020, August 10) PESI UK Announces Free Children and Young People's Mental Health Summit. https://www.pesi.co.uk/bundle/childrens-mental-health-awareness-summit-342?srsltid=AfmBOoqcHeYhNBvxyNpXiquZhnsqyTZuKhcdoU4l6Cs_pMrhZ4IpXwKJ

Powell T., & Acker L. (2016). Adults' experience of an Asperger syndrome diagnosis: Analysis of its emotional meaning and effect on participants' lives. *Focus on Autism and Other Developmental Disabilities, 31*(1), 72–80. https://doi.org/10.1177/1088357615588516

Qian, N., & Lipkin, R. M. (2011). A learning-style theory for understanding autistic behaviors. *Frontiers in Human Neuroscience, 5*, Article 77. https://doi.org/10.3389/fnhum.2011.00077

Rifai, O. M., Fletcher-Watson, S., Jiménez-Sánchez, L., & Crompton, C. J. (2022). Investigating markers of rapport in autistic and nonautistic interactions. *Autism in Adulthood: Challenges and Management, 4*(1), 3–11. https://doi.org/10.1089/aut.2021.0017

Rosenberg, A., Patterson, J. S., & Angelaki, D. E. (2015). A computational perspective on autism. *Proceedings of the National Academy of Sciences of the United States of America, 112*(30), 9158–9165. https://doi.org/10.1073/pnas.1510583112

Sachs, O. (1995). *An Anthropologist on Mars: Seven Paradoxical Tales.* Knopf Doubleday Publishing Group.

Shakespeare, T. (2006). *Disability Rights and Wrongs.* Routledge.

Sheppard, E., Pillai, D., Wong, G. T. L., Ropar, D., & Mitchell, P. (2016). How easy is it to read the minds of people with autism spectrum disorder? *Journal of Autism and Developmental Disorders, 46*(4), 1247–1254. https://doi.org/10.1007/s10803-015-2662-8

Sinha, P., Kjelgaard, M. M., Gandhi, T. K., Tsourides, K., Cardinaux, A. L., Pantazis, D., Diamond, S. P., & Held, R. M. (2014). Autism as a disorder of prediction. *Proceedings of the National Academy of Sciences of the United States of America, 111*(42), 15220–15225. https://doi.org/10.1073/pnas.1416797111

Stein, E. (1989). *On the Problem of Empathy* (3rd ed.; W. Stein, trans.). ICS Publications. (Original work published 1916)

Sterling, P., & Eyer, J. (1988). Allostasis: A new paradigm to explain arousal pathology. In S. Fisher & J. T. Reason (Eds.), *Handbook of Life Stress, Cognition, and Health* (pp. 629–649). Wiley.

Stevanovic, M., Henttonen, P., Koskinen, E., Peräkylä, A., Nieminen von-Wendt, T., Sihvola, E., Tani, P., Ravaja, N., & Sams, M. (2019). Physiological responses to affiliation during conversation: Comparing neurotypical males and males with Asperger syndrome. *PloS One, 14*(9), Article e0222084. https://doi.org/10.1371/journal.pone.0222084

Thompson, M. G. (2005). Phenomenology of intersubjectivity: A historical overview and its clinical implications. In J. Mills (Ed.), *Relational and Intersubjective Perspectives in Psychoanalysis: A Critique* (pp. 35–70). Rowman & Littlefield Publishers.

Treweek, C., Wood, C., Martin, J., & Freeth, M. (2018). Autistic people's perspectives on stereotypes: An interpretative phenomenological analysis. *Autism, 23*(3), 759–769. https://doi.org/10.1177/1362361318778286

Van Boxtel, J. J. A., & Lu, H. (2013). A predictive coding perspective on autism spectrum disorders. *Frontiers in Psychology, 4*, Article 19. https://doi.org/10.3389/fpsyg.2013.00019

Van de Cruys, S., Evers, K., Van der Hallen, R., Van Eylen, L., Boets, B., de-Wit, L., & Wagemans, J. (2014). Precise minds in uncertain worlds: Predictive coding in autism. *Psychological Review, 121*(4), 649–675. https://doi.org/10.1037/a0037665

Vermeulen, P. (2012). *Autism as Context Blindness*. Autism Asperger Publishing Company.

Wallace, A. (2001). Intersubjectivity in Indo-Tibetan Buddhism. *Journal of Consciousness Studies,* 8(5), 209–230.

Wayment, H. A., & Bauer, J. J. (2018). The quiet ego: Motives for self-other balance and growth in relation to well-being. *Journal of Happiness Studies: An Interdisciplinary Forum on Subjective Well-Being, 19*(3), 881–896. https://doi.org/10.1007/s10902-017-9848-z

Zeldovich, L. (2018, November 10). How history forgot the woman who defined autism. *Scientific American*. https://www.scientificamerican.com/article/how-history-forgot-the-woman-who-defined-autism/

Chapter 10:

'It's almost like everybody's just throwing stones in the middle...': Autistic Lived Experiences of Inter-neurotype Communication

Liz Roscoe

Introduction

It is difficult to pinpoint exactly what contributes to social misunderstandings, since every social interaction and how it is experienced is unique. This chapter describes an investigation into the Double Empathy Problem (Milton, 2012) and social communication involving autistic adults, using participatory research methods. The research combined ideas and perspectives from social psychology and the social model of disability, with an explicit consideration of how findings could be applied to improve the lives of autistic people. The research questions being explored were about the extent to which the Double Empathy Problem explains social communication involving autistic adults, how autistic adults communicate with people of the same and different neurotypes and what affects the success of this communication.

The Double Empathy Problem describes how people of different worldviews and outlooks are more likely to misunderstand each other. Differences in social communication between autistic and non-autistic people may arise not because of impairments in the perception of autistic people, but from differences in 'inter-neurotype communication' (Chown et al., 2020). Autistic people may find communication with non-autistic people challenging at times, but non-autistic people similarly lack insight into autistic perceptions – possibly more so, since they have not had to adapt to a society based around a different neurotype. Recent research indicates that processes regarded as 'deficits' in autism are better explained as communication challenges operating bidirectionally between autistic and non-autistic people (Milton, 2012).

This autistic-led study involved semi-structured interviews with a working group of autistic adults (seven female, two non-binary and one male participant) to discuss their lived experiences of social communication. For the ten people in this study, the experiences of misunderstanding others, and being misunderstood, were common occurrences and a large driver of their feelings of social anxiety. Participants discussed their reasons for wanting to become involved in the research, their experiences of enjoyable and unenjoyable social communication, how social communication could be made easier for autistic people in practical ways and their priorities for future research. I would like to sincerely thank all the participants who are driving this research for their honest, moving and invaluable accounts of their lived autistic experiences.

Background to the study

Participatory research was central to this study. It is an approach which is inclusive, seeks to increase social justice and recognizes the value of engaging in the research process those who are intended to be its beneficiaries (Cargo & Mercer, 2008). It involves an active partnership between researchers and the people affected by the issues being investigated, reflecting the belief that this generates better quality research that is more applicable (Macaulay et al., 2011), since the participants' '*real-world knowledge and experiences enhance the researchers''* expertise in theory and methodology (Cargo & Mercer, 2008). The core principles are co-ownership and co-decision making, ensuring that the balance of power is equal throughout and with full participant involvement at each stage.

The language preferences of the autistic community should always inform the type of language used in research. In the UK, many autistic adults have endorsed identity-first language, preferring 'autistic', 'autistic person' and 'person on the spectrum' in greater numbers to 'person with autism' (Bottema-Beutel et al., 2021), reflecting the view that a person's autism is fundamental to their identity and cannot be separated from them in the way that person-first language implies (Sinclair, 2013). The term 'autistic person' was preferred by the majority of the participants in this study and so will be adopted throughout. In terms of language preferences, most of the group preferred the term 'participant', with one person choosing the term 'co-researcher'.

The study involved the researcher talking to participants in semistructured interviews about their views on social communication, answering questions about their experiences with people of different neurotypes and their research priorities. Beforehand, participants identified their chosen method of talking to the researcher, whether that was in person, online, by telephone or in writing and either in a small group or a one-to-one situation; the latter was chosen by all the participants. Two information exchange meetings were subsequently offered to provide background information about the Double Empathy Problem and current research methods, to enable meaningful involvement in the process; these sessions were also offered as videos to provide an alternative way of engaging. The sessions involved explaining existing models of both qualitative and quantitative double empathy research (Chapple et al., 2021; Crompton et al., 2020a; Crompton et al., 2020b; Heasman & Gillespie, 2019a; Morrison et al., 2019). There was particular interest among the group in the finding that autistic people shared information as accurately with each other as non-autistic people did with other non-autistic people, and with greater rapport than mixed-neurotype chains (Crompton et al., 2020b), contradicting the clinical definition of autism as involving deficits in social communication.

Many different reasons for involvement were expressed in the interviews. The main motivation was to highlight the autistic voice and to challenge the stereotype of autistic people as lacking in empathy; many participants described their own strong feelings of empathy. The empowering nature of participatory research was also a large factor for some. A deeper understanding of the Double Empathy Problem and addressing the consequences of not being fully understood by neurotypical, and therefore most, people, were also incentives. Some felt that investigating double empathy would help with self-knowledge and contribute to broader information about autistic social communication, which would benefit autism knowledge in general. An overarching aim was to also demonstrate, through recounting their lived experiences, the uniqueness of each autistic person. Below are some of the key themes that emerged from the discussions.

When is social communication enjoyable?

A desire for conversation that was meaningful and validating was frequently expressed by participants (Ps). There was a sense that these sorts of interactions were very precious and sought after. Enjoyable communication was described as that which felt 'right', with no pressure, being fully heard and understood and not feeling the need to mask. This kind of 'perfect' communication felt natural, nurturing and effortless. It often occurred with close friends, and was often, but not always, an interaction between autistic people.

> *I feel I can just absolutely be myself. I feel she's being herself ... if the pace is right, you can feel it ... being able to listen and being understood and being heard. And that that's being reciprocated, that feels really important ... I think it's felt inside and probably it would be like ... the absence of anxiety.* (P1)

> *It was a stimulating, stretching conversation, and again new perspectives for myself, things to reflect on ... any conversations that are about trying to understand what's going on, why people might be behaving like they're behaving and trying to work out what's going on for me, sometimes, why am I responding in the way I am to particular situations, just really interested in it, and I also think it would be great if everyone did that a bit more...* (P3)

> *I feel like I've really enjoyed a conversation when I feel like I know someone better at the end of it ... Like how they think and how they feel and what drives them and that kind of stuff, because then I feel like some kind of barrier has maybe been removed and we're maybe a little bit closer ... it's connection really that I'm looking for...* (P6)

Aspects which made communication feel easier were using a comfortable pace for the talking and knowing instinctively when to take turns. With these elements in place, communication was enjoyable and a feeling of being authentic and relaxed was generated.

> *...We kind of know whose turn it is to talk ... there's something about if the pace is right, you can feel it.* (P1)

Being able to react to the social cues available was also described as the marker of a successful interaction. Knowing the direction that a conversation was taking, so there was nothing unexpected, was very welcome. One participant described an interesting personal strategy for supporting her social communication. She had created a mental image of a filing cabinet and, since childhood, had been building up a catalogue of information on individual cards which she could withdraw from the cabinet and refer to, when necessary, about what to say in different situations. New experiences were stressful but once experienced, they could be filed away so that a bank of responses was available, ready for the card to be removed when needed. This strategy perhaps indicates a different way of processing information that is more readily accessible and useful for her than simply trying to conjure up a memory.

Autistic-to-autistic communication

The concept of autistic-to-autistic communication feeling easier and more effective than mixed-neurotype communication has long been familiar to autistic people (Crompton et al., 2020b). Communication between autistic people was generally described by participants as being easier and more positive than between people of different neurotypes. It was usually described as being more relaxing and straightforward, without the constant, exhausting set of internal calculations that can accompany mixed-neurotype communication. People felt they could be themselves and that no masking was required; they could be more open about anxieties and habits and behave in an authentic way.

> *…there was that absolutely, that penny dropping moment of well, actually this communication is really easy because that person is autistic and it's like … really clean communication … you're not having to guess what you're having to talk about … in being with other autistic people, I've found my place where like it's like going home…* (P1)

> *I think because you're talking to somebody who you know has a similar world view to you. So you're talking to somebody and often the conversation will go something along the lines of, oh I do this thing, it's a bit weird. I do that too. Do you? Oh that's really interesting…* (P2)

> *I get on with him like a house on fire, I always have…* (P7)

> *…I think autistic communication is very much about passing on information rather than trying to connect with people.* (P4)

> *…There are moments in my conversation … that I enjoy … when I feel I can process the information … their communication is clear…* (P5)

However, the idea that autistic-to-autistic communication is always easier than mixed-neurotype communication is not straightforward and depends very much on the individuals involved. A key point which emerged from the interviews and meetings was that autism is not a way of assigning personalities, preferences and opinions to people; every autistic person is unique and there was a huge desire to increase public understanding of this. A non-autistic person would not assume that their neurotypical status also defined their entire identity, and made them the same as other neurotypical people, yet this misconception can occur around autism. Autistic spaces where everyone is a stranger can therefore be as stressful as any other social situation, which was the experience of several participants. Autistic people have different ways of communicating that they prefer, and these can be at odds with other autistic people's communication styles. One participant commented that she usually enjoyed socializing in autistic groups, but that communication breakdowns or misunderstandings could be much worse in this environment than in mixed-neurotype groups. This was partly, she believed, due to sensory clashes whereby people's diverse needs could not be adequately accommodated in a complex group setting. Another participant had only met one other person she knew to be autistic and felt that their different communication style – the other person was talking a lot more – was very tiring and prevented the reciprocity that she wanted.

Another way in which autistic people may communicate effectively and empathetically with each other may stem from their ability to visualize concepts, which could indicate similarities in processing information for some autistic people. Visualizing as a way of understanding concepts is discussed by several participants. In a chat with an autistic friend, the friend referred to them both imagining the year as a big wheel, with some months bigger than others. This hadn't been discussed before but was exactly how the participant visualized time. They also discussed how they visualized numbers and the imagined position of numbers in relation to other numbers. A non-autistic friend also present was confused by these depictions and didn't share this way of seeing concepts at all; the autistic friends were fascinated by the fact that this type of visualization is probably not done by most people. This could indicate a unique autistic way of processing abstract information as well as a powerful ability to visualize, which has been long documented in autistic people (Grandin, 2009).

Another participant described a system that her and her sister, both finding out about their autism identity later in life, used to categorize their acquaintances during childhood. They put people into two categories: in or out. They never discussed what the categories meant and couldn't articulate it then. She feels now that it was the people they felt comfortable with, or not; were they classifying people according to their neurotype?

> *…looking back on that categorizing people and not being able to say why. It's really strange because we used to explain it to people and some people would just get it and go, 'I know what you mean and I'm one.' It just sounds really unbelievable now.* (P10)

There was an almost universal preference for talking one-to-one or in a small group. Large group conversations were difficult for most of the participants. There was more pressure to react appropriately in those situations and a loss of individual control could be experienced, as there was no structure to the chatting and no way of knowing when a suitable time to have a break or leave the conversation would occur.

> *I prefer to ... have a definite start time and a definite end time and points at which it's clear it's okay to stop. So, kind of get out moments where you can get out of the conversation and it's acceptable and people are okay with it.* (P3)

> *...when it's a big group setting I'm very much like, okay I need to make sure I'm saying the right thing, or am I making the right facial expressions, or being interested in what the person is saying.* (P2)

Sometimes, extra time was needed to get used to the pace of the conversation and to settle into feeling comfortable with it. Knowing when to join in could be stressful, as a large group could be experienced as too noisy and overwhelming, resulting in feelings of exhaustion. One participant commented that she found larger groups easier now compared to years ago, as there was no stress about running out of things to say, although this depended entirely on the group and situation itself.

Specialist subjects

Preferred topics of conversation were wide-ranging. Discussion of topics that participants felt passionate about was important and conversations in which there was a mutual interest were particularly successful. There was a marked preference for the discussion of 'big questions'. Many commented on their interest in psychology – not surprising considering their decision to participate in psychology research – and had researched topics to improve their own knowledge and understanding. There was a desire to discuss important, significant issues and an almost universal dislike of small talk, with one participant expressing a hatred of it. This appeared to be because it was perceived as pointless, irrelevant and at odds with the depth and quality of conversation which most participants enjoyed. It was more like a rehearsed habit for some, rather than a genuine part of an interaction. For one participant, small talk was a way of signalling to her close friend that the more meaningful part of their chat had been completed and that the conversation was drawing to a close.

One participant described an interest in people and social interactions as her 'specialist subject'. Wanting to understand and learn more about other people and making huge efforts to do this was a frequent observation during the interviews.

> *I want to understand things, and I want to understand people, as well. Because I've spent my whole life not understanding other people. So, I like conversations where people sort of are self-reflective, and are looking at why they do the things that they do and just have that element of looking at their own behaviour, or the way that the world works…* (P6)

In summary, social communication was enjoyable to participants when it felt effortless and natural and precluded the urge to mask. The communication was clear and unambiguous and about meaningful topics in which both sides were interested, without small talk. A successful conversation left the participant feeling as though they could understand the other person better and took place as either one-to-one or in a small group. There was enough time to settle into the pace of the conversation and to process information effectively.

When is social communication not enjoyable?

Participants described their experiences of not enjoying social interactions as the most prevalent. Before interacting with non-autistic people, one participant described feeling 'braced and vigilant', which came from a fear of misunderstandings occurring and then often 'bewildered' as the chatting progressed. Having to always adapt to neurotypical communication, which was described by one participant as 'vague and confusing', was seen as ridiculous. Being extremely specific was a strategy employed by several participants in order to minimize the kind of inter-neurotype misunderstandings characterized by the Double Empathy Problem. The pressure to talk in social situations, when the preference was to be a bystander, was unpleasant.

One participant described what a non-autistic person would have to do in order to match his efforts to adapt his communication:

I understand what a neurotypical person needs when you're engaged in conversation or socially. But then they don't understand to anywhere near the degree of what my needs or other autistic people's needs are. We've been forced into learning that because that's how life is, isn't it. That's how the environments are. That's the masking things. Speaking to neurotypical people and say okay, so you would have to mask to satisfy my needs. You'd have to mask your neurotypicality and you would have to pretend to be autistic to speak to me in the way that I would be most comfortable and relaxed. (P7)

He explained that with a neurotypical person, the first few meetings are when he made a mental profile of them and decided whether to even continue talking to them again, based on how comfortable he felt. He would avoid them thereafter if he couldn't cope with their communication style.

The mental gymnastics that occurred during mixed-neurotype interactions were constant and referred to many times. One participant described first a worry about eye contact which became distracting, then a thought that they should reciprocate soon if the other person had asked a question. These thoughts grew into a mental plan which felt formulaic and anxiety-provoking, rather than feeling like a naturally progressing conversation. After a couple of questions, the anxiety could be too much and so she would stop talking, which caused awkwardness about why the conversation had ended. Sometimes, this internal checking by the autistic person was for criticism, judgement or rejection and involved scrutinizing the words and also the body language of the other person at the same time as the ongoing interaction. This process was described as a series of mental questions, often ending in the participant feeling that they were to blame for any difficult moments:

What's happening? What's going on with the other person? What do I need to be doing to make it all OK? (P1)

The participant knew that this interpretation was subjective but also felt that there was no option to change the course of the interaction in these types of social situations, explaining it as pressing a button which led to an inevitable and unstoppable internal reaction. The constant mental checking and calculating that occurred during uncomfortable conversations was exhausting. It added to verbal processing time and could be interpreted by others as aloofness and unfriendliness, whereas it was, ironically, the opposite – a huge effort to stay involved in a conversation which was becoming overwhelming.

This participant described the goal of successful conversation as being, for her, the closing of a communication loop. The aim of her communication was to share some information with the other person and let them know that their information had been understood. When that reassurance of understanding didn't materialize in her mixed-neurotype interactions, the effective communication ended on her part; the information frustratingly did not feel shared and wasn't built upon. No connection was felt; they were not talking in the same communication loop.

> *...with non-autistic people, it's like someone throws something in the middle and it's like left. You just see what happens and it's like has it landed? Hasn't it landed? Have they heard me? Do they understand me? ... it's almost like everybody's just throwing stones in the middle.* (P1)

The clashing of different communication styles and the resulting misunderstandings were bidirectional, as described in the Double Empathy Problem, but the barrier felt insurmountable. Participants believed that it was usually the autistic person, however, who was left feeling as if they were to blame for not being able to adapt their communication style, since they were in the minority.

Several comments were made about how the wrong pace in a conversation led to it remaining very much at a surface level, with what felt like an inability to include deeper, more meaningful topics. This has significant implications for a lack of deep meaning during inter-neurotype communication, which was often experienced by participants as being at an uncomfortable pace. These circumstances could cause participants to shut down emotionally and give up on the communication, which had become overwhelming and pointless. It was also unnerving and disappointing to participants who had tried hard to communicate but felt as though the other person was not listening or paying enough attention to notice their discomfort.

Work situations

Several participants had experienced misunderstandings with work managers, when they had completed the task they were asked to do, and then were met with criticism when the manager challenged them about their actions. This was described as a formulation of assumptions that were different on both sides and a reflection of poor communication that can occur in professional relationships built around power and autonomy. On challenging the misunderstanding in one such situation, the manager insisted on their own decision without a clear acknowledgement of how the miscommunication had occurred. Interactions with doctors and other authority figures were often perceived as unsuccessful, and left the autistic person feeling at fault:

> *I sort of feel like I'm in trouble almost, even though I've not done anything wrong.* (P9)

To summarize, social communication that was not enjoyable for the participants tended to evoke tension due to a fear of possible misunderstandings and lack of meaningful connection. It involved constantly adapting their preferred communication style to suit a non-autistic audience, which was exhausting and added to processing time. This meant that the pace of the interaction was often not well-matched to the autistic person. Pressures to talk and to make frequent eye contact were experienced as uncomfortable, and the content was too vague and imprecise.

How could autistic people be supported around social communication in a variety of settings?

Despite the high levels of self-knowledge and understanding demonstrated by this research group in relation to their interpersonal communication, it was noticeable just from their recollections that their neurotypical acquaintances, who had little experience of autism, were completely unaware of most of the difficulties faced in autistic life and had no knowledge of the Double Empathy Problem. One participant commented on their resentment and discomfiture at having to take on the role of 'educator' in both personal and workplace conversations after disclosing their autism and being faced with a barrage of demanding questions. While the urge of non-autistic people to learn more is to be encouraged, this also reveals the extent of the lack of information and knowledge of many people. First impressions of autistic people improve when non-autistic people have a good understanding of autism together with personal experience of knowing autistic people (Cage et al., 2019; Sasson et al., 2017) but worsen when stigma toward autism is high (Morrison et al., 2019), suggesting that the social experiences of autistic people can be significantly affected by non-autistic beliefs about autism. Cage et al. (2019) reported that people with less open attitudes were more likely to endorse the stereotype of a lack of empathy in autistic people. A study into the effect of autism acceptance training found that a short course increased mutual social interest for both autistic and non-autistic people (Jones et al., 2021). A focus on increasing acceptance and reducing stigma in non-autistic people could therefore be effective in improving autistic social experiences.

The following opinions and suggestions came directly from the participants and are about supporting autistic people in overcoming the Double Empathy Problem in their daily lives. I have included relevant literature to support these views. They cover the kinds of situations which may be difficult to manage due to a lack of autism knowledge among neurotypical people and the way physical environments are usually designed for non-autistic people. These bidirectional communication challenges between autistic and non-autistic people (Milton, 2012) could be reduced with greater public understanding about autism and an acceptance that communication styles, while different, are not necessarily obstacles to social cognition and understanding (Heasman & Gillespie, 2018). This increase in knowledge could modify some non-autistic misconceptions such as the assumption that there is less autistic ability to feel empathy (Dugdale et al., 2021).

Social settings

There needs to be greater awareness about the heterogeneity of autistic people. Autistic people are as diverse as non-autistic people, but their different personalities, opinions and interests can be overlooked. Some autistic people struggle with social cues, take things literally and dislike eye contact, but this is not true for all autistic people and may also be true for many neurotypical people.

More designated quiet places should be provided in social settings, which could benefit people of every neurotype. As one participant commented, improving things for autistic people can improve them for everyone. At organized social events, the order of activities should be provided in advance, as this would reduce stress and unpredictability (for all neurotypes), and have less impact on autistic people's processing energy. There needs to be more awareness that autistic people, like everyone, should be able to sit quietly and listen and not be pulled into conversations. Social situations with a purpose or activity, like a walk or a game, can be easier for some autistic people; this is supported by several studies where a shared activity enabled rapport, humour and mutual understanding to flourish while at the same time reducing social awkwardness (Chapple et al., 2021; Chen at al., 2021; Heasman & Gillespie, 2019b). These studies highlight the way neurodivergent intersubjectivity can thrive given the right opportunities.

Work settings

Knowledge about autism should be increased in all workplaces and organizations, especially amongst managers and decision-makers. In meetings, it could be ensured that only one person is talking at a time and that managers are open to people asking questions to clarify points. Misunderstandings around tasks that work managers have requested could be reduced with clearer and more precise communication; when misinterpretations occur, managers should be open to discussing how the communication could have been better. Knowledge of the Double Empathy Problem, which deals with people of different outlooks, could be useful here considering the power dynamic and potentially different priorities of a manager and their workforce. Possible sensory preferences should be considered when planning work environments, particularly in open-plan settings which do not always provide appropriately calm and quiet working conditions. Advice from medical and health professionals should be considered alongside the autistic person's preferences when providing requested adaptations to working conditions. Better autism awareness has been shown to have a positive impact on attitudes between different neurotypes (Jones et al., 2021), but the effectiveness of autism awareness training on neurotypical attitudes should be followed up at later times to check whether the effects are enduring. A government-funded campaign to raise autism awareness has been advocated by the National Autistic Society in the UK, which could go some way toward providing at least a basic level of knowledge.

Research priorities

Autistic communities have expressed frequent, growing concern over the last decade that most research does not reflect their priorities and needs (Pellicano et al., 2014). They would like more research into issues of 'immediate practical concern' in their daily lives rather than the biomedical focus of most UK work. A Priority Setting Partnership (James Lind Alliance, 2016) identified the top ten priorities in autism research identified by autistic people, family members and professional stakeholders. A high priority was supporting the development of communication and language skills; other priorities implicitly involve communication – they describe reducing anxiety, supporting education, life and social skills, and workplace performance, and how non-autistic people can better understand the experience of being autistic, all of which involve the Double Empathy Problem. Roche et al., (2021) similarly identified key stakeholders' priorities for autism research as applied research to improve the everyday lives of autistic people, such as the development of skills, improved trajectories, more accurate public understanding of autism and the inclusion of autistic people in research and the community.

The research priorities of the participants reflected many of these issues around social communication and the Double Empathy Problem, which can have such a huge impact on everyday life. Better public knowledge and understanding of double empathy was a significant priority which could reduce some of the anxiety and misunderstandings which can affect intersubjectivity between people of different neurotypes. Neurotypical people need to be educated to a level where they understand how to adapt their communication to better suit autistic people and understand that communication challenges are bidirectional, and not the fault of the autistic person. Clearer communication, which is more literal and less ambiguous, would be extremely helpful in all settings to autistic people. It is particularly important that precise language is used in formal situations such as medical appointments, in which a misunderstanding could have serious consequences. Medical appointments and the way they are arranged should be made more accessible and less stressful for autistic people; for example, providing information initially online, so that there is less emphasis on the face-to-face appointment itself, could be helpful. Autistic people's communication styles may be different to that of non-autistic medical professionals but should be regarded as equally valid. Again, training in double empathy could provide better understanding and a more positive experience.

There are still long-standing misconceptions, stereotypes and prejudices about autism which need to be challenged. For example, if people can communicate, behave sociably and work effectively then people with no understanding of masking may believe that they must be neurotypical. Autistic meltdowns can be perceived as bad behaviour, whereas the autistic person is trying to express a valid emotion; this frequently happens with children. Some people inaccurately associate autism with intellectual disability. Better public understanding of autism and double empathy would increase acceptance of autistic people and reduce stigma (Jones et al., 2021).

Conclusion

It is hoped that this research will have a real-world impact on the lives of autistic people. The clear research priorities expressed by this group could benefit not only autistic people, but also people of every neurotype. Improved public understanding of autism, which includes a focus on double empathy, would enable non-autistic people to understand mutual communication challenges better. This would hopefully generate better social communication which causes fewer challenges for autistic people and could lead to more positive inter-neurotype interactions and relationships. It would also reduce stereotypical attitudes and misconceptions, which can be damaging to autistic people. An increased and more sophisticated understanding of autistic communication styles could reduce the Double Empathy Problem in wider society.

References

Bottema-Beutel, K., Kapp, S. K., Lester, J. N., Sasson, N. J., & Hand, B. N. (2021). Avoiding ableist language: Suggestions for autism researchers. *Autism in Adulthood, 3*(1), 18–29. https://doi.org/10.1089/aut.2020.0014

Cage, E., Di Monaco, J., & Newell, V. (2019). *Understanding, Attitudes and Dehumanisation Towards Autistic People.* Sage.

Cargo, M., & Mercer, S. L. (2008). The value and challenges of participatory research: Strengthening its practice. *Annual Review of Public Health, 29*(1), 325–350. https://doi.org/10.1146/annurev.publhealth.29.091307.083824

Chapple, M., Davis, P., Billington, J., Myrick, J. A., Ruddock, C., & Corcoran, R. (2021). Overcoming the double empathy problem within pairs of autistic and non-autistic adults through the contemplation of serious literature. *Frontiers in Psychology, 12*, 708375. https://doi.org/10.3389/fpsyg.2021.708375

Chen, Y., Senande, L. L., Thorsen, M., & Patten, K. (2021). Peer preferences and characteristics of same-group and cross-group social interactions among autistic and non-autistic adolescents. *Autism: The International Journal of Research and Practice, 25*(7), 1885–1900. https://doi.org/10.1177/13623613211005918

Chown, N., Hughes, L., & Baker-Rogers, J. (2020). What about the other side of double empathy? A response to Alkhaldi, Sheppard and Mitchell's JADD article concerning mind-reading difficulties in autism. *Journal of Autism and Developmental Disorders, 50*(2), 683–684. https://doi.org/10.1007/s10803-019-04263-y

Crompton, C. J., Sharp, M., Axbey, H., Fletcher-Watson, S., Flynn, E. G., & Ropar, D. (2020a). Neurotype-matching, but not being autistic, influences self and observer ratings of interpersonal rapport. *Frontiers in Psychology, 11*, 586171. https://doi.org/10.3389/fpsyg.2020.586171

Crompton, C. J., Ropar, D., Evans-Williams, C., Flynn, E. G., & Fletcher-Watson, S. (2020b). Autistic peer-to-peer information transfer is highly effective. *Autism: The International Journal of Research and Practice, 24*(7), 1704–1712. https://doi.org/10.1177/1362361320919286

Dugdale, A., Thompson, A. R., Leedham, A., Beail, N., & Freeth, M. (2021). Intense connection and love: The experiences of autistic mothers. *Autism: The International Journal of Research and Practice, 25*(7), 1973–1984. https://doi.org/10.1177/13623613211005987

Grandin, T. (2009). How does visual thinking work in the mind of a person with autism? A personal account. *Philosophical Transactions of the Royal Society of London. Series B. Biological Sciences, 364*(1522), 1437–1442. https://doi.org/10.1098/rstb.2008.0297

Heasman, B., & Gillespie, A. (2018). Perspective-taking is two-sided: Misunderstandings between people with Asperger's syndrome and their family members. *Autism: The International Journal of Research and Practice, 22*(6), 740–750. https://doi.org/10.1177/1362361317708287

Heasman, B., & Gillespie, A. (2019a). Neurodivergent intersubjectivity: Distinctive features of how autistic people create shared understanding. *Autism: The International Journal of Research and Practice, 23*(4), 910–921. https://doi.org/10.1177/1362361318785172

Heasman, B., & Gillespie, A. (2019b). Participants over-estimate how helpful they are in a two-player game scenario toward an artificial confederate that discloses a diagnosis of autism. *Frontiers in Psychology, 10*, 1349–1349. https://doi.org/10.3389/fpsyg.2019.01349

James Lind Alliance (2016). Autism: Top 10 priorities. https://www.jla.nihr.ac.uk/priority-setting-partnerships/autism

Jones, D. R., Morrison, K. E., DeBrabander, K. M., Ackerman, R. A., Pinkham, A. E., & Sasson, N. J. (2021). Greater social interest between autistic and non-autistic conversation partners following autism acceptance training for non-autistic people. *Frontiers in Psychology, 12* https://doi.org/10.3389/fpsyg.2021.739147

Macaulay, A. C., Jagosh, J., Seller, R., Henderson, J., Cargo, M., Greenhalgh, T., Wong, G., Salberg, J., Green, L. W., Herbert, C. P., & Pluye, P. (2011). Assessing the benefits of participatory research: A rationale for a realist review. *Global Health Promotion, 18*(2), 45–48. https://doi.org/10.1177/1757975910383936

Milton, D. E. M. (2012). On the ontological status of autism: The 'double empathy problem'. *Disability & Society, 27*(6), 883–887. https://doi.org/10.1080/09687599.2012.710008

Morrison, K. E., DeBrabander, K. M., Faso, D. J., & Sasson, N. J. (2019). Variability in first impressions of autistic adults made by neurotypical raters is driven more by characteristics of the rater than by characteristics of autistic adults. *Autism: The International Journal of Research and Practice, 23*(7), 136236131882410-1829. https://doi.org/10.1177/1362361318824104

Pellicano, E., Dinsmore, A., & Charman, T. (2014). What should autism research focus upon? Community views and priorities from the United Kingdom. *Autism, 18*(7), 756–770. https://doi.org/10.1177/1362361314529627

Roche, L., Adams, D., & Clark, M. (2021). Research priorities of the autism community: A systematic review of key stakeholder perspectives. *Autism, 25*(2), 336–348. https://doi.org/10.1177/1362361320967790

Sasson, N. J., Faso, D. J., Nugent, J., Lovell, S., Kennedy, D. P., & Grossman, R. B. (2017). Neurotypical peers are less willing to interact with those with autism based on thin slice judgments. *Scientific Reports, 7*(1), 40700–40700. https://doi.org/10.1038/srep40700

Sinclair, J. (2013). Why I dislike "person first" Language. *Autism Network International.* https://blogs.exeter.ac.uk/exploringdiagnosis/files/2017/03/Sinclair-Why-I-Dislike-First-Person-Language.pdf.

Chapter 11:

A Working Conceptualization of Autistic Sociality in Autistic Spaces and Cultures

Maisie Roberts

The failure to learn your (neurotypical) language is seen as a deficit but failure to learn my (autistic) language is seen as so natural. (Baggs, 2007)

Autistic people have long been deemed to be lacking sociality and social reciprocity. Our different social preferences, embodiments and expressions have been treated as abnormalities to be solved and pitied (Milton, 2014; Sinclair, 1993). However, many of us are highly social, particularly in spaces that are suited to our needs and affirm our identities (Bagatell, 2010; Botha et al., 2022; Crompton et al., 2020). Previous attempts to conceptualize autism as a social communication disorder have wrongly assumed that social difficulties only reside in autistic people, thereby ignoring the relational and contextual underpinnings of social situations (Milton, 2012). When two different neurotypes socialize, a breakdown in social communication may indeed emerge, with social difficulties encountered by *both* autistic *and* neurotypical people, leading to the Double Empathy Problem (Milton, 2012). The Double Empathy Problem (2012) highlights that we are not disordered or deficient in our sociality but, simply, that we embody and express ourselves differently to the current compulsory neuronormative social order.

Our preferred methods of socializing have long been marginalized and inhibited, and we are often pressured to interact in a neurotypical manner (Baggs, 2007). As a result, we often lead dual existences, socializing in a neuronormative form at school, work or other settings and in a more authentic way outside of these spaces, with those with whom we feel comfortable, like friends and family (Harp, 2012). As a result, and not surprisingly, recent accounts have foregrounded the tactics we engage in to survive within this neurotypical world, through masking (Milner et al., 2019; Pearson & Rose, 2021, 2023), passing and camouflaging (Cage & Troxell-Whitman, 2019; Hull et al, 2017), or explored our sociality in relation to neurotypical sociality (Baker-Rodgers, 2017; Rice-Adams, 2023). These survival strategies are essential for many of us to survive, but they are ultimately a product of a society that medicalizes and pathologizes our autistic ways of being. Our own, autistic sense of being in the social world remains unexplored (Brown, 2012). Understanding how we socialize within autistic spaces and cultures is key to understanding how the current inequality we face could be overturned, thereby cultivating a greater sense of autistic culture, joy, solidarity and community. Developing concepts and frameworks to describe what this looks like, is key to generating such possibilities (Pearson & Rose, 2023).

This is not without its challenges. As Williams' (1998a) book title suggests, how do we, as autistic people, become 'somebody somewhere' when we have not been able to be 'someone' in our own geographies, cultures and society? As we are not born into a common autistic culture (Jordan, 1999) and do not always have access to, or feel included within, autistic spaces, it is difficult to differentiate our own and shared sense of sociality from neurotypical sociality (Brown, 2012). Equally, many of us are part of other communities and cultures, which are rarely discussed in relation to their intersection with autism (Cascio et al., 2021). Our social selves are shaped by our identities and too often what is conceived as 'autism' in the media, medical and research communities ignores our other identities, creating a blueprint of what we 'should' be like to be autistic. How do we disentangle ourselves from the narratives imposed by the medical–industrial complex that has pathologized us for so long (and continues to do so), while also recognizing that, within our own autistic communities, we too often view autism as a single-issue identity and struggle (Lorde, 1984)?

This makes it difficult to map our real histories, sense of community and cultures, as many of us still feel quite isolated and disparate from one another. From this perspective, I have found writing about this topic challenging at times, despite engaging (albeit not always successfully) in autistic spaces myself. As a result, I do not write this from an 'expert' point of view. Instead, I write this from a first-hand experience of sometimes struggling at being autistic in autistic spaces. As a white, middle-class, queer, non-binary, autistic ADHDer,[24] I am not attempting to – and know I cannot – provide an all-encompassing narrative or theory of autistic spaces, cultures and socialities in this piece. Alongside my own perspectives, I draw upon intersectional perspectives from neurodivergent and disabled communities. This narrative is a snapshot of my understanding in time. I realise that I

24 I identify as an ADHD-er, rather than a person with ADHD (attention deficit hyperactivity disorder), because I prefer identity-first language.

may have missed important details and I am open to exploring these or any inaccuracies. Overall, I hope this piece can contribute to a wider, emerging conversation around this important topic.

In what follows, I provide an overview of existing autistic spaces and cultures, past and present. From there, I explore the barriers to inclusion in autistic spaces and what is required to create a collective foundation for autistic sociality. This leads me to imagine what autistic spaces and cultures could look like before I start to describe the embodiments and expressions of what we could term autistic sociality.

Autistic spaces and cultures: A brief overview

Autistic people have been meeting for at least 30 years, creating communities, connections, and shared customs and cultures (Sinclair, 2010). The Internet provided the foundation for some of the first autistic spaces. One of the first was Autism Network International (ANI), founded in 1992 by Donna Williams, Xenia Grant and Jim Sinclair (Sinclair, 2005), who set up a penpal list and newsletter (Sinclair, 2010). An online autistic forum called ANI-L was set up in 1994, leading to other online autistic spaces emerging, notably InLv (Independent Living on the Autism Spectrum) (Milton, 2020), set up by Martijn Dekker (Dekker, 1999). These online spaces created an accessible home and meeting point for autistic people. They emerged as a reaction against online spaces dominated by parents of autistic people, notably the St John's University AUTISM mailing list, which epitomized the neurotypical, medicalized and pathologizing world view of autism (Dekker, 1999; 2015). Over time, this approach led to the emergence of a range of advocacy groups, advocating for autistic rights, and often for specific communities including marginalized genders and non-speaking people. These include the Autistic Self Advocacy Network, the Autistic Women and Non-Binary Network, and Communication First, to name but a few.[25] In the last decade, other autistic online spaces have proliferated, through forums, local virtual autistic groups and social media sites such as Facebook, X (formerly Twitter), Bluesky, Reddit, Youtube, Discord and TikTok.

These online autistic spaces allowed for a coming together of autistic people, who found they were a minority in their geographical setting. Online autistic spaces such as forums, groups, mailing lists or channels provide the opportunity to interact via written and text form and move away from face-to-face social interactions and sensory stimuli, departing from neurotypical culture that relies heavily on speech (Botha, et al., 2022; Dekker, 2015; Sinclair, 2010). These kinds of spaces often provide themed discussions around particular interests, which subscribers can opt into and out of (Sinclair, 2010). They might include

25 See Crosman (2019) for a more comprehensive list.

specific areas where parents and professionals can also contribute.[26] Online spaces, such as mailing lists and forums, avoid the need for automatic responses and the pressure to keep up with the fast-paced flow of the conversation found in neuronormative social situations (Dekker, 2015). Now, many autistic discord servers also provide 'slow' channels,[27] which further allows for slower-paced interaction than that found in more typical autistic online spaces. Online spaces might also provide 'infodump vaults' for people to share their interests consensually with others.[28]

Online social meet-ups with small groups of autistic people are also frequently used in the autistic community. Online meet-ups that I have attended at Autism Aim in Leeds, UK will often be facilitated with a 'round-robin' set-up, where everyone has a chance to contribute to the discussion at least once, either by speaking or via the chat box; a particular order is randomly selected and shared in the chat box to provide structure and to avoid one or more people talking for too long. In the neurodivergent staff group I facilitate at work, I have found it helpful to allocate more time to meet-ups, as the conversation inevitably expands and overruns, with the option to leave at any point. Debbie (Aucademy, 2022) notes that to stimulate conversation, she will ask groups to share one good thing from their week, and one not-so-good thing, or have themed discussions on particular topics. However, Farahar and Hunley explain (Aucademy, 2022) that many participants in online socials will choose to just listen, which is respected and affirmed in autistic spaces in general. Putting on personal cameras is also optional and many of us will switch between having our cameras on and off or not at all to avoid sensory and social overload. Farahar (Aucademy, 2022) highlights that private messaging can also be used, to check in on people's well-being or by participants to contact the facilitator. Jack (Aucademy, 2022) also observes that some groups also provide a quiet breakout room, if participants need some space away from the wider group. Hunley and Farahar (Aucademy, 2022) point out that many will also prefer to communicate via the chat box or a combination of speaking or typing, with the chat box accommodating different processing and communications needs. Typically, facilitators will regularly return to the chat throughout the meeting to read out responses. This is common in online autistic social meet-ups, such as those like Aucademy (n.d.b), and is often referred to as a 'voice box' (a designated person who will read out someone's text-based responses so they can be shared with the rest of the group) for those who are non-speaking, minimally speaking or do not want to speak. Farahar (Aucademy, 2022) notes that avatars, filters, costumes or props might also be used to disguise or inhabit different identities to avoid the sense of being observed that might lead to anxiety.[29]

26 For example, some online groups such as Autism Inclusivity (n.d.) have a mixed membership of autistic people and neurotypicals but questions posed in the group will often give preference to autistic people to answer first, to avoid misconceptions being shared, as well as time for autistic people to respond in line with their own processing pace.

27 Such as the Autscape Discord server that is created anew for each Autscape conference.

28 Such as the Aucademy Infodump Vaults Facebook group (Aucademy, n.d.a).

29 The Aucademy YouTube channel has many examples of presenters using filters, props and avatars (Aucademy, n.d.b).

While autistic online social spaces have been the bedrock of social interaction, more physical in-person gatherings have emerged. On the back of ANI's (2009) correspondence lists and forum, Autreat, the first in-person conference run, designed and led by autistic people, was organized in 1996 by ANI (Sinclair, 2010). Inspired by Autreat, Autscape, a yearly in-person three-day conference in the UK was started in 2005, and has led to smaller regional events and international spin-offs.[30] Autreat and Autscape have paved the way for a more distinctive autistic culture comprised of a range of shared customs and practices; many autistic people have described attending these events (or others) as an instant homecoming, or felt as though they were 'finding their tribe' or meeting someone 'from the same planet' as them (Botha et al., 2022; Sinclair, 2010). Farahar (Aucademy, 2022) notes that in the organization of physical events, spaces are designed to ensure the needs of different autistic people are met, which means putting rules in place. This means absolute freedom of expression might need to be tempered somewhat in these spaces (Sinclair, 2010).

These practices are important as, compared to virtual spaces, physical spaces often present more challenges. These include the stress of travelling to the event, the sense of uncertainty around being in a new venue, and interacting with new people and social environments, as well as not being in control of one's sensory environment (Sinclair, 2010). To address these challenges, detailed information is distributed before events, and participants are invited to ask questions via events' online forums or mailing lists to avoid any anxiety (Autscape, n.d.a). This pre-event information makes clear that different autistic social expressions are accepted and anticipated, including more so-called 'atypical', as well as masked, expressions (Autscape, n.d.a). On arrival at Autscape, participants typically take part in an orientation session that explains everything in detail. Alongside this, small 'home' groups, typically of ten people, are also set up to make participants feel more comfortable and allow them to get to know other attendees better (Autscape, 2020). Home groups meet once a day throughout the conference and are hosted by an autistic facilitator. The social environment is also structured to accommodate different needs and socializing is affirmed as being an optional activity. To put this into practice and to respect people's boundaries, a colour-coded badge or lanyard system is typically put in place to signal participants social needs and wants: red signals no interaction is wanted; yellow indicates that prior permission is required before any interaction happens; green highlights that social contact is welcomed; white (or no badge) typically points to the fact the participant feels confident regulating their own contact; and black alerts everyone to the fact that the participant does not want to be photographed (Autscape, n.d.b).[31] Participants' social needs might change throughout

30 Such as Autisticon in Leeds, UK, Autminds in the Netherlands, Autwave in Finland, Autism Conference in Denmark and Autism by Autistic Voices in Portugal.

31 It has been observed by autistic people that events organised by neurotypicals have used stickers or badges in a way that changed the intended meaning of this signalling system. In addition, some autistic people find stickers or small badges do not serve their intended purpose as they are not visible or legible to others at events.

the event. At both Autscape and Autisticon, a one-day autistic-led conference in Leeds, participants are encouraged to alternate their badge colours to reflect their changing needs throughout the event.

To respect a diversity of sensory needs, Autreat also encouraged participants not to use flash photography or scented products, to avoid touching anyone without their permission and to conduct loud activities outside of designated areas (Sinclair, 2010). Quiet rooms are often provided and participants are also encouraged to go outside; Autscape and Autreat are held in quieter, rural settings. Accommodation, as well as meals, are typically provided. Inevitably, the food is not to everyone's taste, but it removes the stress of extra planning. At Autreat, participants could opt out of meals (Sinclair, 2010), and at Autscape special diets can be requested and a quiet dining room is also provided to avoid sensory overload (Autscape, n.d.b). A variety of different and optional presentations are put on to cater to different interests and informal discussion groups and leisure activities are also organized (Sinclair, 2010). Sessions are also streamed in Autscape, so virtual participants can take part too, which merges the physical and virtual social worlds somewhat. A Discord server is set up for both virtual and in-person participants to connect, ask questions, share learning and discuss areas of interest. Virtual 'home' groups are also set up for online participants.

Despite organizing events around autistic needs, interests and preferences, not everyone has always felt included or felt like their voice has been heard in these spaces (Sinclair, 2010). In the next section, I explore some of the challenges and barriers that these spaces and cultures face in creating a collective sense of autistic sociality.

Creating the space, culture and collective foundation for autistic sociality

To encourage and explore our shared sense of autistic sociality, we need spaces and cultures that provide a refuge from the abuse, frustration, confusion, misunderstandings, bullying, victimization, exclusion and inaccessibility that neurotypical-led spaces have imposed on us (Sinclair, 2010). To this end, it is important to highlight the difference between autistic spaces and neurotypical spaces (even if they have been designed by neurotypicals with autistic people in mind). The latter spaces have historically tended to be more pathologizing (Walker, 2021) and 'treatment'-orientated (Dekker, 2015), viewing us as in need of being taken care of (Baggs, 2012a; Sinclair, 2010). They have typically located issues within autistic people, rather than within the spaces, cultures and societies in which autistic people live. Traditionally, these spaces have not incorporated our views or needs into the design and operation of the spaces, reinforcing a dominant neurotypical culture that has marginalized us. Autistic people have: attended autism conferences where autistic access needs have not been accounted for, leading to sensory overload and a sense of exclusion (Sinclair, 2010); taken part in autism research advisory groups, led by neurotypical researchers, without the necessary accommodations to make the group accessible for them as Debbie highlights (Aucademy, 2022); attended social groups led by neurotypicals, which have aimed to normalize neurotypical means of socializing as Hunley shared (Aucademy, 2022); chaired meetings with autism charities and groups where their autistic identity was questioned in an ableist and racist manner (Simmonds, 2023); and been abused by caregivers (Baggs, 2012a) – or detained against their will (Quinn, 2018) – in medical or residential settings not designed for their needs. Our sense of autistic sociality cannot flourish in neurotypical spaces or spaces such as residential or care homes, hospitals, clinics, workplaces and schools designed and supervised by medical professionals, researchers, policymakers, employers and parents of autistic people from a neuronormative and medical perspective. These kinds of spaces force us to hide our autistic selves and are oppressive. So, how do we create the foundation to explore our sociality further?

We not only need refuge from this oppression, but also autistic solidarity to overcome the painful impact of being detached from any sense of community, which for many of us has been absent for most of our lives (Milton, 2014). Disability writer smith [sic] (2020) attests, *'as long as claiming our own ground is treated as an act of hostility, we need our ground'*. 'Crip spaces' can act as a foundation to transcend marginalization, stigma and exclusion (smith, 2020).[32] Crip spaces are revolutionary and subversive spaces that are designed by and for disabled people to create a sense of belonging, community and pride in being disabled in a world that views disability as flawed and taboo (smith, 2020). This entrenched view of disability being taboo mirrors the social perception of autistic people as deviant – the opposite of what is conceived to be as 'normal' (Milton, 2014; Walker, 2021). Only by embracing our so-called 'deviance' – our forms of autistic expression and disabled embodiment – and rejecting any notion of 'normality', can a sense of solidarity and revolutionary change materialize, allowing us to subvert the current dominant social order and create new possibilities. This practice – and identity – is known as the act of neuroqueering, or identifying as neuroqueer (Walker, 2021; Yergeau, 2018). A neuroqueer is:

> *...any individual whose identity, selfhood, gender performance, and/or neurocognitive style have in some way been shaped by their engagement in practices of neuroqueering, regardless of what gender, sexual orientation, or style of neurocognitive functioning they may have been born with...*
> (Walker, 2021, p. 161)

32 Crip is a term that has historically been used to shame and stigmatize disabled people and has been reclaimed by many in disabled communities, to signify pride in their disabled identity.

Being neuroqueer, or practising neuroqueering, has liberatory potential, as anyone can neuroqueer and choose to defy and subvert neuronormativity, heteronormativity and the wider systems of oppression these performances operate within (Walker, 2021). Neuroqueering invites us to be aware of the pathologizing and harmful ingrained practices that have seeped into our ways of being, with the aim of expressing and embodying ourselves in ways that defy those practices, thereby engaging in a process of reclaiming our identities (Walker, 2021). It also provides an opportunity to create spaces that reflect neuroqueering practices (Walker, 2021), thereby creating a new social reality that challenges the current neuronormative order (Yergeau, 2018).[33] Neurotypicals entering these spaces will be invited to 'inhabit our world' (Mingus, 2017). This might make them feel uncertain around how to act, threatened because the spaces are not designed specifically for them (smith, 2020) or confused because the organisation of the spaces might be less formal and bureaucratic (Piepzna-Samarasinha, 2020). The counter-hegemonic nature of neuroqueering mirrors the way disabled communities organize more generally. Disability justice activists have encouraged us to think differently about the spaces where organizing happens. These spaces are not always located in the places where non-disabled people would expect to find them as Piepzna-Samarasinha explains:

> *Disability justice exists every place two disabled people meet – at the kitchen table, on heating pads in bed talking to our loves ... anyone can be part of disability justice if they organize from their own spoons, own bodies and minds, and own communities.* (Piepzna-Samarasinha, 2020, p. 258)

Disability justice emerged through conversations by disabled activists of colour in 2005 including Patty Berne, Mia Mingus, Stacey Milbern, Leroy Moore, Eli Clare and Sebastian Margaret (Berne, 2015). Disability justice centres upon the experiences of those most marginalized by ableism, white supremacy and capitalism within the disabled community, particularly the disabled working class, queer, trans and people of colour: and it is a practice that organizes within these respective communities (Berne, 2015). As a lens for creating revolutionary crip spaces and spaces of organizing, disability justice activists remind us of the words of Lorde (1984), who disassembled the notion of a single-issue struggle, identity or life. Disability is not a single-issue in the sense that ableism is created within other systems of oppression including colonialism, capitalism, white supremacy and heteropatriarchy (Berne, 2015). Likewise, we cannot view autism as a single-issue identity: many of us also belong to other communities, have other identities and are therefore impacted intersectionally by the systems of oppression that encroach on them.

33 For a fuller explanation of how one can neuroqueer, refer to Walker (2021, pp. 161–163) who provides eight different neuroqueering practices.

This point is important because many of us still face difficulties and even exclusion within autistic spaces. We discover that autistic spaces are not always the utopia of autistic joy we might have envisaged and do not resolve our sense of social exclusion within society. We might find it impossible to escape neuronormative structures and also be unfamiliar with autistic customs and cultures, leading us to use neurotypical coping strategies that may be scorned in some autistic spaces (Sinclair, 2010). Alternatively, we could be considered too 'odd', even by autistics (Sinclair, 2010). Or we may have different access needs, interests or experiences of being autistic, due to our other intersecting identities and life experiences, which may lead to us feeling not included or understood. For example, I have felt ignored, invisible and unable to speak in autistic spaces even though I wanted to, much like I often do in neuronormative spaces. This takes me back to my childhood and the trauma of being 'selectively mute', frozen and silenced due to the lack of social accessibility in the space and people around me. Conversely, at other times, I have experienced a new and exciting feeling of being included, with my words rolling off my tongue like they have never done so before. However, in these times I have stopped and noticed others in the same instance who have not shared my sense of autistic joy and, instead, perhaps felt drowned out by my privileges. In my neurodivergent staff group, I, alongside group members, have felt trapped by neuronormative time pressures encroaching on us, our exploratory discussions that follow multiple paths are halted at the hour, forcing us to cram our thoughts at once, leading to multiple interjections and a sense of frustration. With my femme-ness and femme interests, I have sometimes felt like the odd one out in autistic spaces; I have felt the way I articulate, express and present myself is not received as 'autistic' enough, and I sometimes struggle to be taken seriously or have my voice heard. Equally, my 'in-between' non-binaryness and other neurodivergences, traumas and identities that hum along in the background, seem to work against me being perceived as definitively autistic, leading me to question and doubt myself.

White, middle-class and cisgender young men have typically been considered the archetypal autistic people by society, the media and the medical establishment (Giwa Onaiwu, 2017; Simmonds, 2023). Voices from trans, non-binary, queer, Black, Indigenous, and other people of colour, as well as working-class autistic people are often not represented in autistic spaces. This mirrors the wider inequalities in the knowledge production of autism, with autism research typically not including autistic voices (Kapp, 2020; Wood et al., 2018), especially from marginalized groups, thereby perpetuating an infantilized (Milton, 2014), neurotypical, westernized, white, middle-class, male, cisgender view of autism, that favours the speaking (over non-speaking) autistic population (Simmonds, 2023). Just like neuronormative or spaces designed by neurotypicals for autistics have excluded autistic needs and voices, autistic-led social spaces are not immune from this tendency, and they are undoubtedly shaped by the power and privilege the people who form them, particularly in terms of the whiteness of most autistic spaces:

> *I was a minority group within a minority group within a minority group within a minority group! There was no place that I belonged, no place where I could find someone who understood me.* (Giwa Onaiwu, 2017, pp. xiv-xv)

> *I have not felt rejected by the Autistic community because of my cultural background. At the same time, I don't feel included. I see it as another dimension to the third person perspective I find myself in most of the time as an Autistic adult.* (Socialworks, 2017, p. 176)

Autistic people who do not fit the stereotypical image of an autistic person through their intersectional identities, not only find that they need to mask their autism, but also their other identities (Simmonds, 2023). To this effect, what are we doing within autistic spaces to ensure different people can have their voices heard and, in doing so, allow us to embody and express ourselves in ways that reflect our other identities and cultures? I explore this in the next section.

Imagining future autistic social spaces

In envisaging the future direction of autistic spaces and cultures, as a foundation for our sociality, I try to imagine what it could look like. The future autistic space is one where autistic people come together either in person or digitally (or both) to create and organize a culture which is centred upon the diverse identities, interests, and communities, and sensory, social and processing needs and preferences of the autistic community, as defined by them. The space would recognize that autism is not a single-issue identity and that the autistic community is made up of intersecting identities. Linked to this ethos of fluidity and intersectionality, the space would not necessarily need to be for just 'autistic' people. Instead, it would be beneficial to 'open the gates' to avoid unintentionally promoting a rigid stereotype or expectation around what autism looks like that could continue to perpetuate the medicalization of autism and occlude the intersectionality of autism. This is not least because some people might be questioning or exploring their neurotype or do not have access to or resources for diagnosis (Brown, 2016). Such an approach would also encourage others to neuroqueer and explore their full expressions and embodiments of being autistic, which might deviate even against the autistic norm. The space would be open to our disabled and neurodivergent cousins[34] (Dekker, 2015) and we would collectively

34 Autism Network International (2009) referred to 'cousins' as someone who had not been formally identified as being autistic but who had social and communication differences that signified a sense of them being 'autistic-like'. Here, I refer to cousins in a more loosely defined way as people who diverge from accepted social norms in order to acknowledge the expanding diversity of neurodivergence.

work together to meet different access needs to further 'crip' the space (smith, 2020). The space might attract non-autistic participants, who may also feel stifled by the social codes imposed by the dominant neuronormative culture. Non-autistic participants who entered these spaces would be asked to be respectful of – and open to – autistic cultures, and accountable for their own internalized ableism and any other oppressive ideologies. However, it would also be important for us, the autistic community, to do the same, as Brown articulates:

> *So where are our spaces where we can heal not just from the trauma inflicted on us by others but also from the ongoing trauma we inflict on ourselves? Where can we be vulnerable, truly vulnerable, without fearing the consequences of enforced ostracism from 'safe spaces' that privilege an ableist facade of having-it-together and overcoming-internalized-oppression?*
> (Brown, 2016)

Autistic social spaces have typically placed the responsibility for communicating, being 'social', or 'having-it-all together' (Brown, 2016) on 'the individual, not the group' (Sinclair, 2010). The implication here is that, while participation is never obligatory as it is in neuronormative culture, if an autistic person wants to contribute to a social situation, the onus is on them to do so.[35] Individual preference is certainly important and we should never assume any autistic person in an autistic space necessarily wants to contribute or even be part of the group or community (Sinclair, 2010). But what happens if we do want to, but we cannot figure out how to do so on our own? What happens when we do not know what our social access needs are, perhaps because our identities have been denied for so long? Here, the role of the wider autistic community in facilitating participation by its individual members is key. Sometimes, we need to work together to ensure we can all contribute when we want to.

Mingus (2017) advocates for a culture of interdependence, justice and liberation, over one that promotes dependence and individualism which only encourages social isolation, ableism and able-bodied supremacy. Mingus (2011) aptly terms this process as access intimacy, highlighting that it cannot materialize without relationship, connection and community:

35 I have often been in neurotypical social settings where I have been silent and have suddenly been invasively spotlighted by someone, asking me out of nowhere 'Maisie, what do you think?' with everyone peering over to me in expectation. This often feels like a tool to put me back in my place for being non-compliant to the ableist requirement to perform the to-ing and fro-ing stipulated neuronormativity of conversations. I am thankful this pressure has never been put on me in autistic spaces.

> *Access intimacy is interdependence in action … when access intimacy is present, the most powerful part is having someone to navigate access and ableism with. It is knowing that someone else is with me in this mess. It is knowing that someone else is willing to be with me in the never-ending and ever-changing daily obstacle course that is navigating an inaccessible world. It is knowing that I will not be alone in the stunning silence, avoidance and denial of ableism…* (Mingus, 2017)

The future autistic space would therefore encourage a culture of negotiating and renegotiating accessibility and our agency (and privilege) within the context of ableism and the systems of oppression that surround it. It would involve challenging ourselves on the oppression inherent within our communities, building a deep understanding of our needs, identities and communities, and ultimately reimagining our world so that our access needs become woven into the fabric of this new reality (Mingus, 2017). It would also require creating a culture founded on ongoing consent, where we would recognize that some of us are afforded more agency and power than others in different contexts (Barker & Hancock, 2017). By defying the nonconsensual culture that raised us, we could nurture small, microconsent practices into our interactions with others (Barker & Hancock, 2017). This might involve asking someone beforehand if they want to contribute to a conversation, or if it is okay to speak to them on a particular topic. It could also mean checking in with someone throughout a conversation to ask how they feel it is going, to determine whether the pace is suitable for them and to ensure they want to continue. Equally, we might want to check in with ourselves to see if we still feel present in the conversation or, conversely, to ensure we are allowing others to contribute. Another key practice could involve challenging neuronormative and capitalist time conventions by effectively slowing down and stretching out our interactions, conversations and relationships. Barker (2020) refers to this practice as slow relating and notes it consists of collectively agreeing the intensity of contact time in a relationship in terms of frequency and length of time. For example, a group may decide to meet every month for two hours rather than every weekend for an undefined time. Slow relating helps us to connect, build trust and not only ensure that we can have our voice heard at our own pace but also that others can too (Barker, 2020). Overall, this approach involves creating a culture of care, consent and healing, encouraging others to explore and process new parts of their identities and, through this, build boundaries (Pearson & Rose, 2023).

One small, simple and initial step we could take to start practising consent and access intimacy would be to encourage ourselves and others to explore what our needs actually are. This would help us to collectively disentangle ourselves from a culture that has denied and silenced them for so long. Access riders are documents developed by disabled people, which we can use to map our needs and preferences. Templates are downloadable online, and provide a useful framework for recording our access needs (both essential and desirable), as well as emergency contact information and supporting information (Ajayi-Egunjobi, n.d.; Hemsley, n.d.). The access rider could be extended to highlight our social needs, interests and preferences, alongside the social contexts in which we might have more agency and privilege, and thus serve as a useful framework for encouraging ourselves to practise social consent with others. Completing the forms could be a collective task where we support each other. All of this will take time, not least because we are still exploring what our sociality looks like. In the final section of this piece, I will sketch out what autistic sociality looks like.

Autistic sociality

Our sociality is shaped not only by our autistic selves, but also by intersecting identities such as race, sexuality, cultural background, gender, disability, class, age and life experiences. These facets of our lives generate different manifestations of autistic sociality. Here, I draw upon various perspectives and experiences of autistic and neuroqueer sociality, including my own.

Autistic sociality can primarily be conceptualized as a dynamic and embodied relationship with one's environment:

> *My language is not about designing words or even visual symbols for people to interpret. It is about being in a constant conversation with every aspect of my environment ... Far from being purposeless, the way that I move is an ongoing response to what is around me.* (Baggs, 2007)

Baggs (2007) says they communicate through smelling, feeling, tasting, looking at and listening to things in their environment. This takes many forms like touching surfaces, flapping their hands, rubbing against objects, playing with water, and humming a tune. Such practices are often defined as stimming or self-stimulatory practice, which is a way of communicating, and making meaning with and enjoying the environment around us (Bakan, 2015). This might include expressing ourselves through gestures such as flapping, tiptoeing, swirling, humming, jumping, rocking and swinging (Gennai, 2023). These social practices are influenced by the distinctive way we process information (Milton, 2017). Hence, for autistic people, socializing might take an entirely different form to neurotypical forms of interaction (Yergeau, 2018). Communication with people is not privileged over communication with other parts of the wider environment, thereby challenging the meaning of sociality altogether. Williams (1998b) recalls connecting with objects as a child as a safe way for her to communicate. By focusing on the wider environment, we might have a more perceptual and dynamic sense of sociality that is not based on preconceived ideas or 'normative ideologies' (Milton, 2017, p. 57).

Key to our sociality is also the idea that speech is not central to being social (Baggs, 2007; Harp, 2012, Yergeau; 2018), unlike neurotypical social situations where speaking is highly valorized. 'Autistic language' is not necessarily rooted in the spoken word (Baggs, 2012b; Yergeau, 2018). Many of us struggle with speech and feel that speech is not our intuitive way of expressing ourselves (Harp, 2012). Therefore, we might use different tools to communicate, such as writing, drawing, gesturing, stimming (Harp, 2012), vocalizations (Baggs, 2007), assistive technology and text (Baggs, 2012b; Sequenzia, 2012). We might also complete tasks or stim while socializing to aid our sociality (Harp, 2012). Being silent is also a respected aspect of autistic sociality and is based on 'reflection, mediation, and processing' (Yergeau, 2012, p. 304). Unlike typical neurotypical social situations, being silent for autistic people is not a signifier that someone is not communicating (Harp, 2012). In autistic social situations, there is no real expectation to speak. I find communicating by being silent incredibly freeing. However, I know this is not safe or welcomed in neuronormative social situations. As an autistic femme, I have been socialized to fit in, people-please and be subservient. This conditioning has led me to be imprisoned as 'selectively mute' in neuronormative society due to the inaccessible and exclusionary social environments I often find myself in. Likewise, Gennai (2023), a poet and artist, explores their selective mutism within the context of the silencing of their Indigenous and African ancestry in Jamaica; their performances explore this within the context of their different identities, and use this as a foundation for resisting and deconstructing social norms (Gennai, 2021). For non-speaking autistic people, their silence in social situations can also be particularly stigmatizing and imprisoning as Sequenzia recalls:

> *My self-esteem has been severely damaged by years of listening to people talking about me in front of me, calling me names, labelling me 'severe' and 'retarded', even saying I did not have human dignity.* (Sequenzia, 2012, p. 347)

Alternative means of communicating through text and assistive technology can be a powerful way of connecting, particularly since, historically, many autistic therapies, such as applied behavioural analysis or social skills training, have been focused toward getting autistic people to adopt neuronormative approaches to socializing (Silberman, 2015). While silence in neurotypical society oppresses many of us, it can be an act of nourishing self-care and joyful resistance to imposed neuronormativity in autistic spaces and cultures (Bagatell, 2010; Gennai, 2021; Harp, 2012).

There are also verbal practices that autistic people engage in. Echolalia is a common autistic social practice, which involves repeating back words or noises that have been overheard (Baker, 2013). However, echolalia is often disdained by neurotypicals for lacking substance and significance (Anderson-Chavarria, 2021). Contrary to this perception, echolalia acts as a powerful tool for conveying meaning (Anderson-Chavarria, 2021). I have often used echolalia when I do not have the energy to automatically respond to someone with a fully articulated answer, giving me space to process what is being said. I also use echolalia when I am in a playful mood, to mimic a melody or something that has been said. Similarly, many autistic people use echolalia as self-stimulatory practice (Anderson-Chavarria, 2021) or to echo sensorial input (Williams, 1998b). Through echolalia we might collect certain phrases, sounds or sayings that become part of our everyday vocabulary. Certain words might be steeped in and connected to recollections of certain emotions, memories and sensory experiences (Bascom, 2012a). This is known as metaphorical language (Bascom, 2012a; Harp, 2012). Unlike neurotypical social situations where well-known and well-versed figures of speech might be used, autistic people might invent their own sayings and metaphors that reflect their own individual experiences (Baggs, 2012b). Metaphorical language often knits together one experience with another, and autistic conversation is often infused with metaphors (Baggs, 2012b) resulting in puns, riddles and quick-witted quips (Bagatell, 2010). Here, the literal and the nonliteral might merge, leading us to an almost deadpan, comic delivery, as Debbie explains (Aucademy 2022). Metaphorical language is often not reciprocated or may be viewed as confusing, particularly by neurotypical people, and therefore we might reserve this practice for only people we know well (Harp, 2012). Despite this, Farahar highlights (Aucademy, 2022) that asking for clarification is an affirmed social practice in autistic communities to confirm and explore meaning.

Conversely, we might prefer to draw upon more literal, logical and intentional forms of communication (Yergeau, 2018) to communicate honestly and transparently (Beardon, 2017) and to avoid relying on body language or more abstract expressions of speech (Baggs, 2012b). Speaking openly and truthfully can also be an act of social justice and shine a light on inequalities, such as racism and ableism (Robinson, 2017), in a society that does not openly discuss such issues. Some autistic people also socialize using a more verbose, often baroque, form of language in which speakers strive to locate precise words to convey meanings in rich detail (Bascom, 2012b). Direct, intentional language allows some autistic people to convey their knowledge and interests effectively in a monologue (Bascom, 2012b) while also signalling a sense of genuine interest in one another, striving to get to a clear understanding of others' experiences, as Hunley explains (Aucademy, 2022). Monologuing is often linked to our single sense of monotropic attention (Murray et al., 2005; Williams, 1998b) and can be conceptualized as a flow state (Csikszentmihalyi, 1990) in which we become so immersed and engaged in our speech or text that we lose touch with anything else around us (McDonnell & Milton, 2014). The directness and candour of the monologue or flow state contrasts with the neurotypical preference for small talk and social norms, in which we often do not find meaning (Bagatell, 2010). Monologuing feels like an outpouring of our internal stream of consciousness to the wider collective. It ultimately changes the dynamic and structure of 'standard' conversations. Unlike the constant, fast-paced, back and forth interaction of neurotypical conversations, monologuing promotes turn-taking and allows conversants to 'flow' and go into more detail about a specific area of interest, as Busuttil explains (Aucademy, 2022). While others might chime in at times the focus typically remains on listening to the main conversant. Farahar (Aucademy, 2022) notes that this slower and more structured pace gives everyone time to process the information. From this, people then have the option to take over the reins of monologuing, should they want to.

Despite this, Gray-Hammond (Aucademy, 2022) notes that there might be some disjointedness and 'jumping in' to the conversation, particularly if it sparks an immediate thought that the group member wants to share, before the thought or moment passes. I often find that, having had time to process the information, I might want to return to a certain part of a conversation to clarify my understanding, and force the conversation back in time. It might be that the conversation is already over and weeks, months or years later I want to return back to it. Equally, I might draw inferences or references from past conversations to the present conversation, merging ideas asynchronously in a somewhat abstract, nonlinear way. This might be confusing and some people might wonder where my thoughts have originated from or why I have brought it up. The nonlinear way I process information might manifest itself physically when I speak or write, with the words coming out in the wrong order – disjointed, disorganized – as I try to 'process' in the moment. I might pluck out words that are considered the 'wrong' words for the context, words that might not make sense or words from my first language (German), creating a mish-mash of words and languages. Musician, composer and writer, JJJJerome Ellis (2020), explores the intersection of disfluency and stuttering with Blackness. Ellis' music and writing (2020) describes how his speech and communication does not conform to traditional time parameters and structures as defined by a white and ableist world. Operating outside of these frameworks, and embracing the unpredictable dysfluency of his speech, provides possibilities for creating different and liberatory temporalities:

> *Stuttering … creates unpredictable, silent gaps in speech. I call these gaps 'clearings'. Slaves sang in the fields, and whites heard them; but they also sang (and danced) in the woods at night, out of earshot. Undergirding the clearing created by my stutter is that other clearing, in the woods, where my enslaved ancestors stole away to keep healing, resisting and liberating through music – work that I continue today.* (Ellis, 2020, p. 215)

Ellis (2020; 2021) shows us that defying the traditional structures and temporalities of social situations can be a radical act of defiance, healing and neuroqueering against the efficient and seamless performance of white, able-bodied, neuronormative social delivery. Through this, he creates new opportunities for being social that ultimately change our social reality.

These are some of the many ways we might express and embody ourselves within our own spaces and cultures. By practising our sociality in our own terms in spaces and cultures free from neuronormative pressures (and the wider systems of oppression that surround neuronormative ways of being), we can start to conceptualize ourselves in a way that respects our diverse identities and the complexity this brings to our expressions and embodiments.

Concluding comments

Milton's (2012) Double Empathy Problem has shone a light on the fact that we, as a community, are not lacking in empathy, connection and sociality, and that our autistic selves have instead been marginalized by enforced neuronormativity and a medical–industrial complex that actively seeks to pathologize and label our autistic identities as abnormal. By stepping away from this oppressive and harmful narrative, we can start to explore more authentic and meaningful ways of embodying, expressing and healing our autistic selves. One way of doing this might be to recognize that the Double Empathy Problem is not a strict binary between autistic people and neurotypical people (Milton, 2012). Communication breakdowns can happen in any context where the wider forces of power and privilege are ignored. Meaningful social communication and relationships are difficult, regardless of our neurotypes, in a world that divides us and makes it difficult to be ourselves through multiple systems of oppression. We, the autistic community, are not the sealed off islands isolated from the rest of humanity, devoid of empathy, connection and communication that the psychiatrists, psychologists and other autism professionals and organizations have continued to say we are. To further resist this stereotype, we can recognize the liberatory potential of our intersecting autistic socialites and neuroqueering endeavours, which have the potential to create new ways of being and connecting, that blur the boundaries of 'normal' and 'abnormal'. Adhering to a strict single-issue code of what constitutes autistic only damages us and makes us fall prey to the trappings of the medicalization of autism, which controls and holds us back from cultivating our autistic futures. Therefore, it is imperative that we as a community reflect on the differences both within our own autistic selves, and between us and our wider neurokin. By cripping our spaces, we can work collectively to support each other to build communities of consent and understand our own and others' access needs and preferences in a much more interconnected and interdependent way, creating a firm foundation for autistic sociality, community and connection. I hope this piece is a useful starting point for creating a sense of autistic sociality that allows us to move away from an ideology that has suppressed and denied our social needs and preferences for far too long.

References

Ajayi-Egunjobi, M. (n.d.). *Creating Your Own Access Rider.* Unlimited. Retrieved 12 November, 2023, from https://weareunlimited.org.uk/resource/creating-your-own-access-rider/

Anderson-Chavarria, M. (2021). The autism predicament: Models of autism and their impact on autistic identity. *Disability & Society*, *37*(8), 1–21. https://doi.org/10.1080/09687599.2021.1877117

Aucademy (n.d.a). *Aucademy: Infovault Dumps.* [Facebook Group]. Retrieved 26 November, 2023, from https://www.facebook.com/groups/773389976913468/

Aucademy (n.d.b). *Home.* [YouTube page]. YouTube. Retrieved 26 November, 2023, from https://www.youtube.com/@aucademy6195

Aucademy (2022, September 7). *Autistic Social Spaces vs "Autism" Social Spaces: Aucademy Educates.* [Video]. YouTube. Retrieved 4 February, 2025 from https://www.youtube.com/watch?v=xldXLp9I6oM&t=295s

Autism Inclusivity (n.d.). *About This Group.* [Facebook Group]. Retrieved 26 November, 2023 from https://www.facebook.com/groups/autisminclusivity/

Autistic Network International (ANI) (2009, July 19). *ANI-L: An Online Discussion List.* Autreat. https://www.autreat.com/ani-l.html

Autscape (n.d.a). *The Experience.* Autscape. Retrieved 12 November, 2023, from http://www.autscape.org/experience/

Autscape (n.d.b). *Autistic Needs.* Autscape. Retrieved 12 November, 2023, from

http://www.autscape.org/experience/autisticneeds

Autscape (2020, July 26). *Autscape: Countdown Daily Newsletter.* http://www.autscape.org/2020/Countdown2020-1.pdf

Bagatell, N. (2010). From cure to community: Transforming notions of autism. *Ethos: Journal of the Society for Psychological Anthropology, 38*(1), 33–35. https://doi.org/10.1111/j.1548-1352.2009.01080.x

Baggs, M. (2007, January 15). *In My Language.* [Video]. YouTube. https://www.youtube.com/watch?v=JnylM1hI2jc

Baggs, M. (2012a, April 30). BADD: Caregiver abuse takes many forms. *Ballastexistenz.* https://ballastexistenz.wordpress.com/2012/04/30/badd-caregiver-abuse-takes-many-forms/

Baggs, M. (2012b). Untitled. In *Loud Hands: Autistic People Speaking.* (pp. 324–334). Autistic Self Advocacy Network.

Bakan, M. B. (2015). The musicality of stimming: Promoting neurodiversity in the ethnomusicology of autism. *MUSICultures, 41*(2), 133–161. https://journals.lib.unb.ca/index.php/MC/article/view/22914/26599

Baker, D. (2013). Particular polyglots: Multilingual students with autism. *Disability & Society. 28*(4), 527–541. https://doi.org/10.1080/09687599.2012.717883

Baker-Rodgers, J. (2017). *Autism, Sociality and Friendship: A Qualitative Enquiry* (Doctoral dissertation, Sheffield Hallam University). SHURA. https://doi.org/10.7190/shu-thesis-00072

Barker, M. J. (2020, April 21). Slow relating. *Rewriting the Rules.* https://www.rewriting-the-rules.com/self/slow-relating/

Barker, M. J., & Hancock, J. (2017, November 23). Make consent your aim. *Culture Sex Relationships.* https://megjohnandjustin.com/relationships/make-consent-aim/

Bascom, J. (2012a). Metaphors are important. In *Loud Hands: Autistic People, Speaking.* (pp. 293–297). Autistic Self Advocacy Network.

Bascom, J. (2012b). On being articulate. In *Loud Hands: Autistic People, Speaking.* (pp. 343–345). Autistic Self Advocacy Network.

Beardon, L. (2017). *Autism and Asperger Syndrome in Adults*. Sheldon Press.

Berne, P. (2015, June 10). *Disability Justice: A Working Draft by Patty Berne.* Sins Invalid. https://static1.squarespace.com/static/5bed3674f8370ad8c02efd9a/t/6329eb83b478e84b6a2502ba/1663691651875/Patty_Berne_DJ-Working-Draft.docx.pdf

Botha, M., Dibb, B., & Frost, D. (2022). 'It's being part of a grand tradition, a grand counter-culture which involves communities': A qualitative investigation of autistic community connectedness. *Autism (26)*8, 2151–2164. https://doi.org/10.1177/13623613221080248

Brown, L. X. Z. (2012, October 11). The politics of coming out. *Autistic Hoya.* https://www.autistichoya.com/2012/10/the-politics-of-coming-out.html

Brown, L. X. Z. (2016, April 4). Hello, internalized ableism. *Autistic Hoya.* https://www.autistichoya.com/2016/04/hello-internalized-ableism.html

Cage, E. & Troxell-Whitman, Z. (2019). Understanding the reasons, contexts and costs of camouflaging for autistic adults. *Journal of Autism & Developmental Disorders, 49*(5), 1899–1911. https://doi.org/10.1007/s10803-018-03878-x

Cascio, M. A., Weiss, J. A., & Racine, E. (2021). Making research autism inclusive by attending to intersectionality: A review of the research ethics literature. *Review Journal of Autism & Developmental Disorders, 8,* 22–36. https://doi.org/10.1007/s40489-020-00204-z

Crompton, C. J., Ropar, D., Evans-Williams, C. V. M., Flynn, E. G., & Fletcher-Watson, S. (2020). Autistic peer-to-peer information is highly effective. *Autism. 24*(7), 1704–1712. https://doi.org/10.1177/1362361320919286

Crosman, C. (2019, November 28). *Good Autistic Advocacy Organisations vs. Bad Autism 'Charities'.* In the Loop about Neurodiversity. https://intheloopaboutneurodiversity.wordpress.com/2019/11/28/good-autistic-advocacy-organizations-vs-bad-autism-charities/

Csikszentmihalyi, M. (1990). *Flow: The Psychology of Happiness.* Random House Books.

Dekker, M. (1999). *On Our Own Terms: Emerging Autistic Culture.* [Conference Paper] Autism99 online conference, Virtual. http://www.autscape.org/2015/programme/handouts/Autistic-Culture-07-Oct-1999.pdf

Dekker, M. (2015, August 22). *A History of Early Autistic Space.* [Conference paper]. Autscape. http://www.autscape.org/2015/programme/handouts/early-autistic-space.pdf

Ellis, J. (2020). The clearing: Music, dysfluency, Blackness and time. *Journal of Interdisciplinary Voice Studies, 5,* 215–233. https://doi.org/10.1386/jivs_00026_1

Ellis, J. (2021, November 5). *The Clearing.* Bandcamp. https://jjjjjerome.bandcamp.com/album/the-clearing

Gennai, M. (2021). *SNOB – Étape de Travail.* [Video]. Vimeo. https://vimeo.com/682845289

Gennai, M. (2023, August 1). *Selective Mutism and Autistic Gestures on Stage: A Poc Journey.* [Conference paper]. Autscape. http://www.autscape.org/2023/programme/handouts/autscape-2023-selective-mutism.pdf

Giwa Onaiwu, M. (2017). Preface: Austistics of colour: We exist… We Matter. In L. X. Z. Brown, E. Ashkenazy, & M. Giwa Onaiwu (Eds). *All the Weight of Our Dreams: On Living Racialised Autism* (pp. x–xxii). DragonBee Press.

Harp, B. (2012). Are you listening? In *Loud Hands: Autistic People, Speaking.* (pp. 305–304). Autistic Self Advocacy Network.

Hemsley, A. (n.d.). *Access Rider Open Template.* Alexandria Hemsley. Retrieved 12 November, 2023, from http://alexandrinahemsley.com/resources/access-rider-open-template/

Hull, L., Petrides, K. V., Allison, C., Smith, P., Baron-Cohen, S., Lai, M. C., & Mandy, W. (2017). 'Putting on my best normal': Social camouflaging in adults with autism spectrum conditions. *Journal of Autism & Developmental Disorders, 47*(8), 2519–2534. https://doi.org/10.1007/s10803-017-3166-5

Jordan, R. R. (1999). *Autistic Spectrum Disorders: An Introductory Handbook for Practitioners.* Fulton.

Kapp, S. (2020). Introduction. In S. Kapp. (Ed). *Autistic Community and the Neurodiversity Movement: Stories from the Frontline,* (pp. 1–19). Springer Singapore.

Lorde, A. (1984). *Sister Outsider: Essays and Speeches.* Ten Speed Print.

McDonnell, A., & Milton, D. (2014). Going with the flow: reconsidering 'repetitive behaviour' through the concept of 'flow states'. In G. Jones, & E. Hurley (Eds.), *Good Autism Practice: Autism, Happiness and Wellbeing,* (pp. 38–47). BILD.

Milner, V., Mcintosh, H., Colvert, E., & Happe, F. (2019). A qualitative exploration of the female experience of autism spectrum disorder (ASD). *Journal of Autism and Developmental Disorders, 49,* 2389–2402. https://doi.org/10.1007/s10803-019-03906-4

Milton, D. (2012). On the ontological status of autism: The 'double empathy problem'. *Disability and Society, 27*(6), 883–887. https://doi.org/10.1080/09687599.2012.710008

Milton, D. (2014). Embodied sociality and the conditioned relativism of dispositional diversity. *Autonomy, the Critical Journal of Interdisciplinary Autism Studies, 1*(3), 1–7. https://kar.kent.ac.uk/62632/

Milton, D. (2017). *A Mismatch of Salience: Explorations of the Nature of Autism from Theory to Practice.* Pavilion.

Milton, D. (2020). Neurodiversity past and present: An introduction to the Neurodiversity Reader. In D. Milton, D. Murray, S. Ridout, N. Martin, & R. Mills, (Eds.), *The Neurodiversity Reader* (pp. 3-6). Pavilion.

Mingus, M. (2011, May 5). Access intimacy: The missing link. *Leaving Evidence.* https://leavingevidence.wordpress.com/2011/05/05/access-intimacy-the-missing-link/

Mingus, M. (2017, April 12). Access intimacy, interdependence and disability justice. *Leaving Evidence.* https://leavingevidence.wordpress.com/2017/04/12/access-intimacy-interdependence-and-disability-justice/

Murray, D., Lesser, M., & Lawson, W. (2005). Attention, monotropism and the diagnostic criteria for autism. *Autism. 9*(2), 136–156. https://doi.org/10.1177/1362361305051398

Pearson, A. & Rose, K. (2021). A conceptual analysis of autistic masking: Understanding the narrative of stigma and the illusion of choice. *Autism in Adulthood, 3*(1), 52–60. http://doi.org/10.1089/aut.2020.0043

Pearson, A. & Rose, K. (2023). *Autistic Masking: Understanding Identity Management and the Role of Stigma.* Pavilion.

Piepzna-Samarasinha, L. L. (2020). Still dreaming wild disability justice dreams at the end of the world. In A. Wong (Ed.). *Disability Visibility: First-person Stories from the Twenty-First Century* (pp. 250–261). Vintage Books.

Quinn, A. (2018). *Unbroken: Learning to Live Beyond Diagnosis.* Trigger Publishing.

Rice-Adams, E. (2023). Autistic young people's sense of self and the social world: A challenge to deficit-focused characterisations. In D. Milton, & S. Ryan (Eds.), *The Routledge International Handbook of Critical Autism Studies* (pp. 130–149). Routledge. https://doi.org/10.4324/9781003056577-13

Robinson, O. M. (2017). The real truth about expressing myself. In L. X. Z. Brown, E. Ashkenazy, & M. Giwa Onaiwu (Eds.), *All the Weight of Our Dreams: On Living Racialised Autism,* (p. 276). DragonBee Press.

Sequenzia, A. (2012). Loud hands: I speak with my fingers. In *Loud Hands: Autistic People, Speaking,* (pp. 346–351). Autistic Self Advocacy Network.

Silberman, S. (2015). *NeuroTribes: The Legacy of Autism and the Future of Neurodiversity.* Penguin Random House.

Simmonds, M. (2023). Through the lens of (Black) critical race theory. In D. Milton, & S. Ryan (Eds.) *The Routledge International Handbook of Critical Autism Studies* (pp. 97–105). Routledge. https://doi.org/10.4324/9781003056577-10

Sinclair, J. (1993). Don't mourn for us. *Autreat.* Retrieved 2 December 2023, from: https://www.autreat.com/dont_mourn.html

Sinclair, J. (2005, January). *Autism Network International: The Development of a Community and Its Culture.* Autreat. https://www.autreat.com/History_of_ANI.html

Sinclair, J. (2010). Cultural commentary: Being autistic together. *Disability Studies Quarterly. 30*(1). https://dsq-sds.org/index.php/dsq/article/view/1075/1248

smith, s. e. (2020). The beauty of spaces created for and by disabled people. In A. Wong (Ed.), *Disability Visibility: First-person Stories from the Twenty-First Century,* (pp. 271–275). Vintage Books.

Socialworks (2017). World autism interviews; Socialworks/Toronto, Ontario. In L X. Z. Brown, E. Ashkenazy, & M. Giwa Onaiwu (Eds.), *All the Weight of Our Dreams: On Living Racialised Autism* (pp. 169–177). DragonBee Press.

Walker, N. (2021). *Neuroqueer Heresies: Notes on the Neurodiversity Paradigm, Autistic Empowerment and Postnormal Possibilities.* Autonomous Press.

Williams, D. (1998a). *Somebody Somewhere: Breaking Free from the World of Autism.* Jessica Kingsley Publishers.

Williams, D. (1998b). *Nobody Nowhere: The Remarkable Autobiography of an Autistic Girl.* Jessica Kingsley Publishers.

Wood, R., Milton, D., Arnold, L., & Graby, S. (2018). Redefining critical autism studies: A more inclusive interpretation. *Disability & Society. 33*(6), 974–997. https://doi.org/10.1080/09687599.2018.1454380

Yergeau, M. (2018). *Authoring Autism: On Rhetoric and Neurological Queerness.* Duke University Press.

Section 2: Experiential Accounts

Chapter 12:

On the Ontological Status of Autism: An Angry Poetic Response to the Double Empathy Problem

Paul Davies

Abstract

This submission examines double empathy and the violence endemic in autistic people's lives through the medium of poetry. I sought to devise a way to create an academic examination of various forms of systemic and rhetorical violence experienced by Autistic people, using not only my own Autistic voice but also utilising a nontraditional academic methodology. I decided upon a blend of traditional academic discourse, articulated through a modern (neurodivergent) version of the traditional Japanese poetry form, *tanka*.

The poems contain language and themes that tackle problematic interpersonal or professional communication, and actual and rhetorical violence against autistic people taken from 'real life' situations. Often, I utilize sarcasm, contrary to the popular myth of Autistic people not understanding it, to make my point. I am sensitive to the emotive response the content may cause in readers and hereby offer a content warning; some may find the content triggering. It was my aim to speak with sensitivity around the stigma and discrimination against my fellow autistic people, but it is hard to do this and retain the sense of impact I desired. I consider the discussion of various forms of violence against autistic people, often due to communication differences, as both a necessary and urgent task if we are to tackle the shame that surrounds autism.

Communication is a two-way process, but it is so often framed as a deficit in the Autistic person when the real issue is the poor, confused or confusing, opaque or downright misleading communication of the non-Autistic person, people, agency, sector or society. It is hoped that readers will read these poems as an act of academic activism.

Introduction

It is hard to imagine a more important concept than communication within a hyperconnected global society, especially when a theory offers illumination and the opportunity to reach deeper levels of understanding. So-called 'problems' with communication resonate throughout all levels of interpersonal contact within society, but this is primarily due to the failure of all parties involved to accept that dialogue is a two-way process. It is a deceptively simple idea, yet at the same utterly profound and liberating.

Liz Pellicano states, '*Many autistic adults ... advocate approaches that seek both to help individuals themselves deal with the neurotypical world and to accommodate the needs of autistic people by modifying the surrounding environment*' (Pellicano, 2014, p. 768). We live in a neurotypical world, designed for people without the hyper or hypo sensitivities that so many Autistic people experience. Often, our experiences and responses to distressing environments are misunderstood, or worse, misrepresented as deliberate transgressions of social norms. Hastings et al. (2015) claim that the social implications of this alleged 'challenging behaviour' are exclusion brought about by repeated harm to self or harm to others. However, given the ontological status proposed by most professionals of autism as disordered or ab/sub normal, realistically, there is little chance that most autistic people will be fully accepted as part of 'normal society' without a true paradigm shift.

Knowledge about autism has traditionally been generated from an external position. That is, '*expertise and knowledge production are situated in the hands of the, usually, neurotypical professional, clinician and researcher, with autistic subjectivity being marginalised or dismissed*" (Moore, 2020, p. 42; see also Milton, 2014; Milton & Bracher, 2013). However, a great deal of contemporary literature is now available that clearly demonstrates the problems with some of the 'agreed science' of the traditional, outdated, medical, deficit-based model, which excludes our lived experience and legitimate claim to 'expert' status. Other ways already exist and adopt an autism positive approach, but research and practice need to change in line with new ontologies of autism as cognitive difference not disorder. This does not suggest that we should deny the reality of autism as a disability, rather that society should view ALL Autistic people as valued human beings and citizens.

Much of autism research conducted since it was first identified in the early twentieth century has been neurotypical observation about how autistic people are assumed to differ physiologically, psychologically or cognitively. The autistic person usually had little or no participation other than as the 'research object' of the neurotypical 'expert'. Many autistic and autism activists see the clinical model as deeply flawed, focusing on the perceived lack of ability of the child or adult, while ignoring the psychosocial factors which surround the person and impact upon them. Not all people being diagnosed are children, although the power issues are even more significant when it is a child being observed. Viewing the problems an Autistic person faces without acknowledging the role other people or structures play is ableist and an example of what Damian Milton termed the 'Double Empathy Problem' (Milton, 2012).

Milton proposed this persuasive alternative, asserting that in reality it is, '*a disjuncture in reciprocity between two differently disposed social actors which becomes more marked the wider the disjuncture in dispositional perceptions of the lifeworld – perceived as a breach in the "natural attitude" of what constitutes "social reality" for "non-autistic spectrum" people and yet an everyday and often traumatic experience for "autistic people"*'. (Milton, 2012, p. 884). Throughout my life, my natural Autistic 'way of being' has been forced to be kept hidden lest it 'cause problems' for me. On many occasions it has caused issues whereby I have broken some unspoken socially constructed rule or etiquette and, like so many other Autistic people, it has been blamed on me for not conforming.

The 'blame' for the perceived 'lack' is almost always placed firmly with the Autistic person. Indeed, the very diagnosis of autism is based on 'deficits' in interaction and communication, and does not acknowledge the lack of effort shown by society or the neurotypical individual to seek mutually agreeable communication methods. Chapman and Botha state, '*Clinicians should develop a healthy scepticism to pathology paradigm research, which routinely assumes and reproduces negative biases about neurodivergent populations*' (Chapman & Botha, 2022, p. 15). Stereotypes like the 'lack of theory of mind' and the subsequent 'lack of empathy', extreme male brain and weak central coherence remain, despite so many attempts to point out the erroneous theories and the flawed research which, even now, still underpins the majority of traditional autism research (see Gernsbacher and Yergeau [2019] for a detailed critique of the theory of mind). McDonagh (2013) argues that empathy, in Baron-Cohen's 'cognitive' sense, has been taken as a necessary basis upon which economic and social transactions take place. However, he notes that despite being depicted as a quality that is essential to humanity, empathy has no single characterization through history. Autistic individuals are not inherently less empathetic than neurotypical individuals. Instead, the difficulty in understanding and empathizing with others is mutual. Yet, we are still labelled as lacking it. Indeed, this is included in diagnostic criteria and training, and as such is part of a stigmatized ontology and epistemology of a disordered disability.

Support staff of autistic people have a crucial role in changing the dynamics surrounding the autistic human beings they support. The idea that autistic people, and disabled people in general, are actual human beings is still not reflected in the culture of support or society itself. Truly liberatory and empowering support relies entirely on the 'buy in' of all the different individuals involved in the support of the person. This, currently, is still deeply problematic with little consistent training or guidance rejecting the behavioural engineering or modification of applied behaviour analysis (ABA) and its more acceptable face, positive behaviour support (PBS), and genuinely focusing upon basic human rights first. Kupferstein states that, '*Respondents of all ages who were exposed to ABA were 86 percent more likely to meet the PTSD criteria than respondents who were not exposed to ABA*' (Kupferstein, 2018, p. 1).

Anne MacDonald and Peter McGill observe about PBS training, '*It might be logical to assume that changes in staff beliefs, for example, about challenging behaviour may lead to changes in support to individuals. However, there is little evidence to support this assumption*' (MacDonald & McGill, 2013, p. 27). She uses the term, 'train and hope', i.e., hope the staff will make the changes. Orsini (2012) cautions, '*...any approach that tries to accommodate neurological diversity and autistic "ways of knowing" must pay careful attention to how one might reconfigure our current "citizenship regime" to engage the cognitively disabled citizens among us*' (Orsini, 2012, p. 809).

As Milton asked, '*So what exactly are autism interventions intervening with?*' (Milton, 2014). Autistic people have had their natural responses or actions to unacceptable, or problematic environments deemed 'challenging behaviour' for decades without acknowledgement of the part played by external factors. Chronic lack of funding to the health and well-being sector, based on austerity and neoliberal economic ideology, has had an appalling impact on the lives of millions of people. Sadly, often our 'value' must be demonstrated by the level we are able to 'function' within society. Our worth is based upon comparability with nondisabled or neurocommon counterparts. A medical model places the onus on the individual to change, adjust, subdue or eliminate both their autistic behaviour and identity; to become more neurotypical. This is impossible for many, and indeed, should never be required as it perpetuates the normative and 'normalizing' idea of neurotypicality. David Pitonyak states that we, '*need not forget the person's problem behaviors, but we must understand that people have gifts and capacities that eclipse our labels (or, as Herb Lovett has said, our "clinical accusations")*' (Pitonyak, 2005, p. 5). Liberatory approaches, such as the neurodiversity movement and paradigm, along with critical autism studies, offer answers that behavioural psychology simply can't due to its inherent ontological, linguistic and practice limitations and its problematic history.

This is some of the academic and my own practice-based experiential grounding which underpins the poems I have compiled into this one presentation.

The poetic context

Kei (2016) states, '*Tanka is what happens when you turn life into words.*' Many will be more familiar with the slightly shorter form of Japanese poetry, *haiku*, which are three lines long, but both owe their origins in the form of 'Waka' or Japanese poem. The first recorded versions date back to the sacred text, *Kojiki* (or *Records of Ancient Matters*), from the year 712 CE (Hoffman, 1986). Traditional *tanka* (or 'short poems') combine nature imagery with human elements. Martinásková asserts that modernity brings with it a different relationship to nature, and as such so should *tanka*. She states, '*The term nature, or more precisely "new nature", in a slightly broader sense, as follows: "the external world, consisting of plants, animals, things and phenomena, surrounding human beings in their everyday lives, including objects both existing on their own, and those made by people, either within or outside towns and cities." Simply put, everything that surrounds us*' (Martinásková, 2018, p. 218).

I have placed the focus on the 'nature' of autism itself and what that means to the autistic human lived experience within a non-autistic world. While this may challenge a more 'purist' interpretation of *tanka*, McClintock states, '*While poets continue to experiment, the contemporary tanka in English may be described as typically an untitled free-verse short poem having anywhere from about twelve to thirty-one syllables arranged in words and phrases over five lines crafted to stand alone as a unitary, aesthetic whole—a complete poem*' (McClintock, 2003).

Despite this degree of flexibility in the form, the dominant format is still that of 5-7-5-7-7 syllables per line but is coupled with a lack of the usual grammar found in other written English. This restrictive syllable count framework felt somewhat symbolic of the enforced structures that are imposed upon autistic people's communication daily but, when liberated from archaic linguistic rules, therefore felt appropriate. It may initially seem challenging for some, but communication should be able to transcend arbitrary limits. Additionally, I have included some *haiga* within this piece. A *haiga* is either a Japanese *tanka* or *haiku* poem accompanied by an image which complements the words and adds to the aesthetic the words seek to create.

Before his death in 1902, Masaoka Shiki introduced the idea of '*shasei*' to *tanka* poetry, likening it to the realist style of painting, '*writing exactly what you see so the reader could also experience the scene and understand what had moved you*' (cited in Trumbull, 2009). I have tried to offer a personal 'Autistic sketch from my life', aiming to evoke the emotion of the lived subject matter, to create a more rounded and multifaceted account of the link between autism, double empathy and the experience of violence; both physical and rhetorical.

Double Empathy
Theory It's really
simple you don't
understand me even if I shout...
especially then... who's fault

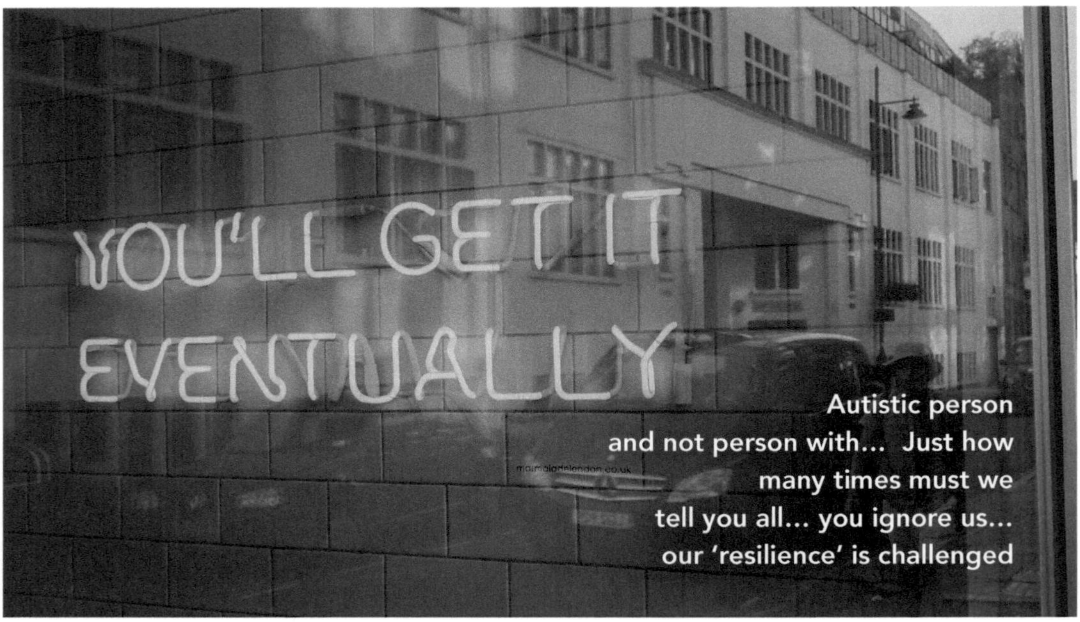
YOU'LL GET IT
EVENTUALLY
Autistic person
and not person with... Just how
many times must we
tell you all... you ignore us...
our 'resilience' is challenged

'very dangerous violent and aggressive be careful with them...' 'the problem with autism is the wide homogeneity'	neurotypical fragility leads to the professionals fear… they assert their dominance and autistic lives denied
they all grieve for me i am not what they wanted or expected but i am here and i hear them i don't know what i did wrong	i don't get asked to play with the other kids as they say i am not nice ... i don't know what to do and they just won't tell me so
'stimming is so bad…' the teacher says …'it is just stereopathy and disruptive' ... the child weeps for ignored communication	practical ableism speech-language pathology ingrained social worth with typical ways seen as superior ... elitism
you enforce change and isolate and ridicule my identity the consequence free triad of neurotypicality	quiet hands are good hands ... make eye contact with me... sit still ... trained teacher and their behaviour ensure the behaviours of concern
you claim to value honesty but then view our radical candour as an attack ... victims of our truth ... how awful for you	neurotypical reasonable adjustments it's fine for us ... it's just you that has a problem... black dog cowers in a ball

article five of the UN convention on the Rights of Persons with Disabilities … may as well be sand in blowing wind	disordered broken problem children disruptive challenging damaged judged stigmatised traumatised all symbolic violence
if you don't have a learning disability then you aren't a person with autism ... say the NT expert autism activists	we use a new form of Positive Behaviour Support … where you have the right to be free subject to our funded approval
the ignorance of epistemic injustice is related to lack of knowledge ... causing the undervaluing of status	self-recognition requires love and acceptance the open violence of structural injustice requires structural response
'people with autism see things in just black and white' where we see the full spectrum … all the experts are locked in binary thinking	electrodes on head to measure where they look… they should look there but they didn't ... that's a disorder... what if they just didn't want to?
it is proven that scientific discourses create knowledge ... but also maintain a tribal community of 'scientists'	slow violence ... is gradual and out of sight across time and space... attritional destruction of all disabled people

i did my best they say but did you really? we know the truth and at night so do you... cut flower promises	Charon my ferry man sits and patiently waits for me broken by icy rejection … far too many kids use his service
daily battles with ongoing hate and ableism and discrimination... why don't you smile more often you're so miserable	iatrogenic harm refers to the harm caused by the therapeutic procedures inflicted on people ... first do no harm
the correlation between iatrogenic harm and dunning kruger effect is high when we are less than human in their eyes	and ... amazingly... being accepted as a human being can enhance one's well-being too... blimey ... who would have thought it
human rights are just a metaphor when we are or have neither with person centred behaviourism	bodies of nature... some say made in the image of their sacred one... why do they then fear us and pray for our soul's salvation
my poor autistic communication issues... 'yes ... when I said weak central coherence i meant that positively...' right then	i'm autistic and i suffer epistemic injustice due to that social identity... and your dismal arrogance

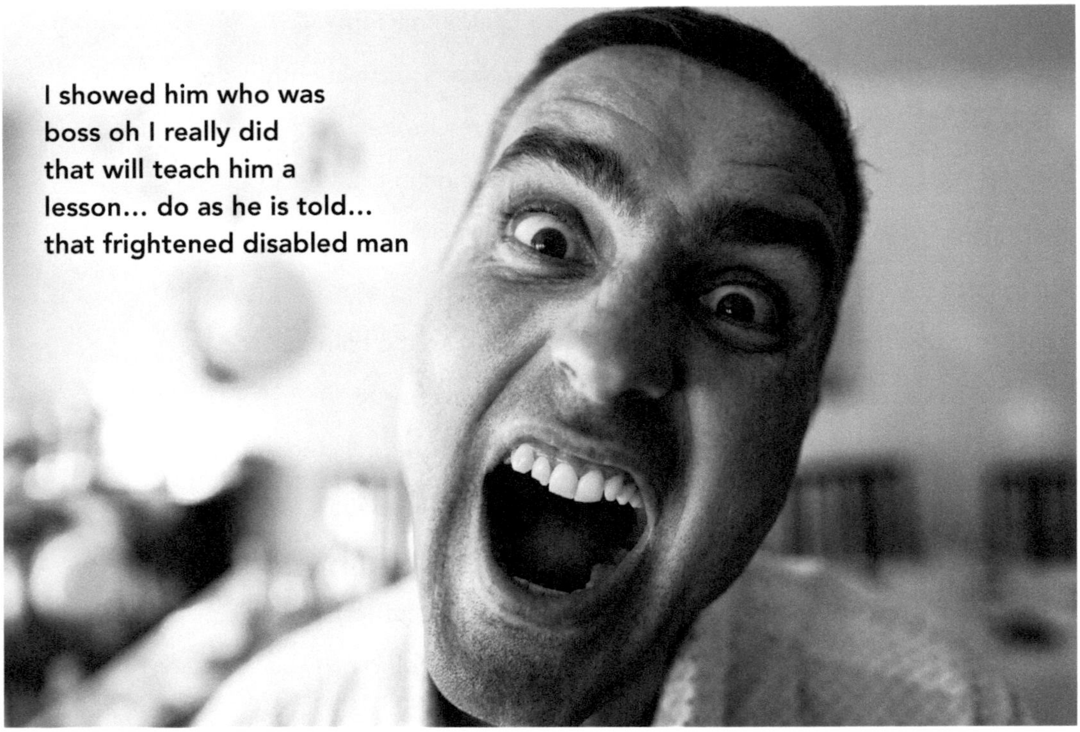
I showed him who was
boss oh I really did
that will teach him a
lesson... do as he is told...
that frightened disabled man

We really love
our child with autism so much...
but could you just make
them a little bit more... you
know... normal...
the child hears them

Asymmetrical
reciprocity is in
the cry... "why can't I
have that too it's not fair they
get more..." rights are not like cake

people with autism don't have relationships or sex ... where do we all come from then ... maybe I just don't understand genetics?	individuals with autism are really smart ... and also they are unintelligent ... and that is true ... we are human
'we can't really work with people with autism because their learning disability makes it hard to control their actions'	'ABA is the most evidence based effective autism intervention...' state the paid therapists who profit from the rhetoric
'people of autism' are you really so scared of the word that you create a fictional place for us weirdos to come from	autistic people have the right to choose in this service ... no ... they have the right to choose what you have decided to approve there
the scientist writes their 25th article on autism where they document our repetitive patterns of behaviour and interests	reinforcers are good... negative and positive... sweets snacks toys precious things if they work then use them... 'Good boy ... sit ... sit ... twirl ... good boy'
if you don't comply they label you difficult and if you question them they call you challenging… but never human being	theory of mind underpinned by false beliefs yet reified by the dogmatic disciples and held as truth ... we know better

it is strange how some individualists will then also adopt a utilitarian approach to justify … eugenics	if you value our human diversity then prove it to us ... and stop trying to cure basic variations in thinking
eons of the human lived experience was based on inclusion and respect for all as part of a group ... then capitalism	if you set me a task and decide how long it will take for me to complete without asking me... then your ableism is showing
you've never seen the real us ... only ever see a mask ... trying to keep our shit together... you just don't know us at all	taught to believe they are stupid or naughty if they think in a way that doesn't conform to the school groupthink ... exclusion starts young
'disabled ... but not really...' microaggression and hostility on a daily basis ... it's no wonder we kill ourselves	'unless you respect me i'm not listening to you...' you demand from me what you refuse to give... typical double standards
'you can't impose your neurodiversity on us ... that's not how we do things ... the system works fine just the way it is thank you'	systems that ignore trauma and harm caused by their ideology are not fit for purpose or were planned that way from the outset

my autism is not science it is rhetoric... fighting structures of meaning ... set systems that hates disability	rhetoric is the means by which ableist culture perpetuates its power and mourns our sad death ...but sees it as a blessing
disabled deaths by COVID... 'but they also had co-existing ill health...' 'oh well that's not so bad then...' lives dismissed as worthless	the whole purpose of symbolic violence is to control autism discourses to uphold the systems of domination
narratives of self-responsibility are pervasive in neoliberal rhetoric... breeding the shame of failure	systemic abuse... what can we do about it when so many of you look the other way and endorse it with your silence
lies are efficient rhetorical devices when they achieve the outcome you need... 'people with autism are burdens to us'	i am bullied and dismissed as less than human because of one thing about me ... my crime is that i am different from you
'don't let anyone else define you ... just be who you really are... accept no compromise and live true...' 'no ... not you ... oh no...'	i don't fear death ... i really don't ... i fear more not having lived an authentic autistic life due to ableism and hatred

Our actually
autistic critique is
iconoclastic
in spirit... it rails against
the systemic injustice

My enduring shame
stems not from your view of me
as lesser than you...
but that for so long...
I believed you completely

Conclusion

It is my belief that the Double Empathy Theory should be placed at the core of all contact, training, education, health care, policy and guidance, legislation and service provision, such is its importance to the lived experience of Autistic and other disabled people. To ignore it is to ignore professional responsibility toward reflective practice and, in some cases, is actually ableist and abusive. Traditional inequal power dynamics weighted in favour of the 'expert' neurotypical within health and social care reflect wider society, perpetuating systems of oppression, while couched in terms of liberation and empowerment. The lived experience of most disabled people is not one of empowerment, it is a daily battle for even the most basic support as #ActuallyAutistic people will attest. Our lives are not valued in the same way as non-autistic people based purely on our perceived ability to 'contribute' to society (or capitalism). This became clear during the ongoing COVID-19 pandemic where hugely disproportionate numbers of disabled people died and many more had 'Do Not Resuscitate' notices added to their personal files without consultation with the individual or family.

I would argue that the Double Empathy Problem has a part to play in all wider levels of society and geopolitics, where lack of flexibility of thinking and a lack understanding different perspectives can ultimately lead to war, conflict and death. Countries ignore the fact that other people have different opinions or experiences and push through and impose their preferred ideology on the more vulnerable or weaker 'opponent'. The parallels are clear. While society and the people and sectors who interact with Autistic people continue to insist on deficit-based terminology and attitudes that discriminate, dehumanize and stigmatize us, then phrases like 'person-centred' remain meaningless at best, or at worst, rhetorical violence. Without a fundamental shift in the focus on the inherent value of the disabled person, and the crucial importance of the role played by family, teachers, professional supporters or carers, employers and health workers, without an acknowledgement of the inherent asymmetrical reciprocity, how can we legitimately claim to provide the best-quality support leading to the best outcomes for the Autistic person?

As it stands, we deserve so much better. Communication is a two-way process, listen to what we are saying, and everybody can benefit.

I hope you appreciate what I was trying to achieve by utilising the tanka to convey short, sharp observations. However, I should point out that, *'If unsuccessful, the limitations are in the poet, not the form'* (Kei, 2016).

References

All images are downloaded from https://unsplash.com/, licence free. I would like to thank the photographers for their talent and generosity in allowing their work to be shared in this manner.

Chapman, R., & Botha, M. (2022). Neurodivergence-informed therapy. *Developmental Medicine & Child Neurology, 65*(3), 310–317.https://doi.org/10.1111/dmcn.15384

Gernsbacher, M. A., & Yergeau, M. (2019). Empirical failures of the claim that autistic people lack a theory of mind. *Archives of Scientific Psychology,* 7(1), 102–118. https://doi.org/10.1037/arc0000067

Hastings, R., Allen, D., Baker, P., Gore, N., Hughes, J. C., McGill, P., Noone, S., & Toogood, S. (2013). A conceptual framework for understanding why challenging behaviours occur in people with developmental disabilities. *International Journal of Positive Behavioural Support, 3*(2).

Hoffman, Y. (1986). *Japanese Death Poems: Written by Zen Monks and Haiku Poets on the Verge of Death.* Charles. E. Tuttle Co.

Kei, M. (2016). *Tanka Compendium by M. Kei.* Octoberblues. https://octoberblues.wordpress.com/2016/02/15/tanka-compendium-by-m-kei/

Kupferstein, H. (2018). Evidence of increased PTSD symptoms in autistics exposed to applied behavior analysis. *Advances in Autism, 4*(1), 19–29..

https://doi.org/10.1108/AIA-08-2017-0016

MacDonald, A., & McGill, P. (2013). Outcomes of staff training in positive behaviour support: A systematic review. *Journal of Developmental and Physical Disabilities,* 25, 17–33. https://doi.org/10.1007/s10882-012-9327-8

Martinásková, S. (2018). "New Nature" in Modern Japanese Tanka and Haiku Poetry. *Silva Iaponicarum.* FASC. LVI/LVII/LVIII/LIX. Special Edition Problems and Perspectives for Japan in a Changing World: THIRTY YEARS OF JAPANES STUDIES IN POZNAŃ edited by Arkadiusz Jabłoński, Justyna Walkowiak Posnaniae, Cracoviae, Toruniae, Varsoviae MMXVIII/MMXIX.

McClintock, M. (2003). Adapted by the author from the 'Introduction'. In M. McClintock, P. Miller Ness, & J. Kacian (Eds.), *The Tanka Anthology.* Red Moon Press. Notes on form, techniques, and subject matter in modern English Tanka. https://www.tankaonline.com/Notes%20on%20Form%20--%20Michael.htm

McDonagh. P. (2013). Autism in an age of empathy: A cautionary critique. In J. Davidson & M. Orsini. (Eds.), *Worlds of Autism: Across the Spectrum of Neurological Difference,* (pp. 31–52). University of Minnesota Press.

Milton, D. (2012). On the ontological status of autism: The 'double empathy problem'. *Disability & Society, 27*(6), 883–887. https://doi.org/10.1080/09687599.2012.710008

Milton, D. (2014). So what exactly are autism interventions intervening with? *Good Autism Practice, 15*(2), 6–14. https://kar.kent.ac.uk/62631/

Milton, D., & Bracher, M. (2013). Autistics speak but are they heard? *Medical Sociology,* 7(2), 61–69.

Moore, A. (2020). Pathological demand avoidance: What and who are being pathologised and in whose interests? *Global Studies of Childhood, 10*(1), 39–52. https://doi.org/10.1177/2043610619890070

Orsini, M. (2012). Autism, neurodiversity and the Welfare State: The challenges of accommodating neurological difference. *Canadian Journal of Political Science/Revue Canadenne de science politique, 45*(4), 805–827. https://doi.org/10.1017/S000842391200100X

Pellicano, E., Dinsmore, A., & Charman, T. (2014). What should autism research focus upon? Community views and priorities from the United Kingdom. *Autism, 18*(7), 756–770. https://doi.org/10.1177/1362361314529627

Pitonyak, D. (2005). *10 Things You Can Do to Support A Person With Difficult Behaviors.* www.dimagine.org. https://positiveaboutautism.co.uk/uploads/9/7/4/5/97454370/10things_you_can_do_about_difficult_behaviour.pdf

Trumbull, C. (2009, August 8). *Crosscurrents East and West: Masaoka Shiki and the Origins of Shasei* [conference presentation]. Haiku North America 2009, Ottawa, Ontario, Canada. https://thehaikufoundation.org/juxta/juxta-2-1/masaoka-shiki-and-the-origins-of-shasei

Chapter 13:
Normative Violence and the Consequences of the Double Empathy Problem

David Gray-Hammond

Autism is spoken of in various ways by wider society. However, there exists a pervasive theme to most discussion on this topic. Society treats autism as though it were a separate entity inhabiting the bodymind of an otherwise neurotypical person. It is approached as something that obscures the true self rather than as the defining factor in our human experience that it is. Autistic people are the only part of autism that actually exists, so why are they denied the opportunity to communicate their experiences and lead the way on knowledge creation about autism? How can we use the Double Empathy Problem to understand our exclusion from knowledge creation? It seems that the most direct measure of what an autistic person is can be drawn from our juxtaposition to non-autistic culture. We are defined by our differences, and subsequently define the so-called 'normal' of normative society by not being a part of it.

What is the Double Empathy Problem and what does it mean for autistic people?

The Double Empathy Problem was first spoken of by Damian Milton in the early 2000s and published into literature in 2012. It positions autistic people as a minority cultural group. The essential basis of the Double Empathy Problem can be understood as thus:

> *Milton's theory of 'double empathy' proposes that Autistic people do not lack empathy.*

> *Milton argues that Autistic people experience the world and express emotions differently to non-autistic people. We communicate, experience and display emotions, interact with others, form relationships, and sense the world around us, differently to non-autistics. That doesn't mean that we don't have emotions or feel empathy.*
>
> *But it makes it difficult for non-autistic people to understand and to empathise with us. And us with them.* (Reframing Autism, n.d.)

This has significant ramifications for how autistic people are perceived by the outside observer. Morrisson et al. (2019) found that perceptions of autistic people were frequently negative in terms of perceived awkwardness. They also found that stigma had a compounding effect, with negative perceptions overall being a major factor in the social experiences of autistic people. Given that we live in a reality built upon our social experiences, it seems reasonable to infer that negative perceptions, driven by the double empathy divide, contribute to the high rates of social trauma in autistic communities.

Reframing autism (2020)

This then allows us to consider the cultural differences between autistic populations and non-autistic populations. Most non-autistic people fail to understand autistic experience and vice versa. This absence of context presents an issue for the autistic person when trying to communicate within power structures that favour non-autistic ways of embodiment and existence. We are labelled as being in deficit because of a pervasive neuronormativity within non-autistic populations.

This presents an issue for both autistic people and non-autistic people when trying to bridge the empathy divide. Neither has a point of reference in the experience of the other. Autistic people will never experience the world from a neurotypical point of view, much in the same way that a neurotypical will never experience the world as an autistic person does. It's not that either group lacks empathy, they lack the prerequisite information required to have an informed opinion on each other's experience. We can both tell you what it is like to trip over, but we cannot tell you what the other's experience of tripping up is.

Why does the Double Empathy Problem exist?

Chapman (2023) explores the history of normativity through the perspective of rising capitalism. It would seem that with the rise of Descartes' machinic body and a shift towards Galtonian worldviews the concept of 'normal' has become more and more restricted. No longer is it enough to fall within the average, one is encouraged to strive for the top of a social hierarchy that is inaccessible to most people. Autistic people, then, are considered not just outliers from the average, but on the lower end of said social hierarchies.

By positioning autistic people as 'less than' we have created a responsibility for autistic people to strive for a higher place in society rather than allow for the diversity they bring to global cultures. Worse still, the emerging discrimination against autistic ways of empathizing and communicating has become a tool of normative violence. Autistic people often find themselves on the wrong side of carceral systems for no reason other than the way they communicate.

This makes me think about the work of Garland-Thompson (1996) and the concept of the normate. The normate presents the issue of a standard of perceived normality that can be accessed by neither the autistic nor the neurotypical person. In the absence of measurable superiority, the double empathy divide has provided a means for those of a predominant neurotype to position themselves higher in society by proximity to arbitrary rules of normativity.

How does neuronormativity unbalance power dynamics for autistic people?

Neuronormativity draws its position largely from Western colonialism (although cultural standards of normativity do differ from group to group) and the belief that one must assimilate into the majority population, becoming a 'productive citizen' within one's socioeconomic system. It creates a strangely reductive notion of one either being helpful or a burden. The existence of neuronormativity can be viewed as logically fallacious in its origins; specifically, it is situated within a fallacy known as *argumentum ad populum*. This means that the argument to support neuronormativity uses its acceptance by the majority as it's evidence base.

This is of significant concern for minority groups. Normative values are often used to suggest that one's humanity is based within a contained and isolated set of values and styles of embodiment. If one need only make an appeal to the masses for something to be true, then almost any dissent from minority groups becomes 'inaccurate' or 'without evidence'. Thus, the power structures of society favour a predominant neurocognitive style over anything that diverges from it.

Another factor to consider here is the impact that reduced access to and unfavourable attitudes toward social welfare systems have on autistic people. Autistic people need adequate support to live and function, not just comfortably but also in a way considered favourable by neuronormativity. Despite this, neoliberal attitudes encourage us to be frugal in our access to the supports we are told we are legally entitled to. Autistic people are seen as a burden for both accessing and not accessing support.

How does the Double Empathy Problem obstruct autistic people from communicating their experiences?

The power imbalances that exist have created a world within which autistic people cannot be correct about their own experience. If one asserts that natural autistic communication is valid, then the majority can simply view that knowledge as inaccurate by virtue of it coming from a minority group rather than the majority. The Double Empathy Problem means that not only can neuronormativity exist, but also the dominant group can't ever fully empathize with how harmful it is.

Not only can dominant groups not understand our experience, but also neuronormativity tells them that neurocognitive styles outside of their understanding are something that need to be corrected. This allows for the mass administration of harmful interventions such as applied behaviour analysis (ABA) and positive behaviour support (PBS), and quack cures like miracle mineral solution (MMS). We are effectively dehumanized by the majority's refusal to step outside the comfort zone of their own worldview, leading to potentially life-threatening consequences.

There is also the issue of demirhetoricity, as set forth by Yergeau (2017), that needs to be considered. Autistic people appear to fall into one of two categories, seemingly at the mercy of the observer. They are either too autistic to effectively communicate their experience, or not autistic enough to have a valid opinion. In either case, the outcome is testimonial injustice.

What does the Double Empathy Problem mean for autistic people in practice?

This gulf between cultural experiences coupled with neuronormative attitudes allows professionals in various multidisciplinary fields to ignore our voices when we advocate for ourselves. In practice, professionals will try to enforce their own opinion of what is needed by the autistic person rather than allow the autistic person to speak their own truth. It is the effective oppression of autistic people contributing to the minority stress that we experience as a minority cultural group.

- Health care professionals don't listen to us.
- Social care professionals don't listen to us.
- Education professionals don't listen to us.

It is a list that I could add to in perpetuity. We are talking about weaponized testimonial injustice that keeps us in a disadvantaged position.

What can autistic people do to combat the fallout of the Double Empathy Problem and neuronormativity?

At this point I might direct your attention back toward the aforementioned minority stress that we experience. This can be understood as the cumulative effect of multiple sources of hostility and oppression within society. The effects of the Double Empathy Problem and neuronormativity have long allowed this minority stress to run wild. Interestingly, Botha (2020) found that community-connectedness acts as a buffer against this.

> *The minority stress model is a social research and public health model designed to help us better understand the lived experiences of people of oppressed communities. The model posits that within the social structure of a particular culture or society, certain (oppressed) groups experience greater incidents of minority stress (based on race, sexuality, gender, disability, etc.) in the form of prejudice and discrimination. As a result of those experiences, members of oppressed communities experience greater negative health outcomes than majority group communities. This leads to large health disparities.*
> (Caraballo, 2019).

Botha (2020) found in their doctoral research that where autistic people were connected with autistic communities, there was an improvement in well-being in nearly every domain explored. It stands to reason then that perhaps the increased confidence in self-advocacy that comes from connection with other autistic people allows us to mitigate the effects of minority stress. For this reason, I strongly believe that one of the most effective things that can be done for newly discovered autistic people is signposting to their community.

It is also vitally important that we shift society away from the current pathology paradigm that is deeply rooted in Galton's concepts of normality. There is no perfect human state to strive for, any assertion to the contrary is an endorsement of colonial capitalism and not a reflection of the communicative abilities of autistic people. Even within our own spaces there remains a wide amount of variability in how we empathize and communicate, and attempting to standardize this constitutes cultural oppression, for which autistic people simply cannot stand.

References

Botha, M. (2020). *Autistic Community Connectedness as a Buffer Against the Effects of Minority Stress* [Doctoral dissertation, University of Surrey] Open Research. https://doi.org/10.15126/thesis.00854098

Caraballo, J. (2019). *Understanding the Minority Stress Model*. Talkspace.com. https://www.talkspace.com/blog/minority-stress-model/

Chapman, R. (2023). *Empire of Normality: Neurodiversity and Capitalism*. Pluto Press.

Garland-Thomson, R. (1996). *Extraordinary Bodies Figuring Physical Disability in American Culture and Literature*. Columbia University Press.

Milton, D. E. (2012). On the ontological status of autism: The 'double empathy problem'. *Disability & Society, 27*(6), 883–887. https://doi.org/10.1080/09687599.2012.710008

Morrison, K. E., DeBrabander, K. M., Faso, D. J., & Sasson, N. J. (2019). Variability in first impressions of autistic adults made by neurotypical raters is driven more by characteristics of the rater than by characteristics of autistic adults. *Autism, 23*(7), 1817–1829. https://doi.org/10.1177/1362361318824104

Reframing Autism (n.d.). Milton's 'double empathy problem': A summary for non-academics. Reframing Autism. https://reframingautism.org.au/miltons-double-empathy-problem-a-summary-for-non-academics/

Yergeau, R. (2017). *Authoring Autism: On Rhetoric and Neurological Queerness*. Duke University Press.

Chapter 14:
Landscapes of an Origami Girl

Josie Green

> *I crossed the border into the Republic of Motherhood*
> *and found it a queendom, a wild queendom.*
> *I handed over my clothes and took its uniform...*
> (*The Republic of Motherhood*, Berry, 2018, p. 1)

It is well documented that many women in late life are identifying as neurodivergent and some of us come to these light bulb moments following the birth of a child and discovering all along there were other people that felt like this too. Current discussions around camouflaging, imitation and masking are considered as possible strategies people adopt to manage their world, to fit in, to survive in the workplace, to protect from discrimination and to hide autistic traits, while also exploring their impact on mental health and general well-being (Hersh et al., 2020). *NeuroTribes* (Silberman, 2015), a history of autism, stopped me dead in my tracks, held me suspended in shock for what felt like an eternity, its stark narrative gave a new depth of meaning to the diagnosis of autism and attention deficit hyperactivity disorder (ADHD) in my family and some perspective on the challenges we were facing. I created a small planet with the plethora of information I had gathered and designed an invisible coat that held the stoicism of my ancestors; it oozed a new language, bygone voices whispered you are not alone, and it urged me to keep going when I was clinging to a single thread. I have a photo in my wallet of my uncle standing with my dad and grandad; for them and all who must have endured so much, in the hope of change I find courage to share.

2010

I was aware of the new parenting narrative; nothing will ever be the same; a new social scene; the economy of parenthood; the importance of breastfeeding; do this, don't do that, and I was both excited and nervous. During the months that followed the birth of my first child I sensed a profound, fundamental shift in my reality, and I assumed it was another one of my naive exposures to a consequence that I was unable to foresee. Quite quickly, I recognized that the room I found myself in seemed different to the new mothers around me; they couldn't reach me, and I could not reach them. The sense of feeling different or on the outside was nothing new and for a while I worked hard on the usual management tasks, monitoring the type of information I shared, how I presented myself, a smile and a joke to get by, the familiar cups of hot water to ease tummy aches, but gradually hours upon hours of breastfeeding, sleepless nights, the immense love that I had for this tiny human, overwhelmed me, I just couldn't tune in to anyone else's station anymore and gave up trying. I had left the communication centre and chronic anxiety had come to join the party. The thin intricate wallpaper that I had spent a lifetime constructing started to fray and peel. I just could not make friends with other mums, and I was grappling with what were once simple tasks. I was worn out, and while I kept up a front to the health visitor as best I could, the walls started to crumble. I experienced prolonged periods of overwhelm and found my inner dialogue became increasingly dissonant with the outside world, and I'm pretty sure sometimes I was not an easy person to be around. Without consent the intensity and atmosphere of my internal space left me with no resource for anything else and the room started to stamp its presence solidly around me, holding me in any state it so wished. I no longer had any of the control I had rehearsed for so long. I no longer recognized myself and understood myself even less. The intricate origami designs that for so long presented a self to the outer world had gone on strike. The paper chain that connected inner and outer worlds strained under the weight, links burst open, and my chin bobbed on the surface of a water not knowing what to do.

Words on paper skin fade as pieces flake off
floating into fragments, dissolving, like the
crepe sea turtles sinking into the moist black eye
(Water Dreams No. 419, from *The Origami Girl*, Green, 2021)

I have found developing meaningful friendships really tricky, but from a young age I found a love of music and the arts, enjoyed playing outdoors, adored our family pets, and loved collecting rubbers, badges and my felt tip pens. From as early as I can remember, I found communicating my experience difficult and general conversation hard. Then, as the teenage years progressed, it became profoundly debilitating and I found it increasingly hard to talk in groups. It often felt like there was a clamp on my throat; I would go to speak, and no sound would come out; sometimes the sound was so quiet no one would respond, other times people would tease me for speaking too softly. I found a voice through music and began performing at school and with a group outside of school, directed by my instrumental teacher. When I began to perform solo pieces at an advanced level, I started to have overwhelmingly strange experiences that I just couldn't make sense of. I went on to study Performing Arts at university, went to my doctor again and this time was prescribed beta blockers for performance anxiety. Now, I realise that when it came to solo performance I experienced sensory overload, the air would pound against my ears, the room would throb forward and back in front of my eyes, my legs went weak like they were going to float away, I felt dizzy, like I was in a haze about to faint, and, now, when I think about it, I start to relive it. Sometimes, a whole performance would go by and I would have been managing a sensory overload the entire time, it would have felt like a dream. When there was a large group of us it would be much easier to cope with, I enjoyed it more, but this eventually became problematic too. Still, the right questions didn't yet exist, and I could never find the right way through as there was no safety net. I held on to everything that challenged me and at therapy in later years found a ball had manifested in my core. Tightly twisted bands of chronic anxiety, low confidence, low self-esteem, rage, depression and self-harm, suspended, entangled below my solar plexus, a floating sphere the size of a small grapefruit. It wasn't until my late 40s that I discovered the discomfort I had held for decades in different body areas could be unravelled through therapy.

I precariously balanced on a double-edged sword between the need to mask and the need to be understood. Unable to communicate my inner world, or deceptively private, as I was once told, meant that I missed opportunities to grow. Not only did I feel misunderstood, but I was also not showing my true self either, which meant that expectations of me were unrealistic and difficult to achieve, and when I did chance being more relaxed or honest about my challenges, or try to hang out with regular girls, the Double Empathy Problem resonates, and I can trace numerous experiences of misunderstanding and confusion back throughout my life. I found most of my good friendships were with men, but that often brought about another set of problems. I was extremely fortunate to be sandwiched between loving siblings, which I believe probably saved my life. The reality of social pain and discomfort and the difficulty processing both personal and professional relationships meant that I spent years watching, analysing and observing others, often overcompensating with either stupid, unsafe or delusional behaviour, and while busy navigating the rocky waves on my tiny rowing boat made of survival tools, I lost huge depths of potential to an ocean of social confusion as I just didn't know which way to row.

Hyper focus mum

Nothing but mum. Hyper focus mum.

Lines curved their way like unruly vines around my feet, pulling me into the centre of the room, hard edges of critical words stuck into my thighs. The music fell quiet as the paper on the walls began to fall away and reveal random letters. White noise would float out of the walls, like steam rising from hot water, only to disappear again. Often the moist bubbles sat inside my ear chanting over and over again the same song lyric, the same film quote, the same line from a book, the same scenario that I had seen or heard before, whether four hours ago or thirty years ago the clarity was the same. Behind the peeling walls letters started to etch and scrape out of the plaster, hints of something different, something not discussed in the books or at parenting groups; we are told it's just another baby finally settling after another round of gentle rocking. Eyes heavy with exhaustion, I lay next to my husband, my best friend, bedraggled in the darkness of night we interlock hands and fall asleep.

While I waited for the room to share its secrets my intuition sensed when something was too loud, too bright, too stimulating, too hot, too this or too that, outdoors and movement, deep pressure; I never thought to ask myself how I knew, I hadn't heard anyone else talk like this, I just accepted that I knew.

> *While numbing (or compensatory sensation seeking) may make life tolerable, the price you pay is that you lose awareness of what is going on inside your body and, with that, the sense of being fully, sensually alive.*
>
> (*The Body Keeps the Score*, Van der Kolk, 2014, p. 272)

The unpredictable ground sometimes swayed me like a standing passenger on a bus, or shook with seismic tremors, sometimes it opened up and I fell through only to cling to the edges of an open hole for days on end, feet swaying in black, endless space, until something pulled me back in, sometimes it would hold me in mid-air, not being able to move, thighs so heavy and pained I could not leave the house, other times I was moved around the room, turned upside down, overheated and I would frantically cut my hair to remove the weight. I was to become very familiar with this room, it was my world. When I slept, the water would come and I began to avoid bedtime; the later I stayed awake the worse it became. I would bend and fold like paper as I tried desperately to save my child from tumultuous waters, night after night. Sometimes, I would wake to a warm hand gently saying, '*it's ok, it's just a dream*'.

Self-harm urges haunted me and drove me to the doctor's room; concerned and kind he gave me some pills and showed me the door to the post-natal depression group. It felt like the wrong room and as I entered the therapist's room, time and time again, it kept feeling like I was still in the wrong room. No one asked the right questions or knew the questions to ask. Until, that is, conversations about autism, attention deficit hyperactivity disorder (ADHD) and neurodiversity landed. With this new information I boarded a rocket of frenetic energy on a relentless quest for answers.

The need to work endlessly on micromanaging my outward impression was what I had learned to do from a young age. It evolved into a self that believed that was just what was necessary to live, it was very stressful and very ingrained, driven by excessive planning and a formidable need to hide the confused and profoundly uncomfortable person inside, even from myself. The collection of negative experiences snowballed from teenage to adult years, the increasing additions of unpleasant side dishes meant a deepening urgency to paint over years of intoxicant abuse and harmful sexualised behaviour and I can now see how the inner and outer world grew further apart. The careful balance of hiding addictions, secret obsessions, compulsions, restrictive eating, sexual assault, sexual harassment and hiding cases of rape led to a deep sense of shame and inadequacy. I was accompanied always by a fear of everything social, a social exhaustion that I could not yet identify and a difficulty expressing myself. After years of being with my husband something triggered in my brain, and I started to experience flashbacks. He helped me find my way to complex post-traumatic stress disorder (C-PTSD) therapy, which took me back to being a teenager and helped me to heal my fragmented self. I was then able to see more clearly and feel whole for what felt like the first time.

1989

When I was 15, I took an overdose of paracetamol. I slept for hours during the day then became really scared and told my sister, who gently insisted she tell my parents. A kind nurse held my hand as my stomach was pumped. When the Unit Sister came in, she terrified me and I stayed silent as she looked at my bruised young face with tubes protruding, telling it you are ungrateful, *pump wretch,* your parents are worried sick outside, *pump wretch,* never be so selfish ever again wasting all of our time, *pump wretch.* I was given some hormone pessaries and did not do it again. However, I did begin to self-medicate at a very young age, although I only named it that in recent years, and I am still rather surprised and grateful that I survived at all. As a teenager, I did return to the doctor on two more occasions to try and unpack my anxiety, but it was always the same answer. You have a loving family, there is nothing to be upset about; it's true, so why is this all so hard. I remember thinking the problem is me, not them. Interestingly, there were no questions about school or friendships. Hiding my tears as I walked home, I decided that I would have to face the fact that I was just a bit less than everyone else, I just couldn't do it and that was that.

over time, the heavy fog dissipates, and the heart abides at ease
with the way things are
(*The Contemplative's Craft,* Ajahn Viradhammo, 2017, p. 166)

2016

'Look at my hands'.

My husband and sister gently reassure me as we sit outside the court room. The Educational Psychologist said something that I did not process while I watched my hands shake vigorously as the panic attack flushed through my body. I had spent time preparing an opening statement and just moments before we were about to enter our solicitor boldly stated, *'you can't read all that, you must just speak naturally, from the heart…'*

The school and local authority were against us; their solicitor was pulling on every possible assumption and stigma to dismiss my son's trauma and protect their budget. Our solicitor could not understand why they were doing this; they refused our request to assess for an Education, Health and Care Plan (EHCP) and all level of need. It was as though we had arrived on the wrong planet and we were being used as an example.

It was apparent that our child could not yet communicate his experience, voice his needs or communicate sensory overload. There was an assumption made that because he was beautifully articulate at times and could understand meanings of words, he could therefore express emotions in a typical way, communicate needs and therefore be able to manage behaviour and any overriding sensory sensitivities. They refuted my explanation of his anger being confusion and distress, scoffed at my commentary on an overloaded sensory world and suggested the anger was based on his home experience, and proposed an anger management programme; this was the ultimate blow for me, and I fell to my knees when I read this. How can they say this when there is so much love. A plea and a cry for help is being ignored, doctors are being ignored and my explanation for his behaviour is being ignored. It was an awful, stressful and drawn-out process; the well-being of this child has been compromised and the early years intervention that we were promised had now passed him by. One afternoon, a staff member covertly approached me and said, *'you need to take him out of this school, please get him out, are you getting him out?'*. Before I could engage, she scuttled away as though she would be in trouble for even talking to me. They stole the happiness of our child's early years, which also stole our happiness, and from his little baby brother, who watched it all from the sidelines. When we received the paperwork which recognized that we had been treated very badly, we received the evidence we needed to go to the right type of school; we never returned.

Everything in my being hopes for humility in the face of difference. For love, for openness, for the space and freedom to feel confident that one can be themselves to grow safely without prejudice and freedom from the barbs of presumptuous stereotypes. The notes still in my ears are sung by voices reaching for insight, freedom, a voice, of courage, for understanding, for validation.

2019

I received a diagnosis of autism spectrum condition/disorder, but ultimately, I am who I am with my own set of stuff.

A notch, a piece
unravelled
creates a resilient spec upon an island
(*The Origami Girl*, Green, 2021)

Social survival became enmeshed in my being and my unusual, quirky, sometimes rebellious tendencies were in fact rebelling against a monumental lack of empathy, and underneath the carefully constructed origami girl were complex patterns that curved and spiralled into endless space, to be lost forever with the leaving tide.

References

Berry, L. (2018). *The Republic of Motherhood* (p. 1). Chatto & Windus.

Green, J. (2021). *The Origami Girl.* [unpublished manuscript].

Hersh, M., Elley, S., Banks, Z., Mery, P., Cowan, D., & Watson, C. (2020). Accessing services and social interaction: strategies used by autistic people. In D. Murray, D. Milton, S. Ridout, N. Martin, & R. Mills (Eds.), *The Neurodiversity Reader* (p. 319). Pavilion Publishing and Media Ltd.

Silberman, S. (2015). *NeuroTribes: The Legacy of Autism and the Future of Neurodiversity.* Allen & Unwin.

Van der Kolk, B. (2014). *The Body Keeps the Score* (p. 272). Penguin.

Viradhammo, A. (2017). *The Contemplative's Craft* (p. 166). Tisarana Buddhist Monastery.

Chapter 15:
The Double Empathy Problem: Approaching from Three Angles

Meghan Wilson Duff

When I introduce the Double Empathy Problem to undergraduate students in courses for people going into mental health and related helping professions, most students approach it head on and come away with 'There is a difference, but not a problem'. They can explain that allistic people have less trouble empathically connecting with other allistic people. Autistic people have less trouble with empathically connecting with other autistic people. It's the cross-group pairings where both sides struggle more, and the difficulty depends on who is connecting with whom. It's a reasonable takeaway. It feels intuitive and noncontroversial. But to me it is also incomplete. They are missing the problem part of the Double Empathy Problem.

What is the problem?

The problem isn't just the lack of understanding between groups. It's that the negative impacts of the Double Empathy Problem or of misunderstanding between cross-group pairings are not shared by both groups. Autistic people have been harmed by allistic assumptions about autistic people. The narratives in society that define what autism is, what autistic people are like and what should be 'done about it' come from the professionals in education, psychology and mental health services. Professional research and training created, and has reinforced, a deficits-based, cure/treatment-focused way of understanding autism and relating to autistic people. If those are the only accessible narratives, the only stories, framing and concerns heard and shared about autistic people, we end up in situations where people tasked with helping can do harm in the name of helping.

When we consider the historical and social context, the allistic group has what Johnson (2006) calls the 'luxury of obliviousness'. I think this is a stronger, more descriptive term than privilege. It is the obliviousness I want to call attention to. The mainstream medical, psychological and educational assumptions about what is normal fit the allistic group better. The 'norm' doesn't chafe people in the allistic group as much because society's default expectation fits them better most of the time. This matters because students I work with are committed to joining helping professions as they genuinely want to decrease people's suffering. Yet, they don't necessarily have enough historical context or awareness to know how the desire to help, and having the professional authority to do so, has never been a safeguard against harming the people they are trying to help. They need to notice the professional perspective they are being socialized into and the assumptions that it makes. We talk about how the medical ethics code and the psychology ethics code have two different principles for 'helping' and 'doing no harm', but they are very abstract.

Together, students and I read and talk about eugenics, medical racism, genocidal state social services policies aimed at destroying Native Americans' cultures and communities and the histories of what has passed as treatment but would no longer be considered ethical. In terms of mental health and disability, we consider how reforms are implemented, proposing a revitalized and more humane form of institutionalizing people with high support needs, only later to have a new wave of exposés about abuse and neglect prompting the next wave of reforms. We talk about the assumptions of behaviourism and applied behaviour analysis (ABA), and early aspirations to convert feminine boys into masculine boys, lest they grow up to be queer. Students are appalled at all of this and seem glad that we're past that now. As the teacher, I have to make things more complicated and ask, *'Are we past this now? Couldn't we too put forth ideas and theoretical frameworks and treatment or intervention protocols, thinking we're helping, but causing harm?'*

The Double Empathy Problem is a problem that is not undone by recognizing both groups can have difficulty with empathic connection with people from other groups. There is danger when one group has so much power over the narrative about the other group and how society is structured. Thinking about this in the context of autistic people is new to many students, though they may have more experience thinking about a similar dynamic around race and racism, mental illness and the stigma associated with it, or how poor people get talked about.

A third angle of approach

I don't spend enough time on the third approach in classes because I'm not sure how to teach it, nor was I taught about it in undergraduate or graduate school. Rather than focusing on the obliviousness of allistic/professional perspectives, or even the negative impact on autistic people, this approach recognizes the existence and vitality of autistic community and culture. This was a personal revelation to me. Having grown up as I did, when I did, I didn't know that so many other people already understood parts of my experience that I struggled with alone, without me even needing to explain or justify myself.

Most of the academic papers or online social media advocacy I initially had access to were autistic people refuting ableist, allistic narratives about autistic people and experience, but there are so many stories, voices, memes and moments of humour, and a sense of joining around these sorts of things, beyond pushing back on the troublesome One Story that got told over and over. Emerging connections and narratives from within community that made sense. It's being able to vent to the appropriate people, the ones understand. I feel like I can let certain things go that make me frustrated when I can tell someone and I know they get it. It's the building buzz of connecting ideas and listening for the reverberation. How do I teach that?

Realizing community

The thing about autistic community is it is hard to know who is part of it or where to find it. Given ableism and its consequences, and the workplace need to perform well, there is a lot of pressure to mask and to not mention being autistic. Depending on a person's age and other aspects of their identity and experiences, there may be other consequences for reaching out or speaking up. So where do you find autistic space? How do you convene? How do you find others?

Recognition

It is hard to recognize autistic community when you don't know or think of yourself as autistic. Mostly, I just thought I was really bad at doing what others seemed to take for granted and I had to keep what I struggled with secret whenever possible. There are many of us who are older, who were growing up when the diagnosis was more restrictive, so we were not recognized. There are probably many of us who wouldn't self-identify because we still largely see it as stigmatizing and have a lot of self-loathing toward ourselves. There are others of us who were never diagnosed or don't recognize ourselves as autistic because of the racism and sexism that made researchers keep looking under the streetlight for white boys with an interest in maths and science and not consider looking elsewhere. We may have been so well behaved no one saw us struggle. People who don't fit the narrow expectations of who is autistic might have received other diagnoses.

Seeking community

What made me seek autistic community and recognize myself as autistic was an upwelling of fear prompted by my children's interaction with providers. I'm a clinical psychologist with a speciality in child and family by training, and I teach. I'm well read in terms of mental health, psychological theory, tests and measures, and therapeutic intervention. It was my children, identified as autistic at a young age mainly because of communication differences, who made the Double Empathy Problem no longer something abstract and intellectual. The power providers have, and the consequences of their framing, became very real to me now. Having read Steve Silberman's (2016) *NeuroTribes* with students every year since it was published, that past is not safely enough in the past to me. I take speech and communication for granted, and without a fairly reliable way for my youngest to explain what happened at school, like being physically held down or being in pain, I think that my fear is reasonable, even though my kids have had a generally positive experience. But whenever there is a new teacher and a new support person, I don't trust them until I've seen them with my kids and have a sense of how well they understand them.

I know from my experience that there are negative consequences to growing up assuming it is my job to accommodate others, but I also know that being a 'good kid' and liked is a powerful desire and reward too. I've been on a bit of a quest to figure out society and how relationships work. I just didn't realize how harmful the rules could be. I know what it is like to be outwardly successful in many ways and inwardly barely holding it together. When school staff say, 'He had a great day' about one of my kids, who then comes home and collapses in tears, I wonder who gets to decide what a great day is? I don't want to teach my kids that they have to bear the cost or feel they need to hide their struggle, just to have people's approval and fit in.

Reading community

> *When I first started learning about autism, I wanted to learn from other Autistic people – from people like me.*
>
> (About section of The Autism Books by Autistic Authors Project. https://autismbooksbyautisticauthors.com/about/)

Reading has always been important to me, so it shouldn't be a surprise that it is my gateway to community. From a young age, books allowed me to meet people and think with them and go on adventures. Reading is blissfully immersive (if I'm left alone). I can stop and pace to think more or stay with a feeling before moving on. I can reread. And reread. Again, and again. The author directs you with sensory details for you to experience, but nothing is ever too loud, too much. It's private and yet intimate and social, even if the author lives across the world or died a hundred years ago. Without getting a chance to read in this way regularly, I start to struggle. This type of reading was how I found autistic community.

I'm not sure what the first book was that I read with a clear intention to find community, rather than just interest in the subject. I deliberately looked up *Loud Hands: Autistic People, Speaking*, which is a collection put together by the Autistic Self Advocacy Network in 2012, because I wanted more voices and diverse voices. Over the years, I wandered into *Autistic Disturbances: Theorizing Autism Poetics from the DSM to Robinson Crusoe* by Julia Miele Rodas (2018) and wrestled my way through *Authoring Autism: On Rhetoric and Neurological Queerness* by Remi Yergeau (2018). I went into it not entirely sure what rhetoric was, as this was not my disciplinary neighbourhood. I read Murray, Milton, Ridout, Martin and Mills' (2020) collection, *The Neurodiversity Reader*, Brown, Ashkenazy and Onaiwu's (2017) *All the Weight of Our Dreams: On Living Racialized Autism*, and *Autistic Community and the Neurodiversity Movement: Stories from the Frontline*, edited by Steven K. Kapp (2020). When seeking lots of voices and perspectives, edited editions are great. After reading *The Autism Industrial Complex: How Branding, Marketing, and Capital Investment Turned Autism into Big Business* by Alicia Broderick (2022), I was prepared for longer conversations about the ascendance of ABA as a treatment gold standard.

But I also love fiction. I started reading Helen Hoang's (2018) *The Kiss Quotient*, since it was described as a gender-swapped *Pretty Woman* with an autistic woman as the main character. That book was not for me, but later I found Larre Bildeston's (2023) *The Space Ace of Mangleby Flat*, which was described as an *'asexual and aromantic love story'*. The protagonist felt very autistic and familiar to me, but it took until later in the book for anyone to even mention autism at all. I love Dahlia Donovan's Motts series, which are cozy mysteries led by an asexual, autistic main character. Science fiction has always been very important to me because I think it allows us to safely explore social themes and dynamics (says the social scientist). *NeuroTribes* has quite a bit of time devoted to autistic community and science fiction. Ada Hoffmann, Jaqueline Koyanagi, Rivers Solomon, Kaia Sønderby, Seanan McGuire/Mira Grant, Al Hess or Kara Jorgensen are some of the folks on my automatic read list.

The first memoir I read was Steven Shores when I was in graduate school. Since then, I've read a lot of autobiographies and memoirs. I appreciate ones where the author reads the audiobook, like Fern Brady's (2023) *Strong Female Character*. I loved Limburg's *Letters to My Weird Sisters: On Autism and Feminism*. I keep a list of books that I wish I could send back to my younger self so that I could imagine other things would be possible in the future.

I may not know these people, but I do like listening and being in their worlds for a while. Community isn't always who is physically present where you live or someone you see regularly. There is great comfort in the familiarity of people's experiences, even if the experiences don't entirely overlap, but that's to be celebrated too. It's the voices. Community, which I often write as communit(ies) because there are so many all at once, and we are part of many.

Online community

Social media was another route for me finding autistic communit(ies). #ActuallyAutistic and related hashtags were helpful for listening to conversations. Usually, I followed authors and through their posts and exchanges found other people, including webs of autistic researchers and academics. Through social media, I learned about Discord servers, which are slower in terms of interaction and number of people. They are also not algorithmically driven, so they don't feed off outrage and divisiveness. I joined academic-leaning communities like the Narratives of Neurodiversity Network, which is '*academics, creatives, and curious folk from all over the world, who have gathered to explore the cultures of neurodiversity*'. I am also part of a server which people often join after Autscape, which is a conference convened by and for autistic people. During the early COVID-19 pandemic, Autscape was only online and I was able to attend. I would love to attend in person. I think a lot of speed of interaction and text-based interaction and the playfulness of some online spaces. I wish I had local community, but I wouldn't trade it for the connections I've made.

How does one teach/share community?

Bringing this back to the classroom, how do I teach the importance of community? How do I present and amplify all the possibilities of autistic community, autistic spaces and culture for students? How do I amplify the lesson from the Double Empathy Problem that resists the pervasive and dominant narratives that limit autistic experience? The two main ways I try are through disclosure and reading. Assigning reading and discussion is a common thing for a university classroom, but disclosure feels like more of a risk.

Disclosure

How would anyone know who is autistic? The person could say, '*I'm autistic*'. Someone else could tell you '*that person is autistic*'. Other than that, we're left with how we read one another and making an assumption. Many students who have disclosed were not a surprise. Often, it's the way their body moves (in person or in synchronous class meetings) or the intensity of their engagement around certain topics. But how would they know that their professor was autistic? Again, maybe they suspect? Being on my best professional behaviour is often about keeping autistic and attention deficit hyperactivity disorder (ADHD) ways of being hidden. But there is something different about having it said and known so people know they have the permission to engage and talk about it. What does it mean for students to not only know their faculty and staff share some of their experience but also the challenges and the joys?

My current style of disclosure in class is roundabout. When talking about autistic people or community I might say, '*Many of us*' or '*For me, …*' Students hear it. I started disclosing in part because I know how many of my colleagues have shared that they have ADHD or dyslexia or anxiety, but students struggling with the clash between their process and way of being and academic expectations and general ableism don't know we're right here. It's the US Family Educational Rights and Privacy Act (FERPA)/Health Insurance Portability and Accountability Act (HIPAA) (in short, school and mental health privacy acts) culture that dissuades people from acknowledging their own experience (it is not a privacy violation to share your own information) and results in the invisibility of certain experiences related to neurodivergence and many disabilities. We learn that certain aspects of our identity make us different and we shouldn't talk about them. You can't know you're part of community if you can't talk about it and connect.

Other ways I passively disclose are the stickers on my office door and the books I keep in my office (since I used to judge my professors based on their bookshelves.) Like the LGBTQIA+ Safe Space training stickers meant to communicate to queer students and queer-questioning students that the office resident should be supportive and affirming, I put up one of Jen White-Johnson's 'Autistic Joy' stickers. Antidiscrimination/safety is a necessary, but very low bar to me. Joy seems to set the tone better. I also have two specific LGBTQIA+ flag stickers for the same reason. Students may never say anything about any of these stickers directly to me, but I know they see them. Also, I've noticed students love stickers, so I have a basket of water bottle stickers ranging from playful, like 'Just Keep Stimming', 'Spicy Autism' and the AD/HD sticker in the AC/DC font, to disability justice stickers, and several queer-affirming ones, too. I love hearing students outside my door talk about the stickers and pick out which ones they want.

Part of what makes my disclosure in professional situations possible is having connections with other neurodivergent (ND) people in higher education who are also committed to supporting students and studying neurodivergence from various disciplinary perspectives. Even if I am the only person in a work meeting to do so, I know that I have a wider ND academic community. I deeply appreciate those connections I have with other academics who are comfortable with connecting around and studying neurodivergence. We need each other, and so do students coming up wondering if college is for them.

It was a shift to go from a therapist's boundaries and limited self-disclosure to being more open with students. As a new faculty member, I was learning how to be a professional in a new field and working to help students socialized to the expectation of mental health services professions. But over time, I heard how much students struggled as they acculturated to college expectations and wondered about future careers. Even those who aren't neurodivergent, and/or disabled, struggle. I want students equipped to resist expectations of doing more and holding themselves to impossible standards. And I tell them so. Though this is not ND students, many students do disclose that they are ND. Students struggle and suffer emotional recrimination for not being able to keep up with an enormous amount of work and expectations, while many of them have caring responsibilities and/or jobs, or a full schedule of extracurricular commitment – and having to adapt to the COVID-19 pandemic. I started to feel obliged to resist out loud to them. I was struggling and still trying to present a confident professional presence. It's not students that are failing. The expectations are no longer reasonable, if they ever were, for many of us.

Disclosure is an invitation for them to ask me questions. Or just know that they can, or that someone else understands a bit more of their experience. If I've said I'm autistic, the quality of the questions they ask shifts because I've made it safe to be direct for any students, but especially for the autistic students.

Reading together and listening well

The first book students and I read together in Abnormal Psychology is *The Collected Schizophrenias* by Esmé Weijun Wang (2019). We learn about her experience of psychotic episodes and mania, the process of diagnosis and what diagnosis means to her, what it has been like to be hospitalized, how her school responded to mental health crises, and how her partner and their families provide support. For many students, they are shocked to be reading memoirs and personal essays rather than psychology journal articles or textbooks. They think the book is a novel and somehow less serious or credible. But by the end of the book and discussions, they understand the value of listening to someone share their experience and that there is a lot to learn about, not just that person's description of their experience of schizoaffective disorder, psychosis and depression, but also system barriers, how the process of diagnosis is expected to work and how it works in practice, and the impact of higher education policies and discrimination.

In that same class, we listen to Professor of Law, Psychology, Psychiatry and the Behavioral Sciences, Elyn Saks's TED Talk about the experience of being diagnosed and treated for schizophrenia. Students are always struck by Saks's sharing how a colleague claimed that being physically restrained didn't hurt psychotic people because '*they can't feel anything*', but Saks knew better from personal experience. Personal experience sticks with students, and I want them to be listening well before they move on to academic and professional texts. That way they are more likely to not accept the distance and well-trod narrative in the professional framing as objectivity. Students may want the hidden parts of expertise, but redirecting listening back to listening well to people talking about their experiences is an important thing for people going into helping professions.

In class, we also wonder about how many stories we don't hear or don't even have access to, even if we tried to find them. Time is short in academic terms, so as a teacher I've had to make decisions about who we listen to in those 15 weeks we work together. Saks and Wang are brilliant thinkers and writers who both acknowledge that they have benefitted from having so much support. They rise to the top in terms of success in a traditional sort of way. What of the voices from their wider communities that don't make it through to the bookshelf?

Around autistic experience, 'Quiet Hands' from Julia Bascom on the Just Stimming blog is a short, powerful read. Students' responses help me understand their experience. Many of them work or have worked in schools, summer camps and childcare. When they read 'Quiet Hands', they are often stuck between the familiarity of repeatedly asking young children to keep their bodies still and pushing them into trying things, and the cruelty of *'people who were much bigger than me with loud echoing voices held my hands down in textures that hurt worse than my broken wrist while I cried and begged and pleaded and screamed'*. It's often the first time that many students recognize they are reading an autistic adult describing their childhood, as if our collective (allistic) imagination was so limited that we weren't sure autistic adults existed. Why have they been so quiet? It's jarring in a positive way, even if the students' realization is troubling. For many autistic students, reading 'Quiet Hands' is familiar and upsetting, providing them a context to respond to their experiences and frustration with how often autistic perspective is absent when talking about autism and autistic people. They know the consequences of being misread for how their bodies move, for how they express themselves, for what they notice and how they think. They have a lot to say about it and, for some, this is the first time they are sharing in an academic context through a reading reflection shared with a teacher.

We also watch Communication First's documentary, *Listen*, which is written by and features nonspeaking autistic people. For many of the students, this documentary is the first time they have realized that nonspeaking people communicate or have something to say, or like them, appreciate being listened to. Occasionally, students will mention that they might even know nonspeaking people, but don't realize it because their relationship takes place online through typed words and memes.

In Counseling Diverse Populations, we listen to podcasts, documentaries and performances, and read personal essays and memoirs. I select as much as I can, often opting for shorter pieces so I can get a wider representation of communities, cultures, identities and experiences. What is overwhelming is trying to do any justice to human diversity in

15 weeks. We talk about how to keep expanding your engagement with communities you are not part of. Who are you listening to? Whose books and movies and music are you consuming? How will you continue after class is over?

Then we return to the language of professionals, and most of the students can hear it. They can hear the limitations. I tell the students over and over that there is more diversity within groups than the distinction between them, and both aspects of diversity and difference matter. Which is to say, it's not enough to listen to one or two autistic people to understand autistic community. You have to keep listening, and perhaps, join in the conversation with your own experience.

References

Autistic Self Advocacy Network (2012). *Loud Hands: Autistic People, Speaking*. The Autistic Press

Bildeston, L. (2023). *The Space Ace of Mangleby Flat.*

Brady, F. (2023). *Strong Female Character*. Octopus Publishing Group.

Broderick, A. A., (2022). *The Autism Industrial Complex: How Branding, Marketing, and Capital Investment Turned Autism into Big Business*. Stylus Publishing.

Brown, L. X. Z., Ashkenazy, E., & Onaiwu, M. G. (2017). *All the Weight of Our Dreams: On Living Racialized Autism*. DragonBee Press.

Hoang, H. (2018). *The Kiss Quotient*. Jove.

Kapp, S. K. (Ed.) (2020). *Autistic Community and the Neurodiversity Movement: Stories from the Frontline*. Palgrave Macmillan.

Limburg, J. (2021). *Letters to My Weird Sisters: On Autism and Feminism*. Atlantic Books.

Murray, D., Milton, D., Ridout, S., Martin, N., & Mills, R. (2020). *The Neurodiversity Reader: Exploring Concepts, Lived Experience and Implications for Practice*. Pavilion.

Rodas, J. M. (2018). *Autistic Disturbances: Theorizing Autism Poetics from the DSM to Robinson Crusoe*. University of Michigan Press.

Silberman, S. (2016). *NeuroTribes: The Legacy of Autism and the Future of Neurodiversity*. Avery.

Wang, E. W. (2019). *The Collected Schizophrenias: Essays*. Graywolf Press.

Yergeau, R. (2018). *Authoring Autism: On Rhetoric and Neurological Queerness*. Duke University Press.

Chapter 16: Double Empathy and Professional Scrutiny of Autistic Families

Alice Running

My experiences of navigating 'supportive' services for my autistic children led me to question why I was being regarded with suspicion by the many and varied children's professionals involved with our family. The scrutiny of my family (by professionals) began when my children were intensely struggling in mainstream primary school. At that time, I had queried the possibility that they may be autistic but was ignorant to the fact that I was also autistic. Professional scrutiny continued throughout their childhood and intensified following the diagnostic outcomes for both me and my children (we are all autistic, and all have diagnoses as such). I began to understand my interactions with our involved professionals in terms of discrimination and blame toward myself, as both an autistic parent and lone mother.

Despite professionals framing the challenges my children were facing in accessing educational settings outside of our home as lax parenting (and later, neglectful parenting) and presenting this as an individual problem centred within myself, I understood that many parent-carers were experiencing similar nationwide.

Returned data from a survey of over 1000 parent-carers of autistic children (Running & Jata-Hall, 2023) suggests that neurodivergent parent-carers may be more vulnerable to the instigation of safeguarding procedures (due to assumed parental failings) by professionals involved with their autistic children. The survey found that 52.5% of respondents identified as being neurodivergent. Of the 10.93% of respondents who had been subjected to formal safeguarding procedures (because of their autistic children's presentations), 76.57% of those parent-carers were neurodivergent.

Neurodivergent parent-carer respondents to this survey shared their experiences of interacting with professionals, detailing how their neurodivergent presentations were often misunderstood, or misrepresented, by involved professionals. Running and Jata-Hall report that one autistic mother shared that, '*I was accused by the Senco of having an unfortunate manner*' (Running & Jata-Hall, 2023, p. 30). Another autistic/attention deficit hyperactivity disorder (ADHD) mother shared that '*apparently, my black and white views of things get in the way*' (Running & Jata-Hall, 2023, p. 30). Indeed, Benson writes about autistic mothers that '*evidence suggests that they may be at a substantially increased risk of involuntary social work interventions*' (Benson, 2023, p. 1445), stating that '*indicators of neurodivergency in both mothers and children are considered perplexing and assigned malign meanings*' (Benson, 2023, p. 1445).

> *More recent research around 'The prevalence and impact of allegations of fabricated or induced illness (Fii)' (Clements & Aiello, 2023) supports that autistic parents are more vulnerable to this specific type of misaligned scrutiny with authors summarizing that 'over 50% of respondents who had experienced an accusation of Fii … identified as a disabled person … over 40% of these respondents identified as autistic'* (Clements & Aiello, 2023, p. 29).

This is certainly my personal experience. I have had my autistic presentation noted as concerning by professionals and subsequently used to inform child services assessments. Professionals from specialist disability-related services (education settings, child and adolescent mental health services [CAMHS], disability children's services) chose to record innate features of my autistic presentation – alternative eye contact, adherence to schedules, auditory processing differences, environmental sensory discomfort, detail focus – as both mental health 'red flags' and obstructive behaviour impacting upon my children's 'progress'. I was not made party to this analysis of my presentation until the point at which serious allegations were presented. This leads me to consider how different matters could have been if the involved professionals had chosen to discuss this directly with myself from the outset.

Benson writes, '*if I could encapsulate my interactions with professionals … I would choose "perplexing" … as an autistic woman … [perplexing] describes both the way I am perceived by others and my own feelings about the way others respond to me*' (Benson, 2023, p. 1446).

So how far does a lack of understanding between (non-autistic) professionals and (autistic) parent-carers impact professional (over)scrutiny of autistic families?

As an individual, I have fallen under professional scrutiny both as an undiagnosed and diagnosed autistic adult. The disability-specific professionals involved with assessment and support for my autistic children made additional (and undisclosed) assessments of my own presentation based on their early impressions of how I interacted in and around the meeting environment. My need for order and preparation ahead of meetings (such as requiring advanced details and requesting agenda inclusions) led to professionals labelling me as controlling. My articulation of acquired knowledge around special education needs and disability (SEND) processes and autism in general, led to professionals recording that I had placed myself in the role of expert (which in turn they argued, obstructed their ability to make 'progress' with my child). This is in stark contrast to non-autistic parent-carers who, in positions of expertise, were not viewed in negative terms by involved professionals. The study *Parental Blame and the PDA Profile of Autism* (Running & Jata-Hall, 2023) summarized that '*where parent-carers have higher status or autism-relevant professions … parent-carer professional status is seemingly respected … [however] where a parent-carer with a high status/autism-relevant profession is … neurodivergent … the profession of the mother is seemingly used against her and identified as a safeguarding concern*' (Running & Jata-Hall, 2023, p. 37).

That non-autistic parent-carers in related 'expert' roles are respected within their position as expert, rather than viewed in the negative (as per the experiences of some autistic parent-carers), may suggest that non-autistic professionals form their initial impressions less around factors of parental expertise or professional status but more around how an autistic parent may present themselves while doing so.

Crompton et al. (2021) write that '*it really seems that it is how autistic people appear and sound, and not what they talk about, that leads non-autistic people to judge … autistic people*'.

I was oblivious to the negative impression our involved professionals had made of me and remained so until receiving copies of my child's records. This failure to reach a shared understanding within parent–professional interactions had seemingly enabled the non-autistic professionals to form a negative early impression of myself (an autistic person), without critically analysing why they had done so.

Of one meeting it was recorded by professionals that I had presented myself in an aggressive manner, but no further details were given when I subsequently queried this description (I had not behaved inappropriately and had my own personal recording of the meeting to attest to this), other than professionals stating that it was their impression. I asked what specifically had led them to describe me in this way – gestures, words or tone? They couldn't provide me with an adequate response.

Memmott (2023) advocates that *'many autistic people get told, "I don't like your tone" or "why are you so angry", or similar. But they weren't feeling anything negative at the time … somehow, many non-autistic people hear negativity/anger/sarcasm in autistic voice tones … when that's not what we meant. At all.'*

In this specific example from my individual experience, there was a missed opportunity whereby professionals could have chosen to engage with me in a conversation around why they perceived my presentation to be aggressive – there was an opportunity for the non-autistic professionals to consider matters from my perspective also, to employ a double-empathy approach. Instead, a further 'red flag' was recorded detailing my inability to understand why I had been perceived as such.

Memmott (2023) summarizes such judgement; *'so many autistic people find themselves in situations where those around us truly believe we're angry, nasty sorts, because they are "misreading" a genuine difference in how we sound…'*

Professional opinion of myself did not improve upon the disclosure of my diagnostic status. In fact, involved professionals used my disclosure as a basis to investigate whether my parenting skills were impeded on account of my being an autistic person. I was subjected to many interviews where professionals sought to 'un-pick' how 'my autism impacted my parenting'. How did I interact with others? Did I have friends? Did I struggle to leave the house? How did I cope with demand avoidance? It felt very much as if these professionals were trying to establish that the challenges my child was facing when trying to interact with a world hostile to his autistic presentation were due to myself being autistic. The professionals involved within this work were universally deferred to as 'autism experts', having spent large parts of their own careers working with autistic people, and yet they did not deviate from analysing my autistic presentation as a deficit – as something intrinsically lacking in myself that was directly causing problems for my son's 'progress' and his 'sought-after assimilation' into non-autistic, standardized, behavioural patterns.

Milton (2018) explains that *'from the position of the non-autistic onlooker, autistic people can seem to have an impaired understanding of social life and other people'*, and this certainly was how non-autistic professionals came to view myself upon learning about my neurodivergence. The decision to share my diagnosis with the professionals working with my family was taken primarily to gain reasonable adjustments. However, this too was problematic. Requests of me (to meet with a professional for coffee at a local café) were still implied (apparently, I should have known that this was to formally discuss issues relating to my child) rather than presented directly and then subsequently recorded as refusal to engage. In this situation, not only did I not pick up on the social cues that a non-autistic person may have done, but also the non-autistic professional did not consider that an autistic person may not recognize or acknowledge the indirect information given in this exchange.

Reaching a shared understanding within an exchange between autistic parent-carers and non-autistic professionals can be further impeded through differences in language use and language comprehension. Overuse of professional 'jargon' and technical language excludes many parent-carers from fully participating in dialogue with professionals, regardless of neurodivergent status. However, when disability professionals with recognized autism expertise create inaccessible spaces through overuse of metaphor, or fast-paced speech patterns, for example, a barrier is created whereby autistic parent-carers are excluded from participating equally. Again, this is something that I have experienced, and my subsequent 'difficulty' in processing verbal information at their speed was then recorded as evidence of how my being autistic impacted my ability to parent, rather than taken as an opportunity to improve inclusion. As Milton explains, '*it is a double problem as both people experience it, and so it is not a singular problem located in any one person*' (Milton, 2012, p. 886). Yet, it was only me that was deemed to be 'less than' within this exchange.

This leads me to consider the balance of power held by each social actor within an exchange. Interactions between parent-carers and social workers, for example, are not balanced in terms of the power wielded by each participant. In my situation the professional (with power in respect to child safeguarding) was able to place fault for the lack of shared understanding exclusively with myself (the person with little power within the exchange). This creates an added layer of significance, as the ramifications of mutual misunderstanding fall solely on the person with less power in the exchange – the parent-carer – creating potential for serious outcomes (child removal).

Milton considers that '*if one can apply a label on the "other", locating the problem in them, it also resolves the applier of the labels "natural attitude" of responsibility in their own perceptions*' (Milton, 2012, p. 886). By placing fault for such shared interactions with autistic parent-carers, professionals can avoid taking any responsibility for their own (non-inclusive) communication which, I believe, can further extend into absolving services of their requirement to provide correct and useful support for autistic families (children, in particular) – if the parent-carer has been viewed to be at fault, then there is no need for the acquisition of disability-specific services.

By labelling an autistic parent-carer as the person at fault within a situation or interaction, the misbelief that autistic parent-carers are also to blame for their child's disability presentation is (potentially) extrapolated by involved professionals by way of explanation as to why an autistic child is not adhering to expected norms. Running and Jata-Hall suggest that parental blame '*is not happening in a small selection of instances … professionals [are] using similar phrases that blame, and parents [are] reporting similar experiences of blame across the UK (and beyond) … this cannot, therefore, be a problem located within the individual parent – parental blame appears to be a systemic way of dealing with parents seeking support*' (Running & Jata-Hall, 2023, p.35).

Professionals, in a safeguarding/children's services context, are positioned as the only perspective that holds value. They hold the role of assessor and expert and so in any given exchange, can lock out the potential for two-way understanding (because they hold ultimate control within the exchange), leading to the misidentification of autistic presentations as safeguarding concerns.

In a study of social work practice with autistic mothers of autistic children, Benson found that '*without a shared understanding to draw on, there was a tendency to interpret perplexing presentations using a neuro-normative lens through which autistic traits were reconfigured as 'suspicious', suggestive of harm or damage*' (Benson, 2023, p. 1453). The interpretation of 'perplexing', autistic presentations (by non-autistic professionals) seemingly extends further than forming negative initial impressions of autistic parent-carers and mislabelling autistic presentations as harmful, into a lack of shared understanding and acceptance of autistic lifestyle. Professional scrutiny of autistic families allows for the assessment of autistic lifestyle adaptations to be judged against non-autistic benchmarks. For example, an autistic child may find one social, extracurricular activity a week satisfactory, whereas an assessing professional may deem this not to be suitable based on non-autistic beliefs and values around what constitutes an acceptable lifestyle for well-being. Safeguarding assessment frameworks employ key assessment categories that assess parents and families against areas such as social integration, employment and family functioning – all of which may look very different for autistic families due to autistic needs differing from non-autistic needs, but when compared against a non-autistic benchmark could be interpreted by the assessing professional as harmful. Safeguarding assessment frameworks, I believe, are constructed in such a way that they are intrinsically biased against autistic families. Government (Welsh Assembly) published frameworks, for example, analyse parental capacity around behaviours such as the overt display of '*appropriate physical contact, cuddling, warm regard, praise and encouragement*' (National Assembly of Wales, Home Office, 2001, p. 23). My children do not overly enjoy cuddling, nor receiving overt statements of praise and to provide an environment for them which is not tortuous I forgo such behaviours and replace them with other demonstrations of love. Many aspects of the adaptations I make to provide a more inclusive home environment for my children were also judged against non-autistic standards by assessing professionals. For example, my cooking meals to suit sensory requirements was labelled as allowing my child to exert too much control. My placing throws over the sofa instead of reprimanding my child for seeking out proprioceptive feedback by bouncing on the sofa was presented as my not creating appropriate boundaries. My provision of toys that my child found stimulating was labelled as 'infantilizing' due to the non-autistic social work expert deeming the toys to not be 'age-appropriate'.

In my opinion, the safeguarding assessment frameworks provide rigidity and exclusion. Despite Government (Welsh Assembly) assessment frameworks stating that '*children and families' differences must be approached with knowledge and sensitivity in a non-judgemental way*' (National Assembly of Wales, Home Office, 2001, p. 28) many professionals fail to do so, subsequently failing to elicit a shared understanding around the lifestyle adaptations autistic families may need to survive within a non-autistic society. It places professionals in a position whereby they are, from the outset, not seeking to understand the differences presented but are instead seeking out deviations from the non-autistic rulebook of parenting.

This does not always encourage professionals to question how their own behaviour or participation in an interaction may impact the ability of an autistic participant to engage. Benson considers this and summarizes one example of professional scrutiny of an autistic family as such, '*the social worker had failed to consider the role that they had played in Lilly's visible distress or why an unexpected intrusion into the family home might have been particularly distressing for an autistic family*' (Benson, 2023, p. 1453).

It is concerning to me that the propensity for autistic parent-carers (most notably mothers) to be subjected to the most extreme aspects of child safeguarding (child removal) has been raised as an issue for some time. Amelia Hill (2016), for *The Guardian* newspaper, presented an investigative article focusing upon the experiences of autistic mothers, highlighting '*the numbers of autistic women whose attempts to get help for their children … are greeted with hostility, combativeness and ultimately, the removal of their children*'.

There are multiple examples of Family Court judgements in which autistic mothers (diagnosed or undiagnosed) have had their children removed, with involved professionals commenting upon some aspect of an autistic or neurodivergent presentation.

In a fact-finding hearing, published via the British and Irish Legal Information Institute (BAILII) (2023) and regarding allegations of emotional harm and fabricated or induced illness (FII) made in respect of the mother (a parent to an autistic child and for whom she had attempted to seek disability-specific support), a professional witness stated that '*during the three telephone calls I have had with [the mother], I have been concerned with her presentation. During calls her speech has been pressured and meandering. Throughout, she has been extremely fixated on what she sees as institutional failings to address her and her children's needs … the emails she has sent have been rambling and bizarre in content…*'

This analysis of a neurodivergent presentation is similar to an account shared by a respondent to the survey *Parental Blame and the PDA Profile of Autism*. Running and Jata-Hall point to a parent-carer who had been criticized by involved professionals for writing long emails – '*the HSLW [health support worker] even gave written examples to justify "her professional opinion" about how my "anxiety" presented – e.g. I wrote long emails*' (Running & Jata-Hall, 2023, p. 29). This respondent categorized her neurodivergence as 'autistic with ADHD'.

As an autistic person I have deliberately adjusted my email output to professionals to avoid such misaligned criticism, but my innate need to include all details in written communication remains – to provide a thorough and detailed communication is my default 'normal'. For me, and other autistic people, detailed communication is not unusual, but because it is a less common communication style for non-autistic professionals, it becomes a point to record. That 'normal', autistic communication styles can be presented as evidence of emotionally harmful behaviour within legal proceedings is terrifying and demonstrates (to me) how little progress many professionals involved within the safeguarding of children have made in relation to understanding interactions and issues from an autistic perspective.

Without the implementation of a double-empathy approach among disability-specific professionals, and safeguarding professionals, the perpetuation of trauma (that occurs when autistic needs are not met, and further, when unnecessary safeguarding interventions are applied) for those autistic families who fall under professional scrutiny, is likely to continue.

In the context of professional scrutiny, a lack of double empathy is also combined with an imbalance of power, in that the relationship between autistic parent-carer and non-autistic professional is not one of equality. In my opinion (by way of lived experience), it is much harder for a parent-carer to apply legal processes to ensure disability equality is achieved than it is for a professional to wield safeguarding power. It is my opinion that autistic people are regularly stripped of power through the consistent neglect with regard to having their legal rights met, and that this boosts the ability of professionals to systematically misinterpret or misrepresent autistic communication, presentation and lifestyle. For me, this demonstrates a need for all-level professional practice to consistently utilize a double-empathy approach.

References

BAILII (2023, March 24). S and T (care – fact finding – FII – emotional abuse) EWFC 195. https://www.bailii.org/ew/cases/EWFC/HCJ/2023/195.html

Benson, K. (2023). Perplexing presentations: Compulsory neuronormativity and cognitive marginalisation in social work practice with autistic mothers of autistic children. *The British Journal of Social Work, 53*(3), 1445–1464. https://doi.org/10.1093/bjsw/bcac229

Clements, L., & Aiello, A. (2023). *The Prevalence and Impact of Allegations of Fabricated or Induced Illness (FII)*. Cerebra. https://cerebra.org.uk/wp-content/uploads/2023/11/FII-Final-report-2023-Nov-01.pdf

Crompton, C., DeBrabander, K., Heasman, B., Milton, D., & Sasson, N. (2021). Double empathy: Why autistic people are often misunderstood. *Frontiers*. https://kids.frontiersin.org/articles/10.3389/frym.2021.554875

Hill, A. (2016, December 25). Autism: 'Hidden pool' of undiagnosed mothers with condition emerging. *The Guardian*. https://www.theguardian.com/society/2016/dec/26/autism-hidden-pool-of-undiagnosed-mothers-with-condition-emerging

Memmott, A. (2023). I don't like your tone. *Ann's Autism Blog*. https://annsautism.blogspot.com/2023/06/i-dont-like-your-tone.html?m=0

Milton, D. (2012). On the ontological status of autism: the 'double empathy problem'. *Disability and Society*, 27 (6), 883–887. https://doi.org/10.1080/09687599.2012.710008

Milton, D. (2018). *The Double Empathy Problem*. National Autistic Society. https://autism.org.uk/advice-and-guidance/professional-practice/double-empathy

National Assembly for Wales, Home Office (2001). *Framework for the Assessment of Children in Need and their Families*. The Stationery Office.

Running, A., & Jata-Hall, D. (2023). *Parental Blame and the PDA Profile of Autism*. PDA Society. https://www.pdasociety.org.uk/resources/parental-blame-and-the-pda-profile-of-autism/

Chapter 17:

Double Empathy and Spiritual Abuse: The Importance of Creating Church Cultures that Validate Autistic Social and Communication Differences

Sarah Douglas

Spiritual abuse (SA) is a uniquely damaging phenomenon and although the majority of research and publications to date are framed by US culture and experience, there is a growing awareness of its malign presence in the UK. The impact of UK-based SA is becoming increasingly reported, researched and supported,[36] but as yet, there is little in the way of academic enquiry into, or understanding about, how autistic people of faith experience this intensely traumatic form of abuse. I am hoping to begin to fill this gap by exploring my own neurodivergent (ND) experiences of SA in my autoethnographic MRes, by engaging in wider fieldwork for my future PhD and also, here in this article, by taking a closer look at how the Double Empathy Problem can exacerbate this kind of trauma for autistic survivors. SA is not confined to Christianity and there is plenty of evidence of controlling cultic practices in other faiths, as well as in secular settings such as workplaces and interest groups, but this is outside of my current knowledge base and my immediate

36 Examples include: https://www.youtube.com/results?search_query=Spiritual+abuse; Jenkinson, G. (2023). *Walking Free from the Trauma of Coercive, Cultic and Spiritual Abuse: A Workbook for Recovery and Growth*. Routledge; Replenished Life and Survivors Voices, which are UK-based support charities for SA survivors; and Safe Spaces which is a national church-related abuse support service for victims of SA in the Church of England, the Catholic Church of England and Wales or the Church in Wales.

aim is to produce work that feeds into external support services, adapts existing pastoral systems and embeds measures in Christian church life that create healthy safe places of worship and belonging for ND survivors. So, for now, I will write about what I know and focus on exploring the connection between the Double Empathy Problem and trauma in the context of my lived experiences of SA in a Christian church setting, and the deep wounds it has inflicted on my autistic soul, spirit and self.

Autistic folk suffer from higher instances of multiplex abuses than the neuromajority, both from post-traumatic stress disorder (PTSD) criteria events recognized in the *Diagnostic and Statistical Manual of Mental Disorders*, 5th edition (DSM-5; American Psychiatric Association, 2013) and from the chronic additional daily microaggressions of living in an unfriendly world (Rumball et al., 2020). Victimization is normalized, expected and, anecdotally, complex PTSD is frequently reported in the autistic community (Pearson et al., 2022). Given this background, I do not think that it is unreasonable to suspect that SA is not only disproportionately more common for autistic people of faith, but also that the impact of SA and the characteristics of these experiences may be qualitatively distinct from those of non-autistic survivors. I have no empirical evidence to back up this theory as the work has yet to be done and any possible reasons will no doubt be intersectional and complex, but what I do have is my lived experience that I can autoethnographically weave around the little research about autistic trauma that we know to date. There is not enough space or time to discuss the many other possible factors that have an impact here, but I believe that autistic social and communication differences, and the resulting blame, shame and stigma from a normative society, contribute a great deal to an autistic person of faith's experiences of SA.

As yet, there are no specifically ND definitions of SA, and although the following is written from a neuronormative perspective, it does resonate with aspects of my own lived experience and emphasizes the expansive and far-reaching nature of spiritually abusive behaviour.

> *Spiritual abuse is coercion and control of one individual by another in a spiritual context. The target experiences spiritual abuse as a deeply emotional personal attack. This abuse may include: manipulation and exploitation, enforced accountability, censorship of decision making, requirements for secrecy and silence, pressure to conform, misuse of scripture or the pulpit to control behaviour, requirement of obedience to the abuser, the suggestion that the abuser has a 'divine' position, isolation from others, especially those external to the abusive context.* (Oakley & Kinmond, 2013, p. 21)

All forms of abuse can have devastating outcomes in terms of biopsychosocialspiritual well-being, irrespective of the context in which they are perpetrated. My experiences of child sexual abuse (CSA) and sexual abuse, both without and within a religious setting, have been utterly traumatizing, and in a church community this type of violence not only clearly intersects with SA, but SA can also be experienced and defined as being something distinct. A survivor of intimate partner victimization can suffer from controlling or manipulative behaviour, which has similarities with behaviour that can occur within a religious setting or community. With SA there can be complex additional layers of abuse and complicity from individuals, sections of or from the entirety of a church community, as well as from a co-opted, disapproving God. Toxic religiosity and a culture of bad theology can also result in unexpected trauma when, for example, a trusting congregant bravely discloses previous external abuse only to be met with shame and victim-blaming, *'Not only can a survivor be abused in church, but they can also be re-abused in church for being previously abused'.*[37]

It is important to point out that I am not advocating for SA to be treated as being at the pinnacle of traumatic experience or that anyone who has had the misfortune to be subjected to it somehow occupies a position of pain supremacy. There is no hierarchy of trauma, and all of our experiences are valid, but nonetheless, there is something qualitatively different about experiencing a kind of trauma that occurs in a place of perceived safety or divine sanctuary and from people in a particular position of trust. A church community can be difficult to navigate, and relationships can be awkward and challenging as the body of Christ works out how to travel on their faith journey together, settle disputes and accommodate differing and sometimes conflicting needs – but SA is a different thing entirely. When it occurs, SA can rob a person of their self-identity, their senses of autonomy, worth and agency, and causes extreme isolation and distrust in very place that should be an experience of growth and being loved, respected and accepted within a supportive church family. The effects can be long-lasting and have profound outcomes for faith, both personal and collective, as well as for relationships with others, the self and the divine. Peppiatt (2007, p. 9) writes about shame being one of the most commonly reported experiences of SA survivors, which is unsurprising as this is also echoed by survivors of many other kinds of abuse, but Oakley and Humphries (2019a) reach deeper into the trauma of the spiritually abused by exploring the effect that SA-induced shame has on survivors when they frame their experience as being part of God's plan. It is a holistic sense of being cast adrift from everything, everyone and the beyond, which is why SA has qualities to it that are so uniquely devastating. No wonder Oakley and Humphries (2019b) explains that, *'so many survivors of spiritual abuse … can no*

37 In conversation with Jane Chevous, co-founder of Survivors Voices, October 2023.

longer trust spiritual leaders or any spiritual organisation' and that recovery will need, '*significant long-term support and non-judgemental investment*', if the abused person is ever going to be able to trust others or themselves again.

There is so much here that speaks to me, but possibly because it is framed by research and findings that have not consciously considered the experiences of folk who are neurodivergent, it does not tell my whole story. It does not speak of the impact of the trauma that had accumulated before I was subjected to SA, much of which revolved around my social and communication differences as an undiagnosed autism and attention deficit hyperactivity disorder (AuDHD) person in a time when there was a lack of understanding about autism, and nothing like the growing autistic and neurodiversity affirming culture that exists today. In DSM-II (1968), published the year before I was born, autism was still associated with childhood schizophrenia and the 1987 revision, DSM-III-R, describes autism in terms of being a disorder marked by unresponsiveness to other people, which could never have been applied to my desperately masked self who had a deep desire for connection. DSM-IV (1994) came too late for me, as by then I was 35 and multiply traumatized by the years of confusion through growing up different, but not knowing why. From an early age, I experienced so much bullying, rejection and abuse as I hovered on the edge of the party, not knowing how to be invited, and, consequently, never feeling that I belonged or that I was good enough. This clever, weird, bespectacled, overweight child, who was outwardly gregarious and talkative, didn't know how to make friends in a neuronormative world and was never going to be accepted by it. I didn't understand others, as hard as I tried to, nor could I fit in with their ways of doing things, and they didn't understand me. The difference though, is that they didn't want to. I was an outsider; a social outcast, and my heart still breaks today for my lonely, younger self.

My home life offered no relief as there was no communication, no discussion, just announcements that expected compliance. In one such scene, my brothers and I were, without warning, informed that our parents were getting a divorce, and it gave me PTSD flashbacks for decades until I had eye movement desensitization and reprocessing (EMDR) therapy. If I went into a room that had the same carpet or a similar pattern to the one in the lounge where the announcement had been made, I would feel sick, panicky and tearful, but would also mask these trauma responses, as I had learned that emotional outbursts were not acceptable in my family. After weeks of silence, emotional torment and confusion, my mother mentioned in passing that my parents weren't in fact, splitting up, but that we were going to move to the Isle of Wight instead, and initially without one of my brothers, who because he was in his final year of O-Levels, was going to be left behind with neighbours until he completed them. Nobody thought that it would be a good idea to communicate these huge changes supportively and gradually, or involve my siblings and I in any of the planning or discussions. They were just landed on us with no warning. A cruel way of going about things for any child, regardless of neurotype, but for autistic children, who need truth and transparency, utter torture.

This dysfunction was also characterized by a rejection of difference; steeped in stigma and discrimination. My father was a deeply racist, classist and misogynistic parent whose toxic upward mobility was driven by his resentment that instead of going to university, he chose a career in banking, accompanied by marriage and children. Keen to escape his working-class roots, he was the quintessential snob, considering himself to be a rightful member of a superior, white, upper middle class. I recall at least one local family not being deemed good enough for us to associate with when I was young because they were, it was claimed, lacking sufficient social standing. In more recent years, I was informed that had my husband been a person of colour, he wouldn't have been welcome in the family and alongside this colonial racism was a post-war generation's refusal to face emotional or mental difficulties. My paternal grandfather's mental health episodes were rarely spoken of, and my mother was mocked for her struggles with ulcerative colitis. Unsurprisingly then, when my nephew was diagnosed with Asperger syndrome and attention deficit hyperactivity disorder (ADHD) in the 1990s, he was framed as being a naughty, undisciplined child who was the product of bad parents, who were blamed for his unacceptable social and communication differences. The glaring irony is that my father, like most of the rest of my blood family, is almost certainly autistic himself, but in all likelihood will never be able to contemplate this probability as for him, with all his prejudices, being autistic would be shameful, stigmatizing and deficient.

My father's lack of empathy and refusal to accept difference was, and still is, reflected in wider society, which is why many neurodivergent folk work hard for a better future for our intersectional minority. Understanding that neuromajority might is not right, and that autistic folk are not wrong simply because we are fewer in number, is a crucial factor in deconstructing damaging normative ways of being and creating a healthier, more inclusive and kinder society. Autistic social and communication preferences may seem weird and confusing to typically wired folk, but the reverse is also true. The injustice though is that it is the neurominority that is always expected to twist, turn and contort ourselves into ill-fitting masks before we are allowed to play in an unfair world. I am fortunate to have had post-diagnostic therapy, and as well as continuously learning about the wonder of being wired differently, I am beginning to bend back into my fearfully and wonderfully created shape and emerge from my chronically masked state. I can now allow myself to consider my social and communication needs, decline invitations or request adaptions with growing confidence and enjoy working in research environments that strive for neuroaffirmative acceptance and support. I have survived a life full of the devastating consequences rooted in a lack of understanding about the reality of double empathy and fully understand the importance for society's need to change, but I am now beginning to thrive and I am grateful that the years the locusts have eaten are being restored. Older generations have not had this opportunity and I wonder how much of the trauma I experienced growing up was projected generational pain. Was my grandfather's poor mental health partly due to living as an undiagnosed autistic man, and my father's home life influenced by a strict need to be seen as being respectable in a more rigid society? I know he felt as though his brother was favoured over him, so did he also learn to internalize his parents' cruelty and rejection of difference as they attempted to normalize their own differences? I will probably never know as I have chosen to be estranged from family members who have caused me harm, but I do catch myself thinking about whether generations of autistic people in my family lived their lives hiding their authentic selves out of fear of judgement, shame and stigma.

By the time I had become involved with the Brethren, an independent, extreme, Evangelical Church, with no governing body, my mental health, which had begun to deteriorate from a young age, had plummeted. I was regularly self-harming and had developed patterns of disordered eating that grew worse as I got older. All of this was done in secret as I had learned my family values of diminishing, masking and internalizing extremely well. Following years of therapy, I came to understand that I had not felt safe enough to express my distress, which was made much worse by not being believed when I disclosed one of my experiences of serious sexual assault, but at the time I had no idea just how multiply traumatized I was. I knew that I was unhappy, but was completely unaware that I had little of the self-identity, autonomy, worth or agency that SA takes away left to give and I was already feeling isolated, unloved and unimportant, so I was horribly exposed and vulnerable to what was to come. It is so hard to write about these things that have left their toxic mark deep within me for more than 35 years and I am only now really starting to unpack the trauma. I thought that my MRes would spur me into action; expensive therapy, if you like, but what has happened, after a promising start, is weeks of avoidance and inertia. Discovering that one of the youth leaders at the Gospel Hall had received a suspended sentence for sexual assault in 2014 brought back so much repressed pain, particularly as this individual had also behaved in an abusive way to me 25 years previous to this conviction and I ground to a halt. My supervisors have been very supportive and by taking a few weeks out and tentatively dipping my toe here, as well as becoming involved with a SA survivor community, I feel in a better place to begin writing about my experiences.

I attended my first meeting at the Gospel Hall during my first year in sixth form with a peer who had been brought up in a Brethren family. I wore the obligatory head covering and was greeted by one of the elders who remarked that they were going to have trouble with me because I was apparently good looking. I didn't spot the obvious red flag, but I know now that this is because I had been conditioned to be compliant, obedient and inferior to men and had also internalized the belief that I had lied about my rape. I should have run a mile, but my mother had taught me well, so I did my best to smile, be worthy and took my place in one of the rows of hard wooden chairs. Prayers were said by the Elders and following a hymn, the preaching began. I was so desperate to be wanted and included that I lapped it up, hanging on to every word. It confirmed what I already painfully knew – that everything about me was wrong. It was all my fault and not only was I unacceptable to my peers and family, but I was also condemned by a God who had kept a record of all of my sins and would only save me from the very real fiery pit of hell if I accepted the Lord Jesus Christ into my life. I did so and was hooked. I began reading the recommended King James Bible, prayed, attended meetings, as they were called, and became involved with the main Brethren families. They were hospitable and outwardly kind, but cracks that were imperceptible to me at the time, began to show. Socializing with other Christians was frowned upon as their ideas were tainted by the lies of the world. The Brethren were the sole recipients of the truth and anything to do with what they considered to be worldly, was anathema. Wearing makeup and jewellery was considered immodest and evidence of a 'Jezebel' spirit. Music other than classical was devilish and because I wanted to be a good Christian and please these people who had taken an interest in me, I destroyed my record collection and resolved not to listen to the Sisters of Mercy, The Damned or Duran Duran again. Slowly, but surely, what was left of my creative self was diminished and replaced with guilt, self-recrimination and a half life lived in tension between what I loved and yearned to do and what was deemed acceptable. It was an appalling imposed hypocrisy that only served to isolate me even further. Peers at school could not only see me veering between wanting to do regular teenage stuff like pubs, clubs, boyfriends and gigs, but also being an insufferably judgemental prig, which only added to my perceived weirdness and existence on the periphery. I even had a song written about my confused religiosity by one of the cool kids whose band performed it on the school stage one lunchtime. Everybody knew that it was going to happen, but not me, and as utterly devastating as it was, I could also see the painful truth of it and hated myself even more as a result.

My isolation and the control that the Brethren had over me increased after I ran away from where I lived with my mother and stepfather and the only place I could go was to the dominant family in the meeting. I stayed with them for a few weeks and then moved into a flat, restarted my A-Levels and lived by myself, as neither of my parents, who had both remarried, wanted me to live with them. I had visitations from the Elders, checking up to see if I was living modestly and when I spent time with the family I had stayed with, was thrown into even more confusion by their condemnation of my father, who they saw as immoral and neglectful. They weren't wrong, but their self-righteousness only served to add more guilt and trauma onto my already overburdened shoulders. My studies were disapproved of as education for a female was not deemed suitable, which caused even more tension as getting to university was the only option that my father considered for me, but go I did and I finally left the Isle of Wight and my marriage after my first year studying Theology and Religious Studies. The marriage was abusive, but I stayed far longer than I should have done because it had been drummed into me that divorce was sinful, and a

Christian wife should serve her husband before her own needs. There is a lot more that I could write, but as I check in with myself, I know that, for now, I do not have the capacity to do so. Needless to say, I was left utterly broken by these experiences and terrified by the years of constant preaching that focused on the horrors of Revelation, the End Times and Dispensational Tribulation. I knew nothing about divine love, grace or joy and it is only now, after nearly 27 years of marriage to my warm, kind and not-remotely-toxic Christian second husband and 12 years post autism diagnosis that I am able to lance the SA boil, extract its deeply festering poison and work out what authentic spirituality looks like to me.

So far, I have learned that I engage with faith atypically and, now, do so on my own terms. I pray arrow prayers as my brain hates being still and meditating. I only attend church when I feel that I can, and I am careful to decompress and rest following the physical socializing and sensory onslaught of a service or event. I refuse to evangelize, am avoidant about reading the Bible and am vocal about pro-LGBTQ and disability rights. Had I known that my way of socializing and communicating was just as valid as anyone else's and that I did not have to mask and destroy myself to fit an unfriendly world, then I may have been better equipped to recognize this SA for what it is. Theological arguments about the human condition aside, I did not need to be saved from my differences and I shouldn't have had to be so ashamed of myself that I felt that I needed the tolerance and acceptance from those who had heaped this shame upon me. All these years later, I no longer want to join in with the party I was so desperate to be invited to, but was excluded from. I am surrounded by the love from so many who like me for who I am, and have the collective power and support of creative community groups, and although I am fearful of confronting the pain, the surface of which I know has been merely scraped, I am determined, through my work as a Practical Theologian, to shine a light on toxic church cultures that feed the evils of SA and to construct better theologies and pastoral supports that honour neurodivergence. An Au-theology or Neu-theology that focuses on a competent working knowledge of the Double Empathy Problem could go a long way to equipping and encouraging churches to create healthy and safe community cultures for autistic congregants where communication differences are fully included, valued and celebrated, and my hope is that my offering here can, in some way, contribute to this.

References

American Psychiatric Association (2013). *Diagnostic and Statistical Manual of Mental Disorders*, 5th edition. American Psychiatric Association.

Oakley, L., & Humphreys, J. (2019a, p. 69). *Escaping the Maze of Spiritual Abuse: Creating Healthy Christian Cultures*. SPCK, quoting Skedgell, K. (2008). *Losing the Way: A Memoir of Spiritual Longing, Manipulation, Abuse, and Escape*. Bay Tree Publishing.

Oakley, L., & Humphreys, J. (2019b, p. 67). *Escaping the Maze of Spiritual Abuse: Creating Healthy Christian Cultures*. SPCK, quoting Diederich, F. R. (2017). *Broken Trust: A Practical Guide to Identify and Recover from Toxic Faith, Toxic Church, and Spiritual Abuse*. Createspace Independent Publishing Platform.

Oakley, L., & Kinmond, K. (2013). *Breaking the Silence on Spiritual Abuse*. Palgrave Macmillan.

Pearson, A., Rose, K., & Rees, J. (2022). 'I felt like I deserved it because I was autistic': Understanding the impact of interpersonal victimization in the lives of autistic people. *Autism, 27*(2), 500–511. https://doi.org/10.1177/13623613221104546

Peppiatt, G. E. (2007). *Integrating Shame, Christianity and Cognitive Behavioural Psychotherapy: A Hermeneutic Study* [Unpublished thesis]. M.Ed. Counselling, University of Derby.

Rumball, F., Happé, F., & Grey, N. (2020). Experience of trauma and PTSD symptoms in autistic adults: Risk of PTSD development following DSM-5 and Non-DSM-5 traumatic life events. *Autism Research, 13*(12), 2122–2132. https://doi.org/10.1002/aur.2306

Chapter 18:

'I couldn't describe to you this pain that I've lived with for so long': How the Double Empathy Problem and Hermeneutical Injustices Contribute to Autistic Adults' Disparate Health Care Access

Kathryn Williams

Introduction

The Double Empathy Problem is increasingly recognized within health care literature as contributing to autistic adults' poor health care access and health outcomes (e.g., Strömberg et al., 2021; Weir et al., 2022). Coined by Dr. Damian Milton to refute the assumptions of proponents of deficit models of autism, such as autistic people lacking a theory of mind (e.g., Happé, 1993), the Double Empathy Problem occurs when interactions between people with different life experiences and 'ways of being' (Milton et al., 2022) – such as autistic and non-autistic people – break down due to a lack of mutual understanding and reciprocity. The non-autistic social majority perceives this as a 'breach' of social norms (Milton, 2012). Within health care, the Double Empathy Problem can contribute to autistic patients not having their health care needs met as they do not 'perform' illness (see Hillman (2014) for an account of the performance of illness) as expected (Ali et al., 2022; Strömberg et al., 2021), which is then perceived as a 'breach' of the social norms of patient behaviour.

Despite the increasing recognition of the Double Empathy Problem within health care research, the medical model – in which a person with neurological differences and/or physical impairments is seen as inherently disabled and in need of treatment or curing – prevails. Under the medical model, the fault for breakdowns in communication is situated within autistic people. Autistic people are deemed as having an inherent communication 'deficit' or 'disorder', which is often cited as the cause of a lack of reciprocity between autistic and non-autistic communicators (Araujo et al., 2022). Of particular importance to health care communication, some researchers consider autistic people as inherently lacking the ability to determine what information is relevant in conversations (e.g., Papp, 2006). These views construct and reproduce a compulsory communicative normalcy, with those who do not meet it being deemed deviant or in breach of social norms.

Outside of the autism literature, researchers studying communication between health care practitioners and their patients have found breakdowns in relevance and understanding. However, rather than situating this breakdown as a communication deficit within patients, there is recognition that the differing lifeworlds of health care practitioners and their patients – or even between health care practitioners from different clinical specialities – leads to a mismatch in cultural competence and the resulting misunderstanding (e.g., Batten et al., 2019). This mirrors empirical research into the Double Empathy Problem between autistic and non-autistic conversation pairs, which also uses relevance theory to conclude that the breakdown in understanding is mutual and no party is more at 'fault' than the other (G. L. Williams et al., 2021).

The increased use of the Double Empathy Problem in research and practice has also seen an increase in its tenets being misused or misunderstood. For instance, a recent study into communication between autistic teenagers and their health care practitioners referenced the Double Empathy Problem while situating 'challenges in social connection' within the autistic participants (Araujo et al., 2022). The irony of this contributory hermeneutical injustice (Catala et al., 2021) – more on this later – is that the Double Empathy Problem is likely to be partially a result of hermeneutical injustices. This form of epistemic injustice occurs when a speaker (here an autistic person) is disadvantaged or unable to make sense of their experiences in a way that either harms or wrongs them due to a lack of terms or concepts (Annesley, 2020; Carel & Kidd, 2014; Fricker, 2007; Pohlhaus, Jr., 2019). The non-autistic social majority construct and uphold the communicative normalcy and neuronormativity that lead to perceived social 'breaches' through acts of '*willful hermeneutical ignorance*' (Pohlhaus, Jr., 2019, p. 17) in which there is little attempt to acknowledge that there are different ways of experiencing the world or, where it is acknowledged, dismissing or ignoring these differences.

In this chapter, I use data from my study into the telehealth experiences of autistic people to explore instances of the Double Empathy Problem that are problematized within autistic patients to see how they affect medical encounters. I particularly focus on my autistic participants' stories of inability to describe symptoms, pain and emotions. Rather than the idea that autistic adults essentially cannot describe these embodied sensations, I consider that autistic adults might struggle to describe these sensations because non-autistic people's experiences inform the ways things like pain and emotions are conceptualized – both the words used and the expected 'performance' of these experiences. These could be considered examples of hermeneutical injustice. I employ instances of my autistic participants being disbelieved by their health care practitioner (known as testimonial injustice) within their accounts and discuss how these could lead to autistic adults being excluded from contributing to the collective meaning-making which enables shared understanding, known as societal hermeneutical resources, which I believe to be a key contributor to the Double Empathy Problem. If autistic people were enabled to contribute to society's collective hermeneutical resources, there is likely to be an increase in mutual reciprocity and empathy, potentially reducing instances of the Double Empathy Problem.

Methods

The data for this chapter were collected during the summer of 2022 as part of my master's research regarding autistic adults' experiences of ableism during their telehealth appointments. The project received ethical approval from Cardiff University's Social Science Research Ethics Committee, study reference 131. A recruitment advertisement was shared on social media for autistic adults (18 +) to self-refer to the study if they had received an appointment using telehealth – health care by telephone or video call – in the United Kingdom within the past five years. As there is little difference in presentation or research responses, autistic adults could be formally or self-diagnosed and no diagnostic paperwork was requested as 'proof' of diagnosis (Brice et al., 2021; Schalk, 2017).

Participant-facing information included Easy Read versions that were sent to all potential participants without the need for participants to request these. Documents were produced on pale yellow backgrounds to mitigate the visual processing difficulties some autistic people have, as suggested by members of the autistic community who were consulted during the project's conceptualization and design stages. I utilized a three-stage consent process (written consent by pdf or online using Qualtrics, the participant telling me in their own words their understanding of what they were consenting to at the start of each interview, followed by a verbal – spoken or typed – confirmation that they were happy to proceed) to avoid the infantilizing automatic exclusion of autistic people with a co-occurring learning disability. Ten participants completed the consent process and were interviewed by a mode of their choice, either video call (n = 8), synchronous Zoom text chat (n = 1) or email (n = 1). Participants were given a colour-coded copy of the interview guide in advance to prepare what they might like to discuss during interviews. Most participants were White British, with one Pakistani, one Latino, one Mixed White and one White non-British participant. Ages ranged from 26 to 61, with a mean age of 41. Participants spanned the gender spectrum, with four cisgender women, three non-binary people, one transgender woman, one gender-fluid person, and one cisgender man. While all participants primarily discussed their experiences as autistic patients, two participants also consented to be identified in write-ups as health care practitioners. Their accounts give additional perspectives on the difficulties faced during (tele)health care interactions.

Interviews were transcribed and pseudonymized immediately after ending. Participants could choose their pseudonyms to balance the erasure of autistic identity within research literature with the need for anonymity. Data were analysed using Braun and Clarke's (2022) six-phase reflexive thematic analysis:

1. Familiarization through multiple readings of the transcripts, making notes of initial thoughts in the margins and memo writing.
2. Coding, initially using an experiential semantic approach with later coding rounds using a latent, critical approach focusing on how my participants talked about their health care experiences.
3. Generating initial themes and cross-checking them across the dataset.
4. Developing themes, combining similar initial themes and recoding transcripts where themes needed further development.
5. Naming themes to ensure they captured the meaning of each theme.
6. Writing up while maintaining reflexivity and theme construction throughout the writing period.

This chapter focuses on instances of the Double Empathy Problem and epistemic injustices within the original analysis. Before writing this chapter, a further round of deductive coding was undertaken to ensure no missing items and that instances of the Double Empathy Problem and epistemic injustices were found across the dataset. A write-up of the full data analysis can be found in my master's dissertation (see K. Williams, 2022).

The Double Empathy Problem

The difficulties Batten (2019) described in the communication between health care practitioners and their patients have been considered by autistic clinician-researchers, who have theorized that this mismatch of relevance and understanding is another example of the Double Empathy Problem (Shaw et al., 2023), and is something that health care practitioners are aware of and seek to mitigate. Christina, one of the study participants who is also a health care practitioner, provided an account of how they are mindful of potential breakdowns in understanding between health care practitioners and patients, regardless of neurotype:

> *[W]hat a patient understands can be very, very different to what the doctor thinks they understand, and it's really important to keep that in mind on both aspects. And for that reason, a lot of the time, you know, you may call in a patient for a face-to-face just to make sure that they've understood properly, and I've definitely had patients not understand.*

However, this difficulty seems to be more common in communication between autistic patients and (presumed to be) non-autistic health care practitioners. Drs Doherty and Shaw have described this as the triple empathy problem (Shaw et al., 2023). Furthermore, rather than acknowledging that breakdowns are a result of differing cultural competencies (as with non-autistic patients), the breakdown in communication is perceived and talked about as a breach, such as in Daisy's account:

> *And so I've tried to speak in their language and say, 'Oh yeah, take my blood pressure at home. I do have a home blood pressure monitor, but I get stressed when I'm doing it, so it probably doesn't get a good reading, so I'm better to come to the surgery to have my blood pressure done.' But that comes across as I don't like doing it, so I don't know why they wrote I don't like doing it, I thought I got the language just right. To make it sound as if I spoke their language. But that was frustrating.*

Daisy described how she felt that she spoke a 'different language' to her health care practitioner and how she tried to 'speak in their language'. Despite this extra cognitive burden taken on by the autistic participant, Daisy's account of her neurotypical health care practitioner's interpretation of their interaction was that Daisy just '[didn't] like' taking her own blood pressure at home, and this was written as 'fact' into Daisy's medical file.

Despite the Double Empathy Problem being theorized within the autism literature, breakdowns in mutual understanding based on cultural competencies that are perceived as 'breaches' in social norms by the members of the dominant social group can also be found outside of differences in neurotype. For instance, Scragger's account reminds us that the Double Empathy Problem can be experienced between any two (or more) people with differing dispositions, such as those with different ethnic or cultural backgrounds:

> *Yeah, cause if in [European country] if I was crying and a doctor went like this < opens arms wide >, they were, you know I'd give them a hug. They were gonna make me feel better. Here, I did that, and oh my God! Was that the wrong move! The looks I got of, 'What the hell are you doing? Get out of this room!' You know, so that, not knowing how to react to people and trying to, you know, fit in and do the right thing, it all just, I suddenly became incapable of knowing how to act in a doctor surgery and then that anxiety just means I'm at my worst.*

That said, the specificity of difficulties arising with mutual understanding due to conversation partners being cross-neurotype was highlighted in Sarah's account of trying to describe her pain to health care practitioners, in which she thought that I – an autistic non-health care practitioner – would 'get more idea' about her pain than a non-autistic health care practitioner:

> *I couldn't describe to you this pain that I've lived with for so long now, I wouldn't be able to describe it to you properly. Whereas I suppose I, actually, cause you're autistic, you would probably get more idea than a non-autistic person.*

Sarah suggests that as we are both autistic, there would be no breakdown in mutual understanding if she described her pain to me. There would be no 'breach' of 'norms' in her performance or testimony of her pain with an autistic conversation partner. This is likely due to our shared cultural competencies and, therefore, sharing hermeneutical resources regarding autistic expression of pain and ways of being, including how we talk about our experiences. Therefore, I suggest that the Double Empathy Problem is closely linked to epistemic injustice, in which people who belong to a minoritized group's 'capacity as knowers' (Pohlhaus, Jr., 2019, p. 16) are harmed either due to being seen as unreliable knowledge producers (testimonial injustice) or – more relevant to the Double Empathy Problem – by not having the social or cognitive resources to be able to talk about their experiences in a way that is understandable by the social majority (hermeneutical injustice). The rest of the chapter focuses on how the participants' accounts provide examples of where they have been subjected to epistemic injustices. I later return to the Double Empathy Problem to discuss how both it and epistemic injustices are mutually constructed and upheld in a society designed around neuronormativity.

Testimonial injustice

Testimonial injustices occur when a person's knowledge is unduly deemed to be inaccurate or unreliable in a way that harms them due to them belonging to a minoritized group (Fricker, 2007). For instance, autistic people are often subjected to a subset of testimonial injustice known as preemptive testimonial injustice, in which it is assumed that autistic people are inherently incapable of correctly describing their experiences *because* they are autistic, and instead, their parent/carers are engaged with as epistemically more valid knowers (Catala et al., 2021). More commonly discussed, however, are systematic testimonial injustices in which the hearer dismisses a speaker's testimony. While this is often considered to occur at an individual level, systematic testimonial injustices can be structural when 'common-sense' theories of experience – e.g., due to institutions being structured around neuronormativity – mean that it is standard to dismiss the first-person testimony of people from minoritized groups, e.g., autistic people (Catala et al., 2021).

Within health care, women are often subjected to systematic testimonial injustice, for example, having their symptoms of heart attack being dismissed as a less serious condition (such as anxiety) due to their atypical presentation, despite health care practitioners being aware of these atypical presentations appearing more frequently in female patients (Annesley, 2020). For autistic patients, I consider that the Double Empathy Problem and the pathologizing of autistic communication leads to testimonial injustices when autistic patients are communicating with their non-autistic health care practitioners.

In the following example, ACP16 gives an account of their health care practitioner not believing they are autistic:

> *'[H]e demanded to know why I wanted a [specific] referral. Not asked, not enquired, demanded. I explained that I'd already written out in detail in the online application (which he clearly hadn't read. And he told me to explain anyway) so I pointed out 40% of autistic people have [other neurodivergence], to which he retorted, 'Why do you think you have autism?' Uhh … because I'm autistic? I was diagnosed a few years back? Apparently that information was not on my records, and he told me to upload evidence – but he didn't know how to do that – so I had to take a copy of my NHS diagnostics paperwork into the surgery for them to scan on.'*

ACP16's account is interpretable as an example of their health care practitioner deeming them untrustworthy. Indeed, the burden of proving that they are autistic fell on them, despite having a National Health Service (NHS) diagnosis. This extra labour resulting from being or feeling disbelieved is something that Pohlhaus, Jr. has termed 'epistemic agential injustice' (Pohlhaus, Jr., 2019, p. 21). Furthermore, their account provides an example of their health care practitioner not being reciprocal with their language around autism, as ACP16's use of 'autistic' is responded to by their health care practitioner with 'have autism'. This is hearable as a deployment of neurotypical power to construct appropriate communication and vocabulary, while being a manifest example of the Double Empathy Problem as the health care practitioner fails to relate to or empathize with his autistic patient. Furthermore, this experience is not unusual. Sarah describes how her health care practitioner dismissed her pain and other medical symptoms and failed to empathize with her needs by deploying the autistic characteristic of Sarah having sensory processing differences as a reason to reject her testimony:

> *This doctor said, 'You're imagining your pain, and I think what you need to do is go back to your GP and ask for some antidepressants, and the antidepressants will help suppress all the sensory issues that you are experiencing.'*

These instances of testimonial injustice, together with the Double Empathy Problem, can lead to what is known as testimonial smothering, in which a person whose testimony has been dismissed or inappropriately deemed uncredible due to bias stops engaging with the person or structures that have dismissed them (Catala et al., 2021). For instance, Josie described why she seeks private health care where possible due to being 'too weird' for NHS services:

> *I'm always very sceptical that standard health care will actually be able to help quite often. Because so much of my experience has been like, 'Oh, you're too weird for us to know what to do,' or 'Oh, that's not actually a real problem. You're just imagining it.' Like so much of it has just been like, 'We provide health care for these things, and you're just not that.'*

Furthermore, testimonial injustices – including testimonial smothering – can lead to hermeneutical injustices, as those who are deemed credible (in relation to this chapter, non-autistic health care practitioners) are those who create hermeneutical resources. That is, the collective social resources used to determine understanding and meaning (Catala et al.,

2021). In the case of my participants, the dismissal of their lived experience of their health care needs (testimonial injustice) results in a lack of words or concepts for them to be able to describe their experiences in the future effectively and for their 'performance' of illness being misunderstood (hermeneutical injustice), and for a mutual difficulty in empathy and understanding (the Double Empathy Problem).

Hermeneutical injustice

Without dismissing the intrinsic difficulties some autistic people might have in describing how they feel, such as those who have alexithymia (Cassidy et al., 2014; Moseley et al., 2020), I consider that for many autistic people, their struggle to describe bodily sensations might be due to non-autistic people's experiences creating the ways in which pain and emotions are conceptualized – both the words used and the expected 'performance' of these experiences. When all conversation members share hermeneutical resources – such as Christina and Daisy due to them being health care practitioners and autistic patients – there are likely to be fewer communication breakdowns. As Daisy says in her interview, 'I'm a [health care practitioner] too, which helps as I already know how it works, and I can ask for what I need'.

Christina's account provides an example of how important shared hermeneutical resources are, especially when considering the different ways vocabulary can be understood in different cultural contexts:

> *[B]eing medically literate is very helpful because I know the terms to use, whereas other patients will use words that don't have the same meaning in lay terms like 'tender' is a good one, or 'fever'. What people interpret it as, and what fever mean, and feeling feverish and things like that.*

In practice, hermeneutical resources are taken for granted as being intrinsically part of human experience and knowledge rather than acknowledged as being socially constructed. The rapid shift to telehealth during the COVID-19 pandemic reveals how the act of describing medical symptoms is not a straightforward, common-sense act but rather is mutually and situationally negotiated and relies on all parties having access to mutually understandable concepts and vocabulary:

> *It was, yeah, trying to explain things and describe things and explain what your [body part] looks like over the phone. And how exercises hurt, cos usually obviously you go to [joint care] you'll usually say, 'Oh, when I put a [body part] like this, it kind of hurts.' But trying to verbalise that over the phone was difficult. Yeah, trying to explain what the [symptoms] that particularly hurt your [body part]. So you just try to find like terms to describe things like [symptoms]. And just hope that they know what you're talking about*
>
> (Amy)

Amy's extract demonstrates how hermeneutical resources are based on cultural norms. The resources drawn upon to describe joint pain rely on the (previous) cultural norm of in-person health care. Therefore, telehealth revealed a gap in hermeneutical resources: how to describe something you would usually physically demonstrate in an understandable way. The 'typical' way of expressing herself (physically showing the health care practitioner what was wrong with the joint) was impossible. Instead, Amy had to try to find 'terms' to describe something she would typically show, putting her and her health care practitioner at a disadvantage and reducing the efficacy of her health care.

Lyla describes a similar difficulty with telehealth:

> *I don't feel like they were real doctor's appointments cause I was just like talking to someone on the phone, especially if they needed to actually check me physically, or look for something. There's only so much I can do with talking words to describe what – at some point when you're in the room, they get the stethoscope out or, you know, check something or something happens to check you, to make sure you're okay.*

As telehealth was so new at the start of the pandemic, there was a lack of hermeneutical resources to describe something that would have been quite simple face-to-face. As with Amy, Lyla found it difficult to put into 'talking words' embodied sensations. This led to her feeling like telephone appointments were not 'real doctor's appointments', demonstrating how a lack of hermeneutical resources can lead to a perceived lack of credibility.

When there is little to no access to shared hermeneutical resources, as with autistic patients and non-autistic health care practitioners, autistic patients can be subjected to hermeneutical injustices. Here, I focus on three types of hermeneutical injustice:

- **Conceptual:** Conceptual hermeneutical injustices occur when there is a gap in the collective hermeneutical resources to describe or make sense of experience.
- **Contributory:** Contributory hermeneutical injustices occur when minoritized groups have a way to describe or make sense of experience, but dominant social groups – in this case, neurotypicals – either ignore or dismiss these concepts.
- **Expressive:** Expressive hermeneutical injustices occur when the *way* in which something is communicated is implicated in misunderstanding and credibility rather than the semantic content of *what* is being said.

See Catala et al.'s (2021) paper for a detailed description of these and other types of epistemic injustice and how they relate to autistic experiences.

Iestyn's account of his difficulty in using numerical pain scales provides an example of a conceptual hermeneutical injustice:

> *I didn't actually quite know how to respond. Quite often, you know, asking those kinds of questions like you know, 'How much does it hurt?' Well I don't know. I don't know, as we've discussed before, the one to ten pain scales are difficult for a lot of us, like, you know. Certainly difficult for me.*

The assumption that numerical pain scales are helpful for all patients underpins their heavy usage within health care (Karcioglu et al., 2018). Despite autistic people – as with Iestyn – claiming that they are a barrier to them effectively accessing health care (Kalingel-Levi et al., 2022; Nicolaidis et al., 2015), they uncritically remain in use. When asked how his experiences could be improved, Iestyn elaborated on his difficulty using pain scales, first highlighting the lack of shared hermeneutical resources, which contributes to the Double Empathy Problem as health care practitioners fail to understand the difficulty their autistic patients are having. However, he concludes that he is '*just not very good at interpreting what pain is*', which is indicative of Iestyn internalizing the status quo that autistic people inherently struggle to do this rather than it being linked to the lack of shared hermeneutical resources:

> *[T]ime to ask what on earth is meant by moderate ... you know a benchmark to put it against. It's the lack of benchmarks that do my box in with these kind of, you know, quite painful, very painful, not painful at all type of things. You know, I'm just not very good at interpreting what pain is really.*

Pink Princess also provides an account of her experiencing conceptual hermeneutical injustices. She describes being unable to ask for help because, without access to collective hermeneutical resources, there is not a way for her to do it:

> *Yes, but I didn't know what I was asking for. Looking back, I wasn't asking for what I actually went there for. I said I needed confidence, I needed these things. In actual fact, that was probably me starting to come out to say that my [Life event 1], I'm not coping. I need support. But I have none of that vocabulary to be able to ask for it.*

While Iestyn and Pink Princess problematized the breakdown in communication in themselves through their accounts – Iestyn believing that he was unable to describe pain, and Pink Princess saying that she lacks the required vocabulary to seek help – Sarah told a story of her experience of her health care practitioner taking no responsibility for the success or failure of their interaction. Sarah described how she needed to provide contextual information to be able to describe her pain. She explained to her health care practitioner that she needed to give this extra information but she was cut off during her account. Sarah's health care practitioner did not allow her to respond to his question in the way she needed to make sense of, and make intelligible, her experience. Instead, he belittled Sarah as she tried to get help for her painful condition:

> *Then he said to me, 'Would you say your pain is the same as it was?' So it almost felt like I was in a courtroom being examined by a barrister who wouldn't let you give the full answer and it was only what they wanted to hear. So I said, 'Well, when I was referred by my doctor, the pain was different and it was so severe I couldn't cope.' So he said, 'Well, can you cope now?' And I said, 'Well, yes. I've got used to the pain, but when you're autistic your sensory experience is different and I have a very high pain threshold, but that doesn't mean to say I'm not struggling with pain because I've noticed it. You know, the pain has affected my life considerably and that I'm not able to do some things because of what the pain's done.' And then it was just like he kept repeatedly asking me he wanted a yes or no answer. So eventually I just said, I agreed to stop him asking me the same question over and over again because I thought, well maybe he doesn't understand what I'm saying.*

Sarah's account is an example of a contributory hermeneutical injustice. While it is known that health care practitioners subject their patients to epistemic injustices and complain '*that patients' speech is full of irrelevant information*' (Carel & Kidd, 2014), Sarah being openly autistic with her health care practitioner makes her account specifically an example of a contributory hermeneutical injustice. Sarah explained that autistic people are more likely to use more words when communicating due to a fear that they will be misunderstood, sometimes described as 'over-explaining' (Price, 2021). Health care access literature contains several accounts of autistic people being misunderstood during health care interactions (Ali et al., 2022; McMillion et al., 2021; Strömberg et al., 2021), which might lead to an autistic patient 'over-explaining' to be understood. Despite this, Sarah's health care practitioner refused to acknowledge these concepts and required that Sarah meet neuronormative communication standards that were not possible – or warranted – resulting in a failed health care interaction.

Sarah describes how the concepts that she drew on to describe her pain, including her sensory processing differences making her pain threshold higher than typical, were ignored. Instead, her health care practitioner continued to insist that she communicate the way he wanted: only to provide a 'yes' or 'no' answer, implying that the other information she provided was viewed as meaningless (Catala et al., 2021). This dismissal of Sarah's capability as a knower of her pain experiences by her health care practitioner, while he displayed a clear lack of empathy, led to an instance of testimonial smothering. Sarah just '*agreed*' with what the health care practitioner was saying to '*stop him asking [her] the same question over and over again*'. This was also experienced by Iestyn, who wondered if it was '*worth bothering at all*' seeking health care.

Running through most of the participants' accounts were instances of being subjected to expressive hermeneutical injustice. This issue has been researched previously, though not labelled as such, particularly as a non-standard performance of pain meant that it was assumed that autistic people did not feel pain (e.g., Goldschmidt, 2017). This assumption was bolstered by health care practitioners and parent/carer reports of their autistic patients/children, which is suggestive of the link between testimonial injustice – particularly preemptive testimonial injustice – and hermeneutical injustices. Furthermore, I believe that expressive hermeneutical injustice is most likely to be linked to the Double Empathy Problem, as those subjected to it are most likely to be perceived as in a 'breach' of social norms.

Daisy provided an account of her performance of pain leading to her being worried that her health care practitioners are less likely to believe her:

> *I think written appointments would be way more helpful on this because then they'd have to just go on my words. On the phone I sound competent and articulate when I'm on my game, and so if I said I was in pain they might not believe me because I know that I can give birth to children without making a sound or looking distressed, but they don't know that.*

Daisy is describing her fear that the way she 'performs' illness would be seen as illegitimate (Hillman, 2014). As the expected presentation of pain is based on neuronormativity and implied communicative normalcy, Daisy's fear is quite rational, particularly as she is also a health care practitioner and is more aware of these concepts and the idea of legitimized performances. Indeed, there is evidence to suggest that the different presentation of pain and illness from many autistic people is misinterpreted by health care practitioners, leading to poor health care outcomes (e.g., Ali et al., 2022; Knight & Steward, 2021).

Scragger told a story regarding how the way they express their anxiety – and the resulting expressive hermeneutical injustice they faced – led to testimonial smothering:

> *[W]hen I'm anxious and confused and scared they seem to interpret my tone as anger and confrontational very quickly over the phone when, I guess, when they can see me you know they can tell I'm anxious. I mean I still scare some people. I've been kicked out of one clinic because you know they couldn't cope with my stimming but over the phone it's amplified. So I've had situations where I've been told to calm down where I've been told that if I don't control my tone and speak appropriately the call will be ended. I mean, what do you do with that? What do you do when you're just terrified and you're trying to convey? Yeah, I find it hard to explain what's going on in my body anyway. So I always sound anxious when I'm trying to describe something that I find really difficult to describe. So the result is, I do not call the doctors for myself very often at all.*

Scragger provides an account of how conceptual hermeneutical injustice – being confused and struggling to make themself understood during health care appointments – leads to anxiety. The stimming and change in vocal tone that accompanies Scragger's anxiety leads to expressive hermeneutical injustice whereby Scragger's health care practitioner does not correctly interpret their anxiety but instead interprets Scragger's vocal tone as aggressive and threatens to terminate their telephone appointment. This threat and accompanying increase in anxiety, for Scragger, has led to another instance of testimonial smothering; Scragger '*[does] not call the doctors for [themself] very often at all*', an outcome that could be considered an '*epistemically justified mistrust of health care providers*' (Annesley, 2020).

However, Scragger's account is not only an example of epistemic injustices. It is also a clear instance of a health care practitioner demonstrating a lack of empathy for their autistic patient due to a lack of mutual understanding and reciprocity. I believe this indicates the link between epistemic injustice – particularly hermeneutical injustice – and the Double Empathy Problem. Scragger's tone being interpreted as aggressive – a 'breach' of appropriate patient communication – likely stems from the dominant social group (neurotypicals) being sole contributors to the hermeneutical resources determining 'correct' communication and is potentially exacerbated by (un)conscious bias against autistic communication styles. This bias, leading to incorrect health care practitioner interpretation, is suggested later in Scragger's interview when they tell me that they and their husband '*were suddenly being accused with all of these things, and the only thing that had changed was that [they] were now diagnosed autistic*'.

Despite the overwhelmingly negative accounts from my participants, there were some descriptions of good practices which improved their access to shared hermeneutical resources and, therefore, their access to health care. Pink Princess's account of her experiences provides an example of how difficulties in communication between health care practitioners and autistic patients are not due to inherent deficits within the autistic patient. Rather, they are due to a lack of access to shared hermeneutical resources. When this lack is addressed, and there is a shared language and understanding, communication breakdowns are mitigated:

> *If you don't have that vocabulary, you can't ask for the help that you need. So in the EPA one, because it was all around how the [Life event 2] was happening – again, not pleasant – but I knew the vocabulary to use. Whereas before, I didn't, and if you are accessing telecare for the first time without 18 plus months of knowledge and knowing that you need to, you're not going to say the right thing, and the person is not going t... – unless they can crack you, and most people would not open up to you, you're not going to get the right answer.*

Pink Princess talks about her journey of understanding and gaining access to the required hermeneutical resources over the course of 18 months while being supported to access specialist health care services. Through this time, and a willingness from the health care practitioner to accept her testimony and enable Pink Princess to contribute to collective hermeneutical resources, Pink Princess's access to health care was improved. Pink Princess went on to explain that the support she received enabled her to explain that she *does* have emotion, but that it looks different from non-autistic emotion. Before this support, Pink Princess thought she '[didn't] do emotion' and, therefore, her need for emotional support was invalid:

> *But there's a lot of um, for anyone and especially for me who was autistic, who went, 'I don't do emotion.' Er ... I do do emotion, but my emotional bar is a lot higher than other people. So it was like, 'You don't do emotion, you shouldn't be feeling like this, you should just be getting on with life, it doesn't matter, etc.'*

Pink Princess's health care practitioner's empathetic support to enable her to access the concepts and vocabulary needed to seek support for her emotional well-being is an example of an 'epistemically just practice' (Carel & Kidd, 2014). Their good practice avoids the potential for testimonial smothering, as Pink Princess felt supported rather than rejected, and mitigates the potential effect of the Double Empathy Problem through the health care practitioner engaging in 'true reciprocity' (Gernsbacher, 2006).

Conclusions and suggestions for improvements and future research

The Double Empathy Problem, the societal pathologization of autistic communication and societal structures built around neuronormativity cause autistic people to be excluded from collective meaning-making processes through testimonial injustices. This creates hermeneutical injustices that can lead to both autistic patients and their health care practitioners lacking the hermeneutical resources to fully understand their health care needs, resulting in disparate access to health care and poor health outcomes.

The link between testimonial injustices and hermeneutical injustices is discussed in the health care literature (e.g., Annesley, 2020). In the case of autistic patients, I believe that the issue is twofold: autistic patients lack the terms necessary to describe their experiences, such as Iestyn finding it difficult to use pain scales, and health care practitioners lack the hermeneutical resources to understand autistic experiences as described (conceptual hermeneutical injustice). Health care practitioners then dismiss or disbelieve their autistic patients (testimonial injustice); for instance, ACP16's health care practitioner requiring proof of ACP16's autism diagnosis, perpetuated by the assumption that there is a 'correct' way to perform illness and pain to be deemed legitimately in need of health care (Hillman, 2014), a performance standard autistic patients often fail to meet (expressive hermeneutical injustice). Being dismissed or frequently misunderstood by health care practitioners can lead to autistic people choosing not to seek health care or to 'go along' with what their health care practitioner says, resulting in unmet health care needs (testimonial smothering), as seen in the examples from Sarah and Scragger. Furthermore, the lack of empathetic reciprocity seen from health care practitioners toward their autistic patients is also indicative of the link between epistemic injustice and the Double Empathy Problem.

Carel & Kidd (2014) talk about how '*ill people are more vulnerable to hermeneutical injustice*' as it can be difficult to communicate the complexities of illness experiences to those who have no embodied experience of it themselves. This can transfer to autistic people trying to communicate the complexities of autistic experiences. As with the triple empathy problem field (Shaw et al., 2023), this will have a compounding effect, arguably placing autistic patients at even greater risk of being subjected to hermeneutical injustices. To mitigate this, health care practitioners should follow the example of Pink Princess's health care practitioner and aim to become 'testimonially just clinicians' (Carel & Kidd, 2014), whereby they are sensitive to the possibility of a lack of hermeneutical resources being the cause of communication breakdowns between them and their autistic patients and do not dismiss their autistic patients' credibility as knowers. They should not assume that their autistic patients are communicatively incompetent but should also provide reasonable adjustments – such as Daisy's suggestion of written communication – to facilitate reciprocal communication. By supporting patients to understand and talk about their experiences, for example, using tools such as the phenomenological toolkit designed by Carel and Kidd (see Carel & Kidd, 2014), autistic adults' access to health care will likely be improved. Furthermore, health care practitioners need to believe the testimony of their autistic patients; in other words, they need to give them the benefit of the doubt. If autistic patients are not believed, they will not be enabled to contribute to collective hermeneutical resources, meaning that they will continue to be misunderstood, perpetuating the disbelief.

That said, there must be care to ensure that these issues are not solely individualized within health care practitioners, just as communication breakdowns should not be situated in individual autistic patients. Rather, it should be acknowledged that current health care structures uphold and reproduce epistemic injustices (Carel & Kidd, 2014) due to being designed around neuronormativity and communicative normalcy. For autistic people to be understood, neuronormative assumptions need to be made visible and questioned. To do this, future empirical research into the Double Empathy Problem could be conducted using a lens of epistemic injustice, particularly within health care settings. Ideally, this research should be observational to capture the interpersonal nature of communication. To avoid perpetuating hermeneutical injustices, research teams should include autistic members, and all projects should be coproduced with lay members of the autistic community to ensure an emancipatory approach and to redress epistemic injustices within autism research.

Autistic people need to be seen as credible and reliable testimonial agents. They must be enabled to contribute to collective understandings, that is, the hermeneutical resources that both speakers and listeners draw on to ensure mutual understanding. A greater contribution to collective understanding from autistic people will likely result in improved reciprocity, a reduction in testimonial injustices, and fewer instances of the Double Empathy Problem.

References

Ali, D., O'Brien, S., Hull, L., Kenny, L., & Mandy, W. (2022). 'The key to this is not so much the technology. It's the individual who is using the technology': Perspectives on telehealth delivery for autistic adults during the COVID-19 pandemic. *Autism, 27*(2), 1–8. https://doi.org/10.1177/13623613221108010

Annesley, K. (2020). Connecting epistemic injustice and justified belief in health-related conspiracies. *Ethics, Medicine and Public Health, 15*, 100545. https://doi.org/10.1016/j.jemep.2020.100545

Araujo, M., Mophosho, M., & Moonsamy, S. (2022). Communication strategies used by adolescents with autism spectrum disorder and health professionals during treatment. *African Journal of Disability, 11*, 1–8. https://doi.org/10.4102/AJOD.V11I0.811

Batten, J. N., Wong, B. O., Hanks, W. F., & Magnus, D. C. (2019). Treatability statements in serious illness: The gap between what is said and what is heard. *Cambridge Quarterly of Health Care Ethics, 28*(3), 394–404. https://doi.org/10.1017/S096318011900029X

Braun, V., & Clarke, V. (2022). *Thematic Analysis: A Practical Guide*. SAGE Publications Ltd.

Brice, S., Rodgers, J., Ingham, B., Mason, D., Wilson, C., Freeston, M., Couteur, A. L., & Parr, J. R. (2021). The importance and availability of adjustments to improve access for autistic adults who need mental and physical health care: Findings from UK surveys. *BMJ Open, 11*(3), e043336. https://doi.org/10.1136/bmjopen-2020-043336

Carel, H., & Kidd, I. J. (2014). Epistemic injustice in health care: A philosophial analysis. *Medicine, Health Care and Philosophy, 17*(4), 529–540. https://doi.org/10.1007/s11019-014-9560-2

Cassidy, S., Bradley, P., Robinson, J., Allison, C., McHugh, M., & Baron-Cohen, S. (2014). Suicidal ideation and suicide plans or attempts in adults with Asperger's syndrome attending a specialist diagnostic clinic: A clinical cohort study. *The Lancet Psychiatry, 1*(2), 142–147. https://doi.org/10.1016/S2215-0366(14)70248-2

Catala, A., Faucher, L., & Poirier, P. (2021). Autism, epistemic injustice, and epistemic disablement: A relational account of epistemic agency. *Synthese, 199*(3), 9013–9039. https://doi.org/10.1007/s11229-021-03192-7

Fricker, M. (2007). *Epistemic Injustice: Power and the Ethics of Knowing.* Oxford University Press.

Gernsbacher, M. A. (2006). Toward a behavior of reciprocity. *The Journal of Developmental Processes, 1*(1), 139–152.

Goldschmidt, J. (2017). What happened to Paul? Manifestation of abnormal pain response for individuals with autism spectrum disorder. *Qualitative Health Research, 27*(8), 1133–1145. https://doi.org/10.1177/1049732316644415

Happé, F. G. E. (1993). Communicative competence and theory of mind in autism: A test of relevance theory. *Cognition, 48*(2), 101–119. https://doi.org/10.1016/0010-0277(93)90026-R

Hillman, A. (2014). 'Why must I wait?' The performance of legitimacy in a hospital emergency department. *Sociology of Health & Illness, 36*(4), 485–499. https://doi.org/10.1111/1467-9566.12072

Kalingel-Levi, M., Schreuer, N., Granovsky, Y., Bar-Shalita, T., Weissman-Fogel, I., Hoffman, T., & Gal, E. (2022). "When I'm in pain, everything Is overwhelming": Implications of pain in adults with autism on their daily living and participation. *Frontiers in Psychology, 13.* https://doi.org/10.3389/fpsyg.2022.911756

Karcioglu, O., Topacoglu, H., Dikme, O., & Dikme, O. (2018). A systematic review of the pain scales in adults: Which to use? *The American Journal of Emergency Medicine, 36*(4), 707–714. https://doi.org/10.1016/j.ajem.2018.01.008

Knight, J., & Steward, R. (2021, April 28). *I don't know how much pain I'm in* [Radio broadcast]. BBC. https://www.bbc.co.uk/programmes/p09g1jmz

McMillion, A., Van Herwegen, J., Johnson, A., Monteiro, J., Cronin, A., & Remington, A. (2021). Dental experiences of a group of autistic adults based in the United Kingdom. *Special Care in Dentistry, 41*(4), 474–488. https://doi.org/10.1111/scd.12583

Milton, D. (2012). On the ontological status of autism: The 'double empathy problem'. *Disability & Society, 27*(6), 883–887. https://doi.org/10.1080/09687599.2012.710008

Milton, D., Gurbuz, E., & Lopez, B. (2022). The 'double empathy problem': Ten years on. *Autism, 26*(8), 1901–1903. https://doi.org/10.1177/13623613221129123

Moseley, R. L., Druce, T., & Turner-Cobb, J. M. (2020). 'When my autism broke': A qualitative study spotlighting autistic voices on menopause. *Autism, 24*(6), 1423–1437. https://doi.org/10.1177/1362361319901184

Nicolaidis, C., Raymaker, D. M., Ashkenazy, E., McDonald, K. E., Dern, S., Baggs, A. E., Kapp, S. K., Weiner, M., & Boisclair, W. C. (2015). "Respect the way I need to communicate with you": Health care experiences of adults on the autism spectrum. *Autism, 19*(7), 824–831. https://doi.org/10.1177/1362361315576221

Papp, S. (2006). A relevance-theoretic account of the development and deficits of theory of mind in normally developing children and individuals with autism. *Theory & Psychology, 16*(2), 141–161. https://doi.org/10.1177/0959354306062532

Pohlhaus, Jr., G. (2019). Varieties of epistemic injustice. In I. J. Kidd, J. Medina, & G. Pohlhaus, Jr. (Eds.), *The Routledge Handbook of Epistemic Injustice* (first issued in paperback, pp. 13–26). Routledge, Taylor & Francis Group.

Price, D. (2021, November 9). Autism is not my personality. *Medium.* https://devonprice.medium.com/autism-is-not-my-personality-839581682371

Schalk, S. (2017). Critical disability studies as methodology. *Lateral, 6*(1). https://doi.org/10.25158/L6.1.13

Shaw, S., Carravallah, L., Johnson, M., O'Sullivan, J., Chown, N., Neilson, S., & Doherty, M. (2023). *A 'Triple Empathy Problem' Leads to Adverse Health Care Outcomes for Autistic Adults: A Qualitative Analysis.* INSAR 2023, Stockholm. https://doi.org/10.13140/RG.2.2.14181.06889

Strömberg, M., Liman, L., Bang, P., & Igelström, K. (2021). Experiences of sensory overload and communication barriers by autistic adults in health care settings. *Autism in Adulthood, 4*(1), 66–75. https://doi.org/10.1089/aut.2020.0074

Weir, E., Allison, C., & Baron-Cohen, S. (2022). Autistic adults have poorer quality health care and worse health based on self-report data. *Molecular Autism, 13*(1). https://doi.org/10.1186/s13229-022-00501-w

Williams, G. L., Wharton, T., & Jagoe, C. (2021). Mutual (mis)understanding: Reframing autistic pragmatic "impairments" using relevance theory. *Frontiers in Psychology, 12*, 616664. https://doi.org/10.3389/fpsyg.2021.616664

Williams, K. (2022). *'Why Are You Causing Trouble?': Autistic Adults' Experiences of Ableism During Telehealth Appointments* [Unpublished master's dissertation]. Cardiff University.

Section 3: The DEP in Practice

Chapter 19:

Autistic Flourishing and Double Empathy: Guidance on Promoting Autistic Communication and Experience

Alexandra Newson and Spencer Brower

Historically, the Autistic community has been described as 'lacking' empathy or having the inability to understand others in social contexts (*Diagnostic and Statistical Manual of Mental Disorders*, 5th edition [DSM-5]; Harmsen, 2019). Dehumanizing language and ableist assumptions have been perpetuated in research and practice (Botha & Frost, 2020), including the theory of mind work which states the many 'supposed' deficits of Autistic individuals' ability to understand and communicate the intentions and beliefs of others (Baron-Cohen, 2000). This idea of 'Autistic as deficit' has been contributed to and been reinforced by the occurrence of neuronormativity. Neuronormativity is the expectation that every person functions and communicates the same and has the same type of needs (Chapman & Carel, 2022; Huijg, 2020; Milton, 2020). In 2012, Dr Damian Milton provided a radically different way of viewing the disconnect that happens for Autistic folks in communicating with neurotypical folks, by uncovering a problem that other people theorized around. He called it the Double Empathy Problem. The Double Empathy Problem states that social contexts are co-constructed and therefore the onus for miscommunication does not lie solely on the part of the Autistic person, but rather on Autistic *AND* neurotypical people. Basically, it is like a bad game of Telephone, where both parties are misinterpreting and misunderstanding the communicational cues of one another leading to a mutual problem. Milton (2012) points out that research needs to stop prioritizing the neurotypical perspective and instead ask questions about why neurotypical people are unable to understand neurodivergent people. Furthermore, he suggests that by prioritizing neurotypical perspectives we are further disabling and harming neurodivergent folks and reinforcing neuronormativity.

Mitchell and colleagues (2021) delved into describing the harm that can be created by the misperceptions of neurotypical society on Autistic people by focusing on Autistic mental health and well-being. Their findings support that Autistic people want to establish meaningful social connections, but are often excluded or isolated from connection and belonging due to lack of acceptance, social rejection, pressure to mask or camouflage Autistic traits, lack of readability and stigmatizing beliefs of Autism by neurotypical people. This can lead to adverse mental health needs, like depression, anxiety and suicidality for the Autistic individuals, all of which negatively impact well-being and positive identity. With suicide being the second leading cause of death for Autistic individuals (Camm-Crosbie et al., 2019; Cassidy et al., 2020), it is imperative for researchers to follow the suggestions from Mitchell and colleagues around accepting diversity, unlearning ableist notions of autism, and taking time to understand and learn from Autistic people in ways that promote their preferred communication styles, level of socialization and support needs.

Dr Catherine Crompton and colleagues in the United Kingdom have followed these suggestions by taking the Double Empathy Problem from theory to practice. In studies done on Autistic peer-to-peer communication, they have provided clear evidence that individuals from the same neurotype are able to communicate with the same proficiency as the supposed 'neurotypical standard' (Crompton et al., 2020a). Additionally, their research supports the concept that Autistic people find a sense of belonging, understanding, authenticity, happiness and ease with other Autistic peers as compared to allistic relationships (Crompton et al., 2020b). This may be due to what Crompton and colleagues describe as cross-neurotype understanding alongside the minority status that can be felt amongst non-autistic peers, friends and family. Autistic participants reported having to adapt to the majority neurotypical ways of interacting, communicating and socializing, often to the detriment of their own well-being. This led to increased levels of identity-based minority stress, as detailed in Botha and Frost (2018). More work needs to be done to understand how to use the double empathy framework to better understand not only barriers in communication for Autistic individuals, but also spaces of flourishing and connection.

Autistic flourishing

All people deserve to live a life that includes flourishing. Flourishing is a broad idea that refers to the overall physical and psychological well-being of an individual. There are four main conceptualizations of flourishing proposed by researchers, mainly in the field of psychology (Diener et al., 2010; Huppert & So 2013; Keyes, 2002; Seligman, 2011). In a review of the operational definitions of flourishing, Hone and colleagues (2014) highlighted that many of the conceptualizations have common themes of positive relationships, purpose and meaning, self-acceptance and self-esteem, accomplishment/competence and social factors that indicate overall levels for well-being. Unfortunately, many of these constructs are still viewed through a psychopathology lens and do not accept the premise that there are multiple and varied ways to communicate, socialize and find meaning, or how outside factors, like racism and ableism, impact how individuals access flourishing.

Even less is known specifically about what it means for Autistic people to flourish and how to support this process. Traditional medical model-framed research has written about Autistic traits as symptoms that need be fixed through intervention or treatment. This one-sided perception of Autism has led to understandings of flourishing that do not consider or include Autistic experiences and fail to acknowledge Autistic strengths. This viewpoint was also created without Autistic perspective on what constitutes a good life (Pellicano & Heyworth, 2023). Dr Elizabeth Pellicano and Dr Melanie Heyworth suggest a shift toward constructing an understanding of what it means for Autistic people to flourish. They argue that not only will this shift help us understand the many ways flourishing is experienced by Autistic people, but it will also help provide support for Autistic flourishing by creating a more accurate understanding of individual Autistic experiences.

Margaret Janse van Rensburg and Bridget Liang aim to reframe the focus on flourishing from something an individual is responsible for to something we must support. They describe Autistic flourishing as the responsibility of peers, community and institutions through efforts to understand and promote Autistic culture and provide adequate and well-matched supports and accommodations for Autistic youth (Janse van Rensburg & Liang, 2023). Like the Double Empathy Problem, Janse van Rensburg and Liang highlight that lack of flourishing for Autistic people is not their fault, but the result of systems that do not understand and thus cannot adequately support Autistic individuals. However, given the priority bestowed on deficit-based traditional autism research, it is no wonder institutions and the general public often have misconceptions about autism, and the majority of spaces are not yet designed to promote Autistic flourishing.

Autistic belonging

Like flourishing, belonging is a nuanced concept with an understanding that has also traditionally left out Autistic people. Contrary to much of what is written about autism, many Autistic people desire and enjoy friendships, relationships and community with others. And like neurotypical people, Autistic people are introverted, extraverted and in between. Social belonging is linked to well-being regardless of neurotype. Dr Damian Milton and Tara Sims conducted a study looking at the link between belonging and well-being

(Milton & Sims, 2016). They demonstrated that though Autistic experiences of belonging are diverse, many Autistic people find similar experiences of social stigma and the influences of Autistic traits on social interactions and relationships. They also showed that challenges in these areas often impacted social isolation, empowerment and mental health – all of which related to a sense of belonging. Autistic people often report feeling more comfortable in Autistic-to-Autistic social interactions. The Double Empathy Problem shows that this could be because Autistic people may be more likely to share communication styles and preferences, contributing to a bigger sense of belonging and authentic sharing of self (Crompton et al., 2020a). It is important to promote a view of belonging and well-being that seeks to facilitate better aligned experiences and environments for Autistic people rather than focusing on 'within person' deficits that detract from belonging.
It is a community responsibility to better understand Autistic experiences, rather than assuming that the challenges Autistic people face with flourishing and belonging are due solely to their own deficits. A sense of belonging is linked to stronger Autistic well-being, which promotes Autistic flourishing (Chapman & Carel, 2022; Milton & Sims, 2016). Conversely, when belonging is thwarted, it is likely that flourishing languishes (Keyes, 2002; Skrzypiec et al. 2016). Mismatches between neurotype needs and communication preferences can contribute to uncomfortable conversations and feelings of social rejection, but this does not have to be the case. Increasing knowledge of facilitators and barriers to belonging and flourishing in Autistic people will help create more spaces where Autistic people can engage authentically with others. When Autistic support needs and communication preferences are better understood, reduced expectations to mask and lowered stigma or feelings of being 'othered' will create more positive, open spaces of interaction overall.

Double empathy and masking

Within a neurotypical majority world, Autistic people must navigate situations with others where communication styles do not match (Milton, 2012; Mitchell et al., 2021), interests may not align and understandings of what is comfortable or preferred differ between neurotypes. To cope with this, Autistic people may mask their Autistic traits. The term masking is used by the Autistic community to describe how Autistic people hide or change aspects of themselves in order to fit in with the social expectations of their environment (Chapman & Carel, 2022; Hull et al., 2017; Milner et al., 2019). This might look like monitoring facial expressions, tone of voice, or changing or controlling body movements. It might also involve hiding interests, wearing particular clothing or taking on the characteristics of others.

Although masking can help with the in-the-moment navigation of social situations, many Autistic people report negative outcomes such as lowered self-esteem, internalized ableism, decreased mental health, burnout and suicidal ideation (Botha & Frost, 2020; Hull et al., 2020). Autistic people, as a minority neurotype, often find themselves in situations that require masking much more often than neurotypical people, and with many more detrimental effects. Miller and colleagues (2021) studied masking in Autistic, neurodivergent but not autistic, and neurotypical people to explore the similarities and differences between experiences and reasons for masking in different populations. They found that though there were many similarities in masking across neurotypes, Autistic people talked about the exhaustion that comes from navigating communication differences including preferences and style, which often required them to hide their reactions to discomfort, confusion or sensory overwhelm (Miller et al., 2021). Further, a study by Bernardin et al. (2021) that explored adolescent experiences of masking showed differences in the motivations for masking. Their study found that while neurotypical teens masked mostly to fit in and make friends, Autistic teens were more likely to mask to avoid negative experiences or the social stigma that results from the Double Empathy Problem.

The Double Empathy Problem and social stigma make masking a common experience, but masking is also a barrier to tackling the Double Empathy Problem. Autistic people often experience alexithymia which is difficulty identifying and describing feelings. This can make it more difficult to identify when they are masking. Many Autistic people spend their whole lives masking and don't know it, which means many Autistic people may mask because they do not know the neurotype and expectations of the other person in their interaction. Having to constantly engage in neurotypical communication 'just in case' reinforces the need to mask by upholding neurotypical communication as the norm (Cook et al., 2021), which makes it more difficult to reduce the impacts of the Double Empathy Problem. Each person's reason for masking is deeply personal, but common to the experience is the need or desire to conceal one's Autistic traits either for safety, security or social belonging (Chapman & Carel, 2022; Lawson, 2020). For many Autistic people, masking is also exhausting and has negative impacts on many aspects of their lives. This makes belonging and flourishing incredibly difficult and creates contrived interactions, even between Autistic people. Many people don't even know they are masking because they have been doing it all their life and had no idea why they were so tired, anxious, depressed or confused about who they are and what they like.

Individuals with multiple intersectional identities, such as those who are Queer and Autistic or Black and Autistic, may mask aspects of themselves to avoid stigma (Miller et al., 2021). They may also mask in situations where other visible identities create heightened risk, such as in encounters with police (Hutson et al., 2022; Melmed, 2022) or places where one or more of their identities is the minority. In working to support Autistic people with the process of unmasking, it is important we acknowledge the safety implications of unmasking, as well as the fact that not everyone has the ability to mask aspects of themselves in the first place. Rather than reinforcing masking through social skills which can be harmful (Roberts, 2021), it is important to teach explicitly when masking could be useful and why. It is helpful to provide awareness around which times, places and people might make masking necessary so that masking becomes a tool through building autonomy, self-determination and authenticity.

Cook et al. (2023) interviewed Autistic people to explore their perspectives on what made interactions feel authentic. They looked at both cross-neurotype interactions and intraneurotype interactions. Their study uncovered themes that highlighted the importance of embracing differences in communication styles, interests and perspectives, creating mixed neurotype social spaces that were inclusive and co-created, finding ways to reduce miscommunication, and creating interactions that were enjoyable and authentic for all rather than anxiety-producing and exhausting. These findings go beyond inclusion and awareness of Autistic people toward promoting an understanding of Autistic needs to facilitate belonging and flourishing by reducing the necessity of masking. Educating Autistic and non-autistic people, both about masking and the impacts of masking, may increase the agency Autistic people feel. It may also have a positive impact on reducing communication challenges by increasing understanding of Autistic traits and communication preferences, making it more likely that Autistic individuals can show up fully as their Autistic selves.

Eight senses

Traditionally, only five senses are recognized within individuals. These include visual (sight), olfactory (smell), tactile (touch), auditory (hear) and gustatory (taste) senses. However, there are three other senses that can impact how Autistic and non-Autistic people interact with their environment and communicate with others. These include:

- **Proprioception**: the senses we feel in our joints and muscles that dictate our body position, orientation within space and coordination.
- **Interception**: the senses we feel in our internal organs that provide signals for our physical and emotional states. This can dictate our feelings of hunger, thirst, pain, joy, urination, etc.
- **Vestibular**: centred in our inner ear and controlling our sense of balance, posture and movement.

The now eight recognized senses can be either hyper (over) or hypo (under) sensitive, particularly for neurodivergent and Autistic folks. This can mean that individuals are extremely aware of sounds in their environment, have highly attuned taste buds that can tell the smallest differences in taste and have large pangs of hunger or thirst. It can also mean individuals can bump into counters, tables and doors, forget to go to the bathroom or not notice visual changes in the environment. These senses can also change depending on co-occurring mental health needs, disabilities, illnesses or general capacity. This can make it difficult for Autistic individuals to communicate effectively or similarly across settings and across people. A slight change in environment or schedule can disrupt the sensory profile of one person, while being affirming to another. When using the double empathy framework, it is essential to understand how this sensory landscape and response can affect communication abilities, styles and preferences for Autistic folks.

Autistic communication preferences

Autistic communication preferences and styles are distinct from neurotypical ones, but there are also variations across Autistic people. Communication is the words we say to each other and even the body language we use, but it is also more than that. Many people have particular ways of communicating, such as preferring texting over phone conversations, finding eye contact overwhelming or distracting, or preferring to talk about interests over small talk. For Autistic people, their Autistic traits may influence their communication styles and preferences. For example, those who prefer texting or email over phone or in-person conversations may appreciate the time to process the message and the removal of needing to read body language. Specific interests may help reduce social discomfort or provide motivation to connect with others. Howard and Sedgewick (2021) conducted a study to explore communication preferences in Autistic adults which found that communication mode preferences differ widely depending on the scenario. Further, they found that preferences depended on whether that scenario involved people who were known to the Autistic person or whether they were unknown. The study also highlighted the preference for written communication because it reduced the necessity to mask. The challenges and negative effects associated with masking support the need to know more about Autistic communication preferences in order to create more accessible interactions, whether personal or professional.

Because neurotypical people lack lived experience with Autistic traits, challenges in communication often arise because neurotypical people cannot often anticipate the needs of their Autistic conversational partners. It is important to understand differences in communication styles and preferences when addressing the Double Empathy Problem, creating a deeper understanding first that differences exist and then what those differences might be. Autistic people have expressed masking less in an online context (Jedrzjewska & Dewey, 2022). There is also research that suggests that many Autistic people prefer online contexts such as social media, texting and email due to a reduction in sensory and anxiety overwhelm, as well as the opportunity to maintain energy balance. This has important implications for the meaningful inclusion of Autistic individuals in spaces typically designed for neurotypicals such as the workplace or universities. Considering the Double Empathy Problem and communication preferences would serve to reduce the barriers to authentic communication posed by mismatches in communication styles and preferences, and create spaces where communication is approached with curiosity, patience and understanding rather than an assumption that communication will match.

Non-speaking refers to those who do not use vocal verbal speech, as well as those who sometimes use vocal verbal speech, those who sign, those who use augmentative alternative communication (AAC) or any combination of those. Some Autistic people are exclusively non-speaking, while for others, particular factors, such as sensory or environment specifics, influence their access to speech and communication. The Double Empathy Problem also impacts the degree to which non-speaking people are included in research. Lack of understanding of access and support needs, as well as how to create access points in research lead to the design of methods that are inherently inaccessible to non-speaking Autistic individuals. Because of this, research around Autism, including that which provides insight into the Double Empathy Problem, does not include insight from a full variety of Autistic lived experiences. It is also for this reason that research provides little insight into the experiences of being social but non-speaking. It is important to seek insight from spaces other than research, such as online blogs and social media pages, in order to learn from a more representative variety of Autistic voices.

In addition to differences in communication styles, Autistic people may have a distinct experience with social drive and preferences. Social drive refers to the motivation we have to create relationships with others and, like neurotypicals, Autistic people can be introverted and extroverted. The degree to which an Autistic person feels motivated to be social and actually engages in activities with others may be informed by Autistic traits or by the interaction between their Autistic traits and environmental factors, such as how many people are in the space, whether they've already done something social that day or the social demand present in that environment. Individual differences in communication may vary based on comfort, cross-neurotype connection and energy levels ('spoons'), among other things. Cummins et al. (2020) highlight the importance of supporting Autistic individuals in the area of communication. They not only highlight the importance of supporting Autistic individuals but also of creating access and understanding in society so Autistic people can show up authentically in communication situations. Without increasing understanding of, and access for, Autistic individuals, social spaces often become exhausting, stigmatizing, alienating and ultimately reinforce masking, lowered social drive in some and poor mental health (Cummins et al., 2020). It is important to understand the impact that Autistic traits, as well as outside factors such as stigma and accessibility challenges, have on social drive to combat the reductive notion that Autistic people struggle socially because of internal factors alone.

Autistic culture and subcultures

The Autistic community is a diverse constellation of individuals with various co-occurring needs, strengths and identities. Autistics share Autistic culture through social media, art, science, cuisine and writing to better understand our shared experiences, trauma and joy (Dekker, 1999; de Vries, 2021). As described by Farahar (2022), Autistic culture is different from the 'culture of autism'. Autistic culture can serve as a protective factor as it is situated within the neurodiversity paradigm, highlighting strengths, community, understanding and a more three-dimensional view of autism. However, as the saying goes, '*If you meet one Autistic person, you have met one Autistic person*'. When using the Double Empathy Theory, it is important to recognize that each Autistic person has their own sensory profile, cultural identity, communication style, and relationship with social drive and capacity that influences how they interact with the world and other Autistics. Just because someone shares the Autistic identity and can find commonalities within the Autistic culture, does not necessarily mean that they hold all the same subcultures or identities.

Autistic folks can have different subcultures like queer culture or Black culture that deeply affect relationships with others, as well as societal biases and prejudices. This is illustrated in Autism research as Black, Brown and Indigenous people of colour are often shut out or pushed to the margins through what Malone and colleagues describe as 'scholarly neglect' (Malone et al., 2022). They reviewed how research, even on the Double Empathy Problem, has mainly focused on white Autistic folks, with many studies not including race or ethnicity demographic information. This is problematic on many levels, including the perpetuation of the traditional concept that Autistic people are mainly white boys who love trains. Botha and Gillespie-Lynch clearly describe this by stating '*To date, the narratives and rhetoric surrounding autism and autistic people have been intertwined with a pervasive and persisting whiteness, cis-gender, middle-class, straight maleness. These stereotypes that autistic people acknowledge and feel trapped by*' (Botha & Gillespie-Lynch, 2022, p. 96). To counteract this narrative and create space for counternarratives, Oluwatobi Abubakare describes their experiences as a Nigerian non-binary person with co-occurring disabilities and needs (Abubakare, 2022). Her prose highlights the importance of understanding how the intersections of cultural perceptions of autism, access to health care, religious beliefs and communication styles manifests in the creation of the 'unexpected autistic'.

Alyssa Hilary also shared how cultural perceptions change the embodiment of Autism in her chapter titled 'Neurodiversity and cross-cultural communication' (Hillary, 2020). Hilary discusses cross-cultural communication by detailing the distinction of neuronormative white Western culture versus other non-Western cultures. White Western cultures have created their own stories, communication rules, ways to play and social realities that are highly situated within white culture and Western thought. These expectations and rules do not translate to other cultures, including subcultures like home culture, neurotype culture, disability culture and more. Researchers and advocates recommend that more narratives of multiply marginalized individuals be available to support not only cross-cultural communication, but also cross-neurotype communication. This would mean decentring whiteness as the default or 'expected Autistic' and to explore the lived experiences of those with intersecting identities to better conceptualize how communication can vary based on disability, identities, individual characteristics/preferences and societal context.

A framework for action

As researchers, educators and activists, we recognize that while theory is tempting, it is also essential to ground it in practical next steps. We were inspired by Kerry Murphy's Neurodiversity Affirming Zones of Practice, Ibram X. Kendi's (2023) work, *How to Be an Antiracist*, on antiracist zones and Terra Vance's work on the website, NeuroClastic, on Autistic identity and core self, to create our own framework visual that can be utilized by Autistic and allistic people alike to take steps toward the promotion of Autistic flourishing and belonging (Figure 19.1).

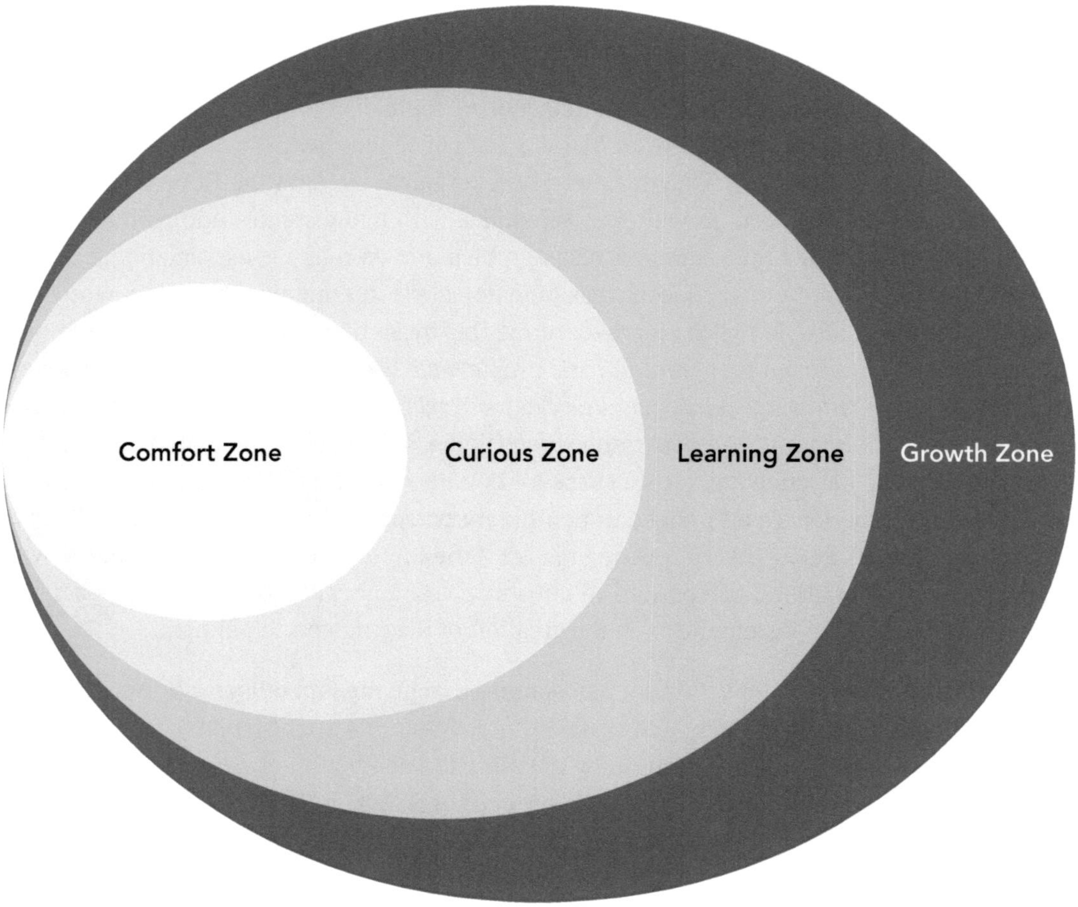

Figure 19.1: A framework visual that can be utilized by autistic and allistic people alike to take steps toward the promotion of autistic flourishing and belonging.

Our goal is to provide nuance to the double empathy framework while facilitating more authentic belonging and meaningful flourishing for Autistic folks in all contexts. As stated previously, when we communicate with others, we may only see one aspect of their identity, whether this is because of masking or different communication styles. This may make it difficult to connect past a superficial level. The framework presented here aims to support the neurodiverse (e.g., neurodivergent and neurotypical) in developing awareness of different styles of communication and of the disconnect that often results from this. The model offers several entry points and relates growing awareness and understanding to: i) Autistic culture, ii) identity subculture, iii) individual characteristics/preferences and iv) context or environmental factors.

We ask that you assess where you are in each of these categories based on the descriptions of each zone. You may have beliefs or actions that lie in multiple zones depending on the category. That is okay! We provide you with reflection questions with the hope of shifting mindsets from the ingrained neuronormative thinking to a neurodiversity perspective informed by the Double Empathy Theory. This calls us to disrupt the notion or normative idea that there is one way, one access point and one type of communication. We must recognize that we interact with individuals from all neurotypes, people with different support needs, people with intersecting identities and more. These identities and needs are not static, but shift and change depending on our surroundings, learning history, past experiences and environment. We also recognize that Autistic people are susceptible to biases and misinformed ways of thinking about themselves and other neurotypes. This work is meant to be done across neurotypes, not just a list to give to the worst neurotypical in your life.

Let's start with the **Comfort Zone.** The Comfort Zone can be familiar or routine as it resides within neuronormative ways of communicating and relating with others. If you are in this space, you may:

Autistic Culture:

- See autism as a monolith

Identity Subculture:

- Not recognize that Autistic people as having intersecting identities

Individual Characteristics:

- View autism through stereotypes (e.g., lack of social skills, lack empathy)

Context and Environment:

- Not understand how environment could affect senses or sense of belonging

Some reflection questions to move out of this space include:

1. Where did I learn about Autism? Who did I learn it from and what was their positionality?
2. What identities do I have? Can I see how my different identities shape the way I interact with the world?
3. How can I listen to the Autistic community more instead of relying on how society or media has portrayed Autistic people?
4. What in the environment makes it difficult for me to be successful or feel like I belong? How do I see this happening for others?

Next is the **Curious Zone.** The Curious Zone is where you may start questioning neuronormativity and traditional medical model descriptions of communication. If you are in this space, you may:

Autistic Culture:

- See Autism through a medical or pathologizing model

Identity Subculture:

- Understand that Autistics have different identities, but not how they influence one another or communication

Individual Characteristics:

- May recognize that Autistic individuals have different preferences but unwilling to adapt or accommodate

Context and Environment:

- Understand how environment impacts Autistic person only when convenient or viewed through your own experiences

Some reflection questions to ask yourself if you are in this zone include:

1. Do I know about the different models of disability? What is the impact of each model on my understanding of disability identity, belonging and flourishing?
2. How do my identities influence the way I communicate and interact with the world?
3. What is preventing me from adapting or accommodating for Autistic preferences or perspectives? Is this an individual bias or systems level issue (e.g., ableist policies, workplace requirements, school expectations)?
4. What barriers are in place that make it difficult for me to empathize with others' needs in an environment? Are these internal biases or influenced by societal prejudices?

The third zone is the **Learning Zone.** This zone is where you explore aspects of neurodiversity and the Double Empathy Theory, with the goal of developing skills that animate spaces of belonging and flourishing for Autistic individuals. If you are in this space, you may:

Autistic Culture:

- Explore and learn about Autistic culture and Double Empathy Theory

Identity Subculture:

- Recognize that certain identities hold privilege and power, while others are oppressed and disadvantaged

Individual Characteristics:

- Be willing to provide individual accommodations if communicated by autistic person

Context and Environment:

- Understand how to accommodate within a physical environment, but not in relation to societal influences

Some reflection questions you can ask yourself to push your perspective are:

1. What sources am I using to learn about Autistic culture/double empathy? Am I including Autistic voices, perspectives or ideas? Am I including Black, Indigenous and people of colour (BIPOC) Autistic voices?
2. What spaces of privilege do I hold? What power do my identities hold? How does that change the way I show up in certain spaces?
3. How can I anticipate or ask about accommodations for Autistic people? Do I understand that needs between people do not always align?
4. How do societal influences (e.g., politics, climate, prejudice, ableism) impact my feelings of belonging and authenticity? How do I see this happening for others?

Lastly there is the **Growth Zone.** The Growth Zone stretches your knowledge and skills to be critical of neuronormative systems of power, while also centring neurodivergence-informed practices that emphasize meaningful Autistic flourishing, authenticity and belonging. If you are in this space, you may:

Autistic Culture:

- Celebrate and acknowledge Autistic culture by learning directly from the Autistic community (advocates, authors, researchers, etc.) with particular attention to those from other historically marginalized identities

Identity Subculture:

- Partner with diverse Autistic individuals to amplify intersectional communication needs

Individual Characteristics:

- Create spaces that are welcoming, affirming and flexible for a range of Autistic people

Context and Environment:

- Be aware of how societal contexts impact sense of belonging, safety and flourishing for Autistic people

In this space it is critical to understand that it is not an endpoint, but rather a continuous growth space, much like antiracist or culturally sustaining work. Some reflection questions you can ask yourself are:

1. Do I gather information from a variety of sources beyond academia? Am I uplifting Autistic culture towards the promotion of Autistic flourishing and belonging?
2. Am I helping for the service of the community or for the service of myself? How do I prevent ableist-creep?
3. How do I create spaces that facilitate agency and disrupt neuronormative communication/interaction expectations?
4. Do I hold myself accountable when I make mistakes or missteps when communicating in environments? Do I consistently show allyship through my actions?

The reflection questions we provide are by no means an exhaustive list. We encourage you to create your own questions to better understand where you lie in the framework.

References

Abubakare, O. (2022). An unexpected autistic. *Autism in Adulthood*, *4*(4), 268–270. https://doi.org/10.1089/aut.2022.0004

American Psychiatric Association (2013). *Diagnostic and Statistical Manual of Mental Disorders* (5th ed.). American Psychiatric Association. https://doi.org/10.1176/appi.books.9780890425596

Baron-Cohen, S. (2000). Theory of mind and autism: A review. *International Review of Research in Mental Retardation*, *23*, 169–184. https://doi.org/10.1016/S0074-7750(00)80010-5

Bernardin, C. J., Mason, E., Lewis, T., & Kanne, S. (2021). "You must become a chameleon to survive": Adolescent experiences of camouflaging. *Journal of Autism and Developmental Disorders*, *51*, 4422–4435. https://doi.org/10.1007/s10803-021-04912-1

Botha, M., & Frost, D. M. (2018). Extending the minority stress model to understand mental health problems experienced by the autistic population. *Society and Mental Health*, *10*(1), 20–34. https://doi.org/10.1177/2156869318804297

Botha, M., & Gillespie-Lynch, K. (2022). Come as you are: Examining autistic identity development and the neurodiversity movement through an intersectional lens. *Human Development*, *66*(2), 93–112. https://doi.org/10.1159/000524123

Camm-Crosbie, L., Bradley, L., Shaw, R., Baron-Cohen, S., & Cassidy, S. (2019). 'People like me don't get support': Autistic adults' experiences of support and treatment for mental health difficulties, self-injury and suicidality. *Autism*, *23*(6), 1431–1441. https://doi.org/10.1177/1362361318816053

Cassidy, S. A., Gould, K., Townsend, E., Pelton, M., Robertson, A. E., & Rodgers, J. (2020). Is camouflaging autistic traits associated with suicidal thoughts and behaviours? Expanding the interpersonal psychological theory of suicide in an undergraduate student sample. *Journal of Autism and Developmental Disorders*, *50*(10), 3638–3648. https://doi.org/10.1007/s10803-019-04323-3

Chapman, R. (2023). Critical psychiatry, mental health, and collective liberation. *Philosophy, Psychiatry, & Psychology*, *30*(2), 129–131. https://doi.org/10.1353/ppp.2023.a899941

Chapman, R., & Carel, H. (2022). Neurodiversity, epistemic injustice, and the good human life. *Journal of Social Philosophy, 53*(4), 614–631. https://doi.org/10.1111/josp.12456

Cook, J., Hull, L., Crane, L., & Mandy, W. (2021). Camouflaging in autism: A systematic review. *Clinical Psychology Review, 89*, 102080. https://doi.org/10.1016/j.cpr.2021.102080

Cook, J. M., Crane, L., & Mandy, W. (2023). Dropping the mask: It takes two. *Autism, 28*(4), 831–842. https://doi.org/10.1177/13623613231183059

Crompton, C. J., Hallett, S., Ropar, D., Flynn, E., & Fletcher-Watson, S. (2020a). 'I never realised everybody felt as happy as I do when I am around autistic people': A thematic analysis of autistic adults' relationships with autistic and neurotypical friends and family. *Autism*, 24(6), 1438–1448. https://doi.org/10.1177/1362361320908976

Crompton, C. J., Ropar, D., Evans-Williams, C. V., Flynn, E. G., & Fletcher-Watson, S. (2020b). Autistic peer-to-peer information transfer is highly effective. *Autism*, 24(7), 1704–1712. https://doi.org/10.1177/1362361320919286

Crompton, C. J., Sharp, M., Axbey, H., Fletcher-Watson, S., Flynn, E. G., & Ropar, D. (2020c). Neurotype-matching, but not being autistic, influences self and observer ratings of interpersonal rapport. *Frontiers in Psychology, 11*. https://doi.org/10.3389/fpsyg.2020.586171

Cummins, C., Pellicano, E., & Crane, L. (2020), Autistic adults' views of their communication skills and needs. *International Journal of Language & Communication Disorders, 55*, 678–689. https://doi.org/10.1111/1460-6984.12552

Dekker, M. (1999, October 17). *On Our Own Terms: Emerging Autistic Culture*. In Conferencia en línea. https://www.autscape.org/2015/programme/handouts/Autistic-Culture-07-Oct-1999.pdf

de Vries, B. (2021). Should autists have cultural rights? *Human Rights Review, 23*(2), 205–219. https://doi.org/10.1007/s12142-021-00642-0

Diener, E., Wirtz, D., Tov, W., Kim-Prieto, C., Choi, D., Oishi, S., & Biswas-Diener, R. (2010). New well-being measures: Short scales to assess flourishing and positive and negative feelings. *Social Indicators Research, 97*(2), 143–156. https://doi.org/10.1007/s11205-009-9493-y

Farahar, C. (2022). Autistic identity, culture, community, and space for well-being. In D. Milton & S. Ryan (Eds.) *The Routledge International Handbook of Critical Autism Studies* (pp. 229–243). Routledge.

Harmsen, I. E. (2019). Empathy in autism spectrum disorder. *Journal of Autism and Developmental Disorders, 49*(10), 3939–3955. https://doi.org/10.1007/s10803-019-04087-w

Hillary, A. (2020). Neurodiversity and cross-cultural communication. In A Stenning (Ed.) *Neurodiversity Studies*. Routledge.

Hone, L. C., Jarden, A., Schofield, G. M., & Duncan, S. (2014). Measuring flourishing: The impact of operational definitions on the prevalence of high levels of wellbeing. *International Journal of Wellbeing, 4*(1), 62–90. https://doi.org/10.5502/ijw.v4i1.4

Howard, P. L., & Sedgewick, F. (2021). 'Anything but the phone!': Communication mode preferences in the autism community. *Autism, 25*(8), 2265–2278. https://doi.org/10.1177/13623613211014995

Huijg, D. D. (2020). Neuronormativity in theorising agency: An argument for a critical neurodiversity approach. *Neurodiversity Studies: A New Critical Paradigm*, (pp. 213–217). Routledge. https://doi.org/10.4324/9780429322297-20

Hull, L., Petrides, K. V., Allison, C., Smith, P., Baron-Cohen, S., Lai, M. C., & Mandy, W. (2017). "Putting on my best normal": Social camouflaging in adults with autism spectrum conditions. *Journal of Autism and Developmental Disorders, 47*, 2519–2534. https://doi.org/10.1007/s10803-017-3166-5

Hull, L., Petrides, K. V. & Mandy, W. (2020). The female autism phenotype and camouflaging: A narrative review. *Review Journal of Autism and Developmental Disorders, 7*, 306–317. https://doi.org/10.1007/s40489-020-00197-9

Huppert, F. A., & So, T. T. C. (2013). Flourishing across Europe: Application of a new conceptual framework for defining well-being. *Social Indicators Research, 110*(3), 837–861. https://doi.org/10.1007/s11205-011-9966-7

Hutson, T. M., McGhee Hassrick, E., Fernandes, S., Walton, J., Bouvier-Weinberg, K., Radcliffe, A., & Allen-Handy, A. (2022). "I'm just different–that's all–I'm so sorry... ": Black men, ASD and the urgent need for DisCrit Theory in police encounters. *Policing: An International Journal, 45*(3), 524–537. https://doi.org/10.1108/pijpsm-10-2021-0149

Janse van Rensburg, M., & Liang, B. (2023). Improving autistic students' experiences in higher education: Developing a community framework for individual autistic student and autistic community flourishing. *Autism in Adulthood*. https://doi.org/10.1089/aut.2022.0079

Jedrzejewska, A., & Dewey, J. (2022). Camouflaging in autistic and non-autistic adolescents in the modern context of social media. *Journal of Autism and Developmental Disorders, 52*, 630–646. https://doi.org/10.1007/s10803-021-04953-6

Kendi, I. X. (2023). *How to Be an Antiracist*. One World.

Keyes, C. L. M. (2002). The mental health continuum: From languishing to flourishing in life. *Journal of Health and Social Behavior, 43*(2), 207–222. https://doi.org/10.2307/3090197

Lawson, W. B. (2020). Adaptive morphing and coping with social threat in autism: An autistic perspective. *Journal of Intellectual Disability-Diagnosis and Treatment, 8*(3), 519–526. https://doi.org/10.6000/2292-2598.2020.08.03.29

Malone, K. M., Pearson, J. N., Palazzo, K. N., Manns, L. D., Rivera, A. Q., & Mason Martin, D. L. (2022). The scholarly neglect of Black autistic adults in autism research. *Autism in Adulthood, 4*(4), 271–280. https://doi.org/10.1089/aut.2021.0086

Melmed, H. H. (2022). *Interactions Between Black, Autistic Students and Law Enforcement Officers in Schools and Beyond: Experiences and Perceptions*. University of California.

Miller, D., Rees, J., & Pearson, A. (2021). "Masking is life": Experiences of masking in autistic and nonautistic adults. *Autism in Adulthood, 3*(4), 330–338. https://doi.org/10.1089/aut.2020.0083

Milner, V., McIntosh, H., Colvert, E., & Happé, F. (2019). A qualitative exploration of the female experience of autism spectrum disorder (ASD). *Journal of Autism and Developmental Disorders, 49*, 2389–2402. https://doi.org/10.1007/s10803-019-03906-4

Milton, D. (2012). On the ontological status of autism: the 'double empathy problem'. *Disability & Society, 27*(6), 883–887. https://doi.org/10.1080/09687599.2012.710008

Milton, D., & Sims, T. (2016). How is a sense of well-being and belonging constructed in the accounts of autistic adults? *Disability & Society, 31*(4), 520–534. https://doi.org/10.1080/09687599.2016.1186529

Milton, D. (2020). Neurodiversity past and present-an introduction to the neurodiversity reader. In: D. Milton, Damian, D. Murray, S. Ridout, N. Martin, & R. Mills (Eds.) *The Neurodiversity Reader* (pp. 3–6). Pavilion.

Mitchell, P., Sheppard, E., & Cassidy, S. (2021). Autism and the double empathy problem: Implications for development and mental health. *British Journal of Developmental Psychology, 39*(1), 1–18. https://doi.org/10.1111/bjdp.12350

Murphy, K. (n.d.). *Neuro Affirming Practice: Early Years from Kerry Murphy*. Teach Early Years. https://www.teachearlyyears.com/a-unique-child/view/neurodiversity-affirming-practice-in-early-years

Pellicano, E., & Heyworth, M. (2023). The foundations of autistic flourishing. *Current Psychiatry Reports, 25*(9), 419–427. https://doi.org/10.1007/s11920-023-01441-9

Roberts, J. (2021, May 27) *Nothing about Social Skills Training is Neurodivergence-Affirming – Absolutely Nothing*. Therapist Neurodiversity Collective. https://therapistndc.org/nothing-about-social-skills-training-is-neurodivergence-affirming/

Seligman, M. E. (2011). *Flourish: A Visionary New Understanding of Happiness and Well-being*. Simon and Schuster.

Skrzypiec, G., Askell-Williams, H., Slee, P., & Rudzinski, A. (2016). Students with self-identified special educational needs and disabilities (si-SEND): Flourishing or languishing! *International Journal of Disability, Development and Education, 63*(1), 7–26.

Chapter 20:
Human Kinds and Neurocultural Mediation

Alice Sodi, Roberto Mastropasqua and Giorgio De Acutis

Abstract

In relation to the politics of inclusion and psychoeducational approaches, we observe that much of the work in supporting relationships between people characterized by significant mutual differences currently consists of translating the 'nonconforming' person, both to themselves and to others, and attempting to enable them to conform to expected relational behaviour. As a result of analyses and insights from social science studies – Heasman and Gillespie (2018); Milton (2012, 2014); Milton et al. (2020); Ochs and Solomon (2010); Ochs et al. (2001, 2004); Sterponi (2004) – we present a proposal to approach relational difficulties from the perspective of what we call neurocultural mediation, which consists of supporting the relationship between people characterized by substantial mutual differences, symmetrically with respect to the parties, with the aim of giving both parties tools for self-awareness and awareness of the variety of human kinds (Hacking, 1986).

In relation to the politics of inclusion and psycho-educational approaches, we observe that much of the work in supporting relationships between people characterized by significant mutual differences currently consists of translating the 'nonconforming' person, both to themselves and to others, and attempting to enable them to conform to expected relational behaviour. As a result of analyses and insights from social science studies – Heasman and Gillespie (2018); Milton (2012, 2014); Milton et al. (2020); Ochs and Solomon (2010); Ochs et al. (2001, 2004); Sterponi (2004) – we present a proposal to approach relational difficulties from the perspective of what we call neurocultural mediation, which consists of supporting the relationship between people characterized by substantial mutual differences, symmetrically with respect to the parties, with the aim of giving both parties tools for self-awareness and awareness of the variety of human kinds (Hacking, 1986).

The conceptualization of neurocultural mediation draws on the principles of intercultural mediation, in which relational and communicative differences stemming from cultural affiliations are addressed through reciprocal mediation aimed at providing parties with tools to contextualize their own perspectives. The challenge is to address perceptual, cognitive, relational and communicative differences, expressions of significant neurobiological differences, through the same approach.

Let us start with an assumption: no one is neutral. Personality, education, experiences, social roles, learning and life contribute to shaping each of our points of view. All these elements make our worldview necessarily partial, oriented and positional. Our fundamental assumption is that even neurotype, given its constitutional potential, which will then be expressed in relation to its interdependence with all other environmental factors, is a positioning element. Elevating a neurotype to a prototypical status and thus considering it the reference norm by which to measure the adequacy of various human expressions in various social contexts proves to be a kind of 'hallucination' that leads us to believe that what cannot be explained and validated according to the reference neurotype's experience is sanctionable and justifies the choice to intervene to reduce the distance from the norm as much as possible.

It is natural to read this cultural legacy in the light of our recent history. Indeed, Quételet devoted himself to applying statistics to the study of human beings, intending to define the characteristics of the *average person* (Quételet, 1835). He argued that *'every quality, within suitable limits, is essentially good; it is only in its extreme deviations from the average that it becomes bad'*. Shortly after, Galton left a profound cultural imprint. Thanks to him, thinking of humans in terms of greater or lesser distance from the 'norm' became the common and shared way to attribute value to them (Galton, 1869, 1883). We can easily trace in our past the steps, the path to naturalizing the idea that there exists a 'prototypical' version of a human being to which one has the moral value to tend, a version that deserves social participation and status as a complete person.

This approach leads to the belief that it is a duty, for the good of the individual and society, to trace and correct the 'error' in nonconforming people. In short, according to this way of interpreting differences, it is natural to think that relational difficulties experienced between autistic and non-autistic individuals should be corrected by the former. Attempting an exercise in cultural deconstruction, we can realise that this imbalanced value attribution, leaning toward adherence to the prototype, is, in fact, arbitrary – just as the existence of the prototype itself and even the criteria that define it. These are the result of a series of choices and events that are not the outcome of an unavoidable path of historical progress but could reasonably have been different, of another make and nature, and have led to a culture that relates to differences in a completely different way. The fact remains that today, it seems absolutely natural to us to divide people into *normal* and *disabled/autistic/ill/foreign/Black*, despite the fact that the boundaries between these categories are constantly shifting, demonstrating precisely the *de facto* arbitrariness of this categorical, and also evaluative and moral, interpretation of humans. This virtual division between conforming and nonconforming individuals to expectations underlies a dichotomous interpretation of society, in which individuals not adhering to expectations represent an exception to the norm – the other, the one-different-from – establishing diversified qualitative standards for different categories of people. We tolerate practices toward, and living conditions for, disabled individuals that would seem unacceptable if applied to non-disabled individuals; we would find them mortifying and detrimental to dignity, yet they appear to us as sad and inevitable consequences of the disabled person's condition rather than administrative choices based on dehumanizing cultural legacies that are by now naturalized.

Returning to autistic individuals, according to common interpretation, the relational difficulties they experience are to be considered their own responsibility. The prototypical interlocutor is automatically relieved of both investigation and the responsibilities of objectively being part of the relational dynamics. In the presence of a particular condition (in this case, autism), the relationship seems to no longer correspond to a shared action involving at least two actors who enter into a reciprocal relationship, balancing and exchanging the roles of senders and receivers. Instead, it becomes a game in which a double standard is predetermined, and the autistic interlocutor will be the only one deemed responsible for any potential failure, while the non-autistic interlocutor will automatically be considered more responsible for any potential success. In reality, trying to step outside our *habitus* (Bourdieu 1990, 2005), we can realise that autistic individuals do experience difficulties in understanding the communication of non-autistic individuals – but at the same time, non-autistic individuals experience difficulties in understanding autistic communication. This has been highlighted by the Double Empathy Problem theory. Crompton and her colleagues, in a study, engage to demonstrate this theory using the 'diffusion chain technique' with three diffusion chains composed solely of autistic individuals, three chains of only non-autistic individuals, and three mixed chains (Crompton et al., 2020). In each chain, detailed and complex information must be verbally passed from one person to another. Afterward, the degree of accuracy to which information is preserved and the number of details that reach the end of the chain are measured. The result of the study shows that communication problems increase when the interaction occurs between different neurotypes, but when interaction takes place between people belonging to the same neurotype it is effective, even when those people are considered nonconforming.

However, we believe it is important to prevent a potential criticality in the interpretation of our proposal. There is a possibility that neurocultural mediation may be understood as a tool to be used solely to address relational difficulties due to constitutional differences that do not have a deficit character. This way of understanding neurocultural mediation can produce the side effect of reinforcing and justifying an othering approach toward conditions that are definitively pathological or characterized by what can be assumed as actual deficits. For example, autistic individuals require mediation not because autism is a non-pathological relational and existential style but because it is a different style. Whether it is pathological or constitutional makes no difference in this case. This perspective is potentially applicable and should be considered even when dealing with conditions that are technically considered pathological from a medical point of view. When these conditions create a distance between a person's experience and that of everyone else, the goal is to address relational difficulties by educating both parties about repositioning their perspectives and becoming aware that they are expressions of an existent typology among many possible ones – deconstructing the automatism of hierarchizing relationships based on the functioning characteristics of the interlocutors.

The same reasoning applies to individuals with complex needs, requiring high levels of assistance and with intellectual disabilities, as all these conditions can determine peculiar and nonconforming ways of experiencing oneself, others and the environment. Positing that those who fall within 'normality' are authorized to consider the use of their interpretative tools as absolutely valid for signifying the experience of all other human types is unethical, as well as inevitably flawed. Everyone is characterized by peculiarities related to sensory perception, attentional orientation and cognitive processes, all of which influence the interpretation of reality and inevitably impact relational styles.

Much has been said about theory of mind (Premack & Woodruff, 1978), the ability to interpret and predict, with reasonable accuracy, the motivations and intentions underlying others' behaviours, which will be influenced by factors such as neurotype and culture. This is characterized as a fundamental relationship tool because it provides a presumably common interpretative basis for interlocutors to navigate, confident of finding correspondence in the other. The criticality of this descriptive model emerges when, still in a dichotomous perspective, there is an attempt to select the theory of mind model to be elected as prototypical. The adequacy of a certain theory of mind can be defined only contingently. The interaction between two people who are non-prototypical, but relatively similar to each other, characterized by a constitutional and experiential baggage adequate to produce reciprocal mirroring, will be effective. Their theory of mind can be considered contextually adequate to the interaction, even if not necessarily effective in interaction with someone very different from them.

A Western person has a theory of mind largely inadequate to understand and predict the intentions and motivations of a person raised in a cultural context profoundly different from theirs, and vice versa. Probably, both would attribute the responsibility for relational failure to the other's ineffectiveness. This is where the cultural mediator comes into play, to facilitate the process of relativizing one's perspective and the awareness that reality does not have a single possible interpretation. Communication can take many valid forms. The relationship can be experienced and cultivated according to different logics, and this does not necessarily make it less meaningful. Applying the theory of the Double Empathy Problem, we must think that between two or more substantially different people (in terms of neurotype, culture, etc.), it is physiological to encounter misunderstandings and relational difficulties. Perhaps, by avoiding an assertion of the legitimacy of a functioning or a culture in relation to its correspondence to an arbitrary prototypical model, we could educate all parties involved in relating to what is different from themselves, helping them realise that each is an expression of only one human typology. Societies are naturally populated by a great variety of different human expressions, each of which experiences the relationship with oneself, others and the environment in a peculiar way.

Let us try to explore the relationship between culture and neurotype, drawing parallels between cultural mediation and neurocultural mediation. What is culture? According to the *Cambridge Free English Dictionary* (2023), it is '*the way of life of a particular people, esp. as shown in their ordinary behavior and habits, their attitudes toward each other, and their moral and religious beliefs*'. The *Oxford Dictionary of Philosophy* (2008, p. 86) similarly defines it as '*the way of life of a people, including their attitudes, values, beliefs, arts, sciences, modes of perception and habits of thought and activity. Cultural features or forms of life are learned but are often too pervasive to be readily noticed from within*'.

Clyde Kluckhohn (1961, p. 73) presented a widely accepted definition that integrated many of these perspectives: '*Culture consists of patterned ways of thinking, feeling and reacting, acquired and transmitted mainly by symbols, constituting the distinctive achievement of human groups, including their embodiment in artifacts; the essential core of culture consists of traditional (i.e., historically derived and selected) ideas and especially their attached values*'.

Cultures have unique systems of meanings that influence the perception and interpretation of the world. For instance, language is not just a means of communication; it shapes our thoughts (Ottenheimer, 2008). The way we articulate a concept influences its perception and the interpretation of reality. Different languages can impact how individuals conceptualize and classify their experiences. Mastering one's native language is independent of our genetic heritage and demonstrates how the environment can program certain brain systems. In the early years of life, exposure to the native language determines the functioning of brain circuits such as Broca's area for language articulation and

Wernicke's area for language comprehension. Growing up in Italy will result in developing an 'Italian brain', and that's why, later on, when we learn a second language, we might retain an Italian accent (Winawer et al., 2007).

One's linguistic environment induces permanent differences in brain structures and functions. When we learn a language during developmental stages, we use the entire Broca's area. However, when we learn a language in adulthood, we use only a subarea. If we are raised bilingually as children, both languages will utilize the same frontal areas. The linguistic and cultural environment determines not only the functioning of brain circuits responsible for language processing but also how we interpret facial expressions and analyse images (Swaab, 2014).

Cultural mediation is useful precisely because our thinking system has a culture-specific structure. Two people belonging to very distant cultures will have rooted conceptualizations, interpretative systems, physical and mental attitudes, and verbal and non-verbal expressive patterns that are partially incompatible. Similarly, two people expressing different neurotypes will have different perceptual styles (sensory processing, attentional orientation) that, in approaching a given situation, will influence the type of experience for both. This, in turn, determines sensations and thoughts consistent with each one's experience, motivating subsequent reactions and behaviours that also influence how they relate to each other. These people may witness the same phenomenon at the same time and attribute potentially contradictory meanings to it. This inevitably produces reactions and behaviours that are mutually incomprehensible or deemed inappropriate in each other's eyes. In such cases, rationalizing that what appears 'natural' to us is the result of the interplay between our constitutional makeup and the culture we have learned helps to understand that the same applies to our interlocutor. Thus, the awareness grows that what previously seemed inappropriate or offensive behaviours may be the outcome of the same process that led us to classify that experience in the way we did, which obviously seemed appropriate to us.

The brain is parsimonious; it naturally tends to save energy. Many of our cognitive processes occur automatically. Culture provides tools to avoid dangers, acquire resources, reproduce, prosper and survive without constantly deepening knowledge of every single phenomenon. It gives us tools to cognitize reality and experience. It establishes mental patterns, prejudices, stereotypes, categorizations, logical (or illogical) processes, guides our abstraction capacity and structures each person's symbolic heritage. It contributes to creating cognitive shortcuts that allow the brain to save time and energy.

The outcomes of encounters between diverse cultures can be so problematic that governments have adopted specific policies. Among policies towards the 'foreigner', we can mention *assimilation* (following the French model), *multiculturalism* (according to the

British model), *segregation* (following the South African model) and *interculturalism* (Bisin et al., 2012; Cesareo, 1997; Zanfrini, 2010). Except for the last one, all respond to ancestral cultural categories of pure/impure, intact/contaminated.

Even the definition of disability fits into a thought pattern that tends to systematize reality through processes of identification and categorization based on binary oppositions: male/female, strong/weak, right/wrong, able/disabled. The concept of ableism governs the able/disabled dichotomy in all its nuances, categorizing functions with reference to a norm. Fougeyrollas (1987) states, '*The idea of disability has [...] an essentially social nature as it is defined in relation to a norm, to a criterion of normality that is also a culturally constructed and strongly ethnocentric notion*'.

The ableist perspective categorizes people based on a deficit and confines them to a condition of lack; the difficulties they experience will be considered the direct effect of such a deficit and will not be related to the contexts in which their lives are lived. In the best case, contextual factors will be considered worsening elements of secondary relevance. An interesting perspective following these reflections comes from ethnopsychiatry and ethnopsychology (Devereux, 1961, p. 1; Ellenberger, 2020), where we find, among the foundational concepts, that of biocultural interaction and the pathogenic cultural factor. Biocultural interaction refers to the interaction between biological and cultural factors and how the latter can influence health and mental illnesses, increasing or minimizing the possibility of developing psychopathological conditions. For example, genetic predispositions to certain mental disorders can be influenced by cultural factors such as stressors or social support systems. Pathogenic cultural factors, on the other hand, refer to those cultural factors, such as social norms, beliefs and practices, that can contribute to the development or exacerbation of mental illnesses. For instance, cultural expectations about gender roles can contribute to higher rates of depression in certain populations.

It seems reasonable to us to hypothesize that, in a given cultural context, certain factors may be neutral or positive for part of the population but may turn out to be pathogenic for another, characterized by peculiarities that interact undesirably or unexpectedly with the same factors. Think about the use of eye contact in Western culture, widely considered one of the determining factors for effective communication (unlike East Asia, where it is seen as disrespectful and out of place). Many autistic individuals report being unable to maintain eye contact with the interlocutor because it generates too much anxiety and cognitive overload due to the need to process too many visual stimuli. Absence of eye contact, in the West, is among the factors that may contribute to the failure of a job interview, as well as an attempt at social interaction, and generally suggests low reliability. This culturally specific expectation, among many others, leads many autistic individuals to be unfairly judged, and contributes to them developing a sense of inefficacy and low self-esteem, often resulting in avoidance behaviours and ultimately social isolation, with negative consequences for mental health. The environment, context and power relationships that characterize them can be disabling and even pathogenic.

In the Italian context, the focus is mainly on the implementation of compensatory measures consisting of direct support to the individual – such as the figure of the educator, the educational assistant, the support teacher, various financial contributions – with the aim of modifying the individual's condition but not the environmental and social contexts.

To ensure a person's access to leisure, assigning an educator to motivate and accompany them is not sufficient; it is necessary to make the contexts where they can spend their leisure time pleasant and easily accessible. Enabling contexts does not only mean taking transformative actions on the physical environment or proposed activities but also, above all, acting in a transformative way on the culture in which they are rooted. Every practice is an expression of the underlying culture. Changing the practice without changing the culture means trying to solve problems while preserving the logic that generated them and that, in one way or another, will influence concrete actions.

But what intentional operations of reduction and 'domestication' of 'other' cultures are there, and what parallels do they offer regarding the 'management' of neurobiological differences? Here are some examples:

- **Folklorization**, or the reduction of foreign cultures to picturesque and exotic elements: the Chinese dragon, Arab couscous, the gypsy violin, Italian pizza. In the context of 'autism culture': counting toothpicks, remembering dates and keeping objects in an obsessive order, encyclopaedic knowledge.
- **Essentialism**, or the reduction of other cultures to some immutable fundamental essence, discarding their complexity, internal conflicts and historical dynamism. For autistic individuals: lack of empathy, self-isolation, expecting them to be either profoundly disabled or profoundly intellectually gifted, fixations.
- **Objectification**, or the transformation of cultures into marble monuments, homogeneous, fixed and immutable. *'In the world of autism, there exists an underlying assumption commonly accepted as a premise: autistic children do not develop like others, they do not mature as they grow, they do not learn – except for maladaptive behaviours. At best, they 'achieve goals' thanks to the hard work that non-autistic individuals will do on them'* (Garofalo, 2023).
- **Stereotyping**, or the confinement of cultures and their interpreters into narrow and often denigrating stereotypes. For example, the autistic person who rocks and repeats nonsensical phrases or the brilliant but socially inept individual.
- **Culturalism**, or the exaltation of the cultural 'given', tends to explain every individual and social behaviour in terms of their belonging culture. Similarly, in autism, there is the

phenomenon of the *prevailing diagnosis*, according to which any phenomenon related to an autistic person is explained through their autism spectrum disorder (ASD) diagnosis: if they scream because they have a stomach ache, it's an autistic crisis. If they bang their head against the wall because of a severe headache, it's an autistic crisis. If they engage in self-harming or aggressive behaviours because they are experiencing profound distress that affects their self-regulation capacity, it's a problematic behaviour to be extinguished, naturally because they are autistic. It is also in this way that significant health problems end up being identified much later in autistic individuals compared to non-autistic ones. Autistic individuals may die from a simple appendicitis, and, on average, they have a life expectancy lower than the average for the general population by 16 years, which becomes 20 if they also have intellectual disabilities. In addition to the prevailing diagnosis phenomenon, it is typical for parents or teachers of an autistic child to seek in their diagnosis an explanation for every behaviour and mood.

The relationship is NEVER solely binary but is, in turn, inserted into a system of hierarchically organized relationships. Power, position and self-perception affect the quality and effectiveness of the relationship. Western culture prefers:

- Extroversion over introversion;
- Big picture thinking over attention to detail;
- Engagement over avoidance;
- Verticality over horizontality (organizes reality into vertical hierarchies);
- Self-control over emotionality;
- Flexibility over rigidity.

It is already evident that the characteristics commonly attributed to autistic individuals are not part of those recognized as positive in Western culture. Quoting Jim Sinclair (1993): '*And autism goes deeper than language and culture; autistic people are "foreigners" in any society.*' But reversing the perspective, we can discover that for Chinese people, Westerners are all the same, we smell like cheese, and we have a giant nose, or that an autistic person may perceive non-autistic individuals as obtuse and superficial. Misunderstanding, therefore, is mutual – but it occurs within a hierarchical and power-based relationship.

One of the fundamental elements to consider is that the narrative of the foreigner or the 'other' is realised through stereotypes. Stereotypes can have negative or positive value, be reassuring or threatening, and are rarely neutral. In any case, they are for the use and consumption of the majority groups and sooner or later become cages to enclose the uniqueness of individuals. For example, Romani people are described as children of the wind according to the positive stereotype or child thieves according to the negative stereotype. Likewise, the positive stereotype of the autistic person as quirky but brilliant contrasts with the negative stereotype of the autistic person as isolated and emotionally detached. If cultural mediation requires being aware of the mechanisms and characteristics of human cultures starting from one's own, neurocultural mediation requires awareness of the variability of neurobiological functions starting from one's own, or else we will be inclined to expect that others experience a situation as we would, feel the emotions we would, react as we would, and we will not understand the legitimacy of different interpretations and reactions.

In the exercise of empathy, it is not enough to think 'how would I feel if I were in your place?'; an extra effort of imagination is necessary, and the question should be 'how would I feel if I were you, in the same situation you are in right now?' Empathy alone is not enough; professionalism is needed. Professionalism alone is not enough; empathy is needed. What is required is conscious empathy. Indeed, neuro-aware empathy.

Just as *cultural relativism* exists, we can also affirm the existence of a certain relativism of constitutional traits, differentiating self-expression even within the context of the same culture. Moreover, we could venture to hypothesize that different cognitive styles may themselves determine a culture or a subculture, as suggested by various authors regarding autism (Davidson, 2008; Rosqvist et al., 2020; Sinclair, 2022; Farahar, 2022).

But what then should a neurocultural mediator do? And how should they do it? The practice of neurocultural mediation must refer to the logics, techniques and tools of intercultural mediation. The cultural mediator does not necessarily have to be a foreigner, just as it is not necessary for them to be perfectly acquainted with the 'two cultures that meet'. Similarly, it is not necessary for the neurocultural mediator to belong to a particular neurotype, nor to have an accurate knowledge of the characteristics of all neurotypes.

The cultural mediator knows the functioning of cultures and understands their underlying mechanisms, is able to affirm cultural relativism, is aware of being an interpreter of culture, and can deconstruct their own reference culture. The neurocultural mediator must be aware that the variety of human expression constitutes the natural fabric of social life, and must understand the mechanisms that establish *habitus* (Bourdieu 1990, 2005), the physiological dynamics of absolutizing one's meanings and the processes of cultural deconstruction and repositioning (Perrenoud, 1996).

The mediator practises disorientation of points of view. They tend as much as possible to be neutral, but more than equidistance, they practise equivicinity. The mediator is not the bridge between two shores but constructs the bridge between the two shores; thus, they are not the one who must ferry the motivations and needs of the respective parties, but instead must provide tools for relationship and deconstruction so that the parties themselves become capable of approaching what they do not understand. The mediator does not replace anyone in the relationship but facilitates it. Mediation is working when it becomes progressively unnecessary. It is not working if it becomes increasingly necessary. The mediator is present in services and encourages their cultural transformation.

The figure of the mediator is hardly compatible with that of the educator/tutor because these two figures play roles that involve different symmetries. An educator is necessarily in an asymmetric relationship with the person they are guiding, they must be. A mediator, to perform their job correctly, must find themselves in a bidirectional symmetric relationship: it is necessary to be in a symmetrical relationship with both interlocutors, always keeping in mind the hierarchical nature of relationships. If the relationship tilts toward one of the two, the characteristics of the mediation relationship are lost, and the intervention returns to the field of tutoring, where the two interlocutors are not necessarily recognized with equal reliability, and where the educator of the nonconforming person will easily have a different kind of relationship with the second interlocutor, tending to reproduce a phenomenon of othering the difference and a dichotomous classification of individual characteristics.

We recognize that there is some resistance to abandoning the idea that an asymmetric approach – of substitution or instruction – is always and in any case necessary in the helping relationship toward nonconforming individuals. On the other hand, mediation involves the delivery of equally distributed tools for cultural deconstruction, just as the distribution of relational responsibility is fair. The tendency to self-preserve one's beliefs, practices, logics and procedural routines is very strong because sometimes these are elements that take on an identity value; thus, deconstructing them means facing the uncomfortable feeling of losing a bit of oneself, temporarily. Hence, a neurocultural mediator can be called such only after they have first gone through their own process of cultural deconstruction.

Reproducing only asymmetric helping relationships, even in those contexts where it is not strictly necessary, is equivalent to assuming that nonconforming individuals cannot be recognized as reliable, ever and in any context – or that they are less generally reliable than their interlocutors. It is an approach that expresses all the paternalism that underlies our approach to differences (Acanfora, 2021, 2022), where, in reality, the only relationship conceived is of an administrative nature. During an anthropology of medicine lecture at the University of Perugia a few years ago, a speaker pronounced, '*Even a person with the most severe intellectual disability can experience a certain degree of agency!*' provided that it is granted to them and – even more so – that we can believe it is possible and necessary; only then will we recognize the opportunity to create spaces for self-determination, where our role is to protect these spaces. The tendency we usually express is to colonize and administer them.

The role of the mediator should not be limited to that of an interpreter, a linguistic translator or addressing the needs of an individual. Resistance to change is a physiological attitude of human beings and is potent in services, and closely linked to bureaucratic processes, habits and professional rigidity. Services often exhibit self-referential tendencies, finding reassurance in routines, not only for autistic individuals.

Existential and cultural differences present a challenge to the status quo, a challenge to which structured systems respond in the direction of self-preservation. The concept of neurocultural mediation aims to be a tool for transforming the logics of the system, starting from the implicit and explicit meanings that drive the individuals participating in it.

Cultural mediation is primarily understood as an activity to promote encounter and knowledge, and to overcome prejudices and stereotypes. It is not exclusively directed at foreign citizens but also at territorial services and society in general. The ultimate goal of mediation in the social context remains the same: to enable people to take advantage of all the opportunities offered by the environment and foster awareness of those that it does not offer. Similarly, the activity of neurocultural mediation is conceived with the perspective of overcoming interventions intended solely or predominantly for autistic individuals, as if they were the sole responsible party for the differences between themselves and others. It is hoped that this mediation extends to services, families, potential interlocutors and all contexts in which the autistic person participates.

The places of neurocultural mediation include schools, workplaces, interpersonal relationships (family/friends/parent training) and socio-health services (among others). The mediator's approach differs from that of an operator who works on the intrinsic abilities of the person. It should also be viewed in the perspective proposed by the *Index for Inclusion* (Booth & Ainscow, 2002), directed at the educational world. When talking about full inclusion, we refer to an approach that rejects the dichotomy between people who include and people to be included. We also emphasize our critical view of the term 'inclusion', which creates cognitive dissonance compared to what it aims to communicate. According to full inclusion, in schools, it should not be the disabled or autistic child who is included by others, as inclusion should not be a charitable operation imposed from above. The exercise of charity is also an exercise of power, implying that, instead of questioning one's privilege and demanding a fair redistribution of that power, the choice is made to administer it. Inclusion should be expressed in processes that tend to reduce power imbalances and dispense power and responsibilities, rights and duties as equitably as possible. Therefore, classmates, teachers and school staff in any capacity are people to whom inclusion should be guaranteed. The same principle applies to the workplace: adopting an inclusive logic means that every person belonging to that context, in any capacity, from the manager to the staff washing windows, is simultaneously included and responsible for including. As Roberto Medeghini (FLC CGIL Toscana, 2021) emphasized during a webinar, '*full inclusion means being able to include oneself in differences*'. We need to stop thinking about society and its contexts dichotomously but realise that we express one of the possible human forms, among many. The same principle applies to the family microsystem: if there are very different neurological expressions at home, there will likely be a different attribution of legitimacy to these expressions. As a result, relational and power asymmetries will not only be determined by specific family roles (parent/child) but also governed by the interpretation of difference as a delegitimizing deviation to be resolved in the person. The same reasoning applies to all interpersonal relationships, as autism and disability, in general, are culturally approached with a logic that produces the pathologization and alterization of degenerate identities (Morel, 1857; Nordau, 1895).

It is curious to note that in Italy, some organizations providing services for autism have eagerly seized the opportunity to articulate their role in terms of mediation, without deeming it necessary to deepen their understanding of the subject. The self-referentiality of services and professionals in the field of care and psychoeducational support is a widespread problem in Italy and proves to be a significant obstacle to individual and collective growth. These attempts to colonize issues and proposals emerging from grassroots initiatives, based on an approach that is decidedly political, more sociocultural than medical–clinical, translate into improbable attempts to rename what should continue to be called by its name: a professional educator. The role of the educator is centrally important and does not need a refreshed image to be valued and recognized. The sad outcome of this self-referential colonization process is to propose training courses on mediation for the social inclusion of autistic or disabled individuals, in which not a single hour is dedicated to the concept, tools and practices of mediation. These are simply courses for educators where the nature of the differences characterizing the target population is discussed (strictly according to the *Diagnostic and Statistical Manual of Mental Disorders* [DSM]). Various intervention techniques on the target population are taught, and at most, activities of 'awareness' to be allocated to schoolmates or colleagues are conceived. It seems appropriate to point out that one of the places that most requires neurocultural mediation is precisely that of services. Operators engaged in care and assistance relationships with disabled individuals not only carry the cultural conditioning that governs their relationship with differences, common to the entire population in society but also, due to their academic and professional training and the role they inevitably play, they are inclined to further radicalize and naturalize the generalization of asymmetry characterizing their relationship with the user. It is as if this were a natural outcome of the user's condition and, above all, without distinguishing the different life contexts: whether it is an educational centre, a school class, a workplace, a restaurant or the kitchen of their own home, the nonconforming person remains trapped in this perpetually and transversally lacking representation, essentializing their identity in the meanings attributed to their deviation from their reference culture.

Currently, we are conducting experimental training in various contexts, from socio-health to work, university and especially advanced training courses for teachers. In these courses, we propose to requalify the role of the support teacher in terms of neurocultural mediation. The aim is to enrich class groups and school operators with a set of critical, interpretative and operational tools for relating to 'the other', and thus, differences. This promotes a vision of society in which differences are understood as the natural fabric of social life.

In the Italian school context, efforts toward inclusion often translate into an attempt to normalize the 'nonconforming' person. There are informational and awareness interventions toward the class group, often of a condescending nature, aiming to stimulate an attitude of 'tolerance'. Additionally, there are training courses for support teachers that are based on medical notions and lists of instructions and procedures on what to do and what not to do with autistic children. In our direct and indirect experience, the support teacher is rarely conceived as a support to the class group to facilitate encounters between different human types. More often, they are seen as mere support for the 'nonconforming' individual.

The support teacher's role is indeed asymmetric concerning students, but – at least on paper – it is intended to be the same with all students. Within an Italian school class, the support teacher is in the perfect position to play the role of a neurocultural mediator. It is already planned and present within the school service; norms dictate that they should facilitate the inclusion of all students without distinction (although their assignment to the class is still conditioned by the certification of disability in one or more children). It is expected that they should be a reference for the entire class and not just for the disabled child. From our point of view, they only need effective tools for cultural deconstruction and mediation to significantly impact the baggage that informs the relationship with the differences of children and adolescents. This will contribute to raising generations that are culturally more inclusive than ours. The goal of understanding the role of educational support in terms of neurocultural mediation is not only to provide a conflict resolution strategy between the class group and the nonconforming person. Rather, it is to educate toward a different cultural approach to relational and expressive differences. This goes beyond explaining the nonconforming person to classmates and aims to translate each person in the room to themselves, highlighting the legitimate differences that set them apart from others and how these differences sometimes create distances.

Preparing mediation tools, within this perspective, for use in the school context does not end with a brief list of more or less rigid indications of what to do and what not to do. It involves developing a mindset as mediation artisans. It is necessary to understand the principles and tools of cultural mediation, apply them to oneself, and be flexible, creative and approach different situations with a clear educational goal of enabling awareness that we are expressions of only ONE human type. This type influences how we perceive, understand and experience ourselves and the world. Each situation will inevitably require tailor-made interventions, and their effectiveness will be directly proportional to the quality of the work the teacher has done on themselves. It depends on how well they have internalized this paradigm shift, not so much conceptually but psychologically and emotionally. The intent of neurocultural mediation in schools is to break the generational transmission of the culture of alienation from difference. It aims to educate future adults to interpret conflicts arising from relational and existential distances as the result of a culturally determined interpretative distortion. This distortion fails to provide functional and effective relationship tools.

Among the most significant experiences of neurocultural mediation experimented with so far, one stands out – the research and intervention project 'Educating Children to Neurodiversity'. Conceived, structured and proposed by the association Neuropeculiar APS and a team of researchers, it involved six third-grade classes from five schools, distributed across three different regions in Italy (south, central and northern Italy). The project included preliminary training for teachers and a 20-hour plan with the children. During this time, we undertook a progressive and interactive journey of discovery and meaning-making of the neurodiversity that characterizes the human race. This diversity is manifested through a wide differentiation of communicative, relational, sensory and cognitive expressions. Throughout the meetings, using games, interactive activities and multimedia material produced by us, the children experienced different sensory perceptions, and ways of paying attention and communicating. Importantly, we dedicated a significant amount of time to open discussions on how these differences influence the meaning of lived experiences, emotions, behaviour and ways of relating to others.

For the research component, we administered a preliminary evaluation test to the class group, assessing parameters identified by the project team. The questionnaire consisted of vignettes depicting possible situations in which some children might find themselves in real life while interacting with diversity. The same survey, with different vignettes, was presented to the children at the end of the project. For teachers, a qualitative survey was conducted at the end of the project and at the midterm.

Data analysis is still ongoing, but we can report some observed elements that we find interesting in the list below:

- During various unexpected experiences, the children raised the question, 'So, what is truly reality?' They were realising that, until that moment, each of them had absolutized their own experience, believing it to be the only possible one. Consequently, they were more inclined to negatively judge those who exhibited reactions and behaviours not in line with this expectation. Our primary goal was not to instruct on the peculiarities of neurodivergences but to achieve a repositioning of each child (and each adult) in the class.
- Empirically, we observed that as the course progressed, the attitude of the children involved, as they became amazed by the differences they discovered, gradually became

more oriented toward identifying the variables that belonged to themselves. They were conducting a path of self-awareness of their own functioning, which, therefore, ceased to be absolute and became individual-specific, like that of everyone else (awareness of neurodiversity).

- At the end of the project, we asked the children if they believed that the adults in their lives would have understood the important things they now knew if they had tried to explain them. The answer was no. We found this data particularly interesting. On the whole, telling an adult that they have experienced differences in how they feel and do things, or that a colour-blind person sees the world in different colours, doesn't seem so complicated. Therefore, we tend to believe that it is the emotional and relational implications that derive from it, the relativization of one's experience, the change in perspective on oneself and the other, that are perceived, rightly so, as difficult to convey. For us, this response was a small confirmation that the children felt they had gained something that adults, without undergoing a similar experience, would not understand. This is what neurocultural mediation should achieve.

In hindsight, also in consideration of discussions with the teachers and their involvement during the project, we deemed it necessary to plan, for the future, a more articulated definition of the teachers' role within the project and more time to be dedicated not only to their training on the neurodiversity paradigm but also to the deconstruction of their views on disability, differences and the nature of the relationship with these elements. We expect that the effects of the project, already observable in the children, need to be supported, encouraged and confirmed over time to ensure that they are taking root and that these effects actually constitute a baggage imprinted in personal history. We have discussed the possible involvement of families several times for the same reason, but for now, we have not found formulas promising enough to involve them, given the logic of the complex Italian school system.

The aim of this proposal is twofold: on the one hand, to help both parties understand the difference that separates them and makes interaction difficult, and on the other hand, to use the neurocultural mediator as a strategic tool for cultural evolution: from a dichotomous view of society, which pits groups of people characterized by particular features (autistic/disabled/migrant, etc.) against the virtual macrogroup of prototypical people, not further characterized (Brekhus, 1998; Zerubavel, 1997, 2018), to a vision that embraces the complexity of human expression and naturalizes awareness of its variety. When people interact with each other they need to understand that their own existential style is only one of many possible styles – this includes professionals – and since they experience the world differently, they need to take these differences into account in order to understand each other, communicate and complete their interaction effectively.

References

Acanfora, F. (2021). *In altre parole. Dizionario minimo di diversità*. effequ.

Acanfora, F. (2022). *Di pari passo: Il lavoro oltre l'idea di inclusione*. Luiss University Press.

Bisin, A., Verdier, T., & Manning, A. (2012). *Cultural Integration of Immigrants in Europe*. Oxford University Press.

Booth, T., & Ainscow, M. (2002). *Index for Inclusion: Developing Learning and Participation in Schools*. Centre for Studies on Inclusive Education (CSIE).

Bourdieu, P. (1990). *The Logic of Practice*. Stanford University Press.

Bourdieu, P. (2005). Habitus. In J. Hillier & E. Rooksby (Eds.), *Habitus: A Sense of Place* (pp. 43–52). Routledge.

Brekhus, W. (1998). A Sociology of the unmarked: Redirecting our focus. *Sociological Theory*, *16*(1), 34–51. https://doi.org/10.1111/0735-2751.00041

Cambridge Free English Dictionary (2023). Culture. Cambridge University Press. https://dictionary.cambridge.org/dictionary/english/culture

Cesareo, V. (1998). Studi e riflessioni per lo sviluppo del dialogo interculturali. In C. Demarchi, N. Papa, & N. Storti, *Per una città delle culture. Dialogo interculturale e scuola, Atti del Convegno Nazionale 8-9 maggio 1997* (Vol. 3, p. 16). Quaderni ISMU.

Crompton, C. J., Ropar, D., Evans-Williams, C. V. M., Flynn, E., & Fletcher-Watson, S. (2020). Autistic peer-to-peer information transfer is highly effective. *Autism*, *24*(7), 1704–1712. https://doi.org/10.1177/1362361320919286

Davidson, J. (2008). Autistic culture online: Virtual communication and cultural expression on the spectrum. *Social & Cultural Geography*, *9*(7), 791–806. https://doi.org/10.1080/14649360802382586

Devereux, G. (1961). Shamans as neurotics. *American Anthropologist*, *63*(5), 1088–1090. https://doi.org/10.1525/aa.1961.63.5.02a00110

Ellenberger, H. F. (2020). Ethnopsychiatry [1965–1967]. In H. F. Ellenberger, *Ethnopsychiatry*. McGill-Queen's University Press. https://doi.org/10.2307/j.ctv1bhg28z.6

Farahar, C. (2022). Autistic identity, culture, community, and space for well-being. In D. Milton, & S. Ryan (Eds.), *The Routledge International Handbook of Critical Autism Studies* (pp. 229–241). Routledge. https://doi.org/10.4324/9781003056577-23

FLC CGIL Toscana (2021, June 23). *Disability studies: Nuove prospettive per l'inclusione scolastica* [video]. Roberto Medeghini starts speech at 01:08:00. YouTube. https://www.youtube.com/watch?v = ER7vTCYvl-s

Fougeyrollas, P. (1987). Normalité et corps différents: regard sur l'integration sociale des handicapés physiques. *Anthropologie et sciences*, *2*, 51–71.

Galton, F. (1869). *Hereditary Genius: An Inquiry into Its Laws and Consequences*. Macmillan Publishers.

Galton, F. (1883). *Inquiries into Human Faculty and Its Development*. Macmillan Publishers.

Hacking, I. (1986). Making up people. In T. C. Heller, M. Sosna, & D. Wellbery (Eds.), *Reconstructing Individualism* (pp. 222–236). Stanford University Press.

Heasman, B., & Gillespie, A. (2018). Neurodivergent intersubjectivity: Distinctive features of how autistic people create shared understanding. *Autism*, *23*(4), 910–921. https://doi.org/10.1177/1362361318785172

Kluckhohn, C. (1961). *Anthropology and the Classics* (p. 73). Brown Publishing Company.

Milton, D. (2012). On the ontological status of autism: The 'double empathy problem.' *Disability & Society*, *27*(6), 883–887. https://doi.org/10.1080/09687599.2012.710008

Milton, D. (2014). Autistic expertise: A critical reflection on the production of knowledge in autism studies. *Autism*, *18*(7), 794–802. https://doi.org/10.1177/1362361314525281

Milton, D., Heasman, B., & Sheppard, E. (2020). Double empathy. In F. R. Volkmar (Ed.), *Encyclopedia of Autism Spectrum Disorders* (pp. 1–9). Springer. https://doi.org/10.1007/978-1-4614-6435-8_102273-2

Morel, B. (1857) *Traité des Dégénérescences*.

Nordau, M. S. (1895). *Degeneration*. D. Appleton & Co.

Ochs, E., & Solomon, O. (2010). Autistic sociality. *Ethos*, *38*(1), 69–92. https://doi.org/10.1111/j.1548-1352.2009.01082.x

Ochs, E., Kremer-Sadlik, T., Sirota, K. G., & Solomon, O. (2004). Autism and the social world: An anthropological perspective. *Discourse Studies*, *6*(2), 147–183. https://doi.org/10.1177/1461445604041766

Ochs, E., Kremer-Sadlik, T., Solomon, O., & Sirota, K. G. (2001). Inclusion as social practice: Views of children with autism. *Social Development*, *10*(3), 399–419. https://doi.org/10.1111/1467-9507.00172

Ottenheimer, H. J. (2008). *The Anthropology of Language: An introduction to Linguistic anthropology*. Cengage Learning.

Oxford Dictionary of Philosophy (2nd ed.) (2008). Culture. Oxford University Press. https://doi.org/10.1093/acref/9780199541430.001.0001

Perrenoud, P. (1996) *Le travail sur l'habitus dans la formation des enseignants*. University of Geneva. https://www.unige.ch/fapse/SSE/teachers/perrenoud/php_main/php_1996/1996_13.html

Premack, D., & Woodruff, G. (1978). Does the chimpanzee have a theory of mind? *Behavioral and Brain Sciences*, *1*(4), 515–526. https://doi.org/10.1017/s0140525x00076512

Quételet, A. (1835). *Sur l'homme et le développement de ses facultés: ou Essai de physique Sociale*. Bachelier.

Rosqvist, H. B., Chown, N., & Stenning, A. (2020). *Neurodiversity Studies: A New Critical Paradigm*. Routledge. https://doi.org/10.4324/9780429322297

Sinclair, J. (1993). Don't mourn for us. *Our Voice*, *1*,(3).

Sinclair, J. (2022). Cultural commentary: Being autistic together. In A. Clarke, J. Boys, & J. Gardner (Eds.), *Developments in Neuroethics and Bioethics: Volume 5 Neurodivergence and Architecture* (pp. 99–128). Academic Press. https://doi.org/10.1016/bs.dnb.2022.08.002

Sterponi, L. (2004). Construction of rules, accountability and moral identity by high-functioning children with autism. *Discourse Studies*, *6*(2), 207–228. https://doi.org/10.1177/1461445604041768

Swaab, D. F. (2014). *We are Our Brains: A Neurobiography of the Brain, from the Womb to Alzheimer's*. Random House.

Winawer, J., Witthoft, N., Frank, M. C., Wu, L. M., Wade, A. R., & Boroditsky, L. (2007). Russian blues reveal effects of language on color discrimination. *Proceedings of the National Academy of Sciences of the United States of America*, *104*(19), 7780–7785. https://doi.org/10.1073/pnas.0701644104

Zanfrini, L. (2010). *Sociologia della convivenza interetnica* (pp. 29-55). Laterza.

Zerubavel, E. (1997). *Social Mindscapes: An Invitation to Cognitive Sociology*. Harvard University Press.

Zerubavel, E. (2018). *Taken for Granted: The Remarkable Power of the Unremarkable*. Princeton University Press.

Chapter 21:
Using the Double Empathy Problem to Reframe Supports for Peer Interaction

Michelle O'Donoghue, Carol-Anne Murphy, Verónica Vidal, Consuelo Martínez, Fiona Ferris and Laura DeThorne

Grant me the dignity of meeting me on my own terms – recognise that we are equally alien to each other and that my ways of being are not merely [a] damaged version of yours.
(Sinclair, 1992, p. 302)

The landscape

Medical model of autism

Despite shifting diagnostic criteria for autism since the 1980s, perceived deficits in social interaction have remained a core feature (Volkmar & Reichow, 2013; Zeldovich, 2018). At present, the *Diagnostic and Statistical Manual of Mental Disorders*, 5th edition (DSM-5) defines autism as 'persistent deficits' in social communication and 'restricted, repetitive patterns of behaviour, interests, or activities' (American Psychiatric Association, 2013, p. 50). This definition is consistent with the concept of autism as a medical condition that needs to be fixed or cured (Straus, 2013). Accordingly, supports for peer interaction have largely treated autistic children as the source of 'the problem', with interventions often aimed at developing non-autistic patterns of behaviour around social skills such as eye contact, joint attention, turn-taking and topic maintenance (Vidal et al., 2018b). Somewhat ironically, however, none of these skills can actually be accomplished alone, and the expectations for such interactions differ based on various aspects of the environment – the participants (e.g., peer versus authority figure), the activity (e.g., circle time versus free play), the available resources (e.g., synchronous in-person versus asynchronous virtual) and the culture at large (e.g., Western versus Eastern or hearing versus Deaf).

Distributed model of communication

In contrast to medicalized models that emphasize what individual skills are needed for communication, social models emphasize the shared and distributed nature of communicative competence. Specifically, Hengst (2015) outlines a model of *distributed communication* as a theoretical framework for building supportive environments for child language development. This framework views communicative competence as shared across communicative partners, inherently multimodal in terms of resources, embedded within activities and environments, and evolving over time (see also Hengst, 2020). A distributed model of communication creates space for the ways that communication partners and other various aspects of the environment (e.g., in/access to augmentative alternative communication [AAC], cultural views) construct communicative in/competence (e.g., DeThorne et al. 2015; Vidal et al., 2023). A commentary provided by Bottema-Beutel et al. (2017) highlighted that such contextual nuances are largely ignored in traditional social skills training for autistic people.

The Double Empathy Problem and autism

Consistent with the idea of communication being distributed/shared across people, Damian Milton (2012) proposed the Double Empathy Problem as a way to frame the social challenges associated with autism. Milton highlighted that empathy is a two-way street, and noted that autistic and non-autistic individuals may have difficulty empathizing with one another due to their different experiences of the world. It might be hard for an autistic person to understand why eye contact is viewed as a form of affection, just as it might be difficult for a non-autistic person to understand the social conventions around infodumping or the painful nature of many everyday sensory experiences. One of the autistic participants in Kimber et al.'s qualitative study of how autistic people experience empathy wrote:

> *It can be more difficult to innately empathize with 'neurotypical people [...] their minds experience things differently thus how they are feeling, what they're thinking, or what their intentions and motivations are will be more alien as compared to those of an autistic mind. [...] However, the very same has happened with roles reversed, with 'neurotypicals' acting callous toward me when I'm upset about something they think is trivial.*
> (Kimber et al., 2023, p. 6)

Although such misunderstandings may be bidirectional in nature, autistic persons are more likely to be stigmatized for their misunderstandings given their neurominoritized status (Sasson et al., 2018). The consequences of such misunderstandings are augmented by the power differential that exists between autistic students and predominantly non-autistic therapists and educators. This power differential between autistic and non-autistic students is exacerbated when interventions privilege non-autistic social behaviours and position non-autistic peers as role models and/or co-therapists.

The neurodiversity perspective

The neurodiversity movement has been central in understanding and building appreciation for autistic sociality. It emerged as a social movement in the 1990s focused on the rights of neurominorities, including those who communicate in non-standard ways and do not have the ability, or access, to narrate their own experiences (Straus, 2013). The term 'neurodiversity' has often been attributed to Australian sociologist, Judy Singer (1999), but the concept has multiple collective origins within autistic and neurodivergent communities (Botha et al., 2024).

Central to this diversity model of autism is the idea that it does not need to be eradicated, corrected or 'cured'. Instead, traits, such as autistic sociality, are viewed as neutral or positive. Connections through the neurodiversity movement, fuelled by ready internet access, have accelerated development of an autistic community and culture around autistic strengths, values and ways of being (Bagatell, 2010; Silberman, 2015; Straus, 2013). The development of community has supported advocacy, which has focused on reducing/eliminating harm, promoting acceptance of differences, and emphasizing accommodation and access (Rattazzi, 2020). Autistic voices and perspectives have become a fundamental part of the social change against the discrimination, stigma and exclusion autistic people often face (AsIAm, 2023; Cadaveira & Waisburg, 2018). Accordingly, neurodiversity activists emphasize the need for greater autistic representation in the decision-making, services and policies that impact them, using the motto '*Nothing about us, without us*.'

The aim of the present chapter is to draw on a distributed model of communication, the concept of the Double Empathy Problem and the neurodiversity movement at large to reframe peer interaction supports for autistic children and youth. Accordingly, the remainder of the chapter is organized into the following sections: i) traditional models of peer-mediated intervention, ii) an alternative approach to supporting peer interactions for autistic children, and iii) application of the alternative approach to a case example.

Peer-mediated intervention

Defining peer-mediated intervention

Peer-mediated intervention (PMI) is a term used to describe a variety of intervention approaches that focus on interaction between an autistic person and their peers, who are typically non-autistic. It includes interventions in which adults scaffold interaction between the autistic and non-autistic children, such as integrated play groups (e.g., Wolfberg et al., 2015). It also includes interventions where the peers are taught strategies to use when interacting with autistic children, such as stay-play-talk (e.g., Goldstein et al., 1997; Ledford & Pustejovsky, 2021). Non-autistic peers may be used as tutors or interventionists to teach specific skills such as initiating social interaction (DiSalvo & Oswald, 2002; Rogers et al. 2000).

Outcomes of peer-mediated intervention

Several reviews conclude that PMI promotes social interaction between autistic children and their peers (Chan et al., 2009; Ledford & Pustejovsky, 2021), including reviews of group studies (Chang & Locke, 2016), preschool-age children (Chapin et al., 2018), inclusive preschool settings (Watkins et al., 2015) and autistic children who are minimally speaking (O'Donoghue et al., 2021). Common outcome measures include the length of time spent in interactions, and the number of initiations made by the autistic child and their peers. There is little evidence of improved quality-of-life measures that are important and relevant to autistic people.

Concerns regarding peer-mediated intervention

Ostensibly, PMI focuses on enhancing interaction between an autistic person and their peer(s). However, an underlying ableist assumption of PMI is that the skills of a non-autistic peer are superior to those of the autistic person and the autistic person will benefit from spending time with a non-autistic peer. Consider, for example, in the integrated play group model outlined by Wolfberg and colleagues (2015), the autistic child is labelled as 'novice' and the non-autistic child as 'expert.' Accordingly, PMIs have largely expected autistic children to meet non-autistic social-communicative expectations. In a review of PMIs for autistic children by DiSalvo and Oswald (2002, p. 198), the authors wrote, '*Peer-mediated strategies typically involve the use of socially competent peers to model and reinforce appropriate social behaviour*' (see also Osborne et al., 2019; Rogers et al. 2000). Privileging non-autistic social skills serves to reinforce existing social stigma associated with autism, thereby teaching non-autistic peers (albeit inadvertently perhaps) that autistic peers have lacking or inferior social skills.

In addition, PMI can include training of the autistic child about non-autistic social interaction (e.g., Dueñas et al., 2021; Kent et al., 2021). This often involves directly or indirectly pressuring autistic students to change their autistic traits and to appear less autistic. This approach prioritizes non-autistic social expectations and fails to recognize or appreciate autistic sociality, thereby encouraging autistic masking, the conscious or unconscious suppression of natural autistic responses. Masking, or camouflaging, starts at a young age (Miller et al., 2021) and is associated with negative mental health outcomes (Beck et al., 2020; Hull et al., 2021; Pearson & Rose, 2021) and autistic burnout (e.g., Mantzalas et al., 2022).

Privileging non-autistic social skills and elevating non-autistic peers to the role of tutor or interventionist establishes a non-egalitarian social dynamic between peers in which the non-autistic peer serves as a role model or tutor (Vidal et al., 2018b). While mentoring relationships can be beneficial, they are not generally conducive to the egalitarian dynamics that define friendship. Finke (2016) stresses that in order for friendship to be achieved as an outcome, the following needs to be considered: equal status among the children, using mutually motivating and authentic opportunities for interaction and planning for frequent interaction opportunities within these activities.

Alternative peer interaction supports

In light of concerns with traditional PMI, we recommend an alternative approach to providing peer interaction supports for autistic children and youth, one that aligns with a distributed model of communication, the Double Empathy Problem particularly, and the neurodiversity movement at large. Specifically, we recommend supports that centre autistic perspectives, focus on strengths and interests, and prioritize environmental change. Given the medicalized nature of the term 'intervention' (e.g., Monk et al., 2022), we will be using the term 'peer interaction supports' to describe this approach.

Centre autistic perspectives

In autism research generally, and in intervention research specifically, the autistic voice is often absent, as are voices of other members of the autism community, including caregivers, educators and peers. Interventions have largely been conceptualized by neurotypical professionals, without incorporating perspectives of the broader autism community. Interventions develop without consultation about people's lived experiences, their priorities, values and real-life implementation contexts. In particular, the voice of the autistic population has been marginalized (Botha & Cage, 2022; Ezzamel & Bond, 2016; Milton & Bracher, 2013).

Partnership with the autism community is required to design and develop interventions that are desirable, beneficial and have a positive impact on autistic people's lives (see Leadbitter et al., 2021; Milton, 2014). The research community needs to adopt participatory approaches to research to include autistic people (Fletcher-Watson et al., 2019; Nicolaidis et al., 2019; Donaldson, 2024). Best practice guidelines on intervention development advocate for collaboration with end users throughout the intervention development process (O'Cathain et al., 2019). Grounding interventions in a sensitive awareness of the perspectives and lives of the people who will use them enables intervention developers to understand how different people, in different situations, may view and engage with the intervention (Yardley et al., 2015). Autistic people and their allies can identify which elements of the intervention seem particularly relevant and useful to them; and which may be rejected. Engaging with end users is critical if effective intervention approaches are to be implemented in real-world education settings (Moir, 2018).

Historically, end users of PMIs have had limited contribution to their development (Ezzamel & Bond, 2016). There is a lack of understanding of what is needed by autistic people, and their peers, educators and parents. In a series of studies, O'Donoghue et al. (2023, 2024) engaged these stakeholders in an iterative process to inform the development of peer interaction supports for minimally speaking autistic children in Irish early childhood education contexts. Autistic adults, early childhood educators (ECEs), parents of autistic and non-autistic children, early childhood sector leaders and policy influencers, and speech and language therapists (SLTs) explored the acceptability and feasibility of peer interaction supports in a series of focus groups, semistructured interviews and document reviews. While peer interaction supports were acceptable to this group of stakeholders, their concept of what it should involve, and how the approach should be conceptualized, deviated from traditional approaches to PMI. Two of the consistent findings across stakeholder groups were the importance of adopting a strengths-based approach which builds on people's interests and making changes to the environment (for full results see O'Donoghue et al., 2023).

Utilize a strengths- and interests-based approach

PMI, like many intervention approaches, is deficits-based. It assumes that there are social skills, such as initiating conversations, that can be improved upon. If social supports are to provide an opportunity for egalitarian friendship building, as outlined by Finke (2016), then a shift is required toward authentic engagement around a topic of mutual interest. These connections can have a powerful effect. A participant in O'Donoghue et al. (2024) describes how connecting with someone at school, based on their interests, felt '*like an electric fence was going through me, I really became alive*' (autistic participant, O'Donoghue et al., 2024). Not surprisingly, autistic people engage more when their interests are incorporated into social activities (Baker et al., 1998; Koegel et al., 2012; Watkins et al., 2019b).

A clinical focus article by Vidal et al. (2018b) outlined three key elements of a supports-based approach to peer interaction, as a contrast to traditional skills-based interventions. The first element was a focus on participation in shared activity, ideally one of mutual interest, where participation is taken up broadly to include multimodal resources. The article outlines an activity-based music programme designed around the interests of a

7-year-old autistic student with AAC and four of his non-autistic classmates, all of whom shared an interest in music. In addition to AAC access, the programme foregrounded non-verbal participation through seating arrangements, interaction with instruments and use of conducting gestures. Other authors have emphasized the role of shared interests in facilitating peer interaction as well (e.g., Baker et al., 1998; Hu et al., 2021; Koegel et al., 2012; Santhanam, 2023). With shared interests as a priority for interactions, educational staff might consider seating accordingly, or take a moment to highlight students shared interests. For example, if an autistic student loves movies, then a great introduction activity might be for everyone to write a favourite movie on their nametag.

Participants in O'Donoghue et al. (2023) conceptualized peer interaction supports as being embedded within the ethos of the early childhood setting. A strength of the approach is that it can be implemented throughout the day, as opportunities arise. It was not a standalone intervention conducted at specific times of the day, as is the case in the implementation of most peer interaction supports (O'Donoghue et al., 2021; Watkins et al., 2019a; Whalon et al., 2015). Rather, its value lies in how it can become part of people's daily routines, *'It's not rocket science. This is just something that you learn to do and [it] will become part of everyday practice'* (autistic participant, O'Donoghue et al., 2023). This requires a workforce who are skilled and ready to implement supports as children require them. This requires environmental change.

Make environmental change

Within a medical model, the aim of intervention is to affect change within an individual. This may be through direct skill-building work with an autistic person or mediated through parents or peers. However, both the distributed model of communication and the neurodiversity paradigm highlight environmental contributions to peer interaction. As an example, a study by Vidal et al. (2023) utilized a situated discourse analysis to illustrate how environmental systems shaped the peer interactions of a minimally speaking autistic child in the classroom, specifically outlining broad macrosystem factors, such as the predominant stigmatizing view toward autism, all the way to microsystem factors, such as how individual interactions were influenced by pacing and use of objects. Vidal et al. (2023, pp. 74–75) also identified limited staff training as a barrier to peer interaction. In particular, the paraprofessional that supported the autistic child in the classroom reported that he had not received any training specific to autism and was doing his best to *'learn on the fly'*.

The stakeholders from O'Donoghue et al. (2024) also recommended the need for environmental changes, such as adopting a whole centre approach where all staff members receive training in peer interaction supports. Such an approach would need to be adaptable to meet the needs of individual early childhood and care settings, meeting educators where they are at in terms of inclusion and their understanding of autism. Integrating peer interaction supports within existing initiatives and utilizing terminology that is familiar to educators would contribute to the feasibility and sustainability of the approach and to the creation of a workforce who are ready to implement supports as autistic children need them, in a child-led manner.

Key areas of training for support personnel that are particularly germane to peer interaction include: i) accessing/integrating AAC (e.g., Donaldson et al., 2023; Robertson, 2010), ii) understanding autistic sensory-motor needs (e.g., Kapp, 2019; Vidal et al., 2020), iii) recognizing/appreciating autistic sociality (e.g., Heasman & Gillespie, 2019; Jaswal & Akhtar, 2018; Jaswal et al., 2020; Ochs & Solomon, 2010), and iv) re-examining one's role as a bidirectional facilitator (e.g., Vidal et al., 2018a). With regard to the latter, Wolfberg (2008) has described the adult role in facilitating peer interaction as a 'stage director' who sets up the environment, assigns roles and narrates the lines as needed. Vidal et al. (2018a) offered and illustrated the term 'behavioural interpretation' as a strategy to foster understanding between autistic and non-autistic peers for behaviours and expectations that might be unclear.

Because of the inherent power imbalance that often favours non-autistic children in institutional settings, such as school, direct training for non-autistic peers may be particularly warranted (Bottema-Beutel, 2017). Of interest, an experimental group study by Kasari et al. (2012) compared two interventions for autistic students (aged 6–11 years): one focused on the autistic children and the other focused on their non-autistic peers. After six weeks of intervention, the group that directed intervention toward the non-autistic peers offered better social outcomes for the autistic students.

It is worth noting that the Double Empathy Problem does not automatically discount the need for autistic students to focus on understanding or targeting non-autistic social skills. The process of masking/camouflaging/passing can serve important safety and accessibility functions. However, Shaw et al. (2023) note that autistic people often develop a greater understanding of non-autistic social interaction than the reverse, given that autistic people have little choice but to develop such an understanding to survive in a non-autistic world. However, it is important to help clients balance the potential benefits of masking with the additional cognitive load and mental health consequences that autistic adults have reported in association with such efforts (e.g., Cage & Troxel-Whitman, 2019; Cassidy et al., 2020; Hull et al., 2021; Miller et al., 2021). The autistic community has offered other priorities for support, including agency, self-determination and communication access (e.g., Donaldson et al., 2021; Donaldson et al., 2023; Robertson, 2010). In sum, supports need to tip the scale toward change in the environment, including peers and educators, over asking autistic students to shoulder more of the burden.

Case Example

Introducing Aaron

Given the need to centre autistic voices, embrace a strength- and interest-based approach, and focus on environmental change, how do we translate this into social supports for autistic children and youth within current educational settings? We aim here to illustrate one case example of how these elements can be applied, focusing on a single student, referred to here by the pseudonym 'Aaron', who has been studied in prior research (i.e., DeThorne et al., 2015; Vidal et al., 2018a; Vidal et al., 2018b). Although the case is situated within the US, we have focused on systemic aspects of support (e.g., eligibility determination, goal-writing and accommodations) that are similar across our three countries (i.e., Chile, Ireland and the US).

Aaron is a White 7-year-old minimally speaking autistic student from a university affiliated school in the midwestern United States. His communication practices included some spoken words, signs, a speech-generating augmentative alternative communication (SG-AAC) device, and a bound set of printed pages from his SG-AAC device. Aaron's peer interactions are considered limited and intentionally constrained, in part by teachers, due to his history of hitting others for reasons that were often not clear.

Assessment and eligibility processes

Across many Western countries, obtaining disability-related supports begins with an assessment and eligibility determination process. For autistic students in the US, this eligibility determination process occurs within the public schools and is focused on meeting pre-established criteria for eligibility categories, including autism, that are framed from a very medicalized perspective (e.g., 'impairment in reciprocal social interaction'). This focus often leads toward assessment reports that reflect a highly pathologized narrative focused on deficits in the child.

Despite such systemic constraints, written assessment results can still incorporate autistic perspectives, and build on strengths/interests and relevant environmental factors. For example, Aaron's perspective as the autistic student could be gathered through modified interview procedures (Harrington et al., 2014), supplemented by input from trusted caregivers, and direct observation of Aaron's regulation and preferences throughout the school day. In addition, seeking out direct input from autistic people can elicit useful insights on unusual behaviour and provide suggestions for less stigmatizing language (Bottema-Beutel et al., 2021; Monk et al., 2022). For example, a statement such as *'Aaron lacks eye contact'*, can be reframed as *'Consistent with autistic sociality, Aaron tends to rely on fleeting and peripheral eye gaze for social information'*.

Direct observation and autistic input also help in recognizing and documenting relevant environmental factors and related needs, accommodations or supplementary supports. Resulting reports might make note of such environmental factors as teachers' approaches, peers' abilities to recognize his autistic sociality, accessibility of AAC and/or aspects of the sensory environment. For example, one might note in Aaron's report that his social engagement appears to be facilitated by side-by-side seating with shared interest in an object rather than face-to-face positioning. Not only does this statement acknowledge his autistic sociality, but it also helps non-autistic people understand how best to engage him, thereby providing ideas for goals and supplementary supports.

Goal-writing and supplemental supports

Once eligible for services in the US, school personnel lead development of the Individualized Education Plan (IEP) that specifies setting, services and goals. Again, this process should centre the autistic student's perspective. Perhaps a student such as Aaron could be given the opportunity to 'try out' a couple of different settings or services, observed for indicators of comfort/distress, and directly asked about preferences with related pictures on his AAC supports.

Goal-writing provides another important opportunity to communicate respect for autistic sociality, leverage strengths and interests, and integrate environmental support (see DeThorne & Searsmith, 2020). As an example, Aaron's parents and teachers reported his interest in musical activities and when asked whether he likes music, he selected 'want music' on his talker paired with non-verbal signs of enthusiasm. Consequently, musical activity seems like a strong context for facilitating positive peer interactions and can be specified in a goal, as can access to his AAC devices or other environmental supports. An example of such a goal would be, '*With access to AAC and at least one selected peer, Aaron will engage in at least one instance of shared positive affect during 85% of musical activities*'. In addition to leveraging his interest in music and his preference in specific peers, this example goal focuses on shared enjoyment (no words needed) and helps ensure Aaron's access to his AAC supports. Ari Ne'eman (2023), at a recent symposium presentation, proposed two relevant criteria for intervention: i) the outcome should not be focused on making the student seem less autistic and ii) the outcome should be accomplished in the least burdensome means for the autistic person.

In the US, the IEP also includes a section dedicated to accommodation and supplementary supports. Although such sections may not carry the same degree of administrative oversight as goals/objectives, they offer an important opportunity to specify needs for environmental change (see DeThorne & Searsmith, 2020). Accordingly, examples of environmental factors that may have supported Aaron's peer interactions in the classroom include peer and staff training on topics such as neurodiversity, autistic sociality and AAC. Other common support needs expressed by members of the autistic community include access to AAC, sensory accommodations (e.g., noise-cancelling headphones, non-fluorescent lighting), frequent breaks, visual/written information and simplified text.

Conclusions

While our case example focused primarily on how educators and therapists can work within existing systems to reframe social interaction supports for autistic students, there is clearly need for broader reform, including policy change (McVey et al., 2023). There are reasons to be hopeful. Despite recent political turmoil in the US federal landscape, language from the neurodiversity paradigm has been shaping academic writing since the 2000s (Vidal et al., 2024). The Autistic Self Advocacy Network (ASAN), which formed in 2006, publicly comments on legislation and professional guidelines that impact autistic people on a regular basis, including persistent lobbying against harmful practices (see Autistic Self Advocacy Network, 2023).

During recent years in Chile, a group of autistic advocates and autistic organization leaders formed the Interregional Autism Table (MILA, its acronym in Spanish) to raise their voices to claim rights for autistic communities. Based on this community work, an autistic law was published during 2023 (TEA Law, 2023). This law ensures equal opportunities and social participation of autistic individuals, eliminating any form of discrimination. While several attempts have been made before from a professional stand, this initiative, which was implemented in practice from 2024, is a reflection of advances in policy and structural changes that need to be originated from the community.

In Ireland, an Autism Bill, first proposed in 2017, has been revived and debated within government houses in 2022 and 2023 (Houses of the Oireachtais, 2023). This bill is a step toward enacting legislation, which would enshrine certain rights for autistic people in Ireland. While the bill is debated, a parallel process to ensure the inclusion of and influence of autistic individuals in public life, through the development of an Autism Innovation strategy, is underway; and to date has involved a public consultation process which includes the perspectives of autistic people (Department of Children, Equality, Disability, Integration and Youth [DCEDIY], 2023). The recommendations arising include the use of identity first language, a move away from damaging behavioural therapies and the implementation of neuroaffirmative supports and frameworks in health and education (DCEDIY, 2023).

While seemingly far removed from the day-to-day supports for peer interaction, such legislative influences exemplify the significant ways that autistic voices are shaping the macrolevel environment for current and future autistic students across three continents. Whether in the legislature or the classroom, the key to reframing social supports for autistic peer interaction is to seek out autistic perspectives, to build on strengths and interests, and to work toward the environmental change necessary to help peers meet autistic children and youth on their own terms.

References

American Psychiatric Association (2013). *Diagnostic and Statistical Manual of Mental Disorders* (5th ed.). American Psychiatric Association. https://doi.org/10.1176/appi.books.9780890425596

AsIAm (2023). *Same Chance Report 2023*. AsIAm. https://cdn.prod.website-files.com/6537ebfefba7b3c24a18e646/65f3343217c192300579e67b_Same-Chance-Report-2023-for-web-1.pdf

Autistic Self Advocacy Network (2023). Action Center. Autistic Self Advocacy Network. https://autisticadvocacy.org/actioncenter/

Bagatell, N. (2010). From cure to community: Transforming notions of autism. *Journal of the Society for Psychological Anthropology, 38*(1), 33–55. https://doi.org/10.1111/j.1548-1352.2009.01080.x

Baker, M. J., Koegel, R. L., & Koegel, L. K. (1998). Increasing the social behavior of young children with autism using their obsessive behaviors. *Research and Practice for Persons with Severe Disabilities, 23*(4), 300–308. https://doi.org/10.2511/rpsd.23.4.300

Beck, J. S., Lundwall, R. A., Gabrielsen, T., Cox, J. C., & South, M. (2020). Looking good but feeling bad: "Camouflaging" behaviors and mental health in women with autistic traits. *Autism: The International Journal of Research and Practice, 24*(4), 809–821. https://doi.org/10.1177/1362361320912147

Botha, M., & Cage, E. (2022). "Autism research is in crisis": A mixed method study of researcher's constructions of autistic people and autism research. *Frontiers in Psychology*, 13, 1050897. https://doi.org/10.3389/fpsyg.2022.1050897

Botha, M., Chapman, R., Giwa Onaiwu, M., Kapp, S. K., Stannard Ashley, A., & Walker, N. (2024). The neurodiversity concept was developed collectively: An overdue correction on the origins of neurodiversity theory. *Autism: The International Journal of Research and Practice, 28*(6), 1591–1594. https://doi.org/10.1177/13623613241237871

Bottema-Beutel, K. (2017) Glimpses into the blind spot: Social interaction and autism. *Journal of Communication Disorders, 68*, 24–34. https://doi.org/10.1016/j.jcomdis.2017.06.008

Bottema-Beutel, K., Kapp, S. K., Lester, J. N., Sasson, N. J., & Hand, B. N. (2021). Avoiding ableist language: Suggestions for autism researchers. *Autism in Adulthood, 3*(1). https://doi.org/10.1089/aut.2020.0014

Bottema-Beutel, K., Park, H., & Kim. S.Y. (2017). Commentary on social skills training curricula for individuals with ASD: Social interaction, authenticity, and stigma. *Journal of Autism and Developmental Disorders, 48*, 953–964. https://doi.org/10.1007/s10803-017-3400-1

Cadaveira, M. & Waisburg, M. (2018). *Autismo: guía para padres y profesionales [Autism: a guide for parents and professionals]*. Paidós.

Cage. E. & Troxell-Whitman, Z. (2019). Understanding the reasons, contexts and costs of camouflaging for autistic adults. *Journal of Autism and Developmental Disorders, 49*, 1899–1911. https://doi.org/10.1007/s10803-018-03878-x

Cassidy, S. A., Gould, K., Townsend, E., Pelton, M., Robertson, A. E., & Rodgers, J. (2020) Is camouflaging autistic traits associated with suicidal thoughts and behaviours? Expanding the interpersonal psychological theory of suicide in an undergraduate student sample. *Journal of Autism and Developmental Disorders, 50*(10), 3638–3648. https://doi.org/10.1007/s10803-019-04323-3

Chan, J.M., Lang, R., Rispoli, M., O'Reilly, M., Sigafoos, J. & Cole, H. (2009). Use of peer-mediated interventions in the treatment of autism spectrum disorders: a systematic review. *Research in Autism Spectrum Disorders, 3*(4), 876–889. https://doi.org/10.1016/j.rasd.2009.04.003

Chang, Y-C., & Locke, J. (2016). A systematic review of peer-mediated interventions for children with autism spectrum disorder. *Research in Autism Spectrum Disorders, 27*, 1–10. https://doi.org/10.1016/j.rasd.2016.03.010

Chapin, S., McNaughton, D., Boyle, S., & Babb, S. (2018). Effects of peer support interventions on the communication of preschoolers with autism spectrum disorder: A systematic review. *Seminars in Speech and Language, 39*(5), 443–457. https://doi.org/10.1055/s-0038-1670670

Department of Children, Equality, Disability, Integration and Youth (2023). *Autism Innovation Strategy Analysis of Initial Public Consultation Submissions*. Report prepared for the Government of Ireland.

DeThorne, L. S. & Searsmith, K. (2020). Autism and neurodiversity: Addressing concerns and offering implications for the school-based speech-language pathologist. *Perspectives of the ASHA Special Interest Groups, 6* (1), 184–190. https://doi.org/10.1044/2020_PERSP-20-00188

DeThorne, L. S., Hengst, J. A., Valentino, H. A., & Russell, S. A. (2015). More than words: Examining communicative competence through a preschool-age child with autism. *Inclusion, 3*(3), 176–196. https://doi.org/10.1352/2326-6988-3.3.176

DiSalvo, C. A. & Oswald, D. P. (2002). Peer-mediated interventions to increase the social interaction of children with autism: Consideration of peer expectancies. *Focus on Autism and Other Developmental Disabilities, 17*(4), 198–207. https://doi.org/10.1177/10883576020170040201

Donaldson, A.L. (2024) 'Participatory Research: New Insights in Speech, Language, and Hearing Sciences', *Seminars in speech and language, 45*(5), 443–444, available: https://doi.org/10.1055/s-0044-1795071.

Donaldson, A. L., corbin, e., & McCoy, J. (2021). "Everyone deserves AAC": Preliminary study of the experiences of speaking autistic adults who use augmentative and alternative communication. *Perspectives of the ASHA Special Interest Groups, 6*(2), 315–326. https://doi.org/10.1044/2021_PERSP-20-00220

Donaldson, A., corbin, e., Zisk, A.H., & Eddy, B. (2023). Promotion of communication access, choice, and agency for autistic students. *Language, Speech and Hearing Services in Schools, 54*(1), 140–155. https://doi.org/10.1044/2022_LSHSS-22-00031

Dueñas, A. D., Plavnick, J. B., & Goldstein, H. (2021). Effects of a multicomponent peer mediated intervention on social communication of preschoolers with autism spectrum disorder. *Exceptional Children, 87*(2), 236–257. https://doi.org/10.1177/0014402920953761

Ezzamel, N., & Bond, C. (2016). How have target pupil, peer and school level outcomes related to peer-mediated interventions for pupils with ASD been evaluated?, *European Journal of Special Needs Education, 31*(4), 440–457. https://doi.org/10.1080/08856257.2016.1194568

Finke E. H. (2016). Friendship: Operationalizing the intangible to improve friendship-based outcomes for individuals with autism spectrum disorder. *American Journal of Speech-Language Pathology, 25*(4), 654–663. https://doi.org/10.1044/2016_AJSLP-15-0042

Fletcher-Watson, S., Adams, J., Brook, K., Charman, T., Crane, L., Cusack, J., Leekam, S., Milton, D., Parr, J. R., & Pellicano, E. (2019). Making the future together: Shaping autism research through meaningful participation. *Autism: The International Journal of Research and Practice, 23*(4), 943–953. https://doi.org/10.1177/1362361318786721

Goldstein, H., English, K., Shafer, K., & Kaczmarek, L. (1997). Interaction among preschoolers with and without disabilities: effects of across-the-day peer intervention. *Journal of Speech, Language, and Hearing Research, 40*(1), 33–48. https://doi.org/10.1044/jslhr.4001.33

Harrington, C., Foster, M., Rodger, S., & Ashburner, J. (2014). Engaging young people with Autism Spectrum Disorder in research interviews. *British Journal of Learning Disabilities, 42*(2), 153–161. https://doi.org/10.1111/bld.12037

Heasman, B., & Gillespie, A. (2019). Neurodivergent intersubjectivity: Distinctive features of how autistic people create shared understanding. *Autism, 23*(4), 910–921. https://doi.org/10.1177/1362361318785172

Hengst, J. A. (2015). Distributed communication: Implications of cultural-historical activity theory (CHAT) for communication disorders. *Journal for Communication Disorders, 57*, 16–28. https://doi.org/10.1016/j.jcomdis.2015.09.001

Hengst, J. A. (2020). *Understanding Everyday Communicative Interactions: Introduction to Situated Discourse Analysis for Communication Sciences and Disorders*. Routledge.

Houses of the Oireachtais (2023, October 3). *Autism Spectrum Disorder Bill 2017: Discussion*. Government of Ireland. Joint Committee on Children, Equality, Disability, Integration and Youth. Houses of the Oireachtas. https://www.oireachtas.ie/en/debates/debate/joint_committee_on_children_equality_disability_integration_and_youth/2023-10-03/4/

Hu, X., Lee, G. T., Watkins, L., & Jiang, Y. (2021). Combining preferred activities with peer support to increase social interactions between preschoolers with ASD and typically developing peers. *Journal of Positive Behavior Interventions, 23*(4), 272–287. https://doi.org/10.1177/1098300720987547

Hull, L., Levy, L., Meng-Chuan, L., Petrides, K.V., Baron-Cohen, S., Allison, C., Smith, P., & Mandy, W. (2021). Is social camouflaging associated with anxiety and depression in autistic adults? *Molecular Autism, 12*(13). https://doi.org/10.1186/s13229-021-00421-1

Jaswal, V. K., & Akhtar, N. (2018). Being versus appearing socially uninterested: Challenging assumptions about social motivation in autism. *Behavioral and Brain Sciences, 42*, E82. https://doi.org/10.1017/S0140525X18001826

Jaswal, V. K., Dinishak, J., Stephan, C., & Akhtar, N. (2020). Experiencing social connection: A qualitative study of mothers of nonspeaking autistic children. *PLOS One, 15*(11), e0242661. https://doi.org/10.1371/journal.pone.0242661

Kapp, S. K. (2019). How social deficit models exacerbate the medical model: Autism as case in point. *Autism Policy & Practice, 2*(1), 3–28.

Kasari, C., Roheram-Fuller, E., Locke, J., & Gulsrud, A. (2012). Making the connection: Randomized controlled trial of social skills at school for children with autism spectrum disorders. *Journal of Child Psychology and Psychiatry, 53*(4), 431–439. https://doi.org/10.1111/j.1469-7610.2011.02493.x

Kent, C., Cordier, R., Joosten, A., Wilkes-Gillan, S., & Bundy, A. (2021). Can I learn to play? Randomized control trial to assess effectiveness of a peer-mediated intervention to improve play in children with autism spectrum disorder. *Journal of Autism and Developmental Disorders, 51*, 1823–1838. https://doi.org/10.1007/s10803-020-04671-5

Kimber, L., Verrier, D., & Connolly, S. (2023). Autistic people's experience of empathy and the autistic empathy deficit narrative. *Autism in Adulthood, 6*(3), 321–330. https://www.liebertpub.com/doi/abs/10.1089/aut.2023.0001

Koegel, L. K., Vernon, T. W., Koegel, R. L., Koegel, B. L., & Paullin, A. W. (2012). Improving social engagement and initiations between children with autism spectrum disorder and their peers in inclusive settings. *Journal of Positive Behavior Interventions, 14*(4), 220–227. https://doi.org/10.1177/1098300712437042

Leadbitter, K., Buckle, K. L., Ellis, C., & Dekker, M. (2021). Autistic self-advocacy and the neurodiversity movement: Implications for autism early intervention research and practice. *Frontiers in Psychology*, 12, 635690. https://doi.org/10.3389/fpsyg.2021.635690

Ledford, J. R., & Pustejovsky, J. E. (2021). Systematic review and meta-analysis of stay-play-talk interventions for improving social behaviors of young children. *Journal of Positive Behavior Interventions, 25*(1), 65–77. https://doi.org/10.1177/1098300720983521

Mantzalas, J., Richdale, A., & Dissanayake, C. (2022). A conceptual model of risk and protective factors for autistic burnout. *Autism Research, 15*(6), 976–987. https://doi.org/10.1002/aur.2722

McVey, A. J., Jones, D. R., Waisman, T. C., Raymaker, D. M., Nicolaidis, C., & Maddox, B. B. (2023). Mindshift in autism: A call to professionals in research, clinical, and educational settings. *Frontiers in Psychiatry, 14*, 1251058. https://doi.org/10.3389/fpsyt.2023.1251058

Miller, D., Rees, J., & Pearson, A. (2021). "Masking is life": Experiences of masking in autistic and nonautistic adults. *Autism in Adulthood: Challenges and Management, 3*(4), 330–338. https://doi.org/10.1089/aut.2020.0083

Milton, D. (2012). On the ontological status of autism: the 'double empathy problem'. *Disability and Society, 27*(6), 883–887. https://doi.org/10.1080/09687599.2012.710008

Milton, D. E. (2014). Autistic expertise: A critical reflection on the production of knowledge in autism studies. *Autism, 18*(7), 794–802. https://doi.org/10.1177/1362361314525281

Milton, D., & Bracher, M. (2013). Autistics speak but are they heard? *Medical Sociology online, 7*(2), 61–69.

Moir, T. (2018). Why is implementation science important for intervention design and evaluation within educational settings? *Frontiers in Education (Lausanne), 3*(61). https://doi.org/10.3389/feduc.2018.00061

Monk, R., Whitehouse, A., & Waddington, H. (2022). The use of language in autism research. *Trends in Neurosciences, 45*(11), 791–793. https://doi.org/10.1016/j.tins.2022.08.009

Ne'eman, A. (2023, October 20). *Operationalizing Neurodiversity: How Should the Neurodiversity Model Shift Autism, Autism-Service Provision, and Research?* [symposium presentation]. Project Comparative Autism Research Effectiveness. On-line.

Nicolaidis, C., Raymaker, D., Kapp, S. K., Baggs, A., Ashkenazy, E., McDonald, K., Weiner, M., Maslak, J., Hunter, M., & Joyce, A. (2019). The AASPIRE practice-based guidelines for the inclusion of autistic adults in research as co-researchers and study participants. *Autism: The International Journal of Research and Practice, 23*(8), 2007–2019. https://doi.org/10.1177/1362361319830523

O'Cathain, A., Croot, L., Duncan, E., Rousseau, N., Sworn, K., Turner, K. M., Yardley, L., & Hoddinott, P. (2019). Guidance on how to develop complex interventions to improve health and healthcare. *BMJ Open, 9*(8), e029954–e029954. https://doi.org/10.1136/bmjopen-2019-029954

O'Donoghue, M., O'Dea, A., O'Leary, N., Kennedy, N., Forbes, J., & Murphy, C. A. (2021). Systematic review of peer-mediated intervention for children with autism who are minimally verbal. *Review Journal of Autism and Developmental Disorders, 8*(1), 51–66. https://doi.org/10.1007/s40489-020-00201-2

O'Donoghue, M., Kennedy, N., Forbes, J., & Murphy, C. A. (2023). Stakeholder perceptions of the acceptability of peer-mediated intervention for minimally speaking preschoolers on the autism spectrum. *Journal of Autism and Developmental Disorders*, 54, 1774–1791. https://doi.org/10.1007/s10803-023-05928-5

O'Donoghue, M., Kennedy, N., Forbes, J., & Murphy, C. A. (2024). Feasible peer-mediated intervention for autistic children using minimal speech: A qualitative intervention development process. *American Journal of Speech-Language Pathology, 33*(3), 1337–1355. https://doi.org/10.1044/2024_AJSLP-23-00303

Ochs, E., & Solomon, O. (2010). Autistic sociality. *Ethos, 38*(1), 69–92. https://doi.org/10.1111/j.1548-1352.2009.01082.x

Osborne, K., Ledford, J. R., Martin, J., & Thorne, K. (2019) Component analysis of stay, play, talk interventions with and without self-monitored group contingencies and recorded reminders. *Topics in Early Childhood Special Education, 39*(1), 5–18. https://doi.org/10.1177/0271121418815236

Pearson, A., & Rose, K. (2021). A conceptual analysis of autistic masking: Understanding the narrative of stigma and the illusion of choice. *Autism in Adulthood: Challenges and Management, 3*(1), 52–60. https://doi.org/10.1089/aut.2020.0043

Rattazzi, A. (2020). *Sé amable con el autismo. guía de navegación para todos [Be kind to autism: everyone's navigation manual]* (2nd ed.). Grijalbo.

Robertson, S. M. (2010). Neurodiversity, quality of life, and autistic adults: Shifting research and professional focuses onto real-life challenges. *Disability Studies Quarterly, 30*(1). http://dx.doi.org/10.18061/dsq.v30i1.1069

Rogers, S. (2000). Interventions that facilitate socialization in children with autism. *Journal of Autism and Developmental Disorders, 30*(5), 399–409. https://doi.org/10.1023/a:1005543321840

Santhanam, S. (2023). An interaction and neurodiversity-affirming approach to communication supports for autistic students through video gaming. *Speech, Language and Hearing Services in Schools, 54*(1), 120–139. https://doi.org/10.1044/2022_LSHSS-22-00027

Sasson, N. J., Faso, D. J., Nugent, J., Lovell, S., Kenned, D. P., & Grossman, R. B. (2017). Neurotypical peers are less willing to interact with those with autism based on thin slice judgements. *Scientific Reports, 7*, 40700. https://doi.org/10.1038/srep40700

Shaw, S. C. K., Carravallah, L., Johnson, M., O'Sullivan, J., Chown, N., Neilson, S., & Doherty, M., (2023). Barriers to healthcare and a 'triple empathy problem' may lead to adverse outcomes for autistic adults: A qualitative study. *Autism, 28*(7), 1746–1757. https://doi.org/10.1177/13623613231205629

Silberman, S. (2015). *NeuroTribes: The Legacy of Autism and the Future of Neurodiversity*. Penguin Random House.

Sinclair, J. (1992). Personal essays. In E. Schopler & G. E. Mesibov (Eds.) *High Functioning Individuals with Autism* (pp. 289–306), Springer.

Singer, J. (1999). 'Why can't you be normal for once in your life?' From a 'problem with no name' to the emergence of a new category of difference. In M. Corker & S. French (Eds.), *Disability Discourse* (pp. 59–67). McGraw-Hill Education.

Straus, J. (2013). Autism as culture. In L. J. Davis (Ed.), *The Disability Reader* (4th ed., pp. 460–484). Taylor & Francis.

TEA Law (2023), Law 21.545, Chile. https://www.bcn.cl/leychile/navegar?idNorma = 1190123

Vidal, V., Ernat, C., & DeThorne, L. (2018a). "I think he wants you to play the guitar": Use of behavioral interpretation as a strategy for facilitating peer interaction across autistic and non-autistic peers. *Perspectives of the ASHA Special Interest Groups, 3*, 68–83. https://doi.org/10.1044/persp3.SIG1.68

Vidal, V., Robertson, S., & DeThorne, L. (2018b). Illustrating a supports-based approach toward friendship with autistic students. *American Journal of Speech-Language Pathology, 27*, 592–601. https://doi.org/10.1044/2018_AJSLP-17-0075

Vidal, V., McAllister, A., & DeThorne, L. (2020). Communication profile of a minimally verbal school-age autistic child: A case study. *Language, Speech, and Hearing Services in Schools, 51*(3), 671–686. https://doi.org/10.1044/2020_LSHSS-19-00021

Vidal., V. G., Wachholtz, D. P., Mattie, L. J., & DeThorne, L. S. (2023). It takes a community: How environmental systems construct (in)competence in autistic peer interactions. *Language, Speech and Hearing Services in Schools, 54*(1) 63–81. https://doi.org/10.1044/2022_LSHSS-22-00028

Vidal, V., Urra, P., Cerda Diez, M. F., Becerra León, C., Ramos Alarcón, M. C., & Cortés, J. P. (2024). Revealing conflicting ideologies: A critical discourse analysis of autism terminology in academic journals. *Topics in Language Disorders, 44*(1), 5–24. https://doi.org/10.1097/TLD.0000000000000334

Volkmar, F. R., & Reichow, B. (2013). Autism in DSM-5: Progress and challenges. *Molecular Autism, 4*(1), 13. https://doi.org/10.1186/2040-2392-4-13

Watkins, L., Ledbetter-Cho, K., O'Reilly, M., Barnard-Brak, L., & Garcia-Grau, P. (2019). Interventions for students with autism in inclusive settings: A best-evidence synthesis and meta-analysis. *Psychological Bulletin, 145*(5), 490–507. https://doi.org/10.1037/bul0000190

Watkins, L., O'Reilly, M., Kuhn, M., Gevarter, C., Lancioni, G. E., Seafood, J., & Lang, R. (2015). A review of peer-mediated social interaction interventions for students with autism in inclusive settings. *Journal of Autism and Developmental Disorders, 45*(4), 1070–1083. https://doi.org/10.1007/s10803-014-2264-x

Watkins, L., O'Reilly, M., Kuhn, M., & Ledbetter-Cho, K. (2019). An interest-based intervention package to increase peer social interaction in young children with autism spectrum disorder. *Journal of Applied Behaviour Analysis, 52*(1), 132–149. https://doi.org/10.1002/jaba.514

Whalon, K. J., Conroy, M. A., Martinez, J. R., & Werch, B. L. (2015). School-based peer-related social competence interventions for children with autism spectrum disorder: A meta-analysis and descriptive review of single case research design studies. *Journal of Autism and Developmental Disorders, 45*(6), 1513–1531. https://doi.org/10.1007/s10803-015-2373-1

Wolfberg, P. J. (2008). Including children with autism in the culture of play with peers. In C. Forlin & J M.G. Lion (Eds). *Reforms, Inclusion and Teacher Education: Towards a New Era of Special Education in Asia-Pacific Regions*. Center for Advancement in Special Education, Hong Kong University.

Wolfberg, P., DeWitt, M., Young, G. S., & Nguyen, T. (2015). Integrated play groups: Promoting symbolic play and social engagement with typical peers in children with ASD across settings. *Journal of Autism and Developmental Disorders, 45*(3), 830–845. https://doi.org/10.1007/s10803-014-2245-0

Yardley, L., Ainsworth, B., Arden-Close, E., & Muller, I. (2015). The person-based approach to enhancing the acceptability and feasibility of interventions. *Pilot and Feasibility Studies, 1*(1), Article 37. https://doi.org/10.1186/s40814-015-0033-z

Zeldovich, L. (2018, May 9). The evolution of 'autism' as a diagnosis, explained. *Spectrum*. https://www.spectrumnews.org/news/evolution-autism-diagnosis-explained/

Chapter 22:
Authentic Autistic Play: A Double Empathy Problem?

Elise Guthrie Stirling

We all express ourselves through play, to play is to be human. However, we have a very different approach to play as autistic individuals, and this is regularly misinterpreted by non-autistics. My doctoral research is centred around authentic autistic play. I could not have anticipated how much of a dearth there would be in literature on true acceptance of the play preferences of autistic children. It was there, I found it, eventually, but when I started my doctorate it seemed like I was searching for the impossible. So, to start, I wrote about my own experiences of play growing up autistic. Before that, I had never expressed these experiences 'out loud', as it were, and in doing so I was able to process 'what went wrong' and even why I stopped playing at the end of primary school. It came down to the way that others interpreted my play. Not my family, necessarily, but my peers, my teachers, even casual onlookers. I was openly mocked for my play choices and so I stopped choosing them. That makes me quite sad to think about, and as the mum of three autistic girls, I am absolutely determined not to let anyone throttle the wonders of autistic play out of them.

My middle daughter, for example, is extremely playful – she's energetic, curious, very witty and loves a pun – play with her is an absolute delight. She needs no guidance, support or intervention to play, her way of life is just playful through and through. Yet for some reason when she started school, her Individualized Education Plan (IEP) included the target '*T will play appropriately with her peers*' and she was expected to achieve this by '*accessing the playroom and learning to play a variety of games once a week for 8 weeks*'. The staff in the class intended to '*take T and a peer to the playroom once a week*' where '*games would be taught and T would be supported to play with another pupil*'. Furthermore, '*T would be encouraged to state her emotions during and after playing the games; and a social story would be used*'. She was 5. This was in a 'specialist' autism provision. This was their plan for her. The other 'targets' were equally as inane, but this one jumped out at me as the most utterly ludicrous target to set for a 5-year-old, any 5-year-old. I asked them *'who decides what is "appropriate" play? Surely play/interaction is individual. It is ableist to assume it's not "appropriate"'* and this did not go down well. No one had pointed this out to them before, apparently.

She did not last long at that school, unsurprisingly, and by the middle of her second year at school she was in an alternative 'specialist' placement. When they pitched their 'play-based curriculum' to me it was appealing, and the (then) headteacher seemed to really understand the challenges we faced in having such a clever little cookie who struggled so badly with a number of challenges as a result not only of her disabilities but also from the post-traumatic stress disorder (PTSD) she experienced after being at the last school. Sadly, that headteacher left and a new one joined the school before my daughter had even begun her transition. Everything seemed fine at first, she had a loosely play-based curriculum that seemed unchallenging but we initially put this down to easing her in after such a traumatic school experience. After the first year, though, she was still unchallenged and becoming bored. She felt that no one understood her, they just gave her 'baby work' to pass the time, and the rest of the time she was given things to 'play' with though this never appeared to be anything that she particularly chose or wanted but often planned around resource availability or timetabling. Her play-based curriculum was not play-based because she did not find it overly appealing or playful. I began to understand the extent of the problem when I received a newsletter from the school about their 'play' developments. It read *'our deputy headteacher is undergoing Froebel training this year and we are excited about embracing Froebelian principles'* and I thought *'Great! At last, someone understands individualised child-centred play!'* But I read on, and immediately took it back. It stated *'X class is going to be doing treasure baskets'* and *'Y class will be doing block play'* – I felt my brain facepalming itself. Froebelian principles are all about being autonomous, learning best through choice and independence; creativity and representing children's own ideas; children having ownership over their play. Dictating what children access for fun and manufacturing whole-class activities is not exactly what Frederick Froebel had in mind for play.

My daughter left that school not long after, but I had started to detect a pattern by that point. Even autism 'specialist' schools struggled to recognize that autistic children are perfectly capable of playing in their own way, using their own play tools, and engaging with play partners however they choose. What hope is there, then, for the mainstream schools who don't claim to be autism specialists? I have met more than a few teachers, support workers and early years practitioners, whether in mainstream or additional support needs (ASN) settings, who truly value authenticity, autonomy and individual children's interpretations of fun in play, including for autistic children. I have met several who do not quite know how to embrace that yet, but are keen to learn and reflect on their practice.

Sadly, however, the overwhelming majority of people I have met who work with autistic children are unwaveringly certain that autistic play is deviant, ineffective and cannot possibly be acceptable. This, in my experience, leads to two scenarios:

- Any autistic child who demonstrates outwardly different play is pathologized and assessed, with the intention of rectifying the issue, and/or;
- Any autistic child who does *not* demonstrate outwardly different play, is determined to be non-autistic, because if they were autistic they could never do these things so well.

The latter happened recently to my youngest daughter at her nursery. The early years practitioners were adamant that she could never be autistic because she was able to use her imagination and chat during play activities, among other markers of 'normal' play. They failed to notice that her 'chat' was echolalia, scripted and memorized from the YouTube videos she enjoys, using the same kind of toys as she enjoyed at nursery. They failed to realise that having a good imagination is entirely possible, and in fact quite common, in autistic girls. They also failed to notice how she lined and sorted everything, repeated the same activities over and over, and flitted from task to task with little follow through. I told them we had noticed this from a young age along with her other, more sensory-based types of play, such as climbing everything and anything, flapping excitedly and dancing on her tiptoes so often that I called her Twinkletoes as she was like a little ballerina. But they remained adamant that her play was not indicative of being autistic, and that she was not autistic.

What I have noticed is that the autistic grown-ups we have in our lives (of which there are many, I tend to only socialize with other neurodivergent adults for reasons that may become clear as I go on) could all recognize immediately that her play behaviours were, apart from being adorable, unmistakably autistic. The neurotypical people in our lives, few of whom we are particularly close with anyway, seemed to assume I was seeing autism because I wanted to see autism. After all, the rest of the family are autistic so I was just dragging her down with the rest of us, right? Wrong. I am an autistic mother, recognizing autistic play in my autistic child because we share a neurotype and have an understanding of how and why she does these things, even if I never actually did these things myself. Adults who do not share the neurotype did not seem to automatically have an awareness of this, never mind understanding it. This interpretive dissonance is no coincidence. It is all down to the Double Empathy Problem.

The Double Empathy Problem is the 'disjuncture' between two individuals who share different neurotypes, and therefore approach interactions and engagements differently to each other (Milton et al., 2018). This is usually down to the norms and expectations that each person holds of themselves and others, which become problematic when the issue is seen to reside with one person (the autistic person, in most cases) rather than being seen as a mutual dissonance. This often leads to tension and misunderstandings during or following social interactions, as a result of the mismatch between '*different dispositional outlooks and personal conceptual understandings … involving autistic and non-autistic people*' (Milton et al., 2018, p. 1).

Before I knew about this phenomenon, in the mid-2010s, it never occurred to me that having empathy for my eldest child's play behaviours meant that I could also potentially miss her differences to the extent that it created almost total denial. I was studying my Masters degree in the inclusive education of autistic pupils when my eldest daughter got her autism diagnosis. I had worked with autistic pupils for a while in different settings, though primarily older boys who were minimally verbal at the time. My little 2½-year-old girl was wonderfully quirky, with a fantastic memory for song lyrics and movie lines, and a vocabulary to rival a pocket dictionary. I knew nothing about hyperlexia or echolalia, and even less about sensory issues which went completely unnoticed at the time, other than her sheer terror around mechanical toys and her penchant for tiny objects that fit in her mouth. So, when her nursery (a different nursery, I might add) indicated that they believed her to be autistic, and noted the play behaviours that created this 'concern', I was completely taken aback. So what if she said the exact same thing every time they turned the lights on, so what if she flicked through the book to get to her favourite bit, so what if she chose to run round and round in circles while repeating '*round, round, round, round*' over and over? None of this seemed particularly odd to me, it was just her way of having fun. But when they told me this, and said she would need a referral to speech and language and educational psychology, I went into a blind panic. I contacted everyone I knew who might be able to help, I wanted to rush the diagnosis so I could stop things from getting too bad before she started school. The panic lasted for at least a year. Eventually, I stopped arguing for intervention and started arguing for support that allowed her to be herself. The only thing that changed in that time was that I got my own autism diagnosis that same year. I started to educate myself on what this meant, including filling the gaps in my knowledge as to why it had taken so long for me to get my diagnosis (despite being diagnosed with attention deficit hyperactivity disorder [ADHD] over a decade prior), and realising that the things I had missed in my girls were the things that others had missed in me. I started being a lot more compassionate and forgiving of the 'deficits' we all had, eventually after a number of years feeling able to celebrate the differences instead. This may be a familiar journey to some.

When our third child came along, she was born into a neurodivergent-friendly household, and she never had to experience the quandaries we previously faced as parents about 'fixing' our children. There was nothing to fix, and we just let her be. I believe it was for this reason that her autistic play was so pronounced, that in our experience (almost) anyone could see it a mile off. But not her nursery staff. Because they believed they knew what autistic play looked like, and that was not it, apparently. Thankfully, two professionals who fell into the category of valuing authenticity and autonomy in play, immediately recognizing her autistic quirks while simultaneously marvelling at her wonderful imagination and incessant chattiness, were the professionals who assessed her for her autism diagnosis and she got it, despite the arguments from nursery to the contrary. It was such a relief to have that validation and recognition, ahead of applying for schools, but I know from personal experience that this was not a naturally inherent understanding of autistic play, like our neurodivergent friends, but an acquired education that developed over a number of years. I know this because the same speech and language therapist who confidently diagnosed my youngest (whose nursery workers were vocally adamant she was *not* autistic) based on her unique play style, eight years prior had told people that my eldest daughter (whose nursery were equally as vocal about her *definitely* being autistic) did not appear to demonstrate any obvious features of autism in her play or otherwise. Two entirely different children both very alike in their play, albeit eight years apart, and two completely different interpretations from the same professional. That is quite a leap in understanding and acceptance, even if it did take the better part of a decade to come about. So, although I have increasingly become aware of the interpretive dissonance surrounding play between non-autistic and autistic people, there seem to be some good examples of how time and education can bridge that gap somewhat, and therefore non-autistic adults can potentially 'learn' empathy toward children's authentic autistic play. Rolemodeling this empathy may lead to the child's peers becoming equally as understanding and accepting, potentially leading to improved outcomes for that child.

Having an understanding of the state of mind behind autistic play may go some way in improving these outcomes, in both play observations and play experiences. King (2023) describes the phenomenon of play 'flow' as a natural, expected state of mind and body that all children can experience when absorbed and immersed in free play. What is often pathologized as aloofness and egocentrism in autistic play, is instead phrased by King as being perceived in general as '*total involvement … in which the activity has an autotelic quality*' (King, 2023, p. 182) with the child being '*lost in their play*' (King, 2023, p. 183) – presumably being aimed at normative (non-autistic) play actors. This illustrates the differences in interpretations of play between neurotypes, but can give insight into how we support a better understanding of autistic play among non-autistic adults and autistic children, as well as non-autistic children and autistic children. According to Wolfberg et al.,

> *Without a framework of understanding, typical peers perceive children with autism as being of limited social interest or as deviant in their behavior. Consequently, children with autism are especially likely to be ignored by tolerant and benevolent peers and taunted or bullied by those more intolerant and malevolent.*
>
> (Wolfberg et al., 2012, p. 59)

Therefore, it seems that the Double Empathy Problem in play between autistic and non-autistic people extends further than just the adult–child exchanges of play, it exists when children play with or around their peers, too. Often, play among children requires a sort of 'social synchronization' in order for the children to maintain an enjoyment of the activity together (Morgan, 2019). This synchronization tends to centre around a common set of group norms that, for autistic children, will almost inevitably be different from their non-autistic peers. Often, on a superficial level, autistic children may appear to be engaging in mutual appreciation of the same activity or types of activity as their non-autistic peers, but they may be masking or camouflaging an entirely different set of play preferences in order to 'fit in' or go unnoticed among the group. Kasari et al. (2013) suggest that autistic children might use their 'best guesses' to figure out a logical way to use play objects that visibly passes as pretend play in a superficial performance but on closer inspection is still qualitatively different to their non-autistic peers. At other times, according to Wolfberg et al. (2012), autistic children may clearly demonstrate their desire to play in a different way to their peers, offering fewer overt initiations of play to peers, and responding less consistently to peers' play initiations. In most cases, this is viewed as problematic, and skewed to neuronormative expectations, for example:

> *While typically developing children need little motivation or guidance to play with peers, children with autism encounter significant obstacles gaining equal access to and benefits from inclusion in peer-play experiences.*
>
> (Wolfberg et al., 2012, p. 55)

Where, in general terms, children appear free to fully absorb themselves in the throes of free play, total immersion in their activity for no purpose, reward or goal other than the play activity itself and adults can observe, partake or merge in the play according to the preferences of the child based on their cues (King, 2023), autistic children's free play preferences, such as sensory involvement in object play and repetition of play actions, are perceived as 'unusual' and '*interfering with their development … and more functionally appropriate play*' (Kasari et al., 2013, p. 4). Why are children in general allowed to play without perceived function and purpose and it gets called 'flow' and yet autistic children play without perceived function and purpose and it gets called 'unusual'? It seems that the default assumption about autistic people is that, even in our most free flow and natural of states, we are just too different to be considered 'usual'. Yet, according to Eisele and Howard (2012), to play is to be human, and so to deny autistic children their own authentic play, is dehumanizing. It amounts, in essence, to a breach of human rights in the sense that '*failure to acknowledge [this]... as play would be at odds with legislation that protects children's rights to play*' (Eisele and Howard, 2012, p. 148). Having, or working with, a child who engages in authentic autistic play, and not fully understanding why they do this, is of course acceptable due to the interpretive dissonance. Having, or working with, a child who engages in authentic autistic play, and not allowing this, is not acceptable and is a breach of their human rights. Making the choice to embrace and encourage their authentic play is the only humanizing choice to make in the circumstances.

There are a number of accounts in the literature, of family members who themselves are not autistic, but welcome an autistic child's play even if they do not understand it. Mitchell and Lashewicz give accounts of fathers of autistic children who accepted their child's play, where they positively described their child's 'quirky' play '*without attempting to mould or change the play and accepted their children's natural proclivities*' (Mitchell & Lashewicz, 2018, p. 1131). Not all of the accounts shared by fathers in this study were as accepting, but some stories illustrated the way they resisted dominant discourses of autistic play as deficient and re-evaluated what we might define as 'fun' or 'functional' (Mitchell & Lashewicz, 2018). Similarly, Conn and Drew shared recollections from non-autistic individuals about their memories of playing with autistic siblings, who 'happily participated' in their sibling's chosen play. This is in contrast to regular accounts of others '*struggling to understand … experiencing him or her as enigmatic, unknowable, and an outsider … and feeling frustrated, annoyed, or angered by it*' (Conn & Drew, 2017, p. 854). This demonstrates well the choice made by those who may be more fondly remembered in childhood to engage with the autistic child in qualitatively different play that was sensitive to their preferences, as opposed to wider accounts in the literature on non-autistic perceptions of autistic play that

> *desaturate the real-life presence of people, their humanity, their unique interests and experiences, and the individuality with which they engage.*
>
> (Conn & Drew, 2017, p. 865)

Autistic individuals are similar to non-autistic people in the sense that they too desire social relationships, including friends as well as family members, but that this is not necessarily a positive experience for them if they feel they cannot be themselves around non-autistic people – sometimes leading to negative self-image, mental distress and depression (Crompton et al., 2020). These reactions tend not to be an issue when interacting with fellow autistics, and Crompton et al. reported autistic individuals having an increased '*sense of comfort and belonging when spending time with their autistic family and friends*' (Crompton et al., 2020, p. 1446), being part of that community gave them a sense of happiness, acceptance and authenticity that was not experienced around non-autistic people, and that everyone in the community was mutually valued and respected in this way. Even when engaging in play with strangers, autistic individuals potentially have more positive interactions with autistic strangers than with non-autistic strangers, according to Heasman and Gilliespie (2019).

The importance of lived experience of play in relationship to friendship, too, cannot be underestimated – specifically, how autistic individuals perceive play and friendship as phenomena – as the accounts of parents, siblings, teachers and health professionals have been well documented in research, but have mostly fallen short of the mark in terms of understanding their true nature (Black et al., 2022). Black et al. recorded a number of positive qualities of friendship as perceived by autistic individuals, such as physical and emotional support and shared interests and conversations (or 'doing the same things together'), but little connection was made between friendship and play. Watson (2019) attempts to disrupt the assumption that children should automatically equate play with friendship through a post-structural lens, by considering the preferences of 'children with a diagnosis' (phrasing that indicates a clumsy attempt, perhaps, to reject the medical model but at the same time ignoring that the overwhelming majority of autistic people use identity-first language) to play alone or differently to others. In Watson's view, '*Children, through play, marginalise and isolate, include and exclude, using societal power relations to maintain the status quo*' (Watson, 2019, p. 257). Watson positions normative play expectations as a political, societal discourse that 'children without a diagnosis' internalize and perpetuate, othering those who do not participate in this illusion of normality. They see their 'friends' with typical play as true friends, but any 'friends' outside of this typicality they perceive as being grudgingly compulsory 'friends' that they have to be 'friends' with because the adults make it a rule to do so. While I disagree that non-autistic children only play a certain way because society tells them to (to an extent, there are obvious gender stereotypes that Watson refers to that are undeniably influenced by society), I do value this observation that for these children '*friendship comes from the act of doing friends, in playing*' (Watson, 2019, p. 259) in comparison to Black et al.'s obvious lack of 'playing together' in the priorities of autistic children. This, to me, demonstrates a potential mismatch in the very foundations of why autistic and non-autistic children play. This, while potentially the tip of the iceberg, may go some way to explaining how such an interpretive dissonance in play has come about. Double empathy theorists suggest that autistic people (both children and adults) may have a greater 'affinity' for other autistic people and have the potential to better understand each other in comparison to how non-autistic people understand them (Milton et al., 2018). The social synchronicity that Morgan (2019) noted as vital for children to enjoy an activity together, appears to be not only present in autistic–autistic interactions but also actually flourishes in a coordinated and cooperative fashion, according to Milton et al. (2018). This positions the dominant discourse of autistic play as being 'arcane', 'less advanced' and '*in sharp contrast to the richly diverse social and imaginary pursuits of typical children*' (Wolfberg et al., 2012, p. 57) as an outdated, outmoded and misdirected notion that is now being more widely discredited as autistic- and ally-led research begins to give a voice to the autistic players of the past, present and future.

References

Black, M. H., Kuzminski, R., Wang, J., Ang, J., Lee, C., Hafidzuddin, S., & McGarry, S. (2022). Experiences of friendships for individuals on the autism spectrum: A scoping review. *Review Journal of Autism and Developmental Disorders*, *11*, 184–209. https://doi.org/10.1007/s40489-022-00332-8

Conn, C., & Drew, S. (2017). Sibling narratives of autistic play culture. *Disability & Society, 32*(6), 853–867. https://doi.org/10.1080/09687599.2017.1321526

Crompton, C. J., Hallett, S., Ropar, D., Flynn, E., & Fletcher-Watson, S. (2020). 'I never realised everybody felt as happy as I do when I am around autistic people': A thematic analysis of autistic adults' relationships with autistic and neurotypical friends and family. *Autism*, *24*(6), 1438–1448. https://doi.org/10.1177/1362361320908976

Eisele, G., & Howard, J. (2012). Exploring the presence of characteristics associated with play within the ritual repetitive behaviour of autistic children. *International Journal of Play*, *1*(2), 139–150. https://doi.org/10.1080/21594937.2012.692202

Heasman, B., & Gillespie, A. (2019) Participants over-estimate how helpful they are in a two-player game scenario toward an artificial confederate that discloses a diagnosis of autism. *Frontiers in Psychology*, *10*, 1349. https://doi.org/10.3389/fpsyg.2019.01349

Kasari, C., Chang, Y. C., & Patterson, S. (2013). Pretending to play or playing to pretend: The case of autism. *American Journal of Play*, *6*(1), 124.

King, P. (2023) Flow and the play cycle: A theoretical consideration of the importance of flow in established play cycles. *American Journal of Play*, *15*(2), 179–195.

Milton, D., Heasman, B., & Sheppard, E. (2018). Double empathy. In F. Volkmar (Ed.), *Encyclopedia of Autism Spectrum Disorders*. Springer.

Mitchell, J., & Lashewicz, B. (2018). Quirky kids: Fathers' stories of embracing diversity and dismantling expectations for normative play with their children with autism spectrum disorder. *Disability & Society*, *33*(7), 1120–1137. https://doi.org/10.1080/09687599.2018.1474087

Morgan, H. (2019). Connections between sensory sensitivities in autism: The importance of sensory friendly environments for accessibility and increased quality of life for the neurodivergent autistic minority. *PSU McNair Scholars Online Journal*, *13*(1), 11. https://doi.org/10.15760/mcnair.2019.13.1.11

Watson, K. (2019). 'We are all friends': Disrupting friendship play discourses in inclusive early childhood education. *Contemporary Issues in Early Childhood*, *20*(3), 253–264. https://doi.org/10.1177/1463949118772575

Wolfberg, P., Bottema-Beutel, K., & DeWitt, M. (2012). Including children with autism in social and imaginary play with typical peers: Integrated play groups model. *American Journal of Play*, *5*(1), 55–80.

Chapter 23:
Beyond Mind: The Embodied Double Empathy Problem

Jill Corbyn and Kay Louise Aldred

Introduction

This chapter examines the persistence of the Double Empathy Problem in embodied experience and provides practical guidance on how the gap can be addressed.

Milton's (2012) Double Empathy Theory identifies that fault for misunderstanding and miscommunication in autistic/non-autistic interactions does not rest solely with the autistic person but is a two-way process with both parties struggling to understand and empathize with people with a different neurotype. Double empathy research is largely focused on an intellectual and cognitive-based understanding and bridging of thinking, communication and exchange differences.

In this chapter, we are moving 'the problem' beyond mind. We are focusing on the less explored embodied experience of the Double Empathy Problem. When people with different experiences of embodiment (emotionality, sensation, feelings, nervous system and regulation states) interact with each other they may struggle to empathize and comprehend the experience of each other. There is little understanding, awareness or discussion of different experiences of embodiment. We explore this primarily in an inpatient context, a location that Shaw et al. (2023) identifies as creating a 'triple empathy' problem due to the addition of the medical/non-medical cultural divide.

Double empathy-related research has largely focused on intellectual and mind-based understanding between two people – often in neurodivergent and neurotypical communication and exchange. In our work with mental health inpatient services, we have supported teams to understand neurodivergent communication and norms to bridge the Double Empathy Problem. However, we noticed a gap in understanding embodied experience. An embodied Double Empathy Problem.

Our experience shows that where there are different experiences of embodiment and regulation, the Double Empathy Problem persists. We believe that this difference is an often overlooked yet key aspect that impacts individual's experience within inpatient mental health services. One that perpetuates the functionalized ideals of normalcy that have dominated autism studies (Milton, 2014) and is characterized by the medical model. It is further exacerbated by the structural and cultural power dynamics present in health services, and particularly in staff–patient relationships (Nimmon & Stenfors-Hayes, 2016).

Staff in mental health services often have different experiences of the world, of embodiment and of regulation than their neurodivergent patients. The lack of understanding and knowledge of autistic people, and appropriate treatment and support contributes to high suicidality (Camm-Crosbie et al., 2019). We identified that staff sometimes struggle to understand, interact and provide effective support and co-regulation to dysregulated autistic patients. As has been reported in the literature, the '*locus of the problem has traditionally been seen to reside in the brain of the neurodivergent person*' (Milton et al., 2022). This misunderstanding is perpetuated and exacerbated when the neurodivergent person is also an inpatient in a mental health ward.

Our work with mental health inpatient service teams demonstrates how embodied connection can facilitate understanding, communication and co-regulation with neurodivergent, as well as neurotypical, folks in their care. We provide information about dysregulation and experiences of disembodiment, alexithymia, hyposensitivity, hyperempathy and emotionality, and hypersensitivity centring learning, understanding and humility in the face of embodied difference.

We provide a framework of understanding and outline activities to support co-regulation, connection and empathy across neurotypes, and between people with different lived and regulatory experiences. In presenting information about the nuances of the lived, embodied and nervous system experience of autistic individuals, we facilitate a shared understanding and help begin to bridge the Double Empathy Problem.

The authors, Jill Corbyn and Kay Louise Aldred, are part of the Neurodiverse Connection Team, a Community Interest Company, which specializes in supporting translation between neurotypes. We work to elevate the voices of neurodivergent people to help them to flourish. Both authors are late-diagnosed autistic and have lived personal and professional experiences about the contents of the chapter.

In this chapter, we explore the embodied experience of the Double Empathy Problem, neurodivergent norms and embodied experiences, understanding regulation, polyvagal theory and window of tolerance, and understanding embodiment in mental health settings before suggesting an approach to address the embodied Double Empathy Problem.

We don't assume that all patients are neurodivergent, or that all staff are neurotypical. However, we focus on differences in the embodied relationship between neurodivergent patients and neurotypical staff. In our experience, inpatient hospital environments are barriers for many neurodivergent staff members (though we have met and worked with some), and neurodivergent people are overrepresented in mental health inpatient settings.

Additionally, we note that ideas of hyper (over) and hypo (under) sensitivity are based on neurotypical norms. We don't yet have neurodivergent-centred descriptors of these experiences, though this work continues to evolve, and we eagerly await further developments.

The embodied experience of the Double Empathy Problem

Embodiment, as we define it, is feeling safe enough to be fully in our body: to think, feel and emote, without shame. These are responses that work somatically – with the body and its intelligence, centring the body and the person. These responses move away from pathologizing sensation and emotion. The sociology of embodiment has developed in response to the '*failure to incorporate the voices of bodies as they are experience[d] or lived*' (Nettleton, 2021, p. 51). Our work aligns with this approach.

In our work with mental health inpatient services and educators, we have supported teams to understand neurodivergent communication and norms to bridge the 'mind-based' Double Empathy Problem. In doing so, we noticed a gap in understanding embodied experience and have developed work to facilitate understanding, to bridge this gap and to address the Double Empathy Problem in embodied understanding.

By example, in our work reviewing mental health inpatient sensory environments, we identify common sensory stressors such as bright lights that create glare and multiple reflections on other surfaces, or the constant rumble from air conditioning or heating. Often, the neurotypical staff that show us around have never noticed the things that we identify as challenging, distressing and cumulatively overwhelming. They live in a different sensory reality to us and need support to understand the reality of our embodied experience.

Gaudion (2014) describes how she identified and overcame the embodied Double Empathy Problem (though she does not label it as such). In her design process, working with autistic adults, she notes that she had to shift her perception and externalize her thoughts to understand how the autistic people she was designing for experienced their home. Prior to this, her assumptions led to misinterpretation of his actions and experiences. Gaudion notes that she had to understand how she felt about things and what her emotional response was before she could empathize and understand another perspective.

Where different experiences of embodiment and regulation are not explored, shared and understood, the Double Empathy Problem persists. To bridge the gap, we must first be embodied.

Regardless of neurotype, there is a disconnect between mind and body throughout society – we are collectively mind-dominant, thought-based and body-phobic. The body is not part of how we are taught to 'know' things. Descartes' theory of mind–body dualism and separation and the supremacy and independent existence of the mind persists. We do not receive education on how to reference our gut instinct and our intuition in school. Knowledge is in books, in words, not the body. Scholars have reflected on how social institutions regulate, control and monitor bodies (Nettleton, 2021; Turner, 1992), facilitated by the disciplinary power of social institutions (Foucault, 1976). The body is taught to be still for hours a day, bound to a desk and computer – which is not its natural habitat. Bodily needs are taboo – as the only recent introduction of menopause policy into the workplace attests (Department for Work and Pensions, 2022). In school and the workplace bodily needs – the toilet, thirst and hunger – are secondary to lessons and meetings (Lynden, 2022). There is no space to follow our natural body rhythm. Emotions of any depth are often deemed unprofessional or pathologized.

Regardless of neurotype, many people assume that everyone else has a similar experience to them – a perspective that Husserl (1913) terms the 'natural attitude'. That they see yellow where we see yellow. When they look at the green carpet, they can taste it in the same way that we do (for those with synaesthesia), they find the lights dazzling and overwhelming, they find unexpected social interactions in narrow corridors anxiety-inducing, etc. However, as our senses detect information about our environment, this information is processed to interpret and make sense of it. The process of perception is a '*creative act of interpretation*' (Seth, 2022). Many autists have limited understanding of their own sensory and social processing differences and aren't able to articulate their experiences because, living in a neuronormative world, they may never have had the support to understand it.

> *I always thought that other people were having the same experience as me, but that they were managing better. I thought I wasn't trying hard enough. I didn't realise that their processing differences meant that they lived in a very different world to me.*
>
> (Jill, personal correspondence, 2023)

Bodies and nervous systems are impacted by the cultural landscape and often the co-occurrence of neurodivergence and eating disorders and mental illness, poverty and abuse, trauma (especially post COVID-19), intersectionality (the interconnected nature of social categories such as race, class and gender as they apply to a given individual or group, creating overlapping and interdependent systems of discrimination or disadvantage, adds to trauma, stress and dysregulation) and structures of society – which are neuronormative.

Neurodivergent norms and embodied experience

Research has found that over 90% of autistic people have atypical sensory processing (Crane et al., 2009) with many experiencing a higher perceptual capacity, or taking in more sensory information, than non-autistic people (Brinkert & Remington, 2020).

Many neurodivergent individuals process the world in a bottom-up, body- and sensation-first way (Amso et al., 2014). For example, sensing the mood and emotions of others. They pattern process and sense perceive, somatically and energetically. Often, neurodivergent individuals experience significant dysregulation due to the sensory trauma caused by living in a world and structures not built for them (Fulton et al., 2020).

Many autists experience hyper (increased) or hypo (decreased) sensitivity – or often a mix of both – in their external and internal senses (Lefebvre et al., 2022). For someone experiencing hypersensitivity (increased sensitivity), hypervision may mean that light flickers create dysregulation. Olfactory hypersensitivity may result in a gagging reflex at certain smells, while hyperhearing can result in a startle response or overwhelm by sudden noises, buzzes or larger crowds. Hypertactile individuals can experience touch as panic-inducing and may be temperature-sensitive or textile-intolerant. Vestibular hypersensitivity can result in an everchanging gait or movement, and difficulty walking, while proprioceptive hypersensitivity can present as the difference in how the body is held, or fine motor skills being a challenge.

Someone experiencing hyposensitivity (reduced sensitivity) may seek additional sensory input. For example, people who have hypovision may touch objects to regulate or are attracted to bright lights. Olfactory hyposensitivity may result in the pull to chew or smell everything or mix foods. Hypohearing can present in seeking out or stimulating noise, such as banging or tapping, while hypotactile individuals might seem immune to cold, hot or pain so may be more frequently injured or prefer tight clothes. Vestibular hyposensitivity can lead to individuals wanting to spin, sing, rock or create circle movements to regulate, while proprioceptive hyposensitivity can result in leaning or bumping into objects or a weakened grasp.

This also applies to internal, emotional and sensation differences. If interoceptive awareness is too amplified, feelings and sensations are just too big and overwhelming. If interoceptive awareness is 'offline', if the individual is experiencing alexithymia, feelings and sensations are absent or hard to feel and understand. These differences in embodied experience require exploration, understanding and empathy.

The term 'neuroception' was introduced to emphasize an automated process that evaluates environments to assess risk and safety (Porges, 2017). However, Elisabeth (2022) identifies that some aspects of polyvagal theory are neuronormative and pathologize autistic ways of being – for example, prosocial behaviours like soft gaze, expressive face, eye contact, smiling and vocal resonance are identified as key indicators of safety. Porges claims that faulty neuroception, or the detection of danger where it does not exist, contribute to psychiatric conditions. Elisabeth suggests an alternative, neurodivergent affirming approach.

> *I'd much rather see us discussing highly attuned or sensitive neuroception, when a person's neuroception is incredibly sensitive and thus responsive to stimulus that might not even register for someone else. Sensitive neuroception much more accurately describes how the Autistic brain interacts with the internal and external environment ... The only time I feel it is accurate to talk about faulty neuroception is when someone is perceiving safety in a situation that is actually dangerous. Due to social naivete, Autistic people may not pick up on danger signals and may unknowingly put themselves in unsafe situations. It is much less subjective to say a situation was actually dangerous and we did not perceive it correctly than to say a situation was perfectly safe and we did not perceive it correctly. Safety is far too relative for us to decide what is or is not a safe experience for someone else.*
>
> (Elisabeth, 2022)

Understanding regulation

The nervous system is an automated response that guides our bodily reactions and engagement with life. To understand these concepts, we refer to the work of Dr Stephen Porges and his polyvagal theory model of the autonomic nervous system and Dr Dan Siegel's (2020) theory of the window of tolerance.

Regulation is the ability to tolerate stressors – to process, digest and complete sympathetic activation (fight, flight), the stress or survival response, without moving beyond capacity or what we can tolerate. Dysregulation is when the nervous system is out of capacity and prepared to take action to ensure safety and survival. This is when stressors can't be processed, where emotions and sensations can't be contained and where there is an increased likelihood of management strategies that may be considered harmful. It may present as impulsive behaviour, mutism, glazed-over eyes, sudden emotional intensity, inability to settle, avoidance and inability to think or make decisions (Porges, 2017).

The polyvagal theory has faced and refuted some criticisms (Porges, 2023), including insufficient experimental evidence, too much emphasis on and centring of vagal tone, an oversimplification of social behaviour and lacking nuance. However, it has been useful in practice and relevant in our work in understanding and working with emotional regulation and the stress and trauma response in a 'whole body' way (Giroux et al., 2023).

The work of Hans Seyle on the stress response, the impact on the body and the concept of the general adaptation syndrome is widely accepted and we have found the polyvagal theory to be a useful application and framework for supporting the resolution of the detrimental effects stress can have on physical and mental health. Selye (1956) famously identifies three factors that universally lead to stress: *uncertainty, the lack of information* and *the loss of control*. Arguably, these factors are all exacerbated for those who are detained in mental health services and may disproportionately impact neurodivergent patients.

There is no well-being without the cultivation of nervous system regulation, we can't think our way into regulation – we feel our way through and to it. For many neurodivergent people, the feeling is big and made bigger and more dysregulated by the sensory environment. Interventions which bypass the body may have little impact therapeutically if regulation isn't supported and restored first.

Polyvagal theory

Dr Stephen Porges' theory explains that our nervous system has parts, the sympathetic and parasympathetic. The social engagement aspect of the parasympathetic part of the nervous system is the place of safety, where we feel connected to others and our environment in the here and now. We are meant to be in this part of our nervous systems for most of the time. Here we are curious and here we learn and connect. We rest and digest and our immune system works well.

The fight and flight stress responses occur in the sympathetic portion of the nervous system. This is activated in response to stress or a perceived threat. We need some sympathetic activation in our nervous system to support action and thinking but if we spend too long in activation, we start to experience an escalation of emotions and body symptoms, anxiety, and panic (flight, moving away from the threat), anger and rage (fight, moving toward the threat aggressively). Blood pressure, heartbeat and adrenaline increase, pupils dilate, we feel sweaty, digestion and immunity slow down, and we feel less connected to others. We can't fully access high-order thinking skills here or connect with others and creativity is impaired.

Finally, if we feel we cannot escape the stress of threat we move into freeze and fawn. Here, the body immobilizes and collapses (freeze) and/or merges with others' views and people pleases (fawn). We are completely overwhelmed, feel helpless, numb and depressed, and can dissociate. In freeze we also shut down – heartbeat, blood pressure, body temperature, eye contact, immunity and social connection decrease, and we feel shame, and trapped, and the body prepares for death. Impactful learning or therapeutic support cannot take place here – memory and thinking are impaired, and creativity can't be accessed.

Window of tolerance

Dr Dan Seigel explains that the window of tolerance is our zone of resilience, where we can deal with day-to-day living and stressors and is where the nervous system can process nervous system arousal, also known as the stress or survival response. In effect, this is the window of regulation.

Our windows of tolerance, or zones of regulation, vary according to neurobiology, childhood experiences, current environment, social support and coping skills. Many neurodivergent individuals' window of tolerance is further reduced because of sensory and social processing differences. Sensory-processing demands (such as bright lighting, beepers, alarms, scratchy bedsheets and disinfectant smells) and social-processing demands (such as big groups, eye contact, lots of questions and too much text) might all reduce our window of tolerance or zone of regulation.

Regardless of neurotype, we are all, as humans, as mammals, trying to regulate – to restore balance and flow into our system, move ourselves back toward rest and digest, to calm, connection, curiosity and well-being. Our bodies are working to soothe the pain of dysregulation and the stress response – whether that be sensory pain, emotional pain or physical pain. Attempts to regulate are attempts to gain mastery and a sense of control over these painful experiences of embodiment and to resolve them. We regulate using resources, things, actions or sounds. The body is working to cease the pain of dysregulation and feel soothed. Stimming, emoting, making sounds, rocking and flapping are all normal and healthy, embodied, attempts to regulate.

> *I found that, if given appropriate guidance, human beings can and do shake off the effects of overwhelming events and return to their lives using exactly the same procedures that animals use.*
>
> (Levine, 2008, p. 30)

Without supportive environments or relationships to do this in or with, or if we are pushed beyond what our regulation tools can support, humans will seek other ways to regulate – these include strategies and methods which may be harmful or considered 'disordered' such as restrictive or binge eating, alcohol and drug use, self-harm, smoking or excessive working.

When dysregulated, the automatic nervous system 'fight', 'flight' and 'freeze' responses may all be misunderstood as bad behaviour and met with behavioural interventions. In our work, we regularly support teams to understand how sensory and social overload contribute to dysregulation, which might present as fight or flight (meltdown) or freeze (shutdown). We encourage them to adapt their responses. Instead of behavioural interventions, they work to reduce stressors and support regulation, connection and collaboration.

Nervous system arousal and embodied distress impact the individuals' ability to interact or engage with therapeutic intervention and require an empathetic embodied response from the care provider and practitioner. When these embodied nervous system states are happening, no therapy can take place – there is no higher-ordered thinking or cognition/logic. The body and nervous system are seeking regulation and safety. In these instances, co-regulation is vital – supporting containment and soothing via resourcing and self-holding. This shift in understanding supports teams in identifying how they can de-escalate and enables them to respond differently to distress, reducing restrictive practices and supporting regulated responses.

Elisabeth (2022) reflects on neurodivergent application of these theories:

> *Ventral supremacy is a big problem. Due to the hierarchical way that the polyvagal ladder is presented, it can be easy to assume that being in ventral social engagement as often as possible is our goal. However, the reality is that our world is dysregulating. Safety is a limited resource in this society. Our bodies evolved to become dysregulated in the face of real stressors. It's okay to be dysregulated some of the time … Stress responses are adaptive. They only become traumatic when we get stuck in them. Releasing the chaotic energy of sympathetic activation is important. Allowing some space for disconnection and avoidance is important.*

Understanding the body and nervous system, understanding dysregulation and facilitating co-regulation to support self-regulation is transformative work.

There are two ways to restore balance. The first is to increase the tools that can be used in response to stress. The second is to reduce the source of dysregulation. Empathy for embodied difference supports both parts – understanding of stressors, and the identification of additional tools of response. Empathy for embodied difference means seeking to understand what is going on emotionally, sensation- and feelings-wise for another person and then imagining what it would be like to experience that.

Understanding embodiment in mental health settings

Autistic people are at high risk of mental health problems, self-injury and suicidality (Camm-Crosbie et al., 2019), and autistic women are 13 times more likely to die by suicide than the general population (Hirvikoski et al., 2016). It is critical, then, that health care providers understand autistic perspectives and experiences and make adjustments to accommodate sensory sensitivities (Doherty et al., 2022).

It is inevitable, due to the natural variation of neurodiversity, that there will be different perspectives on the world, embodiment and regulation among mental health service staff compared to their neurodivergent patients. A lack of understanding and knowledge about embodiment generally, along with insufficient neurodivergent-affirming interventions and support, contributes to high rates of suicidality (Camm-Crosbie et al., 2019). Our work with mental health services has revealed that staff frequently struggle to comprehend, engage with and effectively support or co-regulate dysregulated autistic patients. As noted by the

Double Empathy Problem, the issue has traditionally been framed as residing within the neurodivergent individual's brain. This misconception is further reinforced and intensified when the neurodivergent person is an inpatient in a mental health ward.

Top-down approaches to mental health intervention, treatment and recovery do not consider embodiment full stop, never mind differences within embodied experience.

Differences in embodied experience and a misunderstanding of, and lack of, empathy from neurotypical staff can cause more dysregulation and overwhelm for neurodivergent patients. We have experienced this leading to self-harm as neurodivergent patients try to self-regulate and self-soothe, gain mastery and control over feelings and sensations, and process or express them.

The neurodivergent staff we have worked with have described their dissociation and disembodiment as a response to the challenging culture and physical environment in which they are working. If they are dissociated and disembodied, they may not be any better placed than their neurotypical peers to support embodied understanding and connection with patients who are experiencing sensory distress.

Inpatient services are a huge challenge in terms of sensory and social processing which add to the harm and distress for autistic people detained. The *Manchester Evening News* (Slater, 2023) reported on Lauren Bridges' inquest. Lauren, who was 20, had died in a Psychiatric Intensive Care Unit. Giving evidence at Lauren's inquest, Consultant Psychiatrist Dr Ince defined 'iatrogenic deterioration' as '*harm caused by a setting, placement of treatment that's afforded to a person*' and that '*if that person wasn't subject to that placement, treatment or setting then that harm would not occur*'. He said ... '*Inpatient psychiatric wards are noisy, busy, unstructured environments ... They produce significant sensory demands. They are often associated with high levels of emotional distress due to the nature of the patients that are there. They are often under-staffed and inappropriately staffed, due to the nature of the demands of the patients that are there*'.

Barriers to understanding

Our work with services has identified numerous barriers to connection, understanding and co-regulation between services and patients. The primary and fundamental barrier to understanding and effective support is the embodied Double Empathy Problem – differences in lived and embodied experience for (often) neurotypical staff and their neurodivergent patients. This is exacerbated by power differences, overwhelmed and dissociated service providers, the pathologizing of natural sensations and feelings, a focus on mind-based interventions, and a deficit in training and support to staff.

The freeze and dissociation in service providers, understandable due to the overwhelm and overload of the system and services, creates additional challenges. Dysregulated staff and services don't have the headspace to learn something new – they are surviving, teetering on burnout. The services themselves are in survival mode – high sympathetic activation – verging on and oftentimes in freeze. There is no room to explore, or connect, if the staff or caregiver feel unsafe, dysregulated or overwhelmed. Staff are in mind, dissociated, and to empathize would mean opening to their feelings, which would require them to have a safe space and their therapeutic support to regulate. Hence, there is a primary need for a wholesale culture shift and movement from '*having to go home, lie in a darkened room, after a day's work*' – offered to us by a member of the multidisciplinary team – being a norm.

The pathology of sensation and feelings is coupled with a reluctance to accept the magnitude of the stress and trauma experienced by patients. Our work has demonstrated that support for staff delivered in a regulated way that seeks connection with care providers as humans, with their own needs, delivered from our own lived experience and with heart, is met with a wide variety of responses. They include squirminess, fear, defensiveness, eye-rolling, sarcasm, attempts to close down or diminish, discomfort, relief and hope, but the primary response is curiosity and a pull for something different, things to change to improve outcomes for patients and working conditions for staff alike. Yet others have 'leant in', breathed a sigh of relief to be seen as a living and feeling being, and expressed shock and distress, at the disconnection they sustain to survive in the workplace.

The focus on mind-based, talking interventions is a further barrier to body-based expression, connection and regulation. One psychologist reflected to us, that talking interventions particularly do not work well for children and young people. This reflection is supported by research. Hancock et al. (2022) identified that traditional talking therapies were inaccessible and ineffective for children and young people with speech, language and communication needs, and mental health difficulties.

Additionally, we have noted a training deficit for many frontline staff that work directly with patients. While all staff must attend mandatory training, this is often limited and doesn't often include more progressive or body-based modalities. Staff have identified in our work that when they are dissociated, distracted, overwhelmed and in crisis mode, it limits engagement. In survival mode, the 'thinking' or intellectual parts of the brain are offline. When additional training is provided, staff are not always able to attend due to staff shortages, communication issues or urgent care demands. In 2023, NHS England identified that staffing shortages remain the main constraint to improving services, with vacancy rates in inpatient mental health services up to and around 20% plus (House of Commons Committee on Public Accounts, 2023).

Addressing the embodied Double Empathy Problem in mental health services

So, what is the solution?

The solution is a shift in culture to a focus on the well-being of all and an individualized well-being journey of meaning-making around embodiment.

This may be facilitated by:

- Education about the nervous system, the variety of embodied experiences and somatic (body-based) approaches.
- A suspension of judgement and assumption around embodied experience, the development of curiosity and exploration.
- A movement from behaviour to relational focus – to enquiry and curiosity to learn about the inner landscape and bodily experience of the individual to identify alternative strategies for regulation, including somatic approaches.
- Presence, connection, collaboration and kindness.

These recommendations align with Hartley et al.'s (2022) exploration of the experiences of young people, family members and nursing staff. The researchers identified six key themes that would support the reform and quality improvement in inpatient services. Those themes are '*therapeutic relationships are the treatment, cultivating connection, knowledge is power, being human, the dance, and it's tough for all of us in here*'.

The key is to de-pathologize and normalize how the stress response manifests visibly and in an embodied way. This reduces blame, stigma and shame and moves the focus to how to create safer environments for all bodies. We have found that through authentic relating, through bringing compassion and heart to discussions with services, through empathizing with the stress and trauma of everyone involved (one care provider realised during our training that after years working in mental health services, she didn't have a thick skin – but was actually in the freeze response herself, due to vicarious trauma) there has been a softening and vulnerability in caregivers and staff, which opens the doorway to empathy and a recognition of shared embodied experience, nervous system-wise, regardless of neurotype.

This shift in approach is supported in the recent document jointly published by the World Health Organization and the UN Human Rights Office *Mental Health, Human Rights and Legislation: Guidance and Practice* (World Health Organization, 2023). This guidance suggests a step away from the medical model of mental health (which posits that mental distress is an illness, resulting from brain abnormality, genetics or biochemical imbalances, to be treated with psychiatric drugs, restraint and detention) and steps instead toward social models (which suggest that mental distress is due to socioeconomic, cultural and environmental oppression, stigma and social exclusion), human rights and trauma-informed approaches.

Our experience is that developing language and understanding of nervous system responses and autistic sensory experiences is transformative. It facilitates self-management and identification and support with others, enabling individuals to share their experiences and learning, moving out of isolation and into connection and collaboration. It aligns with the shift from judging and seeking to control observable behaviour, to understanding the internal drives and experiences that have characterized the autistic self-advocacy and neurodiversity movement (Leadbitter et al., 2021).

We recognize that most people have been doing the best they can in services and a societal structure which is inherently dysregulated and disembodied, which overrides and pushes all of us, patients and staff alike, out of our window of tolerance. Acknowledging this can create connection and a bridge of empathy, built out of this shared experience.

The solution is person-centred. There is no one-size-fits-all in terms of embodiment. We advocate for holistic, individualized programmes of mind, body and energy approaches – seeing well-being as a journey of exploration and meaning-making. Meaning-making, as we define it, is making sense of and finding purpose within the lived experience of being alive, now, in this body, experiencing what it has and is experiencing. This is especially important in the case of neurodivergence, due to us living in a world, not made or structured for us, and because of this it is hard to find and live our purpose.

Outstanding support and care are natural outcomes of embodied and regulated caregivers, which starts with embodied regulated leaders, which starts with embodied regulated service structures. The culture sets the tone of the support and care received. However, change begins with us – all of us, individually – building more capacity and regulation into our nervous system, creating more safety in our bodies first. Grassroots change, a bottom-up approach, is aligned with these principles. Individual change ripples out and creates a resonance of safety and embodiment which vibrates throughout the organization.

Whatever the nature of disembodiment or dysregulation – whether it be due to ill health, trauma or neurodivergence, such as autistic sensory or social-processing differences – core support and intervention based on co-regulation, safety and connection is a solution which supports mental and physical health and meets needs.

Our work with mental health inpatient service teams highlights how embodied connection can enhance understanding, communication, and co-regulation for both neurodivergent and neurotypical individuals in their care. By providing information on dysregulation, disembodiment, alexithymia, hyposensitivity, hyperempathy, heightened emotionality and hypersensitivity, we foster learning, deeper understanding and humility in recognizing and respecting embodied differences.

We offer a framework for understanding and practical activities designed to foster co-regulation, connection and empathy across neurotypes and diverse lived experiences of regulation. By sharing insights into the nuanced lived, embodied and nervous system experiences of autistic individuals, we help build mutual understanding and address the challenges of the embodied Double Empathy Problem.

Understanding and empathizing with the issues enables teams to work differently with patients to reduce stressors and to identify resources and solutions. For example, telling someone to calm down is not always the best option. Sometimes, we need to match their energy and understand the importance of anger as a deactivation process from freeze. This isn't often understood as a good thing, and staff may require support to learn how to be present with people to do this safely and not shut it down, so they return to freeze. Flight and fight are normal, healthy responses to perceived threats and stressors.

Regulation is supported through co-regulation and limbic resonance. A culture that supports embodiment is well-being-centred and focused on supporting regulation in leaders and practitioners, so they create a resonance of it being safe to be in the body for those they offer care to. The resonance is limbic and emotional. Regulated adults support regulation in patients – they create a resonance which is limbic and emotional, and they create a 'safety' contagion. Through modelling, space holding, containment – through co-regulation – patients can master physiology and build the capacity to stay present to feeling and sensation, and so improve health in their mental and physical well-being. If there is incongruence between what is being said and embodied by care providers, this can create a felt sense of unsafety.

Therapeutic interventions which support being with the body benefit everybody, regardless of neurotype These include orienting, following (biological impulse), resourcing (bringing the nervous system 'down', building capacity to connect to internal and external environment), self-holding and soothing, potent posture and following the breath. Other somatic exercises such as 'containment' and ABC (anchor, breathe, connect) de-escalate and reduce nervous system activation.

Coaching approaches that connect thoughts, feelings and sensations bridge the embodied Double Empathy Problem. What are you thinking? Can your face and body show me how you feel? Can you tell me or show me what is going on inside your body? Co-regulation through embodied relating and relationship is the backbone of recovery, and therapeutic and service provision success. Co-regulation is a bottom-up, body-first process, built on establishing a felt sense of safety first. Emotional and nervous system education, increasing body awareness, self-soothing and bespoke adaptation of the sensory environment happen through effective therapeutic relationships. Both practitioner and recipient understand their embodiment.

An activity to support regulation

So, where to start in organizations or as an individual? One basic, simple and core practice to implement is a three-step pause process of check, need and adjust, which is practised at the start of each interaction.

Practise pausing and being fully there for yourself and for those you space hold, facilitate or teach. Witness yourself and them while meeting your own needs and encouraging them to do the same in the moment – so creating more capacity, safety, and comfort – more pleasure is the antidote to stress and trauma.

Create a pause to practise this three-step process – check, need and adjust – at the start of each day, in addition to each session or lesson. By modelling this behaviour, you can help yourself and others to develop a greater sense of embodiment.

In addition, if you find you don't feel anything in your body, try the ABC exercise before you begin. Remember – less is more. Titrate. Go slowly. Stop if you need to.

The key to success is the practitioner practising humility in the face of embodied difference, building rapport and bridging the disconnect in service users from their body, regulation and window of tolerance. Creating a felt sense of safety is paramount – checking in, asking, listening, acting, adapting and amending. Helping individuals create a narrative and story of the body, make meaning of it, its sensation and feeling, befriend the body and tend to its needs, with self-compassion and care, is the solution.

Conclusion

Double empathy-related research has largely focused on intellectual and mind-based understanding between two people - often in neurodivergent and neurotypical communication and exchange. We have explored the persistence of the Double Empathy Problem in embodied experience. Where there are different experiences of embodiment and regulation, the Double Empathy Problem persists. In our work with mental health services, a neurotypical majority of staff and a high proportion of neurodivergent patients have different sensory and embodied realities. This difference in experience is not explored or understood, and patient distress is too often misunderstood as behavioural and met with a behavioural response. Additionally, we have found that systemic dysregulation is a barrier to creating regulated spaces.

We recommend supporting a shift in culture to a focus on the well-being of all and an individualized well-being journey of meaning-making around embodiment. We suggest that this may be best supported by fostering a deeper understanding of the nervous system and the diversity of embodied experiences. This involves adopting a curious, exploratory approach that avoids assumptions of sameness, shifting the focus from behaviour to relationship. It also includes helping individuals identify alternative regulation strategies, particularly somatic approaches grounded in presence, connection, collaboration and kindness.

Much of our learning and application has been in inpatient services, but, as with the Double Empathy Problem, we believe that the embodied Double Empathy Problem has a much wider application. This learning may be particularly beneficial in education settings and other support provisions.

References

Amso, D., Haas, S., Tenenbaum, E., Markant, J., & Sheinkopf, S.J. (2014). Bottom-up attention orienting in young children with autism. *Journal of Autism and Developmental Disorders, 44*(3), 664–673. https://doi.org/10.1007/s10803-013-1925-5

Brinkert, J., & Remington, A. (2020). Making sense of the perceptual capacities in autistic and non-autistic adults. *Autism, 24*(7), 1795–1804. https://doi.org/10.1177/1362361320922640

Camm-Crosbie, L., Bradley, L., Shaw, R., Baron-Cohen, S., & Cassidy, S. (2019). 'People like me don't get support': Autistic adults' experiences of support and treatment for mental health difficulties, self-injury and suicidality. *Autism, 23*(6), 1431–1441. https://doi.org/10.1177/1362361318816053

Crane, L., Goddard, L., & Pring, L. (2009). Sensory processing in adults with autism spectrum disorders. *Autism, 13*(3), 215–228. https://doi.org/10.1177/1362361309103794

Department for Work and Pensions (2022). *Menopause and the Workplace: How to Enable Fulfilling Working Lives: Government Response* [Policy paper]. https://www.gov.uk/government/publications/menopause-and-the-workplace-how-to-enable-fulfilling-working-lives-government-response/menopause-and-the-workplace-how-to-enable-fulfilling-working-lives-government-response

Doherty, M., Neilson, S., O'Sullivan, J., Carravallah, J., Johnson, M., Cullen, W., & Shaw, S. C. K. (2022). Barriers to healthcare and self reported adverse outcomes for autistic adults: a cross-sectional study. *BMJ Open, 12*, e056904. https://doi.org/10.1136/bmjopen-2021-056904

Elisabeth, J. (2022, April 3) A neurodiversity paradigm lens on polyvagal theory. *Trauma Geek*. https://www.traumageek.com/blog/a-neurodiversity-paradigm-lens-on-polyvagal-theory

Foucault, M. (1976). *The Birth of the Clinic: An Archaeology of Medical Perception*. Tavistock.

Fulton, R., Richardson, K., Jones, R., & Reardon, E. (2020). Sensory trauma: Autism sensory difference and the daily experience of fear. https://www.researchgate.net/publication/351918786_Sensory_Trauma_-_autism_sensory_difference_and_the_daily_experience_of_fear

Gaudion, K. (2014). Design and wellbeing: Bridging the empathy gap between neurotypical designers and autistic adults. https://www.researchgate.net/publication/277330616_Design_and_Wellbeing_Bridging_the_empathy_gap_between_neurotypical_designers_and_autistic_adults

Giroux, C., Ahlers, D., & Miawotoe, A. (2023). Polyvagal approaches: scientifically questionable but useful in practice. *Journal of Psychiatry Reform, 10*(11). https://journalofpsychiatryreform.com/2023/10/17/polyvagal-approaches-scientifically-questionable-but-useful-in-practice/#:~:text=Critiques%20and%20Alternative%20Explanations,being%20neural%20pathways%20and%20mechanisms

Hancock, A., Northcott, S., Hobson, H., & Clarke, M. (2022). Speech, language and communication needs and mental health: The experiences of speech and language therapists and mental health professionals. *International Journal of Language & Communication Disorders, 58*(1), 52–66. https://doi.org/10.1111/1460-6984.12767

Hartley, S., Redmond, T., & Berry, K. (2022). Therapeutic relationships within child and adolescent mental health inpatient services: A qualitative exploration of the experiences of young people, family members and nursing staff. *PLoS One, 17*(1), e0262070. https://doi.org/10.1371/journal.pone.0262070

Hirvikoski, T., Mittendorfer-Rutz, E., Boman, M., Larsson, H., Lichtenstein, P., & Bölte, S. (2016). Premature mortality in autism spectrum disorder. *British Journal of Psychiatry, 208*(3), 232–238. https://doi.org/10.1192/bjp.bp.114.160192

House of Commons Committee of Public Accounts (2023). *Progress in Improving NHS Mental Health Services: Sixty-Fifth Report of Session 2022–23*, [Report, together with formal minutes relating to the report]. House of Commons. https://committees.parliament.uk/publications/40960/documents/199502/default/

Husserl, E. (1913/1982). *Ideas Pertaining to a Pure Phenomenology and to a Phenomenological Philosophy—First Book: General Intro-duction to Pure Phenomenology*. Trans. F. Kersten. Nijhoff.

Leadbitter, K., Buckle, K. L., Ellis, C., & Dekker, M. (2021). Autistic self-advocacy and the neurodiversity movement: Implications for autism early intervention research and practice. *Frontiers in Psychology*, 12, 635690. https://doi.org/10.3389/fpsyg.2021.635690

Lefebvre, A., Tillmann, J., Cliquet, F., Amsellem, F., Maruani, A., Leblond, C., Beggiato, A., Germanaud, D., Amestoy, A., Ly-Le Moal, M., Umbricht, D., Chatham, C., Murtagh, L., Bouvard, M., Leboyer, M., Charman, T., Bourgeron, T., Delorme, R., Dumas, G. & EU-AIMS LEAP group. (2022). Tackling hypo and hyper sensory processing heterogeneity in autism: From clinical stratification to genetic pathways. *Autism Research, 16*(2), 364–378. https://doi.org/10.1002/aur.2861

Levine, P. A. (2008). *Healing Trauma: A Pioneering Program for Restoring the Wisdom of Your Body*. Sounds True Inc.

Lynden, A. (2024, October 6). School toilets: Should you allow access during lessons? *The Headteacher*. https://www.theheadteacher.com/attainment-and-assessment/teaching-practice/to-wee-or-not-to-wee

Milton, D. E. M. (2012). On the ontological status of autism: The 'double empathy problem'. *Disability & Society, 27*(3), 883–887. https://doi.org/10.1080/09687599.2012.710008

Milton, D. (2014). Embodied sociality and the conditioned relativism of dispositional diversity. *Autonomy, the Critical Journal of Interdisciplinary Autism Studies, 1*(3), 1–7.

Milton, D., Gurbuz, E., & López, B. (2022). The 'double empathy problem': Ten years on. *Autism, 26*(8), 1901–1903. https://doi.org/10.1177/13623613221129123

Nettleton, S. (2021). The sociology of the body. In W. C. Cockerham (Ed.), *The Wiley Blackwell Companion to Medical Sociology*, (pp. 105–124). Wiley. https://doi.org/10.1002/9781119633808.ch6

Nimmon, L., & Stenfors-Hayes, T. (2016). The "handling" of power in the physician-patient encounter: Perceptions from experienced physicians. *BMC Medical Education, 16*, 114. https://doi.org/10.1186/s12909-016-0634-0

Porges, S.W. (2017). *The Pocket Guide to the Polyvagal Theory: The Transformative Power of Feeling Safe*. WW Norton.

Porges, S.W. (2023). *Dr. Porges Responds to Polyvagal Theory Critiques*. Polyvagal Institute. https://www.polyvagalinstitute.org/vagal-paradox#:~:text=CRITICISM%3A,the%20polyvagal%20theory%20is%20untenable

Selye, H. (1956). *The Stress of Life*. McGraw-Hill.

Seth, A. (2022, July 4). Do we all perceive the world the same way? *BBC*. https://www.bbc.co.uk/ideas/videos/do-we-all-perceive-the-world-the-same-way/p0cjqx25

Shaw, S. C., Carravallah, L., Johnson, M., O'Sullivan, J., Chown, N., Neilson, S., & Doherty, M. (2023). Barriers to healthcare and a 'triple empathy problem' may lead to adverse outcomes for autistic adults: A qualitative study. *Autism, 28*(7), 1746–1757. https://doi.org/10.1177/13623613231205629

Siegel, D. J. (2020). *The Developing Mind: How Relationships and the Brain Interact to Shape Who We* (3rd ed.). Mind Your Brain.

Slater, C. (2023, August 16) Lauren Bridges was suffering 'harm' and 'trauma' after being locked in ward 'wholly ill-equipped to meet her needs' before her death, inquest hears. *Manchester Evening News*. https://www.manchestereveningnews.co.uk/news/greater-manchester-news/lauren-bridges-suffering-harm-trauma-27533430

Turner, B. S. (1992). *Regulating Bodies: Essays in Medical Sociology*. Routledge.

World Health Organization (2023, October 9). *Mental Health, Human Rights and Legislation Guidance and Practice*. World Health Organization. https://www.who.int/publications/i/item/9789240080737

Chapter 24:
A Measure of Self-Empathy

Katherine Arrowsmith

Introduction

My first experience of the adult autism diagnostic process was blocked out of my mind for years. It was following a mental crash in my mid-twenties, what I now understand to have been autistic burnout. Three and half hours into the clinical psychologist's questioning, my Mum intervened to ask if I could have a break. He agreed I was 'on the spectrum' but later withdrew it, saying, '*well, there aren't any support services for autistic adults, so there's not much point*'.

I was left in a place of limbo and self-doubt, knowing I was autistic but not having that 'official' backup or indeed support services. Climbing out of the mental health system and back into employment, I was hesitant to disclose my self-diagnosis for fear of rejection and losing my job. At times I found I could be very empathic with other people, but this made me question my autism – autistic people don't have empathy! – what was I thinking? I just needed to try harder to fit in! However, by continuing to mask my autism coupled with this 'imposter syndrome' and hitting perimenopause, I found myself in counselling, which led to my autism diagnosis 20 years after being initially assessed.

I was asked to fill out the Empathy Quotient (EQ) test (Baron-Cohen & Wheelwright, 2004), a screening tool used as a standard part of the Adult Asperger Assessment (AAA) (Baron-Cohen et al., 2005) as recommended by the National Institue for Health and Care Excellence, (NICE, 2012). This is a test designed on the basis that autistic people lack empathy and is used in conjunction with the Autism Quotient (AQ) test.

While there is no clear definition of empathy, its '*status has never been higher*' (Baron-Cohen, 1997, p. 7), being in demand both socially and economically. Society values it so much we even have an 'Empathy Day', and it is held up as '*the most valuable resource in the world'* by Simon Baron-Cohen (2012, p. 107), who co-authored the EQ, and has also described it as a human ability that autistic people *'fail to develop'* (Baron-Cohen, 1997, p. 7). Empathy is continually used as a concept to separate us out as not being fully human (Barnbaum, 2008). This opposition of autism and empathy is dehumanizing and objectifies autistic people (Gernsbacher, 2007; Yergeau, 2013). There is plenty of evidence to show that autistic people can empathize, (Fletcher-Watson & Bird, 2020; Stenning, 2020) and that the issue is a bidirectional 'mismatch' of communication between autistic and non-autistic people (Milton, 2012), as is the basis for this collection.

In this essay, I ask seven questions that relate to gold standards of best practice that could not only be applied to the EQ but also to any tool used in adult autism identification, with particular consideration of autism research priorities and the diagnostic process itself.

Whatever our ability to empathize with others is, I suggest that empathy with ourselves must be nurtured at the time of autism identification rather than what the EQ implies, that of being branded with a low quotient of humanity.

Q1: Is it based on research that is inclusive of autistic people?

The dominant cognitive theories of autism are primarily based on research by non-autistic researchers and are not inclusive of autistic people. They come from a medical model perspective seeking treatments and cures rather than the priorities of autistic people themselves of seeking to improve their quality of life (Benevides & Cassidy, 2020; Fletcher-Watson et al., 2019; Roche et al., 2021). The inclusion of autistic expertise in knowledge production about us would not only provide better theory and, therefore, practice but is also an ethical necessity (Chown et al., 2017; Milton, 2014; Milton & Bracher, 2013; Milton et al., 2014). Inclusive research is also shown to be less ableist (Botha & Cage, 2022). Theories from autistic researchers, such as monotropism (Murray et al., 2005) and the Double Empathy Theory (Milton, 2012), resonate strongly with autistic people. These theories focus on differences rather than being deficit-based and pathologizing (Bottema-Beutel et al., 2021; Woods & Waltz, 2019).

Autism research has often been, in reality, tokenistic in the sense that its involvement of autistic people has been more for the researchers' own esteem rather than involving the autistic person in a meaningful way that might enrich their own life, and this is particularly the case when it does not recognize intersectionality and co-conditions (Michael, 2021). Seeking to address this in the article 'Cutting our own keys' (Bertilsdotter Rosqvist et al., 2022), the authors talk about the benefits of working together more equally as autistic and non-autistic researchers. This requires the 'sharing of narratives' with methodologies and concepts based on *'our own embodied experiences and the social worlds we inhabit'* (Bertilsdotter Rosqvist et al., 2022, p. 1) rather than the 'us and them' reductionist and medicalizing approach that has persisted in previous neurocognitive autism research.

The original theory of mind study was done in 1985 with a small sample of autistic children and concluded that autistic people lack the ability to mentalize, interpret the motivations of others and function 'normally' in a social environment due to this core deficit of a lack of empathy. While it has been pulled apart methodologically, it remains a 'sacred cow' of autism research (Gernsbacher & Yergeau, 2019). Its proponents have continued to peddle it, with its latest incarnation being a 'disequilibrium' of empathy (Shalev et al., 2022). Interventions based on this theory have shown little benefit to autistic people (Fletcher-Watson et al., 2014), and the lack of understanding of autistic theory of mind by the predominant neurotype (PNT) (Beardon, 2021), has meant that interventions that cause harm have come about, for example, applied behavioural analysis (Kupferstein, 2018). Far from being included in the research that the EQ is based on, many autistic people and researchers have felt ignored and dehumanized by it (Cohen-Rottenberg, 2013; Holt et al., 2022; Yergeau, 2013) arguing that it constitutes 'research-based violence' (Botha, 2021).

Q2: Is it relevant to autism identification (content validity)?

The 'diagnosing' of autism is contentious as many argue it should not be categorized as a medical disorder and is better described as a *'difference that needs acknowledgement'* (Beardon, 2018). A formal identification of autism can, however, bring personal relief in terms of better self-understanding and acceptance (Arnold et al., 2020), and it is therefore essential that a tool used to identify autism is accurate and relevant.

Emotional experiences can be overwhelming for autistic people and cause us to shut down and appear as if we lack empathy when we have too much. As Cohen-Rottenberg (2013) writes in her blog, *'many of our problems with sensory and emotional overload derive from an excess of this ability'*. To measure empathy in a fixed amount, scoring people from low to high, is far too blunt a tool here, if there is a need to measure it at all. Far more beneficial to an autistic person may be to look at factors which may affect our ability and capacity to interact socially (Chown & Beardon, 2014), such as differences in how we process information. Techniques for filtering out the emotions of other people may even be useful for an autistic person to develop.

When assessing autistic traits like those the EQ attempts to measure, relevant to emotional and social settings, context is crucial (Gernsbacher et al., 2017). Autistic people may empathize better with other autistic people (Crompton et al., 2020). Therefore, our answers may differ depending on whether we are involved in autistic-to-autistic communication or autistic-to-non-autistic (or vice versa). For example, autistic people may prefer honesty and directness over 'social niceties'. We may experience barriers to social interaction with non-autistic people precisely because of the experience of lack of understanding from them (Sheppard et al., 2016), as it has been shown that non-autistic people struggle to empathize with autistic people (Edey et al., 2016; Rifai et al., 2022; Sheppard et al., 2016).

If we apply monotropism theory to empathy, as in autistic people may feel more intense empathy, but on fewer subjects, our answers will be very context-dependent. If our attention is on someone or something we intensely care about, our response will be different to the polytropic-brained respondent, who will be more able to 'read the room'. For example, in answer to question 6, '*I really enjoy caring for other people*', it may depend on which people and our mental capacity at that time. Many autistic people love animals and the natural world (Stenning, 2020). If we genuinely wanted to measure empathy, there should be a question on empathy for a pet or a cause close to our heart. Question 2, '*I prefer animals to humans*', is classified as a 'filler' question which has no score attached, but it is one clearly loaded with the view that autistic people lack empathy. If there was a scored question on the love of animals, for example, '*sometimes I prefer the company of my cat over anyone else*', we might get a point or two.

Part of the problem with the EQ is that it mixes cognitive empathy (ability to understand the motivations and predict the behaviour of others) with affective empathy (relating more to understanding others' emotional states), while in his book *Zero Degrees of Empathy* Baron-Cohen (2012) separates the two. He describes autistic people as 'zero positive' in that we are at level 'zero' on his empathy spectrum, but gives us credit as having affective empathy, i.e., we can be upset if someone else is upset. He suggests that this 'moral code' has been developed via our ability to systemize, to see patterns in behaviour that we learn to adopt. Systemizing is known to be a trait of autism, yet as Chapman (2019) observes, this may be a stress reaction rather than some inherent gift. If our affective empathy is 'intact', as it is according to Baron-Cohen, then why are we being tested on it in the EQ? Cognitive and affective empathy being lumped together in the EQ is problematic. As Fletcher-Watson and Bird (2020) point out, '*if we do not separate feelings of empathy from these other social and cognitive factors, then we will underestimate empathy in autistic people*'.

Q3: Does it have the person's well-being at heart?

Autistic people are at a higher risk of suicide (Hirvikoski et al., 2016; Kirby et al., 2019) and experience mental health issues, particularly anxiety and depression, as co-conditions (Cooper et al., 2017). These can be related to the need to mask our autistic traits (Cassidy et al., 2020; Pearson & Rose, 2021). In their paper on autistic masking, authors Pearson and Rose emphasize the need to '*acknowledge masking as a self-protective mechanism rather than a necessarily conscious choice*' (Pearson & Rose, 2021, p. 55) against bullying, victimization and stigma. This overcompensation can be exhausting and lead to burnout (Raymaker et al., 2020). Whether or not an autistic person has a diagnosis, they can experience shame from the sense of being different and from that difference often being minimized as a kind of 'reverse stigma' (Gates, 2022). *'Repeated experiences of stigma'* (or 'microaggressions') *'related to various forms of invalidation can become emotionally damaging events and a source of complex trauma'* (Gates, 2019, p. 18).

Before coming to a diagnosis, the length of time is significant in how long we have experienced the oppression of this layering of shame and stigma. Self-empathy in this respect is probably more pertinent when a diagnosis is received later in life. Age, as well as other intersectionalities, such as race and class, can also make it less safe to unmask (Pearson & Rose, 2023). Practice must be sensitive to this and be an empathic port in a storm. A screening tool is a gateway, an initial signpost for someone feeling low self-worth and potentially in an identity crisis. Getting the tone right is vital in bringing balance to an experience that focuses on identifying impairment with a need also to recognize a person's strengths.

Good practice in terms of empathy would be to encourage validation of the autistic person's experience and self-compassion. It is crucial to understand that our sensory differences are not a choice and that often we are in a heightened state of anxiety because of them, which can look like 'challenging behaviour' (Reardon & Fulton, 2022). Sensory processing differences in autism are sometimes treated as an 'add-on' to the 'core-deficits', but Fulton et al. (2020) argue that this should be at the forefront of autism identification. They suggest that autistic difficulties with social interaction may be due in part to how our *'information pick-up in any given environment tends to prioritise sensory affordances over social ones'* (Fulton et al., 2020, p. 44). How this balances with Double Empathy Theory, in that autistic people may not experience any social struggles when with their own sociality rather than with PNT sociality, is something to be further explored.

Post-diagnostic support, in my view, would include identifying sensory differences and supporting the person to be able to advocate for themselves to reduce the stress of navigating challenging sensory environments and to learn how to self-regulate in preparing for before and after such an event. In this way, we can predict our *own* behaviour so that we can function better. This is not to place responsibility on the individual – there is much to be done from a social model perspective on autism, but strategies and tools to give us a fighting chance do not go amiss.

Understanding the role of the environment in our ability to function aligns with Beardon's Golden Equation of *Autism + Environment = Outcome* (Beardon, 2021). Self-knowledge is important for the ability to unmask but as Pearson and Rose argue *'masking is situated in an ecological framework'* that must also take some of the weight of it in order to reduce the toll on the autistic person of communicating in the unequal playing field that Double

Empathy Theory outlines. If we mask less in autistic-to-autistic communication then peer support should be encouraged to nurture a sense of belonging, positive social identity and empathy with each other.

Q4: Is it reliable and consistent in applying to a wide range of individual experiences?

The theory that the EQ and much of autism practice is based on, and the measurement tools used in identifying it, need to reflect the lived experience of autistic people. This means recognizing our heterogeneity and diversity of experience – we are not just one type of mind. While we may look for commonalities with autism that are helpful in identification, in practice, the mantra of monotropism, '*meet the person where they are*' (Murray, 2018a), also has its place.

Most of the research that autism practice is based on (including the EQ) was done with a very narrow demographic, primarily (White male) children, and therefore does not apply well to adults. Its reductionist methods focus on 'the mind' and are criticized for ignoring our bodies (Yergeau, 2013) and co-conditions that make it devoid of being holistic (Michael, 2021). The adage '*when you've met one autistic person, you've met one autistic person*' is true; we are all different and come with intersectional identities. Many women, myself included, have been missed and misdiagnosed (Gould & Ashton-Smith, 2011). Baron-Cohen's 'male brain' theory (Baron-Cohen, 2002) has alienated women from autistic identification and gendered autism in a very unhelpful way. Identification tools must reflect the diversity of the population they aim to apply to, especially minority and oppressed groups.

Q5: Does it use language that is autistic-friendly and non-pejorative?

Much of the language around autism is negative and pathologizing (Bottema-Beutel et al., 2021), and dehumanizing to us (Fletcher-Watson & Bird, 2020). By talking more in terms of strengths and differences, we can improve the well-being of autistic people and the narrative around us. In communication, clear and direct language is preferred, and non-literal language should be avoided as it can be open to misinterpretation by autistic people. A sense of 'speaking the same language' is found when autistic people are together (Chapman, 2019), and it would be good practice to involve autistic people in the wording of self-report tools such as the EQ (Ratto et al., 2022) to ensure they are accessible.

As mentioned earlier, many questions in the EQ are ambiguous and without context. They are also open to literal interpretation, for example, question 22, '*I find it easy to put myself in someone else's shoes'*. The questions in the EQ don't use pathologizing words, but those used around it in the AAA (Baron-Cohen et al., 2005), such as 'informant', 'impairment' and 'symptoms' do. 'Informant' is used to describe someone who may accompany a person to their assessment, such as a partner or parent, to give further information that might be relevant. While having the support of someone close has been invaluable to me and others going through it, the term 'informant' implies they are there to report some shameful secret knowledge to prevent it from going on.

A screening tool described as a 'red flag' (Allison et al., 2012) gives the impression of a danger warning rather than someone needing support. The idea of one person applying a 'quotient' of something so nebulous as empathy to another is condescending and part of a framework ('diagnosis') that medicalizes autism. The EQ is part of the AAA and was developed prior to the amalgamation of terms such as 'Asperger syndrome', 'autism spectrum condition' and 'higher functioning autism'. It is preferable to use the term autism consistently, as the use of different terms and subcategories is confusing (Beardon, 2021).

Q6: Does it contribute to a positive and realistic understanding of what autism is?

Other people's perceptions of autism can be internalized by us, leading to depression and other mental health problems (Cage et al., 2018). The stigma associated with being autistic can be experienced whether or not we disclose our autistic identity (Botha et al., 2022). Stereotypes related to autism, such as that we are 'weird', not only harm us through internalized disablement but can also cause discrimination against us, for example, in employment (Baldwin et al., 2014; Treweek et al., 2019). A positive autistic social identity can improve self-esteem and mental well-being (Cooper et al., 2017).

What a person takes away about themselves from the identification process is significant in terms of their self-image (Arnold et al., 2020) and in what and how they disclose their identity to others. Feelings of stigma and shame can prevent disclosure (Botha et al., 2022) and perpetuate masking. An identification process that informs both a realistic and positive sense of self can enable a more positive cycle where confidence in disclosure dispels stereotypes in the minds of others. This, in turn, can create a safer environment to 'come out' and, therefore, a 'collective self-esteem' (Cooper et al., 2017) conducive to better mental health.

As it stands, '*ableism is entangled with our measurements of autism – we create deficit focused measures, which only could measure deficits*', confirming the idea of autism as a deficit and from which '*we create deficit narratives that pervade almost all conversations of autism*' (Botha, 2021, p. 8). Internalization of stereotypes such as that we lack empathy mean that an autistic person might self-report '*empathy deficits even when they frequently experience empathic feelings*' (Fletcher-Watson & Bird, 2020, p. 4). The EQ does nothing to counter this. Instead, it muddies the waters of empathy, mixing not only affective with cognitive empathy but also with psychopathy, as in question 18, '*when I was a child I enjoyed cutting up worms*'. Baron-Cohen places us with psychopaths at the same level of zero on his empathy scale and 'redefines' evil in his books as 'the erosion of empathy' (Baron-Cohen, 2012, p. ix). Weaving this connection between autism and empathy into popular culture in such a negative correlation further harms autistic people (McDonagh, 2013).

Q7: Do practitioners have quality autism training?

Any practitioner involved in diagnosing autism should have specialist training on autism, such as an appropriate postgraduate award in autism that includes delivery by autistic people themselves, so that they can see the diagnostic process from the autistic person's perspective. Consistent practice is also preferred, so clinicians would ideally go on training together to achieve this. Awareness of Double Empathy Theory, especially where the practitioner is non-autistic, would be essential, and ideally, the practitioner would be autistic themselves.

Having an awareness of the broader sociopolitical issues surrounding autism and of the neurodiversity movement would help the practitioner to empathize with the autistic person and the context of what they are facing. Identification could be made by an autism specialist who wasn't clinically trained if there are no mental health co-conditions as in the 'triage-based autism identification pathway' suggested by Beardon and Chown (2014). More people qualified to do non-clinical assessments would also counter long waiting lists allowing for earlier identification (Chown & Beardon, 2014).

Perhaps the only aspect of the EQ that I regard as good practice is its self-reporting nature which means it can be done in an environment chosen by the autistic person without entering any medical setting. Self-reports are cheap and easy for researchers, and many have been designed by autistic people themselves, such as Samantha Craft's Autistic Traits Checklist (Craft, 2022), which addresses the way autism may present differently in women. Fergus Murray's *Six Starting Points* (Murray, 2018b) from monotropic theory is also useful for understanding autism from an autistic perspective.

A measure of self-empathy

The EQ test does not meet these gold standards for good practice, so I suggest a different approach regarding empathy for practitioners involved in diagnosing or assessing autistic people. To look for an alternative is also the recommendation of Harrison et al. (2022), who conclude that the EQ has insufficient criterion validity and finds no evidence for its content validity either. Some measure of empathy, I argue, is good practice, but not a 'quotient' to be handed out or withheld. I argue that the focus of empathy in adult autism assessment is with the person's empathy for themselves, especially in later life where over time masking and other forms of damaging coping mechanisms, such as substance abuse, have led to burnout or complex trauma.

Theory of mind was thought to extend to theory of *own* mind (Frith & Happé, 1999) in that an autistic person's lack of ability to empathize with others meant that we also lack this capacity with ourselves. Although alexithymia (ability to recognize our own emotional states) has been put forward as a reason for difficulties in emotional reciprocity shown by autistic people (Bird & Cook, 2013), and is common among autistic people, it is not unique to us, nor is it found to be universal (Kinnaird et al., 2019).

Whatever capacity we have for self-empathy, it is to be nurtured in a therapeutic setting, in this case, the diagnostic process, to aid well-being. Alexithymia is associated with risk-taking behaviour and other mental health problems (Kinnaird et al., 2019), which is even more of a reason to look at issues with this person-centred approach. Awareness of what environments are challenging for us and how to navigate them can enable us to prevent meltdowns, shutdowns and burnout. (Kinnaird et al., 2019). '*Difficulty identifying one's own emotions can make it difficult to self-regulate, that is, not realising that stress is increasing until you are at breaking point*' (Pearson & Rose, 2021, p. 55). This is illustrated by Roz Blackburn (McMahon, 2021, 14:32), describing autism as 'an end result' of suddenly feeling overwhelmed and out of her depth. She says it is 'the going wrong', her behaviour, that has told her she hasn't coped rather than her emotions preceding to alert her to put boundaries there.

Autistic bloggers, such as Nicola Rathbone (autisticvillage, 2021a, 2021b), explore how the sense of interoception affects our emotional state into the 'lost connections' between interoception and masking (The Autistic Advocate, 2018). 'Altered' interoception in autistic people has also been found to correlate with our social cognition (Yang et al., 2022). A low level of interoception may be a big factor in burnout for autistic people. Learning how our body functions in a sensory way, how to unmask and how to set boundaries all require a degree of self-compassion and confidence that post-diagnostic support could provide. Exercises such as journaling, making a sensory profile and how to use stimming to regulate sensory experience may be useful in relation to this and help us better advocate for our well-being. How the individual experiences empathy, for example, as a passionate interest in a subject or ways of feeling 'autistic joy' can also improve well-being. We know that anxiety reduces the ability to function, so if we know what its triggers are and how to manage them, then we can reduce the likelihood of burnout and the trauma that it may cause.

How much self-understanding a person has may itself be an indicator of autism; therefore, being able to measure or identify this in some way may help in autism assessment.

Is it time to get rid of the EQ test?

The EQ is based on flawed theory, lacks relevancy and is even harmful to autistic people, so, in my opinion, it reflects a non-autistic view of empathy in which we are set up to fail, is not conducive to well-being and serves no purpose in improving the lives of autistic people. More research needs to be done with autistic people into how we experience empathy before some such tool can be designed and used effectively. My perspective on empathy as a late-diagnosed autistic adult is one that seeks to empower autistic people in navigating the world as a neurominority. Through sharing our experience, autistic people can move from a position of shame to one of pride, similar to that experienced historically by Deaf and Queer communities.

Receiving a diagnosis of autism can not only bring relief but also the *grief* of missing out on all that self-awareness. The autistic community provides valuable peer support for self-understanding and validation (Chapman, 2019; Crompton et al., 2022). Research that is inclusive of autistic adults' lived experience would give a better understanding of autism that will enable earlier identification and so provide earlier access to this.

Knowing how different sections of the autistic community experience autism will also improve practice and provide more consistency in diagnostic methods if needed. Broader understanding and acceptance of autism that is less deficit-based would enable easier disclosure as it wouldn't carry so much shame and stigma (Botha et al., 2022) and therefore require less masking of it (Pearson & Rose, 2021). Also, behaviours that allow self-regulation, such as stimming, would be more acceptable, the 'language' of which '*may assist with learning to recognise the inner emotional states of autistic adults*' (Kapp et al., 2019).

A diagnostic tool with an autistic empathy-based approach that can be built on through post-diagnostic support would increase self-esteem and confidence with self-determination and self-advocacy skills, for example, in employment, health care and relationships (Cook & Purkis, 2022). Questions around it could be included as part of a revised AQ, which is also a self-report tool. A self-empathy approach would be more constructive by improving our quality of life rather than looking for where we don't 'measure up' in relation to a so-called 'norm'.

Holding up empathy so highly and simultaneously asserting that autistic people lack it, the EQ is part of the '*normalisation agenda and the psycho-emotional disablement of autistic people*' (Milton, 2012). This binary view of the medical model in its 'abstraction' of autism, creation of empathy 'types' and lack of quantifiability of such, perpetuates its commodification (Mallett & Runswick-Cole, 2012). The emergence in the US of 'Cassandra syndrome' seems to be providing further profiteering on the idea of the gendered view of autism and conflating it with a lack of empathy (only US$99 for NT [neurotypical] 'ladies' recovering from the emotional deprivation of being with an autistic husband to join a Skype meeting for mutual support) (Hutten, n.d.).

Autistic participation in knowledge production about us is essential to counter us being 'a product' of the autism industry (Milton, 2012) in this way. Looking for what we share rather than what divides us may help dissolve the binary view of autism and empathy.

Conclusion

Although empathy is not easy to define, it is a powerful and compelling concept. The EQ test lacks validity (Harrison et al., 2022), is driven by a theory that is not inclusive of autistic people and reflects research priorities that are focused on treatment and cure rather than on improving the lives of autistic people. More participation and collaboration are needed '*working across the double empathy divide*' (Milton in Offord, 2021) to have a broader understanding of '*what it's like*' (Frith & Happé, 1999) to be autistic. Autistic people are best placed to identify our traits in collaboration with researchers of mixed neurologies (Ratto et al., 2022)

NICE (2012) recommend using the EQ in the diagnostic process for autism. The EQ drives the concept of autistic people lacking empathy further into popular culture, making autism the 'other' and the 'anti-human'. The stigmatizing and shaming this does to autistic people is detrimental to our well-being. For these reasons, I do not regard the EQ as good practice, and dispensing of it would go some way to reversing this trend. The NICE (2012) '*general principles*' for working with autistic adults include (building) '*a trusting, supportive, empathic and non-judgemental relationship as an essential part of care*'. In my opinion, the opposite is true of the EQ – that it is judgemental and unempathic to autistic people.

It would be more beneficial to autistic people for the diagnostic practitioner to encourage the autistic person to have empathy with themselves rather than look for gaps in their understanding of non-autistic communication, as well as encourage better understanding in the general population. Tools that support the autistic person to develop a realistic and positive sense of self to understand their difference, I argue, should begin and be part of the diagnostic process rather than the EQ test.

References

Allison, C., Auyeung, B., & Baron-Cohen, S. (2012). Toward brief "red flags" for autism screening: The short autism spectrum quotient and the short quantitative checklist in 1,000 cases and 3,000 controls. *Journal of the American Academy of Child & Adolescent Psychiatry, 51*(2), 202–212.e7. https://doi.org/10.1016/j.jaac.2011.11.003

Arnold, S. R. C., Huang, Y., Hwang, Y. I. (Jane), Richdale, A. L., Trollor, J. N., & Lawson, L. P. (2020). "The single most important thing that has happened to me in my life": Development of the impact of diagnosis scale—preliminary revision. *Autism in Adulthood, 2*(1), 34–41. https://doi.org/10.1089/aut.2019.0059

The Autistic Advocate (2025, 2 May) Online Autism Training https://theautisticadvocate.com/onlinelearning/.

autisticvillage (2021a, June 17). Making sense of the senses – Part 2 – The secret agents of interoception and proprioception. *Autistic Village.* https://autistic-village.com/2021/06/17/making-sense-of-the-senses-part-2-the-secret-agents-of-interoception-and-proprioception/

autisticvillage (2021b, July 15). The other side of the mirror – Explaining autistic emotions. *Autistic Village.* https://autistic-village.com/2021/07/15/the-other-side-of-the-mirror-explaining-autistic-emotions/

Baldwin, S., Costley, D., & Warren, A. (2014). Employment activities and experiences of adults with high-functioning autism and Asperger's disorder. *Journal of Autism and Developmental Disorders, 44*(10), 2440–2449. https://doi.org/10.1007/s10803-014-2112-z

Barnbaum, D. R. (2008). *The Ethics of Autism: Among Them, But Not of Them.* Indiana University Press.

Baron-Cohen, S. (1997). *Mindblindness: An Essay on Autism and Theory of Mind* [First MIT Press paperback edition]. MIT Press.

Baron-Cohen, S. (2002). The extreme male brain theory of autism. *Trends in Cognitive Sciences, 6*(6), 248–254. https://doi.org/10.1016/S1364-6613(02)01904-6

Baron-Cohen, S. (2012). *Zero Degrees of Empathy: A New Theory of Human Cruelty and Kindness.* Penguin Books.

Baron-Cohen, S., & Wheelwright, S. (2004). The Empathy Quotient: An investigation of adults with Asperger syndrome or high functioning autism, and normal sex differences. *Journal of Autism and Developmental Disorders, 34*(2), 163–175. https://doi.org/10.1023/B:JADD.0000022607.19833.00

Baron-Cohen, S., Wheelwright, S., Robinson, J., & Woodbury-Smith, M. (2005). The Adult Asperger Assessment (AAA): A diagnostic method. *Journal of Autism and Developmental Disorders, 35*(6), 807–819. https://doi.org/10.1007/s10803-005-0026-5

Beardon, L. (2018, July 17). Luke Beardon: Profile. *Perspectives on Autism.* https://blogs.shu.ac.uk/autism/?doing_wp_cron=1619099974.3495130538940429687500

Beardon, L. (2021). *Autism in Adults.* Sheldon Press.

Beardon, L., & Chown, N. (2014). Identification of adults on the autism spectrum: A suggested pathway and good practice principles. *Good Autism Practice (GAP), 15*(1), 34–46.

Benevides, T. W., & Cassidy, S. A. (2020). Measuring what matters in autism research and practice. *Autism in Adulthood, 2*(1), 1–3. https://doi.org/10.1089/aut.2020.29009.twb

Bertilsdotter Rosqvist, H., Botha, M., Hens, K., O'Donoghue, S., Pearson, A., & Stenning, A. (2022). Cutting our own keys: New possibilities of neurodivergent storying in research. *Autism, 27*(5), 1235–1244. https://doi.org/10.1177/13623613221132107

Bird, G., & Cook, R. (2013). Mixed emotions: The contribution of alexithymia to the emotional symptoms of autism. *Translational Psychiatry, 3*(7), Article 7. https://doi.org/10.1038/tp.2013.61

Botha, M. (2021). Academic, activist, or advocate? Angry, entangled, and emerging: A critical reflection on autism knowledge production. *Frontiers in Psychology, 12.* https://www.frontiersin.org/articles/10.3389/fpsyg.2021.727542

Botha, M., & Cage, E. (2022). "Autism research is in crisis": A mixed method study of researcher's constructions of autistic people and autism research. *Frontiers in Psychology, 13.* https://www.frontiersin.org/articles/10.3389/fpsyg.2022.1050897

Botha, M., Dibb, B., & Frost, D. M. (2022). 'Autism is me': An investigation of how autistic individuals make sense of autism and stigma. *Disability & Society, 37*(3), 427–453. https://doi.org/10.1080/09687599.2020.1822782

Bottema-Beutel, K., Kapp, S. K., Lester, J. N., Sasson, N. J., & Hand, B. N. (2021). Avoiding ableist language: Suggestions for autism researchers. *Autism in Adulthood, 3*(1), 18–29. https://doi.org/10.1089/aut.2020.0014

Cage, E., Di Monaco, J., & Newell, V. (2018). Experiences of autism acceptance and mental health in autistic adults. *Journal of Autism and Developmental Disorders, 48*(2), 473–484. https://doi.org/10.1007/s10803-017-3342-7

Cassidy, S. A., Gould, K., Townsend, E., Pelton, M., Robertson, A. E., & Rodgers, J. (2020). Is camouflaging autistic traits associated with suicidal thoughts and behaviours? Expanding the interpersonal psychological theory of suicide in an undergraduate student sample. *Journal of Autism and Developmental Disorders, 50*(10), 3638–3648. https://doi.org/10.1007/s10803-019-04323-3

Chapman, R. (2019). Autism as a form of life: Wittgenstein and the psychological coherence of autism. *Metaphilosophy, 50*(4), 421–440. https://doi.org/10.1111/meta.12366

Chown, N., Robinson, J., Beardon, L., Downing, J., Hughes, L., Leatherland, J., Fox, K., Hickman, L., & MacGregor, D. (2017). Improving research about us, with us: A draft framework for inclusive autism research. *Disability & Society, 32*(5), 720–734. https://doi.org/10.1080/09687599.2017.1320273

Cohen-Rottenberg, R. (2013, January 11). A critique of the Empathy Quotient (EQ) test: Conclusion. *Autism and Empathy.* https://autismandempathyblog.wordpress.com/a-critique-of-the-empathy-quotient-eq-test-conclusion/

Cook, B., & Purkis, Y. (2022). *The Autism and Neurodiversity Self-Advocacy Handbook: Developing the Skills to Determine Your Own Future.* Jessica Kingsley Publishers.

Cooper, K., Smith, L. G. E., & Russell, A. (2017). Social identity, self-esteem, and mental health in autism. *European Journal of Social Psychology, 47*(7), 844–854. https://doi.org/10.1002/ejsp.2297

Craft, S. (2022). Samantha Craft's Autistic Traits Checklist. *My Spectrum Suite.* https://the-art-of-autism.com/females-and-aspergers-a-checklist/

Crompton, C. J., Hallett, S., McAuliffe, C., Stanfield, A. C., & Fletcher-Watson, S. (2022). "A group of fellow travellers who understand": Interviews with autistic people about post-diagnostic peer support in adulthood. *Frontiers in Psychology, 13.* https://www.frontiersin.org/articles/10.3389/fpsyg.2022.831628

Crompton, C. J., Ropar, D., Evans-Williams, C. V., Flynn, E. G., & Fletcher-Watson, S. (2020). Autistic peer-to-peer information transfer is highly effective. Autism, 24(7), 1704–1712. https://doi.org/10.1177/1362361320919286

Edey, R., Cook, J., Brewer, R., Johnson, M. E., Bird, G., & Press, C. (2016). Interaction takes two: Typical adults exhibit mind-blindness towards those with autism spectrum disorder. *Journal of Abnormal Psychology, 125*(7), 879–885. https://psycnet.apa.org/record/2016-41993-001?doi = 1

Fletcher-Watson, S., Adams, J., Brook, K., Charman, T., Crane, L., Cusack, J., Leekam, S., Milton, D., Parr, J. R., & Pellicano, E. (2019). Making the future together: Shaping autism research through meaningful participation. *Autism, 23*(4), 943–953. https://doi.org/10.1177/1362361318786721

Fletcher-Watson, S., & Bird, G. (2020). Autism and empathy: What are the real links? *Autism, 24*(1), 3–6. https://doi.org/10.1177/1362361319883506

Fletcher-Watson, S., McConnell, F., Manola, E., & McConachie, H. (2014). Interventions based on the Theory of Mind cognitive model for autism spectrum disorder (ASD). *Cochrane Database of Systematic Reviews*, 3. https://doi.org/10.1002/14651858.CD008785.pub2

Frith, U., & Happé, F. (1999). Theory of mind and self-consciousness: What is it like to be autistic? *Mind & Language, 14*(1), 82–89. https://doi.org/10.1111/1468-0017.00100

Fulton, R., Reardon, E., Richardson, K., & Jones, R. (2020). *Sensory Trauma: Autism, Sensory Difference and the Daily Experience of Fear.* Autism Wellbeing Press.

Gates, G. S. (2019). *Trauma, Stigma and Autism: Developing Resilience and Loosening the Grip of Shame.* Jessica Kingsley Publishers.

Gates, G. (2022, September 23). Autism and Stigma. https://autism-explained.teachable.com/p/online-summit-free

Gernsbacher, M. A. (2007). On not being human. *APS Observer, 20*(2), 5–32.

Gernsbacher, M. A., Stevenson, J. L., & Dern, S. (2017). Specificity, contexts, and reference groups matter when assessing autistic traits. *PLOS One, 12*(2), e0171931. https://doi.org/10.1371/journal.pone.0171931

Gernsbacher, M. A., & Yergeau, M. (2019). Empirical failures of the claim that autistic people lack a theory of mind. *Archives of Scientific Psychology, 7*(1), 102. https://doi.org/10.1037/arc0000067

Gould, J., & Ashton-Smith, J. (2011). Missed diagnosis or misdiagnosis? Girls and women on the autism spectrum. *Good Autism Practice (GAP), 12*(1), 34–41.

Harrison, J. L., Brownlow, C. L., Ireland, M. J., & Piovesana, A. M. (2022). Empathy measurement in autistic and nonautistic adults: A COSMIN systematic literature review. *Assessment, 29*(2), 332–350. https://doi.org/10.1177/1073191120964564

Hirvikoski, T., Mittendorfer-Rutz, E., Boman, M., Larsson, H., Lichtenstein, P., & Bölte, S. (2016). Premature mortality in autism spectrum disorder. *The British Journal of Psychiatry, 208*(3), 232–238. https://doi.org/10.1192/bjp.bp.114.160192

Holt, A., Bounekhla, K., Welch, C., & Polatajko, H. (2022). "Unheard minds, again and again": Autistic insider perspectives and theory of mind. *Disability and Rehabilitation, 44*(20), 5887–5897. https://doi.org/10.1080/09638288.2021.1949052

Hutten, M. (n.d.). Recovery from emotional deprivation for neurotypical partners in neurodiverse relationships. *Cassandra Syndrome Recovery.* https://www.cassandrasyndromerecovery.com/2021/08/recovery-from-emotional-deprivation-for.html

Kapp, S. K., Steward, R., Crane, L., Elliott, D., Elphick, C., Pellicano, E., & Russell, G. (2019). 'People should be allowed to do what they like': Autistic adults' views and experiences of stimming. *Autism, 23*(7), 1782–1792. https://doi.org/10.1177/1362361319829628

Kinnaird, E., Stewart, C., & Tchanturia, K. (2019). Investigating alexithymia in autism: A systematic review and meta-analysis. *European Psychiatry, 55,* 80–89. https://doi.org/10.1016/j.eurpsy.2018.09.004

Kirby, A. V., Bakian, A. V., Zhang, Y., Bilder, D. A., Keeshin, B. R., & Coon, H. (2019). A 20-year study of suicide death in a statewide autism population. *Autism Research, 12*(4), 658–666. https://doi.org/10.1002/aur.2076

Kupferstein, H. (2018). Evidence of increased PTSD symptoms in autistics exposed to applied behavior analysis. *Advances in Autism, 4*(1), 19–29. https://doi.org/10.1108/AIA-08-2017-0016

Mallett, R., & Runswick-Cole, K. (2012). Commodifying autism: The cultural contexts of 'disability' in the academy. In D. Goodley, B. Hughes, & L. Davis (Eds.), *Disability and Social Theory: New Developments and Directions* (pp. 33–51). Palgrave Macmillan.

McDonagh, P. (2013). Autism in an age of empathy. In J. Davidson, & M. Orsini (Eds.), *Worlds of Autism: Across the Spectrum of Neurological Difference* (pp. 31–51). University of Minnesota Press.

McMahon, T. (2021, April 23). Logically illogical: An interview with Ros Blackburn with special guest Sigourney Weaver. *Uniquely Human: The Podcast.* https://uniquelyhuman.com/2021/04/23/logically-illogical-an-interview-with-ros-blackburn-with-special-guest-sigourney-weaver/

Michael, C. (2021). Is being othered a co-occurring condition of autism? *Autism in Adulthood, 3*(2), 118–119. https://doi.org/10.1089/aut.2021.0019

Milton, D. (2012). On the ontological status of autism: The 'double empathy problem'. *Disability & Society, 27*(6), 883–887. https://doi.org/10.1080/09687599.2012.710008

Milton, D. E. (2014). Autistic expertise: A critical reflection on the production of knowledge in autism studies. *Autism, 18*(7), 794–802. https://doi.org/10.1177/1362361314525281

Milton, D., & Bracher, M. (2013). Autistics speak but are they heard? *Medical Sociology Online, 7*(2), Article 2.

Milton, D., Mills, R., & Pellicano, E. (2014). Ethics and autism: Where is the autistic voice? Commentary on Post et al. *Journal of Autism and Developmental Disorders, 44*(10), 2650–2651. https://doi.org/10.1007/s10803-012-1739-x

Murray, D., Lesser, M., & Lawson, W. (2005). Attention, monotropism and the diagnostic criteria for autism. *Autism, 9*(2), 139–156. https://doi.org/10.1177/1362361305051398

Murray, F. (2018a, November 30). Me and Monotropism: A unified theory of autism. *BPS.* https://www.bps.org.uk/volume-32/august-2019/me-and-monotropism-unified-theory-autism

Murray, F. (2018b, December20). Theories and practice in autism. *Medium.* https://oolong.medium.com/theories-and-practice-in-autism-5a168dd4fafc

National Institute for Health and Care Excellence (NICE) (2012). *Autism Spectrum Disorder in Adults: Diagnosis and Management* [Clinical guideline CG142]. NICE. https://www.nice.org.uk/guidance/cg142

Offord, J. (2021, May 1). The Double Empathy Problem [podcast]. *Different Minds.* https://anchor.fm/differentminds/episodes/The-Double-Empathy-problem-e101guu

Pearson, A., & Rose, K. (2021). A conceptual analysis of autistic masking: Understanding the narrative of stigma and the illusion of choice. *Autism in Adulthood, 3*(1). https://doi.org/10.1089/aut.2020.0043

Pearson, A., & Rose, K. (2023). *Autistic Masking: Understanding Identity Management and the Role of Stigma.* Pavilion Publishing.

Ratto, A. B., Bascom, J., daVanport, S., Strang, J. F., Anthony, L. G., Verbalis, A., Pugliese, C., Nadwodny, N., Brown, L. X. Z., Cruz, M., Hector, B. L., Kapp, S. K., Giwa Onaiwu, M., Raymaker, D. M., Robison, J. E., Stewart, C., Stone, R., Whetsell, E., Pelphrey, K., & Kenworthy, L. (2022). Centering the inner experience of autism: Development of the self-assessment of autistic traits. *Autism in Adulthood, 5*(1). https://doi.org/10.1089/aut.2021.0099

Raymaker, D. M., Teo, A. R., Steckler, N. A., Lentz, B., Scharer, M., Delos Santos, A., Kapp, S. K., Hunter, M., Joyce, A., & Nicolaidis, C. (2020). "Having all of your internal resources exhausted beyond measure and being left with no clean-up crew": Defining autistic burnout. *Autism in Adulthood, 2*(2), 132–143. https://doi.org/10.1089/aut.2019.0079

Reardon, E., & Fulton, R. (2022, September 23). Sensory Trauma. https://autism-explained.teachable.com/p/online-summit-free

Rifai, O. M., Fletcher-Watson, S., Jiménez-Sánchez, L., & Crompton, C. J. (2022). Investigating markers of rapport in autistic and nonautistic interactions. *Autism in Adulthood, 4*(1), 3–11. https://doi.org/10.1089/aut.2021.0017

Roche, L., Adams, D., & Clark, M. (2021). Research priorities of the autism community: A systematic review of key stakeholder perspectives. *Autism, 25*(2), 336–348. https://doi.org/10.1177/1362361320967790

Shalev, I., Warrier, V., Greenberg, D. M., Smith, P., Allison, C., Baron-Cohen, S., Eran, A., & Uzefovsky, F. (2022). Reexamining empathy in autism: Empathic disequilibrium as a novel predictor of autism diagnosis and autistic traits. *Autism Research, 15*(10), 1917–1928. https://doi.org/10.1002/aur.2794

Sheppard, E., Pillai, D., Wong, G. T.-L., Ropar, D., & Mitchell, P. (2016). How easy is it to read the minds of people with autism spectrum disorder? *Journal of Autism and Developmental Disorders, 46*(4), 1247–1254. https://doi.org/10.1007/s10803-015-2662-8

Stenning, A. (2020). Understanding empathy through a study of autistic life writing. In H. Bertilsdotter Rosqvist & N. Chown (Eds.), *Neurodiversity Studies: A New Critical Paradigm* (pp. 108–124). Routledge, Taylor & Francis Group.

The Autistic Advocate (2018, August 10). We are not OK. *The Autistic Advocate.* https://theautisticadvocate.com/2018/08/we-are-not-ok/

Treweek, C., Wood, C., Martin, J., & Freeth, M. (2019). Autistic people's perspectives on stereotypes: An interpretative phenomenological analysis. *Autism, 23*(3), 759–769. https://doi.org/10.1177/1362361318778286

Woods, R., & Waltz, D. M. (2019). The strength of autistic expertise and its implications for autism knowledge production: A response to Damian Milton. *Autonomy, 1*, 6.

Yang, H.-X., Hu, H.-X., Zhang, Y.-J., Wang, Y., Lui, S. S. Y., & Chan, R. C. K. (2022). A network analysis of interoception, self-awareness, empathy, alexithymia, and autistic traits. *European Archives of Psychiatry and Clinical Neuroscience, 272*(2), 199–209. https://doi.org/10.1007/s00406-021-01274-8

Yergeau, M. (2013). Clinically significant disturbance: On theorists who theorize theory of mind. *Disability Studies Quarterly, 33*(4), Article 4. https://doi.org/10.18061/dsq.v33i4.3876

Chapter 25:

1:1 Collaborative Character and Narrative Drawing as a Way for Autistic Children and Young People to Communicate Visually and Construct Their Own Experiences

Caehryn Tinker

Introduction

Visual creative methods, for example, art or photography, create ways for autistic children and young people to express their thoughts and feelings without the need to use language (Ellis, 2016). They have the potential to overcome some of the challenges that result from communication differences between autistic and non-autistic people, as identified in Damian Milton's Double Empathy Problem (Milton, 2012). In addition, visual creative methods can support autistic individuals to understand their experiences and construct new ways of being that do not conform to neurotypical expectations (Milton, 2014). These autistic ways of being challenge the power imbalances highlighted in the Double Empathy Problem (Milton, 2017).

This chapter will discuss 1:1 collaborative character and narrative drawing as a visual creative method that I am developing as part of my ongoing PhD study at the University of

Brighton, UK. The research aims to understand the ways that autistic children and young people who experience demand avoidance participate in the collaborative drawing method. Demand avoidance is understood in the research as being the action of finding requests difficult. There may be just one or many areas of a child or young person's life where pressures and expectations feel difficult, for example, the demand of verbal interaction, resulting in situational mutism.

Research drawing sessions take place in school, where the researcher (myself) draws with each child or young person individually, creating characters and narratives together. An issue is then introduced into the narrative for the drawn characters to respond to. The drawing method aims to be a way to encourage expression of thoughts and feelings, and construct ideas about how the characters deal with situations within the drawn narrative.

By asking how the characters might respond to the issue in the narrative, the drawing method aims to reduce the demand of asking the child or young person direct verbal questions about their personal experiences and the challenge of finding a response. It is hoped that this type of drawing, as a visual way to communicate between autistic children and young people and non-autistic practitioners working with them, could be a way to reduce some of the communication and interaction challenges identified in the Double Empathy Problem (Milton, 2012).

By developing ideas about how the characters might respond to issues in the drawing, the drawing method could be a way for practitioners to support children and young people to construct their own values and ideas about what would be helpful in their lives, instead of conforming to neurotypical expectations. In this way, the drawing method also incorporates the premise of the Double Empathy Problem, that autistic ways of being are different and not lesser than those of non-autistic people (Milton, 2012).

Background and context

As a neurodivergent person and artist, drawing is a particular interest that I can become absorbed in and achieve a sense of inner balance. McDonnell and Milton (2014) refer to this focus as 'flow state'. Drawing is also something I have control over, that is mine. When things don't work out in the world, I can rely on creating drawing to feel good about myself again. Drawing is a kind of safe space, a retreat from the outside world, where I create my own world within the boundaries of the paper. I like the immediacy of drawing and the connection between body, mind, through to hand, pencil and paper. I also enjoy the familiar sameness of using pencil (8B to be precise!) and paper, as well as the routine of expressing my feelings through drawing at the end of the day. Drawing feels a comfortable way to communicate, where experiences and emotions become embodied in the marks made. It is a relief from the misunderstandings that often occur in verbal and written communication. All of this helps maintain my well-being.

Over many years supporting autistic children and young people in various job roles, drawing together has been a successful and enjoyable way to interact and connect. By following the child's motivations while drawing, power imbalances were reduced, and trust and rapport created. With autistic children with learning disabilities, who did not use language to communicate, intensive interaction methods (Intensive Interaction Institute, 2023) could be extended into drawing. Toy trucks were pushed through paint and driven across large sheets of paper on the classroom floor to create large drawings. With another child, I drew similar images to their drawings on my own sheet of paper, which led to creating drawings together on shared paper.

In more recent years, when supporting verbal autistic children and young people with their well-being, I noticed that asking questions about their experiences and emotions often felt uncomfortable for them and were often avoided. With some children, I found that it was possible to create a rapport again through drawing. I created a method where we each drew a character on separate paper, then drew an environment where the characters could meet on shared paper. It was then possible to introduce issues into the shared drawing for the characters to deal with. This sometimes led to children discussing their own experiences without being asked. The drawing method developed into the 1:1 collaborative character and narrative drawing method I am now developing in my PhD research.

The 1:1 collaborative character and narrative drawing method

A small selection of mark makers and colours (pencils, felt-tip pens, biros, pastels or graphite blocks), and paper to draw on, is provided. The practitioner and the child or young person each create a character on their own sheet of paper. Prompt questions can be offered if needed – is the character human, animal or imaginary? Other characteristics can also be suggested, for example, hair colour, a tail, particular clothes. Background information could also be added, for example, the character's name, age, where they live, interests, dislikes, superpowers.

When the characters have been created, and if the child or young person is happy to move on to a shared drawing, choices can be offered about the type of environment the characters could meet in. Is the place real or imaginary? City or countryside? Further choices within the drawing could be, forest or mountains. If it is hard to make choices, options can be written on paper, turned over and randomly chosen. Alternatively, the child or young person may have their own ideas and not need any options offered for the character or the environment.

Next discuss who will draw the environment or whether this will be done jointly. The characters can then be drawn into the environment. It may be helpful to suggest drawing the characters in a simplified way in the shared drawing. Issues or challenges for the characters can then be introduced, for example, there is a loud noise, or someone new arrives in the drawing. The child or young person can choose an issue or create their own. Further drawings illustrate what the characters might think and feel about the issue and what they might do about it. The narrative can then be continued or concluded.

Important points

Reassure the child or young person about any pressures or insecurities they may feel about drawing (Lyon, 2020). Emphasize that there is no right or wrong way to draw, it's just about having fun. It can be useful to demonstrate how simple the drawings can be by drawing a stick person or just a simple pair of eyes.

The practitioner should always be flexible to adapt and follow the child or young person's motivations, so they feel in control and want to stay engaged in drawing. The practitioner should be vigilant to observe the child's direction while drawing and offer choices. Do they have their own ideas or would prompts to create drawings be useful? Do they want to do most of the drawing or prefer the practitioner to draw their ideas?

The drawing method should be seen as a very flexible framework, rather than a fixed set of rules. It is a starting point that the child and young person can adapt or completely dismiss if they prefer to draw another way. They may also just want to participate in the first part of the method where characters are created on individual paper, rather than a shared drawing or introducing an issue. It's about following their lead.

Collaborative drawing as a way to express and understand thoughts and emotions

The 1:1 collaborative character and narrative drawing method builds on other collaborative drawing methods that have been used as visual approaches to supporting autistic children and young people to understand their experiences and express thoughts and feelings. Carol Gray (Gray, 1994) is well known for developing comic strip conversations, where the practitioner draws simple cartoons with the child or young person as a visual way of retelling and understanding their social experiences, then constructing new ways forward. Gray's method is a very structured way of drawing, for example, specific colours, style and symbols are used (Gray, 1994), instead of supporting the child or young person to develop their own ways of expressing thoughts and feelings. This type of direction could be felt by some autistic children as constraining their creativity and expression, as well as being a demand.

A few practitioners in the field of art therapy have developed collaborative drawing methods that follow the autistic child's own way of expressing their thoughts and feelings (Bragge & Fenner, 2009; Evans & Dubowski, 2001). Some art therapists have also introduced ideas or issues relevant to the child's personal experience into the shared drawing for them to consider (Epp, 2008; Round et al., 2017). The pressure to reflect directly on personal experience, however, may feel uncomfortable and difficult for some autistic children and young people, particularly if they struggle to identify their emotions.

Antoniou and Charalambous-Darden (2022) have also developed a collaborative drawing method as a way of communicating and interacting with autistic children in educational settings. Like the examples above, the practitioner follows the child's lead, then introduces ideas relevant to them. Some illustrations have also included imaginary social situations instead of the child's direct personal experiences (Antoniou et al., 2019).

Introducing issues indirectly through the characters and narratives as a way to construct new ways of being

To reduce the pressure of referring directly to personal experience, the 1:1 collaborative character and narrative drawing method emphasizes creating other characters. The option of spending time creating and developing the characters and the place they meet in depth is encouraged. The drawing method aims to be an enjoyable art activity, where the focus is not solely on the issue introduced into the drawing.

As the narrative is developed, thoughts and feelings can be expressed through the characters. An issue introduced for the characters to consider could be the main focus of the narrative or a small part of a bigger narrative. It is an indirect way for the child or young person to express their own ideas and construct new thought patterns. Responses to the issue in the narrative may be in thought, discussion, writing or drawing. They could include thinking of practical solutions to the issue or the characters might become more confident by overcoming a challenge. Responses could either be within the narrative as an initial way of developing thinking, or the child or young person may choose to reflect more personally on their own thoughts or experiences.

If the practitioner suggests an issue, it is important to consider how generalized or close to the child or young person's experience it is. Despite being introduced into a fictitious narrative, an issue that is closer to lived experience may feel too difficult for some children or young people to consider. The aim of creating characters and a narrative is for the drawing to be a safe space. It is also a playful space where ideas are considered without the pressure of referring to personal experiences or real-life consequences (Greenstein, 2013).

Being asked to refer to direct experiences could feel uncomfortable or possibly create a sense of feeling exposed. Autistic writer Donna Williams discussed finding it helpful to talk through objects as a way to reduce the sense of exposure she felt when referring directly to personal experiences (Williams, 2003). By not being asked direct personal questions in the drawing method, children and young people are not asked to take off a mask which they may have developed to feel socially accepted (Pearson & Rose, 2023). Personal questions could feel like a pressure if they don't feel safe to be their authentic selves. The drawn characters offer an alternative type of protection and way to express thoughts and feelings, as well as develop new ideas more comfortably. With the pressure of personal questions reduced, it may feel possible to refer to personal experiences. In creative methods, children are empowered by being in control of how much they choose to disclose about themselves, if at all (Pimlott-Wilson, 2012).

Creative methods like drawing can also be empowering for children and young people as a safe space to consider ideas and make choices, because there is no judgement about what is right or wrong. It is therefore a way to reduce conformity and power imbalances, especially in schools (Greenstein, 2013). Karan Barad's theory of agential realism describes power as creating force and pressure on the body (Barad, 1998). These pressures can be felt particularly strongly by autistic people trying to exist within the confines neuronormative physical spaces and social interactions (Yergeau, 2018).

It is particularly important that autistic children and young people feeling empowered to construct their own ideas about their lives and social values as a way to challenge the power imbalances experienced by autistic people (highlighted in the Double Empathy Problem [Milton, 2012]). Autistic people are often viewed by non-autistic people as just being a collection of external observable traits without the ability or agency to create meaningful decisions about their lives (Yergeau, 2018). In a paper 'Autistic development, trauma and personhood: Beyond the frame of the neoliberal individual' (Milton, 2017), Damian Milton discussed creative methods as a way to challenge these imbalances and construct new ways of being. In a personal project, old family photographs were used to reflect on past events and create new understanding. Milton linked this approach to personal construct theory (PCT) (Kelly, 1955/1991), where individuals have agency to enact change by re-evaluating themselves or events and develop new ways of being. He also referenced drawing projects where autistic children were supported to reflect on current experiences, then create ideal visions of their future: Moran (2006), creating the 'ideal self', and Williams and Hanke (2007), 'imagining the ideal school'.

Autistic children and young people participating in the 1:1 collaborative character and narrative drawing method are also supported to construct their own ideas and values. This practical process of constructing new realities through the action of doing, relates to the theoretical framework of phenomenology. In collaborative drawing, new ideas are created through the process and flow of interactions between the child or young person and the practitioner during drawing exchanges. Thought is also developed through the physical and visual exchanges between mind, body, pencil and paper during the drawing process (Cain, 2010; McGuirk, 2010).

1:1 collaborative character and narrative drawing method as a visual way to interact and communicate

The 1:1 collaborative character and narrative drawing method, as a visual way of interacting could reduce the demands of verbal communication, as well as the challenges and misunderstandings (identified in the Double Empathy Problem [Milton, 2012]) between autistic children and young people, and non-autistic practitioners. Instructions in the drawing method are practical and straightforward. They can be spoken or written during drawing sessions. Structured choices for creating drawings can be useful as a prompt for some children and young people, as well as reducing the anxiety of being asked open questions (Ellis, 2016). Offering written or pictorial choices can also be useful for children and young people who do not communicate with spoken words.

Visual approaches may also suit many autistic children and young people who are visual thinkers or find that visual information provides a sense of clarity (Ellis, 2016; Grandin, 2009; Round, et al., 2017). It may be preferable to express thoughts and emotions visually instead of using words (Spyrou, 2011). In addition, it can be difficult to respond to questions about emotions if a child or young person has challenges with interoception (reflecting on the self) or alexithymia (recognizing and describing emotions).

Drawing together as a shared activity provides a joint focus between the practitioner and child or young person, which could reduce some of the social pressures and anxiety of interacting (Evans, 1998; Ellis, 2016). They can sit next to each other while drawing, which may feel more relaxing than sitting opposite during a conversation (Scott Barrett et al., 2019). This also reduces pressure to understand and respond with facial expressions (Scott Barrett et al., 2019) and eye contact, which can feel uncomfortable and distracting for many autistic people (Madipakkam et al., 2017). While drawing together, the focus is away from the child or young person, which can make it easier for them to express feelings in words or through drawing (Fidler & Christie, 2019). If they choose to discuss something personal, the child or young person can return back to the safety of drawing the characters and narrative at any time (Bragge & Fenner, 2009). In addition, embodying experiences into drawings creates something external, which is visual and concrete, and can be a useful reference point for further thought, drawing or discussion in more depth (Winstone et al., 2014).

Collaborative drawing can be a way to develop trust and rapport with autistic children that is not reliant on verbal communication (Evans & Dubowski, 2001). It is important that trust and rapport are established before further aspects of drawing are introduced (Evans & Dubowski, 2001), for example, introducing an issue into the narrative for consideration (Antoniou & Charalambous-Darden, 2022). Building trust and rapport also reduces power imbalances between the child and young person, and the practitioner. It creates a sense of safety, enabling them to express thoughts and feelings. Power imbalances are reduced further by the practitioner being on the inside of the drawing process, with the child or young person, rather than observing and instructing on the outside while they are drawing (Bragge & Fenner, 2009). The flow of drawing and social interactions could also reduce the demand of introducing an issue into the drawing for consideration.

In the 1:1 collaborative character and narrative drawing method, the practitioner follows the child or young person's lead and motivations, which means that monotropic focused attention (Murray et al., 2005) can be accommodated. This allows the time and space needed to think about and express experiences, leading to constructing new ways of thinking and being, which may positively impact their well-being.

Benefits of 1:1 collaborative character and narrative drawing for autistic children and young people who experience demand avoidance and drawing safety

The emphasis in my ongoing PhD research is to create a method for practitioners to use with autistic children and young people who experience demand avoidance. Methods often used with autistic children can create pressure and barriers to participation for those that struggle with demands (O'Nions et al., 2019). Many aspects of the collaborative 1:1 character and narrative drawing method correspond with advice for working with autistic children and young people who have pathological demand avoidance (PDA). This includes having a collaborative approach, building trust and connection, and being flexible to adapt to the child or young person's interests, needs and motivations, as well as giving them choice and control within an activity (Fidler & Christie, 2019). Drawing can feel comfortable as a safe space where the child is in control, when discussion would have felt like too much pressure. In addition, drawing characters and narratives is helpful as an indirect way to express and reflect on emotions and personal experiences (Christie et al., 2012).

There is always the possibility that uncomfortable memories could occur while drawing. Christie et al. (2012) have discussed that if practitioners are not trained therapists, it may still be possible to draw with children who have PDA if you know them well and follow their pace and lead, as well as being sensitive to respond to their feelings and needs.

Conclusion

The 1:1 collaborative character and narrative drawing method could provide a safe space for autistic children and young people to express their thoughts and feelings, as well as construct new ideas. If they choose not to introduce an issue into the drawing, there may still be benefits from developing trust and rapport with a practitioner, as well as expressing thoughts and feelings through drawing. Despite being a flexible framework for children and young people to adapt however they choose, it may still feel too demanding for some, while others may simply not be interested in this type of drawing.

It has been discussed above that the drawing method may be a way to overcome some of the challenges identified in the Double Empathy Problem (Milton, 2012). Interacting visually could be a way to overcome some of the communication differences between autistic children and young people, and non-autistic practitioners. When trust and rapport have been developed with practitioners, children and young people can be supported to develop their own ideas about new ways of being through drawing. This could be empowering as a way to challenge the existing inequalities between autistic and non-autistic people (Milton, 2012).

References

Antoniou, P. & Charalambous-Darden, N. (2022). Collaborative drawing with children with autism spectrum disorder. In *Learning Through Art #3 International Pictures of Practice,* (pp. 379–383). The International Society for Education Through Art. https://www.insea.org/learning-through-art-3-international-pictures-of-practice/

Antoniou, P., Charalambous-Darden, N., & Kouvou, O. (2019, February). *Drawing with Children with Autism Spectrum Disorder* [Conference presentation abstract]. Creating Spaces: Inclusivity, Ethics and Participation in Art and Design Education. https://www.researchgate.net/publication/344306075_Drawing_with_children_with_Autism_Spectrum_Disorder

Barad, K. (1998). Getting real: Technoscientific practices and the materialization of reality. *Differences: A Journal of Feminist Cultural Studies, 10*(2), 87–128. https://doi.org/10.1215/10407391-10-2-87

Bragge, A. & Fenner, P. (2009). The emergence of the 'Interactive Square' as an approach to art therapy with children on the autistic spectrum. *International Journal of Art Therapy, 14*(1), 17–28. https://doi.org/10.1080/17454830903006323

Cain, P. (2010). *Evolution of the Practitioner.* Intellect.

Christie, P., Duncan, M., Fidler, R., & Healy, Z. (2012). *Understanding Pathological Demand Avoidance Syndrome in Children: A Guide for Parents, Teachers And other Professionals.* Jessica Kingsley Publishers.

Ellis, J. (2016). Researching the social worlds of autistic children: An exploration of how an understanding of autistic children's social worlds is best achieved. *Children & Society, 31*(1), 23–36. https://onlinelibrary.wiley.com/doi/abs/10.1111/chso.12160

Epp, K. (2008). Outcome-based evaluation of a social skills program using art therapy and group therapy for children on the autism spectrum. *Children & Schools, 30*(1), 27–36. https://doi.org/10.1093/cs/30.1.27

Evans, K. (1998). Shaping experience and sharing meaning art therapy for children with autism. *International Journal of Art Therapy: Inscape, 3*(1), 17–25. https://www.tandfonline.com/doi/abs/10.1080/17454839808413055

Evans, K., & Dubowski, J. (2001). *Art Therapy with Children on the Autistic Spectrum: Beyond Words*. Jessica Kingsley Publishers.

Fidler, R., & Christie, P. (2019) *Collaborative Approaches to Learning for Pupils With PDA: Strategies for Education Professionals*. Jessica Kingsley Publishers.

Grandin, T. (2009). How does visual thinking work in the mind of a person with autism? A personal account. *Philosophical Transactions Royal Society London Biological Science, 364*(1522), 1437–1442. https://www.ncbi.nlm.nih.gov/pmc/articles/PMC2677580/

Gray, C. (1994). *Comic Strip Conversations*. Jenison Public Schools.

Greenstein, A. (2013) Today's learning objective is to have a party: playing research with students in a secondary school special needs unit. *Journal of Research in Special Educational Need, 14*(2) 71–81. https://doi.org/10.1111/1471-3802.12009

Intensive Interaction Institute (2023). https://www.intensiveinteraction.org/

Kelly, G. (1955/1991). *The Psychology of Personal Constructs, volumes 1 and 2*. Routledge.

Lyon, P. (2020). Using drawing in visual research: Materializing the invisible. In L. Pauwels, & D. Mannay (Eds.), *The SAGE Handbook of Visual Research Methods* (2nd ed., pp. 297–308). SAGE.

Madipakkam, A. R., Rothkirch, M., Dziobek, I., & Sterzer, P. (2017). Unconscious avoidance of eye contact in autism spectrum disorder. *Scientific Reports, 7*(1) 13378. https://www.ncbi.nlm.nih.gov/pmc/articles/PMC5645367/

McDonnell, A., & Milton, D. (2014). Going with the flow: reconsidering 'repetitive behaviour' through the concept of 'flow states'. In G. Jones, & E. Hurley (Eds.), *Good Autism Practice: Autism, Happiness and Wellbeing* (pp. 38–47). BILD. https://kar.kent.ac.uk/id/eprint/62647

McGuirk, T. (2010). Heidegger's Rift: The epistemological significance of drawing. *Studies in Material Thinking, 4*. https://materialthinking.aut.ac.nz/sites/default/files/papers/TomMcGuirk.pdf

Milton, D. (2012). On the ontological status of autism: the 'double empathy problem'. *Disability & Society, 27*(6) 883–887. https://kar.kent.ac.uk/62639/1/Double%20empathy%20problem.pdf

Milton, D. (2014). Fragments: putting the self back into the picture. In G. Jones, & E. Hurley (Eds.), *Good Autism Practice: Autism, Happiness, and Wellbeing* (pp. 58–63). BILD. https://kar.kent.ac.uk/62648/

Milton, D. (2017). Autistic development, trauma and personhood: Beyond the frame of the neoliberal individual. In K. Runswick-Cole, T. Curran, & K. Liddiard (Eds.), *The Palgrave Handbook of Disabled Children's Childhood Studies* (pp. 461–476). Palgrave Macmillan.

Moran, H. (2006). A very personal assessment: Using personal construct psychology assessment technique (drawing the ideal self) with young people with ASD to explore the child's view of the self. *Good Autism Practice, 7*(2) 78–86.

Murray, D., Lesser, M., & Lawson, W. (2005) Attention, monotropism and the diagnostic criteria for autism. *Autism, 9*(2), 139–156.

https://journals.sagepub.com/doi/epdf/10.1177/1362361305051398

O'Nions, L., Happé, F., & Viding, E. (2019) Extreme/'pathological' demand avoidance. *British Psychological Society DECP Debate. 160*, 1–5.https://explore.bps.org.uk/content/bpsdeb/1/160/18

Pearson, A., & Rose, K. (2023). *Autistic Masking: Understanding Identity Management and the Role of Stigma*. Pavilion.

Pimlott-Wilson, H. (2012). Visualising children's participation in research: Lego, Duplo, rainbows and clouds and moodboards. *International Journal of Social Research Methodology, 15*(2), 135–148. https://doi.org/10.1080/13645579.2012.649410

Round, A., Baker, W., & Rayner, C. (2017). Using visual arts to encourage children with autism spectrum disorder to communicate their feelings and emotions. *Open Journal of Social Sciences, 5*(10) 90–108. https://www.researchgate.net/publication/320349771_Using_Visual_Arts_to_Encourage_Children_with_Autism_Spectrum_Disorder_to_Communicate_Their_Feelings_and_Emotions

Scott-Barrett, J., Cebula, K., & Florian, L. (2019). Listening to young people with autism: Learning from researcher experiences. *International Journal of Research & Method in Education, 42*(2) 163–184.https://www.tandfonline.com/doi/abs/10.1080/1743727X.2018.1462791

Spyrou, S. (2011). The limits of children's voices: From authenticity to critical, reflexive representation. *Childhood, 18*(2) 151–165. https://journals.sagepub.com/doi/10.1177/0907568210387834

Williams, D. (2003). *Exposure Anxiety: The Invisible Cage*. Jessica Kingsley Publishers.

Williams, J., & Hanke, D. (2007). Do you know what sort of school I want? Optimum features of school provision for pupils with autistic spectrum disorder. *Good Autism Practice, 8*(2) 51–61.

Winstone, N., Huntington, C., Goldsack, L., Kyrou, E., & Millward, L. (2014). Eliciting rich dialogue through the use of activity-oriented interviews: Exploring self-identity in autistic young people. *Childhood, 21*(2) 190–206. https://journals.sagepub.com/doi/abs/10.1177/0907568213491771

Yergeau. M. (2018). *Authoring Autism/on Rhetoric and Neurological Queerness.* Duke University Press.

Chapter 26:

Autistic, Hysteric: Inequity in Health Care for Autistic People Assigned Female at Birth in the United Kingdom

Gemma L. Williams, Rebecca Ellis, Harriet Axbey and Aimee Grant

Abstract

When the Double Empathy Problem affects communication with medical professionals, the consequences can be dire. This is evidenced by the significantly reduced life expectancy of Autistic people compared to our non-Autistic peers and the far poorer physical and mental health we experience on almost every metric. At the same time, people assigned female at birth (AFAB)[38] are known to experience a 'gender health gap' in modern medicine. We consider this to be at least in part due to centuries of medical misogyny, where much of what ailed women was attributed to 'hysteria' and their reproductive organs. These days, women in the UK have longer life expectancies than men but spend more of their life in poor health or chronic pain with conditions left undiagnosed for longer. This is particularly pronounced within the specialisms of gynaecological and reproductive care. For those

38 As a collective of authors, we have a transinclusive stance. This is reflected in our use of transinclusive terminology throughout this chapter. However, when referencing findings or facts we will use the language of original studies to ensure accuracy in our reporting.

from racialized and additionally minoritized groups, the health gap is even greater. In this chapter we – a collective of Autistic AFAB researchers[39] from the UK – explore how the Double Empathy Problem intersects with structural misogyny within health care, leading to dangerously inadequate services for Autistic AFAB people and an urgent need for more research.

Introduction

Communication differences have had a central role in descriptions of Autism since its earliest conceptions. Historically, Autistic people have been thought of as having inherent 'impairments' when it comes to social communication, in particular in terms of their ability to intuit or infer the mental states and emotions of others: known as having a 'theory of mind' (Chown, 2017). However, research now supports what Autistic advocates have been saying for some time: that the issue is better described as a communication incompatibility, or a 'Double Empathy Problem' (Milton, 2012; Milton et al., 2018). We now have extensive evidence, for example, that non-Autistic people experience difficulty in inferring the emotional and mental states of Autistic people (Brewer et al., 2016; Edey et al., 2016; Heasman & Gillespie, 2017; Hubbard et al., 2017; Sheppard et al., 2016). Conversely, Autistic people often experience high levels of mutual understanding and rapport when interacting with other Autistic individuals (Crompton et al., 2019a, 2019b, 2020; Heasman & Gillespie, 2019; Morrison et al., 2019; Williams et al., 2021). Likewise, it isn't true (as has been suggested by some Autism theorists) that all Autistic people struggle to empathize – in fact, many are hyperempathic (Kimber et al., 2023) – but more that divergent ways of experiencing and processing the world cause gaps in mutual understanding between neurotypes that take extra efforts to overcome (Williams, 2021).

The Double Empathy Problem can occur in all areas of life, but when it impacts communication between Autistic people and their medical care providers, the consequences can be dire (Doherty et al., 2022; Shaw et al., 2023; Williams et al., 2022). For example, life expectancy for Autistic people is significantly reduced, with Autistic individuals dying 16–30 years younger compared to their non-Autistic peers (Doherty et al., 2022; Hirvikoski et al, 2016). In addition, Autistic people's physical and mental health is far poorer, with Autistic people more likely to die from almost all medical conditions (Hirvikoski et al., 2016). Serious medical conditions, such as diabetes and hypertension, are far more prevalent among Autistic people (Doherty et al., 2022), as are mental health conditions such as depression (Buck et al., 2014) and anxiety (Uljarević et al., 2020), along with increased instances of both self-injurious behaviours (Hedley et al., 2018a) and suicidal ideation (Hedley et al., 2018b). In addition to systemic and social pressures, such as stigma and minority stress (Botha & Frost, 2018), affecting the well-being of Autistic

39 We are a mix of cisfemale and gender nonconforming AFAB individuals.

people, practical issues, such as unmet access requirements to primary care services, communication barriers between Autistic patients and clinicians, and symptoms not being believed or picked up soon enough – often on account of atypical ways of experiencing and expressing pain – contribute to poorer health care experiences and uptake (Doherty et al., 2022; Shaw et al., 2023; Williams et al., 2022). Difficulties in patient–doctor communication are long acknowledged. When combined with the challenges with mutual understanding that often trouble cross-neurotype communication (the Double Empathy Problem), it is plausible that the negative effects on health care experiences and outcomes will be magnified for Autistic health care users, a phenomenon referred to by Shaw et al. (2023) as the 'triple empathy problem'.

In the following few pages, we take a broader look at health care provision for women and people with wombs in the UK and explore how the Double Empathy Problem intersects with structural misogyny within health care. We draw on the history of women cast as 'hysterics' on account of their 'wandering wombs', and the pervasive emphasis on 'sanitation' and 'hygiene' in the patriarchal-capitalist approach to menstrual and vaginal care. We ask the question: how does the Double Empathy Problem intersect with a larger, systemic, cisheteronormative, misogynistic and racist ableism?

The gender health gap

All AFAB people – both neurodivergent and neurotypical – are known to experience a 'gender health gap' in modern, Western medicine (Department of Health and Social Care, 2022). Women in the UK have longer life expectancies than men but spend more of their life in poor health or chronic pain with conditions left undiagnosed for longer (Department of Health and Social Care, 2022). One study, for example, found that women have a striking 50% higher chance of receiving a wrong diagnosis following a heart attack than men (Wu et al., 2018). Another study highlights the markedly poorer care that women with dementia in UK receive compared to men with the same condition (Cooper et al., 2017). In one large-scale review of over 700 diseases from diabetes to cancer, women were found to be receiving diagnoses on average four years later than men (Westergaard et al., 2019).

Troublingly, but unsurprisingly, in a public survey called to inform the 2022 Women's Health Strategy for England Policy Paper (Department of Health and Social Care, 2022), 84% of over 100,000 women responding felt that their health concerns had not been listened to by health care professionals. Of these, many reported dismissive attitudes toward their reports of serious pain, particularly in relation to gynaecological pain. This fits into a wider picture of inequity toward gynaecological and reproductive health care in the UK. For example, endometriosis is a painful and debilitating disease affecting around 10% of people of reproductive age with wombs, yet the current wait time for an initial diagnosis is around 8 years (All-Party Parliamentary Group on Endometriosis, 2020). Alongside this, polycystic ovary syndrome (PCOS) impacts 5–10% of women of reproductive age, but the existing diagnostic criteria are not evidence-based, relying instead on the weaker evidence of clinician consensus, due to lack of research in this area (Rao & Bhide, 2020).

Autism and the gender health gap

For Autistic AFAB people, this gender gap in health care compounds with the Double Empathy Problem. Autistic people often have highly divergent sensory and bodily perceptual experiences, impacting both on how pain is and isn't perceived and on interoception – the internal sense responsible for registering internal bodily states such as hunger or temperature (Mason et al., 2019, Williams et al., 2022). This likely has a bearing on how Autistic people experience and report ill health and yet, thus far, very few research efforts have been dedicated to exploring this.

More recently, Talcer and colleagues (2023) have highlighted the additional sensory challenges that Autistic mothers often experience during the perinatal period that frequently go unsupported, impacting their mothering, social lives, work lives, mental health and energy levels. In a systematic review, led by one of our co-author group (Aimee Grant), of qualitative research into Autistic women's views and experiences of infant feeding, the researcher team found that only eight peer-reviewed papers had been published covering this topic (Grant et al., 2022). In another systematic review (by this present co-authoring team, led by Rebecca Ellis), looking at Autistic people with wombs' experiences of menstruation (Ellis et al., 2025), we found a similarly sparse number of sources (N = 12) on the topic. Very few of these featured the Autistic voice, centring parents' experiences instead. In terms of Autistic people's experiences of maternity care, this is still a new area being explored. Research so far has highlighted that Autistic birthing people feel that they were not listened to and were treated as a problem by staff (Grant et al., 2025). Autistic AFAB people report high levels of breastfeeding[40] motivation and satisfaction (Grant et al., 2023a) – despite significant feeding-related sensory issues (Grant et al., 2022) – but lower satisfaction with infant feeding support compared to non-Autistic AFAB people (Hampton et al., 2023).

Also important to note is that just as not all women have wombs, not all people who have wombs – and need gynaecological care – are women. Some increased correlation has been observed between being Autistic and being trans or non-binary (e.g., see George and Stokes, 2018) although, as Kourti (2021, p. 17) highlights, this relationship has been researched from a perspective that '*[has] been notably cisgender and neurotypical, starting with the assumption that being neurotypical and cisgender are, and should be, desirable states*'. Regardless, it probably is the case that there are a higher number of Autistic trans and non-binary people.

40 We use the term *breastfeeding* here, but we acknowledge and respect the fact that others may refer to this as *chestfeeding* or *bodyfeeding*.

Trans people in the general population not only already face substantial barriers in accessing gender-affirming treatment in the UK, but also encounter additional obstacles (including transphobic discrimination from staff) when seeking non-gender-related health care within the National Health Service (NHS) (London Assembly Health Committee, 2022). In a recent qualitative systematic review (Sbragia & Vottero, 2020) of the experiences of transgender men seeking gynaecological and reproductive health care, the authors found that trans men experience specific additional barriers in accessing health care, including a binary-gendered health care system that doesn't easily admit them. This issue was unfortunately exemplified in a recent article in a British newspaper (Chantler-Hicks, 2023) reporting on Conservative Party proposals *'aimed at restoring 'common sense' to the NHS'* by banning trans women from female hospital wards. For the many Autistic trans and non-binary people that exist we can only imagine these health care gaps will be wider. And while some others (e.g., Strauss et al., 2021) have also surmised that the systemic barriers that trans and Autistic individuals independently face in accessing health care might compound for those who are both trans *and* Autistic, investigation into this is, thus far, absent from the literature.

A brief history of medical misogyny

You see, he does not believe I am sick! And what can one do?

If a physician of high standing, and one's own husband, assures friends and relatives that there is really nothing the matter with one but temporary nervous depression – a slight hysterical tendency – what is one to do?

(Charlotte in Perkins Gilman, 1892/1995)

There is an undeniable thread of misogyny within modern medicine, that runs its roots through a history where women were cast as 'hysterics'[41] (Agarwal, 2022) on account of their 'wandering wombs' (Cleghorn, 2022). At the dawn of modern, Western medicine, the ancient Greeks imagined the womb (or, uterus) as a troublesome 'animal within an animal' that was able to move around the body at will, causing all kinds of ills which male medical authority was tasked with controlling:

Medical writers of ancient Greece and Rome held many different views on the wandering womb. But the uterus, as the dominant force behind so many illnesses, diseases, and

41 The root of the word *hysteric*, of course, being *hyster-*, deriving from ὑστέρᾱ, the ancient Greek word for (you guessed it!) *womb*.

symptoms of women, was woven into them all. Women were under the dominion of male authority, and medical discourse legitimized this by making women's bodies subordinate to the whims of the very organ that defined their social purpose. (Cleghorn, 2022, p. 15)

Treatment for the various pathologies attributed to migrating uteruses was – perhaps unsurprisingly – a strong prescription for early marriage, plentiful marital sex and lots of babies (Cleghorn, 2022).

During Medieval and Renaissance times in Europe (c. 1066–1603), the view persisted that women's 'emotional states and nervous disposition' (in turn emanating from the unruly uterus) were usually the sources of their physical ailments (Agarwal, 2022, p. 118). Again, remedies included recommendations of participation in orgies and sex with young men (Agarwal, 2022). Not only was there misinformation and obfuscation around women's bodies and gynaecological health, but also a fear of women possessing knowledge about how to support other women, demonstrated in the fifteenth-century witch-hunter's guidebook, *The Malleus Maleficarum*, which declared that '*[n]o one does more harm to the Catholic Church than midwives*' (Henricus Institoris & Jacobus Sprenger, 2006, p. 164). Indeed, in the seminal (*or: 'ovoid'?*) second-wave feminist radical pamphlet 'Witches, Midwives and Nurses', authors Ehrenreich and English (1974) map the origins of patriarchal dominance over modern health care and draw parallels with the persecution of (usually) women denounced as 'witches', highlighting how (male) physicians benefitted from the suppression of (female, lay) competitors.

In the introduction to a revised, second edition (Ehrenreich & English, 2010), they provide a reflective context for the original publication. At the time of writing (in the seventies), the authors describe a status quo whereby:

> *...as healthcare professionals, women were largely confined to subordinate roles as nurses and aides. As consumers of care, we found ourselves subject to both insensitive and hazardous treatment: unnecessary hysterectomies, over medicalised-childbirth, insufficiently tested contraceptives, involuntary sterilizations, and the almost universal condescension of male doctors.* (Ehrenreich & English, 2010, p. 8)

One further way in which women, as consumers of care, experienced dangerous treatments founded in misogynistic thinking was during the burgeoning contraceptive movement in the 1920s and 1930s. To advertise birth control products for private sale was illegal, but manufacturers of suppositories, foaming tablets, vaginal jellies and liquids, and antiseptic douches got around the issue by marketing them euphemistically as 'feminine hygiene' products (Tone, 2002). The antiseptic douche soared in popularity in the 1940s, no doubt influenced by large adverts in newspapers and magazines emphasizing how grateful a woman's husband will be that she was keeping herself 'fresh'. However:

> *[s]cores of douching preparations, though advertised as modern medical miracles, contained nothing more than water, cosmetic plant extracts, and table salt. On the other hand, many others, including the most popular brand, Lysol disinfectant, were soap solutions containing cresol (a constituent of crude carbolic acid, a distillate of coal and wood), which, when used in too high a concentration, caused severe inflammation, burning, and even death. The Lysol douche did not prevent pregnancy…*
> (Tone, 2002, p. 170)[42]

Thankfully, Lysol products are no longer for sale. However, present day menstrual products retain euphemistic names, such as 'sanitary towels' (which carry the tacit implication that menstruation is 'unsanitary'). There also remains a flourishing female sexual and reproductive wellness industry (valued globally at around US$4.5trillion in 2018: Patton et al., 2022) which promotes non-medical remedies to AFAB people. Without the benefit of regulation, products which cause definite harm to AFAB people's bodies continued to be marketed to them. One contemporary example might be the Goop 'jade vaginal egg', which is now advertised as harnessing '*the power of energy work, crystal healing, and a Kegel-like physical practice*' (Goop Wellness, 2023) for the benefit of vaginal health. Originally, however, it was advertised as a tool to '*balance hormones, regulate menstrual cycles, prevent uterine prolapse, and increase bladder control*' (Patton et al., 2022, p. 19) until Goop was fined by the California Food, Drug and Medical Device Task Force for false advertising and medical risk (Patton et al., 2022).

AFAB people of all backgrounds experience medical misogyny and barriers to healthy reproductive care. However, it is AFAB people with additional marginalizations that often experience even poorer care and harm by neglect of their needs. *Reproductive justice* is a rights-based, intersectional feminist activist movement and framework, founded in the 1990s by Black women in the US with the aim of redressing this imbalance and injustice (Onwuachi-Saunders et al., 2019). The reproductive justice movement continues to advocate for equitable access to reproductive and sexual health care for all AFAB people, but particularly so for Black AFAB people who still endure racialized oppression within the health care sector.

---

42 While it may not have had had success as a method of birth control, *Lysol* was an excellent cleaning solution for the garbage pail and toilet bowl.

Medical misogynoir and systemic racism in health care

Misogynoir is the term given to the particular blend of anti-Black racism and misogyny that is uniquely enacted against Black AFAB people, taking the form of '*stereotypes, violence [and] disregard for bodily integrity, and physical or emotional suffering*' (Edmonds et al., 2023, p. 16). In the UK, AFAB people who are Black face increased health disparities compared to white AFAB people. For example, in a recent review of maternal, newborn and infant clinical outcomes in the UK, Black women were, shockingly, found to be nearly four times more likely to die than white women (34 women per 100,000 giving birth [MBRRACE-UK, 2022]). While Black AFAB people are uniquely victimized by medical misogynoir, AFAB people who are Brown or from other minoritized ethnic backgrounds also contend with racism within the health care system that often intersects with medical misogyny. For example, in the same MBRRACE-UK (2022) study, Asian women were found to be nearly twice as likely to die than white women (16 women per 100,000 giving birth).

Systemic racism within gynaecological (and obstetric) care can be traced back to the discipline's origin story. Dr J. M. Sims, the 'father of gynaecology', developed his craft through regular experimentation on enslaved Black women: operating, for example, on one young woman called Anarcha – in a time before the use of anaesthesia was commonplace – 29 times before eventually resolving how to fix a vaginal fistula (Rol, 2018). In addition, as Roberts (2014, p. 6) reflects in the introduction to her book *Killing the Black Body*, '*regulating Black women's reproductive decisions has been a central aspect of racial oppression in America*'. On the one hand, Black women's reproduction and childbearing became '*central to the economic enterprise of chattel slavery*' (Edmonds et al., 2023, p. 16) following a law change in the 1600s ensuring that children born of enslaved Black women be born into slavery (no matter who the father was). The impact of Black enslaved women being required to 'wet nurse' white infants continues to impact on Black women's breastfeeding today (Freeman, 2017). On the other hand, up until as late as the 1970s in the US, Black, Hispanic and Indigenous women (along with, to a lesser extent, poor white women and women with so-called 'cognitive impairments') were routinely sterilized without consent:

> *They were told their tubes would be "tied," implying an easy untying, or they were not told at all that a hysterectomy or tubal ligation had been performed. The secret procedure was so common, it was euphemistically referred to as a "Mississippi appendectomy." Fannie Lou Hamer, a voters' rights and Civil Rights icon, fell victim herself to such a hysterectomy at the hands of a [w]hite physician in 1961.* (Rol, 2018, np)

In addition to the systemic barriers it creates, misogynoir shows up in health care contexts in many ways, including as judgemental stereotypes (e.g., that Black women are 'aggressive', 'stupid' or 'promiscuous' [Edmonds et al., 2023, p. 16]), and clinically dangerous false beliefs about biological differences, including that Black people experience less pain (Hoffman et al., 2016). For Black Autistic AFAB people who may already experience atypical sensory processing of their pain and internal states, there is an even greater risk of receiving inadequate or even harmful care. This is complicated further by the fact that Black and Brown people in the UK face significant biases within the Autism diagnostic system and remain under-included in Autism research (Begeer et al., 2009; Cascio et al., 2020). While a formal Autism diagnosis does not – in any way – guarantee accommodative health care (although, legally, it should according the UK's The Equality Act, 2010 and The Autism Act, 2009), the absence of one leaves even greater room for misinterpretations of seemingly atypical behaviour that, in the case of Black Autistic AFAB people, may be incorrectly interpreted as aggression (Williams et al., 2022).

The Double Empathy Problem for autistic people assigned female at birth seeking health care

Breakdowns in cross-neurotype understanding are borne out again and again in Autistic people's descriptions of their health care experiences. In one online survey of UK Autistic birthing parents' experiences of infant feeding (Grant et al., 2023a), 82 (of a total of 193; only three-quarters of whom had received support) participants reported negative interactions with at least one health professional, describing services as '*absent*', '*lacking*', '*poor*', '*rubbish*', '*outdated*' and '*terrible and unhelpful*', and – tellingly – staff as '*useless*' and '*judgemental and [...]unable to understand Autistic communication*' (Grant et al., 2023a, p. 11). In a further online survey of 200 Autistic adults, investigating their experiences of the treatment and support they received for mental health problems (Camm-Crosbie et al., 2019), 89 participants reported negative experiences. Many described the practitioners they had seen as having a '*very poor knowledge of autism*' and felt professionals needed to be '*better trained in autism*' to '*realise it may not always be possible to accurately read a person with autism*' (Camm-Crosbie et al., 2019, p. 1435). It is not, it should also be noted, just Autistic people themselves who have noticed these barriers to mutual understanding. In a recent systematic review of health care professionals' knowledge, self-efficacy and attitudes toward working with Autistic people (Corden et al., 2022), the researchers found that health care professionals themselves reported poor working knowledge of Autism and low confidence in working effectively with Autistic patients.

Despite governmental reviews and policy commitments (e.g., Department of Health and Social Care, 2019; Department of Health and Social Care and Department for Education,

2021; NHS England, 2019; The Health and Care Act, 2022) to address these service failures and communication breakdowns, little impact has been felt within day-to-day service provision. In England, a promising new Oliver McGowan Mandatory Training in learning disability and Autism was introduced in 2022 with the ambition to increase '*understanding of people's needs, resulting in better services and improved health and wellbeing*' (Health Education England, 2022, p. 1). While this has in some ways been a laudable effort, its impact on services is as yet unclear and it has met with some criticism relating to the quality of training packages and theoretical content (National Development Team for Inclusion, 2022). In 2022, a new National Autism Trainer Programme for health care and education professionals has also begun to roll out, which was co-produced by the Anna Freud centre and Autistic-led organization, AT Autism, and so far seems promising.

At a more grassroots level, some ground has been covered by various collectives of Autistic-activist scholars and medics (including *Autistic Doctors International*)[43] and some neurodiversity-affirming mixed neurotype groups in the creation of Autistic-led toolkits designed to support practitioners to provide higher-quality care for their Autistic patients. These include the AASPIRE Healthcare toolkit (Nicolaidis et al., 2016), More Than Words (Williams et al., 2022), It's Not Rocket Science (National Development Team for Inclusion, 2021) and most recently the SPACE Framework[44] (Doherty et al. 2023) which highlights the importance for practitioners to consider sensory needs, provide predictability and acceptance, adapt their communication and offer empathy. Ensuring these toolkits reach practitioners so as to be able to influence service provision, however, is not always easy. Finally, at present, there remains a dearth of research investigating the specific health experiences and health care needs of Autistic AFAB people. As such, in addition to the double empathy gap that Autistic individuals can experience with their health care providers, there is a larger, systemic empathy gap that shapes the kind of care that is (and more often, isn't) available. This should be addressed with urgency.

Absence of data

In order to understand problems, we need to be able to measure them. One significant issue when trying to determine the effect of the Double Empathy Problem on Autistic AFAB people's health care needs is the dearth of data currently available. In the influential MBRRACE-UK (2020) report, for example, which is an important indicator of misogynoir, no data relating to disability of any kind was included among the sociodemographic characteristics collected of women who died. As such, we cannot establish how many Autistic AFAB people may have died in childbirth in the UK. It is plausible, however, to assume this number may be not insignificant, following one Swedish cohort study which found that Autistic mothers were more likely to have preterm births and adverse pregnancy outcomes (Sundelin et al., 2018, p. 1816), and analysis of the SAIL databank identified

43 https://autisticdoctorsinternational.com/

44 SPACE = Sensory needs, Predictability, Acceptance, Communication and Empathy.

that 0.79% (approximately 1 in 125) births in Wales, UK in 2020 were to those who had a diagnosis of Autism listed on their health or education records (personal correspondence with Professor Sinead Brophy).

Aggravating the issue of lack of data are the poor rates of Autism diagnoses for AFAB people (Lockwood Estrin et al., 2021). Figures suggest that in some parts of the UK, around three-quarters of Autistic people are undiagnosed (Grant et al., 2023b) while many others sit on waiting lists for assessment that last years (Westminster Commission on Autism, 2021), obscuring them from view. There are also a number of Autistic people who refrain from disclosing their diagnosis to health care professionals due to fear of perceived stigma or worse treatment (Doherty et al., 2021).

Finally, research has found that even when Autistic individuals do have a recorded Autism diagnosis, doctors in both primary care and hospitals often underestimate the number of Autistic patients they have (Doherty et al., 2021; Zerbo et al, 2015). And, while Autism health passports (AHPs) were introduced in the UK, and recommended in National Institute for Health and Care Excellence (NICE) clinical guidance, with the aim of describing and thus improving health care accessibility needs, a recent review found that there was no evidence of any AHP introduced anywhere around the world fulfilling its aims (Ellis et al., 2023).

A material risk to Autistic people assigned female at birth

It is now understood that Autistic people face serious barriers to accessing adequate health care; one recent study found that of the 507 Autistic people asked, 80% reported challenges visiting a general practitioner (GP) in any circumstance and 56% described having difficulties communicating with their doctors (Doherty et al., 2022). Raymaker and colleagues (2017, p. 7) also found that '*autistic adults experience many similar barriers to healthcare access as people with other types of disabilities; however, they experience them at higher rates, and also experience unique autism-specific barriers that may be less likely to be addressed in modern healthcare systems*'.

We currently lack sufficient data about Autistic AFAB people's experiences of health and health care to make definitive conclusions. However, we can infer from the general population's gender health gap and from the little research that does exist that there are likely to be additional challenges for Autistic AFAB people when trying to access health care. What we *do* already know is that when services fail Autistic people at times when they need support the most, this often triggers a cycle of involvement with poor-fit mental health services (Camm-Crosbie et al., 2019) that can, ultimately, lead to escalating crisis situations resulting in restraint, seclusion and long-term segregation (Care Quality Commission, 2020). For example, in her book, *Unbroken*, Alexis Quinn (2018, p. 36) describes being '*incarcerated in the NHS*' postnatally, following a mental health admission through her local crisis team where she experienced dehumanizing and harmful treatment and wasn't permitted to keep her baby with her. The case of another young Autistic woman, Bethany, came to prominence recently in the news when she was finally released from living all her teenage years in solitary confinement under a Mental Health Act detainment, following the long-term advocacy of her father and Autistic advocates and activists (Joshi, 2020)[45]. Yet, Alexis and Bethany's stories are not rarities. An NHS England (2020) report found that the number of Autistic people detained long-term in inpatient mental health hospitals in the UK rose from 800 in 2015 to 935 in 2020, despite the national effort to 'Transform Care' (NHS England, 2017) and support previously detained Autistic people to live in the community.

This dangerously poor care during times of mental distress has potentially even more bearing on the lives of Autistic AFAB people, given the role of the menstrual cycle hormones on mental health. Some studies have begun to find that Autistic AFAB people are more likely to experience reproductive hormone-related complications than non-Autistic AFAB people. For example, Lever and Geurts (2016) found that almost 21 % of Autistic women – compared with 3 % of non-Autistic women – suffered from premenstrual dysphoric disorder (PMDD): a severe form of premenstrual syndrome during the luteal phase of the menstrual cycle that often involves extreme mood swings and suicidal ideation. In another study, researchers found that Autistic women experience higher levels of menopausal symptoms than non-Autistic women, often associated with higher rates of depression and an increase in Autistic traits (Groenman et al., 2022)[46]. Furthermore, Moseley and colleagues (2021) also looked at Autistic women's experiences in menopause and found a deterioration in quality of life during this life stage, troubled by typical menopausal challenges in addition to an increased propensity to experience extreme emotional lability and increased frequency of meltdowns, concluding that there are significant '*healthcare access problems and unmet needs for autistic women at midlife*' (Moseley et al., 2021, p. 710). Taken in the context that Autistic people live significantly shorter lives than non-Autistic people and die by suicide far more frequently (Hirvikoski et al, 2016), the compounded care gap that Autistic AFAB people face by virtue of experiencing both increased and atypical reproductive hormonal complications, and the Double Empathy Problem within health care settings, is especially alarming. Moreover, none of these studies report on the race or ethnicity of participants, but it is likely that the vast majority of participants were white, as in common in Autism research (Jones et al., 2020). For Black, Brown, Asian and other ethnically minoritized Autistic AFAB people the already unacceptable care gap is almost certainly even wider.

45 Thankfully, Bethany now lives comfortably at home with her family, enjoying '*going for walks, caring for her pets and experimenting with new hairstyles and clothes*' (National Development Team for Inclusion, 2021).

46 Of course, an apparent increase in Autistic traits may well mean that in these instances Autistic women are masking less, or finding it harder to mask.

Conclusion

As things currently stand, anyone with a minoritized identity – AFAB people, Black, Brown and other ethnically minoritized people, trans people, disabled people, neurodivergent people, people with lower economic status, LGBTQ+ people, ex-offenders, refugees, people with larger body sizes, insecurely housed people, etc. – faces biases in and barriers to medical care that keep them in pain and reduce their lifespan (Robards et al., 2018). The more intersecting identities (Crenshaw, 1989) an individual has, the greater the compounded impact on their access to non-harmful health care. For those who are Autistic, additional communication barriers in the form of the Double Empathy Problem complicate this even further.

Finally, within the SPACE framework (Doherty et al., 2023) is *E* for *empathy*: the notion also at the heart of the Double Empathy Problem. The health care system in the UK, under years of Conservative austerity cuts and within an already historically patriarchal system, isn't fit for purpose for many, but especially not for Autistic people (Grant et al., 2023b). It is often the extra efforts – and the empathy and care – of health care professionals that keep the crumbling system running. Greater diligence in routinely offering meaningful and person-centred reasonable adjustments (Doherty et al., 2021, 2023; Williams et al., 2022) when providing health care to Autistic AFAB people will make a difference, as will an empathic and open-minded approach toward those who are different and practitioner training in Autism and co-occurring health conditions. Research into the health care needs of Autistic AFAB people is also clearly and urgently indicated. However, it is the health care system itself – shaped by the funding and policy whims of the government – that needs to change more than anything in order to ensure a service that supports Autistic AFAB people to thrive.

References

Agarwal, P. (2022). *Hysterical: Exploding the Myth of Gendered Emotions.* Canongate

All-Party Parliamentary Group on Endometriosis (2020). *Endometriosis in the UK: Time for Change, APPG on Endometriosis Inquiry Report* (October, 2020). https://www.endometriosis-uk.org/sites/default/files/files/Endometriosis%20APPG%20Report%20Oct%202020.pdf

Begeer, S., El Bouk, S., Boussaid, W., Terwogt, M. M., & Koot, H. M. (2009). Underdiagnosis and referral bias of autism in ethnic minorities. *Journal of Autism and Developmental Disorders, 39*(1), 142–148. https://doi.org/10.1007/s10803-008-0611-5

Botha, M., & Frost, D. (2018). Extending the minority stress model to understand mental health problems experienced by the autistic population. *Society and Mental Health, 10*(1), 20–34. https://doi.org/10.1177/2156869318804297

Brewer, R., Biotti, F., Catmur, C., Press, C., Happé, F., Cook, R., & Bird, G. (2016). Can neurotypical individuals read autistic facial expressions? Atypical production of emotional facial expressions in autism spectrum disorders. *Autism Research*, 9(2), 262–271. https://doi.org/10.1002/aur.1508

Buck, T. R., Viskochil, J., Farley, M., Coon, H., McMahon, W. M., Morgan, J., & Bilder, D. A. (2014). Psychiatric comorbidity and medication use in adults with autism spectrum disorder. *Journal of Autism and Developmental Disorders,* 44(12), 3063–3071. https://doi.org/10.1007/s10803-014-2170-2

Camm-Crosbie, L., Bradley, L., Shaw, R., Baron-Cohen, S., & Cassidy, S. (2019). 'People like me don't get support': Autistic adults' experiences of support and treatment for mental health difficulties, self-injury and suicidality. *Autism, 23*(6), 1431–1441. https://doi.org/10.1177/1362361318816053

Care Quality Commission (2020). *Out of Sight – Who Cares? A Review of Restraint, Seclusion and Segregation for Autistic People, and People with a Learning Disability and/or Mental Health Condition.* Care Quality Commission. https://www.cqc.org.uk/sites/default/files/20201218_rssreview_report.pdf

Cascio, M. A., Weiss, J. A., & Racine, E. (2020). Making autism research inclusive by attending to intersectionality: A review of the research ethics literature. *Review Journal of Autism and Developmental Disorders, 8,* 22–36. https://doi.org/10.1007/s40489-020-00204-z

Chantler-Hicks, L. (2023, October 3). Tories announce plan to ban trans women from female hospital wards. *Evening Standard.* https://www.standard.co.uk/news/politics/trans-women-hospital-wards-tory-conservative-party-conference-steve-barclay-b1110934.html

Chown, N. (2017). *Understanding and Evaluating Autism Theory.* Jessica Kingsley Publishers.

Cleghorn, E. (2022). *Unwell Women: Misdiagnosis and Myth in a Man-Made World.* Penguin/Dutton.

Cooper, C., Lodwick, R., Walters, K., Raine, R., Manthorpe, J., Iliffe, S., & Petersen, I. (2017). Inequalities in receipt of mental and physical healthcare in people with dementia in the UK. *Age and Ageing, 46*(3), 393–400. https://doi.org/10.1093/ageing/afw208

Corden, K., Brewer, R., & Cage, E. (2022). A systematic review of healthcare professionals' knowledge, self-efficacy and attitudes towards working with autistic people. *Review Journal of Autism and Developmental Disorders, 9*(3), 386–399. https://doi.org/10.1007/s40489-021-00263-w

Crenshaw, K. (1989). Demarginalizing the intersection of race and sex: A black feminist critique of antidiscrimination doctrine, feminist theory and antiracist politics. *University of Chicago Legal Forum,* 1(8), 139–167. https://chicagounbound.uchicago.edu/cgi/viewcontent.cgi?article = 1052&context = uclf

Crompton, C. J., Fletcher-Watson, S., & Ropar, D. (2019a). "I never realised everybody felt as happy as I do when I am around autistic people": A thematic analysis of autistic adults' relationships with autistic and neurotypical friends and family. *Autism, 24*(6), 1438–1448. https://doi.org/10.1177/1362361320908976

Crompton, C. J., Fletcher-Watson, S., & Ropar, D. (2019b). Autistic peer to peer information transfer is highly effective. *Autism, 24*,(7) 1704–1712. https://doi.org/10.1177/1362361320919286

Crompton, C. J., Sharp, M., Axbey, H., Fletcher-Watson, S., Flynn, E. G., & Ropar, D. (2020). Neurotype-matching, but not being autistic, influences self and observer ratings of interpersonal rapport. *Frontiers in Psychology, 11,* 2961. https://doi.org/10.3389/fpsyg.2020.586171

Department of Health and Social Care (2019). *'Right to be Heard': The Government's Response to the Consultation on Learning Disability and Autism Training for Health and Care Staff.* Department of Health and Social Care. https://assets.publishing.service.gov.uk/government/uploads/system/uploads/attachment_data/file/844356/autism-and-learning-disability-training-for-staff-consultation-response.pdf

Department of Health and Social Care (2022). *Policy Paper: Women's Health Strategy for England.* Department of Health and Social Care. https://www.gov.uk/government/publications/womens-health-strategy-for-england/womens-health-strategy-for-england

Department of Health and Social Care and Department for Education (2021). *The National Strategy for Autistic Children, Young People and Adults: 2021 to 2026.* Department of Health and Social Care and Department for Education. https://www.gov.uk/government/publications/national-strategy-for-autistic-children-young-people-and-adults-2021-to-2026

Doherty, M., Haydon, C., & Davidson, I. A. (2021). Recognising autism in healthcare. *British Journal of Hospital Medicine, 82*(12), 1–7. https://doi.org/10.12968/hmed.2021.0313

Doherty, M., Neilson, S., O'Sullivan, J., Carravallah, L., Johnson, M., Cullen, W., & Shaw, S. C. K. (2022). Barriers to healthcare and self-reported adverse outcomes for autistic adults: a cross-sectional study. *BMJ Open, 12*(2), e056904. https://doi.org/10.1136/bmjopen-2021-056904

Doherty, M., McCowan, S., & Shaw, S. C. (2023). Autistic SPACE: A novel framework for meeting the needs of autistic people in healthcare settings. *British Journal of Hospital Medicine, 84*(4), 1–9. https://doi.org/10.12968/hmed.2023.0006

Edey, R., Cook, J., Brewer, R., Johnson, M. H., Bird, G., & Press, C. (2016). Interaction takes two: Typical adults exhibit mind-blindness towards those with autism spectrum disorder. *Journal of Abnormal Psychology, 125*(7), 879–908. https://doi.org/10.1037/abn0000199

Edmonds, B. T., Sharp, S., & Walker, V. P. (2023). Mitigating misogynoir: inclusive professionalism as a health equity strategy. *Clinical Obstetrics and Gynecology, 66*(1), 14–21. https://doi.org/10.1097/GRF.0000000000000768

Ehrenreich, B., & English, D. (1974/2010). *Witches, Midwives, & Nurses: A History of Women Healers* (2nd edition). The Feminist Press at CUNY.

Ellis, R., Williams, K., Brown, A., Healer, E., & Grant, A. (2023). A realist review of health passports for Autistic adults. *PloS One, 18*(9), e0279214. https://doi.org/10.1371/journal.pone.0279214

Ellis, R., Williams, G., Caemawr, S., Crane, M., Holloway, W., Williams, K., Shaw, S., & Grant, A. (2025). Menstruation and autism: A qualitative systematic review. *Autism in Adulthood.* https://doi.org/10.1089/aut.2024.0307.

Freeman, A. (2017). Unmothering Black women: Formula feeding as an incident of slavery. *Hastings Law Journal, 69*(6), 1545–1606.

George, R., & Stokes, M. A. (2018). Gender identity and sexual orientation in autism spectrum disorder. *Autism, 22*(8), 970–982. https://doi.org/10.1177/1362361317714587

Goop Wellness (2023). Jade Egg. Goop. https://shop.goop.com/shop/products/jade-egg?country=GBR

Grant, A., Jones, S., Williams, K., Leigh, J., & Brown, A. (2022). Autistic women's views and experiences of infant feeding: A systematic review of qualitative evidence. *Autism, 26*(6), 1341–1352. https://doi.org/10.1177/13623613221089374

Grant, A., Griffiths, C., Williams, K., & Brown, A. (2023a). "It felt like I had an old-fashioned telephone ringing in my breasts": An online survey of UK Autistic birthing parents' experiences of infant feeding. *Maternal & Child Nutrition, 20*(3), e13581. https://doi.org/10.1111/mcn.13581

Grant, A., Williams, G. L., Williams, K., & Woods, R. (2023b) Unmet need, epistemic injustice and early death: How social policy for Autistic adults in England and Wales fails to slay Beveridge's Five Giants. In C. Ruggero, M. Rose, & A Jolly (Eds.), *Social Policy Review 35: Analysis and Debate in Social Policy, 2023*, (pp. 239–257). Policy Press.

Grant, A., Griffiths, C., Williams, K., & Brown, A. (2025). "I just gritted my teeth to get through it all": An online survey of autistic people's experiences of maternity care in the United Kingdom. *Autism in Adulthood.* https://doi.org/10.1089/aut.2024.0275

Groenman, A. P., Torenvliet, C., Radhoe, T. A., Agelink van Rentergem, J. A., & Geurts, H. M. (2022). Menstruation and menopause in autistic adults: Periods of importance? *Autism, 26*(6), 1563–1572. https://doi.org/10.1177/13623613211059721

Hampton, S., Allison, C., Baron-Cohen, S., & Holt, R. (2023). Autistic people's perinatal experiences ii: a survey of childbirth and postnatal experiences. *Journal of Autism and Developmental Disorders, 53*(7), 2749–2763. https://doi.org/10.1007/s10803-022-05484-4

Health Education England (2022). The Oliver McGowan Mandatory Training in Learning Disability and Autism. https://www.hee.nhs.uk/our-work/learning-disability/current-projects/oliver-mcgowan-mandatory-training-learning-disability-autism

Heasman, B., & Gillespie, A. (2017). Perspective-taking is two-sided: Misunderstandings between people with Asperger's syndrome and their family members. *Autism, 22*(6), 740–750. https://doi.org/10.1177/1362361317708287

Heasman, B., & Gillespie, A. (2019). Neurodivergent intersubjectivity: Distinctive features of how autistic people create shared understanding. *Autism, 23*(4), 910–921. https://doi.org/10.1177/1362361318785172

Hedley, D., Uljarević, M., Wilmot, M., Richdale, A., & Dissanayake, C. (2018a). Understanding depression and thoughts of self-harm in autism: A potential mechanism involving loneliness. *Research in Autism Spectrum Disorders, 46*, 1–7.https://doi.org/10.1016/j.rasd.2017.11.003

Hedley, D., Uljarević, M., Foley, K. R., Richdale, A., & Trollor, J. (2018b). Risk and protective factors underlying depression and suicidal ideation in Autism Spectrum Disorder. *Depression & Anxiety, 35*(7), 648–657. https://doi.org/10.1002/da.22759

Henricus Institoris, O. P., & Jacobus Sprenger, O. P. (2006). *The Malleus Maleficarum*, Vol. 11. Trans. and ed. C. S. MacKay. Cambridge University Press.

Hirvikoski, T., Mittendorfer-Rutz, E., Boman, M., Larsson, H., Lichtenstein, P., & Bölte, S. (2016). Premature mortality in autism spectrum disorder. *British Journal of Psychiatry, 208*(3), 232–238. https://doi.org/10.1192/bjp.bp.114.160192

Hoffman, K. M., Trawalter, S., Axt, J. R., & Oliver, M. N. (2016). Racial bias in pain assessment and treatment recommendations, and false beliefs about biological differences between blacks and whites. *Proceedings of the National Academy of Sciences, 113*(16), 4296–4301. https://doi.org/10.1073/pnas.1516047113

Hubbard, D. J., Faso, D. J., Assmann, P. F., & Sasson, N. J. (2017). Production and perception of emotional prosody by adults with autism spectrum disorder. *Autism Research, 10*(12), 1991–2001. https://doi.org/10.1002/aur.1847

Jones, D. R., Nicolaidis, C., Ellwood, L. J., Garcia, A., Johnson, K. R., Lopez, K., & Waisman, T. C. (2020). An expert discussion on structural racism in autism research and practice. *Autism in Adulthood, 2*(4), 273–281. https://doi.org/10.1089/aut.2020.29015.drj

Joshi, A. (2020). Autistic teen who was locked up 24/7 now loves hair dye, gardening and fishing one year on. *Sky News*. https://news.sky.com/story/autistic-girl-who-was-locked-up-24-7-now-loves-hair-dye-gardening-and-fishing-one-year-on-12087199

Kimber, L., Verrier, D., & Connolly, S. (2023). Autistic people's experience of empathy and the autistic empathy deficit narrative. *Autism in Adulthood, 6*(3). https://doi.org/10.1089/aut.2023.0001

Kourti, M. (Ed.) (2021) *Working with Autistic Transgender and Non-Binary People: Research, Practice and Experience*. Jessica Kingsley Publishers.

Lever, A. G., & Geurts, H. M. (2016). Psychiatric co-occurring symptoms and disorders in young, middle-aged, and older adults with autism spectrum disorder. *Journal of Autism and Developmental Disorders, 46*, 1916–1930. https://doi.org/10.1007/s10803-016-2722-8

Lockwood Estrin, G., Milner, V., Spain, D., Happé, F., & Colvert, E. (2021). Barriers to autism spectrum disorder diagnosis for young women and girls: A systematic review. *Review Journal of Autism and Developmental Disorders, 8*(4), 454–470. https://doi.org/10.1007/s40489-020-00225-8

London Assembly Health Committee (2022). *Trans Health Matters: Improving Access to Healthcare for Trans and Gender-Diverse Londoners*. London Assembly Health Committee. https://www.london.gov.uk/sites/default/files/health_committee_-_report_-_trans_health_matters.pdf

Mason, D., Ingham, B., Urbanowicz, A., Michael, C., Birtles, H., Woodbury-Smith, M., Brown, T., James, I., Scarlett, C., Nicolaidis, C., & Parr, J. R. (2019). A systematic review of what barriers and facilitators prevent and enable physical healthcare services access for autistic adults. *Journal of Autism and Developmental Disorders, 49*(8), 3387–3400. https://doi.org/10.1007/S10803-019-04049-2

MBRRACE-UK (2022). *Saving Lives, Improving Mothers' Care: Lessons Learned to Inform Maternity Care from the UK and Ireland Confidential Enquiries into Maternal Deaths and Morbidity 2017–19*. MBRRACE-UK. https://www.npeu.ox.ac.uk/assets/downloads/mbrrace-uk/reports/maternal-report-2021/MBRRACE-UK_Maternal_Report_2021_-_FINAL_-_WEB_VERSION.pdf

Milton, D. (2012). On the ontological status of autism: The double empathy problem. *Disability & Society*. *27*(6), 883–887. https://doi.org/10.1080/09687599.2012.710008

Milton, D., Heasman, B., & Sheppard, E. (2018). Double empathy. In F. Volkmar (Ed.) *Encyclopedia of Autism Spectrum Disorders*. Springer.

Morrison, K. E., DeBrabander, K. M., Jones, D. R., Faso, D. J., Ackerman, R. A., & Sasson, N. J. (2019). Outcomes of real-world social interaction for autistic adults paired with autistic compared to typically developing partners. *Autism, 24*(5): 1067–1080. https://doi.org/10.1177/1362361319892701

Moseley, R. L., Druce, T., & Turner-Cobb, J. M. (2021). Autism research is 'all about the blokes and the kids': Autistic women breaking the silence on menopause. *British Journal of Health Psychology, 26*, 709–726. https://doi.org/10.1111/bjhp.12477

National Development Team for Inclusion (2021). *It's Not Rocket Science*. Commissioned by National Quality Improvement Taskforce for children and young people's mental health inpatient services. https://www.ndti.org.uk/resources/publication/its-not-rocket-science

National Development Team for Inclusion (2022). Evaluation of the Oliver McGowan Mandatory Training Trial in Learning Disability and Autism. https://www.ndti.org.uk/resources/publication/evaluation-of-the-oliver-mcgowan-mandatory-training-in-learning-disabilities-and-autism-final-report

NHS England (2017). *Transforming Care. Model Service Specifications: Supporting Implementation of the Service Model*. NHS England.https://www.england.nhs.uk/wp-content/uploads/2017/02/model-service-spec-2017.pdf

NHS England (2019). *The Long Term Plan*. NHS England. https://www.longtermplan.nhs.uk/publication/nhs-long-term-plan/

NHS England (2020). DAPB2007: *Assuring Transformation (Information Standard)*. NHS England. https://digital.nhs.uk/data-and-information/information-standards/information-standards-and-data-collections-including-extractions/publications-and-notifications/standards-and-collections/dapb2007-assuring-transformation#about-this-information-standard

Nicolaidis, C., Raymaker, D., McDonald, K., Kapp, S., Weiner, M., Ashkenazy, E., Gerrity, M., Kripke, C., Platt, L., & Baggs, A. (2016). The development and evaluation of an online healthcare toolkit for autistic adults and their primary care providers. *Journal of General Internal Medicine, 31*, 1180–1189. https://doi.org/10.1007/s11606-016-3763-6

Onwuachi-Saunders, C., Dang, Q. P., & Murray, J. (2019). Reproductive rights, reproductive justice: Redefining challenges to create optimal health for all women. *Journal of Healthcare, Science and the Humanities, 9*(1), 19–31.

Patton, C., McVey, M., & Hackett, C. (2022). Enough of the 'snake oil': Applying a business and human rights lens to the sexual and reproductive wellness industry. *Business and Human Rights Journal, 7*(1), 12–28. https://doi.org/10.1017/bhj.2021.51

Perkins Gilman, C. (1892/1995). *The Yellow Wallpaper*. Penguin Classics.

Quinn, A. (2018). *Unbroken: Learning to Live Beyond Diagnosis*. Welbeck Publishing Group.

Rao, P., & Bhide, P. (2020). Controversies in the diagnosis of polycystic ovary syndrome. *Therapeutic Advances in Reproductive Health, 14*, 2633494120913032. https://doi.org/10.1177/2633494120913032

Raymaker, D. M., McDonald, K. E., Ashkenazy, E., Gerrity, M., Baggs, A. M., Kripke, C., Hourston, S., & Nicolaidis, C. (2017). Barriers to healthcare: Instrument development and comparison between autistic adults and adults with and without other disabilities. *Autism, 21*(8), 972–984. https://doi.org/10.1177/1362361316661261

Robards, F. Kang, M., Usherwood, T., & Sanci, L. (2018). How marginalized young people access, engage with, and navigate health-care systems in the digital age: Systematic review. *Journal of Adolescent Health, 62*(4), 365–381. https://doi.org/10.1016/j.jadohealth.2017.10.018

Roberts, D. (2014). *Killing the Black Body: Race, Reproduction, and the Meaning of Liberty*. Vintage.

Rol, A. (2018). "Mississippi Appendectomy" and other stories: When silence is complicity. *Hektoen International, A Journal of Medical Humanities*, 10(2). https://hekint.org/2018/01/10/mississipi-appendectomy-stories-silence-complicity/

Sbragia, J. D., & Vottero, B. (2020). Experiences of transgender men in seeking gynecological and reproductive health care: A qualitative systematic review. *JBI Evidence Synthesis, 18*(9), 1870–1931. https://doi.org/10.11124/JBISRIR-D-19-00347

Shaw, S. C. K., Carravallah, L., Johnson, M., O'Sullivan, J., Chown, N., Neilson, S., & Doherty, M. (2023). Barriers to healthcare and a 'triple empathy problem' may lead to adverse outcomes for autistic adults: A qualitative study. *Autism, 28*(7), 1746–1757. https://doi.org/10.1177/13623613231205629

Sheppard, E., Pillai, D., Wong, G. T. L., Ropar, D., & Mitchell, P. (2016). How easy is it to read the minds of people with autism spectrum disorder? *Journal of Autism and Developmental Disorders, 46*(4), 1247–1254. https://doi.org/10.1007/s10803-015-2662-8

Strauss, P., Cook, A., Watson, V., Winter, S., Whitehouse, A., Albrecht, N., Toussaint, D. W., & Lin, A. (2021). Mental health difficulties among trans and gender diverse young people with an autism spectrum disorder (ASD): Findings from Trans Pathways. *Journal of Psychiatric Research, 137*, 360–367. https://doi.org/10.1016/j.jpsychires.2021.03.005

Sundelin, H. E., Stephansson, O., Hultman, C. M., & Ludvigsson, J. F. (2018). Pregnancy outcomes in women with autism: A nationwide population-based cohort study. *Clinical Epidemiology, 10*, 1817–1826. https://doi.org/10.2147/CLEP.S176910

Talcer, M. C., Duffy, O., & Pedlow, K. (2023). A qualitative exploration into the sensory experiences of autistic mothers. *Journal of Autism and Developmental Disorders, 53*(2), 834–849. https://doi.org/10.1007/s10803-021-05188-1

The Autism Act (2009). https://www.legislation.gov.uk/ukpga/2009/15/contents

The Equality Act (2010). https://www.legislation.gov.uk/ukpga/2010/15/contents

The Health and Care Act (2022). https://www.legislation.gov.uk/ukpga/2022/31/contents/enacted

Tone, A. (2002). *Devices and Desires*. Hill and Wang.

Uljarević, M., Hedley, D., Rose-Foley, K., Magiati, I., Cai, R. Y., Dissanayake, C., Richdale, A., & Trollor, J. (2020). Anxiety and depression from adolescence to old age in autism spectrum disorder. *Journal of Autism and Developmental Disorders, 50*, 3155–3165. https://doi.org/10.1007/s10803-019-04084-z

Westergaard, D., Moseley, P., Karuna Hemmingsen Sørup, F., Baldi, P., & Brunak, S. (2019). Population-wide analysis of differences in disease progression patterns in men and women. *Nature Communications, 10*(1). https://doi.org/10.1038/s41467-019-08475-9

Westminster Commission on Autism (2021). *Support Surrounding Diagnosis: An Inquiry into Pre- and Post- Support for the Autism Diagnosis Pathway*. https://www.bath.ac.uk/publications/resources-for-researchers-and-the-autism-community/attachments/support-surrounding-diagnosis.pdf

Williams, G. L. (2021). Theory of autistic mind: A refreshed relevance theoretic account of so-called autistic pragmatic 'impairment'. *Journal of Pragmatics, 180*(1), 121–130. https://doi.org/10.1016/j.pragma.2021.04.032

Williams, G. L., Wharton, T., & Jagoe, C. (2021). Mutual (mis)understanding: reframing autistic pragmatic 'impairments' using relevance theory. *Frontiers in Psychology. Autism: Innovations and Future Directions in Psychological Research, 12*, 616664. https://doi.org/10.3389/fpsyg.2021.616664

Williams, G. L., Adams, J., Bull, P., Cave, H., Chown, N., Doherty, M., Forrest, K., Foster, R., Fricker, R., Godfree, B., Keaveney-Sheath, K., Knight, J., Marrable, T., Murray, R., Shaw, S. C. K., Ventour-Griffiths, T., & Wood, J. (2022). *More*

Than Words: Supporting Effective Communication with Autistic People in Health Care Settings. Economic and Social Research Council https://www.england.nhs.uk/south-east/wp-content/uploads/sites/45/2022/10/More-than-words-supporting-effective-communication-with-autistic-people-in-health-care-settings-3.pdf

Wu, J., Gale, C. P., Hall, M., Dondo, T. B., Metcalfe, E., Oliver, G., Batin, P. D., Hemingway, H., Timmis, A., & West, R. M. (2018). Editor's Choice-Impact of initial hospital diagnosis on mortality for acute myocardial infarction: A national cohort study. *European Heart Journal: Acute Cardiovascular Care, 7*(2), 139–148. https://doi.org/10.1177/2048872616661693

Zerbo, O., Massolo, M. L., Qian, Y., & Croen, L. A. (2015). A study of physician knowledge and experience with autism in adults in a large integrated healthcare system. *Journal of Autism and Developmental Disorders, 45*(12), 4002–4014. https://doi.org/10.1007/s10803-015-2579-2

Chapter 27:
With or Without Interpersonal Disparities: Taking Up Theatre and Improv

Nathan Keates

Overview

In this chapter, I will explore the connection between autistic theatre performers and the Double Empathy Problem (Milton, 2012). The focus is on interpersonal disparities that could be experienced by autistic performers. This will include those that are new to performance and or performing and those who have experienced interpersonal disparities within their career (such as actors, dancers, clowns, improvisers, stand-up comedians, etc.). Moreover, I will discuss non-autistic performers as well as autistic experiences of theatre, and, at times, specifically improv comedy/theatre. There are various facets that are inclusive of improv comedy or theatre which are of interest in relation to interpersonal disparity or the Double Empathy Problem. It is necessary to highlight performers and neurodiversity; arts as a profession and a hobby; and improv and theatre as social arts. Additionally, imagined and perceived space are crucial to understanding the experiences of theatre makers and performers, and how they are related to autistic people. A brief discussion of social masking will also be included. Consequently, the Double Empathy Problem is a factor that identifies the natural dispositional diversity existent in theatre and the non-fictitious world.

Theatre and improv

Theatre is a collaborative form of fine art involving live performers to present the experience of a real or imagined event (such as a story) through acting, singing and/or dancing before a live audience in a specific place (Carlson, 1986; Kaye, 2013). The performers may communicate this experience to the audience through combinations of speech, gesture, mime, puppets, music, dance, sound and spectacle — indeed any one or more elements of the other performing arts. Elements of design and stagecraft are used to enhance the physicality, presence and immediacy of the experience. Theatre has a long and rich history, dating back to ancient Greece, and nowadays, theatre is enjoyed by people all over the world (Carlson, 1993). Improv is a form of theatre whereby there is no script (Frost & Yarrow, 2007; Halpern et al., 1994; Johnstone, 2012). The performers rely on their own creativity and imagination to react to each other and to the audience. Broader theatrical improvisation includes, among others, playback theatre, fools, Butoh and theatre of the oppressed (Keates & Beadle-Brown, 2022). A small subset of theatrical improvisation could be suggested to be improv where facets of the above improvisational art forms are less prominent; for example, both playback theatre and theatre of the oppressed use different structures and purposes compared to improv. There are many different types of improv, including short-form improv (a type of improv that is typically structured around shorter presentations of improvisation, commonly a series of games) and long-form improv (a type of improv that is typically more free-flowing and unstructured) (Kozlowski, 2002). These can be linear narrative improv, where the improvisation is designed to tell a story, or non-linear, that explores other options to the theatrical presentation (Halpern, 2006; Kozlowski, 2002). Theatre is typically more formal than improv, and it often has a higher production value. Improv is typically more relaxed and informal, and it is often more spontaneous.

Performers and neurodiversity

Engagement in theatre and performance seems to be valuable no matter your neurotype (Balfour & Freebody 2018; Gruzelier, 2018; Keates & Beadle-Brown, 2023; Walmsley, 2013). However, when considering the lived experience of neurodivergent people and specifically autistic people, Turner's (1967, 1969, 1977) concept of liminality becomes important. Liminality is the affordance of respite from the day-to-day existence; thus, this is the in-between of the mundane and the imaginary fictional worlds. Theatre has facilitated this well, with social spaces in which people (including autistic people) have partaken in this liminal existence/life. In fiction, hierarchies are suspended external to the pretended fiction (Kim et al., 2015). Theatre seems to provide this liminality that proffers opportunities for personal and collective change due to the liberation of usual constraints (Hughes & Wilson, 2004; Schechner & Appel, 1990). When theatre is constructed for marginalized people, such as decolonializing theatre, the results can be more sensitive to cultures, the cohort of people and the needs present (Magni, 2020). In considering this ideal, theatre should reflect all societies, including disabled people. Disabled people's source of creativity tends to be the very aspect of them that is deemed to restrict them (Whitfield, 2019). Marrero (2012) discusses music and creativity, in which they identify that the performance from autistic people is on their own terms. Once more, this liberation and freedom from the social world provides respite.

Neurodivergent theatre companies and practitioners exist, for example, NeuroSpace theatre (originally Stealth Aspies). In their theatre and rehearsal space, there is no need to comply with neurotypical expectations (Catchpole, 2022). In this theatre company, they engaged in a practice whereby they could be themselves acting, and playing out other characters. Being an autistic performer could have various strengths, such as studying 'normal' expressions that inform autistic actors playing characters that would produce this form of communication (Buckley et al., 2021a). Similarly, a different way of perceiving the world can be presented through humour, profiting from being an outsider regarding social interactions to offer this observation and insight (Brady, 2022). Another prospective, positive strength is that autistic people can have perfect pitch, and a natural ability for mimicry (Brady, 2022). Nonetheless, there can be negative experiences for autistic performers. These can consist of having feelings of isolation in the industry, and the need for professional advice on both career and being neurodivergent in the arts (Buckley et al., 2021b, 2022).

However, learning about theatre and developing relevant skills have been suggested as offering autistic people improvement in their self-esteem, empathetic abilities and comfort with others (Kim et al., 2015). In addition, there could be developments in communication and socialization skills, yet these must be aligned to how non-autistic people also develop in these areas. One example of this development is with improv comedy, whereby all neurotypes interviewed stated how they developed communication and social skills (Keates & Beadle-Brown, 2023). Neurotypical improvisers discussed developing cognitive empathy, and neurodivergent improvisers mentioned turn-taking (specifically from autistic improvisers) and a framework for interactions and building friendships.

The arts as a profession and a hobby

It could be assumed that neurodivergent performers existed, even in times when diagnosis was not possible (see Happé & Frith [2020] regarding diagnosis). There are numerous ways in which anyone can engage in the theatre, or the arts more widely. These include as a career being employed in the arts or creative cultural industries in some manner, or through engaging in a more community-based approach, whereby people may explore their interest in the arts either aligned to being a hobby, or semi-professionally. For instance, in the heyday of Commedia dell'arte, performers were a collective group of professionals who were contracted or hired to perform, with the money being shared and the companies' use of cash requiring consensus (Crick & Rudlin, 2002). The range of engagement within the arts, has been, and remains, quite wide.

The interpersonal of the social arts

Theatre requires interpersonal relations (Grainger, 2014). It is a social art, however, the extent to which it is social could differ between the forms of theatre. For example, dance requires an embodied experience of the communication – it is a shared language of those that connect with it. This includes the audiences, who may understand and interpret the movements. Therefore, it is additionally possible that theatre is a social art due to the collective creativity of the theatre-makers and the audience (Wartemann, 2009). In any case, it can easily be acknowledged that there is an interplay between the actors resulting in social art, yet this can be furthered. In improv, communication is heightened and requires greater metacommunicative comprehension (Keates & Beadle-Brown, 2022). Therefore, the interaction between characters and performers is what creates this *social* art (Engelberts, 2004). For improvisers, the metacommunication occurs through group mind and flow to result in cohesive co-creation (Keates & Beadle-Brown, 2022). I posit that improv requires a greater quality of this interpersonal relation, and the reason is due to the improvisers not knowing what they are due to perform. Hence, when on stage, improvisers must engage in creating live, based on each other's contributions, and moment to moment. They may create scenes, songs and, broadly, anything that could be in a theatrical production. Nothing about the production being created extemporaneously is directly expressed. In improv, the production is frequently created based on suggestions provided by the audience. Fortier (2010) claims that the audience transforms from relative outsiders to insiders with a shared, common experience due to the collective construction of the performance. According to Sawyer (1993), everyone relates spontaneously throughout each day in everyday adult life; however, this is amplified on stage. The main difference between life and stage is the condensed space and time (Wunder, 2007). Similarly, live moments in scripted or devised theatre, whereby actors opt to ad-lib (or perceivably do so), create what the audience would deem a unique instance shared with them in that moment (Jellicoe, 1967). Regardless of ad-libbing, theatre is a live performance, and the uniqueness of the predetermined production will be shared between the audience and the performers.

Theatre as a social space for autistic people would come with caveats of practice, if the (physical and social) environment are designed to be inclusive. As Fletcher-Watson & May (2018) suggest regarding the Autism Arts Festival, autistic needs are not static nor homogeneous; therefore, there is a requirement for autistic people to enact self-regulation. This lesson derives from autistic-led autism conferences, such as Autscape and Autreat (Owren, 2013). At the Autism Arts Festival, the social rules were explicit, and expectations were set (Fletcher-Watson & May, 2018). Inclusive practices were adopted, and this was perceptively due to the festival being or becoming an 'autistic space', at least from the perspective of some of those attending and performing. It would make sense to suggest that autistic theatre companies and practitioners themselves should transform their practice into an autistic space. When I interviewed autistic improvisers, some of them worked in the arts as professionals. One story from these interviews was that one performer/improviser attended an Equity (the performing arts and entertainment trade union) event and began to talk to another person. They found that they both had similar interests and ways of expressing themselves, which led to them collaborating on a theatre project. It was found out that the person met at the Equity event was also neurodivergent.

The dangers in theatre

I am not seeking to claim that theatre is a sanctuary nor a cause of harm for autistic people. It could be either of these for some of the people that engage in it. However, there are possible dangers that should be highlighted. In Keates & Beadle-Brown (2023), it was found that some autistic people found theatre a problematic sector. This was both professionally and within a community setting. The false nature of networking and professional friendships made one participant of the study dislike the arts, albeit that they remained performing. They alluded to noticing that some people within the arts can seem fake and adopt performative behaviours that are focused on obtaining their own goals over collaboration. Additionally, there could have been normative ideals that underpin these behaviours. Another participant identified how they were not welcome in the local community theatre productions. Both participants contrasted this with the safer nature of improv, and that it was more the general theatre community that were less accepting. All participants identified how accepting improv can be, which could be due to the unconditional positive regard that underpins improv (Bermant, 2013). This is not to suggest that improv is completely safe, as this is not true. Nonetheless, these participants clearly found more helpful components to improv than not, and comparative to general theatre. Admittedly, experiences of theatre, and improv specifically, are likely heterogeneous.

Social relations and dispositional disparities

Having outlined theatre and improv as social art and requiring interpersonal relations, it is necessary to link this to dispositional disparities. The social relations that occur can create outsiders, which sometimes positions the marginalized in an out-group (Carr, 2003; Goffman, 1963). Autistic people are an enduring outsider group. This disparity is through the marginalization of people due to personal characteristics. The propagation of the outsider *based on a way of being*, or their 'humankind', leads to a disposition diversity. By which, I mean to suggest that the autistic way of being is the disposition which causes them to become disregarded or ostracized (Milton et al., 2023). The dispositional marginalization of people is the disparity in which we are interested. Societies spawn normed practices and cultures to which certain groups are unable to conform, resulting in this dispositional disparity (e.g., Brinker, 1985; Fehr & Schurtenberger, 2018). In other words, due to the structural and systemic creations of people, the subsequent dispositional disparities result in prejudice, such as ableism for autistic people (Milton et al., 2023; Yergeau, 2018).

People create various practices in which we base our lives. One of them is how we develop children into adults. Within the educational system in the UK, the foundation stage is constructed based on a lifespan model of child development with a normed practice of play that staff promote (Department for Education, 2018/2022). The way in which children play is judged to be correct or not based on a levelled understanding of what they are supposed to be able to do. In doing so, this positions one mode of play better or more appropriate for a child than another. Recognizing this disparity becomes an interesting consideration when we identify that autistic people experience life and the world differently, and this seems to result in more pleasure and satisfaction with parallel engagement than in engagement with non-autistic people (Burch, 2022; Pritchard et al., 2023). I am not suggesting the education system is completely unjust or wrong, but there are insights emerging. Therefore, such thoughts are being furthered in other levels of schooling (Wood, 2019, 2021; Wood & Happé, 2023).

Inevitably, the mutual disjuncture between the system and the autistic person is due to the dispositional disparities, which are between the normed practice and autistic needs. Consequently, a problem within the wider system, and not just interpersonal relations, is made apparent when considering these issues. For example, the route to obtaining work is based on accessing job interviews and presenting oneself as capable through normed expectations. Albeit that the social relations are at the forefront of what people encounter on a daily basis, the disparity or disjuncture is what is frequently experienced. An exemplary situation of disjuncture for autistic people is the physical environment in all realms of life (work, shopping, hospitals, etc.), which is not adapted to meet autistic needs. In other words, comparing micro versus macro perspectives of the social world would suggest that the micro aspects of day-to-day living are more prominent. An example of the micro or day-to-day living that has a long-term impact is consistently overcoming communication barriers and misinterpretations. This does not mean to suggest that the macro aspects of systemic and structural barriers are not important; in fact, I am suggesting the system in which autistic people live could be considered more impactful.

Nonetheless, I will currently remain discussing the micro aspects, which are more pertinent to the topic of the chapter. The consequence of a mixed neurotype (people from different neurotype groups) seems to operate less well than both autistic only and non-autistic only groups. The consequence of a mixed neurotype group has been found within creativity and within communication. For example, Axbey et al. (2023) found less similarity between the mixed neurotype and the same neurotype groups. The findings from the study could be interpreted to indicate that when an autistic only and a non-autistic only group used creative problem-solving (building a tall tower), they resulted in similar towers or perceptively more cohesion. In communication between neurotypes, Crompton et al. (2021) found that the weakest chain was the mixed neurotype chain, according to data collected from their study using the telephone game. This further highlights how challenges across neurotypes can persist due to the natural dispositional diversity. Nonetheless, theatre may overcome these well, or theatre practitioners or performers may find other neurodivergent people.

Theatre and improv agents

In theatre, there are numerous areas that include social relations. There are the onstage social interactions that are guided by rehearsal (whether scripted or improvised), the offstage interactions and arrangements (i.e., organizing oneself for the next scene), and the real-world interactions of social, informal networking or formal professional development. Nevertheless, performers and theatre practitioners have a diversity of experiences. By which, I mean, across neurotypes, that the events and practices are diversely felt and understood by the individuals. Autistic people will obviously encounter some level of dispositional disparity, whether nearly no issues or to a great extent.

Where could autistic people be successful? It seems like many autistic people have felt they thrive or fit well within comedy, especially stand-up comedy (Brady, 2022; Fox, 2018; Keisalo, 2018). I have spoken to various autistic comedians over the years and they report the social communication with stand-up comedy clubs to be easy. There is a community of stand-up comedians that they can opt to talk with if they have the capacity in the moment, or not. Theatrical professionals can also be advocates and speakers for the autistic community in general, and the most successful of these presenters use comedy. There could be a cross-over with this, but this is not studied and merely a possibility. Nonetheless, in both of these professions, the autistic individual has full control over their performance, and need not engage others outside of this if they so desire. In improv, this is different, but the ethos of it is laden with unconditional positive regard (Bermant, 2013); it would be expected that if someone did not wish to stay to socially engage that no one would judge. However, this specific prospect did not arise in my study where I interviewed autistic improvisers in Keates & Beadle-Brown (2023). The paucity of difficulties discussed in the study would suggest that there are limited issues about meeting autistic needs within the improv community.

One example from Keates and Beadle-Brown (2023) is when an autistic improviser understood their own needs and had the self-knowledge to realise what would help. They were in a theatre space during a rehearsal and lights were too bright and the autistic improviser knew they had less capacity to be under intense theatre lights. The person running the session just accommodated the request without question. This example demonstrates the affordance available that may not always be possible for autistic people. There are often issues in life for autistic people, when they do not understand their own needs and reasons for them; by which, I mean to suggest that without knowledge, the result can be self-blame (Chapman & Carel, 2022). For example, an autistic person may not be lazy and instead it could be inertia. There is much to be said for self-compassion, and knowledge. Knowing how to overcome issues, and particularly within the industry, has immense value. Such issues, related to dispositional disparities, can entail employability, including access to performing, networking and friendship-building in the industry.

Employability, agents and access to theatre and improv

Autistic theatre professionals exist and have been in the industry for decades, as denoted by famous actors disclosing over recent years. This implies that, famous or not, autistic performers can succeed in theatre as a professional.

Theatre has gatekeepers, for example, casting directors, agents and management companies, theatre directors and trade union rules. In theatre, agents will find work for professional actors. This has many issues, for instance, an actor needs theatre work in order for an agent to watch them perform, which then results in the agent hiring them and thereafter seeking work for the actor. Many industries have this type of catch-22. In any case, we can consider the disparities autistic people can face, and the thin-slice judgements whereby autistic people are rapidly perceived more negatively than non-autistic people (Heasman & Gillespie, 2019; DeBrabander et al., 2019; Morrison et al., 2020; Sasson et al., 2017). These judgements are termed 'thin-slice' due to the speed at which they are made leading to a decisions (based on norms) that are non-conducive to a population that are already marginalized by 'society'. These thin-slice judgements further the disparities felt by autistic people (Crompton et al., 2021; Scheerer et al., 2022). Consequently, accessing the right to perform may be difficult, as found in Keates & Beadle-Brown (2023) when one participant detailed how they were not welcome in their local amateur dramatics (amdram) or community theatre, prospectively due to a thin-slice judgement. This may be different for improv, but only to the extent that the gatekeepers are required to practice the philosophies integral to improv. It is known that prejudice exists in improv, so ableism and discrimination is possible (maybe even likely). However, fortunately for the autistic improvisers I have interviewed, they did not experience improv negatively.

Networking

We should consider how creatives obtain commissions or gain roles as actors in productions. As with most fields of work, the answer tends to be about who the person knows and networking. For autistic people, when the norms are a barrier to engagement with others, networking can be a problem. In the arts, this is no different, and potentially even more troubling (Buckley et al., 2021). Exclusionary practices are not just felt by autistic people, but by disabled performers more generally (Kuppers, 2017). It is clear that autistic performers (professional and amateur) encounter many challenges (Buckley et al., 2021). Nonetheless, in improv this might be slightly different, or at least for some autistic improvisers. When interactions are guided by the ways in which an autistic performer could meet a contact, networking can be slightly easier. For example, the first time one might meet other improvisers could be after watching their performance, or perhaps after improvising with them onstage before a 'real-life' meeting. In addition, the possibility of initiating conversation could be easier due to a central topic, which could be general improv, or specific events or scenes. This provides autistic people with a structure and shared practice from which they can network.

Friendship-building

Autistic friendships (between like-minded people, seemingly often neurodivergent but not necessarily always) may well operate differently to those of non-autistic people (Black et al., 2022; Calder et al., 2013; Finke et al., 2019; Sosnowy et al., 2019). For example, autistic friends may prefer to text message or use social media on their phone (Ryan et al., 2021). Therefore, an autistic preference seems to be this direct approach to friendship, whereas ambiguity may play an important part for some non-autistic friendships. Thus, when autistic people's way of being is normalized, this seems to result in more cross-neurotype friendships (Sosnowy et al. 2019), which is a possible reason why there is more need for homophily within autistic friendship interactions (Black et al., 2022). Additionally, there is a drive for less 'hanging out' and more activity-based interaction (Finke et al., 2019), meaning that friendship for autistic people might operate in a way that meets this need for clear goals and boundaries. In addition, those with similarities in their disposition are more likely to feel closeness, acceptance and a sense of gaining help (Bolis et al., 2021; this study investigated autistic traits). Sosnowy et al. (2019) found that autistic friendship formed when social norms were not expected, which directly relates to reduction in dispositional disparity. Their grounded theory study of semistructured interviews included 20 autistic young adults (mean age 23.5, age range 18–29, 55% male, 35% female, 10% non-binary), and data from 21 parents and 11 service professionals. In theatre, this reduction of norms of practice would similarly be required.

How social contact is enacted would impinge on how autistic theatre professionals can maintain a collegial, friendship-based social contact. Within improv, whereby most of the improv around the world is not professional, but community-driven, autistic improvisers might encounter difficulties with accessing stage-time. Maintaining and building collegial friendships may be a possible barrier to stage time due to the difference in how friendships operate for autistic people (see Bertilsdotter-Rosqvist et al., 2020; Heasman & Gillespie, 2019). In general, it has been suggested that a self-directed, prearranged social engagement that is about a shared interest could facilitate socialization (Bottema-Beutel et al., 2019).

The social, imagined space

The space in which social contact and any disparities that may be felt underpins our connections with one another. This is true across the demographic characteristics and identities that people hold. The way in which we are treated impacts what we feel able to do and how we perceive people, events and situations that occur. Autistic people, as well as other marginalized groups within the diverse human population, are subject to discriminatory practices, which can have a long-lasting impact (even after these are removed or deemed to be eradicated). Therefore, it can affect participation and engagement with theatre, much like all aspects of life.

Stigma

For this section, we will begin by discussing the stigmatization of the outsider. In discussing stigma, we must identify the multiple ways in which this occurs. People can experience felt stigma (i.e., self-stigma or self-blame), courtesy or affiliative stigma (i.e., stigma by association with an outsider), and public stigma (i.e., discriminatory attitudes toward a person with an outsider identity) (Allport et al., 1954; Corrigan et al., 2006; Goffman, 1961/1968; MacRae, 1999; Scambler, 2006, 2009). There can also be self-ableism, which affects those that embody the narrative around their outsider identity. For example, depreciating one's social preferences for those of the normed social skillset. In relation to autistic people, stigma is due to having an outsider identity or 'blemished' identity (Goffman, 1961/1968), whereby autistic people have the outsider identity that is othered by society (Han et al., 2022; Milton, 2013). Self-blame regarding dispositional disparities can lead to self-stigma (Botha et al., 2022; Moore et al., 2022). Conversely, it is necessary to state that not all autistic people experience stigma.

Massa et al. (2020) investigated whether people performing theatre could reduce stigma. Autistic actors played the autistic characters, and the non-autistic actors played the other roles in the production. They found that the audience gained knowledge about autistic people and stigma reduced. However, as identified in Keates & Beadle-Brown (2023), theatre remains stigmatizing. This could even be to the extent that one autistic improviser in this study could have become self-stigmatized. Their acceptance of being ostracized from their local community as having inadequate social skills to participate in the theatre is clear from data reported in the study.

Obviously, autistic people can participate in improv, and have done over the years since 'modern improvisation' began with Jacob Levy Moreno in 1912 (see Moreno, 1947); admittedly, I cannot state whether there were autistic people engaging in improv as early as Moreno. Yet, we do know there are currently famous autistic actors due to their disclosure, and they have been in the cultural and creative industries for many decades; thus, it is easy to assume that other autistic creatives could have existed. In a study of live-action role-playing (LARP), it was detailed how autistic differences were accepted and became an asset. Being autistic in this environment was not stigmatized (Fein, 2015). It was further identified that the LARPers were mirroring their lived experience during the role-play. Literature about broader theatrical improvisation and autistic people (Keates & Beadle-Brown, under review) seems to identify an availability for reduction of stigma for autistic people (although most literature is not with regard to liberation but intervention). This seemed to be through demonstrable similarities between autistic and non-autistic people. In this sense, theatrical improvisation seems to be less polarizing for autistic people due to their differences, and everyone is viewed as an 'oddball'. In Keates & Beadle-Brown (2023), there was substantial discussion that indicated acceptance of the autistic person according to the participants' experiences.

Space, place and the imaginary

The imaginary is not about imagination, but I wish to use it as a noun. The 'imaginary' is an interesting framework with which to embed understanding of the autistic life. The imaginaries in relation to space are a social product (Lefebvre & Nicholson-Smith [trans.], 1991). This can be understood through conceiving an imaginary as a triadic concept: first, the perceived element or the spatial practices that are materialistic identifies what is in the space; second, the conceived element, or how space is believed to be, refers to the aspect of the space that is social or idealistic (what it is ideally conceived to be for); and third, the lived space or how the space is used is the aspect that bridges to the other elements – it is about human experiences of that space (Peet, 2000; Zhang, 2006). An example of this is, for teenagers, the local shop, a space in which they buy sweets or other products, but it is conceived to be a social meet-up space, and the lived experience of it can be a space where stories form. These social attributions occur for everyone, including autistic people. Therefore, the lived experience of a place is crucial to our understanding of disparities and people's lives more generally. Hence, place includes the physical, social, political and symbolic space (Lefebvre & Nicholson-Smith [trans.], 1991). There is a shared or collective understanding of a particular space that includes the practices of living in that space.

There is likely a distinct contrast between autistic and non-autistic space. This is because of the residual imagination of a space which remains, regardless of the alteration that may exist in a space. In relation to autistic people, there is an analogous version of a Lipsitz (2007) comment about space for Black people; he stated, '*not all blacks consciously embrace the black spatial imaginary, even though all blacks are subjected to it*'. This is the same for autistic people as not all autistic people embrace autistic imaginaries, although they subjected to it. Another available analogy to be made from Lipsitz (2011) is from his statement about Black people being subjected to '*...humiliating and dehumanizing segregation ... [but can form into an] exhilarating and rehumanizing congregation*'. We can also query the formation of autistic space: where are autistic people allowed to be?

In theatre, many autistic people can equate their experiences of space as similar to autistic space; however, this is not likely to be widespread. Nonetheless, improv has been positioned as more accessible and more akin to autistic space than general theatre (Keates & Beadle-Brown, 2023). Considering the common narrative about autistic people and theatre being predominantly based in a deficit narrative, it is possible to understand that the perceived space is not one that always accommodates autistic performers and theatre-makers. In addition, there is the dichotomy of liberation versus remediation noticeable in literature about autistic people and theatre. This is not academically problematic as such, due to the requirement to understand the effects of one variable on another. Yet, in practice, the desire to intervene with autistic people based on neuronormative ideology is not instantaneously credible or valuable.

Space is subject to the past, present, and prospective or perceived future. This is due to the imaginary, from which numerous autistic people face negative experiences that infringe on the sense of safety. Albeit that this might be overcome with the right people, the best space and a correct environment (socially and physically), it is noteworthy to understand the impact of the imaginary.

Enacted space (from perceived to the actual)

Consequently, the enacted space for autistic people is key to a productive theatre environment. Enacted space is the actual practice that is implemented within the space itself. If the practice is felt to be accommodating and the actual implementation of the theatre activities succeed, then the perceived and the actual are well aligned. This is regardless of what practice or experience is under discussion, as the difference between the perceived and the actual seems to always matter; this also includes the extent to which, in the long-term, the actual *remains* fitting to what was perceived. In other words, one's perception of the space must remain positive no matter the actual practice. In the long-term, the actual implementation of the practice must fit the perceived (or the perception about it) for the practice to sustain a positive outlook from the autistic individuals involved.

Trust with autistic people can easily and quickly be broken. For example, when considering dispositional disparities, the imaginary and stigmatization, Maurer et al.'s (2018) findings indicate how autistic people may maintain caution to alter their judgement on the trustworthiness of others. They found that autistic people continued to use their initial judgements on trust, whereas non-autistic people would update their prior judgements about others. In practice, this is more about experience of memory, where autistic people can ruminate on or recall untrustworthy occurrences of the recipient (albeit that past research can frame this as deficits: Boyd-Johnson, 2017; Dallman et al., 2022; Fuld, 2018; Jordan, 2008; Sharma, 2014); this will be a heightened response to the world-space in which an autistic person is situated, meaning the impact on them of stigma, etc. The enacted space within a theatre practice must support autistic performers well, in order to maintain a good, professional (and successful) relationship. At times, the relationship could be based more on their own past, negative experiences than the actual practice within the space. This is another factor to consider regarding the perceived-to-actual space. A key element of the enacted space is this interaction between the real, and how the space and practice are perceived. The consequence of the issue is that trust can be blighted or eradicated. Conversely, successful theatre experiences in themselves may lead to increased trust from autistic people (Kim et al., 2015). Therefore, when engagement and interactions go well, there can be a productive exchange that increases trust.

Presentation management, dispositional disparities and theatre

Regardless of the perceived, autistic people manage how they present themselves in the world (Ai et al., 2022). Considering stigma, and the imaginary, it is clear why this would be the case.

Masking and theatre

There is an important, and currently unanswerable question about masking and theatre. Masking is when autistic people consciously or unconsciously hide their autistic selves or behaviour (Lai et al., 2017). The need for autistic people to mask is apparent in the neuronormative social world (Cook et al., 2021). Pearson and Rose (2021) query how the shifting identities impact autistic people through the fluctuation of identities within the differing contexts encountered. The impact of this fluctuation is like cognitive dissonance, or the discrepancy between two beliefs (about ones' identities) that results in stress. This is explored by Pearson and Rose in their paper, where they state how this is what Black scholars discussed regarding the need to see oneself through someone else's perception.

Specifically, they mention Du Bois (1903/1999), who wrote about Black people in America being a 'double consciousness'. This translates well to autistic people in the neuronormative social world.

It is my belief that there is likely another form of masking because theatre does not seem to negatively impact autistic people. Masking in life has a clear negative impact, and non-literal masks of characters in theatre does not seem to have the same effect. Therefore, this other type of mask is clearly different. In my own research, I have found, when interviewing improvisers across neurotypes, that the experience of masking or hiding themselves through self-presentation management was phenomenologically different. Neurotypical improvisers (to distinguish from neurodivergent participants including autistic people within the study) expressed roles and it is a different side of them, whereas autistic people discussed the impact of needing to be other than themselves in life. This had no connection to performing in theatre.

Dissecting the various presentation management systems employed by people that could relate to masking has little clarity when considering the complexities of why and when presentation management is required. I have identified how roles may not be (or were not deemed) impactful for neurotypical improvisers. Therefore, there are seemingly three or more related presentation management systems that are implemented for different reasons. In theatre, the use of non-literal masks is to perform as someone else by choice.

The explanation may well arrive from the Double Empathy Problem. The control of presentation management lies within the individual, the theatre being made is shared in improv between those involved. Therefore, there is a qualitative difference between needing to mask in life and choosing to play in theatre that seems apparent, albeit not fully elucidated in research as yet. This is a topic requiring further investigation.

Conclusion

Whether performers across neurotypes engage in theatre as a hobby or profession, it can be valuable with the liminal experiences of respite from day-to-day existence through the imaginary fictional worlds. Autistic performers engage in this social art of theatre, which requires consideration of the practice. It has been noted that some autistic people have experienced theatre poorly, although improv has been suggested to be easier. The philosophy of improv being about unconditional positive regard may be a reason that this distinction could occur. However, with limited research, and known issues within improv (sexism, institutional racism), it is possible ableism does exist in practice (and is not yet identified in the research). The way in which autistic people are in life is the disposition in which they live life, and, as such, the divergence from non-autistic people creates scope for disparity. In theatre, this would impact rehearsals (whether scripted or improvised), the offstage interactions and arrangements (i.e., organizing oneself for the next scene), and the real-world interactions of social, informal networking, or formal professional development. Autistic people can thrive in the industry, with some people having stated to me that the social relations in stand-up comedy work well for them. However, we must consider thin-slice judgements and gatekeepers to work and access to performing across theatre. These aspects would impact networking and making new friends in the industry. Obviously, it could be easier with other neurodivergent performers, and others with a similar disposition. The social interaction that autistic people engage in within theatre is underpinned by their lived experiences, such as stigma, and the imagined and enacted space. I also propose masking in theatre as being different to the current understood version of this phenomenon. Fundamentally, theatre professionals can use inclusive practices that are better for autistic people, but this might not always exist. The Double Empathy Problem indicates an important factor regarding the natural dispositional diversity that exists within theatre, as well as in the non-fictitious world.

References

Ai, W., Cunningham, W. A., & Lai, M. C. (2022). Reconsidering autistic 'camouflaging' as transactional impression management. *Trends in Cognitive Sciences, 26*(8), 631-645. https://doi.org/10.1016/j.tics.2022.05.002

Allport, G. W., Clark, K., & Pettigrew, T. (1954). *The Nature of Prejudice*. Addison-Wesley Publishers.

Axbey, H., Beckmann, N., Fletcher-Watson, S., Tullo, A., & Crompton, C. J. (2023). Innovation through neurodiversity: Diversity is beneficial. *Autism, 27*(7), 2193–2198. https://doi.org/10.1177/13623613231158685

Balfour, M., & Freebody, K. (2018). Theories of change: Cultural value and applied theatre. In K. Freebody, M. Balfour, M. Finneran, & M. Anderson (eds.), *Applied Theatre: Understanding Change*, (pp. 19–31). Springer.

Bermant, G. (2013). Working with (out) a net: Improvisational theater and enhanced well-being. *Frontiers in Psychology, 4*, 929. https://doi.org/10.3389/fpsyg.2013.00929

Bertilsdotter-Rosqvist, H. B., Örulv, L., Hasselblad, S., Hansson, D., Nilsson, K., & Seng, H. (2020). Designing an autistic space for research: Exploring the impact of context, space, and sociality in autistic writing processes. In H. Rosqvist, N. Chown, & A Stenning (Eds.) *Neurodiversity Studies* (pp. 156–171). Routledge.

Black, M. H., Kuzminski, R., Wang, J., Ang, J., Lee, C., Hafidzuddin, S., & McGarry, S. (2022). Experiences of friendships for individuals on the autism spectrum: A scoping review. *Review Journal of Autism and Developmental Disorders, 11*(1), 184–209. https://doi.org/10.1007/s40489-022-00332-8

Bolis, D., Lahnakoski, J. M., Seidel, D., Tamm, J., & Schilbach, L. (2021). Interpersonal similarity of autistic traits predicts friendship quality. *Social Cognitive and Affective Neuroscience, 16*(1–2), 222–231. https://doi.org/10.1093/scan/nsaa147

Botha, M., Dibb, B., & Frost, D. M. (2022). 'It's being a part of a grand tradition, a grand counter-culture which involves communities': A qualitative investigation of autistic community connectedness. *Autism, 26*(8), 2151–2164. https://doi.org/10.1177/13623613221080248

Bottema-Beutel, K., Malloy, C., Cuda, J., Kim, S. Y., & MacEvoy, J. P. (2019). Friendship expectations may be similar for mental age-matched children with autism spectrum disorder and typically developing children. *Journal of Autism and Developmental Disorders, 49*, 4346–4354. https://doi.org/10.1007/s10803-019-04141-7

Boyd-Johnson, S. A. (2017). Does emotional valence of personal events influence their recall in typical development and autism?

Brady, M. (2022). Onstage and behind the scenes: Autistic performance and advocacy. *Studies in Social Justice, 16*(2), 429–446. https://doi.org/10.26522/ssj.v16i2.2666

Brinker, R. P. (1985). Interactions between severely mentally retarded students and other students in integrated and segregated public school settings. *American Journal of Mental Deficiency, 89*, 587–594.

Buckley, E., Pellicano, E., & Remington, A. (2021a). “The real thing I struggle with is other People’s perceptions”: The experiences of autistic performing arts professionals and attitudes of performing arts employers in the UK. *Journal of Autism and Developmental Disorders, 51*, 45–59.

Buckley, E., Pellicano, E., & Remington, A. (2021b). Higher levels of autistic traits associated with lower levels of self-efficacy and wellbeing for performing arts professionals. *PloS One, 16*(2), e0246423. https://doi.org/10.1177/27546330241245354

Buckley, E., Pellicano, E., & Remington, A. (2022). “Knowing that I’m not necessarily alone in my struggles”: UK autistic performing arts professionals’ experiences of a mentoring programme. *Journal of Autism and Developmental Disorders, 52*(10), 1–20. https://doi.org/10.1007/s10803-021-05394-x

Burch, J. (2022). Don’t Change Autistic Play. Join In. *AshaWire*.https://leader.pubs.asha.org/do/10.1044/leader.MIW.27112022.slp-antiableist-play.22/full/

Calder, L., Hill, V., & Pellicano, E. (2013). ‘Sometimes I want to play by myself’: Understanding what friendship means to children with autism in mainstream primary schools. *Autism, 17*(3), 296–316. https://doi.org/10.1177/1362361312467866

Carlson, M. (1986). Psychic polyphony. *Journal of Dramatic Theory and Criticism, 1*(1), 35–47.

Carlson, M. A. (1993). *Theories of the Theatre: A Historical and Critical Survey from the Greeks to the Present*. Cornell University Press.

Carr, S. C. (2003). *Social Psychology: Context, Communication and Culture*. Wiley.

Catchpole, J. (2022). Acting out neurodiversity. *The Lancet Psychiatry, 9*(7), 545–546. https://doi.org/10.1016/S2215-0366(22)00109-2

Chapman, R., & Carel, H. (2022). Neurodiversity, epistemic injustice, and the good human life. *Journal of Social Philosophy, 53*(4), 614–631. https://doi.org/10.1111/josp.12456

Cook, J., Hull, L., Crane, L., & Mandy, W. (2021). Camouflaging in autism: A systematic review. *Clinical Psychology Review, 89*, 102080. https://doi.org/10.1016/j.cpr.2021.102080

Corrigan, P. W., Watson, A. C., & Barr, L. (2006). The self-stigma of mental illness: Implications for self-esteem and self-efficacy. *Journal of Social and Clinical Psychology, 25*(8), 875–884. https://doi.org/10.1521/jscp.2006.25.8.875

Crick, O., & Rudlin, J. (2002). *Commedia dell’arte: A Handbook for Troupes*. Routledge.

Crompton, C. J., DeBrabander, K., Heasman, B., Milton, D., & Sasson, N. J. (2021). Double empathy: why autistic people are often misunderstood. *Neuroscience, 9*(554875), 4–11. https://doi.org/10.3389/frym.2021.554875

Dallman, A. R., Bailliard, A., & Harrop, C. (2022). Identifying predictors of momentary negative affect and depression severity in adolescents with autism: An exploratory ecological momentary assessment study. *Journal of Autism and Developmental Disorders, 52*, 291–303. https://doi.org/10.1007/s10803-021-04935-8

DeBrabander, K. M., Morrison, K. E., Jones, D. R., Faso, D. J., Chmielewski, M., & Sasson, N. J. (2019). Do first impressions of autistic adults differ between autistic and nonautistic observers? *Autism in Adulthood, 1*(4), 250–257. https://doi.org/10.1089/aut.2019.0018

Department for Education (2018/2022). *Early Years Foundation Stage Profile Handbook*. Department for Education.

Du Bois W. E. B. (1999). *The Souls of Black Folk*. H. L. Gates, & T. H. Oliver (Eds.). Norton Critical Editions (Original work published 1903).

Engelberts, M. (2004). ‘Alive and Present’: Theatresports and Contemporary Live Performance. *Theatre Research International, 29*(2), 155–173. https://doi.org/10.1017/S0307883304000306

Fehr, E., & Schurtenberger, I. (2018). Normative foundations of human cooperation. *Nature Human Behaviour, 2*(7), 458–468. https://doi.org/10.1038/s41562-018-0385-5

Fein, E. (2015). Making meaningful worlds: Role-playing subcultures and the autism spectrum. *Culture, Medicine, and Psychiatry, 39*, 299–321. https://doi.org/10.1007/s11013-015-9443-x

Finke, E. H., McCarthy, J. H., & Sarver, N. A. (2019). Self-perception of friendship style: Young adults with and without autism spectrum disorder. *Autism & Developmental Language Impairments, 4*, 2396941519855390. https://doi.org/10.1177/2396941519855390

Fletcher-Watson, B., & May, S. (2018). Enhancing relaxed performance: Evaluating the Autism Arts Festival. In C. Conroy, A. Ong, & D. J. Rodricks, *On Access in Applied Theatre and Drama Education*, (pp. 72-86). Routledge.

Fortier, B. (2010). *Long-form Improvisation: Collaboration, Comedy and Communion*. LAP LAMBERT Academic Publishing.

Fox, K. (2018). Standing up to false binaries in humour and autism: A dialogue. In H. Davies, & S. Ilott, *Comedy and The Politics of Representation: Mocking the Weak*, (pp. 171–188). Palgrave Macmillan.

Frost, A., & Yarrow, R. (2007). *Improvisation in Drama.* Palgrave Macmillan.

Fuld, S. (2018). Autism spectrum disorder: The impact of stressful and traumatic life events and implications for clinical practice. *Clinical Social Work Journal, 46*(3), 210–219. https://doi.org/10.1007/s10615-018-0649-6

Goffman, E. (1961/1968). *Asylums: Essays on the Social Situation of Mental Patients and Other Inmates.* Aldine Transaction.

Goffman, E. (1963). *Stigma: Notes on the Management of Spoiled Identity.* Prentice-Hall.

Grainger, R. (2014). *Theatre and Encounter: The Psychology of the Dramatic Relationship.* Trafford Publishing.

Gruzelier, J. H. (2018). Enhancing creativity with neurofeedback in the performing arts: Actors, musicians, dancers. In S. Burgoyne (Ed.), *Creativity in Theatre: Theory and Action in Theatre/Drama Education,* (pp. 223–245). Springer.

Halpern, C. (2006). *Art by Committee: A Guide to Advanced Improvisation.* Meriwether Publishing.

Halpern, C., Close, D., & Johnson, K. H. (1994).. *Truth in Comedy: The Manual of Improvisation.* Meriwether Publishing.

Han, E., Scior, K., Avramides, K., & Crane, L. (2022). A systematic review on autistic people's experiences of stigma and coping strategies. *Autism Research, 15*(1), 12–26. https://doi.org/10.1002/aur.2652

Happé, F., & Frith, U. (2020). Annual Research Review: Looking back to look forward–changes in the concept of autism and implications for future research. *Journal of Child Psychology and Psychiatry, 61*(3), 218–232. https://doi.org/10.1111/jcpp.13176

Heasman, B., & Gillespie, A. (2019). Neurodivergent intersubjectivity: Distinctive features of how autistic people create shared understanding. *Autism, 23*(4), 910–921. https://doi.org/10.1177/1362361318785172

Hughes, J., & Wilson, K. (2004). Playing a part: the impact of youth theatre on young people's personal and social development. *Research in Drama Education, 9*(1), 57–72. https://doi.org/10.1080/1356978042000185911

Jellicoe, A. (1967). *Some Unconscious Influences in the Theatre.* CUP Archive.

Johnstone, K. (2012). *Impro: Improvisation and the Theatre.* Routledge.

Jordan, R. R. (2008). Practical implications of memory characteristics in autistic spectrum disorders. In J. Boucher, & D. Bowler (Eds.), *Memory in Autism: Theory and Evidence,* (pp. 293–310). Cambridge University Press.

Kaye, N. (2013). *Art into Theatre: Performance Interviews and Documents.* Routledge.

Keates, N., & Beadle-Brown, J. (2022). The benefits of participating in improvisational comedy: a global confirmatory survey study. *Comedy Studies, 13*(2), 161–174. https://doi.org/10.1080/2040610X.2022.2091719

Keates, N., & Beadle-Brown, J. (2023). Improvisers' experiences across neurotypes of participating in improv comedy. *Advances in Autism, 9*(3), 253–265. https://doi.org/10.1108/AIA-09-2022-0047

Keates, N., & Beadle-Brown, J. (under review). Theatrical improvisation and autistic people: A scoping review. University of Kent.

Keisalo, M. (2018). Perspectives of (and on) a comedic self: A semiotics of subjectivity in stand-up comedy. *Social Analysis, 62*(1), 116–135. https://doi.org/10.3167/sa.2018.620108

Kim, A. J., Stembridge, S., Lawrence, C., Torres, V., Miodrag, N., Lee, J., & Boynes, D. (2015). Neurodiversity on the stage: The effects of inclusive theatre on youth with autism. *International Journal of Education and Social Science, 2*(9), 27–39.

Kozlowski, R. (2002). *The Art of Chicago Improv: Short Cuts to Long-Form Improvisation.* Heinemann Drama.

Kuppers, P. (2017). *Theatre and disability.* Bloomsbury Publishing.

Lai, M. C., Kassee, C., Besney, R., Bonato, S., Hull, L., Mandy, W., Szatmari, P., & Ameis, S. H. (2019). Prevalence of co-occurring mental health diagnoses in the autism population: a systematic review and meta-analysis. *The Lancet Psychiatry, 6*(10), 819–829. https://doi.org/10.1016/S2215-0366(19)30289-5

Lefebvre, H., & Nicholson-Smith, D. [trans.] (1991). *The Production of Space.* Blackwell.

Lipsitz, G. (2007). The racialization of space and the spatialization of race: Theorizing the hidden architecture of landscape. *Landscape Journal, 26,* 10–23. https://doi.org/10.3368/lj.26.1.10

Lipsitz, G. (2011). *How Racism Takes Place.* Temple University Press.

MacRae, H. (1999). Managing courtesy stigma: the case of Alzheimer's disease. *Sociology of health & illness, 21*(1), 54–70. https://doi.org/10.1111/1467-9566.t01-1-00142

Magni, S. (2020). *Virtual Theatre of Neurodiversity: A Workbook for Educators, Facilitators and Performers with Disabilities* [Doctoral dissertation, Faculty of Environmental Studies in partial fulfillment of the requirements for the degree of Master in Environmental Studies, York University, Toronto].

Marrero, E. (2012). *Performing Neurodiversity: Musical Accommodation by and for an Adolescent with Autism*. The Florida State University.

Massa, A., DeNigris, D., & Gillespie-Lynch, K. (2020). Theatre as a tool to reduce autism stigma? Evaluating 'Beyond Spectrums'. *Research in Drama Education: The Journal of Applied Theatre and Performance, 25*(4), 613–630. https://doi.org/10.1080/13569783.2020.1732810

Maurer, C., Chambon, V., Bourgeois-Gironde, S., Leboyer, M., & Zalla, T. (2018). The influence of prior reputation and reciprocity on dynamic trust-building in adults with and without autism spectrum disorder. *Cognition, 172*, 1–10. https://doi.org/10.1016/j.cognition.2017.11.007

Milton, D. E. (2012). On the ontological status of autism: The 'double empathy problem'. *Disability & Society, 27*(6), 883–887. https://doi.org/10.1080/09687599.2012.710008

Milton, D. (2013). 'Filling in the gaps': A micro-sociological analysis of autism. *Autonomy, the Critical Journal of Interdisciplinary Autism Studies, 1*(2).

Milton, D. E., Waldock, K. E., & Keates, N. (2023). Autism and the 'double empathy problem'. In F. Mezzenzana, & D. Peluso, *Conversations on Empathy: Interdisciplinary Perspectives on Empathy, Imagination and Othering*, (pp. 78–97). Routledge.

Moore, I., Morgan, G., Welham, A., & Russell, G. (2022). The intersection of autism and gender in the negotiation of identity: A systematic review and metasynthesis. *Feminism & Psychology, 32*(4), 421–442. https://doi.org/10.1177/09593535221074806

Moreno, J. L. (1947). *The Theatre of Spontaneity*. Beacon House.

Morrison, K. E., DeBrabander, K. M., Jones, D. R., Faso, D. J., Ackerman, R. A., & Sasson, N. J. (2020). Outcomes of real-world social interaction for autistic adults paired with autistic compared to typically developing partners. *Autism, 24*(5), 1067–1080. https://doi.org/10.1177/1362361319892701

Owren, T. (2013). *Autreat and Autscape: Informing and Challenging the Neurotypical will and Ability to Include* [Masters dissertation]. University of Bergen, Norway.

Pearson, A., & Rose, K. (2021). A conceptual analysis of autistic masking: Understanding the narrative of stigma and the illusion of choice. *Autism in Adulthood, 3*(1), 52–60. https://doi.org/10.31219/osf.io/6rwa5

Peet, R. (2000). Culture, imaginary, and rationality in regional economic development. *Environment and Planning A, 32*(7), 1215–1234. https://doi.org/10.1068/a3250

Pritchard, E. J., de Lemos, C., Howard, K., & Gibson, J. L. (2023). Social play as a "double-edged sword": Exploring the experience of autistic play from the perspective of autistic adults. *Autism in Adulthood, 6*(2). https://doi.org/10.1089/aut.2023.0008

Ryan, C., Coughlan, M., Maher, J., Vicario, P., & Garvey, A. (2021). Perceptions of friendship among girls with Autism Spectrum Disorders. *European Journal of Special Needs Education, 36*(3), 393–407. https://doi.org/10.1080/08856257.2020.1755930

Sasson, N. J., Faso, D. J., Nugent, J., Lovell, S., Kennedy, D. P., & Grossman, R. B. (2017). Neurotypical peers are less willing to interact with those with autism based on thin slice judgments. *Scientific Reports, 7*(1), 1–10. https://doi.org/10.1038/srep40700

Sawyer, K. R. (1993). The pragmatics of play: Interactional strategies during children's pretend play. *Pragmatics. Quarterly Publication of the International Pragmatics Association (IPrA), 3*(3), 259–282. https://doi.org/10.1075/prag.3.3.01saw

Scambler, G. (2006). Sociology, social structure and health-related stigma. *Psychology, Health & Medicine, 11*(3), 288–295. https://doi.org/10.1080/13548500600595103

Scambler, G. (2009). Health-related stigma. *Sociology of Health & Illness, 31*(3), 441–455. https://doi.org/10.1111/j.1467-9566.2009.01161.x

Schechner, R., & Appel, W. (Eds.). (1990). *By Means of Performance: Intercultural Studies of Theatre and Ritual*. Cambridge University Press.

Scheerer, N. E., Boucher, T. Q., Sasson, N. J., & Iarocci, G. (2022). Effects of an educational presentation about autism on high school students' perceptions of autistic adults. *Autism in Adulthood, 4*(3), 203–213. https://doi.org/10.1089/aut.2021.0046

Sharma, S. (2014). Appraisal, coping and negative affect: Comparative evaluation between typically developing and children with high-functioning autism. *Journal of Psychology and Psychotherapy, 4*(6), 1–7. https://doi.org/10.4172/2161-0487.1000165

Sosnowy, C., Silverman, C., Shattuck, P., & Garfield, T. (2019). Setbacks and successes: How young adults on the autism spectrum seek friendship. *Autism in Adulthood, 1*(1), 44–51. https://doi.org/10.1089/aut.2018.0009

Turner, V. W. (1967). Betwixt and between: The liminal period in Rites de passage. In V. Turner (Ed.), *The Forest of Symbols: Aspects of Ndembu Ritual* (pp. 93–111). Cornell University Press.

Turner, V. W. (1969). *The Ritual Process: Structure and Anti-Structure*. Routledge & Kegan Paul.

Turner, V. (1977). Variations on a theme of liminality. In S.F. Moore & B. Myerhoff (Eds.), *Secular Ritual*, (pp. 36–52). Van Gorcum.

Walmsley, B. (2013). "A big part of my life": A qualitative study of the impact of theatre. *Arts Marketing: An International Journal, 3*(1), 73–87. https://doi.org/10.1108/20442081311327174

Wartemann, G. (2009). Theatre as interplay: Processes of collective creativity in theatre for young audiences. *Youth Theatre Journal, 23*(1), 6–14. https://doi.org/10.1080/08929090902851528

Whitfield, P. (2019). *Teaching Strategies for Neurodiversity and Dyslexia in Actor Training: Sensing Shakespeare*. Routledge.

Wood, R. (2019). *Inclusive Education for Autistic Children: Helping Children and Young People to Learn and Flourish in the Classroom*. Jessica Kingsley Publishers.

Wood, R. (2021). Autism, intense interests and support in school: From wasted efforts to shared understandings. *Educational Review, 73*(1), 34–54. https://doi.org/10.1080/00131911.2019.1566213

Wood, R., & Happé, F. (2023). What are the views and experiences of autistic teachers? Findings from an online survey in the UK. *Disability & Society, 38*(1), 47–72. https://doi.org/10.1080/09687599.2021.1916888

Wunder, A. (2007, April 12–14). *Positive Feedback: A Model for Developing Creative Improvisers* [Conference Presentation]. Improvisation Continuums: Theorising Practice Across Disciplines, Cardiff, Wales, United Kingdom. https://mmd.research.southwales.ac.uk/news-and-events/events/improvisation-continuums-theorising-practice-across-disciplines/

Yergeau, M. R. (2018). *Authoring Autism: On Rhetoric and Neurological Queerness*. Duke University Press.

Zhang, Z. (2006). What is lived space. *Ephemera, 6*(2), 219–223.

Chapter 28:

Autistic Self-Advocacy: Understanding the Complexities

Emine Gurbuz and Siva priya Santhanam[47]

Maya is an undergraduate student in Chemistry; she is bright, curious and loves to learn. She always participates in all activities in class and asks engaging questions. Maya finds participating and learning in Chemistry lab-based activities quite challenging. Despite Maya's sincere efforts to learn, Maya's professor finds Maya rather rude and disruptive during the lab. Maya is autistic; her professor is not. The professor struggles to recognize if Maya follows directions in the lab and whether she is paying attention during the class. The professor is unable to interpret Maya's facial expressions. The professor also struggles to understand Maya's intonation in speech; she complains that Maya speaks in a monotone. The professor complains that Maya responds to questions in a single word often and does not provide elaborations. For these reasons, the professor perceives Maya to be rude and discourteous. Maya finds lab activities to be fast-paced, but she generally likes the professor and enjoys Chemistry class.

In this scenario, there is a miscommunication between the professor and Maya. The professor wants to support Maya and Maya wants to earn good grades in her class. They both mean well. The professor perceives Maya to be rude although Maya does not intend to, and keeping up with the pace of the lab activities is challenging for Maya. It is likely that Maya struggles to understand the professor's facial expressions and intonation of speech. Maya, like many other autistic individuals, uses fewer inflections in her speech. Maya does not use exaggerated facial expressions while speaking. According to Maya, she

47 Both authors contributed equally to this chapter.

smiles when needed and has a steady facial expression at other times. Maya also chooses to respond in single words in situations where she thinks elaborations are unnecessary. Maya prefers writing over speaking.

Non-autistic people, like Maya's professor, often find it challenging to understand and interpret autistic communication differences. Non-autistic communication conventions and styles are quite different from autistic communication and sociality, which sometimes creates misunderstandings between autistic and non-autistic people (Milton et al., 2023). Enhancing mutual understanding in communication can be achieved by expressing one's interaction style and preferences, a task that involves the cultivation of effective self-advocacy skills. In this chapter, we discuss self-advocacy as it relates to double empathy. In addition, we discuss the complexities associated with self-advocacy and elaborate on barriers to autistic self-advocacy.

Autistic self-advocacy and the Double Empathy Problem

The Double Empathy Problem means communication breakdown between two partners with different interaction/communication styles and preferences (Milton et al., 2022). The Double Empathy Problem may often be observed in interactions between autistic and non-autistic people. Autistic individuals who use speech as their primary modality of communication, display social communication differences. They may demonstrate differences in gestural communication (De Marchena et al., 2019) such as a difference in direct eye gaze (Ma et al., 2021). Autistic individuals may prefer alternate modalities of communication, such as emails and texting, over using the phone (Howard & Sedgewick, 2021). Similarly, in a study conducted by Rifai et al. (2022), autistic individuals used backchanneling (e.g., saying 'mmh' to show acknowledgement) and looking at each other during a conversation differently when compared to non-autistic peers. These communication differences make interactions between autistic and non-autistic peers challenging because non-autistic people rely heavily on eye contact; they have difficulties interpreting autistic people's mental states and facial expressions (Edey et al., 2016; Sheppard et al., 2016), and overestimate autistic egocentricity (the condition of thinking only about yourself and what is good for you) (Heasman & Gillespie, 2018).

While miscommunication and misunderstandings are common between speaking autistic and non-autistic peers (Crompton et al., 2021), about 25–30% of autistic individuals do not use speech to communicate; they identify as minimally speaking or semi-speaking (Tager-Flusberg & Kasari, 2013). This alternate communication choice among many autistic people can pose a bigger challenge for non-autistic communication partners, who are typically not familiar with non-speech communication modalities. The absence of a shared communication modality (speech in this situation), makes it difficult for many non-autistic individuals to understand the autistic person's expressed needs and preferences. A study conducted by Kim and Gillespie-Lynch (2023) comparing stigma toward autistic individuals in the US and South Korea, found that in the South Korean group, a non-autistic person's stigma toward a non-speaking autistic character with high support needs was heightened when compared to a non-speaking character with low support needs. There were no differences in the US group in terms of stigma towards a non-speaking autistic character with low versus high support needs.

One way to bridge the gap in social communication and increase mutual understanding is through self-advocacy. Self-advocacy is crucial to accomplish the goal of increasing knowledge, understanding and acceptance of autistic communication differences among non-autistic communication partners. By advocating for their own needs and preferences and explaining their communication styles, autistic individuals aim to foster better communication and mutual understanding with non-autistic individuals. However, one needs an environment that supports self-advocacy. Not all autistic individuals are strong self-advocates, and that is not because they cannot be one, but because they do not have the environmental support to be one (Santhanam & Bellon-Harn, 2022). In the next section, we describe self-advocacy and how it benefits autistic people. Subsequently, we discuss factors that may make some autistic individuals more equipped for self-advocacy than others.

What is self-advocacy?

Self-advocacy is defined as the ability to assert one's needs, wants and rights, make informed decisions about the supports needed and pursue them (Field et al., 1998; Martin & Marshall, 1995). It is the ability to 'speak up' for one's wants and needs, as well as for others (Ryan & Griffiths, 2015). According to Test et al. (2005), the three elements of self-advocacy are: knowledge of self and rights, communication and leadership. This framework of self-advocacy can be applied to the life of an autistic individual. Within the context of an autistic person's life, the self-advocacy framework translates to: (i) awareness and recognition of social, communication, learning and sensory preferences, strengths and needs; (ii) the ability to communicate about these differences to non-autistic peers and professionals and to seek out needed supports; and (iii) the willingness and ability to advocate for autistic peers who share similar life experiences (Santhanam & Bellon-Harn, 2022).

Describing self-advocacy solely as the capacity to 'speak up' might be limiting, as it suggests that self-advocacy is confined to expressing desires and requirements through verbal communication alone. Mel Baggs, a disabled writer and activist, emphasizes that self-advocacy is also about communicating what one does *not* want, and not only with words, but also through actions (Baggs, 2012). Baggs contends that when an autistic child rejects instructions and, in response to being disregarded, resorts to biting the staff, the child asserts self-advocacy. Baggs also emphasizes that non-compliance, communicating 'against' as well as 'for', should be considered when thinking about self-advocacy. The ability to say 'no', either through words or alternate means of communication, is an important part of self-advocacy. Self-advocacy doesn't have to conform to status-quo-preserving standards; it can be disorderly as a means to challenge the entrenched power imbalances and inequalities between disabled individuals and those who are not disabled.

A strong self-advocate recognizes their own strengths and challenges, and believes in their ability to achieve their chosen goals. They communicate these strengths and challenges to others while asserting their preferences and the supports they need to overcome challenges. They engage in collaborative negotiation and problem-solving to meet their goals. Ultimately, a strong self-advocate is an ally; they advocate not just for themselves but also for others who face similar challenges, thereby contributing to collective advocacy.

The focus on self-advocacy within the autistic community is rather recent with the advent of the Autistic Self-Advocacy Network (ASAN) and the association of self-advocacy with the neurodiversity movement (Cook & Purkis, 2022). Professionals, including educators and clinical service providers, have begun showing an increased interest in supporting autistic self-advocacy in recent years (Santhanam & Bellon-Harn, 2022). Participatory approaches to intervention are emerging and children are being involved as active members of their Individualized Education Plans (IEPs) within the US (Macleod et al., 2017) to make decisions regarding their clinical goals and outcomes.

How is self-advocacy related to self-determination?

Self-advocacy is part of a broader construct of self-determination; self-determined individuals consistently advocate for themselves. Wehmeyer defines self-determination as '*the attitudes and abilities required to act as the primary causal agent in one's life and to make choices regarding one's actions free from undue external influence or interference*' (Wehmeyer, 1992, p. 305). Wehmeyer provides a non-exhaustive list of indicators of self-determination, which includes attributes such as '*choice-making, decision-making, problem-solving, goal-setting and attainment, self-observation, evaluation and reinforcement, an internal locus of control, positive attributions of efficacy and outcome expectancy, self-awareness, self-knowledge and self-advocacy*' (Wehmeyer, 1992, p. 4). Self-determined individuals exercise personal autonomy; they influence their life circumstances through goal-directed action. Self-determination is a predictor of a disabled person's overall quality of life (Shogren et al., 2015).

How is self-advocacy beneficial to the autistic individual?

Self-advocacy is an important skill for disabled people at large, as it empowers them to actively participate in decisions that affect their life, communicate their needs and preferences, and promote inclusion. Self-advocacy skills are associated with an increased perception of social support in the environment, greater academic self-efficacy (Gillespie-Lynch et al., 2017), improved skills for seeking accommodation in college settings (White et al., 2014), an enhanced ability to overcome barriers and challenge oppression in work settings (Skelton & Moore, 1999), and improved future outcomes such as a greater likelihood of continuing higher education, employment and independent living (Zhang et al., 2019). In a study conducted by Mineur et al. (2017), participating in a self-advocacy group contributed to a positive sense of self and identity for students with intellectual disabilities.

Self-advocacy has implications for clinical interventions with autistic people such that any attempt to 'cure' or 'normalize' the autistic individual or autistic traits is problematic (Leadbitter et al., 2021). Instead, the interventions should focus on improving 'the goodness of fit' between the autistic individual and their environment, together with promoting an understanding of autism/autistic experience and neurodiversity in society. Meaningful involvement of autistic people in clinical assessments and developing interventions/supports for autistic, as well as non-autistic, members of our society, can help achieve mutual understanding and address the Double Empathy Problem.

Self-advocacy is also important to fight stigma and misconceptions of autism, which contribute to the Double Empathy Problem occurring in the first place. By advocating for their needs and preferences, autistic people not only promote mutual understanding between themselves and non-autistic partners, but also change the perceptions of the non-autistic community about autism and autistic people. Self advocacy, therefore, can be seen as a 'response' to stigma toward autism and one way to eliminate the Double Empathy Problem between autistic and non-autistic people (Han et al., 2022). Given the diversity of experiences within the autistic community, more autistic people advocating for themselves would mean more awareness, normalization and acceptance of neurodiversity in society. Previous research has shown that learning about autism from social media and blogs written by autistic people compared to learning from professionals and parents is more likely to reduce internalized stigma, as well as encouraging autism identity (Bury et al., 2022). This suggests that self-advocates have an important role in reducing stigma about autism and autistic experience.

While several benefits to self-advocacy have been reported and emphasized among autistic and other disabled communities, little attention has been given to understanding various environmental factors that make self-advocacy challenging for some autistic individuals. In the subsequent section, we elaborate on several issues that hinder autistic self-advocacy.

Issues in self-advocacy

The autistic person as the target of self-advocacy interventions

To a large extent, research on self-advocacy and clinical interventions to promote self-advocacy have targeted the autistic individual with little or no attention to environmental factors that may facilitate or hinder self-advocacy (Santhanam & Bellon-Harn, 2022). Even among other non-autistic disabled individuals, self-advocacy has gained significant attention as an outcome of intervention (Dryden et al., 2017; Schena et al., 2022; Zhang et al., 2019). According to Test et al. (2005), disabled individuals, irrespective of their age or type of disability, can be taught self-advocacy skills. While some training is more rigorous than others, these interventions hardly involve disabled individuals in designing their own intervention plan and/or determining if the outcome of the intervention was personally meaningful to them. Designing self-advocacy goals for autistic people without their involvement is problematic. As Baggs (2012) described in their blog, it is common for everyone, except the autistic individual, to assume what is effective or suitable for them. These assumptions extend to passing judgement on how an autistic person advocates for themselves, deeming them as incorrect and/or inappropriate. When self-advocacy is consistently shaped by the societal norms and perspectives of non-disabled individuals who lack an understanding of the disabled person's life, it reflects a fundamental lack of respect for the autonomy of the disabled individual.

In prior reviews of studies that examine promotion of self-advocacy through intervention or instruction (Test et al., 2005; Roberts et al., 2016; Schena et al., 2022), there has been no mention of the use of participatory approaches. A participatory approach is one in which everyone who has a stake in the intervention participates in the planning, the process and the outcome of intervention (e.g., Leadbitter et al., 2021). Most interventions for self-advocacy are designed by a non-disabled team or are designed by teams whose identities are not disclosed in the published literature. Despite the nature of this training, it shares a commonality in establishing a predetermined set of self-advocacy and/or self-determination skills that are 'taught' to autistic individuals either directly through a coaching model using workshops and a curriculum (e.g., Martin et al., 2006; Rothman et al., 2008; Wehmeyer et al., 2011) or indirectly through participation in support groups (Gilmartin & Slevin, 2010). This type of intervention directed at autistic individuals runs the risk of aligning with the medical model of disability (Heidgerken et al., 2005), which most autistic self-advocates and allies of autistic individuals have been attempting to move away from. Self-advocacy interventions claim to be aligned with the values/principles of the neurodiversity movement in supporting autistic agency and autonomy (Cook & Purkis, 2022). However, much like other interventions that focus on teaching 'non-autistic skills' to autistic persons, self-advocacy interventions run the risk of imposing pre-established expectations and norms of self-advocacy on autistic individuals, especially norms established by non-autistic individuals. In a study by Andrews et al. (2023), higher autistic traits were associated with lower quality of life for autistic adults, and this relationship was partly associated with challenges in self-determination. In other words, fewer autistic traits are associated with better abilities in self-determination and thereby better quality of life. Findings of this nature are important when considering the need for more self-determination supports for autistic individuals. However, the study also reinforces the belief that the ability, or the lack of ability, to be self-determined lies within the autistic individual, implying that failure to develop self-determination skills would lead to negative outcomes for the autistic individual (Bruce & Aylward, 2021).

Disclosure vulnerability

Disclosure and self-advocacy regarding disability-related needs may make disabled individuals vulnerable to misperceptions and negative impressions. Disabled individuals may encounter negative reactions to disclosure or be perceived as increasingly demanding, defensive and difficult, thereby exacerbating their vulnerability (Turnock et al., 2022). Autistic people have to take the risk of being judged by others every time they decide to advocate for themselves or others (Cox et al., 2017). This might also explain why autistic people have to form strategies and engage in selective disclosures (e.g., selecting whom to disclose their autism). For example, according to a scoping review of research on the perceptions and outcomes of disclosure of autism, autistic people are hesitant to disclose due to concerns about negative judgement, discrimination and stigma (Thompson-Hodgetts et al., 2020). They disclose their autistic identity to receive support as they require a diagnosis. Some are concerned about being treated differently once they disclose as others might focus on the diagnosis rather than the person behind it in their interactions (Macleod et al., 2018). On the other hand, some studies showed that disclosing to others might lead to positive outcomes for autistic people (e.g., in employment, higher education, jury service), especially when more information about autism/autistic experience was provided (Blackhurst et al., 2022; Norris et al., 2023). Nevertheless, these findings are not conclusive because improved self-reported attributes toward autism might not be followed by changes in the actual behaviour of others (Heasman & Gillespie, 2019).

Parental advocacy

Most autistic people are diagnosed when they are children. Therefore, parents of disabled individuals, including those on the autism spectrum, provide greater support for their children than parents of non-disabled children and parents have a crucial role as advocates for their autistic children (Rottier & Gernsbacher, 2020). However, non-autistic parents may not always understand the experiences and needs of their autistic child, and the priorities and interests of non-autistic parents and their autistic children may not align (Waddington et al., 2023). Moreover, becoming a parent advocate requires multiple resources (e.g., time, money, knowledge, service availability) and skills (e.g., raising awareness, expressing concern), which may not be available to all parents (Smith-Young et al., 2022). It is important for non-autistic parents and autistic adults to come together and learn from each other and collaborate with the aim of changing policy and support practices for autistic children and adults.

Parental advocacy is even more pronounced among non-speaking autistic children and adults (Chen, 2022). Parents may often assume that they can speak for and about their autistic child, providing fewer opportunities for the child to assert their preferences or needs. Some autistic advocates do not think parents should be the default voice of their autistic child (Bethany, 2022). For example, one the one hand, some non-autistic parents see their autistic kids as too 'impaired' and do not consider their opinions as worthy of value (Rosa, 2018). They are criticized for being focused on 'fixing' their child rather than understanding their rights and needs. On the other hand, other non-autistic parents think speaking autistic advocates do not represent the needs of non-speaking autistic people and they do not understand what it means to be a parent of a non-speaking autistic child. Autistic parents of autistic children might be particularly helpful as advocates of the same neurotype who share the understanding and challenges of their children, making it easier to relate and communicate about their child (Bethany, 2022). These complexities in parental advocacy are an important factor in shaping an autistic person's pathway to self-advocacy.

Professional advocacy

Professional attitudes toward autistic individuals continue to be largely aligned with the medical model (Heidgerken et al., 2005) with an important but small-scale attitudinal shift happening among service providers, including speech-language therapists, psychologists, educators, physicians and others. To a large extent, autistic characteristics are seen as undesirable and in need of modification to mimic non-autistic norms, and both children and adults on the autism spectrum are frequently left out of conversations that centre their life decisions (Fletcher-Watson et al., 2019). Another barrier to self-advocacy lies in situations when professionals, including speech and language therapists, act as gatekeepers to communication access for individuals on the autism spectrum who may be minimally speaking (Zimmerman, 2022). In a study conducted by Donaldson et al. (2021), alternate communication access was not offered to children on the autism spectrum because they produced some speech output. The addition of an aided communication system might have been beneficial to these children, but professionals valued speech output more than alternate modalities of communication, restricting the children's overall sense of agency. We need to acknowledge that access to communication is a human right (Zimmerman, 2022), and that speech is not the only modality of communication. The heightened focus on speech output (Zisk & Dalton, 2019) takes away access to alternative modalities of communication, thereby limiting the person's ability to self-advocate and exercise their communication right, choice and agency.

Lack of opportunities to practice self-advocacy is another barrier. Autistic children often lack models of self-advocates and opportunities to practice or apply knowledge of self-awareness, and leadership skills are rarely available to children on the autism spectrum within the school setting (Roberts et al., 2016; Santhanam & Bellon-Harn, 2022). Roberts et al. (2016) and Santhanam and Bellon-Harn (2022) recommend that service providers intentionally incorporate opportunities to practice self-advocacy through IEP participation, advocacy through writing, self-advocacy support groups and systematic self-assessment of self-advocacy skills.

Last, professionals may be challenged by the lack of resources available to assess self-advocacy skills in students on the autism spectrum. Potential assessment measures include Shogren et al.'s (2015) self-determination inventory, which includes both self-reported and parent-reported versions. The inventories provide a detailed assessment report that can be utilized by teachers and clinicians. For example, Santhanam and Bellon-Harn (2022) provide the self-advocacy questionnaire adapted for use with autistic adults using a participatory approach.

Economic barriers to self-advocacy

Financial resources are important influencers of self-advocacy. Economic barriers bring another roadblock to self-advocacy, especially when advocacy extends to the entire disabled community. People who identify as self-advocates and become activists, often invest a significant amount of unpaid time toward advocacy initiatives and ongoing advocacy-based efforts. According to Petri et al. (2021), autistic and intellectually disabled individuals face economic challenges in advocating for themselves. Poverty, unpaid positions and limited access to resources hinders self-advocacy, especially within disability movements and disabled peoples' organizations that are still largely controlled by parents and professionals who do not identify as disabled (Petri et al., 2020). Additionally, autistic people, and those with intellectual disabilities, continue to be involved in a tokenistic way in these organizations (Petri et al., 2017).

Within advocacy-based organizations, self-advocates often need to rely on their personal resources to cover the costs associated with their advocacy work, including transportation, communication and other related expenses. While some advocacy organizations may offer paid positions, the availability of such roles is often limited. Many self-advocates engage in grassroots advocacy efforts or volunteer positions, which may not provide monetary compensation. This situation compels them to use their personal time and resources to participate in advocacy activities while juggling other responsibilities. In addition, serving in a self-advocacy role may increase the likelihood of being discriminated against, thereby losing employment or opportunities for employment for many disabled self-advocates.

More recently, self-advocates have volunteered their time and worked at an individual level through platforms such as social media and community presentations; they are not part of organizations. These individual-level roles pinch on personal time and resources.

Cultural differences in self-advocacy

Self-advocacy and self-determination are rooted within individualistic ideologies (Podlucká, 2020) that align with a Western and urban mindset. Our knowledge of autistic self-advocacy mostly comes from a Western context, mainly the US and the UK, and therefore, reflects and addresses the sociocultural and political circumstances and concerns of these countries (Cheng et al., 2023). Narratives of autistic self-advocacy are largely prevalent in the Western, educated, industrialized, rich and democratic (WEIRD) communities. Autistic self-advocates, several of whom are advocates of the neurodiversity movement, also identify as cisgender-male, White and English-speaking. We do not know much about existing practices and resources for self-advocacy among racially/ethnically diverse autistic individuals, and we know less about self-advocacy practices in non-Western populations, especially the Global South. We are unaware of what self-advocacy looks like in these communities and what underlying reasons contribute to the lack of need for self-advocacy in some cultures. Given the universality of the values associated with the neurodiversity paradigm and self-advocacy such as equality, dignity and respect for all people, one would assume that autistic people in non-Western countries are also engaged in self-advocacy. However, the need for self-advocacy can be shaped by community priorities and sociopolitical and family-level differences.

Globally, self-advocacy may be perceived differently by different communities depending on cultural underpinnings and cultural expectations. Hierarchical communities may not place as heightened a value on self-advocacy as individualistic cultures do. In non-Western cultures, self-advocacy may not be appreciated as an essential life skill because very early on in their life, people are taught and expected to be humble and grateful with what they have. They are not expected to, or even allowed to, speak up for themselves (Vannavuth, 2016). Members of the family in a hierarchical position, often the father or the grandfather, hold the right to make important decisions about their child's life irrespective of whether the child is disabled or not. This may be more true of disabled individuals who are often taught interdependence, relationship-building and collective well-being as opposed to achieving independence or acquiring attributes for independent living (Podlucká, 2020). Therefore, when disabled individuals advocate for themselves or others, they might be perceived as an anomaly to social conformity and familial expectations. While there are issues associated with patriarchal familial structures and the inherent ableism within these structures (Cherney, 2011), the focus on building a support system for the autistic child lies at the core of their cultural values. As a result, parents of autistic and other disabled children in non-Western cultures, may be the earliest and most important allies for their children.

Another cultural factor that may influence self-advocacy is the existing disparity in access to services and supports. Prior research suggests that racial and ethnic minorities advocate less for themselves in health care settings in the US. For example, Black and Hispanic individuals were less likely to ask their doctors for lower cost medications than White individuals, even when controlling for socioeconomic factors (Delavar et al., 2023). Contributing factors could be poor patient–provider communication, lack of understanding and awareness of the conditions to advocate for, and lack of support/training for self-advocacy (Thomas et al., 2023). Moreover, as discussed earlier, inadequate financial resources might be another barrier to engaging in self-advocacy in families from marginalized cultural and linguistic backgrounds.

Other barriers to self-advocacy may include access to diagnosis/assessments, financial resources and class differences, and stigma associated with autism in non-Western cultures. Autistic people and their families might further restrict autistic communities from coming together and standing up for their rights in society (Cheng et al., 2023). Implementation of participatory, emancipatory research that is in line with the neurodiversity paradigm and social model of disability should be encouraged in non-Western countries and the research should consider all the barriers we discuss in this chapter in collaboration with local communities. More importantly, we need to pay attention to intersectionality and the need for an increased representation of autistic people's experiences from diverse cultural, linguistic and economic backgrounds.

Advocacy fatigue

Self-advocacy can be effortful. Advocacy fatigue is defined as '*the increased strain on emotional, physical, material, social, and wellness resources that comes from continued exposure to system inequities and inequalities*' (Basas, 2015, p. 39). People of marginalized identities are likely to experience advocacy fatigue due to being represented less (Strolovitch, 2006). Several factors may contribute to increased exhaustion associated with advocating for oneself. First, most disabled individuals are marginalized in society (e.g., Pillai & Janardhanan, 2021), and they may be relentlessly fighting for their rights; they may face stigma, discrimination and systemic barriers that impact several aspects of their daily living (e.g., Emerson et al., 2009). Constant advocacy and combating with slow-moving systems of change can lead to emotional exhaustion and a sense of hopelessness among disabled individuals, which might subsequently lead to burnout (Raymaker et al., 2020). Tangible outcomes take time. Therefore, disabled individuals may feel disillusioned and may question the possibility of seeing meaningful change.

It is hard to feel part of a community or a collective when you are over-reliant on individual identity and self-advocacy at the individual level. For example, in higher education, the student has to have individual skill and desired independence to engage in required acts of self-advocacy as part of the accommodation processes (Bruce & Aylward, 2021). This means the burden to ensure inclusive practices at university is placed on the student. Second, self-advocacy often requires sharing of highly personal life experiences with others, some of which may be trauma-inducing. Continuously reliving these experiences in order to raise awareness and enact change can lead to emotional fatigue and burnout. Another contributing factor to advocacy fatigue could be the presence of intersectional identities. An autistic person from a racially/ethnically marginalized community is likely to experience compounded challenges and discrimination due to the intersection of their identities as they are often required to navigate complex power dynamics and systemic inequalities simultaneously (Botha & Gillespie-Lynch, 2022; Jones, 2023). Therefore, even though advocacy of autistic people with intersectional identities is crucial as their experiences might be different to others, they may also be at higher risk for mental exhaustion and burnout.

The need for allyship

Considering the highly complex nature of self-advocacy, we suggest allyship as a potential mechanism to address existing issues and barriers. Allyship redistributes the task of self-advocacy from the autistic individual to those who actively support and advocate on their behalf. Allyship entails a shared commitment, wherein allies assume some of the emotional load and responsibility associated with self-advocacy and lighten the effort for autistic individuals. An ally is someone who advocates for and supports the rights, dignity and well-being of autistic individuals. An ally recognizes, empathizes and takes action in addressing the everyday challenges faced by autistic individuals by working collaboratively to create inclusive and safe environments. Allies can and do speak up against discrimination related to autistic individuals; they educate themselves and others about existing barriers and roadblocks to autistic well-being; they promote cross-neurotype understanding and appreciation of communication differences, and they actively contribute to system-level policy changes.

Allyship can happen within families; service providers and educators can be allies. Friends, coworkers and community members can also serve as allies of autistic individuals. We need to teach allyship to non-autistic people instead of, or in addition to, teaching advocacy to the autistic person. We can shift the focus from intervention for improving self-advocacy of autistic individuals to intervention for non-autistic people on allyship models (Gensic & Brunton, 2022). Initiatives that educate the non-autistic community about allyship are also in line with the Double Empathy Problem in autism.

Conclusion

In this chapter, we discuss self-advocacy as a response to the Double Empathy Problem in autism and the complexities of being an autistic self-advocate. Our core argument is to lift the burden of self-advocacy from the autistic person, especially given all the barriers and the emotional cost of self-advocacy, to addressing barriers in the environment that are likely to make self-advocacy challenging and present it as the only way forward. By prioritizing self-advocacy as the outcome of intervention that solely places the autistic individual as responsible for achieving the outcome, we continue to uphold deficit-focused approaches and reinforce ableist perspectives. We argue that autistic well-being requires communal work and the allyship of members within every autistic person's life. Genuine self-advocacy, as opposed to misguided impositions, is characterized by a commitment to respecting and listening to the experiences and voices of disabled individuals. It rejects the notion of controlling narratives or imposing restrictive conditions, emphasizing the importance of recognizing and valuing the diverse perspectives within the disabled community.

We need to closely examine existing barriers and question attitudes and models that promote individual-level independence and place the burden of self-advocacy on the autistic individual. Cultural expectations, hierarchical structures, familial roles and disparities in access to services contribute to varying perceptions and practices of self-advocacy globally. We may possess valuable insights to share and valuable lessons to glean from non-Western cultures and communities. We need culturally sensitive approaches that prioritize intersectionality, and acknowledge and appreciate various family- and community-level factors that influence self-advocacy. Our priority must shift to educating individuals who are not on the autism spectrum – parents, educators, service providers, coworkers and friends – about the complexities associated with autistic self-advocacy and the need for partnership and allyship with autistic individuals. Finally, we must move beyond understanding and acceptance, and *anticipate* differences and diversity in every part of society. Achieving these objectives could lead to a future where the *demand* for self-advocacy among autistic individuals decreases, thereby diminishing the risk of advocacy fatigue and burnout.

References

Andrews, H. E., Hedley, D., & Bury, S. M. (2023). The relationship between autistic traits and quality of life: Investigation of indirect effects through self-determination. *Autism in Adulthood, 6*(2). https://doi.org/10.1089/aut.2022.0117

Baggs, A. (2012). The meaning of self-advocacy. In J. Bascom (Ed.), *Loud Hands: Autistic People, Speaking,* (pp. 223–225). The Autistic Press.

Basas, C. G. (2015). Advocacy fatigue: Self-care, protest, and educational equity. *Windsor Yearbook of Access to Justice, 32*(2), 37.

Bethany, S. (2022, August 11). Who Speaks for Autistic Non-Speakers? https://www.stephaniebethany.com/blog/who-speaks-for-autistic-non-speakers

Blackhurst, T., Hartley, C., Turner, P., & Warmelink, L. (2022). Jurors' judgements of an autistic defendant are influenced by awareness of autism, knowledge of psychological conditions and trait-empathy. *Journal of Intellectual Disabilities and Offending Behaviour, 13*(3/4), 90–101. https://doi.org/10.1108/JIDOB-09-2022-0007

Botha, M., & Gillespie-Lynch, K. (2022). Come as you are: Examining autistic identity development and the neurodiversity movement through an intersectional lens. *Human Development, 66*(2), 93–112. https://doi.org/10.13140/RG.2.2.33966.02881

Bruce, C., & Aylward, M. L. (2021). Disability and self-advocacy experiences in university learning contexts. *Scandinavian Journal of Disability Research, 23*(1), 14–26. https://doi.org/10.16993/sjdr.741

Bury, S. M., Haschek, A., Wenzel, M., Spoor, J. R., & Hedley, D. (2022). Brief report: Learning about autism: Is the source of autism knowledge associated with differences in autism knowledge, autism identity, and experiences of stigma. *Journal of Autism and Developmental Disorders, 54,* 4346–4353. https://doi.org/10.1007/s10803-022-05823-5

Chen, R. S. Y. (2022). *Being Non-Speaking in a Speaking World: Surfacing the Improvisations of Autistic Individuals* (Order No. 30244514). Available from ProQuest Dissertations & Theses A&I; ProQuest Dissertations & Theses Global. (2884077197). https://www.proquest.com/dissertations-theses/being-non-speaking-world-surfacing-improvisations/docview/2884077197/se-2

Cheng, Y., Tekola, B., Balasubramanian, A., Crane, L., & Leadbitter, K. (2023). Neurodiversity and community-led rights-based movements: Barriers and opportunities for global research partnerships. *Autism, 27*(3), 573-577. https://doi.org/10.1177/13623613231159165

Cherney, J. L. (2011). The rhetoric of ableism. *Disability Studies Quarterly, 31*(3). https://doi.org/10.18061/dsq.v31i3.1665

Cook, B., & Purkis, Y. (2022). *The Autism and Neurodiversity Self Advocacy Handbook: Developing the Skills to Determine Your Own Future.* Jessica Kingsley Publishers.

Cox, B. E., Thompson, K., Anderson, A., Mintz, A., Locks, T., Morgan, L., Edelstein, J., & Wolz, A. (2017). College experiences for students with autism spectrum disorder: Personal identity, public disclosure, and institutional support. *Journal of College Student Development, 58*(1), 71–87. https://doi.org/10.1353/csd.2017.0004

Crompton, C. J., DeBrabander, K., Heasman, B., Milton, D., & Sasson, N. J. (2021). Double empathy: Why autistic people are often misunderstood. *Neuroscience, 9*(554875), 4–11. https://doi.org/10.3389/frym.2021.554875

De Marchena, A., Kim, E. S., Bagdasarov, A., Parish-Morris, J., Maddox, B. B., Brodkin, E. S., & Schultz, R. T. (2019). Atypicalities of gesture form and function in autistic adults. *Journal of Autism and Developmental Disorders, 49,* 1438–1454. https://doi.org/10.1007/s10803-018-3829-x

Delavar, A., Saseendrakumar, B. R., Weinreb, R. N., & Baxter, S. L. (2023). Medication affordability and self-advocacy among racial/ethnic minorities in a nationwide cohort. *Journal of General Internal Medicine, 38*(1), 249–251. https://doi.org/10.1007/s11606-022-07685-0

Donaldson, A. L., corbin, e., & McCoy, J. (2021). “Everyone deserves AAC”: Preliminary study of the experiences of speaking autistic adults who use augmentative and alternative communication. *Perspectives of the ASHA Special Interest Groups, 6*(2), 315–326. https://doi.org/10.1044/2021_PERSP-20-00220

Dryden, E. M., Desmarais, J., & Arsenault, L. (2017). Effectiveness of IMPACT: Ability to improve safety and self-advocacy skills in students with disabilities—Follow-up study. *Journal of School Health, 87*(2), 83–89. https://doi.org/10.1111/josh.12474

Edey, R., Cook, J., Brewer, R., Johnson, M. H., Bird, G., & Press, C. (2016). Interaction takes two: Typical adults exhibit mind-blindness towards those with autism spectrum disorder. *Journal of Abnormal Psychology, 125*(7), 879. https://doi.org/10.1037/abn0000199

Emerson, E., Madden, R., Robertson, J., Graham, H., Hatton, C., & Llewellyn, G. (2009). *Intellectual and Physical Disability, Social Mobility, Social Inclusion and Health: Background Paper for the Marmot Review.* Center for Disability Research (CeDR). http://eprints.lancs.ac.uk/26403/1/Disability_Social_Mobility_Social_Inclusion.pdf

Field, S., Martin, J., Miller, R., Ward, M., & Wehmeyer, M. (1998). Self-determination for persons with disabilities: A position statement of me division on career development and transition. *Career Development for Exceptional Individuals, 21*(2), 113–128. https://doi.org/10.1177/088572889802100202

Fletcher-Watson, S., Adams, J., Brook, K., Charman, T., Crane, L., Cusack, J., Leekam, S., Milton, D., Parr, J. R., & Pellicano, E. (2019). Making the future together: Shaping autism research through meaningful participation. *Autism, 23*(4), 943–953. https://doi.org/10.1177/1362361318786721

Gensic, J., & Brunton, J. (2022). *The #ActuallyAutistic Guide to Advocacy: Step-by-Step Advice on How to Ally and Speak Up with Autistic People and the Autism Community.* Jessica Kingsley Publishers.

Gillespie-Lynch, K., Bublitz, D., Donachie, A., Wong, V., Brooks, P. J., & D’Onofrio, J. (2017). “For a long time our voices have been hushed”: Using student perspectives to develop supports for neurodiverse college students. *Frontiers in Psychology, 8.* https://www.frontiersin.org/articles/10.3389/fpsyg.2017.00544

Gilmartin, A., & Slevin, E. (2010). Being a member of a self-advocacy group: Experiences of intellectually disabled people. *British Journal of Learning Disabilities, 38*(3), 152–159. https://doi.org/10.1111/j.1468-3156.2009.00564.x

Han, E., Scior, K., Avramides, K., & Crane, L. (2022). A systematic review on autistic people’s experiences of stigma and coping strategies. *Autism Research, 15*(1), 12–26. https://doi.org/10.1002/aur.2652

Heasman, B., & Gillespie, A. (2018). Perspective-taking is two-sided: Misunderstandings between people with Asperger's syndrome and their family members. *Autism, 22*(6), 740–750. https://doi.org/10.1177/1362361317708287

Heasman, B., & Gillespie, A. (2019). Participants over-estimate how helpful they are in a two-player game scenario toward an artificial confederate that discloses a diagnosis of autism. *Frontiers in Psychology, 10*, 1349. https://doi.org/10.3389/fpsyg.2019.01349

Heidgerken, A. D., Geffken, G., Modi, A., & Frakey, L. (2005). A survey of autism knowledge in a health care setting. *Journal of Autism and Developmental Disorders, 35*, 323–330. https://doi.org/10.1007/s10803-005-3298-x

Howard, P. L., & Sedgewick, F. (2021). 'Anything but the phone!': Communication mode preferences in the autism community. *Autism, 25*(8), 2265–2278. https://doi.org/10.1177/13623613211014995

Jones, D. R. (2023). *Intersectional Experiences of Stigma and Their Relation to Mental Health Outcomes Among Black and White Autistic Adults.* [Doctoral dissertation]. The University of Texas at Dallas.

Kim, S. Y., & Gillespie-Lynch, K. (2023). Do Autistic people's support needs and non-autistic people's support for the neurodiversity movement contribute to heightened autism stigma in South Korea vs. the US? *Journal of Autism and Developmental Disorders, 53*(11), 4199–4213. https://doi.org/10.1007/s10803-022-05739-0

Leadbitter, K., Buckle, K. L., Ellis, C., & Dekker, M. (2021). Autistic self-advocacy and the neurodiversity movement: Implications for autism early intervention research and practice. *Frontiers in Psychology, 12*, 782. https://doi.org/10.3389/fpsyg.2021.635690

Ma, X. E., Gu, H., & Zhao, J. (2021). Atypical gaze patterns to facial feature areas in autism spectrum disorders reveal age and culture effects: A meta-analysis of eye-tracking studies. *Autism Research, 14*(12), 2625–2639. https://doi.org/10.1002/aur.2607

MacLeod, K., Causton, J. N., Radel, M., & Radel, P. (2017). Rethinking the individualized education plan process: Voices from the other side of the table. *Disability & Society, 32*(3), 381–400. https://doi.org/10.1080/09687599.2017.1294048

MacLeod, A., Allan, J., Lewis, A., & Robertson, C. (2018). 'Here I come again': The cost of success for higher education students diagnosed with autism. *International Journal of Inclusive Education, 22* (6), 683–697. https://doi.org/10.1080/13603116.2017.1396502

Martin, J. E., & Marshall, L. H. (1995). ChoiceMaker: A comprehensive self-determination transition program. *Intervention in School and Clinic, 30*(3), 147–156. https://doi.org/10.1177/105345129503000304

Martin, J. E., Van Dycke, J. L., Christensen, W. R., Greene, B. A., Gardner, J. E., & Lovett, D. L. (2006). Increasing student participation in IEP meetings: Establishing the self-directed IEP as an evidenced-based practice. *Exceptional Children, 72*(3), 299–316. https://doi.org/10.1177/001440290607200303

Milton, D., Gurbuz, E., & López, B. (2022). The 'double empathy problem': Ten years on. *Autism, 26*(8), 1901–1903. https://doi.org/10.1177/13623613221129123

Milton, D. E., Waldock, K. E., & Keates, N. (2023). Autism and the 'double empathy problem'. In F. Mezzenzana, & D. M. Peluso (Eds.), *Conversations on Empathy: Interdisciplinary Perspectives on Empathy, Imagination and Othering*, (pp. 78–97). Routledge.

Mineur, T., Tideman, M., & Mallander, O. (2017). Self-advocacy in Sweden: An analysis of impact on daily life and identity of self-advocates with intellectual disability. *Cogent Social Sciences, 3*(1), 1304513. https://doi.org/10.1080/23311886.2017.1304513

Norris, J. E., Prosser, R., Remington, A., Crane, L., & Maras, K. (2023). Disclosing an autism diagnosis improves ratings of candidate performance in employment interviews. *Autism, 28*(4), 1045–1050. https://doi.org/10.1177/13623613231203739

Petri, G., Beadle-Brown, J., & Bradshaw, J. (2017). "More honoured in the breach than in the observance": Self-advocacy and human rights. *Laws, 6*(4), 26. https://doi.org/10.3390/laws6040026

Petri, G., Beadle-Brown, J., & Bradshaw, J. (2020). Redefining self-advocacy: A practice theory-based approach. *Journal of Policy and Practice in Intellectual Disabilities, 17*(3), 207–218. https://doi.org/10.1111/jppi.12343

Petri, G., Beadle-Brown, J., & Bradshaw, J. (2021). 'Even a self-advocate needs to buy milk': Economic barriers to self-advocacy in the autism and intellectual disability movement. *Scandinavian Journal of Disability Research, 23*(1), 180–191. https://doi.org/10.16993/sjdr.738

Pillai, M. J., & Janardhanan, K. A. (2021). Challenges faced by person with disability due to marginalization and their solutions: A review. *Turkish Online Journal of Qualitative Inquiry, 12*(7).

Podlucká, D. (2020). Educational goals for college students diagnosed with disabilities: From individualist to transformative activist agenda. *Psicologia da Educação*, (50), 52–64.

Raymaker, D. M., Teo, A. R., Steckler, N. A., Lentz, B., Scharer, M., Delos Santos, A., Kapp, S. K., Hunter, M., Joyce, A., & Nicolaidis, C. (2020). "Having all of your internal resources exhausted beyond measure and being left with no clean-up crew": Defining autistic burnout. *Autism in Adulthood, 2*(2), 132–143. https://doi.org/10.1089/aut.2019.0079

Rifai, O. M., Fletcher-Watson, S., Jiménez-Sánchez, L., & Crompton, C. J. (2022). Investigating markers of rapport in autistic and nonautistic interactions. *Autism in Adulthood, 4*(1), 3–11. https://doi.org/10.1089/aut.2021.0017

Roberts, E. L., Ju, S., & Zhang, D. (2016). Review of practices that promote self-advocacy for students with disabilities. *Journal of Disability Policy Studies, 26*(4), 209–220. https://doi.org/10.1177/1044207314540213

Rosa, S. D. R. (2018, October 11). How 'autism warrior parents' harm autistic kids. *The Establishment*. https://medium.com/the-establishment/how-autism-warrior-parents-harm-autistic-kids-6700b8bf6677

Rothman, T., Maldonado, J. M., & Rothman, H. (2008). Building self-confidence and future career success through a pre-college transition program for individuals with disabilities. *Journal of Vocational Rehabilitation, 28*(2), 73–83. https://doi.org/10.3233/JVR-2008-00406

Rottier, H., & Gernsbacher, M. A. (2020). Autistic adult and non-autistic parent advocates: Bridging the divide. In A. C. Carey, J. M. Ostrove, & T. Fannon (Eds.), *Disability Alliances and Allies (Research in Social Science and Disability, Vol. 12)* (pp. 155–166), Emerald Publishing.

Ryan, T. G., & Griffiths, S. (2015). Self-advocacy and its impacts for adults with developmental disabilities. *Australian Journal of Adult Learning, 55*(1). https://files.eric.ed.gov/fulltext/EJ1059141.pdf

Santhanam, S., & Bellon-Harn, M. (2022). Speech-language pathologist's role in understanding and promoting self-advocacy in autistic adults. *American Journal of Speech-Language Pathology, 31*(2), 649–663. https://doi.org/10.1044/2021_AJSLP-21-00223

Schena, D., Rosales, R., & Rowe, E. (2022). Teaching self-advocacy skills: A review and call for research. *Journal of Behavioral Education*, 1–49. https://doi.org/10.1007/s10864-022-09472-7

Sheppard, E., Pillai, D., Wong, G. T. L., Ropar, D., & Mitchell, P. (2016). How easy is it to read the minds of people with autism spectrum disorder? *Journal of Autism and Developmental Disorders, 46*(4), 1247–1254. https://doi.org/10.1007/s10803-015-2662-8

Shogren, K. A., Wehmeyer, M. L., Palmer, S. B., Rifenbark, G. G., & Little, T. D. (2015). Relationships between self-determination and postschool outcomes for youth with disabilities. *Journal of Special Education, 48*(4), 256–267. https://doi.org/10.1177/0022466913489733

Skelton, J., & Moore, M. (1999). The role of self-advocacy in work for people with learning difficulties. *Community, Work & Family, 2*(2), 133–145. https://doi.org/10.1080/13668809908413937

Smith-Young, J., Chafe, R., Audas, R., & Gustafson, D. L. (2022). "I know how to advocate": Parents' experiences in advocating for children and youth diagnosed with autism spectrum disorder. *Health Services Insights, 15*, 11786329221078803. https://doi.org/10.1177/11786329221078803

Strolovitch, D. Z. (2006). Do interest groups represent the disadvantaged? Advocacy at the intersections of race, class, and gender. *The Journal of Politics, 68*(4), 894–910.

Tager-Flusberg, H., & Kasari, C. (2013). Minimally verbal school-aged children with autism spectrum disorder: The neglected end of the spectrum. *Autism Research, 6*(6), 468–478. https://doi.org/10.1002/aur.1329

Test, D. W., Fowler, C. H., Wood, W. M., Brewer, D. M., & Eddy, S. (2005). A conceptual framework of self-advocacy for students with disabilities. *Remedial and Special Education, 26*(1), 43–54. https://doi.org/10.1177/07419325050260010601

Thomas, T. H., Taylor, S., Rosenzweig, M., Schenker, Y., & Bender, C. (2023). Self-advocacy behaviors and needs in women with advanced cancer: Assessment and differences by patient characteristics. *International Journal of Behavioral Medicine, 30*(2), 211–220. https://doi.org/10.1007/s12529-022-10085-7

Thompson-Hodgetts, S., Labonte, C., Mazumder, R., & Phelan, S. (2020). Helpful or harmful? A scoping review of perceptions and outcomes of autism diagnostic disclosure to others. *Research in Autism Spectrum Disorders, 77*, 101598. https://doi.org/10.1016/j.rasd.2020.101598

Turnock, A., Langley, K., & Jones, C. R. (2022). Understanding stigma in autism: A narrative review and theoretical model. *Autism in Adulthood, 4*(1), 76–91. https://doi.org/10.1089/aut.2021.0005

Vannavuth, S. (2016). *Examining Cross-Cultural Factors Related to Happiness and Gratitude* [Doctoral dissertation]. Alliant International University.

Waddington, H., Minnell, H., Patrick, L., van Der Meer, L., Monk, R., Woods, L., & Whitehouse, A. J. (2023). Community perspectives on the appropriateness and importance of support goals for young autistic children. *Autism, 28*(2), 316–326. https://doi.org/10.1177/13623613231168920

Wehmeyer, M. L., Palmer, S. B., Lee, Y., Williams-Diehm, K., & Shogren, K. (2011). A randomized-trial evaluation of the effect of whose future is it anyway? On self-determination. *Career Development for Exceptional Individuals*, *34*(1), 45–56. https://doi.org/10.1177/0885728810383559

White, G. W., Summers, J. A., Zhang, E., & Renault, V. (2014). Evaluating the Effects of a Self-Advocacy Training Program for Undergraduates with Disabilities. Journal of Postsecondary Education and Disability, 27(3), 229–244.

Zhang, D., Roberts, E., Landmark, L., & Ju, S. (2019). Effect of self-advocacy training on students with disabilities: Adult outcomes and advocacy involvement after participation. *Journal of Vocational Rehabilitation*, *50*(2), 207–218. https://doi.org/10.3233/JVR-181001

Zimmerman, J. (2022). SLPs as AAC gatekeepers. *CommunicationFIRST*. https://communicationfirst.org/slps-as-aac-gatekeepers/

Zisk, A. H., & Dalton, E. (2019). Augmentative and alternative communication for speaking autistic adults: Overview and recommendations. *Autism in Adulthood*, *1*(2), 93–100. https://doi.org/10.1089/aut.2018.0007

Chapter 29:

Specialist Mentoring and the Double Empathy Problem in Autism

Ghafaria Khan

Abstract

For the past five years, I have been working as a specialist mentor supporting higher education students that have mental health conditions and autism. Mentoring, in my experience, is a role with no power hierarchy between myself and the students, rather, as I am not associated with any university, it allows a safe and confidential space for the students to discuss their worries and concerns. My academic background in psychology and mental health studies, as well my own lived experience as a mature neurodivergent student in the UK, allows me to provide science-based strategies and techniques to support the students. This chapter will give some of examples of the Double Empathy Problem at university as experienced by autistic students that I have supported through mentoring.

Introduction to the author

My name is Ghafaria Khan. I am a woman (she/her), a person of colour, my ethnicity is Pakistani and I was raised in the Netherlands with my first language being Dutch. I am also a single mother and a first-generation graduate. I identify myself as autistic (as after being denied a diagnosis through the National Health Services (NHS), I am resisting paying a ridiculous amount to get a private autism diagnosis) and I am late-diagnosed with attention deficit hyperactivity disorder (ADHD), hence neurodivergent. I am an early career researcher at University College London (UCL) in autism and mental health focusing on the South Asian population living in the UK. Reading this chapter, it is important to me that the readers are aware of my many identities, which shape my experiences of reality. In New Zealand, in the Maori language, one introduces oneself not only by name but also referring to what family one belongs to and/or one's identities. We call this; Whakapapa (pronounced as FakkaPapa) meaning genealogy (Mahuika, 2019). This is particularly the case when some aspects of my identities are currently oppressed and/or reflect minorities, such as belonging to a certain race, being a woman and being neurodivergent in the current majority White, neurotypical and patriarchal society in the UK.

What is specialist mental health mentoring?

Mentoring means 'the act or process of helping and giving advice to a younger or less experienced person, especially in a job or at school' (Cambridge University Press & Assessment, n.d.). A specialist mental health mentor provides mentoring that is *'highly specialist, tailored to the individual's needs and diagnosis, enabling students to address barriers to learning created by a particular impairment'* (UMO Services, 2023, p. 31). Autism is a part of the human neurodiversity in which the brain works differently; the diagnostic criteria is having difficulty in social communication, repetitive and restricted behaviours, and sensory sensitivity (Jaarsma & Welin, 2012; Kapp et al., 2013). A mixed methods study with both mentors and mentees evaluated specialist autism mentoring and reported how mentoring can be effective depending on the quality of the mentee–mentor relationship (Lucas & James, 2018).

In 2014–2015 there were 33,500 students in higher education with mental health conditions and 6,845 with autism and/or social communication disorder but by 2021–2022 this had increased to 119,480 students with mental health conditions and 18,820 students with autism and/or social communications disorder, as reported by the Higher Education Statistic Agency (HESA, 2022). According to the Royal College of Psychiatrists, the COVID-19 pandemic is one of the main factors that caused the increase of 14.7% in attendance at mental health, learning disability and autism services in the UK (Royal College of Psychiatrists, 2022). Therefore, not only is mentoring proving to be effective for autistic higher education students but there is also an increased demand for specialist mentors in autism and mental health conditions.

My undergraduate honours degree in Psychology, accredited by the British Psychological Society (BPS), and my MSc in Mental Health Studies, from King's College London, which covered autism, qualifies me, along with comprehensive training in autistic adults through the National Autism Society (NAS) modules, and allows me to work as a specialist mental health mentor (Student Loan Company, 2019). Student Finance England (SFE) provides mentoring support sessions using Disabled Students' Allowance (DSA), or sometimes the university provides mentoring support sessions with their own funding as it is the university's responsibility to ensure the well-being of the students, including their mental health (GOV.UK, n.d.). Once the student has been granted their sessions, they will get booked with me through mentoring agencies such as Diversity and Ability Ltd, Clear-links Ltd and UMO.

The first meeting is crucial to introduce myself, and to get to know the student and what autism means to the student, as well as what mentoring can mean for the student. This session is important to understand the history, medication, therapy and current diagnosis that might have led for the student to get in touch with well-being services at their university. It is also an opportunity to highlight how this space is a safe and confidential space for them to talk about any worries and concerns they might have, as I am not affiliated with their university. Also, I put out the disclaimer that I am not a qualified therapist and that these meetings will not be therapeutic, though I can signpost them to mental health services such as counselling and psychological therapies if needed. For me, there is no power hierarchy between us as I enjoy meeting and learning from the students, which is a common theme for mentors in the study by Lucas and James (2018)., along with the flexibility of meetings as and when they are needed, whether that is weekly, fortnightly or once a month online using Google Meet, Microsoft Teams or Zoom. I have found that this kind of introduction puts the students at ease, knowing that our meetings will be confidential and will not get back to their lecturers or impact their work at university.

What is the Double Empathy Theory?

Coined by Damien Milton (2012) more than ten years ago, 'the Double Empathy Problem' refers to a 'breakdown in mutual understanding' between two people, in this case one is autistic and the other non-autistic (Milton et al., 2022). In 2022, the BPS funded the first Double Empathy Problem seminar series held at Portsmouth University at which I was invited to present my experiences as a specialist mentor supporting autistic adults in higher education. The following parts of the chapter will include some of the examples I presented on the day.

As a specialist mental health mentor, the students that I meet have autism and/or mental health conditions that they are diagnosed with, such as depression and anxiety. The clinical definition of depression is having a low mood for at least two weeks and being unable to '*enjoy ordinary things and experiences*' (National Institute for Health and Care Excellence, 2023). The clinical definition for generalized anxiety disorder (GAD) is when someone's experience is excessively worrying with physiological symptoms such as insomnia, restlessness and headaches (National Institute for Health and Care Excellence, 2023). When students have depression and/or anxiety I have found them to have little understanding of what this means on a biological level and I have spent time explaining the psychoeducation behind these conditions, followed by strategies that they can use to manage their symptoms, for example, breathing techniques and mindfulness, along with the benefits of going for a walk, and writing in their journals to process thoughts and worries. Unfortunately, by the time I meet the student they have developed unhealthy coping strategies such as alcohol abuse, isolating themselves and self-harm. In such cases, we talk about these coping mechanisms and how they can be replaced by healthy coping strategies to manage their symptoms, along with any medication and therapy that they might have in place. Healthy coping strategies usually tend to work. If I find a student is not making improvements, I can signpost them to relevant mental health services.

Communications problems with professionals

The autistic students that I mentor have usually had appalling experiences with mental health services and I use our meetings to validate their feelings and emotions, and end up apologizing for the behaviours of professionals. Mental health professionals have been found not to listen, or take the students' concerns seriously, at times making matters worse (Camm-Crosbie et al., 2019; Crane et al., 2019). Communication problems with mental health professionals are very common among autistic people and, considering the power imbalance between professional and client, it is the professional that needs to be able to sympathize. There is a strong need for professionals to have their knowledge on autism updated as a lot of them still hold on to old information on autism. The compulsory annual continuing professional development (CPD) set by the UK Department of Health (2015) is trying to address this gap along with training on autism for mental health professionals.

Communications problems with lecturers and university administration

At university, autistic students have communications problems not only with peers but also with lecturers and the administration. In the last few years, there have been many strikes at universities where autistic students completely support the reasons for the strikes, but they experience anxiety with last-minute lecture cancellations, and the conflict between crossing the picket lines or not and missing out on lectures. Last-minute lecture cancellations have impacted autistic students a lot as they struggle with sudden change and end up having complete meltdowns of not knowing what to do with the rest of their day, whereas a neurotypical student tends to adapt more easily and make instant plans or perhaps does nothing. Sometimes, autistic students really struggle with communication via email, so we use our session to go over how to write an email, ensuring they get across their main points, or reading the emails of university staff and lecturers. Doing this together, students have reduced their anxiety and ensured they can resolve any issues they might be having with their assignments and lectures. Finally, explaining the reader's perspective and how the lecturers won't know about a concern until you tell them or email them, has been particularly helpful for autistic students.

Communications problems with parents and/or carers

The communication problems autistic students experience when arriving at university also occur with their parents and/or carers. Parents tend to be very overprotective and moving out to live on campus is difficult for both parties. The parents' own anxiety is not helpful for the student and I explain how this usually comes from a place of love and care. Not all autistic students have a good relationship with their parents. As young adults, they feel more comfortable to explore their sexuality, how they dress, or their ambitions for the future. These changes – children growing into adults – can lead to complicated relationships between the parents and students (Van Hees et al., 2018). Christmas holidays are especially difficult for students – they go home, meet their extended families and engage in social events that can be particularly overwhelming for autistic students. Therefore, I use our sessions as a safe space to talk about their worries and concerns, as well as create an action plan so that they can feel more in control of the situation, be more assertive and set boundaries to ensure their own well-being. Personal boundaries are helpful tools to create a safe space for oneself within relationships and I refer to the work and books of Nedra Glover Tawwab, a therapist and author of *Set Boundaries, Find Peace*, who uses very simple sentences to illustrate how to communicate our boundaries. Nedra not only covers boundaries in relationships with family and at work, but also with ourselves. In our mentoring sessions, I often introduce books and other resources to help the students with their personal development and growth, along with ensuring their well-being.

Communication problems with peers

Furthermore, during mentoring meetings with autistic students, the following themes have come up: accommodation issues and communication problems with peers and staff. Autistic people tend to have sensory sensitivity, for example, of noise, whereby at times they have not been able to sleep when at campus because of the choices of their peers to party and/or stay up all night. Shared space, such as a communal kitchen, can also be problematic for some students, as the autistic student would not know when it is their turn to cook, and this is worsened when they do not have good relationships with their peers (McLeod et al., 2019). At times, I have met autistic students who would resort to getting a microwave for their room instead, or order takeaways and fast foods only. During our mentoring meetings, I check in with the autistic students on their daily tasks to ensure they are eating and sleeping properly, as well as taking care of laundry, cooking meals and/or keeping their dorms clean, as executive dysfunctioning means that there can be a deficit in cognitive control processes in autistic people that enables one to plan, decide and complete tasks and cope with new situations (Craig et al., 2016). Answers to these questions are indicators for me to assess their mental health and well-being, whereby I can review how much support they need or signpost them to the relevant services such as talking therapy, counselling or their general practitioner (GP).

Implications in practice for autistic higher education students

This part of the chapter will cover some of the implications that I have found were beneficial in the context of university when supporting autistic students. Some of the academic side of support that I provide through mentoring is to go over the students' assignments and break down the task into smaller and more manageable chunks, as, at times, autistic students can find it overwhelming to manage the weekly tasks of reading before lectures, attending lectures, and working toward their essays and assignments. Through mentoring, I ensure they complete the task before the submission date with strategies to ensure they are organized, and gentle reminders. Neurodivergent students can get hyperfocused or fixated on a particular essay or assignment, which is perceived as an autistic strength whereby one can focus on a particular interest (Dupuis et al., 2022). In our mentoring meetings, we go over assignment grade percentages to get an idea of how much these will weigh toward the final degree, to prioritize which assignments need more time and focus – essentially, zooming out and looking at the bigger picture. There needs to be more autism awareness training in preparation for lectures and for university staff on what it means to be autistic and how to support autistic people. There are things that could be done on an individual level for lectures by university staff, by perhaps reaching out to autistic students, introducing themselves and asking if the students need any specific support during their lectures. When my supervisor, Susana Castro-Kemp, was asked by me to read through the chapter for feedback, she enlightened me on what the Institute of Education (IOE) at UCL, in the faculty of Psychology and Human Development, is doing to ensure students are supported. She explained how this academic year had seen the biggest number of students that needed additional support. *'That's great news!'* I replied as that means less students are masking their needs. Susana ensures she knows each of those 18 students, out of the 80 allocated to her, on a personal level and knows what their needs are. She is working hard with other faculty members, usually working extra hours through back-and-forth email communications, to ensure, for example, that there are videos available of exit routes of the IOE building. This is very helpful for people like myself who are visual learners and once we have seen the route it makes a lot more sense, as well as managing our anxiety levels when attending. Susana shared how there is a lot of awareness among staff and other university members about neurodiversity and that there need to be changes made at institutional and systemic levels, as, at the moment, lecturers and staff members are working above and beyond their paid hours to ensure the right support is available and provided. The notion of being undervalued and overworked on a professional level in the education system here in the UK is so common unfortunately. Hearing Susana's experience as a lecturer who is passionate and working hard to be able to support students, was very eye-opening as a mentor, as I am usually hearing negative experiences from students. I feel relieved and hopeful to know there are people, like Susana, who are ensuring that institutes are inclusive and working hard to pave new ways to support and accommodate the needs of individual students.

In my mentoring meetings, I remind all students to be assertive otherwise there is the assumption that everything is fine according to the lecturers and university staff. During mentoring meetings, I have met and supported autistic students that wanted to belong to the university, and try their best to integrate by living in student accommodation and doing what other students of their age do. Some autistic students did not feel the need to socialize and were rather content with the lectures and academic side of being at university. Therefore, parents, lecturers and university staff need to facilitate and provide the support that meets the autistic student's needs on an individual level. More importantly, universities need to ensure their staff and lecturers are being given support, whether that is pastoral care or providing the right tools and being paid for their hard work and time to ensure inclusivity along with education.

Conclusion

During my mentoring sessions with autistic students, the following issues have been most significant – communication problems with their parents and carers, peers and professionals. In all cases, I have found that the autistic students are usually blamed and considered problematic. This common pattern of victim blaming in autistic people needs to stop (Gibbs et al., 2023; Pearson et al., 2022), although a small shift in our thinking and perception of autism can make a huge difference to a relationship. By being open-minded, empathetic, non-judgemental, not making any assumptions and considering each person as unique as they are by asking them a simple question: '*How can I help and/or support you?*' Finally, my mentoring approach is parallel to the specialist mentoring in autism 'framework for reframing', with key themes of creating a space of safety and connections, and adapting to the individual's needs along with high levels of optimism, as shared by Brian Irvine (Irvine, 2023a, 2023b). In conclusion, on an institutional and systemic level there is a lot more support, training and awareness needed for university staff and students on how to support autistic students. More awareness is needed on available support, such as mentoring and what this can mean for students. On an individual level, we can start by checking in on our own privileges and not to making any assumptions.

References

Cambridge University Press & Assessment (n.d.). Mentoring. https://dictionary.cambridge.org/dictionary/english/mentoring

Camm-Crosbie, L., Bradley, L., Shaw, R., Baron-Cohen, S., & Cassidy, S. (2019). 'People like me don't get support': Autistic adults' experiences of support and treatment for mental health difficulties, self-injury and suicidality. *Autism*, *23*(6), 1431–1441. https://doi.org/10.1177/1362361318816053

Craig, F., Margari, F., Legrottaglie, A. R., Palumbi, R., De Giambattista, C., & Margari, L. (2016). A review of executive function deficits in autism spectrum disorder and attention-deficit/hyperactivity disorder. *Neuropsychiatric Disease and Treatment, 12*(12), 1191–1202. https://doi.org/10.2147/NDT.S104620

Crane, L., Adams, F., Harper, G., Welch, J., & Pellicano, E. (2019). 'Something needs to change': Mental health experiences of young autistic adults in England. *Autism, 23*(2), 477–493. https://doi.org/10.1177/1362361318757048

Department of Health (2015). CPD Curriculum Guide for Social Workers Who Are Working with People on the Autism Spectrum. UK Department of Health. https://assets.publishing.service.gov.uk/government/uploads/system/uploads/attachment_data/file/467394/Pt2_Autism_Guide_Accessible.pdf

Dupuis, A., Mudiyanselage, P., Burton, C. L., Arnold, P. D., Crosbie, J., & Schachar, R. J. (2022). Hyperfocus or flow? Attentional strengths in autism spectrum disorder. *Frontiers in Psychiatry, 13*, 886692. https://doi.org/10.3389/fpsyt.2022.886692

Gibbs, V., Hudson, J. L., & Pellicano, E. (2023). Poly-victimization of autistic adults: An investigation of individual-level correlates. *Autism Research, 16*(12), 2336–2349. https://doi.org/10.1002/aur.3031

GOV.UK (n.d.). *Help If You're a Student with a Learning Difficulty, Health Problem or Disability*. https://www.gov.uk/disabled-students-allowance-dsa

HESA (2022). *Table 15: UK Permanent Address Student Enrolments by Disability and Sex 2014/14 to 2022/23*. HESA. https://www.hesa.ac.uk/data-and-analysis/students/table-15

Irvine, B. (2023a). *A Framework for Specialist (Autism) Mentoring in UK Higher Education* [Doctoral dissertation]. University of Birmingham. https://etheses.bham.ac.uk/id/eprint/13500/

Irvine, B. (2023b, January 6). *Specialist Autism Mentoring at University: A Framework for Reforming*. National Autistic Society. https://www.autism.org.uk/advice-and-guidance/professional-practice/mentoring-university

Jaarsma, P., & Welin, S. (2012). Autism as a natural human variation: Reflections on the claims of the neurodiversity movement. *Health Care Analysis, 20*, 20–30. https://doi.org/10.1007/s10728-011-0169-9

Kapp, S. K., Gillespie-Lynch, K., Sherman, L. E., & Hutman, T. (2013). Deficit, difference, or both? Autism and neurodiversity. *Developmental Psychology, 49*(1), 59–71. https://doi.org/10.1037/a0028353

Lucas, R., & James, A. I. (2018). An evaluation of specialist mentoring for university students with autism spectrum disorders and mental health conditions. *Journal of Autism and Developmental Disorders, 48*,(3), 694–707. https://doi.org/10.1007/s10803-017-3303-1

Mahuika, N. (2019). A brief history of Whakapapa: Māori approaches to genealogy. *Genealogy, 3*(2), 32. https://doi.org/10.3390/genealogy3020032

McLeod, J. D., Meanwell, E., & Hawbaker, A. (2019). The experiences of college students on the autism spectrum: A comparison to their neurotypical peers. *Journal of Autism and Developmental Disorders 49*, 2320–2336. https://doi.org/10.1007/s10803-019-03910-8

Milton, D. E. (2012). On the ontological status of autism: The 'double empathy problem'. *Disability & Society, 27*(6), 883–887. https://doi.org/10.1080/09687599.2012.710008

Milton, D., Gurbuz, E., & López, B. (2022). The 'double empathy problem': Ten years on. *Autism, 26*(8), 1901–1903. https://doi.org/10.1177/13623613221129123

National Institute for Health and Care Excellence (2023a). *Depression.* National Institute for Health and Care Excellence (NICE). https://cks.nice.org.uk/topics/depression/background-information/definition/

National Institute for Health and Care Excellence (2023b). *Generalised Anxiety Disorder.* National Institute for Health and Care Excellence (NICE). https://cks.nice.org.uk/topics/generalized-anxiety-disorder/diagnosis/diagnosis/

Pearson, A., Rees, J., & Forster, S. (2022). "This was just how this friendship worked": Experiences of interpersonal victimization among autistic adults. *Autism in Adulthood, 4*(2), 141–150. https://doi.org/10.1089/aut.2021.0035

Royal College of Psychiatrists (2022, March 15). *Record 4.3 Million Referrals to Specialist Mental Health Services in 2021* [Press release]. https://www.rcpsych.ac.uk/news-and-features/latest-news/detail/2022/03/15/record-4.3-million-referrals-to-specialist-mental-health-services-in-2021

Student Loan Company (2019). *Disabled Students' Allowances (DSAs): DfE Qualification and Professional Body Membership Requirements to Deliver DSA's Fundable NMH Roles (AKA the NMH Matrix)*. Department for Education. https://www.practitioners.slc.co.uk/media/1762/ssin-0919-dsa-mandatory_qualifications_and_professional_body_membership_requirements.pdf

UMO Services (2023). *The Role and Impact Specialist Mental Health Mentoring on Students in UK Higher Education Institutes* [White paper]. UMO Services. https://hubble-live-assets.s3.amazonaws.com/umhan/file_asset/file/92/UMO_White_Paper_The_Role_and_Impact_-_Copy.pdf

Tawwab, N. G. (2021). *Set Boundaries, Find Peace: A Guide to Reclaiming Yourself.* Piatkus Publisher.

Van Hees, V., Roeyers, H., & De Mol, J. (2018). Students with autism spectrum disorder and their parents in the transition into higher education: Impact on dynamics in the parent–child relationship. *Journal of Autism and Developmental Disorders*, *48*(10), 3296–3310. https://doi.org/10.1007/s10803-018-3593-y

Chapter 30:

Double Empathy and the Double Rainbow: Health Care Inequities for Gender Diverse Autistic Adults

Katie Munday

The Double Empathy Problem (Milton, 2012) appreciates that miscommunication – and the blame which can come with it – happens between people of different neurotypes, but what does this mean for Autistic people who are also gender diverse? Transgender identities have been found to be twice as common in Autistic individuals, with this intersection being described as the 'double rainbow' – referring to the colours which represent both queer and neurodivergent identities (Morgan, 2019). Reasons for this significant overlap often conflate gender 'issues' with perceived social and emotional 'deficits' of being Autistic. Unfortunately, this stigma effects our access to health care, as we are often blamed for miscommunications or *disengaging* with services. In this chapter, I explore the Double Empathy Problem between cisgender neuronormative professionals and transgender and gender diverse (TGD) Autistic patients, and how this affects our experiences of health care. I shall also make recommendations to health care professionals on how they can improve the equitability of their practice.

There are many concerns to consider before engaging in health care services, including the ability to take the time off work or caring responsibilities and worries about medical insurance, not to mention the fear of potential diagnosis. Individuals may also worry about being seen to waste doctors' time or being told off for not coming in sooner. For TGD Autistic people there are additional fears that we may: be deadnamed or misgendered; be asked intrusive questions; be seen as 'rude' for not using eye contact; need to take off clothing for physical examinations; experience a meltdown, shutdown or sensory overload. There are many barriers to engaging in health care services for TGD Autistic people; perhaps the biggest is that we cannot be our authentic selves and have our needs supported holistically.

The power dynamics between health care professionals and their patients heavily favours the (usually) more educated and privileged practitioner, meaning those of us with any marginalized identity or experience are in a vulnerable position when engaging with health care. The mismatch in empathy, culture and communication between Autistic patients and non-Autistic health care professionals has been referred to as the Triple Empathy Problem (Shaw et al., 2023). The problem of patient blame within health care is deeply entrenched, and often involves misogyny, transphobia, ableism and ageism, which means the empathy problem in health care may be much more than double or triple.

Complexifying the gender diverse Autistic person

Health care services and practitioners are often inadequately trained on Autistic, and TGD, embodiment, affecting the accessibility of their practice and services. Practitioners may understand TGD *or* Autistic health care needs but rarely both, let alone how they may intersect to create very specific health care needs (Gratton, 2019). Lack of adequate training on gender diverse and Autistic issues means professionals, and their practice, can fall prey to transphobic and ableist ideologies shared in the media. This misinformation leaves gender diverse Autistic people judged on how well we 'person' – how we communicate, look and act according to social norms. These social norms, including transmedicalism (in which transgender people are only considered transgender when we medically transition) centre neuronormativity and are often irrelevant to many Autistic people (Milton, 2021). Our divergence from social norms (sometimes considered 'noncompliance') can affect our care within gender identity health care, as we are perceived as doing (trans)gender *incorrectly* (Bruce et al., 2023; Jackson-Perry, 2020). Going against social norms means our health care needs are labelled as 'complex'; these complexities ease the transition from systemic blame to individual blame. It is *our* fault that we *will not* engage with a service, therefore the change in communication and attitude must come from us. Crucially, for gender diverse Autistic people the Double Empathy Problem is not just a social issue – it is a health issue.

Under the guise of being 'too complex', gender diverse Autistic patients can be moved from one practitioner to another and if we show frustration at being treated as a 'medical marvel' we can be labelled as 'aggressive' or 'over sensitive'. Sadly, this mirrors the gaslighting that so many of us experience in our everyday life and may stop us from advocating for our health care needs altogether. This, coupled with bureaucracy, lack of choice in communication preferences, and overly sensorial environments can add to the reasons we avoid health care settings, as one participant from Munday shared:

> *Because I'm Autistic and I'm in a building with literally thousands of other people, because our hospitals are currently very crowded, and have always been very crowded, so I'm getting overstimulated, I'm getting overwhelmed, my anxiety is shooting through the roof.* (Munday, 2022, p. 18)

This participant explained that accessing an overwhelming health care environment affected his mental health. He reflected that the settings in which he should have been able to find help added to his discomfort and overwhelm. For, as experienced by this participant and many other gender diverse Autistic people, we must choose which part of our bodymind we need to keep the safest – our physical or mental health. Fortunately, there are supportive practitioners who appreciate the needs of Autistic patients, who are well-versed in Autistic and gender diverse experiences. These practitioners value their patients holistically and understand that all elements of a patient interweave to create a full picture of their health care needs. Being supportive and sympathetic makes a big difference to Autistic patients, as one participant in Shaw and colleagues shared:

> *A sympathetic and understanding GP [General Practitioner] means I feel less anxiety at appointments means I will be willing to go to the doctors when needed, and means I attend regular screening check-ups.* (Shaw et al., 2023, p. 1751)

This participant highlighted the importance of a healthy relationship between practitioner and patient, and how this affects a person's ability to organize and attend appointments. Gender diverse Autistic people need sympathetic and understanding practitioners to enable us to use health care services regularly and safely. However, we also need practitioners to have a deep understanding of gender and neuro diversity, or at least the willingness to learn.

The exhaustion of self-advocacy

TGD Autistic health practitioners exist, but not in enough quantity to allow for a greater understanding across services. Additionally, those of us from oppressed groups should not be expected to constantly educate others; our expertise and knowledge should be respected (and paid for). Despite lived experience underpinning practice, Autistic practitioners can also be considered to lack epistemic authority due to supposed biases around Autistic culture and embodiment (Fisher, 2023). Autistic practitioners can be seen as unfair when caring for Autistic patients by giving them preferential treatment. Even TGD Autistic practitioners in a position of power – and there are fewer of them due to inequity in education and employment – can only effect small change, which often drains their resources. Perhaps more worryingly, Autistic patients can be seen as not understanding our bodies, including how we are *supposed* to experience and talk about pain. For both gender diverse Autistic patients and practitioners', epistemic injustice and the Double Empathy Problem interweave framing us as unknowledgeable and unreliable. We are only considered 'lived experience experts' when it suits the power dynamic.

TGD Autistic people must repeatedly advocate for at least one of our identities when engaging in health care due to inconsistent training and ideals of practitioners, as a participant in Munday explained:

> *Services that are targeted towards Autistic people aren't necessarily trans-friendly and vice versa. I'm always nervous when approaching doctors etc. because I never know where each one will fall.* (Munday, 2022, p. 29)

Some practitioners understand and validate Autistic, and gender diverse, needs. However, you 'never know' until you are in the examination room. This puts TGD Autistic people in a precarious position; we must often decide between our mental health and our physical health. This is not a choice anyone should be made to make. Personally, I have experienced second-hand transphobia within my dental care and within my pregnancy care; these experiences make it clear that it is not safe for me to be 'out' in my gender diversity in health care. This has not stopped me from engaging in care. However, I do not bring my whole self into an examination room, which may mean some of my health care needs go unmet.

Bigotry can underpin poor practice; however, it is more likely that a lack of knowledge is creating many of the health care barriers TGD Autistic people experience. Uninformed practice can include heightened sensory environments, unclear information and lack of gender and neuro affirming language. Crucially, the problem of Double Empathy often starts *before* communication takes place – when lights are too bright we are being 'too sensitive'; when inaccessible information is shared we are blamed for misunderstanding 'simple' information. These issues exist between the professional and the patient *and* the systems which govern housing, travel, employment and other essential structures. Many of us carry trauma from past experiences within these different systems; being misunderstood, misgendered, invalidated and judged. When coming into the examination office many TGD Autistic people carry the baggage of transphobia, ableism, misogyny, abuse and neglect. We are vulnerable to these things within our everyday lives and then must choose whether to potentially expose ourselves to more stigma within health care.

How can practitioners improve health care equity for gender diverse Autistic people?

Thankfully, equity and equality in health care in Western countries is moving in the right direction due, in part, to the increase in gender diverse Autistic research, and wider neurodivergent LGBTQIA+ work, from both allies and the community. Work which explores the accessibility of gender identity health care (Bruce et al., 2023; Strang et al., 2019) and general health care (Kourti & Griffin, 2022; Lawson, 2022) shall begin to underpin practice both directly and indirectly. This work highlights the importance of improving the communication and empathy of health care professionals to mitigate the Double Empathy Problem. Practitioners and services which understand Autistic and gender diverse embodiment and experiences, shift responsibility for communication from individual to group. There are many ways that practitioners can continue this shift in responsibility, including:

- Check your privilege and biases – this is a long-term practice and may involve a lot of unlearning. You may be holding onto outdated ideas and stereotypes around Autistic and gender diverse experiences which affect your practice (check the Resources section for cisgender and neurotypical privilege checklists).
- Follow professional guidelines, including *Creating a Safe and Welcoming Clinic Environment* (Deutsch, 2016) and The Academic Autism Spectrum Partnership in Research and Education (AASPIRE; Nicolaidis et al., 2019).
- Check and use the current name and pronouns for your patient. Make sure that they agree for these to be included in their forms and at reception – there may be reasons why a patient may not want their name or pronouns on 'official' documents. These checks need to be an ongoing conversation.
- Send clear and detailed expectations of appointments and procedures – who will be there, what will happen and if there is anything the patient needs to bring with them. This needs to be communicated in their preferred way (phone call, text, email, letter, etc.).
- Clear expectations need to be shared before and during procedures around private areas, including if a person needs to take off a binder. These procedures should only be undertaken when totally necessary and with plenty of information on what the process will look like. The patient may ask for a practitioner of a certain gender for these procedures, and they may want to bring in a support person.

- Encourage patients to provide information on how best to accommodate their needs. Make use of prefabricated toolkits (see Resources) and make your patients aware of how this could help them.
- Allow patients plenty of time for processing information and give them time to answer any questions.
- If the patient brings a support person, all information and communication should still be directed to the patient. Their support person may intervene if the patient becomes overwhelmed, or to ask for clarity on their behalf.
- Make it explicit how and when people can stop or slow procedures – this may be a word or hand signal from the patient which needs to be discussed beforehand. Let patients know when you are going to touch them and that they can say 'no' at any point.
- Give patients the option of practitioners for personal procedures. They may prefer a practitioner of a specific gender or one who they know is a gender and neuro diverse ally.
- Engage in cross-specialism working. Make a network of gender diversity and neurodiversity specialists to ensure your practice is appropriate.
- Engage in training, workshops and webinars by gender diverse Autistic people. There are also many great blogs on this area including those by Wenn Lawson, Yenn Purkis and Laura Kate Dale.

Practitioners can think more critically around holistic and individualized care for gender diverse Autistic people, by staying up to date with information from within medicine and gender diverse Autistic communities. Practice which appreciates the lived experience expertise of gender diverse Autistic patients allows for the growth of knowledge, understanding and empathy for both patients and practitioners, and could help mitigate the Double Empathy Problem in health care.

Resources

AASPIRE Healthcare Toolkit: https://autismandhealth.org

Adams, N., & Liang, B. (2020). *Trans and Autistic*. Jessica Kingsley Publishers.

Autistic Women & Nonbinary Network (2022). Before You Go: Know Your Rights & What to Expect at the Doctor and in the Hospital – Tips and Advice (Life Hacks!) for Autistic Trans People about Finding and Going to Doctors. Autistic Women & Nonbinary Network. https://awnnetwork.org/wp-content/uploads/2022/11/Final-Version-Before-You-Go-Know-Your-Rights-Booklet.pdf

Bev & Community at Square 8. (2009). Checklist of Neurotypical Privilege: New Draft. https://au-ti.com/2022/08/22/the-checklist-of-neurotypical-privilege/

Brown, L. X. Z. (2016, June 22). Gendervague: At the intersection of autistic and trans experiences. *Asperger/Autism Network*. https://www.autistichoya.com/2020/05/gendervague-at-intersection-of-autistic.html

Dale, L. K. (2019). *Uncomfortable Labels: My Life as a Gay Autistic Trans Woman*. Jessica Kingsley Publishers.

Killermann, S. (2011). 30+ Examples of Cisgender Privileges. *It's Pronounced Metrosexual*. https://www.itspronouncedmetrosexual.com/2011/11/list-of-cisgender-privileges/

Kourti, M. (2021). *Working with Autistic Transgender and Non-Binary People: Research, Practice and Experience*. Jessica Kingsley Publishers.

Lawson, W. (2020). The autism spectrum and gender dysphoria. *Build Something Positive*. https://www.buildsomethingpositive.com/wenn/gender.html

Sparrow, M. (2020). *Spectrums: Autistic Transgender People in Their Own Words*. Jessica Kingsley Publishers.

Walker, N. (2021). *Neuroqueer Heresies: Notes on the Neurodiversity Paradigm, Autistic Empowerment, and Postnormal Possibilities*. Autonomous Press.

References

Bruce, H., Munday, K., & Kapp, S. K. (2023). Exploring the experiences of autistic transgender and non-binary adults in seeking gender identity health care. *Autism and Adulthood, 5*(2), 191–203. http://doi.org/10.1089/aut.2023.0003

Deutsch, M. B. (2016, June 17). *Creating a Safe and Welcoming Clinic Environment*. University of California Transgender Care. https://transcare.ucsf.edu/guidelines/clinic-environment

Fisher, J. (2023). Epistemic injustice: The silenced voices. *Mental Health Nursing, 32*(4), 1186–1189. https://doi.org/10.1111/inm.13163

Gratton, F. V. (2019). *Supporting Transgender Autistic Youth and Adults: A Guide for Professionals and Families*. Jessica Kingsley Publishers.

Jackson-Perry, D. (2020). The autistic art of failure? Unknowing imperfect systems of sexuality and gender. *Scandinavian Journal of Disability Research, 22*(1), 221–229. http://doi.org/10.16993/sjdr.634

Kourti, M., & Griffin, E. (2022). Developing a good relationship with an autistic transgender or non-binary person as a professional. In M. Kourti (Ed.), *Working with Autistic Transgender and Non-Binary People: Research, Practice and Experience* (pp. 125–140). Jessica Kingsley Publishers.

Lawson, W. (2022). Reflection on the spectra of autism and gender identity: Consideration for professionals supporting autistic transgender and non-binary people. In M. Kourti (Ed.), *Working with Autistic Transgender and Non-Binary people: Research, Practice and Experience* (pp. 107–124). Jessica Kingsley Publishers.

Milton, D. E. M. (2012). On the ontological status of autism: The 'double empathy problem'. *Disability & Society, 27*(6), 883–887. https://doi.org/10.1080/09687599.2012.710008

Milton, D. E. M. (2021). 'Here comes trouble': Autism and gender performance. In M. Kourti (Ed.), *Working with Autistic Transgender and Non-Binary People: Research, Practice and Experience* (pp. 25–32). Jessica Kinglsey Publishers.

Morgan, N. (2019). Living under the "double rainbow": Colourful LGBTQ+ community with ASD. *Milestones Autism Resources*. https://www.milestones.org/resources/blog/2019/09/30/living-under-the-double-rainbow-the-colorful-lgbtq-community-with-asd

Munday, K. (2022). *Stories from Under the "Double Rainbow": Trans and Non-Binary Autistic Narratives* [unpublished master's thesis]. https://doi.org/10.13140/RG.2.2.34886.75843

Nicolaidis, C., Raymaker, D., Kapp, S. K., Baggs, A., Ashkenazy, E., McDonald, K., & Joyce, A., (2019). The AASPIRE practice-based guidelines for the inclusion of autistic adults in research as co-researcher and study participants. *Autism: An International Journal of Research and Practice, 23*(8), 2007–2019. https://doi.org/10.1177/1362361319830523

Shaw, C. K. S., Carravallah, L., Johnson, M., O'Sullivan, J., Chown, N., Neilson, S., & Doherty, M. (2023). Barriers to healthcare and a 'triple empathy problem' may lead to adverse outcomes for autistic adults: A qualitative study. *Autism, 28*(7), 1746–1757. https://doi.org/10.1177/13623613231205629

Strang, J., Klomp, S. E., Caplan, R., Griffin, A. D., Anthony, L. G., Harris, M. C., Graham, E. K., Knauss, M., & van der Miesen, A. I. R. (2019). Community-based participatory design for research that impacts the lives of transgender and/or gender-diverse Autistic and/or neurodiverse people. *Clinical Practice in Paediatric Psychology, 7*(4), 396–404. https://doi.org/10.1037/cpp0000310

Chapter 31:

Using Universal Design to Reduce the Double Empathy Problem Between Autistic and Non-Autistic Individuals

Larissa Minner

Introduction

The Double Empathy Problem is a communication challenge between people with differing perspectives and experiences that notably takes on a distinctive form between autistic and non-autistic individuals (Jones et al., 2023). This specific type of Double Empathy Problem has gained recognition through recent studies and personal narratives. Rooted in the interplay of divergent communication and social styles, this phenomenon often leads to mutual misunderstandings, making it essential to bridge the gap by fostering understanding from both perspectives. Recent research, including insights from autistic individuals, emphasizes the unique communication approaches of both groups, contributing to the complexity of the Double Empathy Problem (Crompton et al., 2020; Mitchell et al., 2021; Shaw et al., 2023).

Often, the sole burden is on the autistic individual to adapt their behaviour to meet the non-autistic individual's needs, increasing the risk of developing autistic burnout (Raymaker et al., 2020). As an autistic individual who has experienced the Double Empathy Problem first hand, I recognize the importance of finding effective solutions to bridge this communication gap. This chapter delves into the potential of universal design as a strategic tool to mitigate the Double Empathy Problem, particularly among autistic and non-autistic adults, by addressing communication, sensory and cognitive barriers.

Universal design, characterized by its commitment to inclusivity, can create environments where communication and sensory barriers are reduced, and empathy is enhanced for individuals with diverse communication styles.

What is universal design?

Universal design involves making changes that benefit everyone and that everyone has access to. Examples of universal design include wheelchair curb cuts that people with strollers and grocery carts can also use or closed captioning which anyone can enjoy. Universal design provides individuals with accessible environments without the need to disclose a diagnosis or identify as having a disability (Milton et al., 2016). Universal design is different from accessibility and reasonable accommodations but should optimally be incorporated with both. Universal design is proactive and benefits everyone, unlike accessibility and reasonable accommodations, which are reactive and individual-specific.

Common barriers faced by autistic individuals

The following list identifies the types of barriers commonly faced by autistic individuals:

- Attitudinal barriers: ableism, disablism and societal attitudes (Raymaker et al., 2020)
- Accessibility barriers: sensory, cognitive, communication and physical needs
- Programmatic and policy barriers: inaccessibility, underfunding, exclusion and delays in getting benefits and enacting policy changes.

Universal design benefits

Universal design can reduce negative attitudinal barriers toward autism and disability by promoting inclusive environments and fair access. Practices that support belonging contribute to lowered negative attitudes toward disability. If something is inaccessible, then meaningful interaction with people with disabilities, like autistic people will be reduced due to lack of access. In addition, many autistic people do not identify as having a disability, instead, viewing autism as a difference. Others may identify as having a disability or experiencing both a difference and a disability. Universal design helps bridge this gap and honours the diverse ways autistic people understand their identities. When there are supports in place, they also normalize accessibility and access. In addition, incorporating universal design can reduce attitudinal barriers by demonstrating that autistic people and people with disabilities matter. Ideally, universal design should be integrated before a launch and considered from the conception of any project.

Universal design reduces accessibility barriers by providing built-in strategies that reduce these barriers or their effects. For example, allowing every individual in a doctor's office the option to be texted or see their cue in an app, allows an autistic individual to wait in a different area that has reduced sensory input. Asking on a patient questionnaire about communication, sensory and anxiety needs can benefit all patients.

Communication considerations

While the concept of universal design often conjures images of physical accommodations such as elevators and printed materials in large font, it extends far beyond these tangible adjustments. Universal design serves as a comprehensive framework that transcends mere accessibility; it encapsulates an ethos of inclusivity that addresses attitudinal, cognitive, communicative and sensory barriers faced by autistic individuals. Communication is a key challenge in the Double Empathy Problem, and universal design offers strategies to level the playing field. Although an untraditional form of universal design, there are specific communication strategies that can be universally incorporated to reduce accessibility barriers. Use direct language and avoid relying solely on non-verbal body language. For instance, in professional settings, giving clear, sensitive feedback can prevent misunderstandings (Tomczak et al., 2021). Say what you mean and mean what you say. Asking clarifying questions instead of making assumptions can prevent misunderstandings (Wilson & Bishop; 2020). It can also be helpful to explain the purpose behind a question to enhance communication. Incorporating communication strategies into universal design can compensate for the Double Empathy Problem. Ideally, organizations should regularly ask about communication preferences and enable someone to communicate in their preferred method (Milton et al., 2016). Typically, both parties can benefit from being asked clarifying questions and using concise direct language. Offering plain language versions of texts can also mitigate communication breakdown from the Double Empathy Problem.

The application of universal design in job interviews exemplifies its effectiveness in mitigating the Double Empathy Problem. A classic example of universal design is offering all job candidates the opportunity to review the job questions in advance or at least what kinds of questions to expect. This type of universal design can help prevent the Double Empathy Problem by providing communication in writing, and giving the individual time to process the information, as well as time to prepare their answer.

In addition, studies suggest that modifying open-ended questions can benefit both autistic and non-autistic adults' performances in job interviews (Maras et al., n.d.). Modifying open-ended questions for clarity can lessen the impact of the Double Empathy Problem.

Some autistic individuals can benefit from additional processing time, especially in social and high-stress situations (Zapparrata et al., 2023). A universal design approach can be built in by giving extra time for everyone, even if it is just a few additional minutes. Everyone can be asked if they are ready before changing topics or going on to a new question. This approach can mitigate the Double Empathy Problem by lessening the need to use non-verbal communication and allowing for differences in processing information. People who use augmentative alternative communication or screen readers may need additional time to allow for communication, depending on the technology and individual needs (Mathis et al., 2011).

Announcing when small talk is likely to occur in meetings, for instance, near the beginning, and sticking to a schedule can be helpful. For example, it can be announced that optional small talk will happen in the first ten minutes of the meeting. Every individual can be offered the choice to arrive ten minutes late if they choose to do so.

Another workaround for differences in social expectations includes allowing for tactile or visual cues for when people can approach someone when working, when applicable. Some conferences or events utilize a colour-coded badge approach for the level of comfort someone has with being approached or touched.

Last, allowing for performance-based promotions, or promotions not based on social interactions can reduce the Double Empathy Problem's impact on an autistic individual's ability to move forward in the workplace. This ensures that differences in social expectations and communication styles are not inhibiting an autistic individual's ability to receive promotions.

Cognitive considerations

Sometimes differences in processing and understanding tone and language can contribute to the Double Empathy Problem. For example, River, an autistic person, finds it challenging to decipher the tone of voice and body language to deduce that someone is being sarcastic. Individuals interacting with River do not adjust their communication style or notice that River doesn't pick up on the sarcasm. This example of the Double Empathy Problem demonstrates how both parties can contribute to misunderstandings. Consider asking individuals their preferences on sarcasm and humour. Some people find it helpful if they are told when someone is joking or being sarcastic, if this is carried out respectfully. Refraining from figurative language can reduce misunderstandings when there are certain language disabilities present.

Plain language versions are often more inclusive of individuals with cognitive differences (Maaß, n.d.; Riddell & Igarashi, 2021). Providing a scannable QR code with a plain language version can help optimize accessibility.

In addition, providing one step at a time can make multistep instructions more inclusive and can accommodate individuals with executive function challenges. Breaking down complex instructions into a series of one-step instructions can be very beneficial. Moreover, consider offering instructions in multiple accessible formats, based on the person's preference if possible.

Offering visual aids can help individuals who have cognitive considerations that may contribute to the Double Empathy Problem. For example, a visual calendar or schedule can enhance understanding. Often, what may be intuitive to a neurotypical individual may not be apparent to an autistic individual. Allowing for clear cues can lessen the impact of the Double Empathy Problem. For example, it can be helpful to clearly mark where to line up in a setting and indicate where to order and pay in stores (Garner et al., 2022).

Encourage the use of technology tools to compensate for challenges in executive functioning. For example, reminders, calendars and task management apps can be utilized. Using email for meeting reminders can help everyone, including those with anxiety about unexpected changes, those with busy schedules or those with executive function challenges. Provide access to speech-to-text or text-to-speech software to assist with communication and written tasks.

Allow for multiple ways of presenting material to give autonomy and to accommodate diverse learning approaches (Glass et al., 2013; Milton et al., 2016; Rose, 2014).

Sensory considerations

Differences in sensory processing, including but not limited to a reduced tolerance or increased tolerance of sensory stimuli, are common in autistic individuals (MacLennan et al., 2021). Studies suggest the need for sensory-friendly spaces (Manning et al, 2023). A common manifestation of the Double Empathy Problem is that non-autistic adults may voice that a sensory stimulus isn't causing problems. This problem is typically more pronounced when an autistic individual has not yet been identified as autistic. Incorporating sensory universal design can ensure that unidentified autistic individuals are better accommodated. In addition, it can mitigate the need for an autistic individual to be able to convince someone that a sensory stimulus is causing problems.

Sensory universal design considerations include scent-free soaps and cleaning products, and consistent encouragement that people opt for scent-free personal products or refrain from them in certain spaces. Alternatives to fluorescent lighting and adjustable lighting can help (Black et al., 2022). It is important to consider how blinds, curtains and dim lighting might affect someone who is blind or has low vision. Sometimes, autistic individuals simply want to be allowed to wear sunglasses indoors without judgement. Being mindful of sounds and creating safe spaces to retreat to can benefit people with other identities or those that have disabilities. Having less cluttered spaces and clear pathways can benefit autistic people and non-autistic people, as well as people with disabilities. Offering remote or hybrid options enables an individual to be in control of their sensory environment. Offices can provide a quiet space, like a wellness room, for all employees to have access to. Providing safe, quiet spaces to retreat to at events can help. Offering the use of noise-cancelling headphones when possible and safe, for all employees, creates an inclusive environment for those with sensory needs. Classrooms can utilize clear zoning of restorative or escape areas with visual boundaries and other cues that can help students experiencing sensory overload.

Many autistic individuals have endorsed that 'the Deaf clap', in lieu of audience applause, can reduce sensory overload. When I was attending a conference, I experienced sensory overload from the audience repeatedly clapping so I ended up requesting the 'Deaf clap' as an accommodation. Often, a non-autistic person may underestimate the sensory impact of clapping. However, incorporating the 'Deaf clap' into conferences can compensate for the Double Empathy Problem by meeting autistic individuals' needs (Patel et al., 2022).

When universal design is incorporated, it can help make application processes more accessible and may increase success in employment and education.

Self-regulation considerations

Another common Double Empathy Problem is differences in self-regulation, including processing information like active listening.

For instance, some autistic individuals can focus and listen more actively if they do not make eye contact and if they engage in self-regulatory or stimming behaviour while listening. However, most individuals are taught that signs of active listening typically include eye contact and being still, as well as not fidgeting. An autistic individual may experience discomfort when engaging in typical active listening behaviours. Notably, someone may listen more effectively in different ways on different days, and it can even vary moment-to-moment. Universal design can minimize the Double Empathy Problem by incorporating questions or encouraging self-advocacy. For instance, an individual could begin the conversation by acknowledging that individuals may experience active listening differently and that they can let them know if they need to move around or look around. Or conversely, they can say they will assume the individual is listening unless they voice that they are finding it challenging. In addition, someone can periodically ask questions to check for understanding and attention. An interesting consideration is a recent study that suggests that some neurotypical individuals may experience distress when looking at the face of someone avoiding eye contact, but autistic individuals don't experience this distress (Clin & Kissine, 2023).

Finally, repetitive self-regulatory behaviours, or stimming, are often misunderstood by non-autistic individuals, leading to the Double Empathy Problem. For instance, an autistic individual may self-soothe by rocking their body, but a non-autistic individual may misinterpret this behaviour. For example, Bailey, an autistic worker, excitedly flaps their hands when their team wins a sales competition. However, Bailey's colleagues assume that Bailey's mannerisms do not serve any functional purpose and they falsely assume that Bailey is not expressing happiness at the team's success. Bailey's colleagues are comparing Bailey's body language and expressions to non-autistic individuals and are missing the signals that Bailey is happy. However, Bailey doesn't voice what their hand flapping means. Unfortunately, this Double Empathy Problem leads to disconnect and Bailey experiences exclusion at work. A simple universal design solution could be asking clarifying questions and encouraging self-advocacy. Training can also be used to show that individuals can express themselves in many valid ways. Workplaces and educational settings can provide universal access to fidget tools and allow for movement. Both non-autistic and autistic individuals must expand their horizons on the different ways people self-regulate and communicate.

Additional considerations

Anyone can benefit from being informed of changes in plans as soon as they occur. Being told about changes, or the possibility of change and transitions, may alleviate anxiety for some autistic individuals (National Autistic Society, n.d.).

Fostering supportive environments and collaboration

Establish a supportive and understanding work or learning environment where differences are embraced. Cognitive diversity can contribute to an organization's growth and improvement. Studies suggest financial benefits for organizations that fully integrate disability inclusion into their infrastructure (Accenture, 2023; Alemany & Vermuelen, 2023; Lindsay et al., 2018). Encouraging respectful collaboration and peer support to share responsibilities can promote a sense of responsibility.

Conclusion

Reflecting on the Double Empathy Problem, we see that it arises from differences in communication, social expectations and delivery styles often resulting in misunderstandings and social barriers. Yet these challenges can be meaningfully addressed with universal design, when integrated with easy access to accommodations and accessibility. By promoting direct communication, offering various communication methods, allowing extra processing time, creating sensory-friendly spaces and embracing individual differences, universal design bridges the communication gap between autistic and non-autistic individuals.

As we continue to explore the depths of neurodiversity, the integration of universal design principles continues to evolve. Embracing universal design as a multifaceted solution to the Double Empathy Problem requires ongoing advocacy and training. It is crucial to highlight the profound impact that inclusive environments can have on fostering genuine connections between autistic and non-autistic individuals. In embracing universal design, we embark on a journey toward neuro inclusive environments, where differences are not obstacles but pathways to growth and collaboration. Universal design not only fosters inclusivity but also promotes understanding and empathy, paving the way for a more harmonious interaction between autistic and non-autistic individuals. It is through this lens that we can envision a future where the Double Empathy Problem is but a distant memory, and a world where every individual, regardless of neurotype, finds their voice and is heard.

References

Accenture (2023). *The Disability Inclusion Imperative.* Accenture. https://www.accenture.com/content/dam/accenture/final/accenture-com/document-2/Disability-Inclusion-Report-Business-Imperative.pdf

Alemany, L., & Vermeulen, F. (2023). Disability as a source of competitive advantage. *Harvard Business Review, 101*(4), 62–71. https://hbr.org/2023/07/disability-as-a-source-of-competitive-advantageBlack, M. H., McGarry, S., Churchill, L., D'Arcy, E., Dalgleish, J., Nash, I., Jones, A., Tse, T. Y., Gibson, J., Bölte, S., & Girdler, S. (2022). Considerations of the built environment for autistic individuals: A review of the literature. *Autism, 26*(8), 1904–1915. https://doi.org/10.1177/13623613221102753

Clin, E., & Kissine, M. (2023). Neurotypical, but not autistic, adults might experience distress when looking at someone avoiding eye contact: A live face-to-face paradigm. Autism, *27*(7), 1949–1959. https://doi.org/10.1177/13623613221148553

Crompton, C. J., Ropar, D., Evans-Williams, C. V., Flynn, E. G., & Fletcher-Watson, S. (2020). Autistic peer-to-peer information transfer is highly effective. *Autism, 24*(7), 1704–1712. https://doi.org/10.1177/1362361320919286

Garner, A., Burns, P., Carolan, L., Price, T., & Pearson, Z. (2022). Good business: Creating an autism-friendly community using the SERVICE principles. *Disability & Society, 39*(3), 1–24. https://doi.org/10.1080/09687599.2022.2077174

Glass, D., Meyer, A., & Rose, D. (2013). Universal Design for learning and the arts. *Harvard Educational Review 83* (2), 98–119. https://doi.org/10.17763/haer.83.1.33102p26478p54pw

Jones, D. R., Botha, M., Ackerman, R. A., King, K., & Sasson, N. J. (2023). Non-autistic observers both detect and demonstrate the double empathy problem when evaluating interactions between autistic and non-autistic adults. *Autism, 28*(8), 2053–2065. https://doi.org/10.1177/13623613231219743

Lindsay, S., Cagliostro, E., Albarico, M., Mortaji, N., & Karon, L. (2018). A systematic review of the benefits of hiring people with disabilities. *Journal of Occupational Rehabilitation, 28*(4), 634–655. https://doi.org/10.1007/s10926-018-9756-z

Maaß, C. (n.d.). Easy language – plain language – easy language plus. Balancing comprehensibility and acceptability. *Core.* https://core.ac.uk/works/81752793

MacLennan, K., O'Brien, S., & Tavassoli, T. (2021). In our own words: The complex sensory experiences of autistic adults. *Journal of Autism and Developmental Disorders, 52,* 3061–3075. https://doi.org/10.1007/s10803-021-05186-3

Manning, C., Williams, G., & MacLennan, K. (2023). Sensory-inclusive spaces for autistic people: We need to build the evidence base. *Autism, 27*(6), 1511–1515. https://doi.org/10.1177/13623613231183541

Maras, K., Norris, J., Nicholson, J., Heasman, B., Remington, A., & Crane, L. (n.d.). Adapting job interview questions for autistic candidates. University of Bath. https://www.bath.ac.uk/publications/interviewing-an-autistic-person-toolkit-resources/attachments/adapting-job-interview-questions-autistic-candidates.pdf

Mathis, H., Sutherland, D., & McAuliffe, M. (2011). The effect of pause time upon the communicative interactions of young people who use augmentative and alternative communication. *International Journal of Speech-Language Pathology, 13*(5), 411–421. https://doi.org/10.3109/17549507.2011.524709

Meyer, A., Rose, D. H., & Gordon, D. (2014). *Universal Design for Learning: Theory and Practice.* CAST Professional Publishing.

Milton, D., Martin, N., & Melham,P. (2016). Beyond reasonable adjustment: Autistic-friendly spaces and Universal Design. In D. Milton, & N. Martin (Eds.), *Autism and Intellectual Disabilities in Adults. Volume 1, 2016* (pp. 81–86). Pavilion Press.

Minner, L. (TBD) This chapter is adapted from Working title: Preventing Neurodivergent Burnout Through Fostering Neuroinclusive Environments (Unpublished at the time of this writing)

Mitchell, P., Sheppard, E., & Cassidy, S. (2021). Autism and the double empathy problem: Implications for development and mental health. *British Journal of Developmental Psychology, 39*(1), 1–18. https://doi.org/10.1111/bjdp.12350

National Autistic Society (n.d.). *The SPELL Framework.* National Autistic Society. https://www.autism.org.uk/what-we-do/autism-know-how/training/the-spell-framework

Patel, T., Dorff, J., & Baker, A. (2022). Development of special needs classroom prototypes to respond to the sensory needs of students with exceptionalities. *Archnet-IJAR, 16* (2), 339–358. https:/doi.org/10.1108/ARCH-07-2021-0196

Raymaker, D. M., Teo, A. R., Steckler, N.A., Lentz, B., Scharer, M., Delos Santos, A., Kapp, S. K., Hunter, M,, Joyce, A., & Nicolaidis, C. (2020) “Having all of your internal resources exhausted beyond measure and being left with no clean-up crew”: Defining autistic burnout. *Autism in Adulthood. 2*(2), 132–143. https:/doi.org/10.1089/aut.2019.0079

Riddell, A., & Igarashi, Y. (2021). *Varieties of Plain Language.* https://doi.org/10.26615/978-954-452-072-4_133

Rose, D.H., Meyer, A., & Gordon, D. (2014). Universal Design for learning: Theory and practice. CAST Professional Publishing

Shaw, S. C., Carravallah, L., Johnson, M., O’Sullivan, J., Chown, N., Neilson, S., & Doherty, M. (2023). Barriers to healthcare and a ‘triple empathy problem’ may lead to adverse outcomes for autistic adults: A qualitative study. *Autism, 28*(7) 1746–1757. https://doi.org/10.1177/13623613231205629

Tomczak, M. T., Szulc, J. M., & Szczerska, M. (2021). Inclusive communication model supporting the employment cycle of individuals with autism spectrum disorders.*International Journal of Environmental Research and Public Health, 18*(9), 4696. https://doi.org/10.3390/ijerph18094696

Wilson, A. C., & Bishop, D. V. M. (2020). “Second guessing yourself all the time about what they really mean…”: Cognitive differences between autistic and non-autistic adults in understanding implied meaning. *PsyArXiv.* https://doi.org/10.31234/osf.io/f6ksu

Zapparrata, N. M., Brooks, P. J., & Ober, T. M. (2023). Slower processing speed in autism spectrum disorder: A meta-analytic investigation of time-based tasks. *Journal of Autism and Developmental Disorders,* 53, 4618–4640. https://doi.org/10.1007/s10803-022-05736-3

Chapter 32:

Bridging Double Empathy Gaps in the Higher Education Classroom

Lorna G. Hamilton and Ruth Knight

Introduction

In this chapter, we consider the implications of Double Empathy Theory for educational practice, specifically in the context of higher education. We begin by briefly reviewing recent empirical evidence that challenges the former orthodoxy in psychological science as to the nature of 'empathy' across neurotypes. Next, we consider how the Double Empathy Problem (Milton, 2012) may play out in classroom interactions between student and educator. We then present case studies of two third-year modules within a Psychology BSc programme that sought to reduce double empathy barriers in the classroom through the use of universal design for learning (UDL) techniques, interest- and strength-based approaches, and the removal of forced participation. We conclude by recommending adjustments to teaching practice that can help to make higher education more accessible for neurodivergent learners.

Empathy: From intrapsychic to interpersonal

The traditional biomedical approach to neurodevelopmental difference entails the identification and detailed description of (neurocognitive) 'pathology' in order to remediate an individual toward a 'healthy' (neuronormative) ideal. In the case of autism, differences in social communication have thus been explained as stemming from a faulty 'theory of mind', i.e., a difficulty in understanding the mental states of self and others – or cognitive empathy deficit – that is located within the brain of the autistic person (Baron-Cohen, 2000;

Leslie, 1987). This account of autism has been problematized within autistic communities for decades, and more recently also in the academic literature (Milton, 2012; Pellicano & den Houting, 2022). Its characterization of autism as an inherent inability to take the perspective of others has been uniquely stigmatizing, since empathy is often framed as a core feature of being human (Cage et al., 2018). However, many empirical studies now challenge the idea that a theory of mind deficit is either necessary or sufficient to explain autism (Gernsbacher & Yergeau, 2019; Speyer et al., 2021). Emerging transactional (Mitchell et al., 2021) or socioneuroconstructivist (López, 2015) accounts of autism shift from a narrow focus on neurocognitive mechanisms toward a broader conceptualization of person-in-context developing over time. For example, Mitchell et al. (2021) argue that cumulative experiences of exclusion, rejection and stigmatization from early childhood act to reinforce the segregation of autistic people from mainstream society. This renewed acknowledgement of the role of sociocultural context in understanding neurodevelopmental difference has important implications for where and how intervention should be targeted to improve outcomes for neurodivergent people. Interventions that aim to promote acceptance and inclusion of difference are needed in addition to those that seek to ameliorate individual-level difficulties.

The Double Empathy Problem (Milton, 2012; Milton et al., 2022) has provided a powerful challenge to cognitive deficit accounts of autism. Its central insight – that perspective-taking difficulties are relational – has far-reaching implications for the understanding of autism and neurodivergence more broadly. Milton's contention that social communication failure is more likely when two people have widely differing experiences, dispositions and expectations of each other (e.g., across neurotypes) offers a non-pathologizing, interactional account of the social differences associated with autism, which does not situate the locus of the problem solely with the neurodivergent party. There now exists a growing body of empirical evidence in support of the Double Empathy Problem as a theoretical framework; this evidence can be combined with lived experience accounts to shed light on the ways in which (often arbitrary) social norms and stigmatized attitudes contribute to social communication difficulties.

Recent experimental studies indicate that neurotypical people are often poor at taking the perspectives of autistic people, underlining the bidirectional nature of social communication. For example, using videos of autistic and neurotypical people's reactions to a set of events, Sheppard et al. (2016) showed that neurotypical participants interpreted the behavioural reactions of neurotypical actors more successfully than those of autistic actors, despite autistic actors being judged to be equally expressive. Further, Heasman and Gillespie (2018) used a bidirectional methodology to show that family members overestimate the extent to which their autistic relation is constrained within an egocentric perspective. The autistic participants meanwhile anticipated that their family members would rate them poorly on indicators of social competence, while judging the extent of their own social skills more favourably. These findings speak to the fact that neurotypical people often find it difficult to read the behaviours of autistic people and make mistakes in assigning meaning to these behaviours.

As well as showing poor accuracy in reading autistic behaviours, non-autistic people tend to judge autistic people negatively on the basis of scant behavioural information. Non-autistic observers form negative impressions of autistic people following minimal exposure (Sasson et al., 2017). Further, neurotypical people are more likely to say that they dislike autistic than neurotypical actors based on short observations of behaviour, citing awkwardness and 'lack of empathy' as reasons for negative judgements (Alkhaldi et al., 2021). In another study, autistic people were rated as more deceptive and less credible than neurotypical people, although negative judgements were unrelated to direct measures of stereotypically autistic behaviours, such as gaze aversion, repetitive body movements and flat affect (Lim et al., 2022). While some studies suggest that autistic people also form more negative first impressions of autistic than non-autistic actors (Grossman et al., 2019), these first impressions do not impact their willingness to interact, in contrast to neurotypical participants (DeBrabander et al., 2019; Sasson et al., 2017).

The consequences of being misunderstood and negatively judged are not trivial for neurodivergent people. In interviews and focus groups, autistic participants described others' misunderstandings of their behaviours and intentions as pervasive across the lifespan. Acceptance within the social environments where they lived, studied and worked was experienced as the exception rather than the rule, with far-reaching consequences for education, employment and health outcomes (Camus et al., 2022). Contrary to theories that posit a lack of social motivation to be a defining feature of autism (Chevallier et al., 2012), many autistic people express a desire for belonging that can be difficult to achieve in neurotypical-dominated social settings. Concerningly, thwarted belonging and an associated sense of being a burden to society are predictive of suicidality in autistic people (Pelton et al, 2020).

If double empathy barriers are commonly disruptive to interactional flow between autistic and non-autistic people, social communication is more likely (though not guaranteed) to run smoothly in same-neurotype interactions. Increasingly, research has sought to document how autistic communication may qualitatively differ from neuronormative conventions, without being less rich or less successful. In a paradigm in which transfer of information along 'diffusion chains' of eight people was examined, Crompton et al. (2020) showed that information was communicated equally effectively in same-neurotype chains whether all autistic or all non-autistic. However, performance was impaired in mixed-neurotype diffusion chains, in support of the predictions of Double Empathy Theory. Congruently, neurotypical observers rate all-autistic or all-neurotypical social interactions to be equally successful, and both more successful than mixed-neurotype interactions (Jones et al., 2023). Moreover, autistic survey respondents self-reported weaker theory of mind skills only when interacting with non-autistic people (Sheppard et al., 2023).

The impact of more positive interactional experiences with same-neurotype peers can be observed in naturalistic settings. In an observational study in a school club, autistic adolescents were increasingly likely to interact with same-neurotype peers over the five months of the study (Chen et al., 2021). Research suggests that there are measurable differences in friendship preferences and behaviours between autistic and neurotypical adolescents and adults; for instance, autistic people are more likely to enjoy activity-focused interaction over 'hanging out' without a purpose (Finke, 2023; Finke et al., 2019). Unconventional, yet successful and mutually satisfying, social relating between autistic people has been documented during a collaborative gaming activity (Heasman & Gillespie, 2019). In this study, autistic intersubjectivity was characterized by a '*generous assumption of common ground leading to rapid rapport*' (Heasman & Gillespie, 2019, p. 915) and low demands for communicative co-ordination. Similar findings are reported in a fine-grained linguistic analysis of autistic communication, with some autistic participants' communicative competence measurably increasing when in conversation with an autistic interlocutor (Williams et al., 2021). These studies highlight how 'social competence' is mutable and context-dependent.

Taken together, findings from this burgeoning experimental and observational research based on Double Empathy Theory indicate that: (i) social communication difficulties are bidirectional and do not reside solely within the autistic person; (ii) neurotypical people are poor at reading autistic behaviours and liable to ascribe negative meaning to them; and (iii) social communication between autistic people may be unconventional and qualitatively different from neuronormative interactional patterns, but can be equally successful and mutually satisfying. These insights have important implications for inclusive educational practice.

Double empathy in the university classroom

There has been a substantial increase in the number of neurodivergent students accessing higher education internationally in recent years, likely due to various factors including a global increase in the recognition of neurodevelopmental difference and university widening participation initiatives (Clouder et al., 2020). While research on experience and outcomes for this student population is in its infancy, available evidence suggests elevated levels of attrition, reduced belonging at university and more mental health need in comparison with neurotypical peers (Baczewski et al., 2022; Dwyer et al., 2023; Garcha & Smith, 2024). At the same time, employers and policymakers are beginning to recognize the benefits of neurocognitive diversity for problem-solving and innovation (Khan et al., 2023;

Krzeminska et al., 2019). There is, therefore, a pressing need for higher education to adopt neurodiversity-inclusive and -affirming practices, which will allow the widest possible range of learners to succeed and progress to post-university careers that are commensurate with ability (Cheriyan et al., 2021).

In this chapter we focus on addressing double empathy barriers in the classroom as a route to neurodiversity-affirming higher education practice. However, it is important to contextualize pedagogical practice both within the broader systemic context of the sector, and within students' educational journeys over time. Many neurodivergent students arrive at university with many years of negative experience of school that can include bullying and peer rejection (Humphrey & Hebron, 2015), inaccessible teaching practices (Gray et al., 2023), behaviour policies that disproportionately punish neurodivergence (Mesa & Hamilton, 2022), and, in some cases, extended periods of emotionally based school avoidance (Hamilton, 2024). Unsurprisingly then, many neurodivergent university students are often highly anxious, have a negative concept of self-in-education and low expectations that their needs will be met (Hamilton & Petty, 2023; Spaeth & Pearson, 2023).

Structural barriers within university systems can further marginalize neurodivergent students. The onus is often on the student to advocate for accommodations via disability services in order to access the curriculum; fear of stigmatization and confusion about how to navigate institutional structures and processes can inhibit students from self-advocacy (Clouder et al., 2020; Weiting Tan et al., 2023). Reliance on add-on accommodations, rather than universally accessible teaching and assessment practices, also reinforces deficit models of neurodivergence. In a recent interview study in the Australian context, autistic students reported that they had to 'game the system' and 'present in a certain way' in order to be granted accommodations, which lecturers were then not obliged to implement (Weiting Tan et al., 2023). Beyond the academic domain, the sensory environment and intensity of social expectations on campus can be overwhelming and lead students to consider dropping out (Gurbuz et al., 2019; Sarrett, 2018).

Against this backdrop of structural discrimination and high levels of situational anxiety related to education, collaborative efforts to dismantle double empathy barriers within the classroom might be transformational for neurodivergent students' experience at university. Autistic students, for example, are most often taught by non-autistic educators, and typically the burden of closing the communicative gap falls on the student by changing their preferred methods of communication to meet implicit neurotypical norms. In an interview study, autistic students described the anxiety provoked by verbal communication with tutors and fellow students in class, and the mental effort that they dedicated to preparing for and navigating these interactions (Ballentine & Artemeva, 2020). Many preferred communicating in written formats, although this option is rarely available in learning activities outside formal assessments. As educators, maintaining '*humility in the face of difference*' (Milton et al., 2022, p. 1902) might entail reflecting on the communicative demands of our teaching practice, being open to challenge and building in flexibility in how students access and engage with our curricula.

Universal Design for Learning (UDL; Center for Applied Special Technology, 2018) is an approach to pedagogy that involves planning for diversity in the classroom from the start of the design process. Core principles include providing multiple means for students to engage with the curriculum, represent information and demonstrate their learning. Embedding flexibility and choice within higher education curricula has the potential to mimimize the need for bolt-on accommodations for individual neurodivergent students and is likely to be to the benefit of all students (Roberts et al., 2011). Providing agency in how students navigate their way through the curriculum can also facilitate strength- and interest-led learning, which is potentially well-suited to neurodivergent attentional styles (Shaughnessy, 2022; Wood, 2019). UDL practices are not yet widespread in higher education, and the evidence base for their effectiveness in promoting engagement, belonging and attainment for diverse student groups is in development. However, there is increasing interest in how UDL can be harnessed as a neurodiversity-inclusive pedagogy in university settings (Burgstahler & Russo-Gleicher, 2015; Waisman et al., 2023), and initial evidence that such approaches are positively evaluated by neurodivergent students in comparison with traditional pedagogies (e.g., Barrera Ciurana & Moliner Garcia, 2023).

Finally, Milton (2019) highlights the importance of forming communities of practice including a range of stakeholders in creating educational experiences that are appropriate for neurodivergent learners. Collaborative approaches, including co-production of programmes of learning with students, may be effective in creating common ground, bridging double empathy gaps and redressing power imbalances in the classroom (Weiting Tan et al., 2023). In the next section, we present examples from our own teaching practice in which we have tried to implement these principles.

Case studies: Toward neurodiversity-affirming practice at university

In this section, we present case studies of two third-year undergraduate modules within an undergraduate Psychology programme at a small, widening participation university in a city in the north-east of England. In the design and delivery of these modules, we sought to reflect on power imbalances in the classroom, bridge double empathy barriers and enact neurodiversity-affirming pedagogical practice.

Institutional context

Based on the most recent available data, the total student population at York St John University is under 10,000, comprising proportions of disabled (20.5%), female (61.4%),

LGB+ (17.9%) and transgender (1.6%) students that are higher than average in UK higher education (Higher Education Statistics Agency, 2022). Conversely, proportions of global majority (7.3%) and mature (32.8%) students are lower than sector averages. Using the language and taxonomy of the Higher Education Statistics Agency (HESA) disability subcategories, 7.8% of students at York St John University disclose a mental health condition; 5.2% a specific learning disability (which in this classification includes dyslexia, developmental coordination disorder [DCD] and attention deficit hyperactivity disorder [ADHD]); and 1.4% a 'social or communication impairment' (i.e., autism). We note that these figures are likely to be significant underestimates of prevalence, since many students do not disclose their diagnoses at university for fear of negative responses and stigma (Anderson et al., 2018), while others have not received diagnoses by the time they register at university (White et al., 2011).

The Psychology undergraduate provision in the 2022–2023 academic year comprised a suite of four British Psychological Society-accredited BSc programmes. Across the suite, annual cohort size is typically between 200 and 300 students, who study core modules together at Levels 4 and 5 (first and second year) and differentiate into specialist pathways at Level 6 (third year). The two modules outlined in the case studies below are specialist or optional Level 6 modules, with class sizes not exceeding 40 students.

Case Study 1: Harnessing universal design and strength-based assessment

'Neurodiversity in Development' is a core final-year module for students on the BSc Psychology and Child Development programme. The curriculum seeks to combine knowledge from scientific research and lived experience to provide a holistic and non-pathologizing understanding of neurocognitive difference (focusing particularly on autism, ADHD, developmental language disorder [DLD], dyslexia, dyscalculia and DCD). The module is taught over twelve weeks, comprising weekly seminars, online activities and two summative assessment points.

In designing this module, I (LH) was mindful of first-person accounts from neurodivergent students describing higher education curricula that presented a narrowly pathologized model of autism and neurodivergence (e.g., Botha, 2021). Reading such accounts prompted me to reflect on previous teaching experiences when I had approached these topics without careful enough consideration of how the material might be received by a neurodiverse student population. The class for this module included several students with diagnoses of autism, ADHD and/or other neurodivergences; I wanted to co-create a learning environment in which they would feel safe to share their first-hand expertise should they wish to. To that end, a range of communication channels (e.g., anonymous brief questionnaires; in-person or online tutorials) was made available to all students, so that they could suggest additions to the curriculum, challenge content or contribute personal experiences. Qualms about disrupting the traditional classroom power structures were quickly dispelled, as students of all neurotypes contributed and enriched the module.

This was the first time that I had explicitly designed a module using UDL, although many of the individual techniques were familiar as good practice for inclusive teaching. I took as a starting point the Universal Design for Learning Guidelines (Center for Applied Special Technology, 2018), aiming to address all 31 checkpoints. I opted to discuss the principles of UDL explicitly with the students at the start of the module, in order to invite their reflections on what was working well or less well as the weeks progressed and their suggestions of additional techniques that I had not thought of. The principles of UDL are also highly relevant to the module content, allowing students to reflect on the science of neurodiversity as applied to their own learning. Here, I summarize key co-created module enhancements, with a common aim of increasing flexibility, agency and accessibility for all students. No formal evaluation of the implementation of UDL in this module was undertaken; in the reflections presented here, students' feedback gathered via various, iterative mechanisms are used to illustrate the techniques described.

A class contract, drawn up during the first seminar, set out mutually agreed expectations of each other from the start of the module. In terms of students' engagement, my expectations were that they would engage in a way that was comfortable and effective for them. For example, they could communicate with me verbally during classes or in tutorials; in writing during or between classes using the online discussion forum; or anonymously via a Padlet board. For interactive activities in class, they could choose to discuss questions in pairs or small groups or think by themselves. Neurodivergent students tended to work independently or in a small group with each other in the early seminars; I observed a slow increase in communication with other members of the class over the course of the module. Where possible, physical movement was built into class activities; for example, students were assigned topics to research independently, wherever they were comfortable on campus, before returning to share their findings with the class. Students appreciated the flexibility and choice that this offered:

> *It has allowed me to feel able to ask questions and have content explained to me in a way that makes sense to me.*
>
> *The amount of choice made it our module just as much as it is yours.*

While it was expected that students would read academic papers on a weekly basis in preparation for seminars, these could be accessed via text-to-speech software and supplemented by relevant podcasts, videos and infographics. A glossary of key terms, and weekly space in seminars to consolidate the previous week's learning were also designed to facilitate comprehension of core material. These techniques helped students to manage information overload, and seemed to increase motivation to engage with reading academic material:

> *Having podcasts, videos and blogs available to choose from really supported my engagement outside the classroom. I also found I was more likely to do my own further reading following my interests.*
>
> *Made it easier to take in more information without feeling overwhelmed.*

One assessment task for the module required students to translate scientific information for a lay audience. Students were given choice in: (i) the topic (from a short list of options, or an approved topic of their choosing); (ii) the format that the information was presented in (e.g., blog, information sheet, recorded or live presentation, infographic or animation; and (iii) the audience that the information was tailored for (e.g., teachers, clinicians). When submitting this work, students were also given the option to request what they would like their feedback to focus on (e.g., conceptual understanding; appropriateness of communication for the audience) and how they would like to receive feedback (e.g., as usual – written and uploaded to the virtual learning environment; via voice note; or in a tutorial (possible only because of the small class size).

I did not anticipate the diversity and quality of work that students produced for this assessment. Overall, students seemed to relish the opportunity to follow their interests within clear boundaries, and to utilize existing skills that otherwise do not have an outlet in a traditional Psychology degree programme. For instance, one student produced an animation on the topic of monotropism for teachers, while another recorded an illustrated presentation on autism in girls for speech and language therapists. Careful scrutiny of the learning outcomes and assessment criteria, with consideration of how they could be applied for work in different formats, was necessary with the support of internal and external examiners in order to maintain quality standards and equitability. However, the built-in flexibility and choice offered by this assessment seemed to increase students' effort and engagement, while also making marking less onerous and more enjoyable.

Employing UDL and strength-based assessment in this module was a pilot exercise in a small class; scaling up these approaches for larger classes would bring additional challenges. Nonetheless, it resulted in a highly rewarding teaching experience, while seemingly having benefits for all students regardless of neurotype (based on anecdotal feedback and subjective observation in the absence of a formal evaluation). Students' attendance in class was noticeably higher than previous modules I have taught at the same level. All students passed the course. Student satisfaction at midpoint evaluation was very high (4.9/5) and 100% of students agreed that the UDL elements had helped them to engage with the module. In the final seminar, I asked the class whether they would be willing to write more in-depth reflections on their learning experience in this module. Two testimonials are included here:

> *I found it easier to contribute to discussions in this module, because I don't feel pressured to contribute. Being able to choose the format of our assessment has been very helpful for me. I was able to choose a creative format that I have experience with. The sessions include breaks, partner and group discussions, and often group research in the library, which gives me breaks from sitting still and makes it easier to concentrate and take in more content in different ways.* (Student with diagnoses of autism and ADHD)

> *I struggled socially in my first year at university, which was made worse by COVID restrictions. In contrast to others, I enjoyed online learning. Learning at my own pace, online in my own home, was ideal for me. This comfort did not extend to my second year. I found the lights in the lectures too bright, I felt unable to ask for help within large groups, and I often struggled with fatigue resulting in me missing lectures. The structure of this module comes from a place of understanding about neurodivergent brains, which has massively helped me to feel comfortable. I get to follow what I'm interested in and complete the assignment in the best way for me, which I believe has improved the quality of my work. I still struggle with noises from inside and outside the building and the lights still hurt my eyes, but I know that I am not going to be chastised or singled out for wearing my headphones or looking away from the board, which allows me to do the things I need to do to keep learning and stay engaged.* (Student on diagnostic pathway for autism)

Case Study 2: Disrupting neuronormative expectations of participation

'Critical Approaches to Mental Health' is a third-year optional module offered as part of the BSc Psychology programme. Broadly, the curriculum focuses on non-traditional models of mental health through a critical lens. This includes work around co-production in mental health research, the survivor movement and Mad Pride, the role of lived experience in both research and practice, and organizations taking alternative approaches to mental health intervention, such as Converge (free university-based arts education for people struggling with their mental health; Anderson et al., 2022).

As a neurodivergent lecturer, I (RK) approached my first semester of teaching with some apprehension inherited from experiences in my own degree. These were characterized by anxiety around pressure to participate in ways deemed appropriate by institutions, such as verbal responses to questions in class, presentations to other students in seminars and group discussions. For neurodivergent students these typical ways of taking part in learning can be both daunting and inaccessible, pointing to the central Double Empathy Problem within university teaching. That is, lecturers and wider institutions often expect neurodivergent students to learn and respond in neurotypical ways. In order to disrupt this expectation, I aimed to work collaboratively with students to remove expectations around rates and means of participation. The first step in this was explicitly stating in the introductory session that there would be no compulsory participation as part of the module, including presentations, answers to questions or group/class discussions. The next step involved co-producing alternative means of participation that were accessible for different needs. The first iteration of this module included regular office hours online and in-person; an open Padlet page for anonymous contributions; flexibility in class activities (e.g., the option to do a presentation one-on-one, online or in-person, or to record a presentation); time for unstructured conversation at breaks and the end of class sessions; and a clear open email policy, as well as an online discussion forum.

When considering the changes that could be made to a predesigned module to attempt to overcome some of the double empathy barriers in the classroom, my assumption was that removing the compulsory nature of participation would reduce interaction in seminars. This was true for the first one or two sessions in which we gathered as a group: when asking questions to the class as a whole, only a couple of students would reply. The course comprised twelve sessions in total, and by the third session it was notable that group discussions were more active and took longer, and that whole-class discussions around broader questions began to take place. This trend continued for the rest of the course. I was somewhat (pleasantly) surprised that removing the assumption of forced participation actually led to increased voluntary interaction within seminars. We suggest that this is due to a resolution of some of the double empathy barriers that can exist within the classroom, particularly when course content is explicitly focused on mental health.

The response from students to the lack of forced participation was positive. In the introductory session where this principle was set out, students expressed surprise and, to a certain extent, confusion around how seminars would work. Creating a space for these reactions was important, particularly considering the many ways in which this approach diverged from traditional university teaching experiences. Some students were concerned that discussions would not be engaging or that there would be a lack of reciprocity in interactions. There were also some concerns that the seminars would be too much like a lecture. Both mid-module and end-of-module feedback demonstrated that these concerns had not come to fruition, and that students found the lack of pressure both refreshing and encouraging. One student said: *'I like how we're encouraged to feed back to the group but it's not forced. The discussions are handled very sensitively and in a positive manner.'* Concerns around interactivity were also resolved by the midpoint of the module, with one student saying: *'There are many interactive sessions within this module, and this makes it much easier to remember the content. There are always intriguing discussions during the sessions as well as great prompts on the slides.'*

The worries that students had at the beginning of the course mirrored my own, particularly around whether the seminars would revert to one-sided lectures, something I wanted to avoid. There was some hesitation in the first couple of sessions of the seminar course, perhaps because of the lack of neuronormative communication expectations, such as questions being posed and then silence used to encourage students to respond. However, students quickly began to create spaces in which they were comfortable engaging. For some, this was in whole-class discussions scaffolded by me, and for others it was in smaller group discussions. For me, this highlights the importance of allowing students the autonomy and agency to decide on their own engagement styles. Frequently in higher education, we expect students to conform to neurotypical norms around engagement and interactivity, which for many directly conflicts with their own ways of being.

Another student highlighted that the lack of forced participation allows for *'really good discussions, [I] feel comfortable contributing in class'*. This was echoed in other feedback, both written and also in discussions with students. Many pointed out that the lack of forced participation actually facilitated the creation of a safe space within the classroom, which allowed hitherto unconsidered perspectives to be shared: *'The conversation and discussion are really welcoming and a safe space to hear different viewpoints and different ideas, potentially not previously thought about'*. There has been much written around the creation of safe spaces in academia, and the complexities involved in this for both students and educators (VanderStouwe., 2015; Waugh, 2019). It is clear from feedback that, in this instance, students felt that the lack of forced expectations of participation facilitated the creation of a safe classroom environment, where challenging topics and issues could be discussed and grappled with.

In terms of evaluation metrics, 100% of students either agreed or strongly agreed that the lack of forced participation contributed to a better classroom environment, and several commented on the increased attendance among their peers. This was something echoed in my own reflections, as there were far fewer absences than I would have expected, and any absences were always communicated to me. All students passed the module, and there were no fails for either of the assessments.

Conclusions

The growing empirical literature based on Double Empathy Theory highlights the interactional nature of social communication difficulties. To date, most of this evidence base relates to autism; however, the same principles likely apply across other neurotypes. Research from this perspective converges to show how frequent misunderstandings, and hasty negative evaluation, of behaviours perpetuate the stigma and discrimination experienced by neurodivergent people. At the same time, research examining the nature of social communication in same-neurotype contexts demonstrates that neurodivergent communication is often highly effective, functional and mutually satisfying, albeit qualitatively different from neurotypical norms. Given that most education is inherently relational, the implications of these findings for educators working with neurodiverse student populations are profound. To dismantle double empathy barriers in the classroom, the onus is on us as educators to reflect on our teaching practice and seek to create learning environments that are accessible for all of the students we work with.

Neuronormative expectations colour our ideas of what university education should look like, often shaped by our own learning preferences and/or experiences as a student. The Double Empathy Problem challenges us to interrogate our assumptions about what student behaviours in the classroom mean, and to acknowledge that our reading of these behaviours may be inaccurate. Simply becoming aware of this may help us to create more inclusive learning environments. A willingness to relax normative expectations of student engagement and disrupt traditional power dynamics in the classroom can have far-reaching effects on individual students' ability to engage in ways that are accessible for them. Embedding flexibility and choice for students to navigate core course material using UDL is neurodiversity-affirming, but can be beneficial for all students regardless of neurotype. We propose that adapting teaching practice based on understandings of the Double Empathy Problem need not be overly complicated or difficult; in practice, small changes can have significant impact in facilitating an inclusive learning environment.

On the other hand, it is easy to replicate power dynamics that reinforce the Double Empathy Problem: i.e., the lecturer is the locus of knowledge, both about the subject and about how it should be taught and assessed, and students are the recipients of this knowledge. In both case studies, we have outlined practices that deliver more control and autonomy back to the student, trusting that they are the expert in what is accessible for them and effective for their own learning. Such approaches may initially feel uncomfortable for us as educators; however, in the longer term they can promote engagement and reduce anxiety for students, which in turn leads to more rewarding teaching experiences.

As understanding of neurocognitive difference improves, with more research conducted within the neurodiversity paradigm, it is likely that students attending university will be increasingly aware of their own needs. As educators, we can rise to this challenge by reflecting on communicative practices within our teaching, and seeking to make adjustments that make our curricula accessible to the widest range of learners. Incidentally, this may also have the effect of making classrooms more interactive, engaging and fun! It is also worth noting that many educators working in higher education are themselves neurodivergent (Bertilsdotter Rosqsvist et al., 2023; Jones et al., 2023). Creating a campus culture where neurodivergence is acknowledged and welcomed will have the added benefit of facilitating a more hospitable working environment for these colleagues. In a culture where neurodivergent academic staff feel enabled to work authentically and disclose their neurodivergence should they wish to, a virtuous cycle is created; our neurodivergent students can see the value of neurocognitive difference in the professional workplace.

References

Alkhaldi, R. S., Sheppard, E., Burdett, E., & Mitchell, P. (2021). Do neurotypical people like or dislike autistic people? *Autism in Adulthood, 3*(3), 275–279. https://doi.org/10.1089/aut.2020.0059

Anderson, A. H., Carter, M., & Stephenson, J. (2018). Perspectives of university students with autism spectrum disorder. *Journal of Autism & Developmental Disorders, 48*, 651–665. https://doi.org/10.1007/s10803-017-3257-3

Anderson, E., Bell, A., Birch, P., Coleman, L., Gowland, P., Harper-Hardcastle, M., Ingham, E., Ostrowska, B., & Paylor, K. (2022). Rewriting the space between a university and a healthcare provider: The model of Converge. In C. Walker, S. Zlotowitz, & A. Zoli, *The Palgrave Handbook of Innovative Community and Clinical Psychologies*, (pp. 259–276). Springer International Publishing.

Baczewski, L. M., Pizzano, M., Kasari, C., & Sturm, A. (2022). Adjustment across the first college year: A matched comparison of autistic, attention-deficit/hyperactivity disorder, and neurotypical Students. *Autism in Adulthood, 4*(1), 12–21. https://doi.org/10.1089/aut.2021.0012

Ballatine, J., & Artemeva, N. (2020). Reports from autistic university students about their interactions with non-autistic and autistic individuals: A rhetorical gender studies perspective. *Revista da Anpoll, 51*(2). https://doi.org/10.18309/anp.v51i2.1406

Baron-Cohen, S. (2000). Theory of mind and autism: A review. *International Review of Research in Mental Retardation, 23*, 169–184. https://doi.org/10.1016/S0074-7750(00)80010-5

Barrera Ciurana, M., & Moliner García, O. (2023). 'How does universal design for learning help me to learn?': Students with autism spectrum disorder voices in higher education. *Studies in Higher Education, 49*(6), 899-912. https://doi.org/10.1080/03075079.2023.2259932

Bertilsdotter Rosqvist, H., Botha, M., Hens, K., O'Donoghue, S., Pearson, A., & Stenning, A. (2023). Cutting our own keys: New possibilities of neurodivergent storying in research. *Autism 27*(5), 1235–1244. https://doi.org/10.1177/13623613221132107

Botha, M. (2021). Academic, activist, or advocate? Angry, entangled, and emerging: A critical reflection on autism knowledge production. *Frontiers in Psychology*, 12. https://doi.org/10.3389/fpsyg.2021.727542

Burgstahler, S., & Russo-Gleicher, R. J. (2015). Applying universal design to address the needs of postsecondary students on the autism spectrum. *Journal of Postsecondary Education and Disability, 28*(2), 199–212.

Cage, E., Di Monaco, J., & Newell, V. (2018). Understanding, attitudes and dehumanisation towards autistic people. *Autism, 23*(6), 1373–1383. https://doi.org/10.1177/1362361318811290

Camus, L., Macmillan, K., Gnanathusharan, R., & Stewart, M. (2022). 'I too need to belong': Autistic adults' perspectives on misunderstandings and well-being. *PsyArXiv Preprints*. https://doi.org/10.31234/osf.io/5mysh

Center for Applied Special Technology (2018). *Universal Design for Learning Guidelines Version 2.2*. Center for Applied Special Technology (CAST). http://udlguidelines.cast.org

Chen, Y.-L., Senande, L. L., Thorsen, M., & Patten, K. (2021). Peer preferences and characteristics of same-group and cross-group social interactions among autistic and non-autistic adolescents. *Autism, 25*(7), 1885–1900. https://doi.org/10.1177/13623613211005918

Cheriyan, C., Shevchuk-Hill, S., Riccio, A., Vincent, J., Kapp, S. K., Cage, E., Dwyer, P., Kofner, B., Attwood, H., & Gillespie-Lynch, K. (2021). Exploring the career motivations, strengths, and challenges of autistic and non-autistic university students: Insights from a participatory study. *Frontiers in Psychology, 12*, https://doi.org/10.3389/fpsyg.2021.719827

Chevallier, C., Kohls, G., Troiani, V., Brodkin, E. S., & Schultz, R. T. (2012). The social motivation theory of autism. *Trends in Cognitive Sciences, 16*(4), 231–239. https://doi.org/10.1016/j.tics.2012.02.007

Clouder, L., Karakus, M., Cinotti, A. Ferreyra, M. V., Fierros, G. F., & Rojo, P. (2020). Neurodiversity in higher education: a narrative synthesis. *Higher Education, 80*, 757–778. https://doi.org/10.1007/s10734-020-00513-6

Crompton, C. J., Ropar, D., Evans-Williams, C. V., Flynn, E. G., & Fletcher-Watson, S. (2020). Autistic peer-to-peer information transfer is highly effective. *Autism, 24*(7), 1704–1712. https://doi.org/10.1177/1362361320919286

DeBrabander, K. M., Morrison, K. E., Jones, D. R., Faso, D. J., Chmielewski, M., & Sasson, N. J. (2019). Do first impressions of autistic adults differ between autistic and nonautistic observers? *Autism in Adulthood, 1*(4), 250–257. https://doi.org/10.1089/aut.2019.0018

Dwyer, P., Mineo, E., Mifsud, K., Lindholm, C., Gurba, A., & Waisman, T. C. (2023). Building neurodiversity-inclusive postsecondary campuses: Recommendations for leaders in higher education. *Autism in Adulthood*, 5(1), 1–14. http://doi.org/10.1089/aut.2021.0042

Finke, E. H. (2023). The kind of friend I think I am: Perceptions of autistic and non-autistic young adults. *Journal of Autism & Developmental Disorders, 53*, 3047–3064. https://doi.org/10.1007/s10803-022-05573-4

Finke, E. H., McCarthy, J. H., & Sarver, N. A. (2019). Self-perception of friendship style: Young adults with and without autism spectrum disorder. *Autism & Developmental Language Impairments, 4*. https://doi.org/10.1177/2396941519855390

Garcha, J., & Smith, A. P. (2024). Associations between autistic and ADHD traits and the well-being and mental health of university students. *Healthcare, 12*(1), 14. https://doi.org/10.3390/healthcare12010014

Gernsbacher, M. A., & Yergeau, M. (2019). Empirical failures of the claim that autistic people lack a theory of mind. *Archives of Scientific Psychology, 7*(1), 102–118. https://doi.org/10.1037/arc0000067

Gray, L., Hill, V., & Pellicano, E. (2023). "He's shouting so loud but nobody's hearing him": A multi-informant study of autistic pupils' experiences of school non-attendance and exclusion. *Autism & Developmental Language Impairments, 8*. https://doi.org/10.1177/23969415231207816

Grossman, R. B., Mertens, J., & Zane, E. (2019). Perceptions of self and other: Social judgments and gaze patterns to videos of adolescents with and without autism spectrum disorder. *Autism, 23*(4), 846–857. https://doi.org/10.1177/1362361318788071

Gurbuz, E., Hanley, M., & Riby, D. (2019). University students with autism: The social and academic experiences of university in the UK. *Journal of Autism & Developmental Disorders, 49*, 617–631. https://doi.org/10.1007/s10803-018-3741-4

Hamilton, L. G. (2024). Emotionally based school avoidance in the aftermath of the COVID-19 pandemic: Neurodiversity, agency and belonging in school. *Education Sciences*, online first.

Hamilton, L. G., & Petty, S. (2023). Compassionate pedagogy for neurodiversity in higher education: A conceptual analysis. *Frontiers in Psychology, 14*(2), 156. https://doi.org/10.3389/fpsyg.2023.1093290

Heasman, B., & Gillespie, A. (2018). Perspective-taking is two-sided: Misunderstandings between people with Asperger's syndrome and their family members. *Autism, 22*(6), 740–750. https://doi.org/10.1177/1362361317708287

Heasman, B., & Gillespie, A. (2019). Neurodivergent intersubjectivity: Distinctive features of how autistic people create shared understanding. *Autism, 23*(4), 910–921. https://doi.org/10.1177/1362361318785172

Higher Education Statistics Agency (2022). *Higher Education Student Statistics: UK, 2021/22*. Higher Education Statistics Agency (HESA). https://www.hesa.ac.uk/news/19-01-2023/sb265-higher-education-student-statistics

Humphrey, N., & Hebron, J. (2015). Bullying of children and adolescents with autism spectrum conditions: A 'state of the field' review. *International Journal of Inclusive Education, 19*(8), 845–862. https://doi.org/10.1080/13603116.2014.981602

Jones, D. R., Botha, M., Ackerman, R. A., King, K., & Sasson, N. J. (2023). Non-autistic observers both detect and demonstrate the double empathy problem when evaluating interactions between autistic and non-autistic adults. *Autism, 28*(8), 2053-2065. https://doi.org/10.1177/13623613231219743

Jones, S. C. (2023). Autistics working in academia: What are the barriers and facilitators? *Autism, 27*(3), 822–831. https://doi.org/10.1177/13623613221118158

Khan, M. H., Grabarski, M. K., Ali, M., & Buckmaster, S. (2023). Insights into creating and managing an inclusive neurodiverse workplace for positive outcomes: A multistaged theoretical framework. *Group & Organization Management, 48*(5), 1339–1386. https://doi.org/10.1177/10596011221133583

Krzeminska, A., Austin, R. D., Bruyère, S. M., & Hedley, D. (2019). The advantages and challenges of neurodiversity employment in organizations. *Journal of Management & Organization, 25*(4), 453–463. https://doi.org/10.1017/jmo.2019.58

Leslie, A. M. (1987). Pretense and representation: The origins of "theory of mind". *Psychological Review, 94*, 412–426. https://doi.org/10.1037/0033-295X.94.4.412

Lim, A., Young, R. L., & Brewer, N. (2022). Autistic adults may be erroneously perceived as deceptive and lacking credibility. *Journal of Autism & Developmental Disorders, 52*, 490–507. https://doi.org/10.1007/s10803-021-04963-4

López, B. (2015). Beyond modularisation: The need of a socio-neuro-constructionist model of autism. *Journal of Autism & Developmental Disorders, 45*, 31–41. https://doi.org/10.1007/s10803-013-1966-9

Mesa, S., & Hamilton, L. G. (2022). School transitions for autistic young people in mainstream settings: A research report. *Institute for Social Justice*. https://www.yorksj.ac.uk/media/content-assets/research/institute-for-social-justice/School-transitions-for-autistic-pupils-report.pdf

Milton, D. (2012). On the ontological status of autism: The 'double empathy problem'. *Disability & Society, 27*(6), 883–887. https://doi.org/10.1080/09687599.2012.710008

Milton, D. (2019) Difference versus disability: Implications of characterisation of autism for education and support. In R. Jordan, J. M. Roberts, & K. Hume (Eds.), *The Sage Handbook of Autism and Education* (pp. 3–11). Sage.

Milton, D., Gurbuz, E., & López, B. (2022). The 'double empathy problem': Ten years on. *Autism, 26*(8), 1901–1903. https://doi.org/10.1177/13623613221129123

Mitchell, P., Sheppard, E., & Cassidy, S. (2021). Autism and the double empathy problem: Implications for development and mental health. *British Journal of Developmental Psychology, 39*(1), 1–18. https://doi.org/10.1111/bjdp.12350

Pellicano, E., & den Houting, J. (2022). Annual research review: Shifting from 'normal science' to neurodiversity in autism science. *Journal of Child Psychology and Psychiatry, 63(4)*, 381–396. https://doi.org/10.1111/jcpp.13534

Pelton, M. K., Crawford, H., Robertson, A. E., Rodgers, J., Baron-Cohen, S., & Cassidy, S. (2020). Understanding suicide risk in autistic adults: Comparing the interpersonal theory of suicide in autistic and non-autistic samples. *Journal of Autism & Developmental Disorders, 50*, 3620–3627. https://doi.org/10.1007/s10803-020-04393-8

Roberts, K. D., Park, H. J., Brown, S., & Cook, B. (2011). Universal design for instruction in postsecondary education: A systematic review of empirically based articles. *Journal of Postsecondary Education and Disability, 24*(1), 5–15.

Sarrett, J. C. (2018). Autism and accommodations in higher education: Insights from the autism community. *Journal of Autism & Developmental Disorders, 48*, 679–693. https://doi.org/10.1007/s10803-017-3353-4

Sasson, N. J., Faso, D. J., Nugent, J., Lovell, S., Kennedy, D. P., & Grossman, R. B. (2017). Neurotypical peers are less willing to interact with those with autism based on thin slice judgments. *Scientific Reports, 7*(1), 1–10. https://doi.org/10.1038/srep40700

Shaughnessy, N. (2022). Learning with labyrinths. *Critical Studies in Teaching and Learning (CriSTaL), 10*(SI), 127–150. https://doi.org/10.14426/cristal.v10iSI.546

Sheppard, E., Pillai, D., Wong, G. T.-L., Ropar, D., & Mitchell, P. (2016). How easy is it to read the minds of people with autism spectrum disorder? *Journal of Autism & Developmental Disorders, 46*, 1247–1254. https://doi.org/10.1007/s10803-015-2662-8

Sheppard, E., Webb, S., & Wilkinson, H. (2023). Mindreading beliefs in same- and cross-neurotype interactions. *Autism, 28*(7), 1828-1837. https://doi.org/10.1177/13623613231211457

Spaeth, E., & Pearson, A. (2023). A reflective analysis on how to promote a positive learning experience for neurodivergent students. *Journal of Perspectives in Applied Academic Practice, 11*(2). https://doi.org/10.56433/jpaap.v11i2.517

Speyer, L. G., Brown, R. H., Camus, L., Murray, A. L., & Auyeung, B. (2021). Alexithymia and autistic traits as contributing factors to empathy difficulties in preadolescent children. *Journal of Autism and Developmental Disorders, 52*, 823–834. https://doi.org/10.1007/s10803-021-04986-x

VanderStouwe, C. (2015). Combating privilege, regulating language: The struggle to create and maintain university safe spaces. *Journal of Language and Sexuality, 4*(2), 272–287. https://doi.org/10.1075/jls.4.2.42

Waisman, T., Williams, Z. J., Cage, E., Santhanam, S. P., Magiati, I., Dwyer, P., Stockwell, K. M., Kofner, B., Brown, H., Davidson, D., Herrell, J., Shore, S. M., Caudel, D., Gurbuz, E., & Gillespie-Lynch, K. (2023). Learning from the experts: Evaluating a participatory autism and universal design training for university educators. *Autism, 27*(2), 356–370. https://doi.org/10.1177/13623613221097207

Waugh, C. (2019). In defence of safe spaces: Subaltern counterpublics and vulnerable politics. In M. Breeze, Y. Taylor, & C. Costa (Eds.), *Time and Space in the Neoliberal University*, (pp. 143-168). Palgrave Macmillan. https://doi.org/10.1007/978-3-030-15246-8_7

Weiting Tan, D., Rabuka, M., Haar, T., & Pellicano, E. (2023). 'It's a symbolic violence': Autistic people's experiences of discrimination at universities in Australia. *Autism, 28*(6), 1344–1356. https://doi.org/10.1177/13623613231219744

White, S. W., Ollendick, T. H., & Bray, B. C. (2011). College students on the autism spectrum: Prevalence and associated problems. *Autism, 15*(6), 683–701. https://doi.org/10.1177/1362361310393363

Williams, G. L., Wharton, T., & Jagoe, C. (2021). Mutual (mis)understanding: Reframing autistic pragmatic "impairments" using relevance theory. *Frontiers in Psychology, 12*. https://doi.org/10.3389/fpsyg.2021.616664

Wood, R. (2019). *Inclusive Education for Autistic Children: Helping Children and Young People to Learn and Flourish in the Classroom*. Jessica Kingsley Publishers.

Chapter 33:
Dementia and the Double Empathy Problem

Allison Moore

Abstract

In this chapter I will make the argument that it can be beneficial to view dementia through a neurodiversity lens. If neurodivergence is viewed as differences in cognitive, affectual and/or sensory functioning compared to the neurotypical majority, it is possible to see how it might apply to dementia. Under the *Diagnostic and Statistical Manual of Mental Disorders*, 5th edition (DSM-5), dementia is classified as a neurocognitive disorder (major or minor), in which there is a significant cognitive decline in one or more domains – complex attention; executive functioning; learning and memory; language; perception; and social cognition. Understood as neurodivergence, although still acknowledging dementia as pathology, it becomes possible to see how people with dementia experience the Double Empathy Problem whereby 'difficulties' in communication are attributable to their cognitive decline, rather than an interactional failure. In conceptualizing the Double Empathy Problem, Milton also drew on the work of philosopher and feminist theorist, Iris Marion Young, and her concept of asymmetrical reciprocity which posits that '*[I]t is neither possible nor morally desirable for persons engaged in moral interaction to adopt one another's standpoint*' (Young, 1997, p. 340). Young argues that the best we can do is to engage in a process of enquiry, and she proposes asymmetrical reciprocity as '*a communicative ethics that recognizes difference and particularity*' (Young, 1997, p. 340). Based on moral respect and recognition, Young suggests the adoption of a sense of wonder when listening to the perspectives of others. This sense of wonder challenges a wholly deficit model of dementia that assumes a lack of capacity and instead invokes enquiry into better understanding the unique ways that people with dementia see, feel, hear and communicate with the world around them.

Introduction

On 21 August 2020, my mum, dad and I sat in front of a laptop screen in their dining room. We were on a video call listening to a psychiatrist, who we had met only an hour earlier, telling mum that she had dementia. It did not come as a surprise to any of us. Over recent years, she had been getting increasingly forgetful and finding it difficult to recall the 'right' words to use in social interactions. She would joke about this, saying 'I keep getting my worms mixed up', not only intentionally replacing 'words' with 'worms' for comedic effect but also to signify that she was aware of the changes in her memory. Despite her use of humour, the reality was that she had begun to lose her confidence and, as a result, reduced social encounters to only those with people she knew well. However, in March 2020, the UK went into lockdown because of the outbreak of the COVID-19 pandemic and all non-essential contact and travel were prohibited. Gone were her weekly trips to the hairdresser she had been going to for almost 30 years, as were her and dad's twice-weekly visits to the coffee shop where the staff knew their names and always welcomed them. The disruption to her routines and reduction in her opportunities for meaningful interaction contributed to a significant deterioration in her condition.

Over time, I came to see dementia as a form of neurodivergence, which can be understood as a divergence in cognitive, affectual and/or sensory functioning compared to the neurotypical majority. Under the *Diagnostic and Statistical Manual of Mental Disorders*, 5th edition (DSM-5), dementia is classified as a neurocognitive disorder (major or minor), in which there is a significant cognitive decline in one or more domains – complex attention; executive functioning; learning and memory; language; perception; and social cognition. Understood as neurodivergence, although still acknowledging dementia as pathology, it becomes possible to see how people with dementia (PWD) experience the Double Empathy Problem whereby 'difficulties' in communication are attributable to their cognitive decline, rather than an interactional failure.

In this chapter, I will make the argument that it can be beneficial to view dementia through a neurodiversity lens and that understanding the Double Empathy Problem can facilitate more meaningful interactions between those who do not have dementia and those who do. As the condition develops, a person's ways of communicating may change; spoken communication may become difficult or may be lost altogether. The persistence of a largely deficit model of dementia that positions it as a gradual loss of personhood and humanity may lead to the erroneous assumption that these changes mean that a person no longer wants to or is able to engage in communication. However, the desire to communicate remains, so it is incumbent on those around the PWD to find alternative ways of interacting with them. My mum is now in the advanced stages of dementia and her support needs mean she is no longer able to live in her home. We are extremely fortunate that she is in an amazing nursing home with caring and attentive staff. I am unable to understand much of what she now says but we have a beautiful, interactive and meaningful relationship. I visit her most days. Sometimes, we communicate only through touch, but other days we have conversations, she tells me tales and we laugh a lot.

Revisiting the Double Empathy Problem

The Double Empathy Problem is best known for its application to social interactions between autistic and non-autistic people. Originating from his own experiences of being autistic, anecdotal accounts from parents of autistic children and the small body of qualitative research that existed at the time (Milton et al., 2022) Milton developed the Double Empathy Problem; '*a disjuncture between two differently disposed social actors which becomes more marked the wider the disjuncture in dispositional perceptions of the lifeworld*' (Milton, 2012, p. 884). The more different their lifeworlds are, the greater the possibility of misunderstanding and misinterpretation between social actors. As dominant cognitive, behaviourist and neuroscientific discourses continue to position autism as a 'disorder' characterized by deficits in social interaction and communication, it is assumed that any breakdown in communication is seen as the responsibility of the autistic person. However, it is important to recognize that communication is a two-way process (Hacking, 1998; Milton, 2012). A breakdown in communication between an autistic person and a neurotypical person is not attributable to *their* autism. It is a result of both parties' failure to understand each other; a failure in '*reciprocity and mutuality*' (Milton, 2012, p. 884). Hence, it is a 'double problem'.

Milton (2012) also draws on the work of philosopher and feminist theorist, Iris Marion Young, and her concept of asymmetrical reciprocity in relation to the Double Empathy Problem, which posits that '*[I]t is neither possible nor morally desirable for persons engaged in moral interaction to adopt one another's standpoint*' (Young, 1997, p. 340). For Young, one cannot step into someone else's shoes as we can never fully know the other person's perspective or truly understand their life experiences, and to claim one can take the perspective of another obscures differences between us. Further, when there is a power imbalance between social actors, the individual in a position of power and privilege will frequently '*put themselves, with their own particular experiences and privileges*' (Young, 1997, p. 349) into a situation, which can '*reinforce a complementary image of themselves*' (Young, 1997, p. 350). Young argues that the best we can do is to engage in a process of enquiry, and she proposes asymmetrical reciprocity as '*a communicative ethics that recognizes difference and particularity*' (Young, 1997, p. 340). Based on moral respect and recognition, Young suggests the adoption of a sense of wonder when listening to the perspectives of others. This sense of wonder challenges a wholly deficit model of dementia that assumes a lack of capacity and, instead, invokes enquiry into better understanding the unique ways that PWD see, feel, hear and communicate with the world around them.

However, in interactions with PWD it can be tempting for those who do not have dementia to impose normative modes of communication, to '*reinforce a complementary image of themselves*' (Young, 1997, p. 350) rather than meeting the PWD where they are.

Although the Double Empathy Problem has most commonly been applied to autism, there is nothing inherent in the definition that limits it to autism. Indeed, a breakdown in understanding can occur between any two social actors, but it is more likely to happen and to be more pronounced, the more different they are in terms of '*qualia of experience, social lifeworlds, dispositional viewpoints and discursive repertoires*' (Milton et al., 2023, p. 83). In any interaction between people with different neurotypes, there is an increased risk of misunderstanding. If the Double Empathy Problem is to be applied to communication between people who have dementia and those who do not, it would be helpful to consider whether dementia can be considered as a form of neurodivergence.

Can dementia be understood as a form of neurodivergence?

In the introduction to *Neurodiversity Studies: A New Critical Paradigm*, the editors are clear that dementia falls under the neurodivergence umbrella:

> *By de-pathologising neurodivergence and the identities of neurodivergent people, it is possible that what are currently known as autism, ADHD, Tourette's, dyslexia, hearing voices, bipolar disorder, Down syndrome, and dementia, may be recognised as components on a broader continuum of sensory, affectual, and cognitive processing.* (Bertildotter-Rosqvist et al., 2020, p. 2)

Similarly, Steve Silberman, award-winning science writer and author of *NeuroTribes: The Legacy of Autism and How to Think Smarter About People Who Think Differently*, recently posed a question about neurodiversity and dementia. Reflecting on his mother's diagnosis of vascular dementia and her experiences in a care home, he asked '*Could dementia also be considered a form of neurodiversity, while also being a pathology?*' (Silberman, 2023).

Despite this support from some proponents of neurodiversity, there continues to be a reluctance to see dementia as a form of neurodivergence. In part, this is due to the dominant biomedical view of the condition as a neurocognitive disorder characterized by progressive and linear cognitive decline. Also significant is the fact that the concept of neurodiversity has been much misunderstood and/or misinterpreted and has led to several critiques. Here, I wish to address and counter three main criticisms of neurodiversity because they act as barriers to considering its applicability to dementia.

First, neurodiversity is commonly critiqued on the basis of the erroneous assumption that challenging the dominance of the medical model is synonymous with rejecting it and, in so doing, denying embodied experiences of disability and the impact of psychoemotional disablism. It is certainly the case that many view their neurodivergence as central to their identity, as is the case with, for example, autism (Kenny et al., 2016) and attention deficit hyperactivity disorder (ADHD; Nielsen, 2017), and most reject attempts at treatment or cure that aim to normalize behaviours or eliminate their neurotype. In her chapter considering the contribution a neurodiversity paradigm can make to critical dementia studies, Örulv notes, it is difficult to see how an identity-oriented model of minority neurotypes can be applied to dementia. She doubts whether PWD will ever embrace identity-first language and suggests that '*[A] scenario where people living with dementia oppose the idea of a possible cure seems even more far-fetched*' (Örulv, 2023, p. 250). I concur with Örulv's reservation on the issue of cure. However, there is currently no cure, nor is there likely to be one any time soon. Therefore, it seems prudent to consider all contemporary approaches to understanding dementia that challenge the dominant biomedical model and offer more humane ways of working with PWD through deeper authentic engagements, which a neurodiversity approach can engender. The progressive nature of dementia may mean that, even if individuals were to identify with their condition, this identification is necessarily time limited. However, there *are* a growing number of people in the early stages of dementia advocating for themselves, campaigning for the rights of PWD and engaging with others in online communities (Bartlett, 2014; Swaffer et al., 2019). Among this burgeoning dementia activist movement, increasing numbers of individuals are 'coming out' with dementia (Thomas & Milligan, 2018), as well as academics diagnosed with dementia offering perspectives on living with the condition as experts by experience, which challenge biomedical orthodoxy (see, for example, Kate Swaffer, 2014, 2015; Peter Mittler, 2018).

The identity-oriented model of ways of being, like autism and ADHD, also leads to the second false accusation that neurodiversity celebrates 'difference' and denies 'disability'. This is a gross oversimplification. It is entirely possible within a neurodiversity framework to subscribe to a view that the human species is naturally diverse with regards to neurotypes and still recognize that an individual can have an objective disability. However, a neurodiversity lens challenges the dominant, medically informed perspective that cognitive disabilities are 'objectively bad' (Chapman, 2020, p. 57).

The final accusation against neurodiversity, aimed specifically at autistic proponents, is that it has been developed by so-called 'high-functioning' autistics and, therefore, does not represent the needs of those autistic people who require higher levels of support.

The origins of this criticism might lie in the fact that one of the earliest framings of neurodiversity by Judy Singer (2017. See also Lutz, 2023) explicitly advocated that it referred only to what was then known as Asperger syndrome. However, Singer was just one voice among many in the burgeoning neurodiversity movement and this criticism belies the fact that *'from its inception, not only did the neurodiversity movement's values include the most significantly disabled, but that those individuals themselves were among … [the] earliest pioneers'* (Ballou, 2018). There are similarities here with dementia activists in the early stages of the condition who are deemed to have the cognitive ability to advocate for themselves and are not considered to be affected enough by the condition to contribute to knowledge construction about dementia or speak on behalf of those in more advanced stages. At the same time, those in late-stage dementia are deemed either incapable of knowing themselves or of communicating to others because of the difficulties in communication they may experience as the condition develops (Jongsma et al., 2017; Spencer, 2023). Katie Swaffer, an Australian activist and academic, reports her amazement at receiving accusations that she faked her diagnosis of Alzheimer's disease (Swaffer, et al., 2019). The basis of these accusations was that she was capable of writing blogs and articles, as well as presenting public lectures on dementia.

What the various conditions that fall under the neurodiversity umbrella have in common is that they are perceived to have variations in cognitive, affectual and sensory processing compared to the majority neurotypical population. Swaffer (2014, cited in Swaffer et al., 2019) defines dementia as *'a condition causing acquired and progressive cognitive and sensory disabilities'*, a definition entirely in keeping with contemporary understanding of neurodivergence. Dementia does differ from other neurodivergent conditions, like autism, in significant ways, in particular the fact that it is an acquired condition that is progressive and results in increasing support needs over time (Örulv, 2023), and these differences need to be acknowledged. Yet, if neurodivergence is viewed as differences in cognitive, affectual, and/or sensory functioning compared to the neurotypical majority, it is possible to see how it might apply to dementia and, indeed, to other acquired cognitive disabilities. According to the UK National Health Service (NHS) website, common early symptoms of dementia include, *'difficulty concentrating; finding it hard to carry out familiar daily tasks, such as getting confused over the correct change when shopping, struggling to follow a conversation or find the right word; being confused about time and place; mood changes; difficulty finding the right words; difficulty with numbers and/or handling money in shops'* (NHS, 2023). Referring specifically to frontotemporal dementia, symptoms include *'personality changes – reduced sensitivity to others' feelings, making people seem cold and unfeeling; lack of social awareness […]; becoming obsessive – such as developing fads for unusual foods, overeating and drinking'* (NHS, 2023). What marks these cognitive, affectual and sensory behaviours out as 'symptoms' is not just that they represent *'a disruption to the functioning that was already in place'* (Örulv, 2023, p. 250) in the individual, but also that they are seen as aberrant in relation to normative expectations of behaviour.

A neurodiversity lens would allow us to see these 'symptoms' as differences in sensory, affectual and cognitive processing which should be accommodated, either through individual and/or environmental modifications.

What is empathy?

In an expert panel discussion on autism and empathy, Milton (Nicolaidis et al., 2019, p. 5) states '*[D]espite using the term "empathy" myself, in the "double empathy problem" theory, I do have some difficulty with what the concept is really referring to*'. This highlights that there is no consensus over what empathy is and how it should be measured, if indeed it can be measured at all. Dictionary definitions of empathy suggest that it concerns the ability to understand, share and be sensitive to what others are feeling and is often presented as a fundamental and biological human characteristic. However, as Milton also notes through his use of Iris Marion Young's work, it is not possible (and Young would add not desirable) to fully understand what another person is feeling.

Given this definitional diversity, one might ask what the 'empathy' in the Double Empathy Problem refers to and how it might be relevant to dementia. I think it is important to acknowledge that the first conceptualization of the Double Empathy Problem was a critique of theory of mind and the assertion that autistic people lack empathy. It challenged the assumption that autistic people's purported social and empathic deficits lead to a breakdown in social interactions with non-autistic people and instead proposed that all interaction is relational and contextual. Empathy was not defined and, in so doing, the language of theory of mind was employed and critiqued without using its 'cognitivist and individualist' (Ekdahl, 2023, p. 8) accounts of social phenomena. In his development of the Double Empathy Problem, Milton drew on symbolic interactionism, ethnomethodology and phenomenology, as well as philosophy, radical psychiatry and disability studies (Milton et al., 2023). The empathy of the Double Empathy Problem was never limited to being able to 'understand and share the feelings of others' (Nicolaidis et al., 2019, p. 5).

Canadian-American psychologist, Paul Bloom (2017), has recently made a distinction between empathy and compassion. He argues that while empathy *can* be understood as compassion and kindness, it often has a narrower meaning of being able to infer the mental states of others and put ourselves in their shoes. This can lead to in-group bias, as people are likely to identify with and express empathy for those who are similar to them, which in turn can reproduce existing prejudices and inequalities. This correlates with Milton's argument that the greater the dispositional diversity between social actors the more likely that misunderstanding will occur.

Compassion is '*simply caring for people and wanting them to thrive*' (Bloom, 2017, p. 42). In dementia care, a person-centred approach underpinned by compassion, meaningful relationships *'and the ability to view the world from their [PWD] perspective'* (Bickford et al, 2019, p. 2) is the gold standard of support. However, in reality, this is far from the experience of PWD in health and social care settings. In Bickford et al.'s (2019) qualitative study exploring how medical and nursing students understood compassion and the factors that influenced it, three features of compassion were identified: connection, care and respect. Care and respect conform with Bloom's notion of compassion, but connection related to a narrow definition of empathy as *'being able to put oneself in the patient's place and being able to communicate an understanding of their struggle'* (Bickford et al., 2019, p. 3). In relation to factors that impacted compassion, a recurrent theme in participants' responses was that it could be reduced *'if people with dementia are perceived in terms of their being violent, aggressive, frustrated, or distressed'* (Bickford et al., 2019, p. 4). Some respondents said they would avoid a person who was in distress, while others reported indifference toward them because they could see only the dementia and not the person. This illustrates the problems of care predicated on a narrow definition of empathy, whereby participants are unable to identify with patients and by extension unable to empathize with them. The focus on the violence, aggression, frustration or distress of the individual as a barrier to compassion also aligns with the Double Empathy Problem and the notion that a breakdown in communication between people of different neurotypes is attributable to the neurodivergence of one of the parties, in this case because of their dementia. These barriers to compassion and connection are compounded as dementia advances. In a systematic review of research exploring nurses' attitudes toward dementia care, Evripidou et al. (2018) found that negative attitudes toward caring for PWD increased as the condition developed. For many people verbal communication becomes increasingly difficult as the condition progresses but their attempts at non-verbal communication are often misinterpreted as 'challenging behaviour', lacking in meaning, dismissed as a symptom of the condition or simply ignored as some of the participants in Bickford et al.'s (2017) study confirm. The dismissal of someone's distress and mischaracterization of PWD's communicative actions can be understood as a form of psychoemotional disablism, which invalidates their experiences and their very existence.

Psychoemotional disablement and dementia

Writing about the social oppression of autistic people, Milton suggests that the dominance of psych-professions in the (re)construction of autism and autistic people as lacking in social reciprocity can result psychoemotional disablement, *'constraining not only what people can do but also what they can be and become'* (Milton et al., 2023, p. 88). Despite some incorporation of psychological, social and relational perspectives into contemporary understandings of dementia, the biomedical model persists, and knowledge is largely generated from an exterior, rather than an interior, standpoint; that is, what we know about dementia comes from 'dementia professionals', rather than the subjective experiences of

PWD or their family and friends affected by it. Dementia professionals include not only psychiatrists, nurses and social workers, but also dementia charities whose remit is usually to campaign for better understanding of and support for people impacted by the condition.

In March 2024, the UK's Alzheimer's Society released its latest campaign advert. Called *The Long Goodbye*, it depicts a woman's wake at which her son states that following her diagnosis of dementia, his mother's life had been a series of deaths until her life finally ended. This is underscored by a voice over saying '*With dementia, you don't just die once. You die again, and again, and again*'. The advert prompted widespread criticisms across social media and 235 complaints were submitted to the Advertising Standards Agency (ASA). George Rook, activist and blogger, wrote the advert '*played on people's worst, deepest fears about older age and dying*' (Rook, 2024). The advert can be seen as an example of psychoemotional disablism, underpinned by structural ageism and disablism, as societal fears about ageing, impairment and death are projected onto dementia and PWD.

In response to the criticism, the Alzheimer's Society's Chief Executive Office (CEO) claimed the advert '*tells the unvarnished truth about the devastation caused by dementia*'. She attempted to justify the 'hard-hitting' awareness raising campaign because '*Shockingly, only 10% of people know that dementia is the leading cause of death in the UK [...] We're hidden away from dementia being UK's biggest killer*' (Alzheimer's Society, 2024). The ASA ruled 'Not Upheld' on the complaints levelled at the advert. It stated that the references to multiple deaths signified the loss of memory, changes in an individual's personality and being unable to do things they were once able to do, and that viewers would not interpret this as literal death.

Media representations of dementia as death are not unusual. Diagnosis is portrayed as a catastrophe and the condition as '*something worse than death*' (Peel, 2014, p. 885). Ironically, where PWD are dehumanized by discourses that characterize them as dying again, and again, and again, the condition of dementia is given life, constructed as an '*active and agentive [entity], visiting death on large numbers of people*' (Brookes et al., 2018, p. 389). The Alzheimer's Society's CEO's assertion that dementia is the UK's biggest killer, is not only highly emotive but it also positions dementia as the active subject and the PWD as the passive recipient.

Although viewers of the Alzheimer's Society advert may not perceive living with dementia as a literal death, it distorts their understanding, perpetuates prejudicial stereotypes of the condition of it and has harmful consequences for PWD. The 'deaths' referred to in the advert occurred when the mother '*couldn't work out how to prepare her legendary roast anymore*' and '*[S]he died as the Queen of Christmas when she refused to have dinner with the family*'. Of particular relevance to the Double Empathy Problem, '*[S]he died again when she asked me, her son, what my name was*' and '*[S]he died as dad's rock, after 52 years of marriage the day she looked straight through him*'. These latter 'deaths' imply not only a deterioration in memory, but also in interaction and reciprocity. What all four 'deaths' have in common is that they say something about who she was as a person. Their gradual loss implies cumulative loss of personhood, which makes a person vulnerable to being treated as though they are socially dead. I am reminded here of what Pripas-Kapit (2020, p. 23) has called *'Neurodiversity's First Manifesto; Jim Sinclair's appeal to parents of autistic children, Don't Mourn for Us'* (Sinclair, 2012). In 1993, he wrote:

> *You didn't lose a child to autism. You lost a child because the child you waited for never came into existence. That isn't the fault of the autistic child who does exist, and it shouldn't be our burden [...] Grieve if you must, for your own lost dreams. But don't mourn for us. We are alive. We are real. And we're here waiting for you.* (Autism Network International, 2012)

Although Sinclair was referring to autistic children, we could easily replace the word 'autism' with 'dementia' in this excerpt. The ramifications of dementia = death are far-reaching. Sweeting and Gilhooly (1997) were the first to examine the extent to which social death preceded biological death in PWD. They concluded that although they retain a sense of personhood, even in the late stages of dementia, stereotypes and misunderstanding of dementia may result in the PWD being seen *'as a liminal or non-person, who is demonstrably making the transition from life to death'* (Sweeting & Gilhooly, 1997, p. 99). Further, seeing PWD as *'as good as dead'* (Sweeting & Gilhooly, 1997), which social death engenders, has a physiological impact, and accelerates biological death (Ghane et al., 2021). However, if family, friends and professional carers see a PWD as a social actor, their personhood can be maintained.

As my mum's dementia developed, her communication methods changed but she never lost her desire to engage with others. Even now, in the advanced stages of dementia she communicates her preferences, demonstrates her likes and dislikes through her facial expressions and body language, and engages in lengthy conversations. Although she uses vocalizations, there are few discernible words in them, but I know that what she is saying is meaningful to her. While caring for my mum I (and, with a steep learning curve, my dad) have drawn on my knowledge of neurodivergence and especially the Double Empathy Problem in an attempt to provide an optimal environment for her to live well with dementia and to sustain meaningful interaction and communication. I believe that it is this neurodivergent-informed way of supporting my mum that facilitated her independence and enabled her to live in her own home for as long as she did. In the remainder of the chapter, I will identify ways of engaging with PWD that can go some way to mitigating the Double Empathy Problem and reflect on my own experiences of using them.

Overcoming the Double Empathy Problem: Adapting the environment

At the heart of Milton's (2012) conceptualization of the Double Empathy Problem is the contention that all interaction is socially and contextually situated. Writing about autism, Milton et al. (2023) suggest that the social environment around an individual can often have a deleterious impact on them. Therefore, strategies aimed at reducing environmental stressors can reduce the negative consequences of the Double Empathy Problem for autistic individuals. As dementia develops, a person's environment can become highly debilitating for them due to changes in their executive functioning, including their organizational and self-regulatory abilities. In addition, many people will experience changes in sensory skills and PWD can become hyper or hyposensitive to environmental stimuli like sound, light, smell and touch. Hypersensitivity is a heightened reaction to sensory input and can result in a person feeling overwhelmed. Hyposensitivity, however, is a reduced reaction to sensory input, which can lead to self-stimulatory behaviours, such as patting oneself or making repetitive sounds or movements in an attempt to get some environmental feedback which, in turn, can provide a sense of security (Ellis & Astell, 2018). These responses to the environment combined with other changes that can occur in dementia, such as mood and personality changes and sleep disturbances, are frequently referred to as '*challenging behaviour*', '*behaviours of concern*', '*responsive behaviours*' (Gutmanis et al., 2015) or the '*behavioural and psychological symptoms of dementia*' (Feast et al., 2016).

The term 'challenging behaviour' was originally introduced as an attempt to move away from descriptors that located behaviour, its cause and motivation within the individual. Such descriptors included, among others, 'abnormal', 'disordered', 'dysfunctional' and 'maladaptive'. When understood from an individual viewpoint, it is not just the behaviour that is abnormal, disordered and dysfunctional – so too is the individual engaging in that behaviour. The intention behind this linguistic shift was '*to broaden the focus of enquiry by placing individual "pathology" in the social and interpersonal context in which certain acts are deemed problematic*' (Emerson & Einfeld, 2011, p. 5). It was supposed to put an end to the previous, pathologizing descriptors being used as a diagnosis and highlight to providers that the behaviour was a challenge to staff and services.

Challenging behaviour can be classified as 'aggressive' or 'non-aggressive' and herein lies potential for misunderstanding to occur. To understand an act as aggressive carries connotations of intentionality which, by extension, implies that the person engaging in it can control their behaviour. Research has demonstrated that if carers believe an individual is acting intentionally and attribute to them the ability to control their actions, they are less likely to be sympathetic toward them (Dagnan et al., 2004, 2012). Behaviours categorized as 'challenging' can be understood as '*a communication of unmet need*' (Dagnan et al., 2004, p. 501) or a means of expressing preferences or, when non-compliance is seen as a type of challenging behaviour (James & Jackman, 2017), simply saying no by an individual whose social status affords them limited opportunities to exercise agency. It is also important to acknowledge that behaviours that challenge can be a behavioural manifestation of emotions, like fear or anxiety and signify that a person is highly distressed.

Irrespective of why these behaviours are occurring, they are upsetting for carers to witness and are physically and emotionally exhausting for the PWD, and it is therefore preferable to prevent them. In supporting my mum at home and trying to foster a stable and secure environment, I drew on my experience of Studio 3's low arousal approach, which was developed by McDonnell et al. (1994) and is primarily concerned with avoiding crisis situations, but also provides steps to manage them when they happen. The low arousal approach contains four key elements: reducing the demands that are made of people being supported; avoiding triggers, such as eye contact and touch, that may lead to confrontation and stress; avoiding non-verbal communications that might lead to conflict; and challenging staff/carer beliefs about how 'challenging behaviour' should be managed (McDonnell, 2010). The essence of the low arousal approach is that a situation can escalate or deescalate on the basis of the actions of those involved. In other words, it emphasizes the '*social situatedness of social interactions and the responsibility of all involved*' (Milton et al., 2023, p. 89)

There are some people who naturally adopt a low arousal approach and instil a sense of calm to any environment they are in (McDonnell, 2019). My dad was one of those people and there were times when I wondered who was teaching who! While my mum lived at home, we made simple adaptations to the house and her routines to accommodate her changing needs. Her weekly hairdresser trips, with their familiar smells and faces, as well as conversations about the present and past, were a highlight of her week, so much so that dad referred to them as therapy. As her dementia progressed, the things that had brought comfort and a sense of security became overwhelming; it was too loud, there were too many people having conversations at the same time, and we started to book the last slot of the day when she would be the only person there and she had the time she needed to be able to process everything that was happening. She is no longer able to go to the salon, but we have arranged for the hairdresser to come to the nursing home, so the feeling of familiarity can continue for as long as possible.

Following her diagnosis, daily life slowed down, we made fewer demands of her and adapted to her changing relationship to the environment around her. However, despite our efforts at maintaining a low arousal approach, there were inevitably times of distress. During these times, we supported her by not only providing the space and time she needed, but also by meeting her where she was at that moment, even if, at that moment, her subjective reality was different to ours. It is not uncommon for PWD to experience time-shifts, remembering events, places and people from their past and reliving them in their present life (Gibbons et al., 2018). Examples include talking about deceased spouses as though they are still alive, referring to grown-up children needing to be taken to school or pacing around worrying that they are going to be late for work. Time-shifts can, though not necessarily, be distressing: imagine being a parent who 'knows' they must get home to feed their children but is unable to open the door of the nursing home to leave. During time-shifts a PWD is at increased vulnerability of the Double Empathy Problem. The people around them may feel that it is appropriate to correct them, tell them that their children have grown up or that their husband has died. The dispositional disjuncture between subjective reality and objective reality can lead to considerable distress, confrontation and a breakdown in communication between the PWD and their carers. When dementia is understood primarily in terms of progressive memory loss, it is easy to frame this breakdown as a result of the symptoms of dementia, rather than interactional failure.

One way of avoiding the Double Empathy Problem is through a validation approach, a method of communicating with PWD developed by Naomi Feil in the 1960s. It is based on the recognition and validation of a person's subjective reality. Rather than attempting to reorient them to their present reality, caregivers should '*attempt to enter the world of the person with dementia*' (Ellis & Astell, 2018, p. 49) with openness and without judgement. Feil also suggests that time-shifts have meaning and can represent the resurfacing of long-buried emotions or reflect an unmet basic need. By accepting the PWD for who they are and where they are, their feelings and their subjective reality is validated.

Overcoming the Double Empathy Problem: Using adaptive interaction

My mum has always been an animated communicator, with funny exaggerated facial expressions and arms that would wave frantically as she spoke. We used to joke that if we held her hands together, she would not be able to talk. This vibrancy in her communication has never left her and, even without clear words, I know when she is regaling me with fantastical tales as her eyes grow wide and she throws her head back as she laughs. When she is telling me something that needs a bit more discretion, she moves her body toward me and looks around to see who can hear her before she begins to share her information. Because of the way she has, and continues, to communicate, it is easy to demonstrate to her that I understand she is communicating with me and that it is meaningful. I do this in lots of ways; by nodding my head, reflecting similar emotions to those she is expressing and with utterances or words, like '*Oh really?*' or '*I didn't know that*' or something similar. This is not simple imitation of her or, even worse, condescension. I am certain that there is mutual communication taking place evidenced by her vocal responses, her laughter and her reaching out to hold my hand. On one memorable occasion when I responded to a tale she was telling me with '*I didn't know that*', she replied with a level of clarity I had not heard in weeks, '*You did. I told you!*' These interactions contain dialogical conventions – back and forth interaction, turn taking and mirroring of body language. To someone observing from the outside, we would look like a mother and daughter having a 'normal' conversation. This form of interacting with her came intuitively to me, borne out of our close relationship, but as I researched dementia and communication, I realised that I had been engaging in what is known as adaptive interaction.

Adaptive Interaction (AI) has its roots in Intensive Interaction (II) which developed in the 1980s as a means of communicating with individuals with learning disabilities who did not use speech to communicate. We are all born with the ability to communicate, what might be understood as pre-verbal interaction. As we develop, a great deal of our needs continue to be communicated non-verbally, through the use of, for example, facial expressions, hand gestures and body language (Caldwell & Horwood, 2008). Intensive Interaction is an approach that '*uses our partner's own non-verbal body language to get in touch with them*' (Caldwell, 2006, p. 13) and reflects that back to them through techniques like body matching or imitation of sounds. This way, the asymmetry and potential for the Double Empathy Problem between speaking and non-speaking partner can be mitigated to some degree: it is the speaking partner who has to learn the language of the non-speaking partner, it is the non-speaking partner who leads the interaction and all behaviour from the non-speaking partner is interpreted as '*intentionally communicative*' (Astell et al., 2022, p. 2). This does not happen by accident. The pervasiveness and normativity of communication through spoken language requires the speaking partner to step back, adopt a sense of wonder when interacting with others and recognize that one's own means of communication is strange '*because it has been put in relation to others*' (Young, 1997, p. 358).

Although AI emerged from II, it differs insofar as one of the key aims of the II approach is to build upon interactions over time and therefore extend communicative repertoires. However, because of the memory changes associated with dementia, especially as it progresses, a PWD may not be able to remember the nature of their previous interaction or who it was with. As a result, Ellis and Astell (2018), founders of AI, stated that the interaction had to occur in the moment, aiming to re-establish the connection from the previous interaction but being prepared to adapt to the communication needs of the individual at that time. From their research on the efficacy of AI, Ellis and Astell have found that PWD, even those who are in the very advanced stages, have a wider communicative repertoire than caregivers had assumed and engaged in imitation of the speaking partner, and intervention sessions produced more positive social behaviours and more meaningful engagement compared to when standard interaction approaches are used (Astell et al., 2022).

What both AI and the validation approach have in common is that they recognize the subjective reality of the PWD and challenge the dominant 'loss of personhood' narrative. Further, they highlight that subjectivity is embodied and intercorporeal; personhood is not the epitome of the individual, sovereign subject, nor is it determined on the basis of cognitive abilities, but rather '*persons are constituted and affirmed through relations with others*' (Petherbridge, 2019, p. 311). The embodied nature of subjectivity is reflected in the fact that even as the condition develops and cognitive abilities diminish, there is continuity in the way people carry themselves and the bodily comportment they use. In Bourdieusian terms, we can think of this as bodily hexis, habituated forms of communication, using gestures or facial expressions people have always used and are unmistakably 'them' (Boyle, 2014). Rather than 'being lost' to dementia, the person is still very much there, as is their relationship with significant others. Although my mum no longer recognizes me as her daughter at a cognitive level, at an embodied level I am still very much her 'baby girl'. I spend many visits with her stroking my hair, twisting it or separating it into bunches as she did so often when she was getting me ready to go to school. There are other occasions when I have not been able to pick out any identifiable words in her vocalizations, but I know what she is saying is meaningful to her because of her 'mum expressions' and her use of different facial expressions to tell particular kinds of stories; her 'gossip' is accompanied by wide-open eyes and a distinctive eyebrow raise, and her whole face changes when she is telling funny tales, which are punctuated with larger-than-life body movements.

Conclusion

In this chapter, I have argued that dominant constructions of dementia as a disorder characterized by progressive cognitive decline leave PWD vulnerable to the Double Empathy Problem. The lifeworlds of PWD and their family and friends change as the condition develops, which increases the chances for misunderstanding. At best, this can result in miscommunication between those who have dementia and those who do not. However, if assumed to be caused by the dementia, rather than miscommunication between social actors, there is the potential for those around the PWD to withdraw from them socially. At worst, this can lead to social isolation and exclusion because of assumptions that PWD do not want to engage in social interaction. I have also argued that a neurodiversity lens can be helpful for understanding the Double Empathy Problem in relation to dementia and have suggested that if being neurodivergent '*simply means to be outside of the category of people who are considered cognitively "normal"*' (Stenning & Bertilsdotter Rosqvist, 2021, p. 1535), PWD could certainly claim membership of the neurodivergence category. If communication is understood as relational and situational when it occurs between people with different neurotypes, it may be possible to mitigate the Double Empathy Problem with strategies like low arousal, validation approach and AI.

It is almost four years since my mum received her diagnosis and during that time our relationship has changed. However, I am not saying a long goodbye to her, and I am not weighed down by anticipatory grief. I don't have time for that – I am too busy focused on living and being in the moment with her, and creating meaningful and reciprocal interactions for us both. That is not to say that there aren't times when I fail to understand what she is communicating, but I see it as interactional misunderstanding, not a result of her dementia alone. The fundamentals of communication that are present at birth continue throughout life. Rather than not wanting to communicate, PWD are inviting us to interact with them; they see our spoken language as strange and we should adopt a sense of wonder as we learn their unique languages.

References

Alzheimer's Society (2024). *Alzheimer's Society CEO Responds to Criticism of Their Latest TV Campaign.* Alzheimer's Society. https://www.alzheimers.org.uk/news/2024-03-24/ceo-responds-criticism

Astell, A. J., Shoaran, S., & Ellis, M. P. (2022). Using Adaptive Interaction to simplify caregiver's communication with people with dementia who cannot speak. *Frontiers in Communication, 6*, 689439. https://doi.org/10.3389/fcomm.2021.689439

Autism Network International (2012). Introducing ANI. Autism Network International. https://www.autismnetworkinternational.org/intro.html

Ballou, E. P. (2018). What the neurodiversity does – and doesn't – offer. *Thinking Person's Guide to Autism.* https://thinkingautismguide.com/2018/02/what-neurodiversity-movement-doesand.html

Bartlett, R. (2014). The emergent modes of dementia activism. *Ageing & Society*, 34, 623–644. https://doi.org/10.1017/S0144686X12001158

Bertilsdotter-Rosqvist, H., Stenning, A., & Chown, N. (2020). Introduction. In H. Bertilsdotter-Rosqvist, A. Stenning, & N. Chown. (Eds.) *Neurodiversity Studies: A New Critical Paradigm* (pp. 1–11), Routledge.

Bickford, B., Daley, S., Sleater, G., Hebditch, M., & Banerjee, S. (2019). Understanding compassion for people with dementia in medical and nursing students. *BMC Medical Education, 19*, 35. https://doi.org/10.1186/s12909-019-1460-y

Bloom, P. (2017). *Against Empathy: The Case for Rational Compassion.* The Bodley Head.

Boyle, G. (2014). Recognising the agency of people with dementia. *Disability & Society, 29*(7), 1130–1144. https://doi.org/10.1080/09687599.2014.910108

Brookes, G., Harvey, K., Chadborn, N., & Dening, T. (2018). "Our biggest killer": Multimodal discourse representations of dementia in the British press. *Social Semiotics, 28*(3), 371–395. https://doi.org/10.1080/10350330.2017.1345111

Caldwell, P. (2006). *Finding You Finding Me: Using Intensive Interaction to Get in Touch with People Whose Severe Learning Disabilities are Combined with Autistic Spectrum Disorder.* Jesssica Kingsley Publishers.

Caldwell, P., & Horwood, J. (2008) *Using Intensive Interaction and Sensory Integration: A Handbook for Those who Support People with Severe Autistic Spectrum Disorder.* Jessica Kingsley Publishers.

Chapman, R. (2020). Neurodiversity, disability, wellbeing. In H. Bertilsdotter-Rosqvist, A. Stenning, & N. Chown. (Eds.) *Neurodiversity Studies: A New Critical Paradigm* (pp. 57–72). Routledge.

Dagnan, D., Grant, F., & McDonnell, A. (2004). Understanding challenging behaviour in older people: The development of the Controllability Beliefs Scale. *Behavioural and Cognitive Psychotherapy, 32*, 501–506.

Dagnan, D., Hull, A., & McDonnell, A. (2012). The Controllability Beliefs Scale used with

carers of people with intellectual disabilities: Psychometric properties. *Journal of Intellectual Disability Research, 57*(5), 422–428. https://doi.org/10.1111/j.1365-2788.2012.01554.x

Ekdahl, D. (2023). The double empathy problem and the problem of empathy: Neurodiversifying phenomenology. *Disability & Society, 39*(10), 2588–2610. https://doi.org/10.1080/09687599.2023.2220180

Ellis, M., & Astell, A. (2018). *Adaptive Interaction and Dementia.* Jessica Kingsley Publishers.

Emerson, E., & Einfeld, S. F. (2011). *Challenging Behaviour* (3rd ed.) Cambridge University Press.

Evripidou, M., Charalambous, A., Middleton, N., & Papastavrou, E. (2018) Nurses' knowledge and attitudes about dementia care: Systematic literature review. *Perspectives in Psychiatric Care, 55*, 48–60. https://doi.org/10.1111/ppc.12291

Feast, A., Orrell, M., Charlesworth, G., Melunsky, N., Poland, F., & Moniz-Cook, E. (2016). Behavioural and psychological symptoms in dementia and the challenges for family carers: Systematic review. *British Journal of Psychiatry, 208*(5), 429–434. https://doi.org/10.1192/bjp.bp.114.153684

Ghane, G., Shahsavari, H., Zare, Z., Ahmadnia, S., & Siavashi, B. (2021). Social death in patients: Concept analysis with an evolutionary approach. *SSM - Population Health, 14*, 100795. https://doi.org/10.1016/j.ssmph.2021.100795

Gibbons, L., Keddie, G., & James, I. A. (2018). Investigating the phenomenon of time-shifting *Australian Journal of Dementia Care, 7*(1), 32–34.

Gutmanis, I., Snyder, M., Harvey, D., Hillier, L. M., & LeClair, K. (2015). Health care redesign for responsive behaviours—The Behavioural Supports Ontario Experience: Lessons learned and keys to success. *Canadian Journal of Community Mental Health, 34*(1), 45–63. https://doi.org/10.7870/cjcmh-2015-001

Hacking, I. (1998). *Mad Travelers: Reflections on the Reality of Transient Mental Disease.* University Press of Virginia.

James, I. A., & Jackman, L. (2017). *Understanding Behaviour in Dementia that Challenges, Second Edition: A Guide to Assessment and Treatment.* Jessica Kingsley Publishers.

Jongsma, K., Spaeth, E., & Schicktanz, S. (2017). Epistemic injustice in dementia and autism patient organizations: An empirical analysis. *AJOB Empirical Bioethics, 8*(4), 221–233. https://doi.org/10.1080/23294515.2017.1402833

Kenny, L., Hattersley, C., Molins, B., Buckley, C., Povey, C., & Pellicano, E. (2016). Which terms should be used to describe autism? Perspectives from the UK autism community. *Autism, 20*(4), 442–462. https://doi.org/10.1177/1362361315588200

Lutz, A. S. F. (26 June 2023) An Interview with Neurodiversity Originator Judy Singer. *Psychology Today.* https://www.psychologytoday.com/gb/blog/inspectrum/202306/an-interview-with-neurodiversity-originator-judy-singer

McDonnell, A. (2010). *Managing Aggressive Behaviour in Care Settings: Understanding and Applying Low Arousal Approaches.* Wiley-Blackwell.

McDonnell, A. (2019). *The Reflective Journey: A Practitioner's Guide to the Low Arousal Approach.* Studio 3.

McDonnell, A., McEvoy, J., & Dearden, R. L. (1994). Coping with violent situations in the caring environment. In T. Wykes (Ed.), *Violence and Health Care Professionals* (pp. 189–206). Springer.

Milton, D. E. M. (2012). On the ontological status of autism: the 'double empathy problem'. *Disability & Society, 27*(6), 883–887. https://doi.org/10.1080/09687599.2012.710008

Milton, D., Gurbuz, E., & López, B. (2022). The 'double empathy problem': Ten years on.

Autism, 26(8), 1901–1903. https://doi.org/10.1177/13623613221129123

Milton, D. E. M., Waldock, K. E., & Keates, N. (2023). Autism and the 'double empathy problem'. In F. Mezzenzana, & D. Peluso (Eds.) *Conversations on Empathy Interdisciplinary Perspectives on Imagination and Radical Othering* (pp. 78–97). Routledge.

Mittler, P. (2018). Hello, my name is Peter Mittler. *Dementia Alliance International.* https://dementiaallianceinternational.org/blog/hello-my-name-is-peter-mittler

NHS (2023). *Symptoms of Dementia.* National Health Service (NHS). https://www.nhs.uk/conditions/dementia/symptoms-and-diagnosis/symptoms/

Nicolaidis, C., Milton, D., Sasson, H. J., Sheppard, E., & Yergeau, M. (2019). An expert discussion on autism and empathy. *Autism in Adulthood: Challenges and Management, 1*(1), 4–11. https://doi.org/10.1089/aut.2018.29000.cjn

Nielsen, M. (2017). My ADHD and me: Identifying with and distancing from ADHD. *Nordic Psychology, 69*(1), 33–46. https://doi.org/10.1080/19012276.2016.1267916

Örulv, L. (2023). Neurodiversity and dementia pitfalls, possibilities and some personal notes. In R. Ward, & L. J. Sandberg (Eds.) *Critical Dementia Studies: An Introduction* (pp. 247–262). Routledge.

Peel, E. (2014). 'The living death of Alzheimer's' versus 'Take a walk to keep dementia at bay': Representations of dementia in print media and carer discourse. *Sociology of Health and Illness, 36*, 885–901. https://doi.org/10.1111/1467-9566.12122

Petherbridge, D. (2019). Beyond empathy: Vulnerability, relationality and dementia. *International Journal of Philosophical Studies, 27*(2), 307–326. https://doi.org/10.1080/09672559.2019.1594588

Pripas-Kapit, S. (2020). Historicizing Jim Sinclair's "Don't mourn for us": A cultural and intellectual history of neurodiversity's first manifesto. In S. K. Kapp (Ed.) *Autistic Community and the Neurodiversity Movement Stories from the Frontline* (pp. 23–40). Palgrave Macmillan (eBook). https://doi.org/10.1007/978-981-13-8437-0

Rook, G. (2024, March 24). Dear Alzheimer's Society. *George Rook: Living with Dementia as Well as I Can*. https://georgerook51.wordpress.com/2024/03/24/dear-alzheimers-society/

Silberman, S. (2023). How my mother's dementia showed me another side of neurodiversity. *Scientific American*. https://www.scientificamerican.com/article/how-my-mothers-dementia-showed-me-another-side-of-neurodiversity/

Sinclair, J. [1993] (2012). Don't mourn for us. *Autonomy, the Critical Journal of Interdisciplinary Autism Studies, 1*(1). https://www.larry-arnold.net/Autonomy/Vol%201,%20No%201%20(2012).htm

Singer, J. (2017) *Neurodiversity: The birth of an idea*. Judy Singer

Spencer, L. (2023). Epistemic injustice in late-stage dementia: A case for non-verbal testimonial injustice. *Social Epistemology, 37*(1), 62–79. https://doi.org/10.1080/02691728.2022.2103474

Stenning, A., & Bertilsdotter Rosqvist, H. (2021). Neurodiversity studies: Mapping out possibilities of a new critical paradigm. *Disability & Society, 36*(9), 1532–1537. https://doi.org/10.1080/09687599.2021.1919503

Swaffer, K. (2014). Dementia: Stigma, language, and dementia-friendly. *Dementia: The International Journal of Social Research and Practice, 13*(6), 709-716. https://doi.org/10.1177/1471301214548143

Swaffer, K. (2015). Dementia and Prescribed Disengagement™. *Dementia: The International Journal of Social Research and Practice, 14*(1), 3–6. https://doi.org/10.1177/1471301214548136

Swaffer, K., LeBlanc, B., & Mittler, P. (2019). Dementia and as disability. In K. Dube, M. Berghs, T. Chataika, & Y. El-Lahib (Eds.) *The Routledge Handbook of Disability Activism*. Routledge.

Sweeting, H., & Gilhooly, M. (1997). Dementia and the phenomenon of social death. *Sociology of Health & Illness, 19*(1), 93–117. https://doi.org/10.1111/j.1467-9566.1997.tb00017.x

Thomas, C., & Milligan, C. (2018). Dementia, disability rights and disablism: Understanding the social position of people living with dementia. *Disability & Society, 33*(1), 115–131. https://doi.org/10.1080/09687599.2017.1379952

Young, I. M. (1997). Feminism and the public sphere: Asymmetrical reciprocity: On moral respect, wonder, and enlarged thought. *Constellations, 3*(3), 340–363. https://doi.org/10.1111/j.1467-8675.1997.tb00064.x

Other titles from Damian Milton

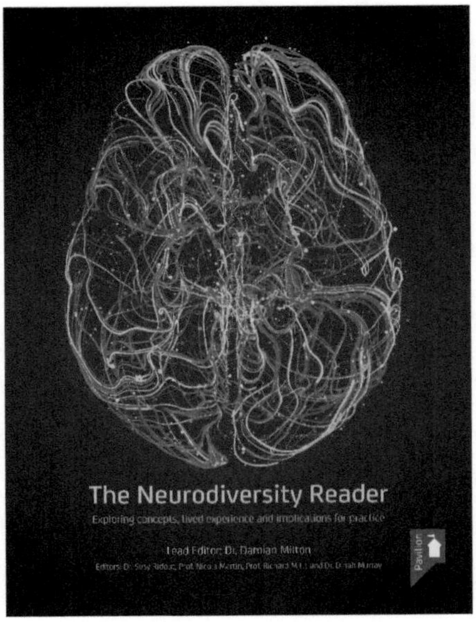

The Neurodiversity Reader

Exploring Concepts, lived experience and implications for practice

Dr Damian Milton (lead ed)

Scan for more information

This collection brings together work from pioneering figures within and beyond the neurodiversity movement to critically explore its associated concepts and how they might be translated into practice. In the 20 years since the inception of neurodiversity as a concept, a strong international movement championing the civil rights of those deemed 'neurodivergent' from idealised norms has grown, alongside an increasing academic interest in the concept of neurodiversity and how such ideas can relate to practice and service provision. This collection will explore the history of the movement, the concepts that have shaped it, and where the future might lead to.

ISBN: 978-1-912755-39-4

A Mismatch of Salience

Explorations of the Nature of Autism from Theory to Practice

Dr Damian Milton

Scan for more information

Bringing together a collection of Milton's writings, this book explores the communication challenges between autistic people and neurotypical people and seeks to re-balance and celebrate this diversity.

ISBN: 978-1-911028-76-5